2016 Football Preview

By: Warren Sharp

SharpFootballAnalysis.com
SharpFootballStats.com

sharp@sharpfootballanalysis.com
@SharpFootball

**Proudly written
& printed in the
USA**

DEDICATION

TO the fans of football who want more meaningful analysis than that which comes from talking heads with uneducated opinions

TO those who share intelligent, factual analysis without casting judgement

TO the decision makers in NFL front offices who exhaust every means to gain an edge because they care about winning – even when it means incorporating input from outsiders with analytics, models and intelligence to make sound suggestions & to the others who will inevitably will follow in their footsteps

TO the good guys who daily fight in the real fights around the world to keep us free – our troops and those who support them

TO anyone who spreads the word

TO my wife & children who allow me a beautiful escape from the working world to remember the true joy in life, and who have allowed me to prove that with intelligent, creative new ideas, insanely hard work & very little sleep, you can achieve anything

THIS IS FOR YOU

TO those overly sensitive fans who hate objective analysis which at time looks down on their favorite football team

TO anyone who thinks they are too elite to appreciate work they actually like but which comes from a source they aren't familiar with

THIS IS NOT FOR YOU

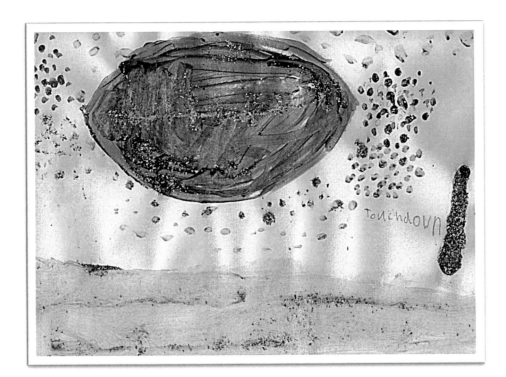

FORWARD

COLUMNS

TEAM CHAPTERS

Artwork courtesy of my children. Logo designs courtesy of Addison Foote of addisonfoote.com

The Mission

The first thing we heard was the rumbling. As we left the courtroom, we saw people gathered by the windows, staring outside. We walked over, looking out into the dark evening sky. Torrential downpours. We looked down from the 7th floor and saw it was causing massive flooding in the city. The roads were jammed, the sidewalks empty. Everyone was bunkered inside office lobbies or standing under awnings. A few brave souls darted around underneath wind driven umbrellas. Our party looked at each other and shook our heads.

The day started extremely early, a docket full of negotiations. At debate were tens of millions of dollars related to a construction project gone horribly awry. With hours spent inside the courtroom without cell reception, we had no idea if the early summer storm would be as bad as they predicted earlier in the day. Turns out it was worse. As we reached the lobby, we saw even people with umbrellas getting destroyed as they walked from building to building. They looked at the traffic. "Even if you make it back to the office, you're not going to get anywhere in this traffic." Seven of the eight of us decided to unwind at the restaurant inside the building and grab a drink. "I'll take my chances, I have to get back", I said, as my umbrella violently popped open and I departed the building. By the time I made it back to my office, I was drenched, from my socks all the way to my suit jacket. The main goal of the umbrella was to keep my electronics dry. It succeeded. A couple of hours later I was home. But my day was just getting started. After a late dinner I worked until 3am on this magazine, grabbed a couple hours of rest, and got ready for another day of negotiations.

As a licensed Professional Engineer from a top 10 engineering school, I have a good background and am proficient at what I do. I've been working in that field for two decades. But like so many others in the working world, my job is not my passion. Analyzing football is my passion. Growing up as an avid athlete, I loved all sports. I played multiple sports for many years competitively, moving from recreational leagues to travel leagues to the best levels available. I was on Olympic development teams in high school, and in high school we won the State Championship. Injuries derailed my chance to play in college. A broken leg followed by rehab and then a shredded knee forced me to wear a knee brace at the start of my freshman year in college. Training with the team that summer, I realized there was no legitimate shot for a future playing sports. So I abandoned that avenue and picked up a new hobby: modeling the NFL to predict game outcomes. When you get to very competitive levels in sports, you understand the elements of the game that many overlook because they can't be measured. Psychological edges, motivational factors and anticipation of certain opponents more than others. Sports science, rest, travel disadvantages and many other aspects.

But to do a better job than linesmakers, you need a computer model to spot their inefficiencies. I spent 4 years building one for football and another few testing it. I've been publicly providing recommendations for 10 years now. My public work is available at SharpFootballAnalysis.com. For over 5 years now, I've also worked for a number of professional betting syndicate groups based in Las Vegas, which entails almost daily communication during the season as I share my recommendations and suggestions.

When asked how I post such strong results, my answer is simple. It's the same answer I would give if someone asked how I created this entire magazine by myself, when other publications literally have dozens of writers and editors. It starts with the right creative ideas, that have not been used before, and combined with a passion that leads to an untiring work ethic, the sky is the limit. You won't have success with a good idea if you don't care to work your ass off to push it all the way to and then beyond the limit. If you are just regurgitating someone else's drivel as opposed to doing something new, even with good work ethic and passion, smart people will see right through it.

So what is the 2016 Football Preview?
-It is not a football betting publication, although reading it will certainly make you more intelligent and better equipped for success in 2016.
-It is not a daily fantasy preview magazine, although there are certain custom analyses which pertain to daily fantasy and as with betting, the more intelligent you are about the teams, players, and the plans forward the more success you are likely to have. Most fantasy football "season preview" magazines spend infinite time on players but rarely discuss team projections, outlook, and even more, advanced metrics, instead focused on basic stats like yardage and touchdowns.
-Most of all, it is not the type of historical almanac you'll find on the shelves of most bookstores which disguise themselves as football preview magazines. Instead of utilizing thoughtful advanced metrics or well versed prediction based on something more than "gut" and player movement, most of those fill their pages with stats over the last 10 seasons, as if that information will help predict the 2016 season. It simply helps them puff up their total page count. This isn't a dumbed down reference tool.

My goal with my 2016 NFL Preview is to break down the teams into their parts, so readers can understand how they are built, how they function, and why they succeed or fail. Once established, it shifts into advanced metrics and analysis from the granular level of player efficiency and performance to how those players fit into their team, draft analysis and roster construction, cap space, 2016 schedule, player health, production, predictions and the most visual, advanced metrics that a season preview magazine has ever attempted to include.

You'll find sections here on game theory, optimal play calling, roster formation, strategy and much more. I hate cumulative stats, such as ranking defenses by total yds allowed. In this publication, I use many of my own, unique stats based on years of research which are predictive in nature, such as my proprietary EDSR metric, which is more correlated to victory than any statistic other than turnovers, but unlike turnovers, is also capable of being modeled predictively to forecast results.

While in theory all of that information sounds great, without proper presentation, it is hard to digest. That is why I spend the same amount of focus on presentation. In particular, this magazine is focused for "visual learners". The ability for the public to consume and "value" statistics is diminished by lack of context as well as the age in which we live. In the newspaper era (from a sports perspective) the only option was targeting "reading/writing learners". Statistics, box scores and standings displayed in columns in a table. Unfortunately, for most sites, that has not changed very much. Most every website displays statistics in a table format. The problem is, in the modern video/app world, most people are becoming "visual learners" (prefer to see info and visualize relationships between ideas) if not "kinesthetic learners" (hands-on, experimental). As such, one goal with this project is to present statistics in a visual and kinesthetic manner through interactive visualizations.

The kinesthetic aspect is not available in a printed magazine. But it is the sole focus of a project I'm excited to launch later this month and that I highly recommend you checking out as soon as you read this page: SharpFootballStats.com. One of the pages in each team chapter comes directly from the data which is shared at Sharp Football Stats. This season, you will be able to "see" the statistic, and then interact with the visualization to create your own impact on it. In turn, this will make the info more understandable, useful and as-such, meaningful.

If you found this magazine because you follow me on Twitter (@SharpFootball) or are a client of mine at SharpFootballAnalysis.com, thank you! If you found this magazine because you have read my articles over at ESPN.com's Chalk section, or over at FOXsports.com's Outkick the Coverage section, thank you and keep tuned in for more analytical work from me at both platforms this offseason and into the 2016 football season.

My hope with this preview is to introduce more "intelligent" statistical analysis to the football population so that everyone can become more astute fans, and potentially parlay that into your own financial gain, whether that is via daily fantasy or sports betting. There is something for everyone in this magazine. As you read this preview, you're getting a glimpse into the ideas, analysis and features which made it to print from months of research to prepare for the 2015 football season. I'll know it was well worth it when you use this publication not only to prep for the season, but you grab it during the season to study up or as a reference tool.

If you like the magazine, please spread the word. If you're on Twitter, feel free to snap a picture of it and tag me (@SharpFootball) and let me know how you like it. And if you like the content, please check out my other projects:

SharpFootballAnalysis.com is where I offer weekly analysis during the football season and detailed, analytical write-ups of game predictions. Last season I recorded my best season in years, winning at a 72% rate on predicting totals through the playoffs. In 10 years, I service I have recorded a record of:

NFL Overall: 1096-766 (59%)
NFL Totals: 433-285 (60%)
College Totals: 612-498 (55%)

The Sharp Football Analysis Podcast over at iTunes (or YouTube) is where I record 2 podcasts weekly, one being a recap show and the other a preview show.
SharpFootballStats.com is the home of my future visualized advanced statistics endeavor, planned to launch in July 2016.

Enjoy the magazine, the upcoming football season, and stay in touch for continued analysis from a different perspective this fall! Best,

4

2016 Season Forecast from NFLproject.com

Two years ago, the NFL Data Science Project was launched. The NFL Data Science Project brings the power of cutting edge machine learning algorithms and big data technology to NFL analytics. Utilizing massive computational power in conjunction with state of the art mathematical techniques, a deeper understanding of the NFL was made available to the common fan.

During the season, www.NFLproject.com, the home of the NFL Data Science Project, released week by week results and analysis from its NFL Season Simulation model. Aspects of the simulation model that represent an edge over the standard industry analysis are:

• A game by game simulation of the entire NFL schedule as it will actually play out
• Ability to map out the complexity of all interactions
related to division and conference rankings
• Implementation of playoff rules in addition to home/away implications
• Inclusion of the most accurate predictive information
available in forecasting the variability of future game
outcomes
• Granular analysis on a team by team basis related to
individual game outcomes,
• personnel changes and their specific effect on season results

To the right are the 2016 predictions from NFLproject.com. Below is a narrative of these projections:

THE PLAYOFF FIELD

From the NFC, the Green Bay Packers will enjoy the return of Jordy Nelson, will see a more svelte Eddie Lacy, and will have a fully healthy Aaron Rodgers. The latter was clearly not himself late in the season and required offseason surgery to bring him back to form. An easier schedule, thanks to their 2nd place finish last year, allowed the Packers to avoid the Carolina Panthers, Arizona Cardinals and the Washington Redskins, and instead they draw the Atlanta Falcons, Philadelphia Eagles and Seattle Seahawks, with their game against the Seahawks coming at home in the cold December air.

That game may foreshadow the 2016 NFC Championship game, as the Seahawks are projected to win the NFC West and secure the last first round bye. Seattle likewise plays a 2nd place schedule. Interestingly, Seattle has slightly better odds to win the Super Bowl, based on the fact GB likely plays Arizona.

The Panthers and the Dallas Cowboys are projected to round out the final division winners, but the NFC Wild Card teams both look to be strong, making Wild Card weekend extremely exciting. If the Panthers host the Cardinals, it will be a repeat of the 2015 NFC Championship game which saw Carolina prevail 49-15. Dallas is the least likely home team to win in the Wild Card round from the NFC, and if Carolina fends

off the Vikings, it will set up a playoff rematch from last season between the Packers and the Cardinals.

In the AFC, the Pittsburgh Steelers are projected to make another deep run in the playoffs. Last season they led the Broncos in Denver before fumbling away their AFC Divisional game. If they meet again, it will be in Pittsburgh.

Earning the other bye, but missing out on the #1 seed in large part because Tom Brady will miss the first 4 games, are the Patriots. Adding Martellus Bennett in free agency will help this offense stay more diverse, as will the reintroduction of their former O-Line coach.

Rounding out the AFC are four teams with plenty of playoff experience. Each made the postseason last year. But this time, the Broncos sneak in as opposed to holding the #1 seed. Meanwhile, the Bengals will look to win their first playoff game under Marvin Lewis, who has led the charge since 2003 but has gone 0-7 in the playoffs.

THE DIVISIONS

Along the road to the playoffs, some teams will be in for smooth seas while others will find the trip much less comfortable.

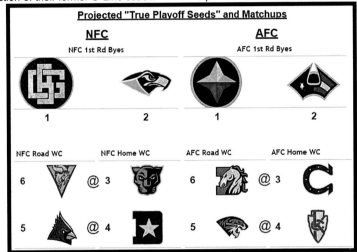

Projected "True Playoff Seeds" and Matchups

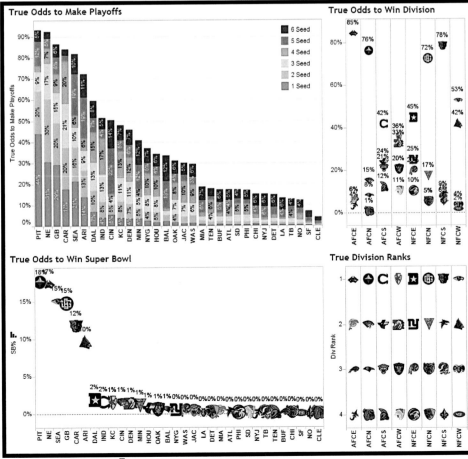

The easiest divisions for the forecast winners appear to be the AFC East and the NFC South. The Buffalo Bills, New York Jets and Miami Dolphins still do not seem to have their act together, and that is exactly what it takes to dethrone the Patriots. And in the NFC South, the Panthers are still projected to win by a margin, despite the Super Bowl runner-up hangover potential.

The most competitive divisions from top to bottom may likely be the AFC South and West. This does not mean that all teams are solid, but there really is not a dominant team in either division, and the race to win the division and secure a playoff spot will be competitive.

The best divisions will likely be the AFC North, the NFC West and the NFC North. The Bengals, Steelers, Cardinals, Seahawks, Packers and Vikings all could find themselves in the postseason. What happens below them is more difficult to say. The Baltimore Ravens could bounce back, the Chicago Bears could take the next step, and either Chip Kelly could work his magic or the Rams and Jeff Fisher could see Jared Goff take this team to a record better than .500. Those last two teams in the NFC West are more of a stretch than the other divisions. In fact, NFLproject.com ranks the

Steelers and Bengals inside the top 5 teams in the entire AFC, and with the Ravens at 9th overall, the AFC North has 3 teams inside the top 9.

In the NFC West, the Cardinals are projected as the team 4th most likely to win the Conference, which shows the power and thus uncertainty of the top 2 teams in the NFC West.

On the prior page, NFLproject's data easily depicts which teams are Wild Card or bust. In the "True Odds to Make Playoffs" which lists teams and seeds, it is apparent that the Vikings most likely route is through the Wild Card based on the Packers strength. The same can be said for the Bengals and the Ravens, as well as all AFC East teams. Meanwhile, for teams like the Jaguars, Texans or Colts, they really must win their division because they are unlikely to qualify as a Wild Card team.

UP AND COMING

Looking at the "True Division Ranks", several teams might finally turn the corner in 2016. Slated to improve their records and finish in 3rd place in their division, the Buccaneers, Raiders and Jaguars are three teams that have younger QBs, have had plenty of good draft value for

years now, and are poised to take that next step while their QBs are still on their rookie deal.

Be sure to check in at NFLproject.com throughout the 2016 season for further analysis and updates on a weekly basis to project key games and forecasted odds for the playoffs.

COMPARISON TO OTHER MODELS

Below, you can see how NFLproject.com's model compares to Pro Football Focus and Football Outsiders in terms of projecting conference standings.

Note that while Football Outsiders takes playoff rules into account (and pegs the Seahawks with the 5th seed despite their record being 3rd best in the NFC), Pro Football Focus does not and ranks teams solely on projected record, regardless of their division.

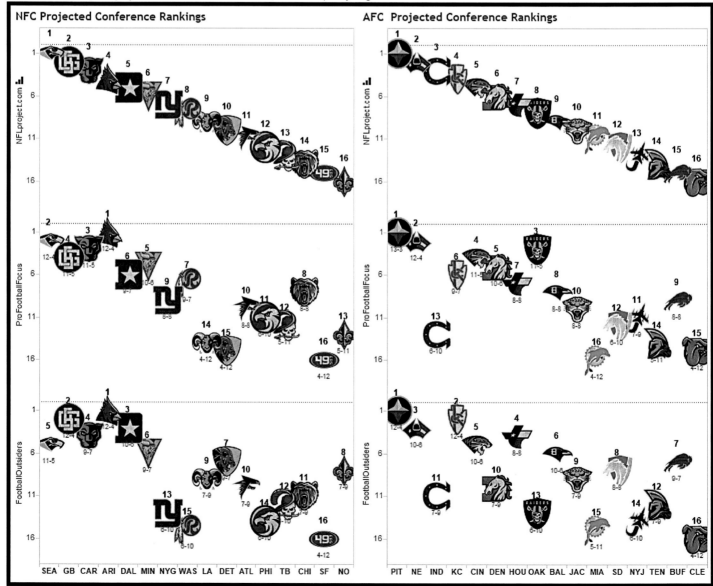

www.sharp football analysis.com

The Forefront of Inventing & Incorporating Custom Advanced Analytics & Metrics into Football Handicapping

Lifetime NFL Record
Totals: 433-285 (60%)
Sides (Personal Plays): 480-351 (58%)

Lifetime NFL Playoffs Record: 115-66 (64%)
Lifetime Super Bowl Record: 15-7 (68%)

Lifetime College Football Record
Totals: 612-498 (55%)

Transparent Record Keeping
All client plays publicly displayed minutes after the start of the game

2015-16 Results:
NFL Totals: 34-13 (72%)
NFL ALL: 76-49 (61%)
CFB Totals: 56-40 (58%)

Respected Analysis
Numerous betting syndicates acquire recommendations & Warren's work is well known by current and former linemakers

NFL's Most Consistent Results
10 Years, 10 Winning Seasons
Emphasizing sound money management, +EV betting opportunities & beating the market

Line Value
Using timed release system, when Warren releases a play to clients, the market reacts giving clients consistent, significant & measurable line value

As currently seen in:

"I noticed Warren was moving some lines around on Wednesdays after he put his stuff up on his site, and he was winning. Instantly, when Warren gives out his play, the books move toward his line. Very rarely will you get a better number than his. He's a consistent winner."

- Professional Bettor & Las Vegas Legend **Bill "Krackman" Krackomberger**

Hear Pro Bettor
Bill "Krackman" Krackomberger:

"Warren's synopsis on game totals is vastly superior utilizing his mathematical formulas, to any preview I have ever seen. His success is two-fold, beating the closing number by up to 3 pts and winning at a clip needed to secure a hefty profit. Getting in early ensures some fantastic middling opportunities."

- **Richie Baccellieri**, former Director of Race and Sports at Caesars Palace, MGM Grand and The Palms, current expert at The Linemakers

Warren Sharp of sharpfootballanalysis.com is an industry pioneer at the forefront of incorporating advanced analytics and metrics into football handicapping after spending years constructing, testing, betting and perfecting computer models written to beat NFL and college football totals.

A licensed Professional Engineer by trade, Warren now works as a quantitative analyst for multiple professional sports betting syndicates in Las Vegas and has parlayed a long-term winning record into selections for clients which move the Vegas line and beat the closing number with regularity.

Pay NOTHING until AFTER the season:
Get all the detailed weekly analysis, write-ups and recommendations now, pay only after the 2016 season! Details at
www . sharp football analysis . com

Layout and Definitions

PAGE 1 - OVERVIEW

<u>2016 Schedule & Week by Week Strength of Schedule</u>: Opponent's are sorted by their forecast 2016 strength, with easy teams in green and difficult teams in red.

<u>Strength of Schedule In Detail</u>: Schedule ranked not on prior season (2015) opponent record, but on predicted (2016) opponent record using season win totals from linesmakers in the betting market.

<u>2015 Play Tendencies</u>: Examination of offensive play calling in various situations. One score is defined as games where the score was within 8 points, thus a team trailing can score once (TD+conversion) to either tie or win the game.

<u>2015 Offensive or Defensive Advanced Metrics</u>: Using my own custom analytics as well as efficiency metrics from Football Outsiders, a look at rankings in offensive metrics from the 2015 season.

PAGE 2 – PERSONNEL & SPENDING

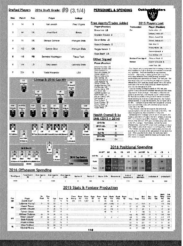

<u>Free Agents/Trades Added</u>: Key players added in free agency or via trade

<u>2015 Players Lost</u>: Key rostered players from 2015 who are no longer with the team in 2016

<u>Other Signed</u>: Additional players signed, generally as undrafted free agents (not inclusive of every player)

<u>Lineup & 2016 Cap Hit</u>: Projected starters in spread offensive package and the respective defenders. Color coded based on 2016 salary cap hit for each player. More expensive players are shaded dark red. SharpFootballStats.com will utilize this layout for visualizations of certain stats during the 2016 season.

<u>Health Overall & by Unit (2015 v 2014)</u>: AGL is a metric created by Football Outsiders and stands for Adjusted Games Lost. Scott Kacsmar has done extensive work in this area. It reflects how healthy (a low number) or injured (a high number) a team was as compared to the rest of the NFL.

<u>2016 Positional Spending</u>: Cap dollars allocated to each position group, as well as the rank as compared to the rest of the NFL. Numbers accurate through 7/1. Also compares the rank in 2015 with that in 2016 to see movement.

<u>2016 Offseason Spending</u>: Contract dollars spent in the offseason by various categories as well as ranks (Rk) as compared to other teams.

<u>2015 Stats & Fantasy Production</u>: Player age, games played, starts, stats, fantasy points scored at Draft King & Fan Duel, and ranking of this production.

PAGE 3 – ODDS & TRENDS

<u>Avg Line</u>: Average line (point spread) of the 15 games that are already lined by CG Technology in Las Vegas.

<u>Pred Wins</u>: Predicted regular season team win totals from the betting market.

<u>Pred Div Finish</u>: The predicted finish in the division based on the betting market.

<u>2016 Weekly Betting Lines (wks 1-16)</u>: Lines on the 15 games already lined, with easy opponents in green and more difficult opponents in red.

<u>2015 Critical and Game-Deciding Stats</u>: Margins and stats for some of the most commonly used statistics which have the greatest impact on wins and losses.

<u>Team Records & Trends</u>: A yearly look at general situational betting results since 2013.

<u>Regular Season Wins: Past Results & Current Proj</u>: A look a team win totals since 2012, the forecast for 2015 and the results achieved in comparison to the projection in 2016.

<u>Close Game Records</u>: Records in games decided by 3 or less points (FG games) or 8 or less points (1 score games). Also includes ranks compared to rest of NFL for win rates in those games, as well as the number of those wins as compared to the total wins the team recorded in the season.

<u>2016 NFLproject.com Forecast</u>: Based on the machine learning algorithm from NFLproject.com and thousands of season sims, the projected rates for teams to win the division, make the playoffs and win the Super Bowl.

<u>Weekly EDSR & Season Trending Performance</u>: EDSR stands for Early Down Success Rate and is a custom metric I invented to study efficiency. I have seen no metric more correlated to wins other than turnovers, but turnovers are not predictive whereas EDSR has proven to be correlated as well as predictive in nature.

PAGE 4 – STATS & VISUALIZATIONS FROM SHARPFOOTBALLSTATS.COM

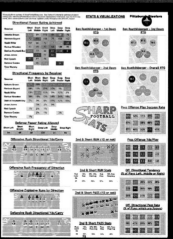

<u>Directional Passer Rating Achieved</u>: Passer rating based on direction, distance and receiver.

<u>Directional Frequency by Receiver</u>: Frequency of receiver targets based on direction and distance.

<u>Passer Rating Cones</u>: Directional passer rating based on short passes (0-14 yds in air) or deep passes (15+ yds in air) on 1st, 2nd, 3rd downs and overall.

<u>Pass Offense Play Success Rate</u>: Plays are graded based on success rate. Definition of which is: 40% of yards-to-go are gained on 1st down; 60% of yards-to-go on 2nd down; or 100% of yards-to-go on 3rd & 4th down. Organized by field location (in 20 yard segments) and by play direction as offense travels from left to right up the field.

<u>Offensive Rush Directional Yds/Carry or Frequency</u>: Yards/carry gained based on runs behind the offensive line in directions depicted. Frequency lists the total number of runs to that direction.

<u>2nd & Short RUN (1D or not)</u>: Run plays called on 2nd and short based on field location, and whether it resulted in a 1st down (green arrow) or not (red X).

<u>2nd & Short RUN Stats</u>: Rank in conversion rate as compared to the NFL average, and run frequency vs avg.

<u>2nd & Short PASS (1D or not)</u>: Same as run, but next to each play is SH or DP for short pass or deep pass att.

<u>Off. Directional Tendency (% of Plays Left, Middle or Right)</u>: Based on field location (20 yard segments), rate of plays that go to the middle, left or right as offense moves up the field (left to right).

<u>Off. Directional Pass Rate</u>: Percentage of plays which are passes, and to which direction they are thrown, as the team moves left to right up the field.

Seattle Seahawks

Coaches

Head Coach: Pete Carroll (7th yr)
OC: Darrell Bevell (6th yr)
DC: Kris Richard (2nd yr)

Forecast 2016 Wins

11

Past Records

2015: 10-6
2014: 12-4
2013: 13-3

Opponent Strength
Easy — Hard

2016 Schedule & Week by Week Strength of Schedule

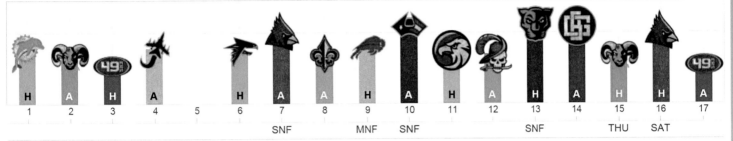

H	A	A	A		H	A	A	H	A	H	A	H	A	H	H	A
1	2	3	4	5	6	7	8	9	10	11	12	13	14	15	16	17

SNF (wk 7), MNF (wk 9), SNF (wk 10), SNF (wk 13), THU (wk 15), SAT (wk 16)

2016 Overview

New frontiers. They can be exciting. They can be refreshing. They can also be challenging. The founders of Seattle found it to be challenging as well. They left Portland, Oregon and sailed to the area, initially attempting to establish a site at Alki Point in the fall of 1851, only to abandon the site the following spring after just one winter. They were unable to deal with the north winds piling up waves in that location, and instead moved to a more protected site on Elliott Bay: what is now the Pioneer Square district in downtown Seattle. Ironically, this site is literally two blocks from Seattle's CenturyLink Field.

For several years now the Seahawks have vigorously defended that turf, and ever since Russell Wilson came to town in 2012, they've never failed to win double digit games or make the playoffs. The first 3 years, Russell Wilson hit the cap annually for between $545k and $817k. He was the biggest bargain the NFL has seen in some time. Knowing they wanted to lock him up long term, Wilson agreed to terms before the 2015 season to a 4 year, $87M deal. However, with a base salary of just $700k in 2015, his cap hit was just $7M. Much like Seattle's founders likely spent the winter of 1851, longing for their protected homes in Portland, for the Seahawks front office and the salary savings afforded by Wilson's first 4 years, those days are long gone. Russell Wilson hits the 2016 cap for $18.5M, 27 times more than his cap hit when Seattle won the Super Bowl in 2013. That cap hit steadily increases over the next 4 years, until it hits $23M in 2019. While many less-deserving QBs may hit the cap for more by that point in time, it doesn't change the fact that Seattle hasn't had to build its cap around a quarterback for many years. After years of struggling, the Seahawks of the early 2000s were at their best when they had a cheap and young Matt Hasselbeck. But after his early success and his 2nd Seattle contract, his cap hit grew, as did his injuries, and the team spiraled downward until Wilson arrived.

The implications of Wilson's deal are easily recognized when examining pre-Wilson-money offensive line vs post-Wilson-money offensive line. When Seattle won the Super bowl with Wilson hitting the cap for only $681k, they had the most expensive offensive line in the NFL. Their offensive line combined to hit the 2013 cap for $28M, the most in the NFL that season. This season, their offensive line is hitting the 2016 cap for $11.7M, the least in the NFL. Their offensive line in 2015 was an issue, ranking 30th in pass protection. Russell Wilson can erase a lot of protection issues. But any time he is called to do that, he generally has to put his body at risk. And while no team wants their QB injured, the implications of seeing a rookie QB injured who has almost no financial commitment is vastly different from an experienced leader who was given $61.5 guaranteed and without whom the team (as currently structured) would be underdogs to perform in the postseason. If Wilson is repeatedly expected to dodge, duck, dip, dive and dodge to avoid free rushers, the clock is ticking until he takes a shot from which he's unable to get up healthy. Assuming Wilson continues to grow and develop as we expect, if the young RBs can carry the load, if Tyler Lockett continues to impress and if their sound defense stays healthy, Seattle can once again pencil in another trip to the playoffs, but it hinges around the offensive line playing as a unit well above their pay grade.

Strength of Schedule In Detail

True Strength of Schedule Rank: 21

Hardest Stretches (1=Hard, 32=Easy)
Hardest 3 wk Stretch Rk: **13**
Hardest 4 wk Stretch Rk: **4**
Hardest 5 wk Stretch Rk: **5**

Easiest Stretches (1=Easy, 32=Hard)
Easiest 3 wk Stretch Rk: **9**
Easiest 4 wk Stretch Rk: **9**
Easiest 5 wk Stretch Rk: **30**

Seattle's end to the year features the 5th most difficult 5-week stretch (wks 10-14) and the 4th most 4-week stretch (wks 13-16), so it no surprise that from week 10 onward, Seattle must play the 5th toughest schedule in the NFL. But Seattle should be in good shape by that point, as they face the easiest first 6 weeks in the NFL (vs MIA, @ LA, vs SFF, @ NYJ, vs ATL and a bye). Their schedule sets up nicely with a tough game vs the Cardinals followed by two easier games (@ NO, vs BUF), then a tough game vs the Patriots followed by two more easier games (vs PHI, @ TB). This theoretically should allow the Seahawks to maintain focus for their hardest opponents and round into form for their late run against strong opposition, so long as they don't overlook one of the easier teams between the tough opponents.

2015 Play Tendencies

All Pass %	52%
All Pass Rk	29
All Rush %	48%
All Rush Rk	4
1 Score Pass %	55%
1 Score Pass Rk	23
2014 1 Score Pass %	50%
2014 1 Score Pass Rk	30
Pass Increase %	5%
Pass Increase Rk	8
1 Score Rush %	45%
1 Score Rush Rk	10
Up Pass %	47%
Up Pass Rk	19
Up Rush %	53%
Up Rush Rk	14
Down Pass %	59%
Down Pass Rk	29
Down Rush %	41%
Down Rush Rk	4

Seattle remained one of the most run heavy teams in the NFL despite paying Russell Wilson and needing him to make more happen for the offense last year. However, in one-score games the Seahawks passed 5% more often in 2016 than 2015, the 8th largest increase in the NFL. It will be interesting to see their philosophy and how it might adjust given their new youth at the RB position, with 2nd year player Thomas Rawls coming off of a season ending injury and rookie CJ Prosise backing him up.

2015 Offensive Advanced Metrics

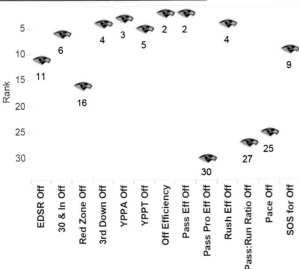

Once again, the Seahawks won with tremendously sound and efficient defense and great offense despite a terrible offensive line. Seattle played a top 10 schedule of opposing defenses, but still ranked top 5 in both pass and rush efficiency. Making their performance more impressive, however, was the injuries they overcame at TE and RB. Marshawn Lynch lasted only 7 games, and rookie RB Thomas Rawls had to take over before he was lost in mid December for the season. The team had to utilize a committee into the playoffs. They also lost star TE Jimmy Graham after 11 disappointing games with just 2 TDs. Thanks to Russell Wilson and the incorporation of Tyler Lockett into the passing attack, the Seahawks offense didn't miss a beat. From weeks 10-17, the offense scored 29+ points in 7 of their 8 games. If the Seahawks can improve their pass protection (30th) and pass rush (15th) in 2016, they will be even more dangerous.

2015 Defensive Advanced Metrics

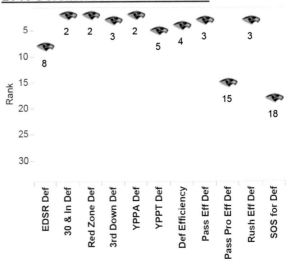

Drafted Players
2016 Draft Grade: #10 (3.1/4)

Seattle Seahawks

Rnd.	Pick #	Pos.	Player	College
1	31	OT	Germain Ifedi	Texas A&M
2	49	DT	Jarran Reed	Alabama
	90	RB	C. J. Prosise	Notre Dame
3	94	TE	Nick Vannett	Ohio State
	97	OT	Rees Odhiambo	Boise State
5	147	DT	Quinton Jefferson	Maryland
	171	RB	Alex Collins	Arkansas
6	215	C	Joey Hunt	TCU
7	243	WR	Kenny Lawler	California
	247	RB	Zac Brooks	Clemson

Lineup & 2016 Cap Hit

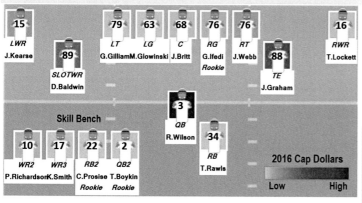

Free Agents/Trades Added

Player (Position)

Bradley Sowell T

Brandon Williams TE

J'Marcus Webb G

Sealver Siliga DT

Other Signed

Player (Position)

Brandin Bryant DT
Christian French DE
David Perkins DE
DeAndre Elliott CB
George Fant TE
Jake Heaps QB
Jamal Marshall CB
Khairi Fortt LB
Lars Koht DT
Lene Maiava T
Montese Overton DE
Pete Robertson LB
Ronnie Shields TE
Steve Longa LB
Taniela Tupou RB
Tanner McEvoy WR
Tre Madden RB
Trevone Boykin QB
Tyler Slavin WR
Tyvis Powell S

2015 Players Lost

Transaction	Player (Position)
Cut	A.J. Francis DT
	Andrew East LB
	Christian French DE
	Clint Gresham C
	Jeff Fuller WR
	Jesse Williams DT
	Lars Koht DT
	Mohammed Seisay CB
	Phillip Sims QB
	Robert Smith S
Declared Free Agent	Brandon Mebane DT
	Bruce Irvin LB
	J.R. Sweezy G
	Ricardo Lockette WR
	Russell Okung T
Retired	Marshawn Lynch RB
	Ricardo Lockette WR

- Seattle's offensive line underwent major changes this offseason. They lost Russell Okung and J.R. Sweezy. In their place, they drafted Germain Ifedi with their first pick (31st overall) and added J'Marcus Webb and Bradley Sowell in free agency. The unit now is the cheapest offensive line in the NFL, as easily depicted by the lineup chart to the left. It's evident how inexpensive the offensive line is compared to the rest of the offense and defense.

- Seattle's strategy defensively has been to build in the secondary and along the line. They continued to do that this offseason as well. Their only two defensive players they drafted are both DTs (Jarran Reed from Alabama and Quinton Jefferson from Maryland). And they re-signed CB Jeremy Lane to a very team friendly deal. As the most expensive members of the secondary age (Richard Sherman, Earl Thomas, Kam Chancellor) it will be important for the Seahawks to monitor their performance and production. With all 3 still in their prime (27 or 28 years old), hopefully Seattle won't need to worry about losing a step for another couple of seasons.

- One of Seattle's issues was their pass protection as well as their pass rush. They ranked 15th in pass rush and 30th in pass protection. Unfortunately they lost Bruce Irvin from their pass rush, as he signed in Oakland this offseason. Seattle will need Frank Clark to take a big step up and will need better play from their 2nd level. LBs K.J. Wright and Bobby Wagner made names for themselves during Seattle's back to back Super Bowl appearances, but need to re-set the bar in 2016 to outperform their 2015 season, particularly Bobby Wagner.

- Thanks to Marshawn Lynch walking away from football, the Seahawks moved from the 6th most expensive RB corps to the 27th in 2016.

- The Seahawks are and have been one of the best teams at identifying young talent and finding players who fit into what they are trying to do. It will be interesting to see them incorporate Jarran Reed & Nick Vannett.

Health Overall & by Unit (2015 v 2014)

2015 Rk	3
2015 AGL	40
Off Rk	9
Def Rk	4
2014 Rk	18
2014 AGL	73

2016 Positional Spending

	All OFF	QB	OL	RB	WR	TE	All DEF	DL	LB	CB	S
2015 Rk	28	21	30	6	24	6	8	7	24	13	1
Rank	31	16	32	27	20	4	4	12	24	8	1
Total	63.4M	19.4M	11.7M	3.7M	15.5M	13.1M	85.7M	27.2M	17.4M	22.6M	18.5M

2016 Offseason Spending

Total Spent	Total Spent Rk	Free Agents #	Free Agents $	Free Agents $ Rk	Waiver #	Waiver $	Waiver $ Rk	Extended #	Sum of Extended $	Sum of Drafted $	Undrafted #	Undrafted $
194M	14	13	60M	15	27	14M	14	2	58M	35M	19	28M

2015 Stats & Fantasy Production

Pos	Player	Ov. Rank	Pos. Rk	Age	Gms	St	Pass Comp	Pass Att	Pass Yds	Pass TD	Pass Int	Rush Att	Rush Yds	Rush YPA	Rush TD	Targ	Recp	Rec Yds	Rec YPC	Rec TDs	Draft King Pts	Fan Duel Pts
QB	Russell Wilson*	21	2	27	16	16	329	483	4,024	34	8	103	553	5	1						353	344
RB	Thomas Rawls		25	22	13	7						147	830	6	4	11	9	76	8	1	132	123
	Marshawn Lynch		56	29	7	6						111	417	4	3	21	13	80	6		86	76
	Fred Jackson		73	34	16							26	100	4		41	32	257	8	2	85	62
WR	Doug Baldwin	15	7	27	16	16										103	78	1,069	14	14	272	230
	Tyler Lockett*+		43	23	16	8						5	20	4		69	51	664	13	6	169	140
	Jermaine Kearse		45	25	16	16										68	49	685	14	5	151	123
TE	Jimmy Graham		16	29	11	11										74	48	605	13	2	124	97
	Luke Willson		45	25	14	7										26	17	213	13	1	47	36

ODDS & TRENDS — Seattle Seahawks

Avg Line	Pred Wins	Pred Div Finish
-5.3	11	#1

2016 Weekly Betting Lines (wks 1-16)

(-) Favorite Underdog (+)
-14.0 ——— +2.0

Avg Line = -5.3

Week	Line	Site
1	-8.5	H
2	-4.0	(ram)
3	-14.0	H
4	+2.0	(away)
6	-10.0	H
7	(underdog)	A
8	-5.0	A
9	-10.0	H
10	(underdog)	A
11	-9.0	H
12	-5.0	A
13	-3.0	
14	+2.0	
15	-10.0	H
16	-3.5	

2015 Critical and Game-Deciding Stats

TO Margin	+7
TO Given	16
INT Given	8
FUM Given	8
TO Taken	23
INT Taken	14
FUM Taken	9
Sack Margin	-9
Sacks	37
Sacks Allow	46
Return TD Margin	+1
Ret TDs	5
Ret TDs Allow	4
Penalty Margin	-23
Penalties	117
Opponent Penalties	94

-Teams that win the turnover battle win 79% of games & cover 79% ATS.
-Teams with more sacks win 71% of games & cover 69% ATS.
-Teams with more return TDs win 75% of games & cover 75% ATS.
-Teams with fewer penalties win 57% of games & cover 54% ATS.

2016 NFLproject.com Forecast

Div RK	1
Div W%	(53%)
Playoffs RK	5
% in Playoffs	(82%)
Super Bowl RK	3
% Win Super Bowl	(15%)

Odds to Win Division
60% — 53%
50% — 42%
40%
30%
20%
10% — 4% 2%
0%
NFCW

Team Records & Trends

	2015	2014	2013
Average line	-5.9	-6.3	-7.9
Average O/U line	43.3	43.7	43.1
Straight Up Record	10-6	12-4	13-3
Against the Spread Record	8-7	10-6	11-5
Over/Under Record	7-9	8-8	6-10
ATS as Favorite	7-6	9-5	10-5
ATS as Underdog	1-1	1-1	1-0
Straight Up Home	5-3	7-1	7-1
ATS Home	4-4	6-2	5-3
Over/Under Home	4-4	4-4	3-5
ATS as Home Favorite	4-4	6-2	5-3
ATS as a Home Dog	0-0	0-0	0-0
Straight Up Away	5-3	5-3	6-2
ATS Away	4-3	4-4	6-2
Over/Under Away	3-5	4-4	3-5
ATS Away Favorite	3-2	3-3	5-2
ATS Away Dog	1-1	1-1	1-0
Six Point Teaser Record	10-6	12-4	12-4
Seven Point Teaser Record	13-3	12-4	13-3
Ten Point Teaser Record	13-2	14-2	14-2

Games Favored
12

Games Underdog
3

Close Game Records

All 2015 Wins: **10**
FG Games (<=3 pts) W-L: **2-2**
FG Games Win %: **50% (#15)**
FG Games Wins (% of Total Wins): **20% (#18)**
1 Score Games (<=8 pts) W-L: **2-5**
1 Score Games Win %: **29% (#27)**
1 Score Games Wins (% of Total Wins): **20% (#32)**

Home Lines (wks 1-16)

Avg Line = -8.5 ... Avg Line = -8.5

1	3	6	9	11	15
-8.5	-14.0	-10.0	-10.0	-9.0	-10.0

Road Lines (wks 1-16)

Avg Line = -1.6 ... Avg Line = -1.6

2	4	8	12
-4.0	-2.0	-5.0	-5.0
	+2.0	+2.0	+2.0

Regular Season Wins: Past Results & Current Proj

	Wins
2012 Wins	11
2013 Wins	13
2014 Wins	12
Proj 2015 Wins	11
2015 Wins	10
Proj 2016 Wins	11

Since Russell Wilson's rookie season in 2012, the Seahawks have always posted double digit wins. Linesmakers predict the same will happen in 2016. Seattle won 10 games last season, but that was despite a lot working against them. While they were +7 in turnover margin, they were -9 in sack margin and -23 in penalty margin. They also went a mere 2-5 in one-score games. That 29% win rate in one-score games was 27th in the NFL. And winning just 2 of 10 (20%) games by one-score was the smallest rate of one-score wins that contributed to total wins for any team last year. They were relatively healthy but did suffer key injuries at positions that hurt worse to a team like Seattle, such as RB and TE. With rebuilding destined to occur in San Francisco and Los Angeles, it likely is another two bird race in the NFC West, and could be very likely that both make the playoffs.

2016 Rest Analysis

Avg Rest	6.5
Avg Rest Rk	3
Team More Rest	4
Opp More Rest	1
Net Rest Edge	3
3 days rest	1
4 days rest	0
5 days rest	1
6 days rest	9
7 days rest	2
8 days rest	1
9 days rest	0
10 days rest	0
11 days rest	0
12 days rest	0
13 days rest	1
14 days rest	0

Weekly EDSR & Season Trending Performance

Week by Week 2015 Results

WEEK	1	2	3	4	5	6	7	8	10	11	12	13	14	15	16	17
RESULT	L	L	W	W	L	L	W	W	L	W	W	W	W	W	L	W
OPP	STL	GB	CHI	DET	CIN	CAR	SF	DAL	ARI	SF	PIT	MIN	BAL	CLE	STL	ARI
SITE	A	A	H	A	H	A	H	A	H	H	H	A	A	H	H	A
MARGIN	-3	-10	26	3	-3	-4	17	1	-7	16	9	31	29	17	-6	30
PTS	31	17	26	13	24	23	20	13	32	29	39	38	35	30	17	36
OPP PTS	34	27	0	10	27	27	3	12	39	13	30	7	6	13	23	6

EDSR Results (W/L) By Week
W=Green
L=Red

Off & Def EDSR Wk & Trend
- Blue=Offense (high=good)
- Red=Defense (low=good)

STATS & VISUALIZATIONS

Seattle Seahawks

Directional Passer Rating Achieved

Receiver	Short Left	Short Middle	Short Right	Deep Left	Deep Middle	Deep Right
Doug Baldwin	106	121	133	74	152	101
Jermaine Kearse	109	144	117	120	13	153
Tyler Lockett	93	155	103	129	79	104
Jimmy Graham	76	95	89	118	118	64
Luke Willson	75	98	103	39	39	118
Cooper Helfet	71	73	82	39		
Kevin Smith	86		118			39
Chase Coffman	39	95	98		0	
Chris Matthews	87	70	85			39
Ricardo Lockette	56		70	158		
B.J. Daniels	91	116				
Kasen Williams			100			
Paul Richardson			118			

Directional Frequency by Receiver

Receiver	Short Left	Short Middle	Short Right	Deep Left	Deep Middle	Deep Right
Doug Baldwin	24%	24%	30%	30%	42%	18%
Jermaine Kearse	26%	12%	14%	38%	13%	18%
Tyler Lockett	17%	13%	13%	19%	21%	38%
Jimmy Graham	14%	27%	17%	3%	17%	13%
Luke Willson	9%	12%	6%	3%	8%	3%
Cooper Helfet	2%	5%	9%	3%		
Kevin Smith	2%		2%			3%
Chase Coffman	1%	3%	3%			3%
Chris Matthews	2%	3%	2%			5%
Ricardo Lockette	2%		3%	3%		
B.J. Daniels	1%	1%				
Kasen Williams			1%			
Paul Richardson			3%			

Defense Passer Rating Allowed

Short Left	Short Middle	Short Right	Deep Left	Deep Middle	Deep Right
82	107	74	78	85	71

Offensive Rush Directional Yds/Carry

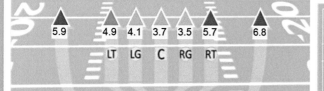

5.9 | 4.9 | 4.1 | 3.7 | 3.5 | 5.7 | 6.8
LT | LG | C | RG | RT

Offensive Rush Frequency of Direction

52 | 70 | 71 | 146 | 42 | 76 | 60
LT | LG | C | RG | RT

Offensive Explosive Runs by Direction

13 | 10 | 7 | 10 | 3 | 11 | 12
LT | LG | C | RG | RT

Defensive Rush Directional Yds/Carry

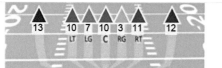

6.3 | 3.7 | 4.3 | 2.4 | 3.3 | 4.6 | 2.6
LT | LG | C | RG | RT

Russell Wilson - 1st Down RTG

128.8 | 125.7 | 135.4
93.6
84.7 | 94.1

Russell Wilson - 3rd Down RTG

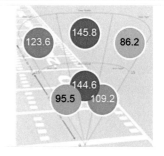

123.6 | 145.8 | 86.2
144.6
95.5 | 109.2

Russell Wilson - 2nd Down RTG

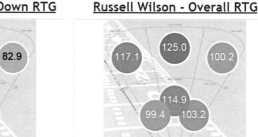

51.0 | 104.2 | 82.9
100.0
119.0 | 109.7

Russell Wilson - Overall RTG

117.1 | 125.0 | 100.2
114.9
99.4 | 103.2

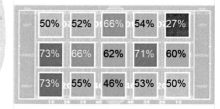

2nd & Short RUN (1D or not)

2nd & Short RUN Stats

Run Conv Rk	1D% Run	NFL 1D% Run Avg	Run Freq	NFL Run Freq Avg
11	75%	69%	78%	64%

2nd & Short PASS (1D or not)

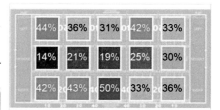

2nd & Short PASS Stats

Pass Conv Rk	1D% Pass	NFL 1D% Pass Avg	Pass Freq	NFL Pass Freq Avg
6	63%	55%	22%	36%

Pass Offense Play Success Rate

50%	52%	66%	54%	27%
73%	66%	62%	71%	60%
73%	55%	46%	53%	50%

Pass Offense Yds/Play

6.2	6.6	11.6	8.2	3.0
9.4	9.1	11.4	12.1	7.1
12.0	8.8	7.4	8.4	4.5

Off. Directional Tendency
(% of Plays Left, Middle or Right)

44%	36%	31%	42%	33%
14%	21%	19%	25%	30%
42%	43%	50%	33%	36%

Off. Directional Pass Rate
(% of Plays which are Passes)

57%	59%	62%	68%	69%
20%	34%	34%	35%	31%
55%	60%	71%	61%	65%

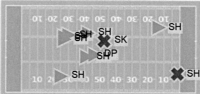

Arizona Cardinals

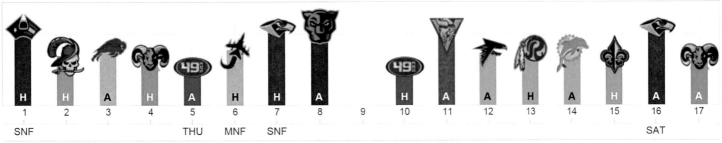

Coaches

Head Coach: Bruce Arians (4th yr)
OC: Harold Goodwin (4th yr)
DC: James Bettcher (2nd yr)

Forecast 2016 Wins

10

Past Records

2015: 13-3
2014: 11-5
2013: 10-6

Opponent Strength
Easy   Hard

2016 Schedule & Week by Week Strength of Schedule

1	2	3	4	5	6	7	8	9	10	11	12	13	14	15	16	17
H	H	A	H	A	H	H	A		H	A	A	H	A	H	A	A

SNF   THU   MNF   SNF   SAT

2016 Overview

Like an aged cigar or liquor, Bruce Arians gets better with time. At Temple, Arians was 21-39 (35%) and struggled. As an NFL offensive coordinator, Arians helped his teams record a 87-57 (60%) record. As an NFL head coach, that record improved further to 32-18 (71%). What has been so successful for Arians in Arizona? The best part about his tenure has been his ability to do what he wants without reproach or being talked out of it by ownership. That has allowed the team to quickly assimilate his personality and style. Aggressive. Leaving no arrow in the quiver. Both offensively and defensively.

Such an approach typically would not lead toward efficiency. It would lead to boom or bust. The opposite of aim small, miss small. Huge plays can change the game quickly. And have a big impact on wins and losses. But boom or bust is not typically correlated to efficiency. Efficiency on early downs is critical, and the Cardinals under Bruce Arians have not been great when trying to run on early downs. "Not great" is actually an upsell. Arizona has gained 3.7 yards per carry on early down runs under Arians, the 2nd worst in the NFL. Sitting a the opposite end are teams like Seattle, Dallas, Kansas City, Minnesota and Green Bay, who have a collective 153 games in those 3 years. Arizona sits with NY Giants, San Diego, Detroit and Cleveland in the bottom 5. Yet while those other teams have won a collective 81 games in those 3 years (an avg of 6.75 per yr), Arizona alone has won 35 games, or 11.7 per year.

Despite the NFL's 2nd worst run offense on early downs, Arizona has excelled in passing efficiency on early downs. Last year, Carson Palmer led the NFL with 8.5 yds/att on early down passing. The team gained new first downs on 38% of first or second down passing, the best rate in the NFL. Bruce Arians has somehow created a deep passing offense which is also the most efficient in the NFL on early downs. That is an extremely dangerous combination. One of Arians next goals needs to be to improve the Cardinals red zone offense, which was one of the offense's biggest Achilles' heels last year. A virtually unstoppable deep passing offense that can't be stopped by opponents is stopped by one thing: the inability to run deep routes near the goal line. From week 4 onward, when passing the ball, 58% of Arians' play calls graded as successful plays, second best in the NFL. But when inside the red zone, that plummeted by almost 20%, and dropped from second best to 26th in the NFL. Everywhere else on the field, Palmer had the 5th best passer rating. But his rating dropped to 22nd in the NFL inside the red zone, even behind young players such as Marcus Mariota's 128, Blaine Gabbert's 124, Kirk Cousins 113, Blake Bortles' 94 and Jameis Winston's 92.

If Bruce Arians is able to fix this, the Cardinals offense will be even more productive in 2016, which is a scary thought. But the defense must improve to take this team all the way to their ultimate goal. Tyrann Mathieu must return quickly and healthy from his torn ACL. The secondary as a whole must play better, and with their propensity to blitz the opposing quarterback, the pass rush led by Chandler Jones must hit home. There is little doubt the Cardinals offense will be strong once again, and could be scary-strong with improved red zone production or early down rushing. As fun as the Arians-led offense is to watch, the key to unlock the ultimate prize might lie on the defensive side of the ball for the 2016 Cardinals.

Strength of Schedule In Detail

True Strength of Schedule Rank: 22

Hardest Stretches *(1=Hard, 32=Easy)*

Hardest 3 wk Stretch Rk:	7
Hardest 4 wk Stretch Rk:	26
Hardest 5 wk Stretch Rk:	28

Easiest Stretches *(1=Easy, 32=Hard)*

Easiest 3 wk Stretch Rk:	11
Easiest 4 wk Stretch Rk:	8
Easiest 5 wk Stretch Rk:	8

Unlike the Seahawks gradual start and tough finish, Arizona starts off immediately with a tough game vs the Patriots in primetime. However, they enjoy several extremely easy stretches. Weeks 2-6 they face the 3rd easiest schedule of any team during those weeks, and from week 12 onward, they play just one team predicted to have a winning record (@ SEA). They also have just one back-to-back road game trip on their schedule.

2015 Play Tendencies

All Pass %	57%
All Pass Rk	23
All Rush %	43%
All Rush Rk	10
1 Score Pass %	59%
1 Score Pass Rk	14
2014 1 Score Pass %	58%
2014 1 Score Pass Rk	14
Pass Increase %	0%
Pass Increase Rk	19
1 Score Rush %	41%
1 Score Rush Rk	19
Up Pass %	50%
Up Pass Rk	13
Up Rush %	50%
Up Rush Rk	20
Down Pass %	71%
Down Pass Rk	6
Down Rush %	29%
Down Rush Rk	27

The Cardinals were a very balanced team from a play tendency perspective. They passed the ball with almost the exact same frequency in 2015 as they did in 2014, and it was right at 59%, 14th in the NFL. They did go more pass heavy when trailing, increasing that rate to 71%, 6th most, but overall, thanks to large leads, the Cardinals were able to call plenty of 2nd half runs. It is hard to envision the winning formula changing in 2016.

2015 Offensive Advanced Metrics

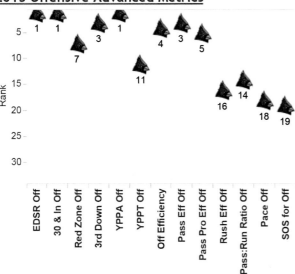

The secret about the 2015 Cardinals was their inability to pressure the opposing QB. As such, it was their only metric that ranked below 15th, but ultimately it showed when playing stronger defenses with capable offenses. Offensively, the Cardinals and the pass game, led by Bruce Arians, was nothing short of magical. Their run game ranked only 16th in efficiency, but thanks to their play calling, balance and pace, the Cardinals were the NFL's best EDSR offense in 2016. However, a major issue for the Cardinals which began to show itself week 4, and that was their offensive inefficiency inside the red zone. The Cardinals were successful on just 39% of red zone plays, 26th in the NFL. It was particularly a problem in the pass game. The rest of the field, the Cardinals had a 58% success rate on pass plays, #2 in the NFL. But it plummeted almost 20%, from #2 down to #26 in the red zone. The deep pass offense was problematic with less real estate.

2015 Defensive Advanced Metrics

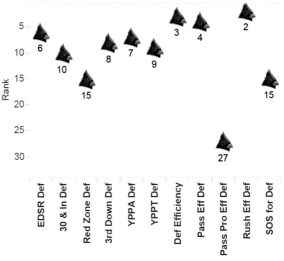

Drafted Players

2016 Draft Grade: #18 (2.9/4)

Rnd.	Pick #	Pos.	Player	College
1	29	DT	Robert Nkemdiche	Ole Miss
3	92	CB	Brandon Williams	Texas A&M
4	128	C	Evan Boehm	Missouri
5	167	S	Marqui Christian	Midwestern State
5	170	OT	Cole Toner	Harvard
6	205	CB	Harlan Miller	Southeastern Louisiana

Lineup & 2016 Cap Hit

PERSONNEL & SPENDING

Free Agents/Trades Added

Player (Position)

Chandler Jones LB

Evan Mathis G

Tyvon Branch S

Other Signed

Player (Position)

Amir Carlisle WR
Chris Hubert WR
Chris King WR
Clay DeBord T
Daniel Dillon TE
Elie Bouka CB
Elijhaa Penny RB
Garrett Swanson P
Givens Price T
Hakeem Valles TE
Jake Coker QB
Jared Baker RB
Jeff Beathard WR
Kameron Canaday DE
Lamar Louis LB
Matthias Farley S
Ronald Zamort CB
Trevon Hartfield CB

2015 Players Lost

Transaction	Player (Position)
Cut	Cory Redding DE
	Coughman, Edawn G
	Damond Powell WR
	Jared Baker RB
	Joel Wilkinson CB
	John Fullington G
	Kevin White CB
	Marion Grice RB
	Mike Reilly LB
	Robert Hughes RB
	Tyrequek Zimmerman S
	Valerian Ume-Ezeoke C
Declared Free Agent	Bobby Massie T
	Jerraud Powers CB
	Rashad Johnson S

- As noted the primary weakness for the 2015 Arizona Cardinals was their pass rush. They addressed that immediately and quickly by acquiring Chandler Jones from New England via a trade. The problem for Arizona wasn't just that they were 27th in pass rush efficiency. Their blitz frequency was incredible. Under Bruce Arians, the Cardinals have blitzed on 46% of opposing dropbacks, far and away the most in the NFL. When you blitz that often, and when such a small percentage of opponent dropbacks result in sacks, it will take a toll on your defensive secondary. Luckily, the Cardinals have Patrick Peterson and Tyrann Mathieu. But they needed someone who would get after the passer with a better frequency, and Jones should accomplish that goal.
- The Cardinals added Robert Nkemdiche, the DT from Ole Miss with their first overall pick, and only selection of the first 90 players. Nkemdiche has a spotted past, and would run into trouble in a number of NFL cities. But in Arizona, with the leadership of Bruce Arians, the veteran presence of team leaders like Larry Fitzgerald and Carson Palmer, and a defensive star who had his share of issues when younger in Tyrann Mathieu, there are few places that would have been a better landing spot than Arizona.
- When you look around the NFL, many teams are built oddly for their strength and strategy. The Cardinals are not one of those teams. Offensively, they have the 2nd most expensive WR corps, which makes sense because their offense is built around an aggressive downfield passing game. The QB position is 10th most expensive and O-Line 15th. They've spent the least at RB (21st) and TE (17th). Defensively, with leads they build and opponent's need to pass, they've built a frequent pass rush team who must cover on the backend. As such, they have the 7th most expensive D-Line, 12th most expensive CB corps and 8th most expensive safeties. They've saved money at the LB position (31st) so they could build the secondary and D-Line.

Health Overall & by Unit (2015 v 2014)

2015 Rk	14
2015 AGL	63
Off Rk	4
Def Rk	25
2014 Rk	17
2014 AGL	73

2016 Positional Spending

	All OFF	QB	OL	RB	WR	TE	All DEF	DL	LB	CB	S
2015 Rk	11	17	4	25	8	21	11	10	26	5	22
Rank	2	11	15	23	2	17	13	7	31	12	8
Total	88.7M	21.5M	26.9M	5.2M	29.0M	6.1M	77.7M	32.8M	9.6M	22.1M	13.2M

2016 Offseason Spending

Total Spent	Total Spent Rk	Free Agents #	Free Agents $	Free Agents $ Rk	Waiver #	Waiver $	Waiver $ Rk	Extended #	Sum of Extended $	Sum of Drafted $	Undrafted #	Undrafted $
93M	32	5	18M	28	22	11M	19	4	10M	22M	19	31M

2015 Stats & Fantasy Production

Pos	Player	Ov. Rank	Pos. Rk	Age	Gms	St	Pass Comp	Pass Att	Pass Yds	Pass TD	Pass Int	Rush Att	Rush Yds	Rush YPA	Rush TD	Targ	Recp	Rec Yds	Rec YPC	Rec TDs	Draft King Pts	Fan Duel Pts
QB	Carson Palmer*	45	5	36	16	16	342	537	4,671	35	11	25	24	1	1						325	320
RB	David Johnson	24	7	24	16	5						125	581	5	8	57	36	457	13	4	223	198
	Chris Johnson		35	30	11	9						196	814	4	3	13	6	58	10		112	104
	Andre Ellington		62	26	10	3						45	289	6	3	24	15	148	10		82	67
WR	Larry Fitzgerald*	29	11	32	16	16										145	109	1,215	11	9	286	226
	John Brown	53	21	25	15	11						3	22	7		101	65	1,003	15	7	212	175
	Michael Floyd		33	26	15	6										89	52	849	16	6	176	147
	JJ Nelson		96	23	11	2						1				27	11	299	27	2	55	45
	Jaron Brown		129	25	16											23	11	144	13	1	34	26
TE	Darren Fells		33	29	14	12										28	21	311	15	3	73	60
	Jermaine Gresham		44	27	15	12										32	18	223	12	1	49	37

14

Arizona Cardinals

Avg Line	-3.6	Pred Wins	10	Pred Div Finish	#2

2016 Weekly Betting Lines (wks 1-16)

(-) Favorite   Underdog (+)
-10.5   +3.5

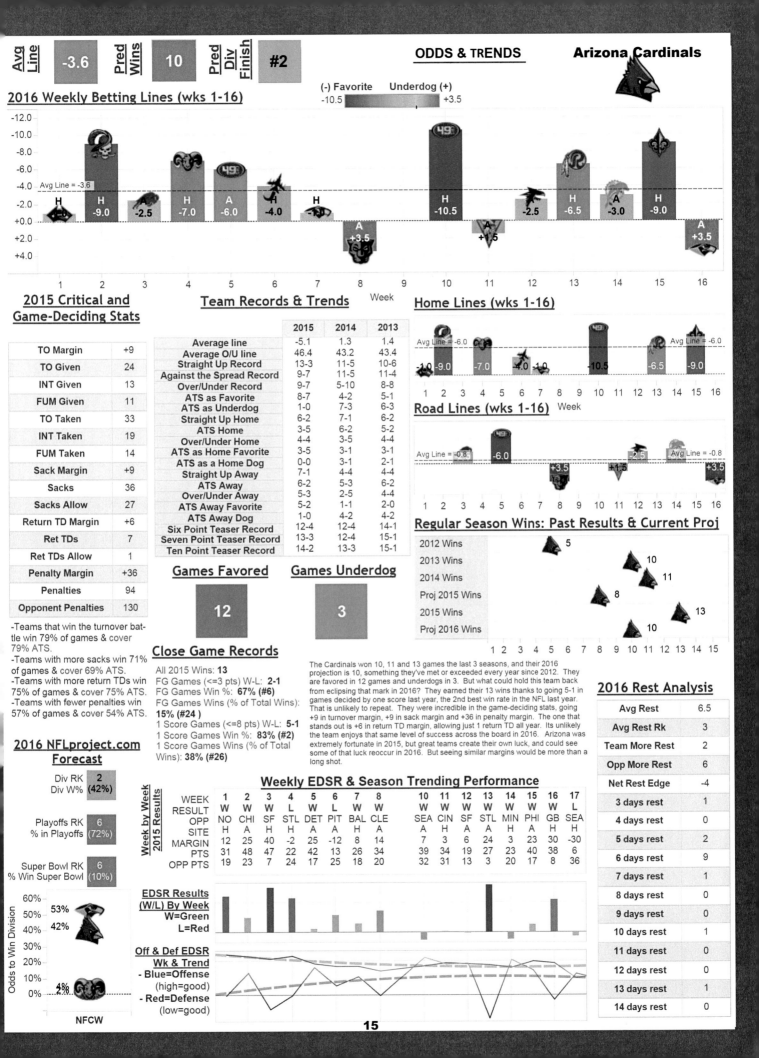

Avg Line = -3.6

Week

2015 Critical and Game-Deciding Stats

TO Margin	+9
TO Given	24
INT Given	13
FUM Given	11
TO Taken	33
INT Taken	19
FUM Taken	14
Sack Margin	+9
Sacks	36
Sacks Allow	27
Return TD Margin	+6
Ret TDs	7
Ret TDs Allow	1
Penalty Margin	+36
Penalties	94
Opponent Penalties	130

-Teams that win the turnover battle win 79% of games & cover 79% ATS.
-Teams with more sacks win 71% of games & cover 69% ATS.
-Teams with more return TDs win 75% of games & cover 75% ATS.
-Teams with fewer penalties win 57% of games & cover 54% ATS.

2016 NFLproject.com Forecast

Div RK	2
Div W%	(42%)

Playoffs RK	6
% in Playoffs	(72%)

Super Bowl RK	6
% Win Super Bowl	(10%)

Odds to Win Division
60%
53%
50%
42%
40%
30%
20%
10%
4%
0%
NFCW

Team Records & Trends

	2015	2014	2013
Average line	-5.1	1.3	1.4
Average O/U line	46.4	43.2	43.4
Straight Up Record	13-3	11-5	10-6
Against the Spread Record	9-7	11-5	11-4
Over/Under Record	9-7	5-10	8-8
ATS as Favorite	8-7	4-2	5-1
ATS as Underdog	1-0	7-3	6-3
Straight Up Home	6-2	7-1	6-2
ATS Home	3-5	6-2	5-2
Over/Under Home	4-4	3-5	4-4
ATS as Home Favorite	3-5	3-1	3-1
ATS as a Home Dog	0-0	3-1	2-1
Straight Up Away	7-1	4-4	4-4
ATS Away	6-2	5-3	6-2
Over/Under Away	5-3	2-5	4-4
ATS Away Favorite	5-2	1-1	2-0
ATS Away Dog	1-0	4-2	4-2
Six Point Teaser Record	12-4	12-4	14-1
Seven Point Teaser Record	13-3	12-4	15-1
Ten Point Teaser Record	14-2	13-3	15-1

Games Favored

12

Games Underdog

3

Close Game Records

All 2015 Wins: 13
FG Games (<=3 pts) W-L: 2-1
FG Games Win %: 67% (#6)
FG Games Wins (% of Total Wins): 15% (#24)
1 Score Games (<=8 pts) W-L: 5-1
1 Score Games Win %: 83% (#2)
1 Score Games Wins (% of Total Wins): 38% (#26)

The Cardinals won 10, 11 and 13 games the last 3 seasons, and their 2016 projection is 10, something they've met or exceeded every year since 2012. They are favored in 12 games and underdogs in 3. But what could hold this team back from eclipsing that mark in 2016? They earned their 13 wins thanks to going 5-1 in games decided by one score last year, the 2nd best win rate in the NFL last year. That is unlikely to repeat. They were incredible in the game-deciding stats, going +9 in turnover margin, +9 in sack margin and +36 in penalty margin. The one that stands out is +6 in return TD margin, allowing just 1 return TD all year. Its unlikely the team enjoys that same level of success across the board in 2016. Arizona was extremely fortunate in 2015, but great teams create their own luck, and could see some of that luck reoccur in 2016. But seeing similar margins would be more than a long shot.

Home Lines (wks 1-16)

Avg Line = -6.0

Avg Line = -6.0

-10.0 -9.0 -7.0 -4.0 -1.0 -10.5 -6.5 -9.0

Week

Road Lines (wks 1-16) Week

Avg Line = -0.8

Avg Line = -0.8

-6.0 +3.5 +1.5 2.5 +3.5

Regular Season Wins: Past Results & Current Proj

2012 Wins	
2013 Wins	
2014 Wins	
Proj 2015 Wins	
2015 Wins	
Proj 2016 Wins	

5
10
11
8
13
10

2016 Rest Analysis

Avg Rest	6.5
Avg Rest Rk	3
Team More Rest	2
Opp More Rest	6
Net Rest Edge	-4
3 days rest	1
4 days rest	0
5 days rest	2
6 days rest	9
7 days rest	1
8 days rest	0
9 days rest	0
10 days rest	1
11 days rest	0
12 days rest	0
13 days rest	1
14 days rest	0

Weekly EDSR & Season Trending Performance

Week by Week 2015 Results	WEEK	1	2	3	4	5	6	7	8	10	11	12	13	14	15	16	17
	RESULT	W	W	W	L	W	L	W	W	W	W	W	W	W	W	W	L
	OPP	NO	CHI	SF	STL	DET	PIT	BAL	CLE	SEA	CIN	SF	STL	MIN	PHI	GB	SEA
	SITE	H	A	H	A	H	H	A	A	A	H	A	A	H	A	H	H
	MARGIN	12	25	40	-2	25	-12	8	14	7	3	6	24	3	23	30	-30
	PTS	31	48	47	22	42	13	26	34	39	34	19	27	23	40	38	6
	OPP PTS	19	23	7	24	17	25	18	20	32	31	13	3	20	17	8	36

EDSR Results (W/L) By Week
W=Green
L=Red

Off & Def EDSR Wk & Trend
- Blue=Offense (high=good)
- Red=Defense (low=good)

STATS & VISUALIZATIONS

Arizona Cardinals

Directional Passer Rating Achieved

Receiver	Short Left	Short Middle	Short Right	Deep Left	Deep Middle	Deep Right
Larry Fitzgerald	105	133	120	64	118	105
John Brown	86	88	102	122	65	115
Michael Floyd	68	87	141	56	94	80
Darren Fells	88	111	118	39	158	145
Jermaine Gresham	83	67	65	87	118	
J.J. Nelson	2	39	87	95	26	135
Jaron Brown	135	9	70	42	45	39
Troy Niklas	152	110	118			
Brittan Golden				87		

Directional Frequency by Receiver

Receiver	Short Left	Short Middle	Short Right	Deep Left	Deep Middle	Deep Right
Larry Fitzgerald	40%	39%	35%	21%	13%	22%
John Brown	25%	11%	20%	19%	31%	27%
Michael Floyd	17%	13%	18%	34%	27%	27%
Darren Fells	3%	17%	6%	2%	4%	5%
Jermaine Gresham	8%	12%	6%	4%	2%	
J.J. Nelson	3%	1%	5%	13%	18%	7%
Jaron Brown	4%	4%	8%	6%	4%	11%
Troy Niklas	1%	2%	1%			
Brittan Golden			1%			

Defense Passer Rating Allowed

Short Left	Short Middle	Short Right	Deep Left	Deep Middle	Deep Right
85	99	80	96	96	23

Offensive Rush Directional Yds/Carry

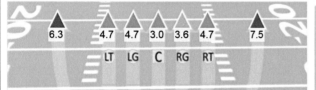

6.3	4.7	4.7	3.0	3.6	4.7	7.5
	LT	LG	C	RG	RT	

Offensive Rush Frequency of Direction

42	78	26	157	32	77	45
	LT	LG	C	RG	RT	

Offensive Explosive Runs by Direction

8	7	4	9	2	11	12
	LT	LG	C	RG	RT	

Defensive Rush Directional Yds/Carry

5.2	3.6	4.6	4.1	4.1	2.4	5.3
	LT	LG	C	RG	RT	

Carson Palmer - 1st Down RTG

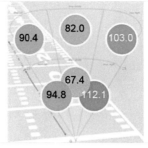

90.4, 82.0, 103.0, 67.4, 94.8, 112.1

Carson Palmer - 3rd Down RTG

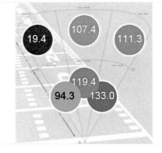

19.4, 107.4, 111.3, 119.4, 94.3, 133.0

Carson Palmer - 2nd Down RTG

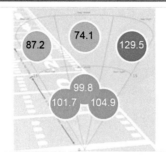

87.2, 74.1, 129.5, 99.8, 101.7, 104.9

Carson Palmer - Overall RTG

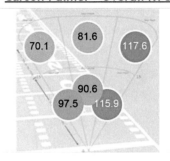

70.1, 81.6, 117.6, 90.6, 97.5, 115.9

2nd & Short RUN (1D or not)

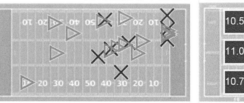

2nd & Short RUN Stats

Run Conv Rk	1D% Run	NFL 1D% Run Avg	Run Freq	NFL Run Freq Avg
25	63%	69%	59%	64%

2nd & Short PASS (1D or not)

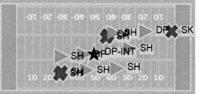

2nd & Short PASS Stats

Pass Conv Rk	1D% Pass	NFL 1D% Pass Avg	Pass Freq	NFL Pass Freq Avg
19	54%	55%	41%	36%

Pass Offense Play Success Rate

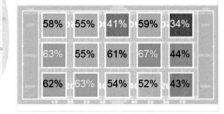

58%	55%	41%	59%	34%
63%	55%	61%	67%	44%
62%	63%	54%	52%	43%

Pass Offense Yds/Play

10.5	8.8	6.1	8.4	4.4
11.0	7.8	7.9	10.3	4.5
10.7	11.2	10.4	7.7	4.3

Off. Directional Tendency (% of Plays Left, Middle or Right)

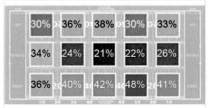

30%	36%	38%	30%	33%
34%	24%	21%	22%	26%
36%	40%	42%	48%	41%

Off. Directional Pass Rate (% of Plays which are Passes)

51%	72%	66%	62%	65%
55%	43%	44%	33%	40%
70%	61%	64%	78%	75%

16

Situational Player Production

Much like the fallacy of looking only at cumulative stats to measure performance, far too often fantasy players don't take context into consideration when forecasting production. Game flow is an essential component, as most professionals understand. It's easy to look from week to week in daily fantasy and anticipate games where a team may be trailing and need to pass the ball more often, or leading and thus can pound the run. But the challenge is more difficult in offseason. Many fantasy players lose sight of the context in which 2015 statistics were achieved, and instead look back to full season numbers sprinkled with "recollection" of how often a team was in those certain situations.

Production in 2014 or 2015 won't predict 2016 production, but understanding the context in which it was achieved helps understand framework for projecting 2016 performance: team philosophy, situational production edges and reasons to discount or accentuate production. As such, I wanted to look at 2015 production to better understand when it was achieved given game situation.

While optimal efficiency is likely to be achieved when refusing to be so wed to binary opposition in analysis, unfortunately most coaches coach rely on black-and-white decision making as opposed to shades of grey. As such, particularly in the 2nd half, most will look at the scoreboard, see if they are ahead or behind, and coach accordingly. They will see if they are up by over 1 score (9+ points) to help aide in their play calling. Thus, examining production based on these simple categories is extremely telling.

Once a player's prior production is thoroughly understood using these methods, it should be applied to the 2016 season based on perceived matchups. Will a player still be trailing as often as they were in 2014 or 2015? Is his team better/worse? Will the team choose to run more because more favorable game flow is projected for their run game?

Between this analysis and the remainder of this 2016 Football Preview magazine, readers should be able to put both pieces together to not only better understand prior production, but better predict 2016 forecasts.

I teamed up with Rotoworld's Evan Silva to utilize his current projections at each position, and overlaid my analysis of situational player production from the last two years. The results are follow. I'll add a few comments on each position group to draw your attention to certain player situations.

Pay close attention to the "VAR RK" column, as it ranks the variance between a player's production in a certain situation and how often the team was in that situation. For instance, while the highest rate, it's not a revelation that Tom Brady recorded 56% of his production when leading, as his team led 55% of all offensive snaps.

Garbage time is defined (for the purposes of this analysis) as the 4th quarter, when one team is ahead or behind by over 10 points.

Name	Evan Silva RK	Team	All Production: Lead	RK	Team %	% VAR	VAR RK	Trail	RK	Team %	% VAR	VAR RK	Large Margin: 9+ Lead	RK	Team %	% VAR	VAR RK	9+ Trail	RK	Team %	% VAR	VAR RK	Garbage Time: No	RK	Team %	% VAR	VAR RK	Yes: Lead	RK	Team %	% VAR	VAR RK	Yes: Trail	RK	Team %	% VAR	VAR RK
Cam Newton	QB1	CAR	39%	9	42%	-4%	22	38%	22	33%	5%	9	19%	6	19%	0%	11	17%	21	17%	0%	16	90%	7	88%	2%	9	3%	9	6%	-3%	21	5%	23	5%	0%	19
Aaron Rodgers	QB2	GNB	44%	3	47%	-3%	20	34%	26	33%	1%	17	19%	5	20%	-1%	12	17%	23	15%	2%	12	92%	6	90%	1%	12	3%	11	6%	-3%	26	5%	22	3%	2%	10
Drew Brees	QB3	NOR	33%	15	34%	0%	11	47%	13	48%	-1%	20	9%	21	11%	-3%	22	24%	13	25%	-1%	18	84%	24	84%	0%	16	3%	10	5%	-2%	15	11%	8	10%	1%	13
Russell Wilson	QB4	SEA	44%	4	46%	-2%	14	38%	23	32%	5%	11	25%	3	28%	-4%	23	13%	25	9%	4%	8	90%	8	87%	3%	7	7%	2	11%	-4%	27	2%	26	1%	1%	17
Andrew Luck	QB5	IND	42%	7	41%	2%	6	42%	17	39%	4%	11	26%	2	20%	6%	1	31%	7	23%	8%	2	83%	26	86%	-3%	24	6%	4	5%	1%	1	12%	6	9%	3%	5
Ben Roethlisberger	QB6	PIT	46%	2	43%	3%	5	35%	25	37%	-1%	22	18%	7	15%	3%	10	18%	20	15%	3%	16	86%	20	86%	0%	23	6%	3	6%	0%	19	5%	20	5%	3%	7
Carson Palmer	QB7	ARI	42%	8	44%	-2%	15	31%	27	34%	-3%	24	15%	12	15%	0%	10	9%	27	12%	-3%	26	95%	1	90%	5%	3	4%	8	6%	-3%	20	2%	28	4%	-2%	25
Tom Brady	QB8	NWE	56%	1	55%	1%	9	25%	28	26%	-2%	23	30%	1	31%	-1%	13	7%	28	8%	-2%	24	90%	9	86%	3%	8	8%	1	11%	-3%	23	2%	27	2%	0%	22
Philip Rivers	QB9	SDG	25%	23	29%	-4%	23	60%	7	54%	5%	7	7%	26	10%	-3%	20	24%	15	22%	-1%	19	89%	10	88%	1%	14	1%	23	2%	-2%	11	10%	13	9%	1%	15
Andy Dalton	QB10	CIN	43%	6	48%	-5%	24	35%	24	30%	6%	5	17%	10	23%	-6%	26	13%	26	14%	-1%	23	93%	3	86%	7%	1	3%	12	8%			28	2%	25	5%	-3%	26
Blake Bortles	QB11	JAX	8%	28	14%	-6%	26	79%	1	67%	12%	1	2%	28	4%	-2%	19	45%	1	32%	12%	1	79%	28	86%	-7%	27	2%	19	2%	0%	4	20%	1	12%	7%	2
Eli Manning	QB12	NYG	28%	18	34%	-5%	25	51%	12	48%	4%	12	10%	17	15%	-5%	25	19%	19	19%	1%	13	87%	19	89%	-2%	22	3%	13	4%	-1%	5	10%	7	11%	-1%	16
Derek Carr	QB13	OAK	23%	25	21%	2%	7	61%	5	62%	-1%	24	8%	22	7%	1%	6	28%	9	31%	-3%	27	87%	17	87%	0%	17	3%	17	4%	-1%	7	11%	7	10%	1%	16
Kirk Cousins	QB14	WAS	35%	13	32%	3%	4	41%	19	46%	-5%	27	16%	11	14%	2%	5	25%	12	25%	-1%	21	89%	11	86%	4%	6	3%	17	4%	-1%	9	8%	16	10%	-1%	23
Tony Romo	QB15	DAL	38%	10	34%	4%	2	39%	20	43%	-4%	26	19%	4	15%	4%	2	17%	22	18%	-1%	26	94%	2	88%	6%	2	2%	21	4%	-3%	19	4%	24	7%		27
Matt Ryan	QB16	ATL	25%	22	28%	-3%	21	62%	4	56%	6%	4	8%	23	10%	6%	24	31%	6	24%	7%	3	88%	12	87%	1%	19	1%	22	3%	-2%	16	11%	9	8%	3%	8
Jay Cutler	QB17	CHI	15%	27	18%	-3%	19	69%	2	64%	5%	6	3%	27	5%	-2%	18	32%	4	28%	5%	7	87%	18	88%	-1%	20	0%	27	2%	-2%	13	13%	4	10%	3%	6
Tyrod Taylor	QB18	BUF	36%	11	35%	1%	8	44%	16	44%	0%	18	10%	16	13%	-3%	21	30%	8	23%	7%	4	83%	25	87%	-4%	26	3%	15	5%	-2%	17	14%	3	8%	6%	3
Marcus Mariota	QB19	TEN	20%	26	22%	-1%	12	60%	6	64%	-3%	25	8%	24	7%	1%	8	33%	3	40%		28	88%	14	84%	4%	5	0%	28	2%	-1%	14	10%	14	14%		28
Jameis Winston	QB20	TAM	24%	24	24%	0%	10	62%	3	61%	1%	15	9%	20	8%	1%	7	36%	2	30%	5%	5	80%	27	87%		28	0%	26	2%	-1%	4	19%	2	10%		
Ryan Fitzpatrick	QB21	NYJ	36%	12	29%	7%	1	46%	15	55%		28	17%	9	14%	3%	3	25%	11	26%	-1%	20	85%	21	86%	-1%	21	4%	6	4%	0%	3	9%	15	9%	0%	21
Matthew Stafford		DET	35%	14	38%	-3%	17	42%	18	43%	-1%	19	13%	14	14%	-1%	16	20%	16	20%	0%	14	87%	16	86%	2%	11	2%	18	5%	-3%	24	10%	12	9%	1%	14
Alex Smith		KAN	44%	5	47%	-3%	18	39%	21	34%	5%	10	18%	8	24%		27	18%	18	15%	3%	9	88%	15	86%	1%	13	5%	5	3%	2%	25	8%	17	6%	2%	11
Teddy Bridgewater		MIN	32%	17			27	47%	14	40%	7%	3	13%	13	14%		24	16%	24	19%	-2%	25	88%	13	88%	0%	18	3%	14	4%	-2%	10	7%	20	7%	0%	20
Ryan Tannehill		MIA	26%	21	27%	-2%	13	57%	9	56%	1%	14	13%	13	14%	-1%	15	32%	5	30%	2%	24	85%	23	88%	-2%	7	4%	7	5%	-2%	12	12%	6	11%	1%	12
Joe Flacco		BAL	26%	20	28%	-2%	16	58%	8	54%	3%	13	9%	19	11%	-2%	17	20%	17	20%	0%	15	92%	4	88%	4%	4	1%	25	3%	-2%	21	6%	18	6%	1%	18
Colin Kaepernick		SFO	25%	27				54%	11	54%	1%	16	8%	25	9%	-1%	14	24%	14	24%	1%	22	87%	4	85%	2%	4	1%	25	2%	-1%	25	8%	18	10%		24
Sam Bradford		PHI	26%	19	38%			56%	10	44%	12%	2	10%	15	19%		28	26%	10	21%	5%	6	86%	22	88%		25	3%	15	5%	-3%	22	10%	10	6%	5%	4

Cam Newton's production was extremely balanced regardless of margin (39% when leading, 38% when trailing), which is ideal. Even when his team was up by a large margin, his production kept pace (6th most at 19%).

Similar to Cam Newton, Aaron Rodgers was balanced but not quite to Newton's extent. Drew Brees was the most similar to his own team's rate of any QB. He produced 33% of production when his team led (34% of snaps) and produced 47% when his team trailed (48% of snaps).

Like Cam Newton, Russell Wilson recorded 5% more production than frequency that his team trailed. When leading in garbage time (11% of snaps), Wilson's production took a 4% hit, 2nd most in the NFL behind Andy Dalton. As such, it's obviously more ideal for Wilson to play outside of garbage time as compared to Andrew Luck or Ben Roethlisberger, whose production didn't diminish as much.

Andrew Luck saw 31% of his total production come when his team trailed by 9+ points. It was by far the most of any top-10 forecast QB, and was especially high because his team was only in these situations 23% of the time. His +8% score was 2nd most, behind only Blake Bortles. However, the red flag that these numbers raise gets lowered by the fact that, when leading by a large margin, Luck still produces 6% more than team frequency. Simply put, the offense doesn't have much choice but to use Luck as the fulcrum for production.

Other observations:
• Clearly Blake Bortles was the biggest beneficiary of deficits and garbage time. When leading, he earned just 8% of his total production. But he gained 79% of his production when trailing, 12% above team frequency, most in the NFL. 45% of his total production came when down by 9+ points. If you believe the Jaguars will be better this year, Bortles will not be nearly the weapon he was in 2015.
• Eli Manning's success came predominantly when trailing. When leading, his -5% variance was 4th worst.
• Andy Dalton was very similar to Manning, and virtually invisible with a lead in garbage time.
• Tyrod Taylor & Jameis Winston's production in garbage time should be a warning if one predicts both teams will be better in 2016.

Name	Evan Silva RK	Team	All Production										Large Margin										Garbage Time														
			Lead	RK	Team %	% VAR	VAR RK	Trail	RK	Team %	% VAR	VAR RK	9+ Lead	RK	Team %	% VAR	VAR RK	9+ Trail	RK	Team %	% VAR	VAR RK	No	RK	Team %	% VAR	VAR RK	Yes: Lead	RK	Team %	% VAR	VAR RK	Yes: Trail	RK	Team %	% VAR	VAR RK
David Johnson	RB2	ARI	62%	4	44%	17%	3	5%	37	34%	[illegible]	37	24%	11	15%	9%	6	2%	35	12%	-10%	27	91%	20	90%	1%	27	9%	7	6%	3%	10	0%	33	4%	-4%	20
Todd Gurley	RB3	STL	49%	8	34%	15%	8	32%	26	49%	-17%	31	15%	24	13%	2%	24	16%	21	26%	-10%	28	89%	27	85%	4%	17	8%	12	4%	3%	8	4%	11	10%	-6%	23
Lamar Miller	RB4	MIA	39%	22	27%	11%	12	46%	15	56%	-10%	22	16%	21	14%	2%	23	14%	23	30%	-16%	34	99%	2	84%	14%	2	1%	34	5%	-5%	35	1%	26	10%	-10%	36
Le'Veon Bell	RB5	PIT	42%	15	43%	-1%	29	43%	18	37%	7%	4	15%	22	15%	0%	25	12%	25	15%	-3%	13	89%	23	89%	1%	30	6%	17	6%	0%	20	3%	17	5%	-2%	11
Jamaal Charles	RB6	KAN	24%	34	47%	[illegible]	37	46%	13	34%	12%	3	17%	20	24%	-8%	35	19%	10	16%	4%	3	88%	28	86%	1%	24	6%	16	8%	-1%	27	6%	6	6%	0%	5
Devonta Freeman	RB7	ATL	26%	31	28%	-2%	31	58%	5	56%	2%	5	7%	34	10%	-3%	31	21%	9	24%	-3%	12	94%	11	89%	5%	14	1%	37	3%	-2%	29	5%	9	8%	-3%	13
Adrian Peterson	RB8	MIN	63%	3	40%	23%	1	21%	31	40%	-19%	32	26%	6	14%	12%	4	10%	27	19%	-9%	25	97%	7	88%	9%	10	2%	29	4%	-3%	31	0%	30	7%	-7%	26
Mark Ingram	RB9	NOR	36%	24	34%	3%	25	45%	17	48%	-3%	12	25%	9	11%	13%	1	16%	20	25%	-9%	26	83%	35	84%	-1%	33	13%	2	5%	8%	3	4%	14	10%	-6%	25
Eddie Lacy	RB10	GNB	48%	10	47%	0%	27	22%	30	33%	-12%	24	26%	7	20%	6%	16	7%	31	15%	-8%	23	92%	16	90%	1%	25	8%	11	6%	1%	14	1%	25	3%	-3%	17
LeSean McCoy	RB11	BUF	46%	13	35%	11%	14	37%	23	44%	-7%	18	20%	15	13%	7%	13	18%	15	23%	-5%	18	92%	15	87%	4%	15	3%	23	5%	-1%	28	5%	10	8%	-3%	18
Doug Martin	RB12	TAM	34%	26	24%	9%	17	50%	9	61%	-12%	25	6%	36	8%	-2%	28	18%	14	30%	-12%	30	97%	5	87%	9%	6	2%	27	2%	0%	19	0%	32	10%	-10%	37
Matt Forte	RB13	CHI	15%	37	18%	-3%	32	60%	4	64%	-4%	13	1%	37	5%	-3%	33	23%	6	28%	-4%	16	90%	22	88%	2%	21	1%	33	2%	-1%	24	8%	5	10%	-1%	7
C.J. Anderson	RB14	DEN	48%	9	49%	-1%	28	34%	25	34%	-1%	10	21%	14	24%	-2%	29	14%	22	14%	0%	8	86%	33	87%	-2%	34	4%	20	7%	-3%	33	4%	12	4%	0%	4
Thomas Rawls	RB15	SEA	66%	1	46%	20%	2	16%	34	32%	-16%	29	35%	2	28%	6%	15	2%	37	9%	-7%	21	89%	25	87%	2%	22	11%	3	11%	1%	16	0%	33	1%	-1%	6
Dion Lewis	RB16	NWE	40%	21	55%	-15%	36	3%	38	26%	-23%	35	29%	4	31%	-1%	27	0%	38	8%	-8%	22	97%	6	86%	11%	3	3%	24	11%	[illegible]	38	0%	33	2%	-2%	12
Carlos Hyde	RB17	SFO	41%	18	29%	11%	11	37%	22	54%	-16%	30	14%	25	9%	5%	18	9%	28	25%	-16%	33	93%	13	87%	5%	12	5%	19	2%	3%	9	0%	31	10%	-10%	34
Latavius Murray	RB18	OAK	37%	23	21%	16%	6	35%	24	62%	[illegible]	36	15%	23	7%	8%	10	13%	24	31%	-17%	36	97%	8	87%	9%	7	2%	26	2%	0%	17	1%	27	10%	-10%	35
Jonathan Stewart	RB19	CAR	46%	12	42%	4%	21	29%	28	33%	-4%	14	18%	17	19%	-1%	26	18%	13	17%	1%	5	97%	3	88%	9%	8	1%	36	6%	-5%	36	2%	20	5%	-3%	19
Matt Jones	RB20	WAS	47%	11	32%	15%	7	25%	29	46%	-21%	34	18%	16	14%	4%	20	12%	26	25%	-14%	31	91%	19	86%	5%	13	8%	9	4%	4%	7	1%	22	10%	-9%	31
Ryan Mathews	RB21	PHI	32%	28	38%	-5%	34	41%	20	44%	-2%	11	8%	33	19%	-10%	37	17%	17	21%	-4%	15	97%	4	88%	9%	9	3%	25	5%	-3%	32	0%	33	6%	-6%	24
Jay Ajayi	RB22	MIA	4%	38	27%	[illegible]	38	87%	1	56%	31%	1	1%	38	14%	[illegible]	38	73%	1	30%	43%	1	99%	1	84%	15%	1	0%	38	5%	-5%	37	1%	23	10%	-10%	33
Duke Johnson	RB23	CLE	25%	33	24%	2%	26	53%	8	60%	-7%	17	18%	18	9%	9%	7	25%	4	28%	-2%	11	74%	36	87%	-14%	38	8%	10	2%	6%	5	15%	2	10%	5%	2
Frank Gore	RB24	IND	44%	14	41%	3%	24	30%	27	39%	-9%	21	12%	31	20%	[illegible]	36	6%	32	23%	-17%	35	96%	9	86%	10%	4	2%	30	5%	-3%	34	1%	21	9%	-7%	28
Jeremy Langford	RB25	CHI	22%	35	18%	3%	22	66%	3	64%	2%	7	13%	26	5%	9%	8	17%	18	28%	-11%	29	89%	26	88%	1%	28	11%	5	2%	9%	2	1%	24	10%	-9%	32
Danny Woodhead	RB26	SDG	41%	16	29%	13%	9	46%	14	54%	-8%	20	12%	30	10%	3%	22	28%	2	24%	3%	4	91%	18	88%	3%	20	2%	31	2%	0%	23	6%	8	9%	-3%	16
DeMarco Murray	RB27	PHI	41%	17	38%	3%	23	39%	21	44%	-4%	15	25%	8	19%	7%	14	18%	16	21%	-3%	14	91%	17	88%	3%	19	7%	15	5%	1%	15	1%	29	6%	-5%	22
Giovani Bernard	RB28	CIN	55%	6	48%	6%	19	15%	35	30%	-15%	28	26%	5	23%	3%	21	9%	29	14%	-5%	17	86%	32	86%	0%	31	8%	8	8%	0%	18	3%	15	5%	-1%	8
Ameer Abdullah	RB29	DET	55%	7	38%	17%	4	12%	36	43%	[illegible]	38	22%	12	14%	8%	9	2%	36	20%	-18%	37	96%	10	86%	10%	5	4%	21	5%	-1%	26	1%	28	9%	-8%	30
Charles Sims	RB30	TAM	40%	20	24%	16%	5	49%	10	61%	-12%	26	13%	28	8%	6%	17	16%	19	30%	-14%	32	89%	24	87%	1%	23	2%	28	2%	0%	22	9%	4	10%	-2%	10
Jeremy Hill	RB31	CIN	58%	5	48%	10%	16	19%	32	30%	-10%	23	31%	3	23%	7%	12	5%	34	14%	-9%	24	87%	31	86%	1%	29	10%	6	8%	2%	12	3%	16	5%	-1%	9
Melvin Gordon	RB32	SDG	20%	36	29%	-9%	35	67%	2	54%	13%	2	6%	35	10%	-3%	32	25%	5	24%	1%	6	93%	14	88%	4%	16	4%	22	2%	1%	13	4%	13	9%	-5%	21
Rashad Jennings	RB33	NYG	32%	29	34%	-2%	30	48%	11	48%	0%	8	12%	29	15%	-3%	30	22%	7	19%	4%	2	87%	30	89%	-2%	35	1%	32	4%	-2%	30	12%	3	7%	4%	3
T.J. Yeldon	RB35	JAX	25%	32	14%	11%	13	47%	12	67%	-19%	33	17%	19	4%	12%	3	5%	33	32%	[illegible]	38	94%	12	86%	8%	11	1%	35	2%	-1%	25	0%	33	12%	-12%	38
LeGarrette Blount	RB36	NWE	66%	2	55%	10%	15	18%	33	26%	-8%	19	44%	1	31%	13%	2	9%	30	8%	1%	7	73%	38	86%	-13%	37	27%	1	11%	16%	1	0%	38	2%	-3%	14
Theo Riddick	RB37	DET	34%	25	38%	-4%	33	45%	16	43%	2%	6	9%	32	14%	-5%	34	18%	12	20%	-1%	10	85%	34	86%	-1%	32	5%	18	5%	0%	21	6%	7	9%	-3%	15
Bilal Powell	RB38	NYJ	33%	27	29%	4%	20	54%	7	55%	0%	9	22%	13	14%	8%	11	26%	3	26%	0%	9	74%	37	86%	-12%	36	7%	14	4%	2%	11	17%	1	9%	9%	1
Isaiah Crowell	RB39	CLE	30%	30	24%	7%	18	54%	6	60%	-5%	16	13%	27	9%	5%	19	22%	8	28%	-6%	19	90%	21	87%	3%	18	7%	13	2%	5%	6	2%	18	10%	-8%	29
Chris Ivory	RB40	NYJ	41%	19	29%	12%	10	42%	19	55%	-12%	27	24%	10	14%	10%	5	19%	11	26%	-7%	20	87%	29	86%	1%	26	11%	4	4%	6%	4	2%	19	9%	-7%	27

David Johnson was more reliant on having a lead than essentially every RB. While the Cardinals led 44% of games and trailed only 34%, Johnson recorded 62% of his production with a lead, but just 5% when trailing.

Todd Gurley likewise saw a drop when trailing, but not nearly as severe (32% production, team trailed 49% of snaps). One could assume with a rookie QB, Gurley should be more productive when trailing in 2016.

RBs who were not impacted by trailing included Le'Veon Bell and Jamaal Charles, both of which recorded tremendous production even when trailing. But when leading, the Chiefs rotated Charles out often, and his production was not nearly as strong.

In Miami, Lamar Miller was criminally underutilized. He was almost never used in garbage time, whether leading or trailing. 99% of his overall production came outside garbage time.

Adrian Peterson is utilized tremendously when leading, his +23% variance led the NFL. But when trailing, the touches went elsewhere.

Mark Ingram saw 25% of his production when leading by 9+ points, but the Saints led by 9+ on only 11% of snaps. His +13% variance was most in the NFL, and could concern given the Saints defensive issues.

(No data for RB1, Ezekiel Elliott)

Name	Evan Silva RK	Team	All Production										Large Margin										Garbage Time														
			Lead	RK	Team %	% VAR	VAR RK	Trail	RK	Team %	% VAR	VAR RK	9+ Lead	RK	Team %	% VAR	VAR RK	9+ Trail	RK	Team %	% VAR	VAR RK	No	RK	Team %	% VAR	VAR RK	Yes: Lead	RK	Team %	% VAR	VAR RK	Yes: Trail	RK	Team %	% VAR	VAR RK
Rob Gronkowski	TE1	NWE	55%	1	55%	0%	8	26%	22	26%	-1%	17	33%	1	31%	2%	4	5%	22	8%	-3%	19	90%	7	86%	4%	5	11%	1	11%	0%	4	3%	21	2%	1%	13
Jordan Reed	TE2	WAS	32%	11	32%	0%	7	49%	12	46%	3%	15	13%	7	14%	-1%	7	27%	8	25%	2%	13	89%	9	86%	3%	7	1%	13	4%	-3%	15	14%	8	10%	4%	8
Tyler Eifert	TE3	CIN	49%	4	48%	1%	5	29%	21	30%	-1%	18	24%	5	23%	1%	5	12%	21	14%	-2%	16	84%	15	86%	-1%	14	6%	5	8%	-2%	12	3%	22	5%	[illegible]	20
Greg Olsen	TE4	CAR	28%	14	42%	-14%	20	46%	14	33%	12%	7	11%	11	19%	-8%	19	24%	13	17%	6%	8	90%	8	88%	2%	9	10%	2	6%	3%	2	16%	5	5%	11%	3
Coby Fleener	TE5	IND	40%	7	41%	-1%	9	45%	15	39%	6%	11	25%	4	20%	5%	3	20%	18	23%	-3%	20	92%	4	86%	6%	3	0%	15	5%	-4%	20	6%	18	9%	[illegible]	22
Travis Kelce	TE6	KAN	50%	2	47%	3%	4	30%	20	34%	-4%	19	18%	6	24%	-6%	15	14%	20	16%	-2%	15	92%	3	86%	6%	2	3%	8	8%	-4%	18	5%	19	6%	[illegible]	17
Antonio Gates	TE7	SDG	25%	16	29%	-4%	11	60%	7	54%	5%	13	3%	19	10%	-6%	18	24%	12	24%	0%	14	87%	12	88%	-1%	15	1%	12	2%	-1%	6	11%	10	9%	3%	10
Ladarius Green	TE8	SDG	21%	17	29%	-8%	15	70%	6	54%	15%	5	7%	14	10%	-2%	9	18%	19	24%	-6%	21	89%	10	88%	0%	11	0%	15	2%	-2%	13	11%	11	9%	3%	11
Gary Barnidge	TE9	CLE	12%	20	24%	-12%	19	74%	4	60%	14%	6	3%	20	9%	-6%	16	37%	4	28%	9%	6	91%	6	87%	4%	6	0%	15	2%	-2%	14	8%	14	10%	[illegible]	19
Julius Thomas	TE10	JAX	43%	6	14%	29%	1	49%	13	67%	[illegible]	22	26%	3	4%	22%	1	23%	14	32%	-10%	22	83%	17	86%	-3%	16	6%	3	2%	4%	1	11%	12	12%	-1%	16
Delanie Walker	TE11	TEN	14%	19	22%	-8%	13	74%	3	64%	10%	9	4%	18	7%	-3%	14	51%	2	40%	11%	3	84%	16	84%	0%	12	0%	15	2%	-2%	9	16%	4	14%	2%	12
Zach Ertz	TE12	PHI	29%	12	38%	-9%	16	50%	11	44%	6%	12	6%	16	19%	[illegible]	20	29%	6	21%	8%	7	94%	1	88%	6%	1	2%	11	5%	-4%	17	4%	20	6%	[illegible]	18
Eric Ebron	TE13	DET	45%	5	38%	7%	3	43%	17	43%	0%	16	11%	12	14%	-3%	13	26%	9	20%	6%	9	82%	18	86%	-4%	18	0%	15	5%	-5%	19	18%	3	9%	9%	4
Austin Seferian-Jenkins	TE14	TAM	7%	22	24%	[illegible]	21	79%	2	61%	18%	4	1%	22	8%	-6%	17	57%	1	30%	27%	1	60%	22	87%	-27%	22	0%	15	2%	-2%	7	38%	1	10%	28%	1
Jason Witten	TE15	DAL	28%	15	34%	-6%	12	53%	10	43%	10%	8	12%	9	15%	-3%	12	22%	15	18%	5%	11	91%	5	89%	2%	8	2%	10	4%	-2%	11	7%	16	7%	0%	14
Zach Miller	TE16	CHI	8%	21	18%	-10%	17	82%	1	64%	19%	3	5%	17	5%	0%	6	25%	10	28%	-3%	17	93%	2	88%	5%	4	0%	15	2%	-2%	8	7%	15	10%	[illegible]	21
Martellus Bennett	TE17	CHI	14%	18	18%	-4%	10	73%	5	64%	9%	10	2%	21	5%	-2%	10	37%	3	28%	9%	5	80%	20	88%	-7%	21	1%	14	2%	-1%	5	18%	2	10%	8%	5
Dwayne Allen	TE18	IND	49%	3	41%	9%	2	31%	19	39%	-8%	21	31%	2	20%	10%	2	28%	7	23%	5%	10	82%	19	86%	-3%	17	3%	9	5%	-2%	10	15%	7	9%	6%	7
Ben Watson		NOR	34%	9	34%	1%	6	43%	18	48%	-5%	20	10%	13	11%	-1%	8	22%	16	25%	-3%	18	86%	13	84%	2%	10	0%	15	5%	[illegible]	21	13%	9	10%	4%	9
Richard Rodgers		GNB	28%	13	47%	[illegible]	22	56%	8	33%	23%	1	6%	15	20%	[illegible]	21	25%	11	15%	10%	4	86%	14	90%	-5%	19	3%	7	6%	-3%	16	11%	13	3%	8%	6
Kyle Rudolph		MIN	33%	10	40%	-8%	14	43%	16	40%	4%	14	12%	10	14%	-3%	11	21%	17	19%	2%	12	88%	11	88%	0%	13	6%	4	4%	1%	3	6%	17	7%	-1%	15
Jimmy Graham		SEA	35%	8	46%	-11%	18	54%	9	32%	21%	2	12%	8	28%	[illegible]	22	33%	5	9%	24%	2	80%	21	87%	-7%	20	4%	6	11%	[illegible]	22	15%	6	1%	14%	2

Rob Gronkowski and Jordan Reed were relatively situationally immune, producing regardless of score. However, Greg Olsen saw one of the biggest hits to production when Carolina led. His 28% production when leading was a -14% variance from his team's situational snaps and the 3rd biggest drop in the NFL. He was heavily utilized when trailing.

You could group Gary Barnidge, Zach Miller and Austin Seferian-Jenkins in the same bucket in that they relied on a ton of production when trailing, but saw large reduction when leading. ASJ recorded 38% of his total production when trailing in garbage time, by far the most in the NFL and should be a huge red flag. The same concerns exist for Jimmy Graham.

Name	Evan Silva RK	Team	All Production										Large Margin										Garbage Time														
			Lead	RK	Team %	% VAR	VAR RK	Trail	RK	Team %	% VAR	VAR RK	9+ Lead	RK	Team %	% VAR	VAR RK	9+ Trail	RK	Team %	% VAR	VAR RK	No	RK	Team %	% VAR	VAR RK	Yes: Lead	RK	Team %	% VAR	VAR RK	Yes: Trail	RK	Team %	% VAR	VAR RK
Antonio Brown	WR1	PIT	48%	7	43%	5%	8	36%	43	37%	-1%	35	20%	13	15%	4%	6	16%	39	15%	1%	31	83%	39	89%	-5%	43	9%	5	6%	3%	4	7%	29	5%	2%	19
Odell Beckham	WR2	NYG	29%	32	34%	-5%	29	51%	22	48%	3%	28	8%	38	15%	-7%	42	15%	42	19%	-4%	42	87%	30	89%	-1%	35	3%	26	4%	-1%	15	9%	20	7%	2%	21
Julio Jones	WR3	ATL	30%	30	28%	2%	13	53%	19	56%	-3%	39	9%	33	10%	-1%	18	23%	27	24%	-1%	38	91%	19	89%	2%	25	0%	42	3%	-2%	31	8%	26	8%	0%	29
A.J. Green	WR4	CIN	36%	19	48%	-13%	46	43%	35	30%	13%	10	20%	9	23%	-3%	26	12%	44	14%	-1%	39	97%	2	86%	12%	1	1%	34	8%	[illegible]	52	1%	50	5%	-4%	47
Dez Bryant	WR5	DAL	43%	11	34%	9%	4	40%	41	43%	-3%	40	15%	16	15%	0%	16	13%	43	18%	-5%	46	91%	17	89%	3%	23	3%	27	4%	-1%	18	4%	36	7%	-2%	40
Allen Robinson	WR6	JAX	10%	51	14%	-4%	27	78%	1	67%	11%	12	0%	51	4%	-4%	31	45%	4	32%	12%	7	80%	45	86%	-5%	42	0%	45	2%	-2%	22	19%	5	12%	7%	8
DeAndre Hopkins	WR7	HOU	34%	21	38%	-4%	26	52%	20	44%	8%	18	20%	8	18%	2%	11	29%	18	22%	7%	17	87%	32	87%	-1%	33	4%	15	7%	-4%	37	10%	18	5%	4%	11
Keenan Allen	WR8	SDG	24%	39	29%	-4%	28	64%	7	54%	10%	17	4%	46	10%	-6%	38	33%	12	24%	9%	10	92%	13	88%	3%	18	0%	45	2%	-2%	26	8%	25	9%	-1%	34
Alshon Jeffery	WR9	CHI	21%	45	18%	2%	14	65%	6	64%	1%	32	2%	50	5%	-3%	25	36%	10	28%	8%	13	86%	35	88%	-2%	37	0%	44	2%	-2%	20	14%	12	10%	4%	13
Brandin Cooks	WR10	NOR	26%	37	34%	-8%	38	52%	21	48%	4%	26	6%	42	11%	-5%	36	28%	19	25%	3%	25	87%	29	84%	3%	19	3%	23	5%	-2%	25	10%	17	10%	0%	31
Jordy Nelson	WR11	GNB	52%	5	47%	5%	9	24%	51	33%	-9%	49	27%	4	20%	7%	3	8%	51	15%	-7%	50	96%	6	90%	6%	10	1%	38	6%	[illegible]	46	3%	39	3%	0%	33
Brandon Marshall	WR12	NYJ	33%	26	29%	4%	11	50%	23	55%	-5%	43	10%	32	14%	-4%	30	30%	14	26%	4%	22	91%	18	86%	5%	11	2%	32	4%	-2%	30	6%	34	9%	-3%	45
Mike Evans	WR13	TAM	22%	41	24%	-2%	19	60%	13	61%	-1%	36	9%	37	8%	1%	13	26%	20	30%	-4%	44	88%	28	87%	0%	32	4%	12	2%	2%	5	8%	27	10%	-2%	39
T.Y. Hilton	WR14	IND	38%	15	41%	-3%	23	42%	37	39%	3%	27	20%	7	20%	0%	17	24%	23	23%	1%	30	96%	8	86%	10%	3	1%	35	5%	-4%	38	3%	40	9%	-5%	50
Demaryius Thomas	WR15	DEN	46%	8	49%	-3%	24	33%	46	34%	-1%	37	20%	11	24%	-4%	27	16%	40	14%	1%	28	91%	20	87%	4%	17	3%	22	7%	-4%	42	5%	35	4%	1%	25
Amari Cooper	WR16	OAK	31%	27	21%	9%	3	50%	25	62%	-12%	50	15%	19	7%	8%	2	9%	49	31%	[illegible]	53	95%	10	87%	8%	7	3%	28	2%	1%	9	2%	46	10%	[illegible]	53
Randall Cobb	WR17	GNB	49%	6	47%	2%	16	29%	48	33%	-4%	41	24%	5	20%	4%	7	15%	41	15%	0%	33	92%	14	90%	2%	27	5%	10	6%	-1%	16	3%	42	3%	-1%	35
Jarvis Landry	WR18	MIA	21%	43	27%	-6%	32	66%	5	56%	11%	14	7%	41	14%	-7%	43	36%	9	30%	7%	18	86%	36	84%	1%	28	1%	36	5%	-4%	43	13%	13	10%	3%	16
Golden Tate	WR19	DET	30%	28	38%	-7%	35	47%	31	43%	4%	24	12%	25	14%	-2%	24	26%	21	20%	6%	19	89%	26	86%	3%	22	2%	33	5%	-3%	33	9%	21	9%	1%	26
Julian Edelman	WR20	NWE	63%	1	55%	7%	7	22%	52	26%	-4%	42	34%	2	31%	3%	9	4%	53	8%	-4%	45	86%	34	86%	0%	31	13%	2	11%	2%	7	0%	52	2%	-2%	37
Jeremy Maclin	WR21	KAN	29%	31	47%	-17%	48	41%	39	34%	7%	20	15%	18	24%	-9%	46	24%	26	16%	8%	15	90%	23	86%	4%	16	4%	18	8%	-4%	39	7%	30	6%	0%	30
Sammy Watkins	WR22	BUF	43%	10	35%	8%	5	38%	42	44%	-6%	44	8%	39	13%	-6%	37	23%	29	23%	0%	34	87%	33	87%	-1%	34	5%	11	5%	0%	10	8%	24	8%	1%	28
Larry Fitzgerald	WR23	ARI	45%	9	44%	1%	18	27%	49	34%	-7%	46	20%	6	15%	6%	4	8%	50	12%	-4%	43	92%	12	90%	2%	24	6%	7	6%	0%	12	1%	48	4%	-2%	41
Eric Decker	WR24	NYJ	23%	40	29%	-5%	30	61%	12	55%	6%	21	10%	31	14%	-4%	29	35%	11	26%	9%	12	83%	40	86%	-3%	39	3%	24	4%	-1%	19	11%	16	9%	2%	22
Kelvin Benjamin	WR25	CAR	18%	46	42%	[illegible]	53	57%	16	33%	23%	3	6%	43	19%	[illegible]	51	41%	7	17%	23%	2	70%	52	88%	-18%	52	0%	45	6%	[illegible]	51	29%	2	5%	24%	2
Doug Baldwin	WR26	SEA	39%	14	46%	-7%	34	43%	36	32%	10%	16	20%	10	28%	-8%	44	18%	36	9%	9%	11	95%	9	87%	9%	5	4%	14	11%	[illegible]	53	0%	51	1%	-1%	36
Donte Moncrief	WR27	IND	29%	33	41%	-12%	44	56%	18	39%	17%	4	15%	17	20%	-5%	35	38%	8	23%	15%	5	80%	46	86%	-5%	44	10%	3	5%	5%	3	9%	22	9%	1%	27
Michael Floyd	WR28	ARI	34%	24	44%	-11%	42	34%	45	34%	0%	33	10%	28	15%	-4%	32	12%	45	12%	0%	32	98%	1	90%	9%	4	0%	43	6%	[illegible]	50	1%	49	4%	-3%	43
John Brown	WR29	ARI	37%	16	44%	-7%	37	47%	29	34%	13%	9	19%	14	15%	4%	5	11%	48	12%	-1%	37	90%	21	90%	0%	30	4%	16	6%	-3%	32	6%	32	4%	2%	20
Jordan Matthews	WR30	PHI	36%	18	38%	-2%	22	48%	28	44%	4%	25	20%	12	19%	1%	15	29%	16	21%	8%	16	75%	51	88%	-14%	51	5%	8	5%	0%	11	17%	8	6%	11%	5
Emmanuel Sanders	WR31	DEN	33%	25	49%	-16%	47	47%	32	34%	13%	11	13%	22	24%	-10%	48	23%	28	14%	8%	14	96%	7	87%	8%	6	2%	29	7%	-5%	44	2%	47	4%	-2%	38
Allen Hurns	WR33	JAX	8%	52	14%	-7%	33	71%	3	67%	5%	22	2%	48	4%	-2%	22	44%	5	32%	12%	8	81%	44	86%	-5%	41	0%	41	2%	-1%	17	19%	4	12%	7%	7
Michael Crabtree	WR34	OAK	34%	22	21%	13%	1	47%	30	62%	[illegible]	52	10%	29	7%	4%	8	16%	38	31%	[illegible]	52	91%	16	87%	4%	14	1%	37	2%	-1%	13	6%	33	10%	-4%	48
DeVante Parker	WR35	MIA	6%	53	27%	[illegible]	51	58%	15	56%	3%	29			14%	[illegible]	53	47%	2	30%	17%	3	76%	49	84%	-8%	47	0%	45	5%	-5%	47	24%	3	10%	13%	3
DeSean Jackson	WR37	WAS	22%	42	32%	-10%	40	61%	10	46%	15%	6	6%	45	14%	-8%	45	20%	31	25%	-5%	47	97%	3	86%	11%	2	0%	45	4%	-4%	40	3%	43	10%	[illegible]	52
Tyler Lockett	WR38	SEA	58%	2	46%	12%	2	15%	53	32%	[illegible]	53	44%	1	28%	16%	1	5%	52	9%	-4%	42	81%	43	87%	-6%	45	17%	1	11%	7%	1	0%	53	1%	-1%	37
Marvin Jones	WR39	CIN	56%	3	48%	7%	6	24%	50	30%	-6%	45	19%	15	23%	-5%	33	11%	47	14%	-3%	40	90%	22	86%	4%	13	2%	30	8%	[illegible]	49	8%	28	5%	3%	15
Dorial Green-Beckham	WR40	TEN	25%	38	22%	4%	12	62%	9	64%	-2%	38			7%	-7%	41	43%	6	40%	4%	23	79%	47	84%	-4%	40	0%	45	2%	-2%	24	17%	7	14%	3%	14
Tavon Austin	WR41	STL	36%	17	34%	2%	15	40%	40	49%	-9%	48	14%	20	13%	1%	14	29%	17	26%	3%	26	79%	48	85%	-6%	46	10%	4	4%	6%	2	11%	15	10%	1%	24
Willie Snead	WR42	NOR	35%	20	34%	1%	17	49%	26	48%	2%	31	9%	34	11%	-2%	23	24%	25	25%	-1%	36	85%	37	84%	0%	29	3%	20	5%	-2%	23	12%	14	10%	3%	18
Torrey Smith	WR43	SFO	34%	23	29%	4%	10	41%	38	54%	[illegible]	51	10%	27	9%	1%	12	22%	30	25%	-3%	41	76%	50	87%	-11%	50	4%	13	2%	2%	6	14%	11	10%	4%	12
Stefon Diggs	WR45	MIN	28%	35	40%	-12%	45	50%	24	40%	10%	15	13%	24	14%	-1%	21	11%	46	19%	-7%	49	93%	11	88%	5%	12	3%	25	4%	-2%	21	4%	37	7%	-3%	42
Markus Wheaton	WR46	PIT	39%	13	43%	-4%	25	48%	27	37%	11%	13	9%	35	15%	-6%	39	16%	37	15%	1%	29	87%	31	89%	-2%	36	4%	17	6%	-2%	28	9%	19	5%	5%	10
Mohamed Sanu	WR50	CIN	42%	12	48%	-6%	31	43%	34	30%	13%	8	14%	21	23%	-10%	47	19%	33	14%	5%	21	88%	27	86%	2%	26	4%	19	8%	-4%	41	6%	31	5%	2%	23
Phillip Dorsett	WR51	IND	18%	48	41%	[illegible]	52	71%	4	39%	32%	1	7%	40	20%	[illegible]	52	67%	1	23%	44%	1	45%	53	86%	[illegible]	53	0%	45	5%	-5%	45	55%	1	9%	47%	1
Vincent Jackson	WR52	TAM	15%	49	24%	-9%	39	75%	2	61%	14%	7	3%	47	8%	-5%	34	45%	3	30%	15%	6	81%	42	87%	-6%	45	1%	39	2%	-1%	14	18%	6	10%	8%	6
Mike Wallace	WR53	MIN	29%	34	40%	-12%	43	56%	17	40%	16%	5	10%	30	14%	-4%	28	18%	34	19%	0%	35	96%	5	88%	8%	8	2%	31	4%	-2%	27	2%	45	7%	-5%	49
Nelson Agholor	WR55	PHI	18%	47	38%	[illegible]	49	35%	44	44%	-8%	47	6%	44	19%	[illegible]	50	24%	24	21%	3%	24	92%	15	88%	3%	20	0%	45	5%	[illegible]	48	8%	23	6%	3%	17
Travis Benjamin	WR56	CLE	13%	50	24%	-10%	41	62%	8	60%	2%	30	2%	49	9%	-7%	40	29%	15	28%	2%	27	84%	38	87%	-3%	38	0%	45	2%	-2%	29	15%	9	10%	5%	9
Brandon LaFell	WR57	NWE	54%	4	55%	-2%	21	31%	47	26%	4%	23	30%	3	31%	-1%	19	18%	35	8%	10%	9	89%	25	86%	3%	21	8%	6	11%	-3%	35	2%	44	2%	0%	32
James Jones		GNB	26%	36	47%	[illegible]	50	59%	14	33%	26%	2	9%	36	20%	[illegible]	49	30%	13	15%	15%	4	82%	41	90%	-8%	48	3%	21	6%	-3%	36	15%	10	3%	12%	4
Pierre Garcon		WAS	30%	29	32%	-2%	20	45%	33	46%	-1%	34	13%	23	14%	-1%	20	20%	32	25%	-6%	48	90%	24	86%	4%	15	5%	9	4%	1%	8	4%	38	10%	-5%	51
Steve Smith		BAL	21%	44	28%	-7%	36	61%	11	54%	7%	19	12%	26	9%	2%	10	25%	22	20%	6%	20	96%	4	90%	7%	9	1%	40	4%	-3%	34	3%	41	6%	-3%	44

Antonio Brown is one of just 3 receivers projected as top-15 who still produce at a high rate even if their team is leading. Brown's 48% production when leading is 5% above his team's average, joining Jordy Nelson and Dez Bryant as the only top-15 WRs whose production exceeds their team's rate of leading by at least 5%.

Like Eli Manning, Odell Beckham drops when leading, joined by only AJ Green and Brandin Cooks as top-15 WRs whose rate drops by at least 5% when leading. Fortunately for Beckham owners, the Giants have trailed 51% of the time, leading to better overall numbers. Interestingly, Beckham was rarely productive with either a large lead or a large deficit. In fact, no other top-35 WR saw negative variance both when down by 9+ or up by 9+ like Beckham did.

Julio Jones was reliable regardless of situation and was clearly a focal point regardless of score.

AJ Green, on the other hand, was on the opposite end of the spectrum. In garbage time of any kind, he was persona non grata. He recorded 97% of his total production outside of garbage time, even if the Bengals were trailing in garbage time. When the Bengals were trailing, AJ Green was open for business. His +13% variance in production when trailing vs team frequency of trailing was the best of any top-20 WR. With many targets leaving this past offseason, Green should see more usage even when leading, but much will depend on the philosophy from the Bengals new offensive coordinator.

Allen Robinson saw the most production of any WR when his team trailed. 78% of his fantasy production came when the Jaguars were down on the scoreboard. Both Allen Robinson and Allen Hurns saw 19% of their production in garbage time when trailing, similar (as expected) to Blake Bortles' 20%.

A positive for DeAndre Hopkins is that even in large margin games, he was still extremely productive, even if leading. He was the only top-10 WR to be at least +2% variance when the Texans were up 9+ points.

Some other comments on other WRs:

- Aaron Rodgers loves hitting Jordy Nelson, regardless of the game score. That element was absent in 2015, but it likely will return with authority in 2016.
- Oddly, Amari Cooper recorded only 50% of his production when trailing, despite the Raiders trailing 62% of snaps. That -12% variance was the worst of any top-30 WR. Likewise, he recorded just 9% production when down by 9+ points. If the Raiders avoid those situations due to a better roster in 2016, it may help Cooper avoid these negative EV situations, as Cooper was +9% variance when the Raiders were leading, the 3rd best of 60 WRs.
- We didn't see him last year, but I wrote just over 1 year ago about Kelvin Benjamin, and I called him "The King of Garbage Time". He recorded 29% of his total production when the Panthers trailed in garbage time. It was by far the most of any top-50 WR, and is incredible considering the Panthers were in garbage time just 5%. That was +24% variance!
- Michael Crabtree was nearly identical to Amari Cooper in terms of production with or without the lead.
- Tyler Lockett was the most scoreboard-proof WR in the NFL last year. He was +12% when leading (2nd), +16% when up by 9+ points, and +7% even when leading in garbage time.

New 2016 Player Production Opportunities

"Opportunities are usually disguised as hard work, so most people don't recognize them." Nothing like a good Ann Landers quote to apply to fantasy football, but the reality is, getting the opportunity to produce does not guarantee success. Players still have to work hard on and off the field to produce. But unfortunately some players will inevitably find themselves in a crowded stable without nearly enough opportunity to produce to their ability.

This study looks at new opportunities for production by team. But it takes it one step further in that it overlays play rate frequency on top of basic opportunity. For example: in the 2015 carries lost infograph, you can see that the Lions lost 25% of their 2015 carries and the Seahawks lost 22%. Very similar. However, the Seahawks called the 10th most run-heavy game plan, while the Lions ranked 22nd. Thus, it would be better to be in Seattle to claim that 22% of a large number is better than 25% of a small number. Similarly, the Texans situation is far more likeable for new RB Lamar Miller than the Saints who lost 14%, because they so infrequently call run plays.

Matt Forte should dominate touches for the slightly better than average run frequency Jets. Meanwhile, the Dolphins lost Lamar Miller, but they ran infrequently last year. However new HC Adam Gase is likely to run more often, so that may not be as big an issue. The question is, will Jay Ajayi put in that hard work to make the most of his opportunity?

Matt Jones showed some spark last year but was more fizzle than firework. He has a huge opportunity to produce in 2016. Ryan Mathews, in Philadelphia, could produce under new HC Doug Pederson.

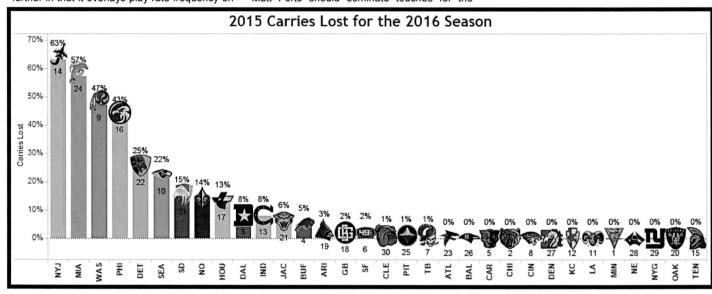

From the receivers, there was more production lost and more teams in interesting positions. The Bengals lost Marvin Jones and Mohamed Sanu in free agency, and Tyler Eifert is not lost but is injured. There is a ton of production available, but the Bengals ranked 25th in pass rate last year. That said, expect more work for AJ Green than historically due to the sheer work available. And whichever #2 WR steps up could be a legitimate low-price option in DFS, but only when the Bengals will be in games that they need to pass to win.

The 49ers likewise have opportunity and Torrey Smith is likely to take advantage of it in Chip Kelly's offense. Kelly ran a very balanced offense in terms of pass v run rate, so I expect his pass rate to increase from 27th.

Meanwhile, three great situations exist in Detroit, Cleveland and for the NY Giants. These teams were pass heavy last year, and all have at least 30% of their production available for new distribution. Corey Coleman could intrigue as the fantasy season progresses in Cleveland, while another rookie in Sterling Shepard should be in solid shape for the Giants offense.

Be cautious about teams like the Bills, Vikings and Panthers. While other sources will look only at targets lost, by overlaying pass frequency, we can easily see that these teams pass only when they need to, and may not be reliable week to week targets. Apart from an uptick from Sammy Watkins, it's hard to feel very confident in Laquon Treadwell or Devin Funchess for season-long leagues due to potential sparse volume.

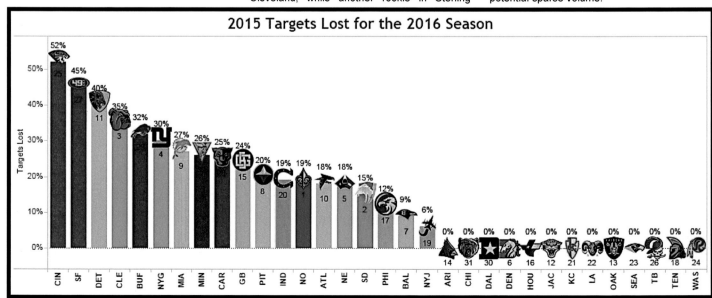

Los Angeles Rams

Coaches

Head Coach: Jeff Fisher (5th yr)
OC: Rob Boras (2nd yr)
DC: Gregg Williams (3rd yr)

Forecast 2016 Wins

7

Past Records

2015: 7-9
2014: 6-10
2013: 7-9

Opponent Strength
Easy — Hard

2016 Schedule & Week by Week Strength of Schedule

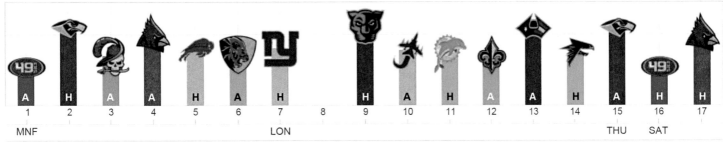

1	2	3	4	5	6	7	8	9	10	11	12	13	14	15	16	17
A	H	A	A	H	A	H		H	A	H	A	A	H	A	H	H

MNF   LON   THU   SAT

2016 Overview

The Rams fell in love with Jared Goff. Like many teams in the last 5 years, the Rams traded up the board in the top 10 to acquire the #1 overall draft pick. It seems like a slam dunk move. At least according to the Rams and the pundits: grab the draft's best QB, regardless of the cost, because he will be worth it. Here is the problem with that logic: it rarely works. I looked at the last 5 years, when the QB position has become even more valuable, and examined all instances of teams trading up to the top 10 to draft players. It happened 10 times the last 5 years, and I examined those teams record post-trade as well as the number of coaches they fired. As it turns out, these 10 posted records combining to win 38% of their games post-trade, with 2 playoff wins in these 5 years between all of them. And they hired a total of 13 new coaches. In other words, teams who make such deals still lose and their coaches are over 6 times more likely to be fired and replaced than to win a playoff game.

But, for the sake of the 2016 Rams season, let's pretend Goff is adequate. Perhaps not a Pro-Bowler but better than Nick Foles or Case Keenum. In that case, the 2016 Rams will be a much better team than the 2015 version which won 7 games. The issue is, can they win enough to make the playoffs given they play the 5th toughest schedule, which includes a division with Seattle and Arizona competing for one automatic berth? Not only do they face divisional foes, but they also must play the Patriots and Panthers, as well as the Jets and a number of teams who underachieved last year that will be hungry this year, such as the Saints, Giants, Lions, Bills and Falcons. However, here is an interesting stat: last year the Rams went 4-2 in the NFC West, and since 2012 they are almost batting .500 in division, at 11-12-1 (48%), going 4-4 against both the Seahawks and the Cardinals. So as bad as the Rams have been for several years, and as good as the Seahawks have been since Russell Wilson came to town and the Cardinals since 2013.

So far, we've spun the positives. Goff comes in and plays well and the team is capable of hanging with the giants of the division (and NFL): Seattle and Arizona. What if the offensive line plays more to its talent and isn't able to replicate the ridiculously strong pass protection from 2015? Last year they played almost 1/3rd of their schedule against teams who finished 26th or worse in pass rush efficiency. What if the issue is wide receiver play in concert with the quarterback? Tavon Austin, Kenny Britt and Brian Quick could look really good as receivers in the Patriots offense a few years ago when their receivers were all injured, but that was with Tom Brady. Will they consistently run the proper routes and use proper releases to get to the spot that Goff needs from them? Will they win one-on-one battles to make Goff's life easier? And then the big question: while the defense should be healthier in 2016 (they were the 4th most injured in 2015), they lost Chris Long, James Laurinaitis, Janoris Jenkins, Nick Fairley and Rodney McLeod this offseason. In that group is two 16-game starters from 2015, including a 15-game starter, 5-game starter (played in 12 games) and one who played in 15 games with no starts (Fairley). We can't automatically assume this defense will continue to make strides. Goff could bring better play from the QB position, but in the ultimate team sport, he will need a lot of help and a lot of questions remain to be answered.

Strength of Schedule In Detail

True Strength of Schedule Rank: 5

Hardest Stretches (1=Hard, 32=Easy)
Hardest 3 wk Stretch Rk:	10
Hardest 4 wk Stretch Rk:	17
Hardest 5 wk Stretch Rk:	11

Easiest Stretches (1=Easy, 32=Hard)
Easiest 3 wk Stretch Rk:	29
Easiest 4 wk Stretch Rk:	32
Easiest 5 wk Stretch Rk:	28

Closing out the top 5 most difficult Strength of Schedule for 2016, Los Angeles does not face any particular rough stretches. The overall caliber of opponent is strong primarily from playing the Cardinals and Seahawks twice in-division, and they also face the Panthers and Patriots, the two teams projected to have the best records in the NFL next year. From a positive perspective, the Rams do not face any of these opponents in back to back weeks. The scheduling committee was also kind in allowing them to travel to Detroit for a game before flying to London to face the Giants week 7. But with the Rams being one of 4 teams to finish the year playing 3 of 4 games at home, and losing a home game to London, in the first 13 weeks the Rams play just 4 game in Los Angeles.

2015 Play Tendencies

All Pass %	53%
All Pass Rk	28
All Rush %	47%
All Rush Rk	5
1 Score Pass %	55%
1 Score Pass Rk	22
2014 1 Score Pass %	55%
2014 1 Score Pass Rk	24
Pass Increase %	1%
Pass Increase Rk	15
1 Score Rush %	45%
1 Score Rush Rk	11
Up Pass %	43%
Up Pass Rk	30
Up Rush %	57%
Up Rush Rk	3
Down Pass %	62%
Down Pass Rk	27
Down Rush %	38%
Down Rush Rk	6

The Rams were the 5th most run heavy team last year, and that percentage didn't change much in one score games. The ranking didn't change much when trailing, still calling run plays the 6th most often. Its unlikely, while working in a rookie QB and with Todd Gurley as RB, that the Rams will pass more often, so they still will rank among the NFL's most run heavy offenses. And that should bode well for Gurley's usage from a fantasy perspective.

2015 Offensive Advanced Metrics

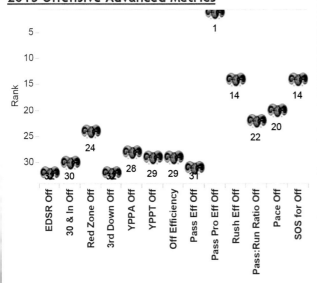

As good as the defense was in most areas, that is how bad the Rams offense was. After their week 6 bye, the Rams went 5-6 to close the season, but were 0-3 in games decided by less than 6 points, losing 3 games by 3 points (twice in OT). Those 3 losses were in games the defense gave up 16, 16 and 18 points in regulation. Their struggles were because the offense was the NFL's worst in EDSR. That translates to a large rate of 3rd down attempts, and they were the NFL's worst offense on 3rd down. That was despite the fact that their run offense was 14th in the NFL. Also interesting is the fact that their defense produced such strong rankings despite facing the NFL's toughest schedule and being the 4th most injured defense last year. Meanwhile, while the offense ranked 32nd in EDSR efficiency, they faced the 14th rated opposing defenses. An improvement by Goff on 3rd down and in the red zone will be massive for the Rams offense in 2016.

2015 Defensive Advanced Metrics

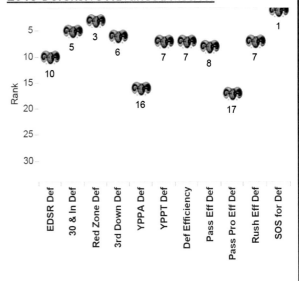

Drafted Players   2016 Draft Grade: #22 (2.6/4)   PERSONNEL & SPENDING   Los Angeles Rams

Rnd.	Pick #	Pos.	Player	College
1	1	QB	Jared Goff	California
4	110	TE	Tyler Higbee	Western Kentucky
4	117	WR	Pharoh Cooper	South Carolina
	177	TE	Temarrick Hemingway	South Carolina State
6	190	LB	Josh Forrest	Kentucky
	206	WR	Michael Thomas	Southern Miss

Free Agents/Trades Added

Player (Position)

Coty Sensabaugh CB

Quinton Coples DE

Other Signed

Player (Position)

Aaron Green RB
Brandon Chubb LB
Brian Randolph S
Cory Littleton LB
D'haquille Williams WR
Darreon Herring LB
Ian Seau DE
J.J. Worton WR
Jabriel Washington CB
Jordan Lomax S
Jordan Swindle T
Kache Palacio DE
MarQuez North WR
Mike Jordan CB
Morgan Fox DE
Nelson Spruce WR
Nicholas Grigsby LB
Pace Murphy T
Paul McRoberts WR
Rohan Gaines S
Taylor Bertolet K
Winston Rose CB

2015 Players Lost

Transaction	Player (Position)
Cut	Chris Long DE
	Isiah Ferguson WR
	James Laurinaitis LB
	Jared Cook TE
	Kache Palacio DE
	Winston Rose CB
Declared Free Agent	Daren Bates LB
	Janoris Jenkins CB
	Nick Fairley DT
	Rodney McLeod S

- The Rams offensively were the NFL's worst red zone passing offense last year. Typically, red zone passing success comes from QB intelligence & decision making, accuracy and play design. Sometimes it is hard to succeed in the red zone when the defense knows your tendency is to pass because your run game is terrible. But that wasn't the case for the Rams: Their run offense was the 2nd most efficient in red zone rushes. If Jared Goff can play even slightly better inside the red zone than Nick Foles' 33% completion rate, 2.8 YPA and 57 rating, worst in the NFL, the Rams can actually be quite intriguing as a red zone offense, and certainly would move up from their 2015 ranking.
- If Goff can improve in the red zone, the other area where he would make an immediate and substantial difference would be in early down passing. The Rams were dead last in EDSR, but they weren't horrible when running the ball. They were, however, horrible when passing. Nick Foles had a 77 passer rating on 1st or 2nd down, with a 2 TD : 5 INT ratio, and inside opposing territory it was even worse: 50% completions, 5.4 YPA and a 57 rating. We know the red zone numbers were bad, but between midfield and the 21, the Rams also had the NFL's least successful passing attack. Goff doesn't have to be superman to have success, he simply needs to be efficient. With a defense and run game like they have, Goff doesn't need to go off to win games, he simply can't be sloppy or error-prone.
- While Goff can make a big improvement, they traded a lot of value to acquire him. It was extreme, and it was a move I routinely disapprove of. The best case scenario is Goff is incredible. But even then, the value the Rams miss out on drafting in the early rounds not just in 2016 but beyond will leave them deficient in talent at various positions. The most likely scenario is Goff is average, as is the case with many players that a particular team falls in love with and moves up the board to grab & it results in coaches getting fired & an even larger step back.

Lineup & 2016 Cap Hit

Health Overall & by Unit (2015 v 2014)

2015 Rk	24
2015 AGL	80
Off Rk	16
Def Rk	29
2014 Rk	13
2014 AGL	64

2016 Positional Spending

	All OFF	QB	OL	RB	WR	TE	All DEF	DL	LB	CB	S
2015 Rk	24	28	22	17	19	2	7	1	30	28	17
Rank	21	18	18	13	19	14	6	3	30	7	11
Total	74.5M	18.7M	23.8M	8.9M	14.7M	8.5M	78.7M	36.2M	9.3M	21.9M	11.3M

2016 Offseason Spending

Total Spent	Total Spent Rk	Free Agents #	Free Agents $	Free Agents $ Rk	Waiver #	Waiver $	Waiver $ Rk	Extended #	Sum of Extended $	Sum of Drafted $	Undrafted #	Undrafted $
187M	16	10	48M	21	1	1M	32	2	63M	41M	22	34M

2015 Stats & Fantasy Production

Pos	Player	Ov. Rank	Pos. Rk	Age	Gms	St	Pass Comp	Pass Att	Pass Yds	Pass TD	Pass Int	Rush Att	Rush Yds	Rush YPA	Rush TD	Targ	Recp	Rec Yds	Rec YPC	Rec TDs	Draft King Pts	Fan Duel Pts
QB	Nick Foles		32	26	11	11	190	337	2,052	7	10	17	20	1	1						109	104
	Case Keenum		41	27	6	5	76	125	828	4	1	12	5	0							50	45
RB	Todd Gurley*	16	5	21	13	12						229	1,106	5	10	26	21	188	9		215	198
	Benny Cunningham		77	25	16	1						37	140	4		36	26	250	10		71	52
	Tre Mason		82	22	13	3						75	207	3	1	25	18	88	5		56	43
WR	Tavon Austin	58	25	24	16	14						52	434	8	4	87	52	473	9	5	207	173
	Kenny Britt		51	27	16	13										72	36	681	19	3	125	104
	Stedman Bailey		121	25	8	3										25	12	182	15	1	39	30
TE	Jared Cook		34	28	16	12										75	39	481	12		91	68
	Lance Kendricks		40	27	15	12										36	25	245	10	2	65	49

ODDS & TRENDS
Los Angeles Rams

<table>
<tr><td>Avg Line</td><td>+1.9</td><td>Pred Wins</td><td>7</td><td>Pred Div Finish</td><td>#3</td></tr>
</table>

2016 Weekly Betting Lines (wks 1-16)

(-) Favorite   Underdog (+)
-5.5   +10.0

Weekly betting lines chart showing values: -2.0, +4.0, +1.0, +7.0, +1.0 (H), +1.0 (H), +3.5 (H), +4.0 (A), -2.0 (H), -3.3, +9.0 (A), -3.0, +10.0 (A), -5.5 (H). Avg Line = 1.9.

2015 Critical and Game-Deciding Stats

TO Margin	+5
TO Given	21
INT Given	11
FUM Given	10
TO Taken	26
INT Taken	13
FUM Taken	13
Sack Margin	+23
Sacks	41
Sacks Allow	18
Return TD Margin	+0
Ret TDs	4
Ret TDs Allow	4
Penalty Margin	-13
Penalties	122
Opponent Penalties	109

-Teams that win the turnover battle win 79% of games & cover 79% ATS.
-Teams with more sacks win 71% of games & cover 69% ATS.
-Teams with more return TDs win 75% of games & cover 75% ATS.
-Teams with fewer penalties win 57% of games & cover 54% ATS.

2016 NFLproject.com Forecast

Div RK
Div W%

Playoffs RK
% in Playoffs

Super Bowl RK
% Win Super Bowl

53%
42%
4%

Odds to Win Division

NFCW

Team Records & Trends

	2015	2014	2013
Average line	1.4	3.1	3.8
Average O/U line	42.1	43.8	43.4
Straight Up Record	7-9	6-10	7-9
Against the Spread Record	7-9	7-9	7-9
Over/Under Record	4-12	8-8	9-7
ATS as Favorite	3-3	2-3	3-1
ATS as Underdog	4-5	5-6	4-8
Straight Up Home	5-3	3-5	5-3
ATS Home	5-3	3-5	5-3
Over/Under Home	3-5	5-3	5-3
ATS as Home Favorite	3-1	1-3	3-1
ATS as a Home Dog	2-1	2-2	2-2
Straight Up Away	2-6	3-5	2-6
ATS Away	2-6	4-4	2-6
Over/Under Away	1-7	3-5	4-4
ATS Away Favorite	0-2	1-0	0-0
ATS Away Dog	2-4	3-4	2-6
Six Point Teaser Record	10-4	10-6	12-4
Seven Point Teaser Record	12-4	10-6	12-4
Ten Point Teaser Record	12-4	10-5	13-3

Games Favored
5

Games Underdog
9

Close Game Records

All 2015 Wins: 7
FG Games (<=3 pts) W-L: 2-3
FG Games Win %: 40% (#20)
FG Games Wins (% of Total Wins): 29% (#13)
1 Score Games (<=8 pts) W-L: 5-4
1 Score Games Win %: 56% (#12)
1 Score Games Wins (% of Total Wins): 71% (#11)

Home Lines (wks 1-16)

Avg Line = -0.6

Road Lines (wks 1-16)

Avg Line = 4.0

Regular Season Wins: Past Results & Current Proj

2012 Wins	7
2013 Wins	7
2014 Wins	6
Proj 2015 Wins	7.5
2015 Wins	7
Proj 2016 Wins	7

The Rams were 2-3 in FG games and 5-4 in one score games, which is theoretically what the long term results for the average team should be: a coin flip in coin flip games. However, a lot of other things went right for the Rams last year as well. They were +23 in sack margin and +5 in turnover margin. They took only 18 sacks, and from a pure metric perspective, ranked #1 in pass protection efficiency. A big factor for any rookie QB is protection and health. It's hard enough trying to make it through your rookie season with protection - ask Marcus Mariota last season. It will be very difficult with games against ARI, SEA, NYJ, CAR and BUF in 5 of your first 9 games as a pro. Last year the defense was one of the most injured in the NFL, and despite that, to close out the season they lost 3 games while holding opponents to 18 or less including two in OT.

2016 Rest Analysis

Avg Rest	6.4
Avg Rest Rk	29
Team More Rest	2
Opp More Rest	2
Net Rest Edge	0
3 days rest	1
4 days rest	0
5 days rest	1
6 days rest	10
7 days rest	1
8 days rest	1
9 days rest	0
10 days rest	0
11 days rest	0
12 days rest	0
13 days rest	1
14 days rest	0

Weekly EDSR & Season Trending Performance

	1	2	3	4	5		7	8	9	10	11	12	13	14	15	16	17
WEEK																	
RESULT	W	L	L	W	L		W	W	L	L	L	L	L	W	W	W	L
OPP	SEA	WAS	PIT	ARI	GB		CLE	SF	MIN	CHI	BAL	CIN	ARI	DET	TB	SEA	SF
SITE	H	A	H	A	A		H	H	A	H	A	A	H	A	H	H	A
MARGIN	3	-14	-6	2	-14		18	21	-3	-24	-3	-24	-24	7	8	6	-3
PTS	34	10	6	24	10		24	27	18	13	13	7	3	21	31	23	16
OPP PTS	31	24	12	22	24		6	6	21	37	16	31	27	14	23	17	19

Week by Week 2015 Results

EDSR Results (W/L) By Week
W=Green
L=Red

Off & Def EDSR Wk & Trend
- Blue=Offense (high=good)
- Red=Defense (low=good)

23

STATS & VISUALIZATIONS

Los Angeles Rams

Directional Passer Rating Achieved

Receiver	Short Left	Short Middle	Short Right	Deep Left	Deep Middle	Deep Right
Tavon Austin	120	87	57	40	39	48
Jared Cook	51	92	54	104	0	46
Kenny Britt	73	17	39	73	141	106
Lance Kendricks	79	31	78	149	0	
Bradley Marquez	91	55	50	39	39	39
Wes Welker	86	93	39		39	
Stedman Bailey	56	58	51	95	118	97
Brian Quick	65	89	50	39	39	39
Cory Harkey	94	39	79			
Chris Givens		95				

Directional Frequency by Receiver

Receiver	Short Left	Short Middle	Short Right	Deep Left	Deep Middle	Deep Right
Tavon Austin	30%	16%	24%	20%	6%	24%
Jared Cook	16%	26%	21%	17%	6%	21%
Kenny Britt	18%	12%	16%	27%	44%	26%
Lance Kendricks	6%	16%	15%	10%	6%	
Bradley Marquez	8%	6%	6%	3%	6%	3%
Wes Welker	8%	12%	3%		6%	
Stedman Bailey	4%	3%	7%	7%	6%	16%
Brian Quick	8%	7%	6%	17%	19%	11%
Cory Harkey	3%	1%	2%			
Chris Givens		1%				

Defense Passer Rating Allowed

Short Left	Short Middle	Short Right	Deep Left	Deep Middle	Deep Right
111	120	79	52	100	57

Offensive Rush Directional Yds/Carry

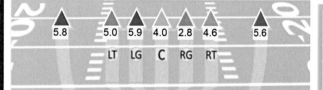

	LT	LG	C	RG	RT	
5.8	5.0	5.9	4.0	2.8	4.6	5.6

Offensive Rush Frequency of Direction

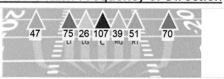

	LT	LG	C	RG	RT	
47	75	26	107	39	51	70

Offensive Explosive Runs by Direction

	LT	LG	C	RG	RT	
10	11	1	10	1	7	16

Defensive Rush Directional Yds/Carry

	LT	LG	C	RG	RT	
5.5	5.4	4.2	3.8	2.6	4.0	4.7

Nick Foles - 1st Down RTG

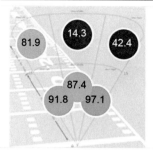

Nick Foles - 3rd Down RTG

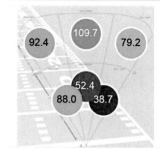

Nick Foles - 2nd Down RTG

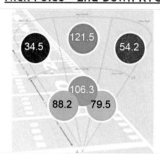

Nick Foles - Overall RTG

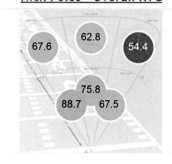

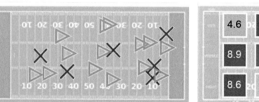

2nd & Short RUN (1D or not)

2nd & Short RUN Stats

Run Conv Rk	1D% Run	NFL 1D% Run Avg	Run Freq	NFL Run Freq Avg
15	70%	69%	77%	64%

2nd & Short PASS (1D or not)

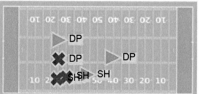

2nd & Short PASS Stats

Pass Conv Rk	1D% Pass	NFL 1D% Pass Avg	Pass Freq	NFL Pass Freq Avg
22	50%	55%	23%	36%

Pass Offense Play Success Rate

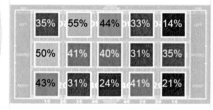

35%	55%	44%	33%	14%
50%	41%	40%	31%	35%
43%	31%	24%	41%	21%

Pass Offense Yds/Play

4.6	9.5	6.3	6.9	3.3
8.9	7.5	7.9	7.9	3.5
8.6	4.0	3.9	5.7	2.4

Off. Directional Tendency (% of Plays Left, Middle or Right)

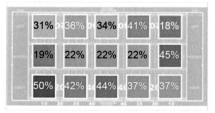

31%	36%	34%	41%	18%
19%	22%	22%	22%	45%
50%	42%	44%	37%	37%

Off. Directional Pass Rate (% of Plays which are Passes)

52%	63%	57%	51%	39%
28%	44%	42%	31%	46%
58%	65%	76%	48%	54%

San Francisco 49ers

Forecast 2016 Wins
6

Past Records
2015: 5-11
2014: 8-8
2013: 12-4

Opponent Strength
Easy _____ Hard

2016 Schedule & Week by Week Strength of Schedule

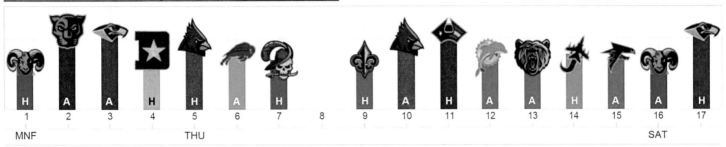

H	A	A	H	H	A	H		H	A	H	A	A	H	A	A	H
1	2	3	4	5	6	7	8	9	10	11	12	13	14	15	16	17

MNF   THU   SAT

2016 Overview

Chip Kelly is a genius and his offense will revolutionize the NFL. That's was said about the Eagles after going from 4 wins in Andy Reid's last season to 10 wins, 1st place in the NFC East, and a playoff berth in Chip Kelly's first season. Two years later, a 6-9 record saw Chip Kelly fired on December 29th. We all remember what happened in 2015 which led to his termination. His personnel management and ego overtook the team and terrible decisions were made heading into the 2015 season. The team cut ties with Nick Foles, LeSean McCoy and Jeremy Maclin among others. They brought in players including Sam Bradford and DeMarco Murray. They had no WRs of threat except for the 2nd year Jordan Matthews, and the team did not utilize the RBs in the most efficient manner possible.

To project the 2016 49ers, forget the 2015 Eagles. Instead, recall the 2013 Eagles. What was right about Chip Kelly and the Eagles in 2013 that allowed the marriage to get off to such a smooth start and see a lot of immediate success, moving from 4 wins to 10? For starters, they were talented. Heading into Andy Reid's last season, the team signed free agent WR DeSean Jackson, G Evan Mathis and LT King Dunlap. The year before, LeSean McCoy was the most efficient running back in the NFL. What happened in 2012 that led to Reid's departure? All-Pro LT Jason Peters tore his Achilles in the offseason and missed the entire year. C Jason Kelse tore up his knee after 2 games. RT Todd Herremans missed the 2nd half of the season with an ankle injury. And McCoy missed 4 games with a concussion. The Eagles in 2012 led the NFL with 37 fumbles. Their opponents had the best starting field position in the NFL, and the Eagles defense in 2012 was the NFL's worst pass defense. That ridiculous combination doomed the team and Andy Reid.

When Chip Kelly walked in the door, their injured players were healthy and they also drafted T Lane Johnson 4th overall in the 2013 draft as well as Zach Ertz in the 2nd round. The combination of returning player health, newer talent that couldn't be fully utilized (Jackson, Mathis) and new draft picks gave the 2013 Eagles a massive upgrade over 2012. They finished 3rd in offensive efficiency. Their pace was unlike anything the NFL had seen & caught teams offguard. The Eagles called an insane 53 plays in the first half of his first game as a head coach. The Eagles were fast tempo but also had fast players, and the combination of Maclin, Jackson and McCoy saw the Eagles post the NFL's best YAC since 1992. They also introduced the zone read in a manner that wasn't seen before. They used zone read runs on 64% of their rushes, including 41 usages in Kelly's first game of the season, for a whopping 245 yards.

It's obvious that the immense talent on the 2013 Eagles, coupled with Kelly's innovation, is what enabled the team to win. The 2016 49ers, however, are absent that level of talent. The offensive line can't be much worse than last year, but they are not getting back pro-bowlers from injury or introducing 4th overall draft picks into the 2016 line. The receiving corps has one fast player (Torrey Smith) but is a far cry from the team speed and talent of the 2013 Eagles. And Kelly's wrinkles have been seen before, and instead of going head to head against the likes of weaker defenses of Washington, Dallas and New York, his offense must go up against the defenses of Seattle, St. Louis and Arizona.

Strength of Schedule In Detail

True Strength of Schedule Rank: 1

Hardest Stretches *(1=Hard, 32=Easy)*
Hardest 3 wk Stretch Rk: 5
Hardest 4 wk Stretch Rk: 2
Hardest 5 wk Stretch Rk: 2

Easiest Stretches *(1=Easy, 32=Hard)*
Easiest 3 wk Stretch Rk: 28
Easiest 4 wk Stretch Rk: 21
Easiest 5 wk Stretch Rk: 13

San Francisco faces the 2nd hardest five-week stretch this season (weeks 2-6: @ CAR, @ SEA, vs DAL, vs ARI, @ BUF). They also are one of ten teams to play back-to-back road games on three separate occasions. As we've seen, Chip Kelly's defenses in his 3 years in the NFL average the most time on the field per game, so starting against a difficult slate of opponents may snowball, throwing a wrench into the 49ers early success. The biggest problem for the 49ers is simply the NFC West, as that means the Seahawks twice and the Cardinals twice, and both teams are projected to be among the best in 2016. Factor in games vs the Panthers and Patriots, and it's the most difficult that any team will face. Even the stretch of easy games they have between weeks 12-16 is made more difficult by the fact that four of five are on the road (@ MIA, @ CHI, vs NYJ, @ ATL, @ STL).

2015 Play Tendencies

All Pass %	60%
All Pass Rk	17
All Rush %	40%
All Rush Rk	16
1 Score Pass %	52%
1 Score Pass Rk	27
2014 1 Score Pass %	52%
2014 1 Score Pass Rk	27
Pass Increase %	1%
Pass Increase Rk	18
1 Score Rush %	48%
1 Score Rush Rk	6
Up Pass %	46%
Up Pass Rk	24
Up Rush %	54%
Up Rush Rk	9
Down Pass %	64%
Down Pass Rk	26
Down Rush %	36%
Down Rush Rk	7

The 2015 49ers tendencies are effectively out the window thanks to Chip Kelly taking over in 2016. The 49ers passed league average, but only because they were trailing so often. When the game was within 1 score, this team wanted to run, passing the 6th least often in the NFL. They passed just 52% in 1 score games. The Eagles under Chip Kelly last year were at 58%, and 58% in his entire tenure in the NFL.

2015 Offensive Advanced Metrics

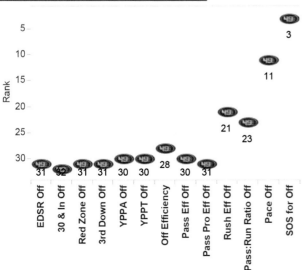

It would be easy to say the 49ers faced the toughest schedule in the NFL last year so naturally their metrics were terrible. But many of the custom advanced metrics I invented are schedule-adjusted, in addition to the efficiency metrics. On top of that, the 49ers play the NFL's most difficult schedule in 2016, so things don't get any easier from that perspective. They need to understand their 2015 deficiencies, their 2016 roster, and ways to get more out of their current group. Offensively, you won't find another team in another year with more 30th-32nd finishes in recent memory. Defensively, they were slightly better in certain key metrics like on 3rd down or inside the red zone, but the 49ers now have a new worry defensively, and that is getting even more worn out if the offense is faster under Chip Kelly but not significantly more efficient.

2015 Defensive Advanced Metrics

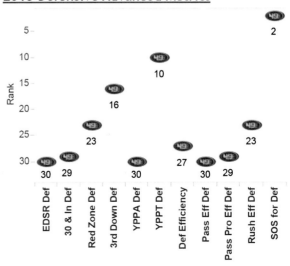

Drafted Players

2016 Draft Grade: #28 (2.3/4)

PERSONNEL & SPENDING   San Francisco 49ers

Rnd.	Pick #	Pos.	Player	College
1	7	DE	DeForest Buckner	Oregon
1	28	G	Joshua Garnett	Stanford
3	68	CB	Will Redmond	Mississippi State
4	133	CB	Rashard Robinson	LSU
	142	DE	Ronald Blair	Appalachian State
5	145	OT	John Theus	Georgia
	174	OT	Fahn Cooper	Ole Miss
	207	QB	Jeff Driskel	Louisiana Tech
6	211	RB	Kelvin Taylor	Florida
	213	WR	Aaron Burbridge	Michigan State
7	249	CB	Prince Charles Iworah	Western Kentucky

Free Agents/Trades Added

Player (Position)

Thaddeus Lewis QB

Wynton McManis LB

Zane Beadles G

Other Signed

Player (Position)

Alex Balducci DT
Blake Muir G
Bryce Treggs WR
Darren Lake DT
Demetrius Cherry DE
Devon Cajuste WR
Jason Fanaika LB
Jered Bell S
John Lunsford K
Kevin Anderson LB
Lenny Jones LB
Norman Price T

2015 Players Lost

Transaction	Player (Position)
Cut	Brian Leonhardt TE
	Corey Acosta K
	Dylan Thompson QB
	Jordan Devey T
	Kendall Gaskins RB
	Kevin Anderson LB
Declared Free Agent	Alex Boone G
	Anquan Boldin WR
Retired	Jarryd Hayne RB

- It was clear the 49ers needed a lot of help. And they had plenty of opportunity in the 2016 draft to add pieces. But while some of these pieces filed needs, others seemed to ignore big issues in the passing game, which due to increased passing under Chip Kelly, could become an issue.

- The 49ers primarily drafted along the lines with their first 7 picks, grabbing 3 offensive linemen and 2 defensive linemen in the process. If you factor in their big free agent acquisition in G Zane Beadles, you have a team that will be able to have competition for position along the offensive line. They addressed a key problem from 2015, which was sack margin, by attacking defensive and offensive linemen this offseason.

- However, whether it ultimately is Colin Kaepernick or Blaine Gabbert under center, the available weaponry is somewhat limited. Anquan Boldin is no longer with the 49ers but was their leading receiver in 2015, catching 69 passes, double that of any other receiver. Torrey Smith is back, along Quinton Patton, Bruce Ellington and newly drafted 6th rounder Aaron Burbridge. Removing Boldin dropped the WR corps from the 13th most expensive in 2015 down to 24th in 2016. And it shows. It will be a challenge for Chip Kelly to accurately evaluate the QB position without moderate WR play. We saw how DeSean Jackson and Jeremy Maclin can elevate the QB in Kelly's offense, making Nick Foles and Mark Sanchez look more than capable at times. But with that position being one of weakness rather than strength, we saw how the offense struggled in 2015.

- Defensively, the 49ers focused on 2 areas exclusively: they drafted nothing but college DEs (2) and CBs (3) in the draft. We know they need to pressure the opposing QB better, and covering better in the secondary helps make that task easier. The 49ers roll into the 2016 season with the 7th most expensive corps of safeties and the 9th most expensive corps of linebackers, but overall the defense is 27th and the offense is 30th.

Lineup & 2016 Cap Hit

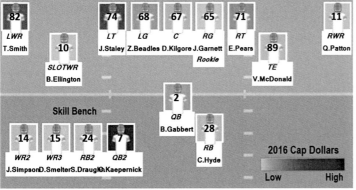

Health Overall & by Unit (2015 v 2014)

2015 Rk	26
2015 AGL	84
Off Rk	28
Def Rk	11
2014 Rk	28
2014 AGL	102

2016 Positional Spending

	All OFF	QB	OL	RB	WR	TE	All DEF	DL	LB	CB	S
2015 Rk	21	10	19	18	13	30	29	28	12	29	13
Rank	30	17	25	26	24	28	27	27	9	26	7
Total	62.8M	19.3M	21.2M	3.7M	13.9M	4.7M	68.5M	20.6M	25.3M	9.1M	13.6M

2016 Offseason Spending

Total Spent	Total Spent Rk	Free Agents #	Free Agents $	Free Agents $ Rk	Waiver #	Waiver $	Waiver $ Rk	Extended #	Sum of Extended $	Sum of Drafted $	Undrafted #	Undrafted $
110M	29	4	15M	30	8	8M	29	4	27M	38M	14	23M

2015 Stats & Fantasy Production

Pos	Player	Ov. Rank	Pos. Rk	Age	Gms	St	Pass Comp	Pass Att	Pass Yds	Pass TD	Pass Int	Rush Att	Rush Yds	Rush YPA	Rush TD	Targ	Recp	Rec Yds	Rec YPC	Rec TDs	Draft King Pts	Fan Duel Pts
QB	Blaine Gabbert	29	26	8	8	178	282	2,031	10	7	32	185	6	1						144	137
QB	Colin Kaepernick	31	28	9	8	144	244	1,615	6	5	45	256	6	1						120	113
RB	Carlos Hyde	55	24	7	7						115	470	4	3	15	11	53	5		84	76
RB	Bruce Miller	103	28	16	5						6	14	2	1	14	10	135	14		34	26
WR	Anquan Boldin	42	35	14	13										111	69	789	11	4	174	135
WR	Torrey Smith	48	26	16	12										62	33	663	20	4	128	109
WR	Quinton Patton	89	25	16	4						1	5	5		57	30	394	13	1	79	61
TE	Vance McDonald	31	25	14	11										46	30	326	11	3	84	66
TE	Garrett Celek	39	27	11	8										28	19	186	10	3	59	46
TE	Blake Bell	57	24	14	5										25	15	186	12		37	26

Avg Line	+5.4	Pred Wins	6	Pred Div Finish	#4

ODDS & TRENDS — San Francisco 49ers

2016 Weekly Betting Lines (wks 1-16)

(-) Favorite   Underdog (+)
+0.0   +14.0

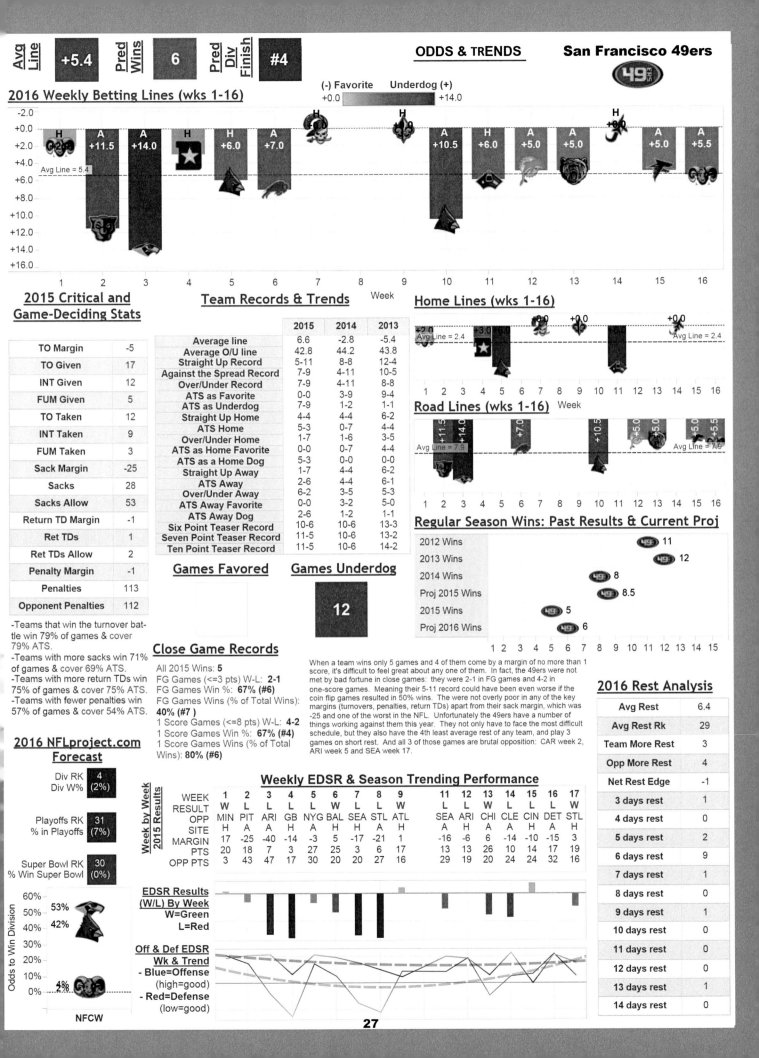

Week	1	2	3	4	5	6	7	8	9	10	11	12	13	14	15	16
Line	H +2.0	A +11.5	A +14.0	H	H +6.0	A +7.0	+0.0		+0.0	A +10.5	H +6.0	A +5.0	A +5.0	+0.0	A +5.0	A +5.5

Avg Line = 5.4

2015 Critical and Game-Deciding Stats

TO Margin	-5
TO Given	17
INT Given	12
FUM Given	5
TO Taken	12
INT Taken	9
FUM Taken	3
Sack Margin	-25
Sacks	28
Sacks Allow	53
Return TD Margin	-1
Ret TDs	1
Ret TDs Allow	2
Penalty Margin	-1
Penalties	113
Opponent Penalties	112

-Teams that win the turnover battle win 79% of games & cover 79% ATS.
-Teams with more sacks win 71% of games & cover 69% ATS.
-Teams with more return TDs win 75% of games & cover 75% ATS.
-Teams with fewer penalties win 57% of games & cover 54% ATS.

2016 NFLproject.com Forecast

Div RK 4
Div W% (2%)

Playoffs RK 31
% in Playoffs (7%)

Super Bowl RK 30
% Win Super Bowl (0%)

Odds to Win Division
60% 53%
50%
40% 42%
30%
20%
10% 4%
0% 2%
NFCW

Team Records & Trends

	2015	2014	2013
Average line	6.6	-2.8	-5.4
Average O/U line	42.8	44.2	43.8
Straight Up Record	5-11	8-8	12-4
Against the Spread Record	7-9	4-11	10-5
Over/Under Record	7-9	4-11	8-8
ATS as Favorite	0-0	3-9	9-4
ATS as Underdog	7-9	1-2	1-1
Straight Up Home	4-4	4-4	6-2
ATS Home	5-3	0-7	4-4
Over/Under Home	1-7	1-6	3-5
ATS as Home Favorite	0-0	0-7	4-4
ATS as a Home Dog	5-3	0-0	0-0
Straight Up Away	1-7	4-4	6-2
ATS Away	2-6	4-4	6-1
Over/Under Away	6-2	3-5	5-3
ATS Away Favorite	0-0	3-2	5-0
ATS Away Dog	2-6	1-2	1-1
Six Point Teaser Record	10-6	10-6	13-3
Seven Point Teaser Record	11-5	10-6	13-2
Ten Point Teaser Record	11-5	10-6	14-2

Games Favored

Games Underdog

12

Close Game Records

All 2015 Wins: 5
FG Games (<=3 pts) W-L: 2-1
FG Games Win %: 67% (#6)
FG Games Wins (% of Total Wins): 40% (#7)
1 Score Games (<=8 pts) W-L: 4-2
1 Score Games Win %: 67% (#4)
1 Score Games Wins (% of Total Wins): 80% (#6)

Home Lines (wks 1-16)

+2.0 Avg Line = 2.4   +3.0 +0.0   +0.0   +0.0   Avg Line = 2.4

| Week | 1 | 2 | 3 | 4 | 5 | 6 | 7 | 8 | 9 | 10 | 11 | 12 | 13 | 14 | 15 | 16 |

Road Lines (wks 1-16)

Avg Line = 7.9   +11.5 +14.0   +7.0   +10.5   +5.0 +5.0   +5.0 +5.5   Avg Line = 7.9

| Week | 1 | 2 | 3 | 4 | 5 | 6 | 7 | 8 | 9 | 10 | 11 | 12 | 13 | 14 | 15 | 16 |

Regular Season Wins: Past Results & Current Proj

2012 Wins	11
2013 Wins	12
2014 Wins	8
Proj 2015 Wins	8.5
2015 Wins	5
Proj 2016 Wins	6

1 2 3 4 5 6 7 8 9 10 11 12 13 14 15

When a team wins only 5 games and 4 of them come by a margin of no more than 1 score, it's difficult to feel great about any one of them. In fact, the 49ers were not met by bad fortune in close games: they were 2-1 in FG games and 4-2 in one-score games. Meaning their 5-11 record could have been even worse if the coin flip games resulted in 50% wins. The were not overly poor in any of the key margins (turnovers, penalties, return TDs) apart from their sack margin, which was -25 and one of the worst in the NFL. Unfortunately the 49ers have a number of things working against them this year. They not only have to face the most difficult schedule, but they also have the 4th least average rest of any team, and play 3 games on short rest. And all 3 of those games are brutal opposition: CAR week 2, ARI week 5 and SEA week 17.

2016 Rest Analysis

Avg Rest	6.4
Avg Rest Rk	29
Team More Rest	3
Opp More Rest	4
Net Rest Edge	-1
3 days rest	1
4 days rest	0
5 days rest	2
6 days rest	9
7 days rest	1
8 days rest	0
9 days rest	1
10 days rest	0
11 days rest	0
12 days rest	0
13 days rest	1
14 days rest	0

Weekly EDSR & Season Trending Performance

WEEK	1	2	3	4	5	6	7	8	9		11	12	13	14	15	16	17
RESULT	W	L	L	L	W	L	L	L	W		L	L	W	L	L	L	W
OPP	MIN	PIT	ARI	GB	NYG	BAL	SEA	STL	ATL		SEA	ARI	CHI	CLE	CIN	DET	STL
SITE	H	A	A	H	H	H	A	H	H		A	H	A	A	A	H	H
MARGIN	17	-25	-40	-14	-3	5	-17	-21	1		-16	-6	6	-14	-10	-15	3
PTS	20	18	7	3	27	25	3	6	17		13	13	26	10	14	17	19
OPP PTS	3	43	47	17	30	20	20	27	16		29	19	20	24	24	32	16

EDSR Results (W/L) By Week — W=Green, L=Red

Off & Def EDSR Wk & Trend
- Blue=Offense (high=good)
- Red=Defense (low=good)

STATS & VISUALIZATIONS San Francisco 49ers

Directional Passer Rating Achieved

Receiver	Short Left	Short Middle	Short Right	Deep Left	Deep Middle	Deep Right
Anquan Boldin	105	78	86	158	118	32
Torrey Smith	83	39	85	129	158	85
Quinton Patton	60	101	83	39		60
Vance McDonald	117	116	83	17	39	39
Garrett Celek	107	129	97	118		39
Vernon Davis	73	118	47	67	39	32
Blake Bell	118	108	44	95	39	
Bruce Ellington	93	56	88	39	39	118
Jerome Simpson	88		68	0	39	39
DeAndrew White	108		100			
Brian Leonhardt			83			

Colin Kaepernick - 1st Down RTG

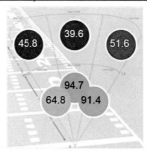

Colin Kaepernick - 3rd Down RTG

Directional Frequency by Receiver

Receiver	Short Left	Short Middle	Short Right	Deep Left	Deep Middle	Deep Right
Anquan Boldin	28%	25%	33%	15%	11%	23%
Torrey Smith	17%	8%	12%	29%	33%	21%
Quinton Patton	14%	19%	14%	6%		23%
Vance McDonald	11%	15%	11%	15%	11%	8%
Garrett Celek	9%	10%	6%	3%		5%
Vernon Davis	6%	5%	9%	9%	11%	10%
Blake Bell	3%	14%	7%	6%	11%	
Bruce Ellington	6%	3%	4%	6%	11%	5%
Jerome Simpson	7%		3%	12%	11%	5%
DeAndrew White	1%		1%			
Brian Leonhardt			1%			

Colin Kaepernick - 2nd Down RTG

Colin Kaepernick - Overall RTG

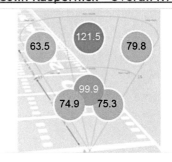

Defense Passer Rating Allowed

Short Left	Short Middle	Short Right	Deep Left	Deep Middle	Deep Right
107	109	80	114	109	65

Pass Offense Play Success Rate

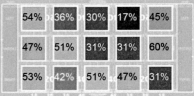

Offensive Rush Directional Yds/Carry

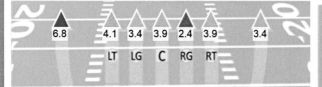

2nd & Short RUN (1D or not)

Pass Offense Yds/Play

Offensive Rush Frequency of Direction

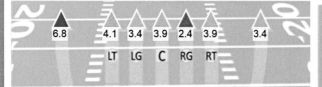

2nd & Short RUN Stats

Run Conv Rk	1D% Run	NFL 1D% Run Avg	Run Freq	NFL Run Freq Avg
17	68%	69%	58%	64%

Off. Directional Tendency (% of Plays Left, Middle or Right)

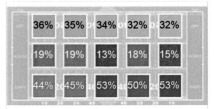

Offensive Explosive Runs by Direction

2nd & Short PASS (1D or not)

Off. Directional Pass Rate (% of Plays which are Passes)

Defensive Rush Directional Yds/Carry

2nd & Short PASS Stats

Pass Conv Rk	1D% Pass	NFL 1D% Pass Avg	Pass Freq	NFL Pass Freq Avg
26	43%	55%	42%	36%

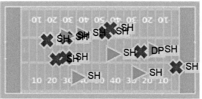

Green Bay Packers

Coaches

Head Coach: Mike McCarthy (11th yr)
OC: Tom Clements (5th yr)
DC: Dom Capers (8th yr)

Forecast
2016 Wins
11

Past Records
2015: 10-6
2014: 12-4
2013: 8-7-1

Opponent Strength
Easy   Hard

2016 Schedule & Week by Week Strength of Schedule

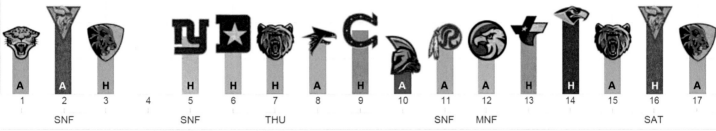

A	A	H		H	H	H	A	H	A	A	A	H	H	A	H	A
1	2	3	4	5	6	7	8	9	10	11	12	13	14	15	16	17
	SNF			SNF		THU			SNF	MNF					SAT	

2016 Overview

In 2015, Aaron Rodgers had a terrible year. And Aaron Rodgers recorded a 93 passer rating. These two statements are completely contradictory for most quarterbacks, but for Aaron Rodgers, it's a testament to his greatness. Aaron Rodgers was hesitant to release the ball last year at times because he lacked confidence in his receivers without Jordy Nelson out there to open up the offense, stretch the field and provide a reliable target. But he missed throws. Announcers and commentators were quick to blame his receivers for not gaining separation. Those same commentators laud Rodgers when hitting covered receivers routinely. You cannot have it both ways. I saw Rodgers struggling & believed it was more than just a lack of confidence. He wasn't playing well, and I thought some of that must have to do with some type of injury. Sure enough, within days of his 2nd playoff game (an OT loss to Arizona), Rodgers had his knee scoped. They may say it was a clean-up from an old injury, but players will resort to surgery as a last alternative. If Rodgers could have avoided the procedure, he would have. If the knee wasn't causing him any issues, it's unlikely he gets it scoped.

Rodgers will rebound, because he's one of the best quarterbacks to have played the game. He is also in an offense that he can run freely, at tempo and use cadence, to dramatically alter the defense's ability to adjust, something that far too few quarterbacks are allowed to do. After going 6-10 in his first year as a starter in 2008, Rodgers has amassed a record as a starter in Green Bay of 74-29 (72%) and has made the playoffs every single one of those 7 seasons. In the salary cap era, the only team with more consecutive playoff appearances was the Peyton Manning-led Colts for 9 straight seasons. The Packers won the Super Bowl in 2010, so that means 6 times Rodgers lost in the playoffs. Three came in overtime on the road. Twice he was defeated by Jim Harbaugh and the innovative zone-read of the Fortyniners, which owned DC Dom Capers. The other loss was to the 2011 Giants, who won the Super Bowl that season. While any great quarterback wants to win it all every single year, it is not as if Rodgers pulled out Andy Dalton playoff clunkers at home. It is not as if Rodgers rarely makes the playoffs, and when he does, almost always goes 1 and done like Matt Ryan. It's not as if Rodgers has a GM who frequently brings in free agent wide receivers, signing them to huge deals so Rodgers can play catch with them. What can the 2016 Packers anticipate with a cleaned up knee, Jordy Nelson and Jared Cook? Hopefully more first half magic. In 2014, Rodgers posted the best first half stat line in the NFL: 120.3 passer rating (#1), built with 25 TDs (#1), 0 Ints (#1), 66% completions and 8.8 yds/att (#1). On deep passes, he posted a 136 rating, which was the NFL's best in at least a decade, as far as I traced the 1st half metric back. That performance led the Packers to score TDs on 40% of their first half drives, 2nd best to only the 2007 Patriots since 1998.

If the Packers want to know an easy way to increase efficiency, they need to simply look to improve their 2nd and short run game. It's the easiest way to convert a first down the NFL has to offer. Yet the Packers converted 9% below average (26th in the NFL) last year, and have consistently ranked well below average for several years now on short yardage running. A few key improvements would there would parlay efficiency across the entire offense. Against an easier schedule, with 8 games against teams who finished bottom-12 in run defense, the Pack should be headed to an 8th consecutive trip to the playoffs.

Strength of Schedule In Detail

True Strength of Schedule Rank: 28

Hardest Stretches *(1=Hard, 32=Easy)*
Hardest 3 wk Stretch Rk:	19
Hardest 4 wk Stretch Rk:	14
Hardest 5 wk Stretch Rk:	16

Easiest Stretches *(1=Easy, 32=Hard)*
Easiest 3 wk Stretch Rk:	13
Easiest 4 wk Stretch Rk:	19
Easiest 5 wk Stretch Rk:	11

For the rest of the NFL, it seems unfair to see such strong teams like the Steelers, Panthers and Packers with easy schedules. But thanks to a schedule that gives Green Bay the AFC South and the NFC East, the hardest part of their schedule is the consecutive travel: they are one of just two teams to play three straight road games (wks 10-12 @ TEN, @ WAS, @ PHI), the first 3 game road trip for the Packers since 2012. However, that difficult is offset by the fact that between September 19th and October 29th, the Packers don't leave Wisconsin as they play 4 consecutive home games and enjoy a bye week. Additionally, late in the season, their 3 most difficult opponents down the stretch (HOU, SEA, MIN) are all at home.

2015 Play Tendencies

All Pass %	59%
All Pass Rk	18
All Rush %	41%
All Rush Rk	15
1 Score Pass %	59%
1 Score Pass Rk	15
2014 1 Score Pass %	56%
2014 1 Score Pass Rk	19
Pass Increase %	2%
Pass Increase Rk	13
1 Score Rush %	41%
1 Score Rush Rk	18
Up Pass %	51%
Up Pass Rk	11
Up Rush %	49%
Up Rush Rk	22
Down Pass %	68%
Down Pass Rk	17
Down Rush %	32%
Down Rush Rk	16

In 2014, with a full compliment of receiving weapons and Aaron Rodgers in the midst of an incredible season, the Packers passed the ball 56% of the time in one-score games, 19th in the NFL. However, last season without Nelson and with Rodgers in the midst of a funk season that saw him require offseason surgery to correct an "issue", the Packers passed the ball 59% of the time in one-score games. They were top 10 in rush efficiency, and likely should have tried to run the ball more often.

2015 Offensive Advanced Metrics

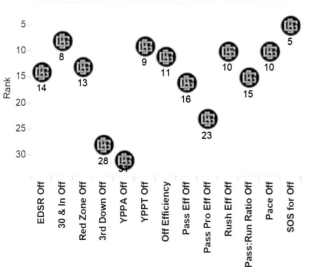

The Packers played a top 5 schedule of opposing defenses and lost their big play receiver who clearly had more impact than many previously realized. It showed, with a 2nd worst rating on yds/pass and their 3rd down offense was 5th worst in the NFL. Those are shocking numbers for Aaron Rodgers and this offense. Their pass protection ranked just 23rd, in part because Rodgers struggled to place the football with receivers not getting open. However, on the flip side, the Packers faced all 5 of the top 5 defenses in pass efficiency last year (DEN, CAR, SEA, ARI, KC), so their schedule really was stacked. Defensively, the team tried to step up to assist the offense, and they were able to do so. They finished 7th EDSR and were very strong against the pass, finishing 6th. In 12 of their 18 games, they held opponents to fewer points than their opponent was projected to score.

2015 Defensive Advanced Metrics

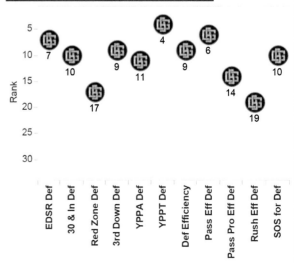

29

Drafted Players

2016 Draft Grade: #15 (3.0/4)

Rnd.	Pick #	Pos.	Player	College
1	27	DT	Kenny Clark	UCLA
2	48	OT	Jason Spriggs	Indiana
3	88	OLB	Kyler Fackrell	Utah State
4	131	ILB	Blake Martinez	Stanford
4	137	DE	Dean Lowry	Northwestern
5	163	WR	Trevor Davis	California
6	200	OT	Kyle Murphy	Stanford

PERSONNEL & SPENDING

Green Bay Packers

Free Agents/Trades Added

Player (Position)

Jared Cook TE

Lerentee McCray LB

Other Signed

Player (Position)

Alstevis Squirewell RB
Beniquez Brown LB
Brandon Burks RB
Brian Price DT
Casey Pierce TE
Cory Tucker G
David Grinnage TE
Demetris Anderson DT
Dennis Parks WR
Devonte Robinson WR
Don Jackson RB
Geronimo Allison WR
Herb Waters WR
Jacob Flores C
Joe Callahan QB
Josh Hawkins CB
Josh James T
Kentrell Brice S
Makinton Dorleant CB
Manoa Pikula LB
Marwin Evans S
Peter Mortell P
Randall Jette CB
Reggie Gilbert LB
Tyler Kuder DT

2015 Players Lost

Transaction	Player (Position)
Cut	David Grinnage TE
	Dennis Parks WR
	Jeremy Vujnovich T
	Josh Boyd DT
	Kowalski, Vince T
	Nate Palmer LB
	Ray Drew DE
	William Campbell G
	Williams, Ryan QB
Declared Free Agent	Andy Mulumba LB
	B.J. Raji DT
	Casey Hayward CB

- While the Packers prefer to be home grown and built through the draft, they made one exception by acquiring TE Jared Cook through free agency. Cook had foot surgery which sidelined him from OTAs, but he was a standout at voluntary practices and should be ready to head into the season. Jared Cook has worked with some atrocious QBs in atrocious offenses before joining Aaron Rodgers and the Packers:
- Old veteran QBs playing out their career with beat-up offenses, such as Shaun Hill, Kerry Collins, Kellen Clemens and Matt Hasselbeck. Middling QBs that have not met potential, such as Nick Foles and Sam Bradford. Less heralded QBs who may never amount to anything like Austin Davis and Case Keenum. And lastly, the trio of Jake Locker, Vince Young and Rusty Smith. Cook should have a tremendous year in Green Bay (if healthy).
- Stats should benefit Aaron Rodgers as well. The last time he had a reliable TE option (Jordan Finley), his stats from Rodgers in the red zone alone: 60% completions, 18 TDs:1 INT and a 104 rating when targeted. He fills a void left in 2013 by TE Jermichael Finley's injury and then retirement. Aaron Rodgers loves throwing to big targets and produces better stats when targeting them. Jared Cook is the biggest starting target Rodgers has ever had to work with. Cook should help to refresh the Packers drop in red zone production, and elevate them back to a top-10 red zone offense (from below-average since Finley left).
- The additions of TE Cook and WR Jordy Nelson, back from injury, will make Aaron Rodgers significantly more comfortable, something he absolutely lacked in 2015.
- The Packers defense, thanks in large part to Clay Matthews, are paying the 2nd most to the LB position, the same rank as in 2015. Thanks to some cost cutting moves at QB, they are actually spending less there in 2016.

Lineup & 2016 Cap Hit

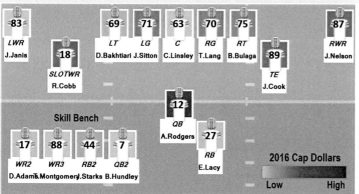

Skill Bench

2016 Cap Dollars Low — High

Health Overall & by Unit (2015 v 2014)

2015 Rk	9
2015 AGL	56
Off Rk	15
Def Rk	14
2014 Rk	3
2014 AGL	42

2016 Positional Spending

	All OFF	QB	OL	RB	WR	TE	All DEF	DL	LB	CB	S
2015 Rk	17	6	15	26	15	28	6	25	2	18	5
Rank	12	13	14	24	12	27	9	26	2	22	10
Total	79.5M	20.7M	27.1M	4.3M	22.2M	5.2M	81.8M	16.8M	35.9M	16.7M	12.5M

2016 Offseason Spending

Total Spent	Total Spent Rk	Free Agents #	Free Agents $	Free Agents $ Rk	Waiver #	Waiver $	Waiver $ Rk	Extended #	Sum of Extended $	Sum of Drafted $	Undrafted #	Undrafted $
124M	25	6	16M	29	12	8M	28	3	31M	28M	26	41M

2015 Stats & Fantasy Production

Pos	Player	Ov. Rank	Pos. Rk	Age	Gms	St	Pass Comp	Pass Att	Pass Yds	Pass TD	Pass Int	Rush Att	Rush Yds	Rush YPA	Rush TD	Targ	Recp	Rec Yds	Rec YPC	Rec TDs	Draft King Pts	Fan Duel Pts
QB	Aaron Rodgers*	52	7	32	16	16	347	572	3,821	31	8	58	344	6	1						311	301
RB	James Starks	76	24	29	16	4						148	601	4	2	53	43	392	9	3	175	145
RB	Eddie Lacy		26	25	15	12						187	758	4	3	28	20	188	9	2	149	131
WR	James Jones	56	23	31	16	15										99	50	890	18	8	194	166
WR	Randall Cobb	31	25	16	15							13	50	4		129	79	829	10	6	212	169
WR	Davante Adams	78	23	13	12											94	50	483	10	1	109	81
WR	Ty Montgomery	116	22	6	3							3	14	5		19	12	136	9		45	35
TE	Richard Rodgers	60	9	23	16	12						1	11	11		85	58	510	9	8	163	131

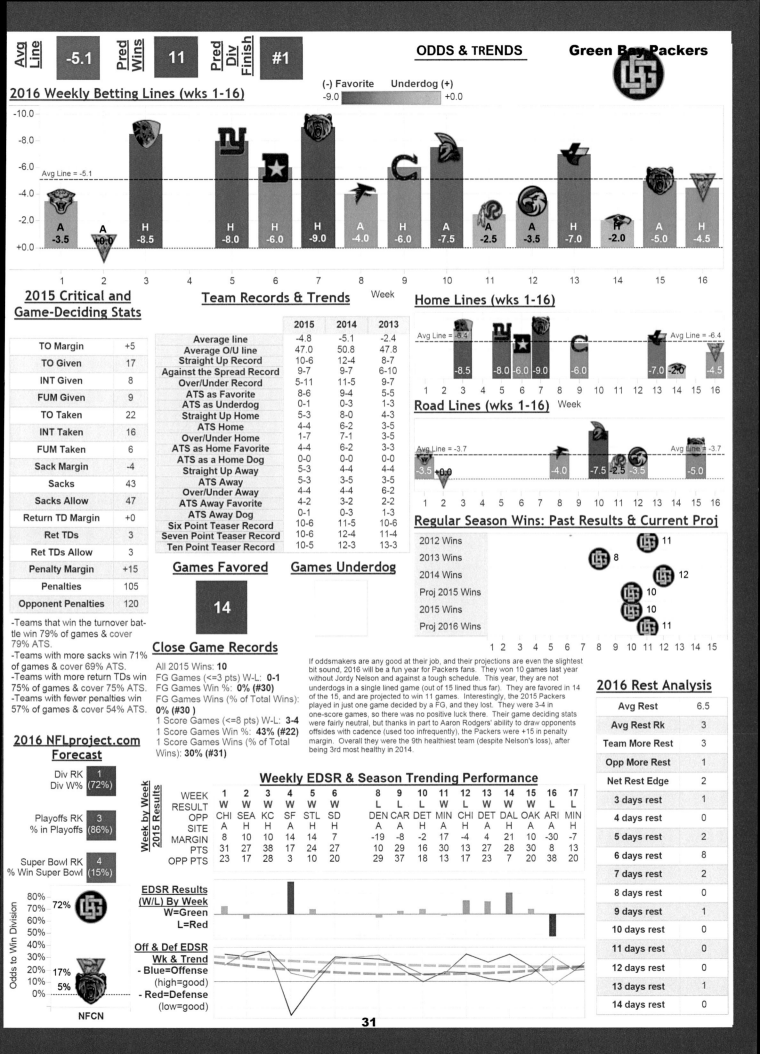

| Avg Line | **-5.1** | Pred Wins | **11** | Pred Div Finish | **#1** | **ODDS & TRENDS** | **Green Bay Packers** |

(-) Favorite   Underdog (+)
-9.0   +0.0

2016 Weekly Betting Lines (wks 1-16)

Week	1	2	3	4	5	6	7	8	9	10	11	12	13	14	15	16
Site	A	A	H		H	H	H	A	H	A	A	A	H	H	A	H
Line	-3.5	+0.0	-8.5		-8.0	-6.0	-9.0	-4.0	-6.0	-7.5	-2.5	-3.5	-7.0	-2.0	-5.0	-4.5

Avg Line = -5.1

2015 Critical and Game-Deciding Stats

TO Margin	+5
TO Given	17
INT Given	8
FUM Given	9
TO Taken	22
INT Taken	16
FUM Taken	6
Sack Margin	-4
Sacks	43
Sacks Allow	47
Return TD Margin	+0
Ret TDs	3
Ret TDs Allow	3
Penalty Margin	+15
Penalties	105
Opponent Penalties	120

-Teams that win the turnover battle win 79% of games & cover 79% ATS.
-Teams with more sacks win 71% of games & cover 69% ATS.
-Teams with more return TDs win 75% of games & cover 75% ATS.
-Teams with fewer penalties win 57% of games & cover 54% ATS.

2016 NFLproject.com Forecast

Div RK	1	
Div W%	(72%)	
Playoffs RK	3	
% in Playoffs	(86%)	
Super Bowl RK	4	
% Win Super Bowl	(15%)	

Odds to Win Division

80% 70% 60% 50% 40% 30% 20% 10% 0%

72%
17%
5%

NFCN

Team Records & Trends

	2015	2014	2013
Average line	-4.8	-5.1	-2.4
Average O/U line	47.0	50.8	47.8
Straight Up Record	10-6	12-4	8-7
Against the Spread Record	9-7	9-7	6-10
Over/Under Record	5-11	11-5	9-7
ATS as Favorite	8-6	9-4	5-5
ATS as Underdog	0-1	0-3	1-3
Straight Up Home	5-3	8-0	4-3
ATS Home	4-4	6-2	3-5
Over/Under Home	1-7	7-1	3-5
ATS as Home Favorite	4-4	6-2	3-3
ATS as a Home Dog	0-0	0-0	0-0
Straight Up Away	5-3	4-4	4-4
ATS Away	5-3	3-5	3-5
Over/Under Away	4-4	4-4	6-2
ATS Away Favorite	4-2	3-2	2-2
ATS Away Dog	0-1	0-3	1-3
Six Point Teaser Record	10-6	11-5	10-6
Seven Point Teaser Record	10-6	12-4	11-4
Ten Point Teaser Record	10-5	12-3	13-3

Games Favored

14

Games Underdog

Close Game Records

All 2015 Wins: **10**
FG Games (<=3 pts) W-L: **0-1**
FG Games Win %: **0% (#30)**
FG Games Wins (% of Total Wins): **0% (#30)**
1 Score Games (<=8 pts) W-L: **3-4**
1 Score Games Win %: **43% (#22)**
1 Score Games Wins (% of Total Wins): **30% (#31)**

If oddsmakers are any good at their job, and their projections are even the slightest bit sound, 2016 will be a fun year for Packers fans. They won 10 games last year without Jordy Nelson and against a tough schedule. This year, they are not underdogs in a single lined game (out of 15 lined thus far). They are favored in 14 of the 15, and are projected to win 11 games. Interestingly, the 2015 Packers played in just one game decided by a FG, and they lost. They were 3-4 in one-score games, so there was no positive luck there. Their game deciding stats were fairly neutral, but thanks in part to Aaron Rodgers' ability to draw opponents offsides with cadence (used too infrequently), the Packers were +15 in penalty margin. Overall they were the 9th healthiest team (despite Nelson's loss), after being 3rd most healthy in 2014.

Home Lines (wks 1-16)

Avg Line = -6.4

1	2	3	4	5	6	7	8	9	10	11	12	13	14	15	16
		-8.5		-8.0	-6.0	-9.0		-6.0				-7.0	-2.0		-4.5

Road Lines (wks 1-16)   Week

Avg Line = -3.7

1	2	3	4	5	6	7	8	9	10	11	12	13	14	15	16
-3.5	+0.0						-4.0		-7.5	-2.5	-3.5			-5.0	

Regular Season Wins: Past Results & Current Proj

2012 Wins	11
2013 Wins	8
2014 Wins	12
Proj 2015 Wins	10
2015 Wins	10
Proj 2016 Wins	11

1 2 3 4 5 6 7 8 9 10 11 12 13 14 15

2016 Rest Analysis

Avg Rest	6.5
Avg Rest Rk	3
Team More Rest	3
Opp More Rest	1
Net Rest Edge	2
3 days rest	1
4 days rest	0
5 days rest	2
6 days rest	8
7 days rest	2
8 days rest	0
9 days rest	1
10 days rest	0
11 days rest	0
12 days rest	0
13 days rest	1
14 days rest	0

Weekly EDSR & Season Trending Performance

WEEK	1	2	3	4	5	6		8	9	10	11	12	13	14	15	16	17
RESULT	W	W	W	W	W	W		L	L	L	W	L	W	W	W	L	W
OPP	CHI	SEA	KC	SF	STL	SD		DEN	CAR	DET	MIN	CHI	DET	DAL	OAK	ARI	MIN
SITE	A	H	H	A	H	H		A	A	A	H	A	H	A	H	A	H
MARGIN	8	10	10	14	14	7		-19	-8	-2	17	-4	4	21	10	-30	-7
PTS	31	27	38	17	24	27		10	29	16	30	13	27	28	30	8	13
OPP PTS	23	17	28	3	10	20		29	37	18	13	17	23	7	20	38	20

Week by Week 2015 Results

EDSR Results (W/L) By Week
W=Green
L=Red

Off & Def EDSR Wk & Trend
- Blue=Offense (high=good)
- Red=Defense (low=good)

Green Bay Packers

Directional Passer Rating Achieved

Receiver	Short Left	Short Middle	Short Right	Deep Left	Deep Middle	Deep Right
Randall Cobb	98	121	84	82	106	47
Richard Rodgers	122	109	81	39	135	48
James Jones	98	35	46	55	113	135
Davante Adams	90	92	74	61	53	51
Jared Abbrederis	32	118	67	39	43	60
Ty Montgomery	129	158	95	39		39
Justin Perillo	83	133	85	118	118	
Jeff Janis	95	66	51	79	135	39
Andrew Quarless	83	95	85			

Directional Frequency by Receiver

Receiver	Short Left	Short Middle	Short Right	Deep Left	Deep Middle	Deep Right
Randall Cobb	27%	32%	26%	16%	30%	15%
Richard Rodgers	24%	27%	17%	2%	7%	12%
James Jones	23%	10%	14%	44%	26%	30%
Davante Adams	10%	16%	26%	19%	11%	24%
Jared Abbrederis	6%	3%	5%	5%	15%	12%
Ty Montgomery	4%	3%	4%	2%		3%
Justin Perillo	3%	5%	1%	2%	4%	
Jeff Janis	1%	2%	5%	11%	7%	3%
Andrew Quarless	1%	1%	2%			

Defense Passer Rating Allowed

Short Left	Short Middle	Short Right	Deep Left	Deep Middle	Deep Right
86	102	68	82	77	75

Offensive Rush Directional Yds/Carry

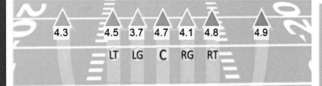

Offensive Rush Frequency of Direction

Offensive Explosive Runs by Direction

Defensive Rush Directional Yds/Carry

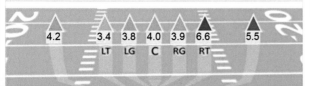

Aaron Rodgers - 1st Down RTG

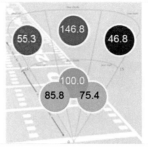

Aaron Rodgers - 3rd Down RTG

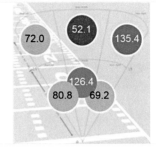

Aaron Rodgers - 2nd Down RTG

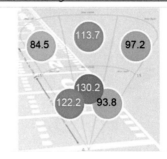

Aaron Rodgers - Overall RTG

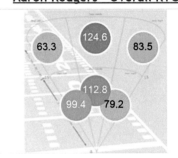

2nd & Short RUN (1D or not)

2nd & Short RUN Stats

Run Conv Rk	1D% Run	NFL 1D% Run Avg	Run Freq	NFL Run Freq Avg
26	60%	69%	63%	64%

2nd & Short PASS (1D or not)

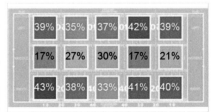

2nd & Short PASS Stats

Pass Conv Rk	1D% Pass	NFL 1D% Pass Avg	Pass Freq	NFL Pass Freq Avg
22	50%	55%	38%	36%

Pass Offense Play Success Rate

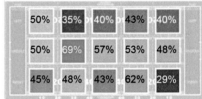

Pass Offense Yds/Play

10.6	5.1	7.3	6.3	3.3
7.4	11.7	9.3	8.9	4.0
4.6	7.1	4.3	9.1	2.0

Off. Directional Tendency (% of Plays Left, Middle or Right)

39%	35%	37%	42%	39%
17%	27%	30%	17%	21%
43%	38%	33%	41%	40%

Off. Directional Pass Rate (% of Plays which are Passes)

60%	61%	55%	59%	74%
34%	55%	51%	37%	46%
57%	58%	66%	65%	75%

Rush to a "Take": The Perils of Ignoring Context

I caught an segment from Colin Cowherd this summer and it was so surprising I had to rewind it and listen to it a few times to let it sink in:

So Aaron Rodgers, now we discover and believe, they have the second best roster in the league. One of the most stable front offices, one of the best GMs, one of the best rosters now. Eight years, one playoff run, no criticism. And for the record he plays in a historically weak division. Chicago's enigmatic, Detroit's historically poorly run and Minnesota runs hot and cold although I do like their young roster. It's amazing to me. Tony Romo, of the Dallas Cowboys, who by the way, has 25 fourth quarter comebacks…. 25! Rodgers has 10. I mean, it's just… it's amazing to me. Pro Football Focus, Green Bay Packers, 2nd best roster in the league. Eight years and for the record, I'll make the argument they've been top 10 Aaron Rodgers' entire run. Where are the playoff pelts?! Where are the playoff wins?! I'm not saying Aaron Rodgers isn't great. He is. Hall of Fame, first ballot, most talented quarterback in a long time, I'm not denying it. But people are so reluctant to say he holds the ball too long, he's not the greatest leader, he can be moody and cocky, he's had wide receivers and tight ends criticize him publicly. Like, even Peter King who I love. Everybody is so reluctant to criticize him. The dude adlibs too much, he doesn't connect with all his teammates, he can be moody, he holds onto the ball too long, and sometimes he's a little too much rock star and not enough coachable.

This isn't anything new for Cowherd. In October last year, he went on a similar rant, and said:

Aaron Rodgers, if anything, is LeBron James. We're in awe of his talent but he hasn't won as much in the postseason as he should win…. Aaron Rodgers is way more LeBron or Durant than he is Michael Jordan…

Later, in November, he came up with the following:

I know a former Green Bay Packer told me Aaron Rodgers can be moody week to week and day to day. He's fought with his head coach, I know that to be true. He's not always gotten along with teammates, I know that to be true. He still holds a grudge against Cal. You ever seem him introduced before a game, you list your alma mater and he says Butte Community College. Awfully juvenile for a star quarterback.

When you get to the point of criticizing his televised intro, labeling it "juvenile", I think it shows the extent of the feelings. It also seems that he only wants to acknowledge the positives after heaping criticism to avoid that "hater" label, though I'm sure many Packers' fans still consider him to be one. Rather than to waste too much time discussing the pettiness of some of this criticism, let's just get it out of the way.

Apparently insiders tell Cowherd that Rodgers is moody and cocky and he clearly believes it to be true. Being moody or cocky is not the reason Aaron Rodgers hasn't lived up to Cowherd's expectations in the postseason, because that is what this boils down to. If Rodgers won as much as Cowherd thinks he should, the moodiness and cockiness goes out the window. It is highly likely that teammates considered Tom Brady or Peyton Manning to be moody or cocky at points in their career. But is it not relevant if they were or were not. Rodgers being a little too much "rock star" is in

the same vein. Cam Newton was plenty "rock star" as he stomped through the regular season and the postseason before losing the Super Bowl. Many of great QBs in recent memory have that same type of rock star mentality.

Before touching on the football specific criticisms of too much adlib and holding the ball too long, let's tie back to the main criticism: the lack of "playoff pelts". I'd start with the idea that Rodgers has never failed to make the playoffs except his first year as a starter, back in 2008. Rodgers has led his team to 7 consecutive playoff appearances from 2009 through 2015. Only one other team has done that: the New England Patriots. That deserves to be mentioned.

Cowherd's retort is likely to be that his division is "historically weak", making it easier to make the playoffs. But that is inaccurate. Playing in non-division games since 2009, the NFC North is joined by only the NFC West as the 2 NFC divisions to have 3 of their 4 teams record an above .500 record against non-division opponents. The Vikings, Bears and Packers all have above .500 records in non-division games. The NFC East has zero teams. The NFC South has two teams.

Over in the AFC, the AFC South has zero teams with winning records outside of their division. The Patriots' AFC East has just 2 teams. The AFC North and the AFC West have 3 teams with winning non-division records, like the Packers. And among the 4 divisions that have had success against non-divisional opponents, the NFC North easily has the best "worst" team: the Lions are 43% against non-division opponents, while the other teams like the Raiders (30%), Rams (33%) and Browns (34%) have been significantly worse.

Thus, trying to prop up easy trips to the playoffs on a weak NFC North holds no water, and as I mentioned, the difficulty of making 7 trips to the playoffs in a row deserves to be mentioned.

As for Rodgers failure to have more "playoff pelts", let's first look big picture before diving into specifics:

In these 7 consecutive trips, Rodgers has a 98 rating, with 27 TDs and 8 INTs. In wins, it was a 109 rating with 15 TDs to 2 INTs. In losses, it was 87, with a 12 TD : 6 INT ratio. (Keep in mind Tom Brady has a 72 rating with a 9 TD : 9 INT ratio in playoff losses.)

If Cowherd wants to ignore his career and look only at his results since winning the Super Bowl in 2010, his rating in losses drops to 80, with a 8 TD : 5 INT ratio. One of those interceptions was in garbage time, down 17. But the other 4 were when the Packers were tied (twice), leading (once) or trailing by no more than 1 point in the first 3 quarters of a game that they went on to lose. Inevitably, these played a role in the loss, but none resulted in immediate points. Of his 5 INTs, opponents scored zero points 4 times on their next drives, and the Packers were in the same position they were prior to the interception. The bigger issue came from the defense in his losses. In the Packers

6 losses, they allowed 35 points on average. It is not as if Aaron Rodgers put up Andy Dalton stat lines, or led the offense to shutouts. The Packers still averaged 26.3 ppg even in the losses. The only team to score more points in playoff losses were the Saints, who averaged 27.7 ppg. In their 7 playoff wins, the Packers averaged 29.4 ppg.

A key point when discussing the lack of "playoff pelts" is the fact that half of his losses came in overtime, all on the road. In regulation, Rodgers is 7-3 in the playoffs, with 3 ties. The last two games that were tied after regulation were tied when the opposing team put up double digit 4th quarter points on the Packers defense. The Packers after 3 quarters on the road as decided underdogs (by at least 1 TD in both games) but the 4th quarter defense was terrible and the home teams tied the game and then won in overtime.

Since winning the 2010 Super Bowl, the Packers have been favored in only 3 of 8 playoff games. They've been underdogs in 5 of the 8. Their one win came when they were underdogs by 1 point. Their 4 losses came when they were underdogs of an avg of over 5 points. Their last two exits, in 2014 and 2015, came on the road, as underdogs of at least 7 points, in games they lost in overtime which involved their opponents outscoring the Packers in the 4th quarter to force the overtime.

The reality of Aaron Rodgers is that he is elite and he has produced tremendous numbers. In large part because of his brilliance, the Packers have a playoff streak only matched by the Patriots, while playing in a division more difficult than the Patriots. In the playoffs, his 98 passer rating on over 450 attempts is only bested by Drew Brees' 103 rating (min 200 att).

He was injured last season and playing without his best WR all year. Even so, I called him out for instances when the blame was more on him than what the talking heads led viewers to believe. The adlib and waiting to throw is part of what makes Rodgers as great as he is – something Cowherd himself believes ("Hall of Fame, first ballot"). But to question his playoff performance and his lack of more playoff "runs", while completely ignoring why or how they lost the games is concerning. The defense, at times, was atrocious. And many games Rodgers was a TD+ underdog on the road yet was poised to win in regulation, only to lose to overtime. Of course there will be plays that Rodgers himself should take the blame for, virtually anyone who has ever played sports will know that they should have performed better at certain times. And hopefully he will in 2016, because he is fun to watch.

But Rodgers has performed at a level good enough to win more playoff games than he has won. The rest of the team must step up in 2016. And if Rodgers makes just 1 or 2 more "+" plays instead of "–" plays, he could erase the Cowherd negativity. Not that he needs to, given how some of it appears to be extremely misguided.

Sharp Football Stats

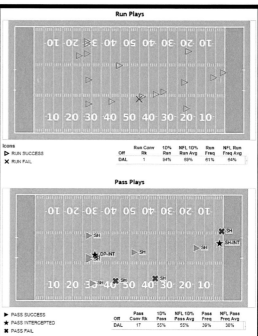

As mentioned in the forward, I believe we are an interesting point in time regarding NFL analysis. More data is being made available to process, but that only increases problems it seems. Some coaches still are scared of the A-word, and are hesitant to utilize analytics. This despite the fact that simply understanding them does not require being wed to them nor forced to use anything that makes the coach uncomfortable. The other issue becomes the sheer volume of information makes processing it and then sharing it in an easy-to-convey and easy-to-understand method extremely challenging.

That is where SharpFootballStats.com comes in. The reality is it takes a unique ability to both understand the metrics that matter and then present them in a manner so the user can understand the implications of the data. With technology all around us, more of us have become "visual learners". The ability for the public to consume and "value" statistics is diminished by lack of context as well as the age in which we live. In the newspaper era the only option was targeting "reading/writing learners": Statistics, box scores and standings displayed in black & white columns in a table. Despite the changing times, most every website displays statistics in a table format. The problem is, in the modern video/app world, most people are becoming "visual learners" (prefer to see info and visualize relationships between ideas) if not "kinesthetic learners" (hands-on, experimental). As such, one goal is to present statistics in a visual and kinesthetic manner through interactive visualizations.

SharpFootballStats.com will launch in July, and it will be a fully interactive site which contains visualizations like you can see on the following two pages, as well as those you have seen on the last page of each team chapter.

Every one to these vizzes are fully adaptable, to sort by team, week, quarter, down, field position, etc. Whether you're an NFL team looking for customized weekly reports or tailored research, a fan frustrated by his team's play calling, a DFS player scouting for matchups and edges, this site will not disappoint. I hope you check it out!

To the left & right are visualizations related to performance on 2nd and short. There is no easier time to convert a first down than on 2nd and short. And run plays are far more efficient in these situations. Despite that, some teams run far too infrequently on 2nd & short, while others desperately need to improve their play calling and execution to make the most of this layup situation. To the left, you can see the field as the Jaguars drive from the left to the right. At the top, run plays receive a green arrow if a first down or a red X if a failure. You can see how much the Jaguars need to improve in this situation, converting just 25% for 1st downs, worst in the NFL & well below the 69% avg. They were exceptional when passing, but passed well above average because of how bad the run game was. But it is unlikely the Jaguars can replicate that short yardage passing success & must improve on the ground. To the right were the Cowboys, the #1 team in the NFL in 2nd & short rush conversion rate. But they still passed the ball above the NFL average, with multiple turnovers. Dallas will be better with Romo, but should more often with success like this.

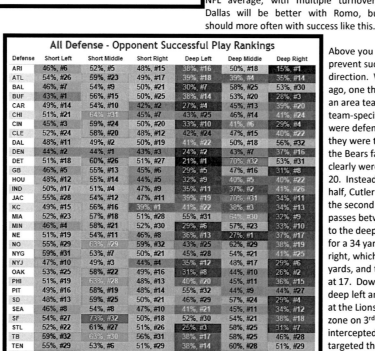

All Defense - Opponent Successful Play Rankings

Defense	Short Left	Short Middle	Short Right	Deep Left	Deep Middle	Deep Right
ARI	46%, #6	52%, #5	48%, #15	38%, #16	50%, #16	15%, #1
ATL	54%, #26	59%, #23	49%, #17	39%, #18	39%, #4	35%, #14
BAL	46%, #7	54%, #9	50%, #21	30%, #7	58%, #25	53%, #30
BUF	43%, #1	56%, #15	50%, #25	38%, #14	53%, #20	28%, #3
CAR	49%, #14	54%, #10	42%, #2	27%, #4	45%, #13	39%, #20
CHI	51%, #21	64%, #31	45%, #7	43%, #25	46%, #14	41%, #24
CIN	45%, #3	59%, #24	50%, #20	33%, #10	41%, #6	29%, #4
CLE	52%, #24	58%, #20	48%, #12	42%, #24	47%, #15	40%, #22
DAL	48%, #11	49%, #2	50%, #19	41%, #22	50%, #18	56%, #32
DEN	44%, #2	44%, #1	43%, #3	24%, #2	43%, #7	37%, #16
DET	51%, #18	60%, #26	51%, #27	21%, #1	70%, #32	53%, #31
GB	46%, #5	55%, #13	45%, #6	29%, #5	47%, #16	31%, #8
HOU	48%, #12	55%, #14	44%, #5	32%, #9	40%, #5	40%, #22
IND	50%, #17	51%, #4	47%, #9	35%, #11	37%, #2	41%, #26
JAC	55%, #28	54%, #12	47%, #11	39%, #19	70%, #31	34%, #11
KC	49%, #15	56%, #16	39%, #1	41%, #22	38%, #3	34%, #13
MIA	52%, #23	57%, #18	51%, #28	55%, #31	64%, #30	32%, #9
MIN	46%, #4	58%, #21	52%, #30	29%, #6	57%, #23	33%, #10
NE	51%, #19	54%, #11	46%, #8	36%, #13	27%, #1	37%, #17
NO	55%, #29	63%, #29	59%, #32	43%, #25	62%, #29	38%, #19
NYG	59%, #31	53%, #7	50%, #21	45%, #28	54%, #21	41%, #25
NYJ	47%, #10	49%, #3	44%, #4	35%, #12	48%, #17	29%, #6
OAK	53%, #25	58%, #22	49%, #16	31%, #8	44%, #10	26%, #2
PHI	51%, #19	63%, #28	48%, #13	40%, #20	45%, #11	36%, #15
PIT	49%, #16	58%, #19	48%, #14	45%, #29	44%, #9	44%, #27
SD	48%, #13	59%, #25	50%, #21	46%, #29	57%, #24	29%, #4
SEA	46%, #8	54%, #8	47%, #10	41%, #21	45%, #11	34%, #12
SF	54%, #27	73%, #32	50%, #18	52%, #30	54%, #21	38%, #18
STL	52%, #22	61%, #27	51%, #26	25%, #3	58%, #25	31%, #7
TB	59%, #32	63%, #30	56%, #31	38%, #17	58%, #25	46%, #28
TEN	55%, #29	53%, #6	51%, #29	38%, #16	60%, #28	51%, #29
WAS	46%, #9	56%, #17	50%, #21	44%, #27	44%, #8	39%, #21

Above you can see defenses ranked by their ability to prevent successful pass plays based on distance and direction. With the hit rules which passed several years ago, one thing is abundantly clear: the short middle is an area teams must target more frequently. But for a team-specific takeaway, notice how strong the Lions were defensing passes to the deep left, but how terrible they were to the deep middle and deep right? When the Bears faced the Lions week 17, these patterns clearly were established. The Bears lost by 4 points, 24-20. Instead of targeting these weaknesses, in the first half, Cutler went deep just one time. Jay Cutler started the second half down 10 points. He threw two deep passes between the 3rd and start of the 4th quarter. One to the deep middle, which was caught by Josh Bellamy for a 34 yard touchdown. The second was to the deep right, which was caught by Deonte Thompson for 45 yards, and the Bears scored 2 plays later to tie the game at 17. Down by a TD with 6 minutes left, Cutler went deep left and it was incomplete. Down by just 4 points at the Lions 37 yard line, Cutler went deep to the end zone on 3rd down, but again went left. This time, it was intercepted, and the Lions ran out the clock. Had Cutler targeted the deep middle or deep right more often, there likely would have been better success.

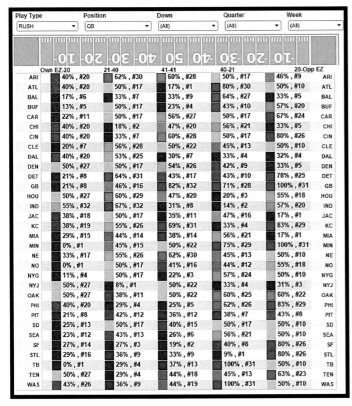

Play Type	Position	Down	Quarter	Week
RUSH	QB	(All)	(All)	(All)

	Own EZ-20	21-40	41-41	40-21	20-Opp EZ	
ARI	40%, #20	62%, #30	60%, #28	50%, #17	46%, #9	ARI
ATL	40%, #20	50%, #17	17%, #1	80%, #30	50%, #10	ATL
BAL	17%, #6	33%, #7	33%, #9	64%, #27	33%, #5	BAL
BUF	13%, #5	50%, #17	23%, #4	43%, #10	57%, #20	BUF
CAR	22%, #11	50%, #17	56%, #27	50%, #17	67%, #24	CAR
CHI	40%, #20	18%, #2	47%, #20	56%, #21	33%, #5	CHI
CIN	40%, #20	33%, #7	60%, #28	50%, #17	80%, #26	CIN
CLE	20%, #7	56%, #28	50%, #22	45%, #13	50%, #10	CLE
DAL	40%, #20	53%, #25	30%, #7	33%, #4	32%, #4	DAL
DEN	50%, #27	50%, #17	54%, #26	42%, #9	33%, #5	DEN
DET	21%, #8	64%, #31	43%, #17	43%, #10	78%, #25	DET
GB	21%, #8	46%, #16	82%, #32	71%, #28	100%, #31	GB
HOU	50%, #27	60%, #29	47%, #20	20%, #3	55%, #18	HOU
IND	55%, #32	67%, #32	31%, #8	14%, #2	57%, #20	IND
JAC	38%, #18	50%, #17	35%, #11	47%, #16	17%, #1	JAC
KC	38%, #19	55%, #26	69%, #31	33%, #4	83%, #29	KC
MIA	29%, #15	44%, #14	38%, #14	56%, #21	17%, #1	MIA
MIN	0%, #1	45%, #15	50%, #22	75%, #29	100%, #31	MIN
NE	33%, #17	55%, #26	62%, #30	45%, #13	50%, #10	NE
NO	0%, #1	50%, #17	41%, #16	44%, #12	55%, #18	NO
NYG	11%, #4	50%, #17	22%, #3	57%, #24	50%, #10	NYG
NYJ	50%, #27	8%, #1	50%, #22	33%, #4	31%, #3	NYJ
OAK	50%, #27	38%, #11	50%, #22	60%, #25	60%, #22	OAK
PHI	40%, #20	29%, #4	25%, #5	62%, #26	83%, #29	PHI
PIT	21%, #8	42%, #12	36%, #12	38%, #7	43%, #8	PIT
SD	25%, #13	50%, #17	40%, #15	50%, #17	50%, #10	SD
SEA	23%, #12	43%, #13	26%, #6	56%, #21	50%, #10	SEA
SF	27%, #14	27%, #3	19%, #2	40%, #8	80%, #26	SF
STL	29%, #16	36%, #9	33%, #9	9%, #1	80%, #26	STL
TB	0%, #1	29%, #4	37%, #13	100%, #31	50%, #10	TB
TEN	50%, #27	29%, #4	44%, #18	45%, #13	63%, #23	TEN
WAS	43%, #26	36%, #9	44%, #19	100%, #31	50%, #10	WAS

On the left is a defensive success by field position graphic. You can easily see which teams were strong at stopping QB runs and which were not. A glaring observation is that designed runs inside your own 40 did not have tremendous success, not nearly as compared to runs in the red zone. Some of that goes to the fact that many runs are more of the scramble when trying to throw, rather than designed runs near the end zone. But another observation is that the Packers were extremely easy to run against, particularly from the 40 to the end zone. It wasn't just that they faced Russell Wilson or Cam Newton, either: Derek Carr had 4 runs for 42 yards (3 for 1D), Teddy Bridgewater had 6 runs for 45 yards. Matthew Stafford had 4 runs for 23 yards (3 for 1D). Jay Cutler and Alex Smith both averaged at least 5 yards per carry against the Packers. They will need to solve that problem or teams should take advantage of the weakness this year.

	Left End	LT	LG	C	RG	RT	Right End
ARI	7	7	9	31	19	9	1
ATL	28	21	14	32	2	27	27
BAL	31	20	26	13	16	22	5
BUF	10	2	16	11	23	1	16
CAR	4	18	4	20	26	7	18
CHI	22	16	11	27	12	25	13
CIN	12	14	16	14	14	26	31
CLE	17	28	22	24	8	12	22
DAL	2	13	10	26	11	19	3
DEN	16	9	18	15	17	18	28
DET	24	26	8	17	27	17	20
GB	22	11	24	2	13	8	15
HOU	18	10	31	18	20	6	30
IND	30	24	7	25	9	24	21
JAC	15	32	3	23	31	5	9
KC	6	1	30	3	3	30	24
MIA	14	8	21	10	5	10	26
MIN	8	29	13	5	1	4	17
NE	9	27	12	28	25	11	8
NO	25	15	5	1	28	29	7
NYG	17	22	10	4	24	15	6
NYJ	21	25	20	6	4	31	2
OAK	19	31	5	19	18	14	13
PHI	20	30	28	7	7	28	23
PIT	1	3	19	8	15	23	19
SD	26	5	23	21	29	32	32
SEA	11	6	15	22	21	2	4
SF	3	17	27	16	32	20	29
STL	13	4	2	12	30	11	10
TB	5	19	1	9	6	16	12
TEN	27	23	6	29	22	3	11
WAS	29	12	25	30	10	21	25

	1	2
ARI	56%, #25	33%, #7
ATL	0%, #1	43%, #14
BAL	43%, #18	47%, #21
BUF	57%, #28	57%, #25
CAR	33%, #8	45%, #18
CHI	89%, #32	69%, #31
CIN	40%, #16	29%, #4
CLE	43%, #18	58%, #27
DAL	57%, #28	43%, #14
DEN	33%, #8	33%, #7
DET	29%, #4	47%, #19
GB	29%, #4	53%, #24
HOU	86%, #31	33%, #7
IND	36%, #12	42%, #13
JAC	46%, #21	63%, #29
KC	50%, #22	60%, #28
MIA	42%, #17	41%, #12
MIN	20%, #3	29%, #4
NE	36%, #13	57%, #25
NO	56%, #25	69%, #30
NYG	29%, #4	25%, #3
NYJ	36%, #13	17%, #1
OAK	33%, #8	44%, #16
PHI	53%, #24	44%, #17
PIT	37%, #15	47%, #20
SD	30%, #7	17%, #1
SEA	43%, #18	30%, #6
SF	60%, #30	38%, #11
STL	0%, #1	33%, #7
TB	50%, #22	72%, #32
TEN	33%, #8	50%, #22
WAS	56%, #25	52%, #23

	1	2
ARI	50%, #11	42%, #8
ATL	83%, #29	67%, #22
BAL	71%, #24	22%, #2
BUF	100%, #31	71%, #26
CAR	33%, #7	83%, #29
CHI	75%, #26	40%, #6
CIN	63%, #21	20%, #1
CLE	45%, #10	40%, #6
DAL	14%, #2	86%, #31
DEN	67%, #22	100%, #32
DET	75%, #26	67%, #22
GB	50%, #11	50%, #11
HOU	50%, #11	57%, #16
IND	30%, #6	54%, #15
JAC	50%, #11	30%, #4
KC	88%, #30	67%, #22
MIA	57%, #20	43%, #9
MIN	100%, #31	50%, #11
NE	50%, #11	67%, #22
NO	40%, #8	80%, #28
NYG	0%, #1	43%, #9
NYJ	50%, #11	50%, #11
OAK	71%, #24	25%, #3
PHI	40%, #8	78%, #27
PIT	25%, #4	38%, #5
SD	50%, #11	50%, #11
SEA	50%, #11	83%, #29
SF	50%, #11	60%, #18
STL	25%, #4	63%, #21
TB	14%, #2	60%, #18
TEN	67%, #22	62%, #20
WAS	80%, #28	57%, #16

The visualization above looks at offensive rushing success based on direction of the run, with the column headers indicating that direction. It is evident how much better the Browns were when running to the right side of their line as compared to the left. Conversely, the Steelers were tremendous when running left, particularly around the left end or behind the left tackle. The Chargers were pretty much terrible running anywhere except the left tackle. The Vikings were the opposite – pretty great everywhere but the left tackle. The Cowboys will hope Ezekiel Elliott will perform better than Darren McFadden in runs up the middle or behind the left guard.

Above, the key is not reading the numbers. That is the beauty of the visualization. Just look at the appearance and the colors. Both tables depict red zone defensive success in the first 2 quarters of the game. I isolated non-first downs. On the left is against pass plays. To the right, is against rush plays. It's clear to see how the defenses perform much worse against the run. There is far more green (indicating offensive success). The fact that defenses get spread out in the red zone, particularly in the 1st half when no game theory is at play based on running out the clock, etc, it is much easier to run in the modern NFL. Yet teams often get far too pass happy. Balance is key, but last year teams passed the ball 857 times, recording a first down on 36% of attempts and turning the ball over on 3.3% of attempts while taking sacks on 5% of attempts. Meanwhile, teams ran the ball just 432 times (almost half), but recorded a first down on 44% (8% better) of those attempts and as importantly, a turnover on just 1.6% of snaps (less than half) and obviously zero sacks.

Above, you will see offensive early down success rates based on field position (score in the end zone on the right) and play type. Pass being on the left, runs on the right. Passes are far more successful deep in your own territory (when teams get conservative & run more) & runs are more efficient in the red zone.

35

Improvement Required: Using Analytics to Increase Efficiency

Looking back on team performances can be extremely depressing. True enough, sometimes great things were done which resulted in amazement. But unfortunately, there was far too much bewilderment at teams failing to make intelligent decisions in their own best interests. Instead, they went with "gut" calls and decisions, which were defensible with quotes of "doing what felt right" or "making the decision by trusting our gut". "Trusting your gut" is the strategy NFL coaches employ in order to avoid intelligent decision making.

While I have notebooks full of isolated team and situation examples of inefficiency and ways they need to improve, there are a number of things the majority of NFL teams should attempt to do better to help league-wide efficiency. I'll share just a small sampling of those ideas in this article, but there are (frustratingly) plenty more of these.

Passing inside your own 20 (and inside your own 40) - 58% of first down plays inside a team's own 40 were graded as successful if they were passes. For a play to be graded as successful on first down, it must gain at least 40% of the yards to go. Thus, in most cases, this would be a 4 yard gain on first down. That doesn't seem unreasonable for a pass in terms of distance it needs to travel. It might seem like such a short distance should enable run plays to be similarly beneficial. But the reality is only 42% of first down run plays inside a team's own 40 were successful. It was a +16% edge to the pass.

Statistically 68% of passes were completed, at an average of 8.1 yds/att. Even factoring in the sacks, the resulting yardage dropped to 7.4 yds/play. The important element here is to avoid turnovers, thus choosing high percentage passes with quick drop backs. But with defenses typically seeing and thus playing run on 1st and 10 with an opponent deep inside their own territory, it is easier to pass on most downs in that location as opposed to run into the teeth of a defense that is playing run.

If we take situational score factors out of the equation, and focus only on the first half: last year passes were 57% successful while runs were 41% successful (still +16%). And yet league wide, teams called 53% runs.

Looking at both first and second down, passes were 53% successful and runs were 40% successful (+13%). Offenses simply must try to build on this efficiency edge. Instead, far too many teams and coordinators get too conservative. They would rather punt the ball than risk a turnover. That may be more reasonable with a lead in the 4th quarter, but it's not an acceptable excuse in the first half. The decision making process on their part assumes that they are unable to design a play creatively enough which minimizes a turnover, and they are unable to coach up their quarterback enough to avoid a negative play. The desire to not pass inside a team's own territory isn't an indication of failings of players. It indicates the failing on the entire process that started with offseason workouts and proceeds through training camp and into the season.

Passing on 1st down - Building on the prior point, particularly with younger quarterbacks, teams feel as if they are protecting their quarterback if they have successful runs on first down. It isn't a problem for teams with great first down run games. But there are not many in the NFL. For the rest of the NFL, it is a big issue. An example is descriptive in this instance:

The Minnesota Vikings and Norv Turner tried to protect the young Teddy Bridgewater by getting extremely conservative on first down. In the first half, 69% of their play calls on first down were run plays. This ultimately became incredibly predictable. Over the course of the season, they gained just 3.66 yds/carry, and recorded a 39% success rate on first down run plays, 24th in the NFL. But by the end of the year, that success rate plunged to 27% (worst in the NFL), gaining less than 2.9 yds/carry.

If a team is trying to help their young quarterback, putting him in predictable and bad situations on 2nd down due to lack of success on first down is never a good thing. Bridgewater recorded an 80 passer rating on 2nd downs in the first half, which ranked 29th of the 33 qualifying QBs. His 57% completion rate was 2nd worst of qualifying QBs, a testament to the tough and predictable situations he was put under.

Running on 2nd and short - Often you will hear announcers suggest that "this is the perfect time for a shot play". They most often say that on 2nd and short. At issue is the deliberation between efficiency and potency. Because while a 2nd and short run play isn't likely to produce the TD potential as a shot play might, a failed shot play sets up 3rd and short, with the opportunity for the defense to substitute in their short yardage package, presuming the pass was not intercepted.

Of any down or distance, the easiest down/distance to convert into a first down is 2nd and short. And it is significantly easier to convert when running the football as opposed to passing. All too often, teams do not understand the importance of efficiency on this particular down and distance, and waste opportunity. A huge 70% of all 2nd and short run plays gain first downs. Also importantly, only 0.8% result in a turnover. Meanwhile, only 52% of pass plays gain first downs, with almost double the turnovers (1.5%) and 2.5% result in sacks.

The conversion rate on runs would be increased even more if teams simply employed tempo and cadence in auto-no-huddle situations on 2nd and short. An 8-9 yard gain and the offense runs to the line of scrimmage, keeps the 1st down package on the field (ideally one which has at least 3 pass catchers including tight ends), deploys in a spread set and runs one of a handful of variants, giving the quarterback full autonomy to audible to whatever run play (including keeping the ball) will work best, as well as utilize cadence to draw the defense offsides or do the opposite and "go" on first sound.

Running in the red zone - In a moment we'll get to one of the types of pass plays which should be used at least once on every trip to the red zone, but the problem is that most teams get far too pass happy in the red zone, when running in the red zone is quite efficient.

On short yardage, as should be obvious, it is particularly effective. Still, on 3rd or 4th and 1-3 yards to go, teams called pass 53% and only 50% were successful in generating a first down. Meanwhile, while teams preferred calling passes, runs in the same situation were successful over 70% of the time. That is a massive +20% edge. Additionally, there were zero turnovers and zero sacks (clearly), whereas over 8% of pass plays were negative (turnover or sack).

But even on early downs, from further out, run plays have a slightly higher success rate than do pass plays. Balance is key, but more important is play calling. Running when the defense is playing pass is far more ideal, and that means running out of spread formations. It also means not bringing in fullbacks to block, let alone defensive tackles. Power running out of one-back formations is effective, especially when every single yard holds such value in the red zone.

Legal pick plays in the red zone - From the prior red zone discussion, there is no reason teams are not running legal pick plays until the rules are enforced differently. These should especially be utilized more often in bad weather or cold weather, which may produce more difficult footing. First and foremost, bad footing will slow a pass rush, making a pass play more ideal regardless. However, on the perimeter, when so much of defending is reacting, the offense must take advantage of knowing the play and where the ball will be going. With the defender a half-step slow, or unable to make the proper cut he would otherwise make on solid footing to avoid the pick, it makes it even more valuable to utilize this play in the red zone in those conditions.

There is a reason why the most unstoppable offense in the NFL last year had trouble producing in the red zone. The Arizona Cardinals pass offense was 29th in successful play frequency on early downs in the first half. Just 33% of their pass plays in that situation graded as successful. The Cardinals were ridiculous offensively over most of the field. They were a deep passing offense, that ate huge chunks at a time. But they were not nearly as efficient inside the confined spaces of the red zone with more defenders in a tighter area. Pick plays should allow free releases to the ball catcher and enable him to use short area quickness to take advantage of the extra couple of steps the pick buys him.

Other easy examples – More play action. Tempo & cadence. First half pace has increased from 28.2 sec/play in 2000 to 27.7 in 2015. It's not just overall pace, but situational pace. Scan for more.

Minnesota Vikings

Coaches

Head Coach: Mike Zimmer (3rd yr)
OC: Norv Turner (3rd yr)
DC: George Edwards (3rd yr)

Forecast 2016 Wins

9

Past Records

2015: 11-5
2014: 7-9
2013: 5-10-1

Opponent Strength
Easy — Hard

2016 Schedule & Week by Week Strength of Schedule

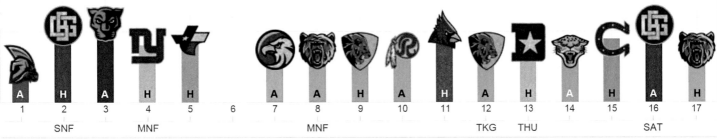

1	2	3	4	5	6	7	8	9	10	11	12	13	14	15	16	17
A	H	A	H	H		A	A	H	A	H	H	H	A	H	A	H
	SNF		MNF				MNF				TKG	THU			SAT	

2016 Overview

The 2015 Vikings were a gambler's paradise, but were frustrating to watch from an efficiency standpoint offensively. The Vikings covered the spread in 14 of 17 games last year, the most covers the NFL has seen and the 2nd best rate (82%), with only the 2004 Chargers at 13-2-2 ATS being slightly stronger. How did they accomplish that feat? For one, they caught the division and overall schedule in a down year. Although the Packers won a playoff game (something the Vikings did not), Green Bay's offense was off all season due to the loss of Jordy Nelson in the preseason. The Bears and the Lions both had down years, with 6 and 7 wins respectively. The Vikings played a non-divisional games vs the AFC West and NFC West. Historically, that would mean tough games vs the Broncos, Chargers, Seahawks, 49ers and Cardinals. But Denver's offense was a shell of itself in 2015, despite winning the Super Bowl, and the Chargers won only 4 games. Meanwhile, while the Seahawks and Cardinals were both strong, the 49ers were an embarrassment. And in their other two NFC games, they drew the Falcons and Giants, neither of which finished with a winning season.

But it wasn't all about schedule. The Vikings played well in metrics that help win games: +5 in turnover margin, +21 in penalty margin, and +6 in return TD margin, while not allowing any on the season. They recorded the 7th most sacks of any team, though their sack margin was -2 due to a porous line. While the Vikings won 11 games & the NFC North, looking closer at the best teams they played last year showed this Mike Zimmer-led team still has a lot of work to do. The best teams they played last year were the Seahawks (twice), the Broncos & the Cardinals. They lost every game. Many were close. But when you factor in the week 11 blowout loss in Minnesota to the Packers (30-13 final) and the week 13 blowout loss in Minnesota to Seattle (38-7 final), its clear the Vikings still have a long way to go. The team must trust Teddy Bridgewater more (and he must deliver) to pass the ball on the early downs to gain more variety and make both the rush and pass attack more potent.

Last year the Vikings ran the ball on 66% of their 1st down plays in the first half. The NFL average was 51%. The next 5 teams in terms of run heavy on first down? STL, CHI, BUF, TB, DAL. No team had a winning season, most had losing seasons. At the other end, are teams who passed the ball more often than the NFL average. Playoff teams like NE, GB, PIT, DEN, KC, ARI, SEA and NYJ. Notice that SEA & NYJ are two of the most run heavy teams in the NFL, but they realized it was smarter to pass more often on 1st down early in games. Making it more odd is the fact that the Vikings were not efficient on 1st down runs, either. They gained just 3.67 YPC (24th) worst of any of the other run heavy teams I listed earlier. The implications of this strategy were as predictable as the play calling: The Vikings recorded 1st downs on 1st or 2nd down play calls just 23% of the time (5th worst). Thus, they faced a lot of 3rd downs, and on those 3rd downs, they passed the ball 88% of the time, 3rd most in the NFL behind only the pass happy Saints and Lions. Being so predictable, they converted just 36.8% of those 3rd downs into 1st down, 7th worst. It's hard to put into words how inefficient that strategy was, or how much more efficient this team could be with more intelligent play calling in 2016. Behind a healthier offensive line, Norv Turner & Mike Zimmer must trust Teddy Bridgewater to pass on the early downs, which could provide the spark for a much more efficient 2016 campaign.

Strength of Schedule In Detail

True Strength of Schedule Rank: 8

Hardest Stretches *(1=Hard, 32=Easy)*
Hardest 3 wk Stretch Rk:	6
Hardest 4 wk Stretch Rk:	5
Hardest 5 wk Stretch Rk:	15

Easiest Stretches *(1=Easy, 32=Hard)*
Easiest 3 wk Stretch Rk:	25
Easiest 4 wk Stretch Rk:	21
Easiest 5 wk Stretch Rk:	25

The Vikings are projected to see 9.5 wins in 2016, with juice making that total slightly north of 9.5. While their schedule is top 10 in difficulty, the worst of it comes weeks 2 through 5, taking on the Packers, Panthers, Texans and Giants. But three of those four games are at home, and after their bye, they play 4 consecutive opponents who are projected to have losing records in 2016. Winning at home and beating opponents they should beat likely will put the Vikings in a great position to make the postseason in 2016, but they may need to win one of their two toughest games after week 5: home vs the Cardinals week 11 or on the road in Green Bay in week 16 (a place they have struggled immensely the last 10 seasons).

2015 Play Tendencies

All Pass %	51%
All Pass Rk	30
All Rush %	49%
All Rush Rk	3
1 Score Pass %	51%
1 Score Pass Rk	32
2014 1 Score Pass %	55%
2014 1 Score Pass Rk	23
Pass Increase %	-4%
Pass Increase Rk	29
1 Score Rush %	49%
1 Score Rush Rk	1
Up Pass %	40%
Up Pass Rk	31
Up Rush %	60%
Up Rush Rk	3
Down Pass %	67%
Down Pass Rk	18
Down Rush %	33%
Down Rush Rk	15

The Vikings called run on 66% of 1st downs in the first half. For comparison, the NFL avg was 50%. The Vikings increased to almost 75% after Thanksgiving in these situations. They were far too predictable on the early downs, which really set up for difficult series on many drives. Overall, they were the most run heavy team in the NFL in one score games. From a play calling perspective, they were the most predictable offense in years.

2015 Offensive Advanced Metrics

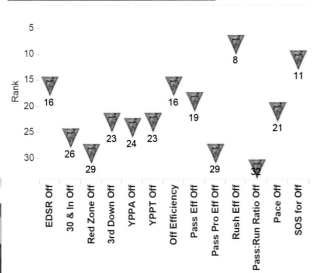

For an 11-win team, the Vikings' metrics are not overly impressive. For a team as run heavy as the Vikings, you might see some obvious issues offensively. But there should be other metrics which are even more efficient. For instance, rushing inside the red zone provides a higher success rate in today's NFL. But the Vikings ranked just 29th in red zone efficiency, and even on runs, those play calls were successful only 43% of the time, good for 23rd in the NFL. Defensively, the Vikings are developing a strong reputation under Mike Zimmer, but despite playing the Packers in a down year offensively, and struggling Bears and Lions offenses for much of the year, the Vikings ranked inside the top 10 in just two metrics. Fortunately they were critical ones: red zone defense and 3rd down defense. Clearly the Vikings need to improve offensively in 2016, with more balance, better protection & better play calling inside the red zone.

2015 Defensive Advanced Metrics

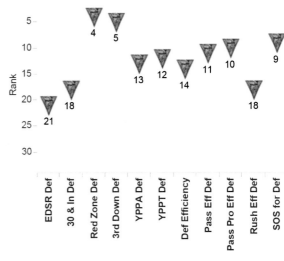

Minnesota Vikings

Drafted Players — 2016 Draft Grade: #6 (3.3/4)

Rnd.	Pick #	Pos.	Player	College
1	23	WR	Laquon Treadwell	Ole Miss
2	54	CB	Mackensie Alexander	Clemson
4	121	G	Willie Beavers	Western Michigan
5	160	ILB	Kentrell Brothers	Missouri
6	180	WR	Moritz Böhringer	Schwäbisch Hall Unicorn
6	188	TE	David Morgan II	UTSA
7	227	OLB	Stephen Weatherly	Vanderbilt
7	244	S	Jayron Kearse	Clemson

PERSONNEL & SPENDING

Free Agents/Trades Added

Player (Position)
- Alex Boone G
- Andre Smith T
- Brian Leonhardt TE
- Emmanuel Lamur LB
- Michael Griffin S
- Travis Lewis LB

Other Signed

Player (Position)
- Brandon Ross RB
- C.J. Ham RB
- Denzell Perine DE
- Eric Rawls CB
- Jake Ganus LB
- Jhurell Pressley RB
- Joel Stave QB
- Keith Baxter CB
- Kyle Carter TE
- Marken Michel WR
- Theiren Cockran DE
- Tre Roberson CB
- Troy Stoudermire WR

2015 Players Lost

Transaction	Player (Position)
Cut	Alex Singleton LB
	Dubose, B.J. DE
	John Lowdermilk S
	Mike Wallace WR
	Ross, Brandon RB
	Terrance Plummer LB
Declared Free Agent	Josh Robinson CB

- The Vikings can blame their protection issues and their heavy run rate on the pre-season offensive line issues if they would like, so long as that predictability does not continue in 2016 now that they've established a stronger line. They will return RT Phil Loadholt and C John Sullivan, and they added T Andre Smith (from CIN) and G Alex Boone (from SF) in free agency, in addition to drafting G Willie Beavers in the 4th round, using their 3rd draft pick on him.
- The Vikings are developing into a very talented and deep roster, one which is likely to go as far as QB Teddy Bridgewater can take them. And with Bridgewater still on his rookie contract, there are substantial cap savings over the next couple of years. However, the Vikings are spending the most of any team at the RB and O-Line positions in 2016. And while washing themselves of Mike Wallace saw the WR corps drop to 28th in cap hit, the TE position is also top 10. As such, the Vikings are the 8th most expensive offense in 2016 based on cap hit. However, that is still better than 2nd which is what they were last year with Wallace.
- Defensively, the unit is getting more expensive, and did so primarily at the safety position, by adding S MIchael Griffin to the flock.
- With a healthy offensive line and the addition of 1st round pick WR Laquon Treadwell, the Vikings should try to pass more often and be more balanced in 2016. That said, although there is a lot of potential and promise at the young WR position, there isn't a lot of history of performance. Their leading WR in 2015 was Stefon Diggs at age 22, and he grabbed 52 receptions but only 4 TDs. The rookie Treadwell certainly has a high ceiling of career potential, but how quickly he assimilates into the offense is not certain. What is certain is they will need him to perform as a rookie starter, because behind him the Vikings have Jarius Wright who is far from a standout and is really difficult to project at anything other than a #3 WR.

Lineup & 2016 Cap Hit

FS H.Smith -22-
SS A.Sendejo -34-
LB A.Barr -55-
LB E.Kendricks -54-
RCB X.Rhodes -29-
SLOTCB C.Munnerlyn -24-
DE E.Griffen -97-
DT L.Joseph -98-
DT S.Floyd -73-
DE D.Hunter -99-
LCB T.Newman -30-

LWR L.Treadwell Rookie -11-
LT M.Kalil -75-
LG A.Boone -75-
C J.Sullivan -65-
RG B.Fusco -63-
RT A.Smith -71-
RWR S.Diggs -14-
SLOTWR J.Wright -17-
TE K.Rudolph -82-
QB T.Bridgewater -5-
RB A.Peterson -28-

Skill Bench
WR2 C.Johnson -95-
WR3 A.Thielen -19-
RB2 J.McKinnon -31-
QB2 S.Hill -13-

2016 Cap Dollars — Low → High

Health Overall & by Unit (2015 v 2014)

2015 Rk	12
2015 AGL	59
Off Rk	17
Def Rk	7
2014 Rk	8
2014 AGL	56

2016 Positional Spending

	All OFF	QB	OL	RB	WR	TE	All DEF	DL	LB	CB	S
2015 Rk	2	27	3	1	10	8	19	9	27	12	29
Rank	8	30	1	1	28	10	12	8	26	21	6
Total	83.1M	6.1M	43.3M	14.0M	10.3M	9.4M	79.1M	31.9M	14.0M	17.6M	15.6M

2016 Offseason Spending

Total Spent	Total Spent Rk	Free Agents #	Free Agents $	Free Agents $ Rk	Waiver #	Waiver $	Waiver $ Rk	Extended #	Sum of Extended $	Sum of Drafted $	Undrafted #	Undrafted $
178M	17	13	54M	16	14	13M	16	2	67M	29M	11	14M

2015 Stats & Fantasy Production

Pos	Player	Ov. Rank	Pos. Rk	Age	Gms	St	Pass Comp	Pass Att	Pass Yds	Pass TD	Pass Int	Rush Att	Rush Yds	Rush YPA	Rush TD	Targ	Recp	Rec Yds	Rec YPC	Rec TDs	Draft King Pts	Fan Duel Pts
QB	Teddy Bridgewater*		23	23	16	16	292	447	3,231	14	9	44	192	4	3						218	209
RB	Adrian Peterson*+	4	2	30	16	16						327	1,485	5	11	36	30	222	7		270	246
RB	Jerick McKinnon		59	23	16							52	271	5	2	29	21	173	8	1	89	73
RB	Zach Line		85	25	16	5						6	10	2	2	9	6	95	16	1	35	32
RB	Matt Asiata		94	28	16							29	112	4		22	19	132	7		49	34
WR	Stefon Diggs		46	22	13	9						3	13	4		84	52	720	14	4	152	123
WR	Mike Wallace		75	29	16	12						1	6	6		72	39	473	12	2	102	79
WR	Jarius Wright		91	26	16	3						1	29	29		50	34	442	13		83	62
WR	Adam Thielen		124	25	16	2						4	89	22		18	12	144	12		38	29
TE	Kyle Rudolph		14	26	16	16										73	49	495	10	5	132	104

Avg Line	-2.1	Pred Wins	9	Pred Div Finish	#2

2016 Weekly Betting Lines (wks 1-16)

(-) Favorite   Underdog (+)
-6.5   +5.5

Avg Line = -2.1

Week 1: A -3.0; Week 2: H; Week 3: A +5.5; Week 4: H -6.0; Week 5: H -6.0; Week 7: -1.6; Week 8: -2.5; Week 9: H -6.5; Week 10: -1.5; Week 12: -2.5; Week 13: H -4.5; Week 14: -2.5; Week 15: H -4.0; Week 16: A +4.5

Weeks: 1 2 3 4 5 6 7 8 9 10 11 12 13 14 15 16

2015 Critical and Game-Deciding Stats

TO Margin	+5
TO Given	17
INT Given	9
FUM Given	8
TO Taken	22
INT Taken	13
FUM Taken	9
Sack Margin	-2
Sacks	43
Sacks Allow	45
Return TD Margin	+6
Ret TDs	6
Ret TDs Allow	0
Penalty Margin	+21
Penalties	88
Opponent Penalties	109

-Teams that win the turnover battle win 79% of games & cover 79% ATS.
-Teams with more sacks win 71% of games & cover 69% ATS.
-Teams with more return TDs win 75% of games & cover 75% ATS.
-Teams with fewer penalties win 57% of games & cover 54% ATS.

2016 NFLproject.com Forecast

Div RK	2	
Div W%	(17%)	
Playoffs RK	12	
% in Playoffs	(41%)	
Super Bowl RK	12	
% Win Super Bowl	(1%)	

Odds to Win Division
80% 70% 60% 50% 40% 30% 20% 10% 0%

72%

17%

5%

NFCN

Team Records & Trends

	2015	2014	2013
Average line	0.0	2.8	4.0
Average O/U line	43.8	45.0	46.3
Straight Up Record	11-5	7-9	5-10
Against the Spread Record	13-3	10-6	9-7
Over/Under Record	4-8	6-10	11-3
ATS as Favorite	7-1	3-1	0-2
ATS as Underdog	5-1	7-4	7-5
Straight Up Home	6-2	5-3	5-3
ATS Home	6-2	5-3	5-3
Over/Under Home	3-4	4-4	5-2
ATS as Home Favorite	6-0	3-1	0-2
ATS as a Home Dog	0-1	2-1	3-1
Straight Up Away	5-3	2-6	0-7
ATS Away	7-1	5-3	4-4
Over/Under Away	1-4	2-6	6-1
ATS Away Favorite	1-1	0-0	0-0
ATS Away Dog	5-0	5-3	4-4
Six Point Teaser Record	13-3	13-3	11-5
Seven Point Teaser Record	13-3	13-3	11-5
Ten Point Teaser Record	13-3	13-3	12-4

Games Favored

12

Games Underdog

2

Close Game Records

All 2015 Wins: **11**
FG Games (<=3 pts) W-L: **2-2**
FG Games Win %: **50% (#15)**
FG Games Wins (% of Total Wins): **18% (#21)**
1 Score Games (<=8 pts) W-L: **4-2**
1 Score Games Win %: **67% (#4)**
1 Score Games Wins (% of Total Wins): **36% (#28)**

Home Lines (wks 1-16)

Avg Line = -4.1

-6.0 -6.0   -6.5   -4.5 -4.0

1 2 3 4 5 6 7 8 9 10 11 12 13 14 15 16

Road Lines (wks 1-16)

Week

Avg Line = -0.4

+5.5   -2.5   -1.6   -2.5   +4.5

1 2 3 4 5 6 7 8 9 10 11 12 13 14 15 16

Regular Season Wins: Past Results & Current Proj

2012 Wins	10
2013 Wins	5
2014 Wins	7
Proj 2015 Wins	6.5
2015 Wins	11
Proj 2016 Wins	9

1 2 3 4 5 6 7 8 9 10 11 12 13 14 15

The Vikings were the 7th healthiest defense last year while their offense was middle of the pack. However, they were fairly healthy during the season given they lost RT Phil Loadholt and C John Sullivan for the year before the season started. Their turnover margin, penalty margin and return TD margin will be hard to improve in 2016, because they were +5, +21 and +6 respectively in those areas. They recorded 43 sacks but finished -2 in margin due to protection issues along the offensive line and Teddy Bridgewater's decision making issues at times. Surprisingly, the Vikings did not play in many close games, with just 4 of their total 11 wins coming by 1 score or less, 28th most in the NFL. They went 4-2 in one score games, 4th best in the NFL, but many of their games saw them win (6 games) or lose (3 games) by double digits.

2016 Rest Analysis

Avg Rest	6.5
Avg Rest Rk	3
Team More Rest	2
Opp More Rest	4
Net Rest Edge	-2
3 days rest	1
4 days rest	0
5 days rest	3
6 days rest	6
7 days rest	3
8 days rest	0
9 days rest	1
10 days rest	0
11 days rest	0
12 days rest	0
13 days rest	1
14 days rest	0

Weekly EDSR & Season Trending Performance

WEEK	1	2	3	4	6	7	8	9	10	11	12	13	14	15	16	17
RESULT	L	W	W	L	W	W	W	W	W	L	W	L	L	W	W	W
OPP	SF	DET	SD	DEN	KC	DET	CHI	STL	OAK	GB	ATL	SEA	ARI	CHI	NYG	GB
SITE	A	H	H	A	H	A	H	A	H	A	H	A	H	H	A	A
MARGIN	-17	10	17	-3	6	9	3	3	16	-17	10	-31	-3	21	32	7
PTS	3	26	31	20	16	28	23	21	30	13	20	7	20	38	49	20
OPP PTS	20	16	14	23	10	19	20	18	14	30	10	38	23	17	17	13

Week by Week 2015 Results

EDSR Results (W/L) By Week
W=Green
L=Red

Off & Def EDSR Wk & Trend
- Blue=Offense (high=good)
- Red=Defense (low=good)

STATS & VISUALIZATIONS

Minnesota Vikings

Directional Passer Rating Achieved

Receiver	Short Left	Short Middle	Short Right	Deep Left	Deep Middle	Deep Right
Stefon Diggs	116	118	97	33	118	69
Kyle Rudolph	78	116	111	135	39	52
Mike Wallace	128	52	59	109	95	0
Jarius Wright	90	94	79	95		103
Adam Thielen	90	42	104	39		118
MyCole Pruitt	109	81	80	74		39
Rhett Ellison	117	42	111			39
Charles Johnson	81		74	48	118	118
Cordarrelle Patterson	79		104			

Directional Frequency by Receiver

Receiver	Short Left	Short Middle	Short Right	Deep Left	Deep Middle	Deep Right
Stefon Diggs	34%	16%	22%	36%	33%	9%
Kyle Rudolph	11%	30%	25%	9%	17%	28%
Mike Wallace	20%	18%	20%	20%	33%	25%
Jarius Wright	14%	18%	13%	14%		25%
Adam Thielen	5%	5%	6%	5%		3%
MyCole Pruitt	3%	5%	6%	7%		3%
Rhett Ellison	8%	9%	5%			3%
Charles Johnson	4%		2%	9%	17%	3%
Cordarrelle Patterson	1%		1%			

Defense Passer Rating Allowed

Short Left	Short Middle	Short Right	Deep Left	Deep Middle	Deep Right
89	103	83	62	123	90

Offensive Rush Directional Yds/Carry

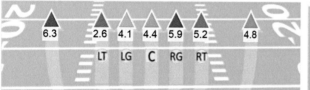

6.3 | 2.6 | 4.1 | 4.4 | 5.9 | 5.2 | 4.8
LT | LG | C | RG | RT

Offensive Rush Frequency of Direction

44 | 47 | 48 | 169 | 54 | 55 | 71
LT | LG | C | RG | RT

Offensive Explosive Runs by Direction

10 | 4 | 5 | 19 | 6 | 10 | 11
LT | LG | C | RG | RT

Defensive Rush Directional Yds/Carry

6.5 | 3.6 | 4.2 | 3.5 | 3.5 | 4.3 | 5.6
LT | LG | C | RG | RT

Teddy Bridgewater - 1st Down RTG

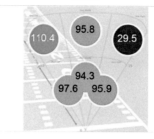

110.4 | 95.8 | 29.5
94.3
97.6 | 95.9

Teddy Bridgewater - 2nd Down RTG

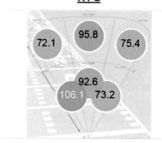

72.1 | 95.8 | 75.4
92.6
106.1 | 73.2

Teddy Bridgewater - 3rd Down RTG

37.0 | 118.8 | 15.3
107.0
113.7 | 115.7

Teddy Bridgewater - Overall RTG

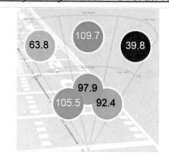

63.8 | 109.7 | 39.8
97.9
105.5 | 92.4

2nd & Short RUN (1D or not)

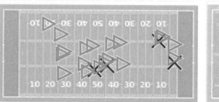

2nd & Short RUN Stats

Run Conv Rk	1D% Run	NFL 1D% Run Avg	Run Freq	NFL Run Freq Avg
7	83%	69%	79%	64%

2nd & Short PASS (1D or not)

SK
SH SH | SH SH | SH

2nd & Short PASS Stats

Pass Conv Rk	1D% Pass	NFL 1D% Pass Avg	Pass Freq	NFL Pass Freq Avg
4	67%	55%	21%	36%

Pass Offense Play Success Rate

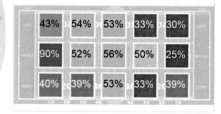

43%	54%	53%	33%	30%
90%	52%	56%	50%	25%
40%	39%	53%	33%	39%

Pass Offense Yds/Play

5.1	9.2	10.3	6.0	3.3
11.7	9.8	9.6	6.9	1.0
5.8	6.1	8.3	5.4	3.6

Off. Directional Tendency (% of Plays Left, Middle or Right)

43%	40%	39%	40%	43%
19%	20%	15%	16%	9%
38%	40%	45%	44%	49%

Off. Directional Pass Rate (% of Plays which are Passes)

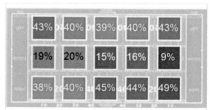

61%	68%	73%	67%	67%
17%	31%	24%	23%	8%
44%	74%	66%	60%	48%

Chicago Bears

Coaches

Head Coach: John Fox (2nd yr)
OC: Dowell Loggins (CHI QB) (1st yr)
DC: Vic Fangio (2nd yr)

Forecast 2016 Wins
7.5

Past Records
2015: 6-10
2014: 5-11
2013: 8-8

Opponent Strength
Easy _____ Hard

2016 Schedule & Week by Week Strength of Schedule

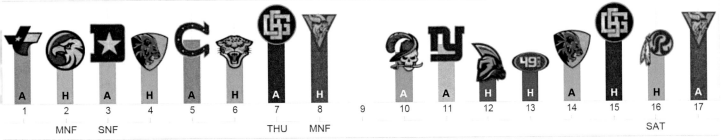

A	H	A	H	A	H	A	H		A	A	H	H	A	H	H	A
1	2	3	4	5	6	7	8	9	10	11	12	13	14	15	16	17
	MNF	SNF				THU	MNF								SAT	

2016 Overview

The Chicago Bears seem as if they are at the brink of something in 2016. It feels like an important year. If the results are strong, it will be a stepping stone for the franchise in John Fox's 2nd season, in the direction he envisioned. If the results are poor, it really throws question on who he chose to replace OC Adam Gase and what the front office's plan is personnel, including paying Jay Cutler but not Matt Forte, and what they'll need to change moving forward. One thing is certain, with half of their first eight games coming in Primetime, the entire nation will see them rise or fall.

Whether they rise or fall will have a lot to do with whether they run or pass. The 2014 Bears were the most pass heavy team in the NFL. They passed 63% of all play calls in one-score games, a 6% increase from 2013 and the 2nd largest jump in the NFL. But then Fox came to town, with Gase in tow, and everything changed. The Bears dropped all the way down to 51% pass in one score games, a massive 12% drop from the prior year. It was the largest drop toward the run of any team. They ran the 3rd most often when losing, the 5th most often when winning, and the 2nd most often in one score games. The identity change was massive. But it paid off big. Ignore the 6 wins for a moment - the Bears went the most run heavy team of any in the NFL, and yet still produced the 5th best rushing efficiency against the 2nd most difficult schedule of opposing defenses. It kept games close and allowed the Bears to be competitive: they lost just 1 game by over 1 score (when Cutler was not injured), as compared to 2014, when they lost 7 games by over 1 score, losing all 7 by 13+ points. But what happened this past offseason was what was most perplexing, and leads me to realize how important 2016 will be for Chicago.

The Bears play calling was clearly limiting Jay Cutler's influence in 2015, despite signing him to a $126.7M deal the year before. They intentionally took the ball out of his hands a lot more, and placed it into the belly of Matt Forte and the rushing numbers took off, as did Chicago's competitiveness in games. But the team lost Adam Gase this past offseason, who helped lead the charge in the 2015 rushing revolution, and then they had no interest in paying Matt Forte. And so the 30 year old Forte was able to sign a very affordable 3 year, $12M deal with the Jets. Somehow, the Jets were able to work a 3 year deal for Forte which has cap hits of $3M, $4M and $5M, while the Bears saw him hit their cap for over $9M last year alone. The 2016 Bears now have Cutler hitting the cap at $17M, Jeffery hitting the cap for $14.6M, and WR Eddie Royal rounding out their top 7 cap hits, at $4.5M. No current RB hits the cap for over $715K.

The question now is, what will the 2016 Bears become with the former QB Coach Dowell Loggins calling plays? Projected starting RB Jeremy Langford was significantly worse than Matt Forte last year in key situations, like rushing on early downs and rushing in the first half. Langford made his hay by rushing for large chunks when the defense was trying to stop the pass and wasn't playing to stop the run, like on 3rd and long or in 2 minute drills. The 2016 Bears made decisions and spent their money as if they plan to turn more back to Cutler and the pass game. But that strategy was a failure in 2014, the year after Cutler signed his new deal. It will be fascinating to see which direction the offense heads in Chicago, but regardless of how that plays out, the defense absolutely must play better (particularly in the secondary) to have any real shot.

Strength of Schedule In Detail

True Strength of Schedule Rank: 24

Hardest Stretches *(1=Hard, 32=Easy)*
Hardest 3 wk Stretch Rk: **21**
Hardest 4 wk Stretch Rk: **15**
Hardest 5 wk Stretch Rk: **19**

Easiest Stretches *(1=Easy, 32=Hard)*
Easiest 3 wk Stretch Rk: **1**
Easiest 4 wk Stretch Rk: **1**
Easiest 5 wk Stretch Rk: **1**

The Bears started 2015 with 3 straight losses to tough teams (GB, ARI, SEA) and never could get back on track. Their 2016 schedule is not nearly as bad, and if they can whether some early difficulty, the back half of their schedule sets up nicely. The issue up front is the fact they alternate home and road games through week 8, but their road slate is quite difficult (@ HOU, @ DAL, @ IND, @ GB) as compared to their home slate (vs PHI, vs DET, vs JAC). After their early bye week, they play 4 home games in 5 weeks with a short trip to Detroit week 14. The Bears actually have more home game back-to-backs than road game back-to-backs. And from week 10 onward, they play the easiest schedule of any team in the NFL. The national audience will get a lot of the Bears early, as for some reason Chicago plays four of their first eight games in primetime.

2015 Play Tendencies

All Pass %	54%
All Pass Rk	25
All Rush %	46%
All Rush Rk	8
1 Score Pass %	51%
1 Score Pass Rk	31
2014 1 Score Pass %	63%
2014 1 Score Pass Rk	3
Pass Increase %	-12%
Pass Increase Rk	32
1 Score Rush %	49%
1 Score Rush Rk	2
Up Pass %	44%
Up Pass Rk	28
Up Rush %	56%
Up Rush Rk	5
Down Pass %	59%
Down Pass Rk	30
Down Rush %	41%
Down Rush Rk	3

It would shock many who forgot, but the Bears were a slow-it-down, run heavy team. Which is why the loss of Matt Forte and Adam Gase mean the 2016 strategy will be much different than 2015. It wasn't just in close games that they wanted to limit Cutler's negative tendencies - even when down, the team ran 41% of the time, 3rd most in the NFL. The Bears previously were pass heavy under Marc Trestman.

2015 Offensive Advanced Metrics

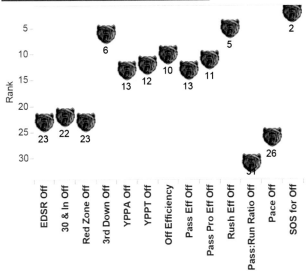

The Bears seemed for a while that they might be on to something with Adam Gase. They started out 5-6 but 7-4 ATS, however they went on to lose 4 of their last 5 and now Adam Gase is gone. The Bears tried their best to limit negativity from Jay Cutler, and they did that simply by not passing the ball. They passed the ball only 51% of the time in one-score games, 2nd fewest in the NFL. They were inefficient in many key metrics, but the slow tempo and run heavy offense was attempting to replicate the Cowboys use of offense to help a terrible defense. It didn't work that well. The Cowboys defense was below average in every statistic, and outright terrible in the ability to rush the passer or get off the field on 3rd down. In the modern era of the NFL, those are two things you can't afford to be terrible in. The Bears offense went up against the 2nd toughest schedule of defenses.

2015 Defensive Advanced Metrics

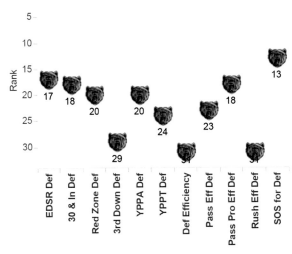

41

Drafted Players

2016 Draft Grade: #2 (3.6/4)

Rnd.	Pick #	Pos.	Player	College
1	9	OLB	Leonard Floyd	Georgia
2	56	G	Cody Whitehair	Kansas State
3	72	DT	Jonathan Bullard	Florida
	113	ILB	Nick Kwiatkoski	West Virginia
4	124	S	Deon Bush	Miami (FL)
	127	S	Deiondre' Hall	Northern Iowa
5	150	RB	Jordan Howard	Indiana
6	185	CB	DeAndre Houston-Carson	William & Mary
7	230	WR	Daniel Braverman	Western Michigan

PERSONNEL & SPENDING

Chicago Bears

Free Agents/Trades Added

Player (Position)
Aaron Brewer LB
Akiem Hicks DT
Bobby Massie T
Brian Hoyer QB
Danny Trevathan LB
Jerrell Freeman LB
Manny Ramirez G
Omar Bolden S
Ted Larsen C

Other Signed

Player (Position)
Adrian Bellard T
Ben Braunecker TE
Ben LeCompte P
Dan Buchholz C
Darrin Peterson WR
Derek Keaton WR
Don Cherry LB
Donovan Williams G
Joe Sommers TE
John Kling T
Kenton Adeyemi DE
Kevin Peterson CB
Kieran Duncan WR
Roy Robertson-Harris LB
Taveze Calhoun CB

2015 Players Lost

Transaction	Player (Position)
Cut	Anthony Jefferson S
	Antrel Rolle S
	Bruce Gaston DT
	D'Anthony Smith DT
	Dan Buchholz C
	Jermon Bushrod T
	Marcus Lucas WR
	Mason, Danny LB
	Matt Slauson G
	Nathan Palmer WR
Declared Free Agent	Jarvis Jenkins DE
	Matt Forte RB
	Vladimir Ducasse G

- There is absolutely no question that John Fox had no intention of taking the 2014 Bears and slowly implementing his strategy. No team in the NFL saw a more dramatic shift from pass to run than the 2015 Bears. And they were remarkably (and surprisingly) efficient when running the ball. They ranked 5th in rush efficiency, they became the 2nd most dependent team on the run, and they slowed the pace. However, several changes this offseason will impact that plan for 2016:
- Matt Forte is gone, and that instantly moved the Bears from spending the 4th most on the RB corps to spending 6th least. The team made moves along the offensive line, ridding themselves of Jermon Bushrod and Matt Slauson among others, and that dropped their offensive line from 24th most cap to 2nd least. And lastly, OC Adam Gase is gone and now, his replacement is the Bears former QB Coach, Dowell Loggins.
- Assuming Loggins listens to Fox and keeps the run heavy approach, the Bears will need to rely on RB Jeremy Langford. The problem is, Langford isn't a primary RB, and averaged just 3.6 YPC last season (as opposed to Forte's 4.1).
- And Langford's numbers are worse on 1st and 2nd down, as he averaged just 3.4 YPC on 1st down and 3.6 on 2nd down. He did most of his damage in 2 minute drills where the defense was expecting pass (6.8 YPC), as well as on 3rd down (5.7 YPC) for similar reasons.
- Forte's numbers looked much different, averaging 4.1 YPC on 1st down, 4.4 YPC on 2nd down, and piling up an impressive 4.5 YPC average on his 129 first half runs (Langford was 3.4).
- The Bears secondary was bad last year, and they didn't do much to help the secondary this offseason. Particularly at the CB position, the Bears will likely run into problems. They currently are spending the least in the NFL at Safety and 24th at Cornerback. Couple that with the 2nd least along the defensive line, and the Bears have the 3rd least expensive defense in the NFL.

Lineup & 2016 Cap Hit

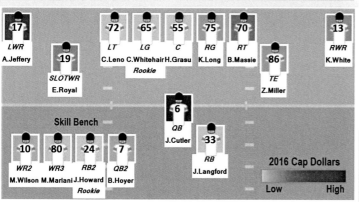

Health Overall & by Unit (2015 v 2014)

2015 Rk	28
2015 AGL	93
Off Rk	30
Def Rk	16
2014 Rk	27
2014 AGL	102

2016 Positional Spending

	All OFF	QB	OL	RB	WR	TE	All DEF	DL	LB	CB	S
2015 Rk	10	13	24	4	16	13	31	32	6	25	15
Rank	23	14	31	28	1	30	30	31	3	24	32
Total	73.2M	19.6M	15.8M	3.5M	28.9M	5.4M	60.5M	11.3M	34.2M	12.2M	2.9M

2016 Offseason Spending

Total Spent	Total Spent Rk	Free Agents #	Free Agents $	Free Agents $ Rk	Waiver #	Waiver $	Waiver $ Rk	Extended #	Sum of Extended $	Sum of Drafted $	Undrafted #	Undrafted $
171M	19	22	100M	8	13	21M	5	0	0M	40M	17	25M

2015 Stats & Fantasy Production

Pos	Player	Ov. Rank	Pos. Rk	Age	Gms	St	Pass Comp	Pass Att	Pass Yds	Pass TD	Pass Int	Rush Att	Rush Yds	Rush YPA	Rush TD	Targ	Recp	Rec Yds	Rec YPC	Rec TDs	Draft King Pts	Fan Duel Pts
QB	Jay Cutler		21	32	15	15	311	483	3,659	21	11	38	201	5	1						247	236
RB	Matt Forte	26	8	30	13	13						218	898	4	4	58	44	389	9	3	222	193
	Jeremy Langford	70	23	24	16	2						148	537	4	6	42	22	279	13	1	154	137
	Ka'Deem Carey		81	23	10	1						43	159	4	2	3	3	19	6	1	41	35
WR	Alshon Jeffery		41	25	9	8										94	54	807	15	4	162	132
	Marquess Wilson		84	23	11	6										51	28	464	17	1	83	66
	Josh Bellamy		101	26	16	3										34	19	224	12	2	56	44
	Eddie Royal		108	29	9	9						1	-1	-1		50	37	238	6	1	70	48
	Marc Mariani		107	28	16	5										33	22	300	14		54	39
TE	Zach Miller		17	31	15	14										46	34	439	13	5	111	91
	Martellus Bennett		26	28	11	11										80	53	439	8	3	118	88

ODDS & TRENDS — Chicago Bears

Avg Line	+1.5	Pred Wins	7.5	Pred Div Finish	#4

(-) Favorite   Underdog (+)
-5.0 ———— +9.0

2016 Weekly Betting Lines (wks 1-16)

Avg Line = 1.5

Values by week: +5.0, +6.0, +3.5, -3.5, +9.0, +2.5, -5.0, -5.0, +4.0, +2.5, +5.0, +0.0

Weeks: 1 2 3 4 5 6 7 8 9 10 11 12 13 14 15 16 — Week

2015 Critical and Game-Deciding Stats

TO Margin	-4
TO Given	21
INT Given	12
FUM Given	9
TO Taken	17
INT Taken	8
FUM Taken	9
Sack Margin	+1
Sacks	35
Sacks Allow	34
Return TD Margin	-7
Ret TDs	0
Ret TDs Allow	7
Penalty Margin	-1
Penalties	99
Opponent Penalties	98

-Teams that win the turnover battle win 79% of games & cover 79% ATS.
-Teams with more sacks win 71% of games & cover 69% ATS.
-Teams with more return TDs win 75% of games & cover 75% ATS.
-Teams with fewer penalties win 57% of games & cover 54% ATS.

2016 NFLproject.com Forecast

Div RK	3
Div W%	(5%)

Playoffs RK	25
% in Playoffs	(15%)

Super Bowl RK	29
% Win Super Bowl	(0%)

Odds to Win Division
72%
17%
5%
NFCN

Team Records & Trends

	2015	2014	2013
Average line	3.9	2.5	-0.1
Average O/U line	44.7	48.6	47.0
Straight Up Record	6-10	5-11	8-8
Against the Spread Record	7-8	7-9	4-10
ATS as Favorite	0-2	2-2	2-3
ATS as Underdog	7-6	5-7	1-5
Straight Up Home	1-7	2-6	5-3
ATS Home	1-6	3-5	1-5
Over/Under Home	4-3	2-6	6-2
ATS as Home Favorite	0-2	2-2	1-2
ATS as a Home Dog	1-4	1-3	0-2
Straight Up Away	5-3	3-5	3-5
ATS Away	6-2	4-4	3-5
Over/Under Away	4-4	5-2	6-2
ATS Away Favorite	0-0	0-0	1-1
ATS Away Dog	6-2	4-4	1-3
Six Point Teaser Record	11-5	8-8	13-3
Seven Point Teaser Record	12-4	8-8	13-2
Ten Point Teaser Record	12-4	10-6	14-2

Games Favored

5

Games Underdog

9

Close Game Records

All 2015 Wins: **6**
FG Games (<=3 pts) W-L: **3-4**
FG Games Win %: **43%** (#19)
FG Games Wins (% of Total Wins): **50%** (#3)
1 Score Games (<=8 pts) W-L: **5-7**
1 Score Games Win %: **42%** (#23)
1 Score Games Wins (% of Total Wins): **83%** (#4)

Home Lines (wks 1-16)

Avg Line = -1.3
Values: -2.5, -3.5, +2.5, -5.0, -5.0
Weeks: 1 2 3 4 5 6 7 8 9 10 11 12 13 14 15 16 — Week

Road Lines (wks 1-16)

Avg Line = 4.6
Values: +5.0, +6.0, +3.5, +9.0, +2.0, +4.0, +2.5
Weeks: 1 2 3 4 5 6 7 8 9 10 11 12 13 14 15 16

Regular Season Wins: Past Results & Current Proj

2012 Wins	10
2013 Wins	8
2014 Wins	5
Proj 2015 Wins	7
2015 Wins	6
Proj 2016 Wins	7.5

1 2 3 4 5 6 7 8 9 10 11 12 13 14 15

The Bears haven't had much luck with injuries, and that bad luck from 2014 carried over to 2015, with the team being 5th most injured, after finishing 6th in 2014. With that came 12 very close games, decided by one score or less. They finished one win shy of flipping-coins, going 5-7. But because they won just 6 games, all but one of those wins was by close margin. For most of the critical metrics, they were close to being neutral, but the one which stands out the most was the -7 return TD margin. The Bears didn't have a single return TD last year but allowed 7. They are currently projected to win 7.5 games in 2015, but are favored in only 5 at the moment. Fortunately, they do have one of the easier schedules in the NFL, and the back-to-back home stand against the Titans and 49ers would be sure to pump 2 more wins into most team's total. And after their bye, they have the easiest schedule of any team in the NFL.

2016 Rest Analysis

Avg Rest	6.5
Avg Rest Rk	3
Team More Rest	4
Opp More Rest	2
Net Rest Edge	2
3 days rest	1
4 days rest	0
5 days rest	2
6 days rest	8
7 days rest	2
8 days rest	0
9 days rest	0
10 days rest	1
11 days rest	0
12 days rest	1
13 days rest	0
14 days rest	0

Weekly EDSR & Season Trending Performance

Week by Week 2015 Results

WEEK	1	2	3	4	5	6		8	9	10	11	12	13	14	15	16	17
RESULT	L	L	L	W	W	L		L	W	W	L	L	L	L	L	W	L
OPP	GB	ARI	SEA	OAK	KC	DET		MIN	SD	STL	DEN	GB	SF	WAS	MIN	TB	DET
SITE	H	H	A	H	A	A		H	A	A	H	A	H	A	H	A	H
MARGIN	-8	-25	-26	2	1	-3		-3	3	24	-2	-4	-6	-3	-21	5	-4
PTS	23	23	0	22	18	34		20	22	37	15	17	20	21	17	26	20
OPP PTS	31	48	26	20	17	37		23	19	13	17	13	26	24	38	21	24

EDSR Results (W/L) By Week
W=Green
L=Red

Off & Def EDSR Wk & Trend
- Blue=Offense (high=good)
- Red=Defense (low=good)

STATS & VISUALIZATIONS

Chicago Bears

Directional Passer Rating Achieved

Receiver	Short Left	Short Middle	Short Right	Deep Left	Deep Middle	Deep Right
Alshon Jeffery	79	155	56	116	118	70
Martellus Bennett	97	28	90	85	87	0
Eddie Royal	87	104	93	39		39
Zach Miller	158	109	86	59	158	95
Marquess Wilson	114	95	75	129	0	59
Marc Mariani	79	118	64		109	39
Josh Bellamy	67	77	76	135	158	53
Cameron Meredith	98		50	50		118
Rob Housler	104	104				
Deonte Thompson				0	118	118
Khari Lee	39		95			39

Directional Frequency by Receiver

Receiver	Short Left	Short Middle	Short Right	Deep Left	Deep Middle	Deep Right
Alshon Jeffery	17%	22%	21%	36%	17%	38%
Martellus Bennett	28%	16%	19%	6%	17%	10%
Eddie Royal	13%	16%	16%	6%		2%
Zach Miller	10%	8%	14%	9%	8%	8%
Marquess Wilson	12%	5%	10%	21%	17%	19%
Marc Mariani	4%	14%	11%		25%	4%
Josh Bellamy	8%	16%	5%	6%	8%	13%
Cameron Meredith	5%		3%	12%		2%
Rob Housler	1%	3%				
Deonte Thompson				3%	8%	2%
Khari Lee	1%		1%			2%

Defense Passer Rating Allowed

Short Left	Short Middle	Short Right	Deep Left	Deep Middle	Deep Right
110	136	83	98	112	106

Offensive Rush Directional Yds/Carry

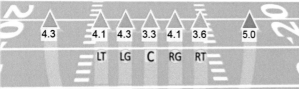

	LT	LG	C	RG	RT	
4.3	4.1	4.3	3.3	4.1	3.6	5.0

Offensive Rush Frequency of Direction

	LT	LG	C	RG	RT	
44	57	74	86	105	59	37

Offensive Explosive Runs by Direction

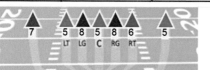

	LT	LG	C	RG	RT	
7	5	8	5	8	6	5

Defensive Rush Directional Yds/Carry

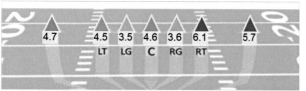

	LT	LG	C	RG	RT	
4.7	4.5	3.5	4.6	3.6	6.1	5.7

Jay Cutler - 1st Down RTG

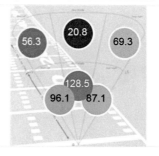

56.3, 20.8, 69.3, 128.5, 96.1, 87.1

Jay Cutler - 2nd Down RTG

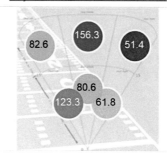

82.6, 156.3, 51.4, 80.6, 123.3, 61.8

2nd & Short RUN (1D or not)

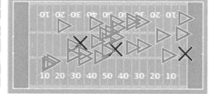

2nd & Short RUN Stats

Run Conv Rk	1D% Run	NFL 1D% Run Avg	Run Freq	NFL Run Freq Avg
2	90%	69%	79%	64%

2nd & Short PASS (1D or not)

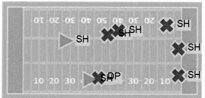

2nd & Short PASS Stats

Pass Conv Rk	1D% Pass	NFL 1D% Pass Avg	Pass Freq	NFL Pass Freq Avg
31	25%	55%	21%	36%

Jay Cutler - 3rd Down RTG

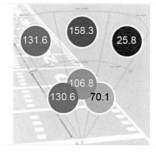

131.6, 158.3, 25.8, 106.8, 130.6, 70.1

Jay Cutler - Overall RTG

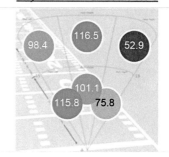

98.4, 116.5, 52.9, 101.1, 115.8, 75.8

Pass Offense Play Success Rate

68%	55%	40%	39%	52%
50%	56%	75%	62%	40%
50%	58%	40%	40%	34%

Pass Offense Yds/Play

15.4	8.2	7.4	6.0	3.8
7.9	12.2	11.7	11.6	3.9
8.0	8.7	5.9	5.4	2.8

Off. Directional Tendency (% of Plays Left, Middle or Right)

40%	42%	44%	36%	38%
14%	13%	10%	12%	13%
46%	45%	46%	50%	49%

Off. Directional Pass Rate (% of Plays which are Passes)

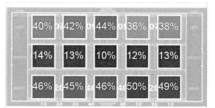
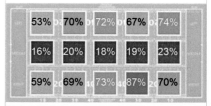

53%	70%	72%	67%	74%
16%	20%	18%	19%	23%
59%	69%	73%	87%	70%

Detroit Lions

Coaches

Head Coach: Jim Caldwell (3rd yr)
OC: Jim Bob Cooter (2nd yr)
DC: Teryl Austin (3rd yr)

Forecast 2016 Wins

7

Past Records

2015: 7-9
2014: 11-5
2013: 7-9

Opponent Strength
Easy — Hard

2016 Schedule & Week by Week Strength of Schedule

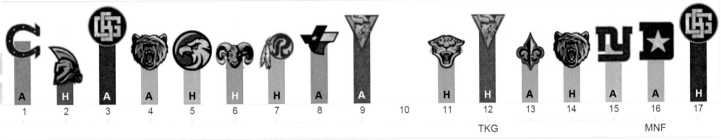

A	H	A	A	H	H	H	A	A		H	H	A	H	A	A	H
1	2	3	4	5	6	7	8	9	10	11	12	13	14	15	16	17

TKG — MNF

2016 Overview

The 2015 Detroit Lions were a fascinating team, in large part because they evolved so much over the course of the year that its extremely interesting trying to forecast what happens in 2016. Picture this: a team plays 6 playoff teams in their first 8 games, including a game against the ultimate Super Bowl champ, and drops 7 of those 8 games, with over half the losses by double digits. Top tier defenses faced included #1 DEN, #3 ARI, #4 SEA, #6 KC and #14 MIN.

In their final 8 games, this team plays 2 games against playoff teams, and wins 6 of 8* (*one of the 2 losses is to an Aaron Rodgers' Hail Mary). Bottom tier defenses faced included #32 NO, #31 CHI, #27 SF, #17 PHI.

As such, its difficult to look at full season stats. Weekly games are not played in isolation - they bleed into one another, and impacts from one week can carry to the next. Playing (without a break) the defenses of the Vikings, Broncos, Seahawks and Cardinals can wear a team down and leave them battered physically and mentally. Initially, I didn't agree with the Lions firing their offensive coordinator mid-season. But it's also hard to not like the results the team's offense got with Jim Bob Cooter.

This offense turned into the #1 offense inside the red zone. Not just based on touchdown rates alone, but play success in general. And even though their run offense was nothing to write home about over the majority of the field, inside the red zone it was the 2nd most successful and between the 21-40, it was the 6th most successful. However, it put up these numbers against poor defense and did so with Calvin Johnson. Johnson, and DET's 52% of all passes 15+ yards in the air that went his way, are gone. Despite signing an 8 yr $131M deal in 2012, Johnson retired. In his absence is the absence of the ability for other receivers to earn man coverage with Johnson doubled. Detroit faces the Herculean task of replacing a player like Johnson in a pass-heavy offense.

In the 8 games that Calvin Johnson was without a catch due to injury since 2009, the Lions offense averaged 14 ppg. The Lions can overpay Marvin Jones ($40M for 5 yrs) but he's not going to scare any defense the way Megatron did. This means it will be more difficult to run and pass. Just ask Tom Brady about missing Rob Gronkowski, as the Patriots are 0-3 dating back to 2013 without his involvement, scoring just 17 ppg.

So where do the Lions turn? They simply must get more out of their rush attack. Ameer Abdullah must be more explosive for more of the season than he was in his rookie year. The newly built offensive line must gel & perform better in run blocking. Because without the threat of a run game, the pass heavy Lions will simply not be able to repeat their early down or red zone efficiency without the coverage-dictating Megatron.

Defensively, the Lions must improve EDSR defense & red zone defense. Being inefficient on the early downs allows frequent 3rd down avoidance and more trips into the red zone. And being poor in red zone conversion rate means the Lions will be playing with a deficit. DC Teryl Austin needs his 9th rated pass rush to help the back-end (20th) even more.

Strength of Schedule In Detail

True Strength of Schedule Rank: 15

Hardest Stretches *(1=Hard, 32=Easy)*

Hardest 3 wk Stretch Rk:	24
Hardest 4 wk Stretch Rk:	30
Hardest 5 wk Stretch Rk:	31

Easiest Stretches *(1=Easy, 32=Hard)*

Easiest 3 wk Stretch Rk:	24
Easiest 4 wk Stretch Rk:	18
Easiest 5 wk Stretch Rk:	21

The Lions have three sets of back-to-back road games, the first of which is in the first four games of the year and features trips to division foes Green Bay and Chicago. But here's an interesting quirk: those 2 games are two of just three games Detroit plays outdoors all year. After week 4, they play just one more game outdoors all year (@ NYG wk 15). Their other road opponents include the Colts, Texans, Vikings, Saints and Cowboys, all dome teams.

2015 Play Tendencies

All Pass %	66%
All Pass Rk	1
All Rush %	34%
All Rush Rk	32
1 Score Pass %	61%
1 Score Pass Rk	11
2014 1 Score Pass %	63%
2014 1 Score Pass Rk	2
Pass Increase %	-2%
Pass Increase Rk	25
1 Score Rush %	39%
1 Score Rush Rk	22
Up Pass %	59%
Up Pass Rk	5
Up Rush %	41%
Up Rush Rk	28
Down Pass %	73%
Down Pass Rk	1
Down Rush %	27%
Down Rush Rk	32

DET was the most pass happy team in the NFL, passing 66% of all play calls including 61% in one-score games. When leading, they still passed 59% (5th most) and when trailing, their 73% pass rate was the largest in the NFL. The team has built itself to see success around its franchise QB but it will be more difficult without Calvin Johnson. Which begs the question: will DET run more or still pass, but to less talented WRs.

2015 Offensive Advanced Metrics

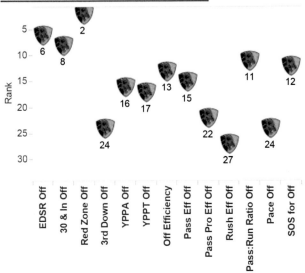

The Lions offense was still a pass first offense primarily because their rushing efficiency was among the worst in the NFL. But examining the efficiency metrics from EDSR, 30 & In TD Rate and Red Zone (the left 3 columns) and the Lions offense was among the best in the NFL, while their defense was among the worst in these metrics. There are so many question marks on both sides of the ball, as the defense needs to see tremendous improvement (and was exceedingly injured last year) while the offense loses one of the biggest mismatches (Calvin Johnson) the NFL has to offer. His loss should immediately impact the Lions performance inside the red zone in a negative manner. That is because once Jim Bob Cooter took over the Lions play calling, 64% of their red zone play calls graded as successful, best in the NFL and well above the 42% NFL average. Without Calvin Johnson, it would be hard to imagine that success being sustainable.

2015 Defensive Advanced Metrics

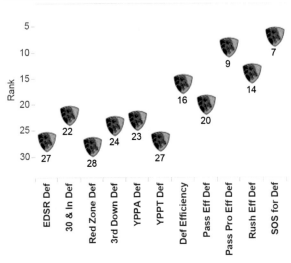

Drafted Players

2016 Draft Grade: #21 (2.6/4)

PERSONNEL & SPENDING

Detroit Lions

Rnd.	Pick #	Pos.	Player	College
1	16	OT	Taylor Decker	Ohio State
2	46	DT	A'Shawn Robinson	Alabama
3	95	C	Graham Glasgow	Michigan
4	111	S	Miles Killebrew	Southern Utah
5	151	G	Joe Dahl	Washington State
5	169	OLB	Antwione Williams	Georgia Southern
	191	QB	Jake Rudock	Michigan
6	202	DE	Anthony Zettel	Penn State
	210	LS	Jimmy Landes	Baylor
7	236	RB	Dwayne Washington	Washington

Lineup & 2016 Cap Hit

FS G.Quin 27
SS R.Bush 25
LB T.Whitehead 59
LB D.Levy 54
RCB N.Lawson 24
SLOTCB Q.Diggs 28
DE E.Ansah 94
DT T.Walker 93
DT H.Ngata 92
DE D.Taylor 98
LCB D.Slay 23

LWR G.Tate 15
LT T.Decker 68 (Rookie)
LG L.Tomlinson 72
C T.Swanson 64
RG L.Warford 75
RT R.Reiff 71
RWR M.Jones 11
SLOTWR T.Jones 13
TE E.Ebron 85

QB M.Stafford 9
RB A.Abdullah 21

Skill Bench

WR2 C.Fuller 10
WR3 J.Kerley 11
RB2 T.Riddick 25
QB2 D.Orlovsky 8

2016 Cap Dollars — Low / High

Free Agents/Trades Added

Player (Position)
Andre Caldwell WR
Darrin Walls CB
Geoff Schwartz G
Jeremy Kerley WR
Johnson Bademosi S
Jonathan Bostic LB
Marvin Jones WR
Rafael Bush S
Stefan Charles DT
Stevan Ridley RB
Tavon Wilson S
Wallace Gilberry DE

Other Signed

Player (Position)
Adairius Barnes CB
Adam Fuehne TE
Andre Caldwell WR
Andrew Zeller G
Charles Washington CB
Chase Farris G
Cole Wick TE
Darius Johnson G
Deonte Gibson DE
Ian Wells CB
Jace Billingsley WR
James DeLoach DE
Jay Lee WR
Louis Palmer DT
Quinshad Davis WR
Zaviar Gooden LB

Health Overall & by Unit (2015 v 2014)

2015 Rk	23
2015 AGL	77
Off Rk	5
Def Rk	30
2014 Rk	15
2014 AGL	68

2015 Players Lost

Transaction	Player (Position)
Cut	Braxston Cave C
	C.J. Wilson DT
	Casey Pierce TE
	Darren Keyton C
	Johnson, Darius G
	Joique Bell RB
	Lamar Holmes T
	Tyrus Thompson T
	Wright, Tim TE
Declared Free Agent	Isa Abdul-Quddus S
	Jason Jones DE
	Manny Ramirez G
Retired	Calvin Johnson WR
	Rashean Mathis CB

- Overnight the Detroit Lions went from having the #1 paid WR corps in the NFL to the league average at 18th when Calvin Johnson retired. If Calvin Johnson was on the Seahawks, Vikings, Bills or Cowboys, it might not be as big an issue, as those teams are run-centric. But the Lions are a pass heavy offense, one of the most pass heavy teams over the last several seasons. Their rush offense has consistently been subpar and they've relied on the huge contracts for Stafford and Megatron to carry the offense.
- With Megatron out the door, the Lions brought in WR Marin Jones in free agency, as well as smaller signings in Jeremy Kerley and Andre Caldwell. Here is the problem: they overpaid Marvin Jones ($27M in first 3 yrs) and Jones did his damage in Cincinnati when playing opposite a true #1 WR in AJ Green. Now he's playing opposite a #2 WR in Golden Tate. Sheer volume alone might be his saving grace from a fantasy perspective, but its highly unlikely he gets targeted on 50% of Stafford's passes 15+ yards downfield, which is the insane volume which was given to Calvin Johnson:
- Of the Lion's 84 passes which traveled 15+ yards in the air last year, 44 (52%) went to Megatron. The next highest WR was Golden Tate with 12 targets (14%) and he caught just 4, none for a touchdown. So Stafford is going to now be targeting Tate more and incorporating Marvin Jones with that massive hole to fill of deep targets.
- The Lions beefed up their offensive line by drafting T Taylor Decker 16th overall and C Graham Glasgow 95th overall, and added G Geoff Schwartz in free agency. The Lions are looking for every way possible to improve protection and open more holes in the run game.
- The Lions lost a big strength in their secondary, S Isa Abdul-Quddus. That won't help a 20th rated pass defense, which was significantly worse before he became a starter.

2016 Positional Spending

	All OFF	QB	OL	RB	WR	TE	All DEF	DL	LB	CB	S
2015 Rk	8	8	32	15	1	12	25	11	20	26	20
Rank	16	6	26	25	18	8	29	19	13	29	12
Total	78.7M	23.7M	19.7M	3.9M	19.7M	11.8M	63.1M	19.8M	23.9M	7.8M	11.6M

2016 Offseason Spending

Total Spent	Total Spent Rk	Free Agents #	Free Agents $	Free Agents $ Rk	Waiver #	Waiver $	Waiver $ Rk	Extended #	Sum of Extended $	Sum of Drafted $	Undrafted #	Undrafted $
153M	20	19	69M	12	9	8M	25	2	14M	37M	17	24M

2015 Stats & Fantasy Production

Pos	Player	Ov. Rank	Pos. Rk	Age	Gms	St	Pass Comp	Pass Att	Pass Yds	Pass TD	Pass Int	Rush Att	Rush Yds	Rush YPA	Rush TD	Targ	Recp	Rec Yds	Rec YPC	Rec TDs	Draft King Pts	Fan Duel Pts
QB	Matthew Stafford	67	9	27	16	16	398	592	4,262	32	13	44	159	4	1	1	1	-6	-6		312	303
RB	Theo Riddick		38	24	16	1						43	133	3		99	80	697	9	3	186	139
	Ameer Abdullah		43	22	16	9						143	597	4	2	38	25	183	7	1	125	105
	Joique Bell		48	29	13	5						90	311	3	4	27	22	286	13		112	95
WR	Calvin Johnson*	27	9	30	16	16										149	88	1,214	14	9	265	217
	Golden Tate		32	27	16	16						6	41	7		128	90	813	9	6	213	164
	Lance Moore		83	32	14	8										43	29	337	12	4	89	70
TE	Eric Ebron		13	22	14	8										70	47	537	11	5	134	107

46

ODDS & TRENDS — Detroit Lions

Avg Line	Pred Wins	Pred Div Finish
+1.5	7	#3

(-) Favorite   Underdog (+)
-5.0   +8.5

2016 Weekly Betting Lines (wks 1-16)

Avg Line = 1.5

Weekly lines by week:
- Wk 1: A +4.0
- Wk 2: H -5.0
- Wk 3: A +8.5
- Wk 5: H -1.0
- Wk 8: A +4.0
- Wk 9: A +6.5
- Wk 11: H -3.5
- Wk 12: H +2.5
- Wk 13: A +1.0
- Wk 14: -2.5
- Wk 15: A +3.0
- Wk 16: A +5.0

Week: 1 2 3 4 5 6 7 8 9 10 11 12 13 14 15 16

2015 Critical and Game-Deciding Stats

TO Margin	-6
TO Given	24
INT Given	14
FUM Given	10
TO Taken	18
INT Taken	9
FUM Taken	9
Sack Margin	-1
Sacks	43
Sacks Allow	44
Return TD Margin	+0
Ret TDs	2
Ret TDs Allow	2
Penalty Margin	-8
Penalties	104
Opponent Penalties	96

-Teams that win the turnover battle win 79% of games & cover 79% ATS.
-Teams with more sacks win 71% of games & cover 69% ATS.
-Teams with more return TDs win 75% of games & cover 75% ATS.
-Teams with fewer penalties win 57% of games & cover 54% ATS.

2016 NFLproject.com Forecast

Div RK	4
Div W%	(5%)

Playoffs RK	27
% in Playoffs	(15%)

Super Bowl RK	20
% Win Super Bowl	(0%)

Odds to Win Division
- 80% 70% 60% 50% 40% 30% 20% 10% 0%
- 72%
- 17%
- 5%

NFCN

Team Records & Trends

	2015	2014	2013
Average line	1.4	-2.3	-2.3
Average O/U line	45.6	45.0	48.9
Straight Up Record	7-9	11-5	7-9
Against the Spread Record	7-9	7-9	6-10
Over/Under Record	9-7	5-11	8-8
ATS as Favorite	3-2	5-6	5-7
ATS as Underdog	3-6	0-3	0-2
Straight Up Home	4-4	7-1	4-4
ATS Home	3-5	5-3	3-5
Over/Under Home	6-2	4-4	5-3
ATS as Home Favorite	2-1	5-3	3-5
ATS as a Home Dog	0-3	0-0	0-0
Straight Up Away	3-5	4-4	3-5
ATS Away	4-4	2-6	3-5
Over/Under Away	3-5	1-7	3-5
ATS Away Favorite	1-1	0-3	2-2
ATS Away Dog	3-3	0-3	0-2
Six Point Teaser Record	10-6	11-4	11-5
Seven Point Teaser Record	10-6	12-4	11-4
Ten Point Teaser Record	14-2	14-2	12-4

Games Favored

6

Games Underdog

9

Close Game Records

All 2015 Wins: **7**
FG Games (<=3 pts) W-L: **2-1**
FG Games Win %: **67% (#6)**
FG Games Wins (% of Total Wins): **29% (#13)**
1 Score Games (<=8 pts) W-L: **5-4**
1 Score Games Win %: **56% (#12)**
1 Score Games Wins (% of Total Wins): **71% (#11)**

Last year 71% of the Lion's wins were in games decided by one score or less. In fact, they won just 2 games by over 8 points (vs SF wk 16 and PHI on Thanksgiving, both at home) while they lost 5 games by 9+ points. They do get a nice schedule from a rest perspective, having more rest than their opponent 4 times. But the Lions were -6 in turnover margin, -8 in penalty margin and -1 in sack margin. If they bring all of those numbers closer to zero at a minimum, they would likely exceed their 7 game win projection, identical to their mark from 2015. But many of those 7 wins came from week 10 onward, when they faced terrible opposing defenses and were tremendous in the red zone. Games against LA, HOU and MIN in a 4 week span will be their offense's biggest test, but going against NO, CHI, NYG and DAL the last 4 weeks of the season should provide better offensive opportunities, despite 3 of the 4 being road games.

Home Lines (wks 1-16)

Avg Line = -1.7

Lines: -5.0, -1.0, -3.5, -2.5

Week: 1 2 3 4 5 6 7 8 9 10 11 12 13 14 15 16

Road Lines (wks 1-16)

Avg Line = 4.3

Lines: +4.0, +8.5, +4.0, +6.5, +2.0, +3.0, +5.0

Week: 1 2 3 4 5 6 7 8 9 10 11 12 13 14 15 16

Regular Season Wins: Past Results & Current Proj

2012 Wins	4
2013 Wins	7
2014 Wins	11
Proj 2015 Wins	8.5
2015 Wins	7
Proj 2016 Wins	7

1 2 3 4 5 6 7 8 9 10 11 12 13 14 15

2016 Rest Analysis

Avg Rest	6.5
Avg Rest Rk	3
Team More Rest	4
Opp More Rest	2
Net Rest Edge	2
3 days rest	1
4 days rest	0
5 days rest	1
6 days rest	10
7 days rest	1
8 days rest	0
9 days rest	1
10 days rest	0
11 days rest	0
12 days rest	0
13 days rest	1
14 days rest	0

Weekly EDSR & Season Trending Performance

	WEEK	1	2	3	4	5	6	7	8	10	11	12	13	14	15	16	17
2015 Results	RESULT	L	L	L	L	W	L	L	W	W	W	L	L	W	W	W	
	OPP	SD	MIN	DEN	SEA	ARI	CHI	MIN	KC	GB	OAK	PHI	GB	STL	NO	SF	CHI
	SITE	A	A	H	A	H	H	H	A	A	H	H	A	A	H	H	A
	MARGIN	-5	-10	-12	-3	-25	3	-9	-35	2	5	31	-4	-7	8	15	4
	PTS	28	16	12	10	17	37	19	10	18	18	45	23	14	35	32	24
	OPP PTS	33	26	24	13	42	34	28	45	16	13	14	27	21	27	17	20

EDSR Results (W/L) By Week
W=Green
L=Red

Off & Def EDSR Wk & Trend
- Blue=Offense (high=good)
- Red=Defense (low=good)

47

STATS & VISUALIZATIONS

Detroit Lions

Directional Passer Rating Achieved

Receiver	Short Left	Short Middle	Short Right	Deep Left	Deep Middle	Deep Right
Golden Tate	100	112	87	59	109	39
Calvin Johnson	115	116	79	105	48	70
Eric Ebron	50	107	106	118	158	39
Lance Moore	107	122	85	65	109	156
T.J. Jones	88	71	50	39	109	39
Tim Wright	47	127	71			39	118
Brandon Pettigrew	58	42	93			39
Corey Fuller	39	39	105	39	118	

Directional Frequency by Receiver

Receiver	Short Left	Short Middle	Short Right	Deep Left	Deep Middle	Deep Right
Golden Tate	27%	38%	32%	19%	14%	9%
Calvin Johnson	41%	18%	26%	65%	36%	55%
Eric Ebron	9%	24%	21%	3%	14%	5%
Lance Moore	10%	6%	10%	8%	14%	18%
T.J. Jones	5%	4%	2%	3%	14%	5%
Tim Wright	4%	3%	4%		5%	5%
Brandon Pettigrew	2%	6%	4%			5%
Corey Fuller	3%	1%	2%	3%	5%	

Defense Passer Rating Allowed

Short Left	Short Middle	Short Right	Deep Left	Deep Middle	Deep Right
94	114	95	68	135	111

Offensive Rush Directional Yds/Carry

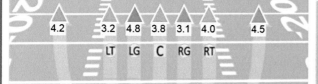

4.2   3.2   4.8   3.8   3.1   4.0   4.5

LT   LG   C   RG   RT

Offensive Rush Frequency of Direction

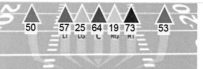

50   57   25   64   19   73   53

LT   LG   C   RG   RT

Offensive Explosive Runs by Direction

6   5   4   7   5   9

LT   LG   C   RG   RT

Defensive Rush Directional Yds/Carry

6.3   6.1   3.4   2.7   5.1   5.8   3.3

LT   LG   C   RG   RT

Matthew Stafford - 1st Down RTG

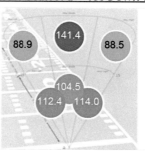

88.9   141.4   88.5   104.5   112.4   114.0

Matthew Stafford - 3rd Down RTG

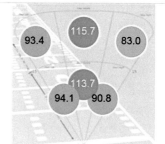

116.4   89.1   81.9   88.8   41.0   72.9

Matthew Stafford - 2nd Down RTG

82.6   92.7   116.7   133.7   100.7   76.0

Matthew Stafford - Overall RTG

93.4   115.7   83.0   113.7   94.1   90.8

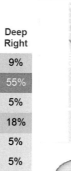

SHARP FOOTBALL STATS

2nd & Short RUN (1D or not)

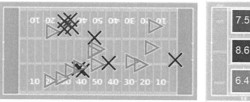

2nd & Short RUN Stats

Run Conv Rk	1D% Run	NFL 1D% Run Avg	Run Freq	NFL Run Freq Avg
27	57%	69%	53%	64%

2nd & Short PASS (1D or not)

2nd & Short PASS Stats

Pass Conv Rk	1D% Pass	NFL 1D% Pass Avg	Pass Freq	NFL Pass Freq Avg
9	58%	55%	48%	36%

Pass Offense Play Success Rate

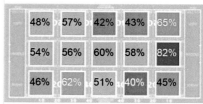

48%	57%	42%	43%	65%
54%	56%	60%	58%	82%
46%	62%	51%	40%	45%

Pass Offense Yds/Play

7.5	8.0	6.0	6.9	4.5
8.6	8.5	9.7	8.3	8.4
6.4	8.8	7.5	3.8	2.4

Off. Directional Tendency (% of Plays Left, Middle or Right)

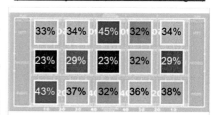

33%	34%	45%	32%	34%
23%	29%	23%	32%	29%
43%	37%	32%	36%	38%

Off. Directional Pass Rate (% of Plays which are Passes)

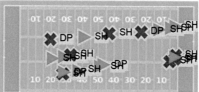

70%	62%	73%	78%	57%
51%	71%	51%	71%	63%
70%	62%	59%	62%	78%

Delta Points: Common Mistakes Made by DFS Players

Many DFS analysts have begun to utilize point spreads in their prognostication on a weekly basis. Often, the goal is to try to avoid negative game script situations, such as playing a RB on the road as an underdog. The logic there is the team may be likely to trail, and would therefore need to produce more through the air, potentially abandoning the run game entirely.

Another method used is to simply take the total and point spread as gospel, and calculate team totals off of those numbers. So if a home team is favored by 7 and the total is set at 47, the projected final score is Home 27, Road 20. The analyst can then back into projected production based on these team total scores.

While implementing this strategy is quick, it is also very dirty. It assumes the totals and spreads are set accurately. As the bettors among us know, that is not true. While linesmakers try their best, they are lining hundreds of games across multiple sports. They are not accurate enough on each and every line. Particularly when they are faced with someone like myself, who focuses solely on the sport of football, and has developed a computer model designed and implemented now for over a decade at attacking inefficiencies in the totals market.

My well documented success in totals is made possible because the lines are often inaccurate. As such, why should they be taken as gospel?

DFS analysts should look at the reverse application of the strategy in their world. Imagine if a sports bettor decided to play DFS, and noticed that there is a dollar amount allocated to each player by the fantasy sites. Converting that dollar amount into projected player points, a sports bettor could simply play weekly DFS and assume each player will score the same as the dollar amount they "cost". Such a strategy would be mocked by the DFS community as far too simplistic and most of all, it does not take into account a judgment as to if the price set is correct or not. It just takes it as gospel. But DFS players know there are inefficiencies in the pricing based on their own evaluation.

I would encourage DFS players to look at the following tables, which show 3 year and 1 year samples of delta points scored or allowed based on the lines. Delta points scored (dps) is simply the team total set by linesmakers less the actual points scored. As an example: the Bengals have frequently exceeded their team total as a dog, going "over" in 11 of 14 games, 2nd best for an underdog. But as a favorite, particularly on the road, they are below average and frequently don't exceed their projection.

2013-2015 Delta Points Scored (Offense) Situational Analysis

	ALL					FAV				HOME FAV				ROAD FAV					DOG				HOME DOG				ROAD DOG				
Team	dps +	dps -	%	RK	Team	dps +	dps -	%	RK	dps +	dps -	%	RK	dps +	dps -	%	RK	Team	dps +	dps -	%	RK	dps +	dps -	%	RK	dps +	dps -	%	RK	Team
ARI	28	19	60%	2	ARI	17	11	61%	5	10	7	59%	9	7	4	64%	10	ARI	11	8	58%	9	4	3	57%	12	7	5	58%	4	ARI
ATL	18	27	40%	28	ATL	8	13	38%	28	5	10	33%	25	3	3	50%	15	ATL	10	13	43%	22	3	4	43%	18	7	9	44%	19	ATL
BAL	23	25	48%	19	BAL	13	13	50%	15	9	8	53%	15	4	5	44%	22	BAL	10	10	50%	14	2	3	40%	20	8	7	53%	11	BAL
BUF	29	19	60%	1	BUF	10	5	67%	2	6	4	60%	6	4	1	80%	3	BUF	18	13	58%	8	9	3	75%	7	9	10	47%	17	BUF
CAR	28	20	58%	3	CAR	18	11	62%	4	13	5	72%	2	5	6	45%	20	CAR	9	8	53%	11	2	3	40%	20	7	5	58%	4	CAR
CHI	23	24	49%	16	CHI	6	6	50%	15	4	6	40%	22	2	0	100%	1	CHI	16	16	50%	14	5	7	42%	19	11	9	55%	10	CHI
CIN	28	20	58%	3	CIN	17	14	55%	10	12	8	60%	6	5	6	45%	20	CIN	11	3	79%	2	3	0	100%	1	8	3	73%	1	CIN
CLE	22	25	47%	20	CLE	5	8	38%	27	5	7	42%	21	0	1	0%	30	CLE	14	17	45%	20	5	4	56%	13	9	13	41%	24	CLE
DAL	24	24	50%	14	DAL	14	8	64%	3	8	6	57%	10	6	2	75%	5	DAL	10	14	42%	23	4	5	44%	17	6	9	40%	25	DAL
DEN	28	20	58%	3	DEN	24	19	56%	8	11	11	50%	16	13	8	62%	11	DEN	4	1	80%	1	2	0	100%	1	2	1	67%	2	DEN
DET	19	28	40%	27	DET	14	13	52%	13	10	8	56%	13	4	5	44%	22	DET	4	10	29%	31	1	2	33%	25	3	8	27%	31	DET
GB	26	22	54%	10	GB	22	15	59%	6	13	9	59%	8	9	6	60%	12	GB	2	6	25%	32					2	6	25%	32	GB
HOU	21	26	45%	22	HOU	8	12	40%	25	3	10	23%	30	5	2	71%	7	HOU	13	12	52%	12	6	3	67%	9	7	9	44%	19	HOU
IND	26	22	54%	10	IND	15	17	47%	20	6	14	30%	27	9	3	75%	5	IND	11	5	69%	3	4	0	100%	1	7	5	58%	4	IND
JAC	18	29	38%	30	JAC	1	5	17%	32	1	5	17%	31					JAC	17	24	41%	25	5	12	29%	27	12	12	50%	15	JAC
KC	26	20	57%	8	KC	16	13	55%	9	8	11	42%	20	8	2	80%	3	KC	9	6	60%	6	2	1	67%	9	7	5	58%	4	KC
MIA	21	26	45%	22	MIA	8	13	38%	28	6	8	43%	19	2	5	29%	26	MIA	11	13	46%	19	4	4	50%	14	7	9	44%	19	MIA
MIN	27	20	57%	7	MIN	9	4	69%	1	8	3	73%	1	1	1	50%	15	MIN	17	12	59%	7	6	2	75%	7	11	10	52%	13	MIN
NE	26	21	55%	9	NE	19	17	53%	12	11	9	55%	14	8	8	50%	15	NE	5	3	63%	5	3	0	100%	1	2	3	40%	25	NE
NO	24	23	51%	13	NO	16	17	48%	18	12	9	57%	10	4	8	33%	24	NO	8	6	57%	10	2	0	100%	1	6	6	50%	15	NO
NYG	25	23	52%	12	NYG	9	11	45%	23	6	9	40%	22	3	2	60%	12	NYG	13	12	52%	12	4	4	50%	14	9	8	53%	12	NYG
NYJ	22	25	47%	20	NYJ	10	11	48%	19	9	4	69%	4	1	7	13%	29	NYJ	12	12	50%	14	3	5	38%	23	9	7	56%	9	NYJ
OAK	19	29	40%	29	OAK	1	4	20%	31	0	3	0%	32	1	1	50%	15	OAK	18	23	44%	21	9	11	45%	16	9	12	43%	22	OAK
PHI	24	24	50%	14	PHI	14	16	47%	21	10	12	45%	18	4	4	50%	15	PHI	8	8	50%	14	0	2	0%	30	8	6	57%	8	PHI
PIT	28	20	58%	3	PIT	14	12	54%	11	12	5	71%	3	2	7	22%	28	PIT	13	6	68%	4	5	1	83%	6	8	5	62%	3	PIT
SD	21	27	44%	24	SD	9	9	50%	15	8	6	57%	10	1	3	25%	27	SD	12	18	40%	26	3	7	30%	26	9	11	45%	18	SD
SEA	23	24	49%	16	SEA	21	20	51%	14	11	12	48%	17	10	8	56%	14	SEA	2	4	33%	30					2	4	33%	30	SEA
SF	20	27	43%	25	SF	12	14	46%	22	5	11	31%	26	7	3	70%	8	SF	8	13	38%	28	3	5	38%	23	5	8	38%	28	SF
STL	23	24	49%	16	STL	8	6	57%	7	7	4	64%	5	1	2	33%	24	STL	15	17	47%	18	7	4	64%	11	8	13	38%	29	STL
TB	17	31	35%	32	TB	3	9	25%	30	3	8	27%	29	0	1	0%	30	TB	14	21	40%	26	2	10	17%	29	12	11	52%	14	TB
TEN	17	30	36%	31	TEN	4	6	40%	25	2	5	29%	28	2	1	67%	9	TEN	12	23	34%	29	4	11	27%	28	8	12	40%	25	TEN
WAS	19	27	41%	26	WAS	4	5	44%	24	3	5	38%	24	1	0	100%	1	WAS	15	21	42%	23	6	9	40%	20	9	12	43%	22	WAS

2015 Delta Points Scored (Offense) Situational Analysis

	ALL					FAV				HOME FAV				ROAD FAV					DOG				HOME DOG				ROAD DOG				
Team	dps +	dps -	%	RK	Team	dps +	dps -	%	RK	dps +	dps -	%	RK	dps +	dps -	%	RK	Team	dps +	dps -	%	RK	dps +	dps -	%	RK	dps +	dps -	%	RK	Team
ARI	10	6	63%	5	ARI	9	6	60%	10	4	4	50%	12	5	2	71%	5	ARI	1	0	100%	1					1	0	100%	1	ARI
ATL	4	10	29%	31	ATL	2	8	20%	26	1	5	17%	27	1	3	25%	19	ATL	2	2	50%	17	1	0	100%	1	1	2	33%	25	ATL
BAL	7	9	44%	17	BAL	4	4	50%	15	3	2	60%	10	1	2	33%	16	BAL	3	5	38%	24	1	2	33%	18	2	3	40%	23	BAL
BUF	11	5	69%	2	BUF	4	3	57%	12	2	2	50%	12	2	1	67%	6	BUF	6	2	75%	5	3	0	100%	1	3	2	60%	11	BUF
CAR	14	2	88%	1	CAR	11	2	85%	1	7	0	100%	1	4	2	67%	6	CAR	2	0	100%	1	1	0	100%	1	1	0	100%	1	CAR
CHI	7	9	44%	17	CHI	0	2	0%	31	0	2	0%	30					CHI	7	7	50%	17	3	3	50%	12	4	4	50%	18	CHI
CIN	10	6	63%	5	CIN	8	4	67%	6	4	4	50%	12	4	0	100%	1	CIN	2	1	67%	7					2	1	67%	6	CIN
CLE	6	9	40%	24	CLE	2	1	67%	6	2	1	67%	7					CLE	3	8	27%	29	1	2	33%	18	2	6	25%	29	CLE
DAL	4	12	25%	32	DAL	2	1	67%	6	1	1	50%	12	1	0	100%	1	DAL	2	9	18%	30	2	3	40%	16	0	6	0%	30	DAL
DEN	7	9	44%	17	DEN	3	9	25%	24	1	5	17%	27	2	4	33%	16	DEN	4	0	100%	1	2	0	100%	1	2	0	100%	1	DEN
DET	7	9	44%	17	DET	4	1	80%	2	3	0	100%	1	1	1	50%	11	DET	3	6	33%	25	1	2	33%	18	2	4	33%	25	DET
GB	8	8	50%	14	GB	7	7	50%	15	3	5	38%	21	4	2	67%	6	GB	0	1	0%	31					0	1	0%	30	GB
HOU	7	9	44%	17	HOU	2	4	33%	23	1	4	20%	24	1	0	100%	1	HOU	5	4	56%	15	1	1	50%	12	4	3	57%	17	HOU
IND	8	8	50%	14	IND	3	5	38%	22	2	4	33%	22	1	1	50%	11	IND	5	3	63%	11	2	0	100%	1	3	3	50%	18	IND
JAC	8	8	50%	14	JAC	1	4	20%	26	1	4	20%	24					JAC	7	4	64%	10	2	1	67%	8	5	3	63%	8	JAC
KC	10	5	67%	4	KC	6	4	60%	10	3	4	43%	20	3	0	100%	1	KC	3	1	75%	5					3	1	75%	5	KC
MIA	5	11	31%	28	MIA	1	5	17%	30	1	3	25%	23	0	2	0%	21	MIA	3	6	33%	25	1	2	33%	18	2	4	33%	25	MIA
MIN	9	6	60%	8	MIN	5	2	71%	3	4	1	80%	4	1	1	50%	11	MIN	3	3	50%	17	0	1	0%	24	3	2	60%	11	MIN
NE	9	7	56%	9	NE	8	7	53%	14	4	4	50%	12	4	3	57%	10	NE													NE
NO	8	7	53%	13	NO	3	3	50%	15	3	2	60%	10	0	1	0%	21	NO	5	4	56%	15	2	0	100%	1	3	4	43%	20	NO
NYG	11	5	69%	2	NYG	5	2	71%	3	4	1	80%	4	1	1	50%	11	NYG	5	3	63%	11	2	1	67%	8	3	2	60%	11	NYG
NYJ	9	7	56%	9	NYJ	6	7	46%	20	5	2	71%	6	1	5	17%	20	NYJ	3	0	100%	1	1	0	100%	1	2	0	100%	1	NYJ
OAK	6	10	38%	27	OAK	1	3	25%	24	0	2	0%	30	1	1	50%	11	OAK	5	6	45%	21	2	4	33%	18	3	2	60%	11	OAK
PHI	5	11	31%	28	PHI	2	8	20%	26	1	6	14%	29	1	2	33%	16	PHI	3	3	50%	17	0	1	0%	24	3	2	60%	11	PHI
PIT	9	7	56%	9	PIT	5	2	71%	3	5	0	100%	1	0	2	0%	21	PIT	4	3	57%	14	1	1	50%	12	3	2	60%	11	PIT
SD	7	9	44%	17	SD	4	2	67%	6	4	2	67%	7					SD	3	7	30%	28	0	2	0%	24	3	5	38%	24	SD
SEA	9	7	56%	9	SEA	7	6	54%	13	4	4	50%	12	3	2	60%	9	SEA	2	1	67%	7					2	1	67%	6	SEA
SF	6	9	40%	24	SF													SF	6	9	40%	23	3	5	38%	17	3	4	43%	20	SF
STL	6	9	40%	24	STL	2	3	40%	21	2	1	67%	7	0	2	0%	21	STL	4	5	44%	22	2	1	67%	8	2	4	33%	25	STL
TB	7	9	44%	17	TB	1	4	20%	26	1	4	20%	24					TB	6	4	60%	13	1	1	50%	12	5	3	63%	8	TB
TEN	5	11	31%	28	TEN	1	1	50%	15	1	1	50%	12					TEN	4	9	31%	27	1	5	17%	23	3	4	43%	20	TEN
WAS	10	6	63%	5	WAS	1	1	50%	15	1	1	50%	12					WAS	9	5	64%	9	4	2	67%	8	5	3	63%	8	WAS

Meanwhile, the NFC North teams from Detroit and Green Bay have been terrible bets offensively when underdogs, failing to hit their team projection in 16 of 22 games combined. To continue the exercise, a team like the Bills, when at home, has performed tremendously against their expectations. They have exceeded the lined total in 9 of 12 games as a home dog and in 6 of 10 games as a home favorite. Combined, that is 15 of 22 games, or 68%.

Keep in mind, this exercise not only may help you with your situational use of team totals for DFS in 2016, it also is perfect evidence of taking team totals as gospel. I will admit, however, nothing is as simple as using a small sample (even if it is 3 years) and suggesting the pattern will continue. Which is why I prefer using detailed, matchup based analysis coupled with my computer models. It is significantly more work, but it is significantly more successful. On this page, we turn to the defensive metrics and look at defenses that have allowed more or less than the linesmakers projected. One team that should jump off the page is the Chicago Bears. Not only have they been terrible for the last 3 years, when they have been favorites in a game, their defense allows the opponent's offense to exceed it's team total 85% of the time (11 of 13 games). Last year, even with John Fox at the helm, it happened both times when the Bears were favored. In a week 13 matchup against the Blaine Gabbert led 49ers, the Bears allowed 75 rush yards 2 total TDs for Gabbert and the 49ers exceeded their team total before the game even went to overtime. I just so happened to be on the over in this game for my clients and it hit.

The following week, the Bears were favorites over the Redskins in a windy, rainy home game in mid December. This time, the Bears allowed Kirk Cousins to go 24/31 for 300 yards, 1 TD and 1 more rushing TD and the Redskins exceeded their team total. Jordan Reed completely abused the Bears, posting 9 receptions for 120 yards and 1 TD.

The Browns have been another defense to target. Opposing offenses have rarely met expectations against the Chiefs defense, exceeding their projected total in a mere 13 out of 48 games the last 3 years (27%). The Falcons have been great to target when they are favored, particularly in their own dome where opposing offenses have exceeded their team total at a 73% clip. But when the Falcons are underdogs, the numbers are no longer in favor of the opposing offense.

Hopefully this analysis changes perspectives on blindly using team totals. Understanding that the linesmakers are typically very wrong on a game to game basis, with some teams scoring considerably more or less than projected, but averaging out in the end. Fortunately, as bettors or DFS players, we don't have to be right about every player or game we bet. We just need to be right on the few that we target. For that reason, I encourage those who want to use team totals to try to forecast their own without worrying what the linesmaker set. And if you don't feel comfortable, at Sharp Football Analysis I specialize in NFL totals of all types and between my podcasts and my client products, there are plenty of tools to assist you in better forecasting team scoring in 2016.

2013-2015 Delta Points Allowed (Defense) Situational Analysis

	ALL					FAV				HOME FAV				ROAD FAV					DOG				HOME DOG				ROAD DOG				
Team	dpa +	dpa -	%	RK	Team	dpa +	dpa -	%	RK	dpa +	dpa -	%	RK	dpa +	dpa -	%	RK	Team	dpa +	dpa -	%	RK	dpa +	dpa -	%	RK	dpa +	dpa -	%	RK	Team
ARI	17	30	36%	2	ARI	10	17	37%	4	6	11	35%	6	4	6	40%	7	ARI	7	13	35%	3	2	5	29%	5	5	8	38%	5	ARI
ATL	26	22	54%	24	ATL	14	7	67%	30	11	4	73%	31	3	3	50%	13	ATL	12	14	46%	11	2	7	22%	3	10	7	59%	23	ATL
BAL	24	23	51%	15	BAL	15	11	58%	26	8	9	47%	14	7	2	78%	28	BAL	8	11	42%	7	2	3	40%	9	6	8	43%	8	BAL
BUF	20	26	43%	7	BUF	7	7	50%	17	4	6	40%	8	3	1	75%	27	BUF	12	18	40%	5	4	8	33%	6	8	10	44%	12	BUF
CAR	19	28	40%	4	CAR	11	17	39%	6	5	13	28%	2	6	4	60%	22	CAR	8	9	47%	12	2	3	40%	9	6	6	50%	17	CAR
CHI	30	18	63%	32	CHI	11	2	85%	32	9	2	82%	32	2	0	100%	29	CHI	18	14	56%	23	9	3	75%	24	9	11	45%	13	CHI
CIN	23	25	48%	12	CIN	15	16	48%	16	10	10	50%	16	5	6	45%	12	CIN	8	6	57%	26	3	0	100%	29	5	6	45%	16	CIN
CLE	28	18	61%	31	CLE	9	4	69%	31	8	4	67%	27	1	0	100%	29	CLE	17	13	57%	25	5	5	50%	11	12	8	60%	24	CLE
DAL	25	22	53%	23	DAL	13	8	62%	27	9	4	69%	29	4	4	50%	13	DAL	11	13	46%	10	5	4	56%	18	6	9	40%	6	DAL
DEN	23	24	49%	13	DEN	20	23	47%	14	11	11	50%	16	9	12	43%	9	DEN	3	1	75%	30	1	1	50%	11	2	0	100%	32	DEN
DET	24	23	51%	15	DET	13	15	46%	13	10	9	53%	24	3	6	33%	4	DET	10	3	77%	31	3	0	100%	29	7	3	70%	30	DET
GB	24	24	50%	14	GB	15	22	41%	9	6	16	27%	1	9	6	60%	22	GB	7	1	88%	32					7	1	88%	31	GB
HOU	26	22	54%	24	HOU	10	11	48%	15	7	7	50%	16	3	4	43%	9	HOU	14	11	56%	22	7	2	78%	26	7	9	44%	11	HOU
IND	25	23	52%	21	IND	16	16	50%	17	8	12	40%	8	8	4	67%	24	IND	9	7	56%	23	3	1	75%	24	6	6	50%	17	IND
JAC	27	19	59%	30	JAC	2	3	40%	7	2	3	40%	8					JAC	25	16	61%	29	11	7	61%	20	14	9	61%	25	JAC
KC	13	35	27%	1	KC	9	22	29%	1	7	14	33%	3	2	8	20%	1	KC	4	11	27%	2	2	1	67%	23	2	10	17%	1	KC
MIA	26	22	54%	24	MIA	12	10	55%	24	10	5	67%	27	2	5	29%	3	MIA	13	11	54%	21	3	5	38%	8	10	6	63%	26	MIA
MIN	21	27	44%	8	MIN	5	9	36%	3	4	8	33%	3	1	1	50%	13	MIN	15	14	52%	18	7	1	88%	28	8	13	38%	4	MIN
NE	22	26	46%	11	NE	19	18	51%	22	8	13	38%	7	11	5	69%	26	NE	2	6	25%	1	1	2	33%	6	1	4	20%	2	NE
NO	24	23	51%	15	NO	17	17	50%	17	11	11	50%	16	6	6	50%	13	NO	7	6	54%	20	1	1	50%	11	6	5	55%	22	NO
NYG	26	21	55%	27	NYG	11	9	55%	25	9	6	60%	25	2	3	40%	7	NYG	14	10	58%	27	4	4	50%	11	10	6	63%	26	NYG
NYJ	27	20	57%	28	NYJ	13	8	62%	27	9	4	69%	29	4	4	50%	13	NYJ	12	12	50%	14	2	7	22%	3	10	5	67%	29	NYJ
OAK	24	23	51%	15	OAK	2	3	40%	7	1	2	33%	3	1	1	50%	13	OAK	21	19	53%	19	12	7	63%	21	9	12	43%	8	OAK
PHI	19	28	40%	4	PHI	13	16	45%	10	9	13	41%	12	4	3	57%	21	PHI	6	10	38%	4	1	1	50%	11	5	9	36%	3	PHI
PIT	21	26	45%	10	PIT	12	14	46%	12	8	9	47%	14	4	5	44%	11	PIT	8	10	44%	8	3	3	50%	11	5	7	42%	7	PIT
SD	21	27	44%	8	SD	9	9	50%	17	7	7	50%	16	2	2	50%	13	SD	12	18	40%	5	2	8	20%	2	10	10	50%	17	SD
SEA	19	28	40%	4	SEA	16	25	39%	5	10	13	43%	13	6	12	33%	4	SEA	3	3	50%	14					3	3	50%	17	SEA
SF	18	29	38%	3	SF	8	17	32%	2	6	9	40%	8	2	8	20%	1	SF	10	12	45%	9	1	7	13%	1	9	5	64%	28	SF
STL	24	23	51%	15	STL	8	7	53%	23	6	6	50%	16	2	1	67%	24	STL	16	15	52%	17	7	4	64%	22	9	11	45%	13	STL
TB	24	23	51%	15	TB	7	4	64%	29	7	4	64%	26	0	0			TB	17	18	49%	13	7	5	58%	19	10	13	43%	10	TB
TEN	28	20	58%	29	TEN	5	6	45%	11	4	4	50%	16	1	2	33%	4	TEN	21	14	60%	28	12	3	80%	27	9	11	45%	13	TEN
WAS	25	23	52%	21	WAS	5	5	50%	17	4	4	50%	16	1	1	50%	13	WAS	19	18	51%	16	8	7	53%	17	11	11	50%	17	WAS

2015 Delta Points Allowed (Defense) Situational Analysis

	ALL					FAV				HOME FAV				ROAD FAV					DOG				HOME DOG				ROAD DOG				
Team	dpa +	dpa -	%	RK	Team	dpa +	dpa -	%	RK	dpa +	dpa -	%	RK	dpa +	dpa -	%	RK	Team	dpa +	dpa -	%	RK	dpa +	dpa -	%	RK	dpa +	dpa -	%	RK	Team
ARI	7	8	47%	11	ARI	6	8	43%	8	4	4	50%	9	2	4	33%	7	ARI	1	0	100%	30					1	0	100%	29	ARI
ATL	6	10	38%	4	ATL	5	5	50%	13	3	3	50%	9	2	2	50%	9	ATL	1	5	17%	1	0	2	0%	1	1	3	25%	6	ATL
BAL	9	7	56%	22	BAL	6	2	75%	27	4	1	80%	25	2	1	67%	16	BAL	3	5	38%	7	2	1	67%	15	1	4	20%	3	BAL
BUF	7	9	44%	7	BUF	4	3	57%	18	2	2	50%	9	2	1	67%	16	BUF	2	6	25%	4	1	2	33%	6	1	4	20%	3	BUF
CAR	7	9	44%	7	CAR	6	7	46%	11	2	5	29%	5	4	2	67%	16	CAR	1	1	50%	13	1	0	100%	22	0	1	0%	1	CAR
CHI	8	8	50%	14	CHI	2	0	100%	30	2	0	100%	29					CHI	6	8	43%	11	4	2	67%	15	2	6	25%	6	CHI
CIN	7	9	44%	7	CIN	5	7	42%	5	4	4	50%	9	1	3	25%	6	CIN	2	1	67%	23					2	1	67%	23	CIN
CLE	11	4	73%	32	CLE	2	1	67%	23	2	1	67%	21					CLE	9	2	82%	29	3	1	75%	21	6	1	86%	27	CLE
DAL	9	7	56%	22	DAL	2	1	67%	23	2	0	100%	29	0	1	0%	1	DAL	6	5	55%	18	3	2	60%	14	3	3	50%	14	DAL
DEN	8	8	50%	14	DEN	5	7	42%	5	3	3	50%	9	2	4	33%	7	DEN	3	1	75%	27	1	1	50%	9	2	0	100%	29	DEN
DET	10	5	67%	31	DET	3	2	60%	20	2	1	67%	21	1	1	50%	9	DET	6	2	75%	27	3	0	100%	22	3	2	60%	21	DET
GB	6	10	38%	4	GB	5	9	36%	4	1	7	13%	2	4	2	67%	16	GB	1	0	100%	30					1	0	100%	29	GB
HOU	7	9	44%	7	HOU	1	5	17%	2	1	4	20%	3	0	1	0%	1	HOU	5	4	56%	20	1	1	50%	9	4	3	57%	20	HOU
IND	9	7	56%	22	IND	5	3	63%	22	3	3	50%	9	2	0	100%	21	IND	4	4	50%	13	1	1	50%	9	3	3	50%	14	IND
JAC	9	6	60%	26	JAC	2	2	50%	13	2	2	50%	9					JAC	7	4	64%	22	1	2	33%	6	6	2	75%	26	JAC
KC	5	11	31%	3	KC	3	8	27%	3	3	5	38%	7	0	3	0%	1	KC	2	2	50%	13					2	2	50%	14	KC
MIA	10	6	63%	27	MIA	3	3	50%	13	2	2	50%	9	1	1	50%	9	MIA	6	3	67%	23	2	1	67%	15	4	2	67%	23	MIA
MIN	3	13	19%	1	MIN	1	7	13%	1	0	6	0%	1	1	1	50%	9	MIN	1	5	17%	1	1	0	100%	22	0	5	0%	1	MIN
NE	8	8	50%	14	NE	7	8	47%	12	2	6	25%	4	5	2	71%	20	NE													NE
NO	10	6	63%	27	NO	6	1	86%	29	5	1	83%	28	1	0	100%	21	NO	4	5	44%	12	1	1	50%	9	3	4	43%	12	NO
NYG	8	8	50%	14	NYG	4	3	57%	18	4	1	80%	25	0	2	0%	1	NYG	3	5	38%	7	1	2	33%	6	2	3	40%	10	NYG
NYJ	9	7	56%	22	NYJ	8	5	62%	21	5	2	71%	24	3	3	50%	9	NYJ	1	2	33%	5	0	1	0%	1	1	1	50%	14	NYJ
OAK	8	8	50%	14	OAK	2	2	50%	13	1	1	50%	9	1	1	50%	9	OAK	6	5	55%	18	4	2	67%	15	2	3	40%	10	OAK
PHI	8	7	53%	21	PHI	4	5	44%	10	2	5	29%	5	2	0	100%	21	PHI	4	2	67%	23	1	0	100%	22	3	2	60%	21	PHI
PIT	4	11	27%	2	PIT	3	4	43%	8	2	3	40%	8	1	1	50%	9	PIT	1	5	17%	1	0	2	0%	1	1	3	25%	6	PIT
SD	8	8	50%	14	SD	4	2	67%	23	4	2	67%	21					SD	4	6	40%	10	1	1	50%	9	3	5	38%	9	SD
SEA	7	8	47%	11	SEA	5	7	42%	5	4	3	57%	20	1	4	20%	5	SEA	2	1	67%	23					2	1	67%	23	SEA
SF	8	8	50%	14	SF													SF	8	8	50%	13	1	7	13%	4	7	1	88%	28	SF
STL	7	8	47%	11	STL	4	2	67%	23	2	2	50%	9	2	0	100%	21	STL	3	5	38%	7	2	1	67%	15	1	4	20%	3	STL
TB	10	6	63%	27	TB	4	1	80%	28	4	1	80%	25					TB	6	4	60%	21	2	0	100%	22	4	4	50%	14	TB
TEN	10	6	63%	27	TEN	2	0	100%	30	2	0	100%	29					TEN	7	6	54%	17	4	2	67%	15	3	4	43%	12	TEN
WAS	6	10	38%	4	WAS	1	1	50%	13	1	1	50%	9					WAS	5	9	36%	6	1	5	17%	5	4	4	50%	14	WAS

Dallas Cowboys

Coaches

Head Coach: Jason Garrett (6th yr)
OC: Scott Linehan (3rd yr)
DC: Rod Marinelli (3rd yr)

Forecast 2016 Wins

9

Past Records

2015: 4-12
2014: 12-4
2013: 8-8

Opponent Strength
Easy — Hard

2016 Schedule & Week by Week Strength of Schedule

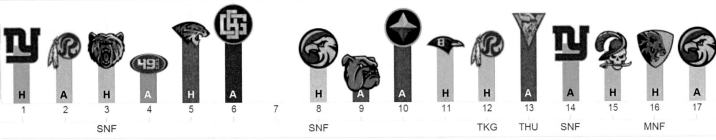

H	A	H	A	H	A		H	A	A	H	H	A	A	H	H	A
1	2	3	4	5	6	7	8	9	10	11	12	13	14	15	16	17
	SNF						SNF				TKG	THU	SNF		MNF	

2016 Overview

In the pass heavy NFL, the Dallas Cowboys tried something very different two years ago and it paid off in a big way. The 2013 Cowboys were the 2nd most pass-heavy team. The Cowboys went 66% pass in one-score games, and DeMarco Murray received only 163 carries, despite averaging 5.4 YPC. The team won just 8 games and decided to make a change. They brought in Scott Linehan from Detroit to help coordinate plays. In an awkward situation, outgoing OC Bill Callahan remained on staff, but the team had Linehan call the plays. The team went run heavy to the extreme. It protected Tony Romo and the Cowboys defense, as it controlled the clock, introduced more efficiency and lessened turnovers. Dallas called run in one-score games 50% of the time, an incredible 16% decrease from the prior year, the largest drop of any team in the NFL by far. Last year, Callahan formally departed and Linehan took over as the full OC, and the team continued the extremely run heavy approach. For many of the same reasons as 2014.

The team drafted their future RB for years to come, taking Ezekiel Elliott 4th overall. It was a pick they received only because their 2015 season ended so terribly (4-12), in large part because they saved money at back-up QB, a move many old school NFL fossils would consider unintelligent. But let's ignore the Elliott in the room for the time being, and discuss the biggest threat to a successful 2016: the Cowboys defense. The plan in 2014 was straight forward for the defense. Play with a second half lead (thanks to the offense), rush the passer and force turnovers against a desperate offense. The 2014 Cowboys' defense held an average lead in the 2nd half of 8.2 points/drive, second best of any team behind the Patriots. Their defense was able to gain takeaways on an insane 23% of opponent's 2nd half drives, most of any team (Denver was #2). But that won't be quite as easy in 2016. Their leading pass rusher, Demarcus Lawrence, is suspended for 4 games (though appealing). Randy Gregory is also suspended for 4 games. Their second leading pass rusher from 2015, Greg Hardy, is gone. That's a lot of pressure off opposing QBs to start the season. And on the backend, the Cowboys have recognizable names, but with questionable performance. They are paying too much for Brandon Carr, they paid too much in draft capital to take Morris Claiborne, and Orlando Scandrick is playing after missing the 2015 season with an ACL tear. These issues raise question marks with the pass rush and the secondary, two of the most critical areas where they need strength when playing with a lead in the second half.

And that brings us back to the Cowboys offense and the Elliott in the room. If the Cowboys offense is going to not only put up enough points themselves to win games, but to also do so in a physical, grinding, time consuming manner to help their defense, they will have to do an even better job than they did in 2014. So there is no doubt the team will be just as run heavy in 2016 as they were in 2014 and 2015, despite Tony Romo and Dez Bryant both coming back to full strength this season. There is little doubt Elliott should be a fantasy stud. Their red zone offense should be tremendous. But they need to control the ball in the 2nd half. That means converting 1st downs. Even last year, the Cowboys were the NFL's smartest (and best) team on 2nd and short, gaining first down on 94% of their run plays. Perhaps the most of any team, how the offense fares in early down success rate (EDSR) will determine how the team fares in wins and losses.

Strength of Schedule In Detail

True Strength of Schedule Rank: 32

Hardest Stretches (1=Hard, 32=Easy)
Hardest 3 wk Stretch Rk: 32
Hardest 4 wk Stretch Rk: 28
Hardest 5 wk Stretch Rk: 27

Easiest Stretches (1=Easy, 32=Hard)
Easiest 3 wk Stretch Rk: 10
Easiest 4 wk Stretch Rk: 13
Easiest 5 wk Stretch Rk: 15

While Dallas does not have any particular empty spots on the schedule, they do play two of the three worst teams based on projections (@ CLE and @ SF). From a scheduling spot, a team should want to play bad opponents on the road, and save the most difficult games for in their own building. Dallas is also slotted to the maximum primetime games (5), and if you factor in a traditional home game for Thanksgiving, 4 of their 6 most high-profile games will be in Dallas. The only downside to their schedule appears to be that their three toughest opponents (GB, PIT, MIN) all will be played on the road. However, after playing in Pittsburgh on November 13th, the Cowboys (a dome-team) play just 2 more games outdoors (@ NYG, @ PHI).

2015 Play Tendencies

All Pass %	58%
All Pass Rk	21
All Rush %	42%
All Rush Rk	12
1 Score Pass %	51%
1 Score Pass Rk	30
2014 1 Score Pass %	51%
2014 1 Score Pass Rk	29
Pass Increase %	1%
Pass Increase Rk	17
1 Score Rush %	49%
1 Score Rush Rk	3
Up Pass %	52%
Up Pass Rk	10
Up Rush %	48%
Up Rush Rk	23
Down Pass %	64%
Down Pass Rk	24
Down Rush %	36%
Down Rush Rk	9

The Cowboys want to run the football. They want to use their strong offensive line to dominate tempo, pace, and keep their weaker defense off the field. In 2014, they passed the ball only 50% of the time in one-score games, moving from 66% (2nd most) in 2013 to 29th most in 2014. That continued in 2015, passing just 51% (again, 29th most) of play calls in one-score games.

2015 Offensive Advanced Metrics

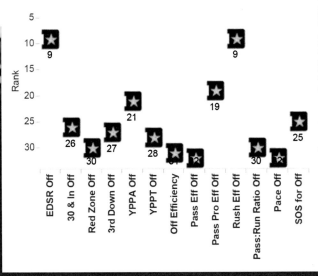

It's difficult to take much away from the 2015 metrics for the Cowboys considering Tony Romo started in only 4 games for the team. No team's defense was aided as much by their offense as was the Cowboys in 2014. So naturally, without the efficiency from the quarterback position, all aspects of the offense will suffer, which in turn will affect the defense. On the positive, the offense was remarkably top 10 in EDSR, and 9th most efficient in running the ball despite very little to fear from the QB / WR, particularly when Dez Bryant was injured. Shockingly, the defensive metrics were not worse, particularly considering Romo started just 4 games but still led the team with 5 TD passes. With so little production and a predictable game plan desire, the Cowboys defense faced many negative EV situations. And yet half of their 12 losses were by 1 score or less. The fact the Cowboys finished 9th in offensive EDSR and 16th defensively was a huge victory.

2015 Defensive Advanced Metrics

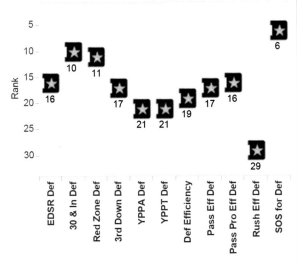

Drafted Players

2016 Draft Grade: #25 (2.4/4)

Rnd.	Pick #	Pos.	Player	College
1	4	RB	Ezekiel Elliott	Ohio State
2	34	OLB	Jaylon Smith	Notre Dame
3	67	DT	Maliek Collins	Nebraska
4	101	DE	Charles Tapper	Oklahoma
4	135	QB	Dak Prescott	Mississippi State
	189	CB	Anthony Brown	Purdue
	212	S	Kavon Frazier	Central Michigan
6	216	RB	Darius Jackson	Eastern Michigan
	217	TE	Rico Gathers	Baylor

PERSONNEL & SPENDING

Dallas Cowboys

Free Agents/Trades Added

Player (Position)

Alfred Morris RB

Cedric Thornton DE

Joe Looney G

Other Signed

Player (Position)

Andy Jones WR
Arjen Colquhoun CB
Austin Traylor TE
Boston Stiverson G
Caleb Azubike DE
Chris Brown WR
David Hedelin T
Deon King LB
Ed Eagan WR
Jake Brendel C
Jason Neill DE
Jeremiah McKinnon CB
Rodney Coe DT
Rolan Milligan S
Ryan Mack T

2015 Players Lost

Transaction	Player (Position)
Cut	Ben Malena RB
	Brandon Hartson TE
	Buddy Jackson CB
	Chris Whaley DT
	Donte Foster WR
	Efe Obada DE
	Neill, Jason DE
Declared Free Agent	Greg Hardy DE
	Mackenzy Bernadeau G
	Matt Cassel QB

- The Dallas Cowboys live with Tony Romo at the helm, or die without him. Since 2006, the team is 9-22 (29%) without him and 80-50 (62%) when he plays the full game through (20+ attempts), including 16-4 (80%) the last two seasons. The team has not had a dependable backup, nor has one presently (Kellen Moor and Dak Prescott will battle for the backup in 2016). But in my view, I'd much rather have that option than the alternative.
- Far too many teams spend too much cap space in a backup QB. They do so because they think he'll be there to win a key game for them if the need it. But the reality is, when Chase Daniel hits the cap for $5M, Chad Henne at $4.75M, Case Keenum at $3.6M, and Shaun Hill at $3.25M, does anyone have confidence they will actually win a game if needed? What about needing to win 3 out of 5 to make the playoffs if the starting QB goes down in week 12?
- Meanwhile, GB is using just $580k, NE just $950k, PIT just $785k & SEA just $455k. Those teams know how to build rosters, and more than most teams, they would actually be likely to be in playoff contention, in need of a backup to deliver in one or a string of games to stay in playoff contention. Yet they've decided (intelligently) to draft young QBs, hope one of them ultimately turns into the franchise replacement, and if they need to use one, there's a solid chance they lose that game, as they likely would with one of the above options, but at a fraction of the cost.
- Then, there is Ezekiel Elliott. Behind that line the RB is going to do well regardless. Darren McFadden (4.6 YPC) & DeMarco Murray(4.7 and 5.2 YPC) thrived & struggled elsewhere. With holes elsewhere the move for Elliott is not primarily about 2016. He'll be the feature back for the next 5 years in Dallas. Romo is 36 and oft-injured. The line may not be nearly as strong in 3 or 4 years. With a healthy Romo & that line, Elliott will feast this year, but he's not the difference maker Dallas needed. But in 2018, 19 or 20, he just might be.

Lineup & 2016 Cap Hit

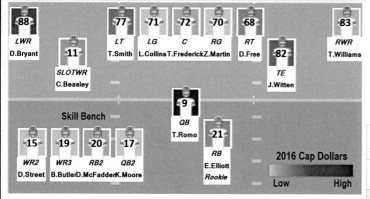

Health Overall & by Unit (2015 v 2014)

2015 Rk	5
2015 AGL	52
Off Rk	11
Def Rk	15
2014 Rk	19
2014 AGL	76

2016 Positional Spending

	All OFF	QB	OL	RB	WR	TE	All DEF	DL	LB	CB	S
2015 Rk	20	11	25	23	21	9	14	16	23	2	30
Rank	6	7	20	10	10	2	20	22	20	2	24
Total	92.6M	22.6M	23.9M	10.0M	22.4M	13.7M	69.7M	15.9M	18.5M	27.8M	7.5M

2016 Offseason Spending

Total Spent	Total Spent Rk	Free Agents #	Free Agents $	Free Agents $ Rk	Waiver #	Waiver $	Waiver $ Rk	Extended #	Sum of Extended $	Sum of Drafted $	Undrafted #	Undrafted $
143M	23	11	49M	20	10	11M	21	2	12M	47M	16	24M

2015 Stats & Fantasy Production

Pos	Player	Ov. Rank	Pos. Rk	Age	Gms	St	Pass Comp	Pass Att	Pass Yds	Pass TD	Pass Int	Rush Att	Rush Yds	Rush YPA	Rush TD	Targ	Recp	Rec Yds	Rec YPC	Rec TDs	Draft King Pts	Fan Duel Pts
QB	Tony Romo		42	35	4	4	83	121	884	5	7	4	13	3							52	48
	Kellen Moore		45	26	3	2	61	104	779	4	6	2	-1	-1							43	39
RB	Darren McFadden	40	14	28	16	10			1			239	1,089	5	3	53	40	328	8		205	176
	Joseph Randle		58	24	6	6						76	313	4	4	10	10	87	9		77	69
	Lance Dunbar		88	25	4							5	67	13		23	21	215	10		52	39
WR	Terrance Williams		44	26	16	13										93	52	840	16	3	157	128
	Cole Beasley		56	26	16	3										75	52	536	10	5	137	106
	Dez Bryant		79	27	9	9										72	31	401	13	3	92	74
	Brice Butler		119	25	7	2										26	12	258	22		41	32
TE	Jason Witten		12	33	16	16										104	77	713	9	3	168	126

ODDS & TRENDS

Dallas Cowboys

Avg Line	-1.5	Pred Wins	9	Pred Div Finish	#1

(-) Favorite   Underdog (+)
-6.0 _____ +6.0

2016 Weekly Betting Lines (wks 1-16)

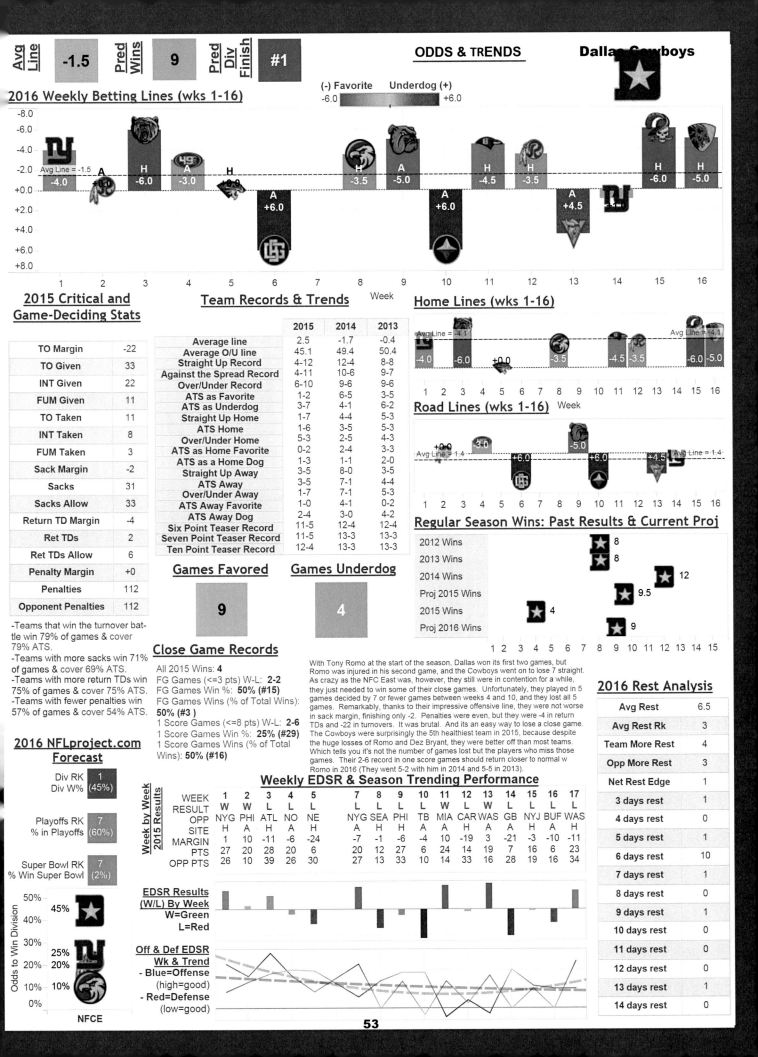

2015 Critical and Game-Deciding Stats

TO Margin	-22
TO Given	33
INT Given	22
FUM Given	11
TO Taken	11
INT Taken	8
FUM Taken	3
Sack Margin	-2
Sacks	31
Sacks Allow	33
Return TD Margin	-4
Ret TDs	2
Ret TDs Allow	6
Penalty Margin	+0
Penalties	112
Opponent Penalties	112

-Teams that win the turnover battle win 79% of games & cover 79% ATS.
-Teams with more sacks win 71% of games & cover 69% ATS.
-Teams with more return TDs win 75% of games & cover 75% ATS.
-Teams with fewer penalties win 57% of games & cover 54% ATS.

2016 NFLproject.com Forecast

| Div RK | 1 |
| Div W% | (45%) |

| Playoffs RK | 7 |
| % in Playoffs | (60%) |

| Super Bowl RK | 7 |
| % Win Super Bowl | (2%) |

Odds to Win Division
50%
40%
30%
20% — 45% ★ ; 25% NYG ; 10%
10%
0%
NFCE

Team Records & Trends

	2015	2014	2013
Average line	2.5	-1.7	-0.4
Average O/U line	45.1	49.4	50.4
Straight Up Record	4-12	12-4	8-8
Against the Spread Record	4-11	10-6	9-7
Over/Under Record	6-10	9-6	9-6
ATS as Favorite	1-2	6-5	3-5
ATS as Underdog	3-7	4-1	6-2
Straight Up Home	1-7	4-4	5-3
ATS Home	1-6	3-5	5-3
Over/Under Home	5-3	2-5	4-3
ATS as Home Favorite	0-2	2-4	3-3
ATS as a Home Dog	1-3	1-1	2-0
Straight Up Away	3-5	8-0	3-5
ATS Away	3-5	7-1	4-4
Over/Under Away	1-7	7-1	5-3
ATS Away Favorite	1-0	4-1	0-2
ATS Away Dog	2-4	3-0	4-2
Six Point Teaser Record	11-5	12-4	12-4
Seven Point Teaser Record	11-5	13-3	13-3
Ten Point Teaser Record	12-4	13-3	13-3

Games Favored

9

Games Underdog

4

Close Game Records

All 2015 Wins: **4**
FG Games (<=3 pts) W-L: **2-2**
FG Games Win %: **50% (#15)**
FG Games Wins (% of Total Wins): **50% (#3)**
1 Score Games (<=8 pts) W-L: **2-6**
1 Score Games Win %: **25% (#29)**
1 Score Games Wins (% of Total Wins): **50% (#16)**

Home Lines (wks 1-16)

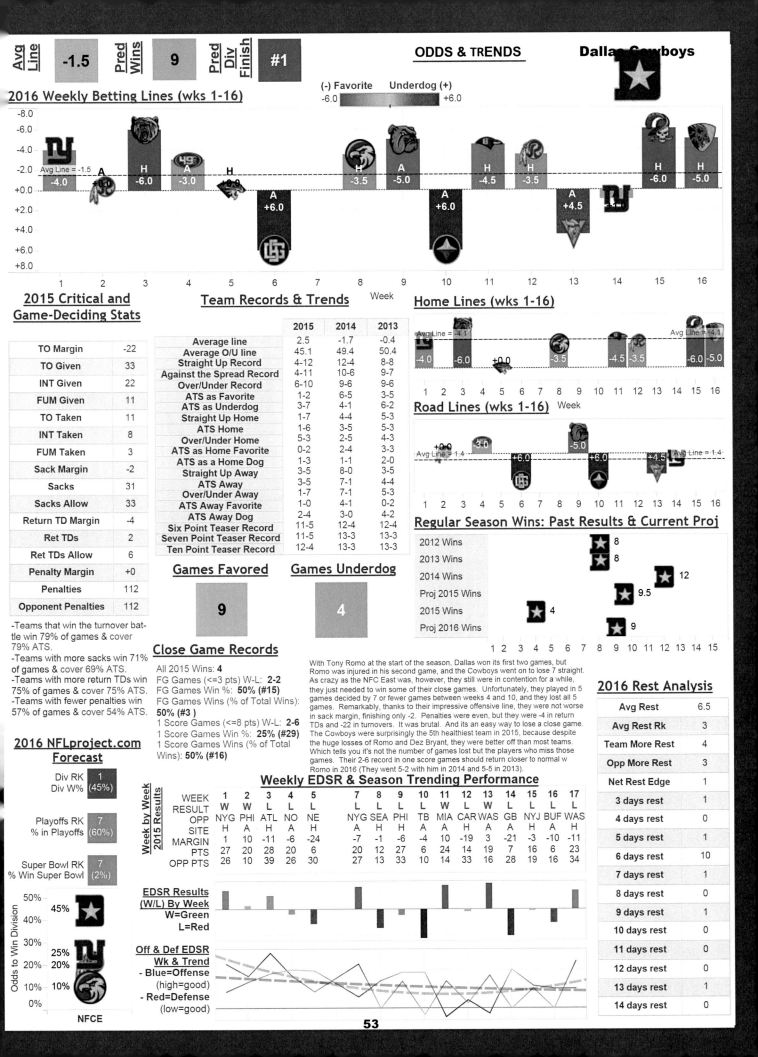

Road Lines (wks 1-16)

Regular Season Wins: Past Results & Current Proj

2012 Wins	★ 8
2013 Wins	★ 8
2014 Wins	★ 12
Proj 2015 Wins	★ 9.5
2015 Wins	★ 4
Proj 2016 Wins	★ 9

1 2 3 4 5 6 7 8 9 10 11 12 13 14 15

With Tony Romo at the start of the season, Dallas won its first two games, but Romo was injured in his second game, and the Cowboys went on to lose 7 straight. As crazy as the NFC East was, however, they still were in contention for a while, they just needed to win some of their close games. Unfortunately, they played in 5 games decided by 7 or fewer games between weeks 4 and 10, and they lost all 5 games. Remarkably, thanks to their impressive offensive line, they were not worse in sack margin, finishing only -2. Penalties were even, but they were -4 in return TDs and -22 in turnovers. It was brutal. And its an easy way to lose a close game. The Cowboys were surprisingly the 5th healthiest team in 2015, because despite the huge losses of Romo and Dez Bryant, they were better off than most teams. Which tells you it's not the number of games lost but the players who miss those games. Their 2-6 record in one score games should return closer to normal w Romo in 2016 (They went 5-2 with him in 2014 and 5-5 in 2013).

2016 Rest Analysis

Avg Rest	6.5
Avg Rest Rk	3
Team More Rest	4
Opp More Rest	3
Net Rest Edge	1
3 days rest	1
4 days rest	0
5 days rest	1
6 days rest	10
7 days rest	1
8 days rest	0
9 days rest	1
10 days rest	0
11 days rest	0
12 days rest	0
13 days rest	1
14 days rest	0

Weekly EDSR & Season Trending Performance

WEEK	1	2	3	4	5		7	8	9	10	11	12	13	14	15	16	17
RESULT	W	W	L	L	L		L	L	L	L	W	L	W	L	L	L	L
OPP	NYG	PHI	ATL	NO	NE		NYG	SEA	PHI	TB	MIA	CAR	WAS	GB	NYJ	BUF	WAS
SITE	H	A	H	A	H		A	H	A	A	H	A	H	A	H	A	H
MARGIN	1	10	-11	-6	-24		-7	-1	-6	-4	10	-19	3	-21	-3	-10	-11
PTS	27	20	28	20	6		20	12	27	6	24	14	19	7	16	6	23
OPP PTS	26	10	39	26	30		27	13	33	10	14	33	16	28	19	16	34

Week by Week 2015 Results

EDSR Results (W/L) By Week
W=Green
L=Red

Off & Def EDSR Wk & Trend
- Blue=Offense (high=good)
- Red=Defense (low=good)

STATS & VISUALIZATIONS

Dallas Cowboys

Directional Passer Rating Achieved

Receiver	Short Left	Short Middle	Short Right	Deep Left	Deep Middle	Deep Right
Jason Witten	97	91	85	118	16	50
Cole Beasley	110	112	94			87
Terrance Williams	74	81	81	7	27	147
Dez Bryant	47	58	60	83	39	39
Brice Butler	17	95	84	104	0	95
James Hanna	105	39	88	39		
Gavin Escobar	79	141	47		89	
Devin Street	46		66	83	118	104
Lucky Whitehead	56		82			
Geoff Swaim			79			
Vince Mayle						0

Directional Frequency by Receiver

Receiver	Short Left	Short Middle	Short Right	Deep Left	Deep Middle	Deep Right
Jason Witten	23%	35%	29%	3%	21%	12%
Cole Beasley	18%	33%	17%			6%
Terrance Williams	15%	15%	22%	33%	26%	52%
Dez Bryant	18%	11%	13%	39%	32%	12%
Brice Butler	10%	2%	3%	14%	5%	6%
James Hanna	4%	1%	5%	6%		
Gavin Escobar	3%	2%	4%		11%	
Devin Street	4%		2%	6%	5%	9%
Lucky Whitehead	3%		3%			
Geoff Swaim			1%			
Vince Mayle						3%

Defense Passer Rating Allowed

Short Left	Short Middle	Short Right	Deep Left	Deep Middle	Deep Right
103	72	82	105	46	139

Offensive Rush Directional Yds/Carry

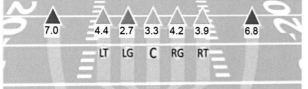

7.0	4.4	2.7	3.3	4.2	3.9	6.8
	LT	LG	C	RG	RT	

Offensive Rush Frequency of Direction

65	64	36	82	51	41	61
	LT	LG	C	RG	RT	

Offensive Explosive Runs by Direction

16	8	1	6	4	2	14
	LT	LG	C	RG	RT	

Defensive Rush Directional Yds/Carry

3.6	2.8	3.7	4.2	4.5	7.0	5.8
	LT	LG	C	RG	RT	

Tony Romo - 1st Down RTG

Tony Romo - 3rd Down RTG

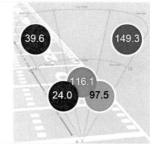

Tony Romo - 2nd Down RTG

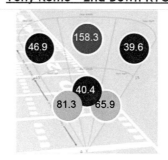

Tony Romo - Overall RTG

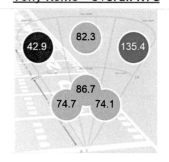

2nd & Short RUN (1D or not)

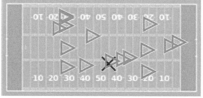

2nd & Short RUN Stats

Run Conv Rk	1D% Run	NFL 1D% Run Avg	Run Freq	NFL Run Freq Avg
1	94%	69%	61%	64%

2nd & Short PASS (1D or not)

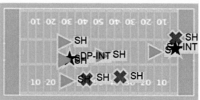

2nd & Short PASS Stats

Pass Conv Rk	1D% Pass	NFL 1D% Pass Avg	Pass Freq	NFL Pass Freq Avg
17	55%	55%	39%	36%

Pass Offense Play Success Rate

54%	57%	47%	29%	28%
45%	55%	44%	65%	48%
55%	47%	56%	38%	15%

Pass Offense Yds/Play

6.2	9.2	7.1	5.1	2.9
6.0	9.0	7.0	10.1	5.0
8.1	7.6	10.2	5.8	1.7

Off. Directional Tendency (% of Plays Left, Middle or Right)

42%	31%	29%	39%	44%
25%	23%	32%	29%	29%
33%	45%	39%	32%	27%

Off. Directional Pass Rate (% of Plays which are Passes)

54%	52%	54%	71%	76%
44%	40%	51%	51%	46%
55%	68%	65%	64%	80%

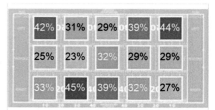

SHARP FOOTBALL STATS

New York Giants

Coaches

Head Coach: Ben McAdoo (NYG OC) (1st yr)
OC: Mike Sullivan (NYG QB) (1st yr)
DC: Steve Spagnuolo (2nd yr)

Forecast 2016 Wins

8

Past Records

2015: 6-10
2014: 6-10
2013: 7-9

Opponent Strength
Easy — Hard

2016 Schedule & Week by Week Strength of Schedule

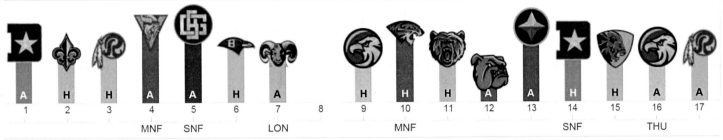

A	H	H	A	A	H	A		H	H	H	A	A	H	H	A	A
1	2	3	4	5	6	7	8	9	10	11	12	13	14	15	16	17
			MNF	SNF		LON			MNF				SNF		THU	

2016 Overview

The 2015 Giants finished with a losing record for the 3rd straight year, and another 6-10 season could not save Tom Coughlin's job. On the positive side, the Giants would have been 9-6 with one tie if games ended after the 3rd quarter. But they went 1-5 in games with a final margin of a field goal or less, and couldn't get out of their own way. Last year, teams who won the turnover margin won 75% of their games, and historically the number is closer to 79%. Instead, somehow the Giants went 4-5 (44%) in these games.

So out went Tom Coughlin, in came Offensive Coordinator Ben McAdoo as Head Coach. Out went a conservative offseason, in came massive deals to free agent DE Olivier Vernon, CB Janoris Jenkins and NT Damon Harrison. Historically, over-spending in free agency does not work but for rare situations. And many of the players signed to lucrative deals get cut following half their planned duration. But let's assume that the Giants and their 30th rated 2015 defense improves to a league average because of the incorporation of these players.

The offense must get better and more balanced. But that is easier said than done. The Giants will spend the 4th most QB cap thanks to Eli Manning's cap hit which jumped form $14.45M last year to $24.2M this year. $10M in cap space doesn't grow on trees, so the Giants trimmed along the offensive line, taking the 12th most paid 2015 unit down to 30th this year. The entirety of the 2016 offensive line is now hitting the cap for $15.9M, 2nd least in the NFL and $9.7M less than they are allocating to the QB position.

What is puzzling, however, is that only the Vikings and Panthers are allocating more to the RB position than the Giants. Why is that strange? Because the Vikings are the NFL's most run-dominant offense, with a remarkable 49% of neutral play calls being passes. The Panthers are at 48%, 5th most. Meanwhile, the Giants are on the opposite end of the spectrum, with 64% of neutral situation play calls being passes, just 1% away from the most pass-heavy team in the NFL.

Inside the red zone, where it pays to be balanced (if not slightly more run dominant vs today's defenses) the Giants called 67% passes last year. Removing the 4th quarter with leads, 70% of the Giants red zone plays were passes, by far the most in the NFL. For comparison, MIN and CAR were both 42% pass. Game theory might suggest that a pass dominant offense would lead to larger gains on the ground due to the defense playing pass. That was not the case for the Giants, who gained 1.86 YPC on their red zone runs, 2nd worst in the NFL and over 40% worse than average.

At the most important position in the NFL, the Giants have the most stable player. Eli Manning has started all 16 games dating back to 2005. The last 5 years, he has made 84 starts for the Giants. Tony Romo has 68, Kirk Cousins has 26 and Sam Bradford has 47 though they may turn to their rookie QB drafted 2nd overall this year. The NFC East should be there for the taking for the Giants. We know their passing game should be tremendous. But their offensive line, particularly the weak right side, must step up & they must run the ball better. And their free agents must earn their deals with immediate and strong impact this year.

Strength of Schedule In Detail

True Strength of Schedule Rank: 31

Hardest Stretches (1=Hard, 32=Easy)
Hardest 3 wk Stretch Rk: **16**
Hardest 4 wk Stretch Rk: **24**
Hardest 5 wk Stretch Rk: **25**

Easiest Stretches (1=Easy, 32=Hard)
Easiest 3 wk Stretch Rk: **20**
Easiest 4 wk Stretch Rk: **15**
Easiest 5 wk Stretch Rk: **19**

Although the Redskins have a very tough schedule having to face the Cardinals and Panthers thanks to their first place finish last year, most other NFC East teams are in great shape. Their third place finish gives the Giants the Saints at home and the Rams on the road (but in London as opposed to LA). The Giants most difficult hurdle is back to back road games in Minnesota and in Green Bay, but fortunately face the Packers early in the calendar. Playing only 3 teams projected to be .500 or better over their last 10 games, the Giants close the year with the 2nd easiest 10 game stretch, though they must be ready to play two NFC East foes on the road to close out the year (@ PHI, @ WAS).

2015 Play Tendencies

All Pass %	62%
All Pass Rk	13
All Rush %	38%
All Rush Rk	20
1 Score Pass %	64%
1 Score Pass Rk	4
2014 1 Score Pass %	59%
2014 1 Score Pass Rk	12
Pass Increase %	5%
Pass Increase Rk	9
1 Score Rush %	36%
1 Score Rush Rk	29
Up Pass %	54%
Up Pass Rk	7
Up Rush %	46%
Up Rush Rk	26
Down Pass %	67%
Down Pass Rk	20
Down Rush %	33%
Down Rush Rk	13

The Giants called 62% passes last year. In one score games, they were the 11th most pass heavy team, and fairly similar to their 2015 ranking. When leading, they still passed the ball well above average (ranking 7th). With the addition of 2nd round pick Sterling Shepard, this rate could further increase, but the Giants would perform more efficiently if they were able to be slightly more balanced, particularly in the red zone.

2015 Offensive Advanced Metrics

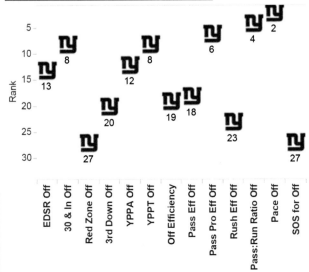

Many of the Giants offensive numbers appear middle of the road. But the bigger issue is that they faced the 27th rated schedule of opposing defenses, so the offensive number should be even better. In particular, a terrible efficiency ranking on 3rd down led to far too many failed drives. If the Giants merely improved on 3rd down, they would have more red zone trips, and with more trips, even a slight improvement in the red zone would be a substantial benefit. Defensively, the Giants tried to upgrade quickly via free agency. Such moves typically don't see long term success, but the Giants would trade short term success, even as a Wild Card seed, knowing that they've done extremely well in the postseason in that role. In particular, ranking 30th in pass rush efficiency will not help any secondary, and ranking dead last in 3rd down conversion rate is a recipe to wear out a defense quickly and give up frequent points.

2015 Defensive Advanced Metrics

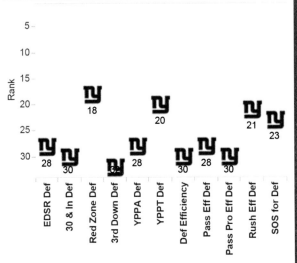

Drafted Players 2016 Draft Grade: #17 (2.9/4)

PERSONNEL & SPENDING

New York Giants

Rnd.	Pick #	Pos.	Player	College
1	10	CB	Eli Apple	Ohio State
2	40	WR	Sterling Shepard	Oklahoma
3	71	S	Darian Thompson	Boise State
4	109	ILB	B. J. Goodson	Clemson
5	149	RB	Paul Perkins	UCLA
6	184	TE	Jerell Adams	South Carolina

Free Agents/Trades Added

Player (Position)
Bobby Rainey RB
Byron Stingily T
Damon Harrison NT
Janoris Jenkins CB
Keenan Robinson LB
Kelvin Sheppard LB
Olivier Vernon DE
Ryan Seymour T
Will Johnson RB

Other Signed

Player (Position)
Andrew Adams S
B.J. Daniels QB
Cedrick Lang TE
Darius Powe WR
Donte Deayon CB
Donte Foster WR
Greg Milhouse Jr. DT
Ishaq Williams DE
Josh Woodrum QB
Kadron Boone WR
KJ Maye WR
Marshaun Coprich RB
Matt Smalley CB
Melvin Lewis DT
Michael Hunter CB
Mike Rose DE
Roger Lewis WR
Romeo Okwara DE
Ryan Malleck TE

2015 Players Lost

Transaction	Player (Position)
Cut	Ben Edwards WR
	Cedrick Lang TE
	G.J. Kinne QB
	Geoff Schwartz G
	James Morris LB
	Jerome Cunningham TE
	Josh Woodrum QB
	Nico Johnson LB
	Uani Unga LB
	Will Beatty T
Declared Free Agent	Prince Amukamara CB
	Robert Ayers Jr. DE
	Rueben Randle WR
Retired	Jon Beason LB

-Eli Manning's increasing contract now puts the Giants at $25M in cap to the QB, 4th most (up from 15th last year). They are also spending significantly more at the defensive line this year. That means there isn't as much to spend elsewhere, and sure enough, the offensive line's cap is 3rd smallest in the NFL this year.

-After bottom 5 rankings in all of the key defensive advanced metrics, the Giants spent in free agency to land several prized players. The well graded Olivier Vernon and Damon Harrison should be immediate improvements along the defensive line as the Giants want to recreate a strong line that propelled them to multiple Super Bowl wins over the Patriots.

-The Giants drafted Eli Apple to play alongside free agent CB Janoris Jenkins. The Giants allowed TEs to wreak havoc up the middle, recording a 156 passer rating w 6 TDs and 0 INTS and a 73% completion rate, while WRs were particularly dominant to the offense's deep right or short left, posting a 112 rating with a 10:2 TD:INT ratio. Signing Jenkins in free agency offset the loss of Prince Amukamara, but the Giants needed CB help even with an improved defensive line via free agency as well (DE Oliver Vernon, DT Damon Harrison). He didn't grade out as best CB available at the time of selection, but time will tell how he fits into the defensive scheme.

-It has been a while since Eli Manning had three threat WRs, but adding Sterling Shepard to that mix would certainly elevate the team to a very dangerous level. Already operating at the 2nd fastest pace of any team last year, in hurry up mode with Odell Beckham Jr, Victor Curz and Shepard plus Shane Vereen as an outlet, this offense can be as dangerous as any. They might continue to operate quickly to keep the defense on its heels and get the ball out of Manning's hands quickly, because they didn't address the OL in the draft and lost G Geoff Schwartz and T Will Beatty this offseason.

Lineup & 2016 Cap Hit

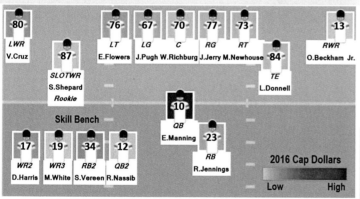

Health Overall & by Unit (2015 v 2014)

2015 Rk	32
2015 AGL	139
Off Rk	31
Def Rk	32
2014 Rk	32
2014 AGL	137

2016 Positional Spending

	All OFF	QB	OL	RB	WR	TE	All DEF	DL	LB	CB	S
2015 Rk	16	15	12	11	11	32	26	18	29	7	32
Rank	22	4	30	3	22	31	16	4	22	17	30
Total	73.3M	25.6M	15.9M	11.2M	17.0M	3.6M	78.8M	36.6M	15.4M	22.1M	4.7M

2016 Offseason Spending

Total Spent	Total Spent Rk	Free Agents #	Free Agents $	Free Agents $ Rk	Waiver #	Waiver $	Waiver $ Rk	Extended #	Sum of Extended $	Sum of Drafted $	Undrafted #	Undrafted $
289M	3	13	209M	2	13	11M	22	2	11M	33M	16	26M

2015 Stats & Fantasy Production

Pos	Player	Ov. Rank	Pos. Rk	Age	Gms	St	Pass Comp	Pass Att	Pass Yds	Pass TD	Pass Int	Rush Att	Rush Yds	Rush YPA	Rush TD	Targ	Recp	Rec Yds	Rec YPC	Rec TDs	Draft King Pts	Fan Duel Pts
QB	Eli Manning*	73	10	34	16	16	387	618	4,436	35	14	20	61	3							309	302
RB	Rashad Jennings	62	20	30	16	16						195	863	4	3	40	29	296	10	1	173	150
	Shane Vereen		37	26	16							61	260	4		81	59	495	8	4	165	129
	Andre Williams		80	23	16							88	257	3	1	3	1	7	7		38	35
	Orleans Darkwa		93	23	16							36	153	4	1	5	3	31	10		30	26
WR	Odell Beckham*	8	5	23	15	15						1	3	3		158	96	1,450	15	13	322	271
	Rueben Randle	72	29	24	16	16										90	57	797	14	8	188	156
	Dwayne Harris		70	28	15	6						2	12	6		57	36	396	11	4	116	95
TE	Will Tye		25	24	13	7										62	42	464	11	3	108	83
	Larry Donnell		41	27	8	8										41	29	223	8	2	66	49

ODDS & TRENDS

New York Giants

Avg Line	+0.3	Pred Wins	8	Pred Div Finish	#2

(-) Favorite   Underdog (+)
-4.5   +8.0

2016 Weekly Betting Lines (wks 1-16)

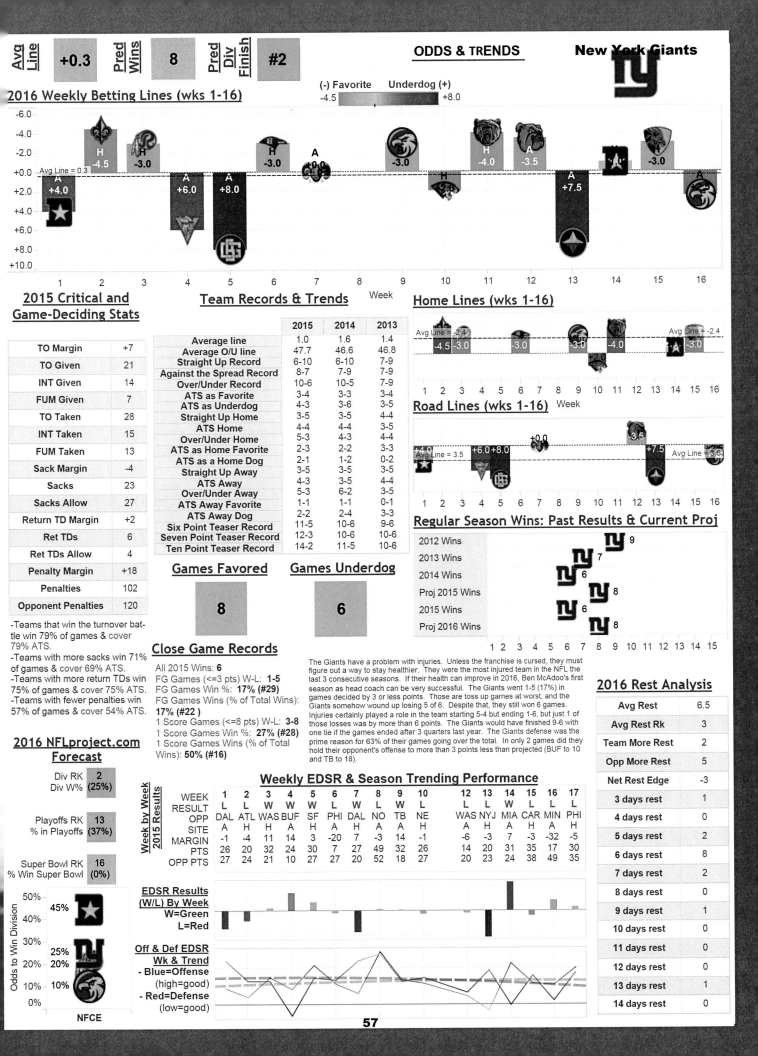

Avg Line = 0.3

H -4.5, H -3.0, A +4.0, A +6.0, A +8.0, H -3.0, A -0.0, H -3.0, H (+), A +7.5, H -4.0, A -3.5, A, H -3.0, A

Week: 1 2 3 4 5 6 7 8 9 10 11 12 13 14 15 16

2015 Critical and Game-Deciding Stats

TO Margin	+7
TO Given	21
INT Given	14
FUM Given	7
TO Taken	28
INT Taken	15
FUM Taken	13
Sack Margin	-4
Sacks	23
Sacks Allow	27
Return TD Margin	+2
Ret TDs	6
Ret TDs Allow	4
Penalty Margin	+18
Penalties	102
Opponent Penalties	120

-Teams that win the turnover battle win 79% of games & cover 79% ATS.
-Teams with more sacks win 71% of games & cover 69% ATS.
-Teams with more return TDs win 75% of games & cover 75% ATS.
-Teams with fewer penalties win 57% of games & cover 54% ATS.

2016 NFLproject.com Forecast

Div RK	2
Div W%	(25%)
Playoffs RK	13
% in Playoffs	(37%)
Super Bowl RK	16
% Win Super Bowl	(0%)

Odds to Win Division

45%
25%
20%
10%

NFCE

Team Records & Trends

Week

	2015	2014	2013
Average line	1.0	1.6	1.4
Average O/U line	47.7	46.6	46.8
Straight Up Record	6-10	6-10	7-9
Against the Spread Record	8-7	7-9	7-9
Over/Under Record	10-6	10-5	7-9
ATS as Favorite	3-4	3-3	3-4
ATS as Underdog	4-3	3-6	3-5
Straight Up Home	3-5	3-5	4-4
ATS Home	4-4	4-4	3-5
Over/Under Home	5-3	4-3	4-4
ATS as Home Favorite	2-3	2-2	3-3
ATS as a Home Dog	2-1	1-2	0-2
Straight Up Away	3-5	3-5	3-5
ATS Away	4-3	3-5	4-4
Over/Under Away	5-3	6-2	3-5
ATS Away Favorite	1-1	1-1	0-1
ATS Away Dog	2-2	2-4	3-3
Six Point Teaser Record	11-5	10-6	9-6
Seven Point Teaser Record	12-3	10-6	10-6
Ten Point Teaser Record	14-2	11-5	10-6

Games Favored

8

Games Underdog

6

Close Game Records

All 2015 Wins: 6
FG Games (<=3 pts) W-L: **1-5**
FG Games Win %: **17% (#29)**
FG Games Wins (% of Total Wins):
17% (#22)
1 Score Games (<=8 pts) W-L: **3-8**
1 Score Games Win %: **27% (#28)**
1 Score Games Wins (% of Total Wins): **50% (#16)**

The Giants have a problem with injuries. Unless the franchise is cursed, they must figure out a way to stay healthier. They were the most injured team in the NFL the last 3 consecutive seasons. If their health can improve in 2016, Ben McAdoo's first season as head coach can be very successful. The Giants went 1-5 (17%) in games decided by 3 or less points. Those are toss up games at worst, and the Giants somehow wound up losing 5 of 6. Despite that, they still won 6 games. Injuries certainly played a role in the team starting 5-4 but ending 1-6, but just 1 of those losses was by more than 6 points. The Giants would have finished 9-6 with one tie if the games ended after 3 quarters last year. The Giants defense was the prime reason for 63% of their games going over the total. In only 2 games did they hold their opponent's offense to more than 3 points less than projected (BUF to 10 and TB to 18).

Home Lines (wks 1-16)

Avg Line = -2.4

-4.5, -3.0, -3.0, -3.0, -4.0, -A-, -3.0

1 2 3 4 5 6 7 8 9 10 11 12 13 14 15 16

Road Lines (wks 1-16)   Week

Avg Line = 3.5

-4.0, +6.0, +8.0, +0.0, -3.5, +7.5, Avg Line = 3.6

1 2 3 4 5 6 7 8 9 10 11 12 13 14 15 16

Regular Season Wins: Past Results & Current Proj

2012 Wins	9
2013 Wins	7
2014 Wins	6
Proj 2015 Wins	8
2015 Wins	6
Proj 2016 Wins	8

1 2 3 4 5 6 7 8 9 10 11 12 13 14 15

2016 Rest Analysis

Avg Rest	6.5
Avg Rest Rk	3
Team More Rest	2
Opp More Rest	5
Net Rest Edge	-3
3 days rest	1
4 days rest	0
5 days rest	2
6 days rest	8
7 days rest	2
8 days rest	0
9 days rest	1
10 days rest	0
11 days rest	0
12 days rest	0
13 days rest	1
14 days rest	0

Weekly EDSR & Season Trending Performance

WEEK	1	2	3	4	5	6	7	8	9	10		12	13	14	15	16	17
RESULT	L	L	W	W	W	L	W	L	W	L		L	L	W	L	L	L
OPP	DAL	ATL	WAS	BUF	SF	PHI	DAL	NO	TB	NE		WAS	NYJ	MIA	CAR	MIN	PHI
SITE	A	A	H	H	A	H	A	A	H	H		A	H	A	H	A	H
MARGIN	-1	-4	11	14	3	-20	7	-3	14	-1		-6	-3	7	-3	-32	-5
PTS	26	20	32	24	30	7	27	49	32	26		14	20	31	35	17	30
OPP PTS	27	24	21	10	27	27	20	52	18	27		20	23	24	38	49	35

Week by Week 2015 Results

EDSR Results (W/L) By Week
W=Green
L=Red

Off & Def EDSR Wk & Trend
- Blue=Offense (high=good)
- Red=Defense (low=good)

57

STATS & VISUALIZATIONS

New York Giants

Directional Passer Rating Achieved

Receiver	Short Left	Short Middle	Short Right	Deep Left	Deep Middle	Deep Right
Odell Beckham Jr.	116	125	91	83	135	90
Rueben Randle	93	95	35	100	156	158
Will Tye	69	97	117	118	116	118
Dwayne Harris	65	134	76	118	149	47
Larry Donnell	22	135	89	89	118	39
Jerome Cunningham	96	39	88	39	39	
Hakeem Nicks	47	58	83	0		
Myles White	56	43	62	56	104	39
Daniel Fells	70	118	91			
Preston Parker	47	39	91			39
Matt LaCosse	83	104				
Geremy Davis				110	39	
Ben Edwards				104	0	

Directional Frequency by Receiver

Receiver	Short Left	Short Middle	Short Right	Deep Left	Deep Middle	Deep Right
Odell Beckham Jr.	25%	33%	36%	39%	32%	48%
Rueben Randle	25%	13%	16%	18%	16%	19%
Will Tye	12%	16%	15%	3%	16%	3%
Dwayne Harris	16%	12%	9%	5%	12%	13%
Larry Donnell	7%	11%	11%	5%	4%	3%
Jerome Cunningham	2%	4%	4%	3%	8%	
Hakeem Nicks	5%	2%	1%	11%		
Myles White	4%	3%	1%	11%	12%	6%
Daniel Fells	1%	1%	3%			
Preston Parker	3%	1%	3%			6%
Matt LaCosse	1%	2%				
Geremy Davis				1%	3%	
Ben Edwards				1%	3%	

Defense Passer Rating Allowed

Short Left	Short Middle	Short Right	Deep Left	Deep Middle	Deep Right
108	104	79	78	104	104

Offensive Rush Directional Yds/Carry

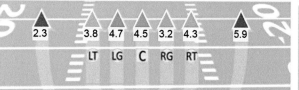

2.3   3.8   4.7   4.5   3.2   4.3   5.9
LT LG C RG RT

Offensive Rush Frequency of Direction

24   58 74 115 71 38   15
LT LG C RG RT

Offensive Explosive Runs by Direction

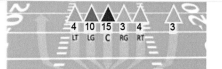

4 10 15 3 4   3
LT LG C RG RT

Defensive Rush Directional Yds/Carry

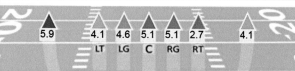

5.9   4.1 4.6 5.1 5.1 2.7   4.1
LT LG C RG RT

Eli Manning - 1st Down RTG

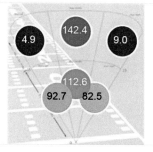

4.9   142.4   9.0
112.6
92.7 82.5

Eli Manning - 2nd Down RTG

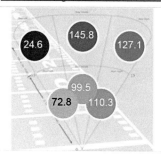

24.6   145.8   127.1
99.5
72.8 110.3

Eli Manning - 3rd Down RTG

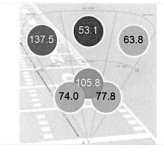

137.5   53.1   63.8
105.8
74.0 77.8

Eli Manning - Overall RTG

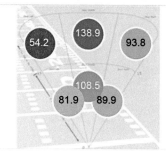

54.2   138.9   93.8
108.5
81.9 89.9

2nd & Short RUN (1D or not)

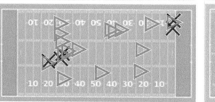

2nd & Short RUN Stats

Run Conv Rk	1D% Run	NFL 1D% Run Avg	Run Freq	NFL Run Freq Avg
10	76%	69%	44%	64%

2nd & Short PASS (1D or not)

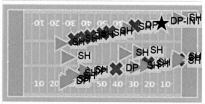

2nd & Short PASS Stats

Pass Conv Rk	1D% Pass	NFL 1D% Pass Avg	Pass Freq	NFL Pass Freq Avg
13	56%	55%	56%	36%

Pass Offense Play Success Rate

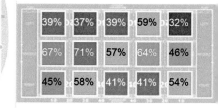

39%	37%	39%	59%	32%
67%	71%	57%	64%	46%
45%	58%	41%	41%	54%

Pass Offense Yds/Play

4.0	6.2	5.7	8.1	3.9
12.1	11.8	10.5	10.1	4.1
8.4	9.6	5.4	4.0	3.9

Off. Directional Tendency
(% of Plays Left, Middle or Right)

29%	35%	44%	42%	31%
23%	28%	28%	31%	27%
48%	37%	28%	26%	42%

Off. Directional Pass Rate
(% of Plays which are Passes)

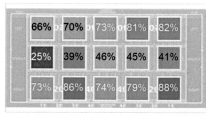

66%	70%	73%	81%	82%
25%	39%	46%	45%	41%
73%	86%	74%	79%	88%

Washington Redskins

Forecast 2016 Wins	Past Records
7	2015: 9-7
	2014: 4-12
	2013: 3-13

Opponent Strength
Easy ——— Hard

2016 Schedule & Week by Week Strength of Schedule

H	H	A	H	A	H	A	H	A		H	H	A	A	A	H	A	H
1	2	3	4	5	6	7	8	9		10	11	12	13	14	15	16	17

LON · SNF · TKG · MNF · SAT

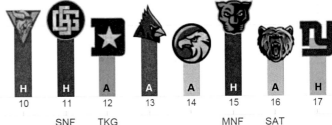

2016 Overview

For the diehard fans of the DC area, the Washington Redskins' 2015 season was uplifting and fun. The team won 9 games, the NFC East, and hosted a playoff game. They finally saw entertaining and efficient quarterback play and an efficient offense which put up a lot of points and productivity. But stepping back and looking at the season with a more tempered lens, several things about 2015 become more clear.

The Redskins beat up a bad schedule of opponents. When they led by 6+ at halftime, they were an undefeated 8-0. But these opponents were not strong at all, and included the Rams, Saints, Bears and Bills, as well as both games vs the Eagles, and a game vs the Giants and the Kellen Moore led Cowboys. However, when leading by less than 6 points at halftime, when tied, or when trailing, the Redskins went 1-8 including their playoff loss to the Packers. Their lone win was a remarkable 24-point comeback to beat the lowly Buccaneers by 1 point.

Aside from that comeback, the Redskins were 1-8 when their opponent held a lead at any point in time larger than 4 points. For a team to make the playoffs despite that type of record was quite telling of how bad the NFC East was in 2015. The Cowboys lost Tony Romo, the Eagles were a mess in Chip Kelly's last season, and the Giants were once again the NFL's most injured team with no clue how to win a close game (NYG went 1-8 in games decided by less than a TD last year).

Despite playing an easy schedule, the defense was a disaster and the run game was non-existent. The team became eternally dependent on the wicked tandem of QB Kirk Cousins and TE Jordan Reed. And to no surprise, they compensated both in a big way this past offseason. Jordan Reed's catch rate is absurd, as he's pulled down 78% of all targets within 15 yards of the line of scrimmage, by far the best rate of any NFL player. He was literally indefensible in the first half of games before opponents began to employ new strategies at halftime. As an example, when targeting Jordan Reed in the 1st half in opposing territory, Kirk Cousins went 28/33 (85%), 10 yds/att, 7 TD : 0 INT and a 149 passer rating, the very best in the NFL by a margin.

GM Scot McCloughan understands the importance of efficiency from the QB position, and is willing to let Kirk Cousins test his repeatability in 2016 with an improved passing arsenal with which to work. Josh Doctson could be an effective weapon for years to come and as Jamison Crowder works the inside with Jordan Reed lining up at various positions, the Redskins passing options are vast and diverse. But 2016 is the money year. DeSean Jackson and Pierre Garcon are in their final contract year. It's unlikely both stay, and possibly both leave. But for 2016, Cousins has all the weapons a QB could ask for at his disposal, and it's his time to shine and earn a long term deal. McCloughan has improved this team dramatically since joining the Redskins. This past offseason, he improved their ability to win passing the football, or by stopping the opposing passing offense. There are holes in this team but if they can excel in their areas of strength, they will be competitive even against a tough schedule in 2016. But predicting no regression to occur would be unwise.

Strength of Schedule In Detail

True Strength of Schedule Rank: 4

Hardest Stretches (1=Hard, 32=Easy)
Hardest 3 wk Stretch Rk:	8
Hardest 4 wk Stretch Rk:	3
Hardest 5 wk Stretch Rk:	4

Easiest Stretches (1=Easy, 32=Hard)
Easiest 3 wk Stretch Rk:	6
Easiest 4 wk Stretch Rk:	5
Easiest 5 wk Stretch Rk:	5

Similar to the Jets, Redskins fans need to be prepared for a roller coaster season in 2016. September sees Washington going up against the 7th most difficult start to the season, with two division foes (vs DAL, @ NYG) after hosting the Steelers on Monday night. After a four-week stretch to start October which sees them playing the Browns and three teams with track records but who struggled in 2015 (@ BAL, vs PHI, @ DET) the Redskins must travel to London to take on a very good Bengals team. Following that bye, the Redskins close the season from weeks 10-17 with the NFL's most difficult schedule. They are one of two teams to play three straight road games, one of which is on a short week (Thanksgiving) vs the Cowboys, and thanks to their #1 finish in the NFC East, they must play the Cardinals and Panthers. The lone bright spot for the Redskins is that of their 6th most difficult opponents, only one (@ ARI) is a true road game. Four are at home (PIT, MIN, GB and CAR) and one is in London (CIN).

2015 Play Tendencies

All Pass %	58%
All Pass Rk	22
All Rush %	42%
All Rush Rk	11
1 Score Pass %	55%
1 Score Pass Rk	24
2014 1 Score Pass %	56%
2014 1 Score Pass Rk	21
Pass Increase %	-1%
Pass Increase Rk	24
1 Score Rush %	45%
1 Score Rush Rk	9
Up Pass %	48%
Up Pass Rk	18
Up Rush %	52%
Up Rush Rk	15
Down Pass %	72%
Down Pass Rk	3
Down Rush %	28%
Down Rush Rk	30

The Redskins tried to be more balanced in 2015 and it paid off. Even when the game was within one score, the team ran just as often (42%) as they did over the entire season. However, when the team trailed they relied on Kirk Cousins and the pass game extensively, calling 72% passes, the 3rd most in the NFL. In the 2nd half when down, they called an NFL high 81% pass plays & that lack of balance was too predictable, as Cousins delivered just an 88 RTG.

2015 Offensive Advanced Metrics

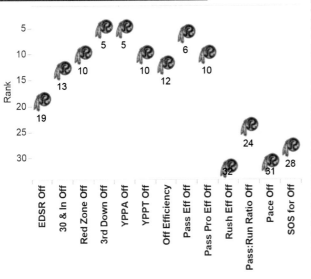

There was no question which unit buttered the bread in the Nation's capital, as the Redskins pass offense carried the torch for the offense, and the offense was the reason for the 2015 success rather than strong defense. With the 6th rated passing offense and the NFL's worst rushing offense, Washington needed strong conversion rates on 3rd down and the red zone to produce enough to compensate for a below average which ranked 26th in yds/pass allowed and 26th in the red zone. The Redskins operated at an extremely slow pace, and that was despite facing the 28th rated opposing defenses. It would make strong sense for the Redskins to test Cousins in this Franchise tag season by running the offense with more tempo to see that will put a much more difficult slate of opposing defenses in more compromised situations. The incorporation of CB Josh Norman should provide strength for the Redskins biggest defensive weakness from 2015.

2015 Defensive Advanced Metrics

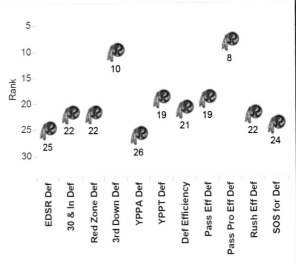

59

Drafted Players

2016 Draft Grade: #5 (3.4/4)

Rnd.	Pick #	Pos.	Player	College
1	22	WR	Josh Doctson	TCU
2	53	LB	Su'a Cravens	USC
3	84	CB	Kendall Fuller	Virginia Tech
5	152	DT	Matt Ioannidis	Temple
6	187	QB	Nate Sudfeld	Indiana
7	232	ILB	Steven Daniels	Boston College
7	242	RB	Keith Marshall	Georgia

PERSONNEL & SPENDING — Washington Redskins

Free Agents/Trades Added

Player (Position)
David Bruton Jr. S
Greg Toler CB
Josh Norman CB
Kendall Reyes DE
Terence Garvin LB
Vernon Davis TE

Other Signed

Player (Position)
Al Bond G
Anthony Lanier DE
Dominick Jackson T
Ejiro Ederaine LB
Joe Gore T
Joe Kerridge RB
Kelsey Young RB
Kevin Bowen T
Lloyd Carrington CB
Mariel Cooper CB
Michael Wakefield LB
Nila Kasitati G
Reggie Diggs WR
Reggie Northrup LB
Rob Kelley RB
Shiro Davis LB
Tevin Carter S
Valdez Showers WR

2015 Players Lost

Transaction	Player (Position)
Cut	Al Louis-Jean CB
	Andre Roberts WR
	Anthony Johnson DT
	Chris Culliver CB
	Christo Bilukidi DT
	Dashon Goldson S
	Derrick Mathews LB
	Desmond Bishop LB
	Jackson Jeffcoat LB
	Jeron Johnson S
	Kamal Johnson DT
	LaRon Byrd WR
	Reggie Northrup LB
	Robert Griffin III QB
	Tevin Carter S
Declared Free Agent	Alfred Morris RB
	Terrance Knighton NT
Retired	Jason Hatcher DE

- With such a strong pass offense from 2015 and such a miserable run offense, at first glance it seems odd the Redskins didn't try to improve the depth or strength of their running back corps or the offensive line. But instead, the Redskins continued to attack the passing phase on both sides of the ball. Offensively, they added WR Josh Doctson who some thought to be a bargain at #22 and potentially the best WR in the draft. They added a ton of help in the secondary, signing CB Josh Norman in free agency and drafting Kendall Fuller from Virginia Tech in the 3rd round. They also added CB Greg Toler and S David Bruton Jr in free agency.
- The Redskins had the 4th most expensive offense in 2015 and it remains the 4th most in 2016, which is primarily a reflection of the Franchise Tag on Kirk Cousins. Defensively, the team is now spending the 4th most of any team on the CB position, and 12th most at the LB position.
- With Alfred Morris now in Dallas, the run game will be spearheaded by the young backfield of the bruiser Matt Jones and the shiftier Chris Thompson. Thompson saw a lot of success last year, gaining over 6 YPC in a limited role (35 total carries) but needs to improve his catch rate (caught only 73% of targets as a RB). Matt Jones was very inefficient last season, and must face significantly stingier run defenses in 2016.
- The Redskins desperately need to improve in short yardage run situations. On 2nd, 3rd or 4th and short runs, the NFL average last year was 65% conversions to first down. The Redskins were 4th worst, converting just 57% of the time and gaining only 2.7 yds/rush. They also fumbled a NFL-high 4 times. In those short yardage situations, when the team passed the ball, Cousins was a lights-out 122 RTG w 6 TDs and 0 Ints. But even so, they converted first downs 56% of the time because its so much easier to convert short yardage runs than passes.

Lineup & 2016 Cap Hit

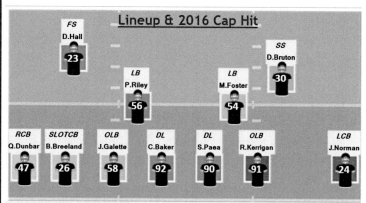

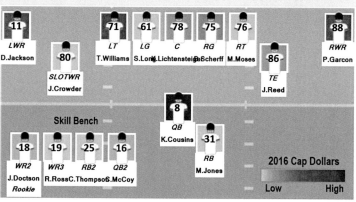

2016 Cap Dollars — Low — High

Health Overall & by Unit (2015 v 2014)

2015 Rk	31
2015 AGL	119
Off Rk	27
Def Rk	31
2014 Rk	24
2014 AGL	90

2016 Positional Spending

	All OFF	QB	OL	RB	WR	TE	All DEF	DL	LB	CB	S
2015 Rk	4	20	5	24	2	19	22	15	16	20	21
Rank	4	10	10	29	4	15	17	18	12	4	31
Total	90.4M	22.2M	30.2M	3.2M	25.4M	9.4M	65.7M	18.1M	24.9M	18.4M	4.3M

2016 Offseason Spending

Total Spent	Total Spent Rk	Free Agents #	Free Agents $	Free Agents $ Rk	Waiver #	Waiver $	Waiver $ Rk	Extended #	Sum of Extended $	Sum of Drafted $	Undrafted #	Undrafted $
239M	7	12	104M	7	18	37M	1	4	59M	27M	21	32M

2015 Stats & Fantasy Production

Pos	Player	Ov. Rank	Pos. Rk	Age	Gms	St	Pass Comp	Pass Att	Pass Yds	Pass TD	Pass Int	Rush Att	Rush Yds	Rush YPA	Rush TD	Targ	Recp	Rec Yds	Rec YPC	Rec TDs	Draft King Pts	Fan Duel Pts
QB	Kirk Cousins	64	8	27	16	16	379	543	4,166	29	11	26	48	2	5						306	300
RB	Matt Jones		40	22	13							144	490	3	3	25	19	304	16	1	124	105
	Alfred Morris		47	27	16	16						202	751	4	1	13	10	55	6		100	92
	Chris Thompson		63	25	13							35	216	6		48	35	240	7	2	99	75
WR	Pierre Garcon		36	29	16	16										111	72	777	11	6	189	150
	DeSean Jackson		60	29	10	9										49	30	528	18	4	109	90
	Jamison Crowder		61	22	16	6				1		2	2		1	78	59	604	10	2	138	104
	Ryan Grant		97	25	16	5										42	23	268	12	2	65	50
	Rashad Ross		120	25	13											13	8	184	23	1	41	34
	Andre Roberts		145	27	9											21	11	135	12		34	25
TE	Jordan Reed	13	3	25	14	9										114	87	952	11	11	249	201
	Derek Carrier		54	25	12	11										22	17	141	8	1	40	29

Avg Line	+1.1	Pred Wins	7	Pred Div Finish	#3

2016 Weekly Betting Lines (wks 1-16)

(-) Favorite   Underdog (+)
-7.5   +6.5

Avg Line = 1.1

Values shown: +3.0, H, A +3.0, H -7.5, A -2.5, -3.0, +1.0, A +4.0, H +1.5, H +2.5, A +3.5, A +6.5, +3.0, A

Week: 1 2 3 4 5 6 7 8 9 10 11 12 13 14 15 16

2015 Critical and Game-Deciding Stats

TO Margin	+5
TO Given	22
INT Given	11
FUM Given	11
TO Taken	27
INT Taken	11
FUM Taken	16
Sack Margin	+11
Sacks	38
Sacks Allow	27
Return TD Margin	+1
Ret TDs	5
Ret TDs Allow	4
Penalty Margin	+8
Penalties	104
Opponent Penalties	112

-Teams that win the turnover battle win 79% of games & cover 79% ATS.
-Teams with more sacks win 71% of games & cover 69% ATS.
-Teams with more return TDs win 75% of games & cover 75% ATS.
-Teams with fewer penalties win 57% of games & cover 54% ATS.

2016 NFLproject.com Forecast

Div RK	3
Div W%	(20%)
Playoffs RK	18
% in Playoffs	(29%)
Super Bowl RK	17
% Win Super Bowl	(0%)

Odds to Win Division
45% ★
25% (NYG)
20%
10%

NFCE

Team Records & Trends

	2015	2014	2013
Average line	3.5	3.1	2.7
Average O/U line	45.2	46.6	49.3
Straight Up Record	9-7	4-12	3-13
Against the Spread Record	9-7	5-11	5-11
Over/Under Record	9-7	8-8	8-8
ATS as Favorite	0-2	1-3	2-2
ATS as Underdog	9-5	4-8	3-8
Straight Up Home	6-2	3-5	2-6
ATS Home	5-3	2-6	3-5
Over/Under Home	3-5	4-4	4-4
ATS as Home Favorite	0-2	1-3	1-1
ATS as a Home Dog	5-1	1-3	2-3
Straight Up Away	3-5	1-7	1-7
ATS Away	4-4	3-5	2-6
Over/Under Away	6-2	4-4	4-4
ATS Away Favorite	0-0	0-0	1-1
ATS Away Dog	4-4	3-5	1-5
Six Point Teaser Record	12-4	10-6	6-9
Seven Point Teaser Record	13-2	10-6	7-8
Ten Point Teaser Record	15-1	11-5	11-5

Games Favored
3

Games Underdog
10

Close Game Records

All 2015 Wins: **9**
FG Games (<=3 pts) W-L: **3-1**
FG Games Win %: **75% (#5)**
FG Games Wins (% of Total Wins): **33% (#8)**
1 Score Games (<=8 pts) W-L: **4-3**
1 Score Games Win %: **57% (#11)**
1 Score Games Wins (% of Total Wins): **44% (#22)**

Home Lines (wks 1-16)

Avg Line = -0.1
-7.5
+1.5
Avg Line = -0.1

Week: 1 2 3 4 5 6 7 8 9 10 11 12 13 14 15 16

Road Lines (wks 1-16)   Week

Avg Line = 2.2
-2.5
+4.0
+3.5 +6.5
0.0
Avg Line = 2.2

Week: 1 2 3 4 5 6 7 8 9 10 11 12 13 14 15 16

Regular Season Wins: Past Results & Current Proj

2012 Wins
2013 Wins — 3
2014 Wins — 4
Proj 2015 Wins — 6
2015 Wins — 10
Proj 2016 Wins — 7, 9

1 2 3 4 5 6 7 8 9 10 11 12 13 14 15

Despite a 9-7 season last year and the hopes and dreams in Washington seeking more, the Redskins are projected to reverse that record and finish 7-9 this year. Why the down turn? Their schedule is exceedingly difficult this year as compared to exceedingly easy last year. 33% of their wins last year came in games decided by 3 or less points, which was the 8th most of any team. And, they won most of the key metrics that decide games, such as turnovers, penalties and sacks. But there are positives. The Redskins were one of the more injured teams last year, particularly on defense (2nd most defensive injuries), and they re-established a home-field edge, going 6-2 in DC after going 5-11 the prior 2 seasons. But they opened as favorites in only 3 games, are projected to win only 7 in total, and worst of all, are favored in just 1 game vs NFC East opposition.

2016 Rest Analysis

Avg Rest	6.4
Avg Rest Rk	29
Team More Rest	2
Opp More Rest	3
Net Rest Edge	-1
3 days rest	1
4 days rest	1
5 days rest	1
6 days rest	8
7 days rest	2
8 days rest	0
9 days rest	1
10 days rest	0
11 days rest	0
12 days rest	0
13 days rest	1
14 days rest	0

Weekly EDSR & Season Trending Performance

WEEK	1	2	3	4	5	6	7		9	10	11	12	13	14	15	16	17
RESULT	L	W	L	W	L	L	W		L	W	L	W	L	W	W	W	W
OPP	MIA	STL	NYG	PHI	ATL	NYJ	TB		NE	NO	CAR	NYG	DAL	CHI	BUF	PHI	DAL
SITE	H	H	A	H	A	A	H		A	H	A	H	A	H	A	H	A
MARGIN	-7	14	-11	3	-6	-14	1		-17	33	-28	6	-3	3	10	14	11
PTS	10	24	21	23	19	20	31		10	47	16	20	16	24	35	38	34
OPP PTS	17	10	32	20	25	34	30		27	14	44	14	19	21	25	24	23

Week by Week 2015 Results

EDSR Results (W/L) By Week
W=Green
L=Red

Off & Def EDSR Wk & Trend
- Blue=Offense (high=good)
- Red=Defense (low=good)

All visualizations courtesy of SharpFootballStats.com. See Table of Contents for definition of stats & coding used. See SharpFootballStats.com for interactive visualizations which break data into more segments, allow customization & user download. Updated weekly throughout the 2016 NFL season.

Directional Passer Rating Achieved

Receiver	Short Left	Short Middle	Short Right	Deep Left	Deep Middle	Deep Right
Jordan Reed	111	135	93	60	158	95
Pierre Garcon	112	62	109	57	99	40
Jamison Crowder	107	114	97	32	39	118
DeSean Jackson	74	100	84	137	95	121
Ryan Grant	56	87	80	104	95	39
Derek Carrier	97	135	59	39		
Andre Roberts	56	77	64	118	54	81
Rashad Ross	100	79	118	95	39	121
Alex Smith		77	39			

Directional Frequency by Receiver

Receiver	Short Left	Short Middle	Short Right	Deep Left	Deep Middle	Deep Right
Jordan Reed	27%	38%	28%	12%	22%	12%
Pierre Garcon	23%	25%	20%	29%	37%	27%
Jamison Crowder	21%	15%	19%	14%	4%	9%
DeSean Jackson	9%	3%	10%	20%	15%	27%
Ryan Grant	10%	6%	11%	10%	7%	9%
Derek Carrier	4%	6%	6%	6%		
Andre Roberts	4%	4%	4%	2%	11%	6%
Rashad Ross	2%	1%	2%	8%	4%	9%
Alex Smith		2%	1%			

Defense Passer Rating Allowed

Short Left	Short Middle	Short Right	Deep Left	Deep Middle	Deep Right
92	93	96	121	100	85

Offensive Rush Directional Yds/Carry

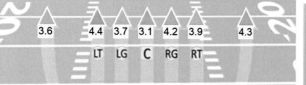

3.6 | 4.4 | 3.7 | 3.1 | 4.2 | 3.9 | 4.3
LT | LG | C | RG | RT

Offensive Rush Frequency of Direction

87 | 56 | 49 | 66 | 48 | 53 | 73
LT | LG | C | RG | RT

Offensive Explosive Runs by Direction

9 | 5 | 2 | 4 | 4 | 3 | 8
LT | LG | C | RG | RT

Defensive Rush Directional Yds/Carry

6.8 | 4.0 | 4.0 | 4.7 | 3.8 | 3.7 | 6.8
LT | LG | C | RG | RT

Kirk Cousins - 1st Down RTG

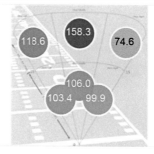

118.6 | 158.3 | 74.6
106.0
103.4 | 99.9

Kirk Cousins - 2nd Down RTG

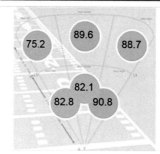

75.2 | 89.6 | 88.7
82.1
82.8 | 90.8

Kirk Cousins - 3rd Down RTG

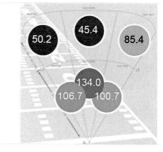

50.2 | 45.4 | 85.4
134.0
106.7 | 100.7

Kirk Cousins - Overall RTG

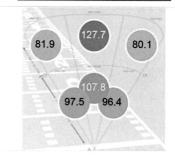

81.9 | 127.7 | 80.1
107.8
97.5 | 96.4

2nd & Short RUN (1D or not)

2nd & Short RUN Stats

Run Conv Rk	1D% Run	NFL 1D% Run Avg	Run Freq	NFL Run Freq Avg
22	64%	69%	64%	64%

2nd & Short PASS (1D or not)

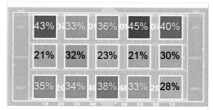

2nd & Short PASS Stats

Pass Conv Rk	1D% Pass	NFL 1D% Pass Avg	Pass Freq	NFL Pass Freq Avg
29	38%	55%	36%	36%

Pass Offense Play Success Rate

50%	49%	63%	50%	45%
35%	58%	88%	68%	54%
36%	46%	57%	44%	46%

Pass Offense Yds/Play

8.0	8.7	8.7	7.2	2.9
5.5	9.4	12.6	9.5	5.6
6.6	7.1	8.8	7.0	4.0

Off. Directional Tendency (% of Plays Left, Middle or Right)

43%	33%	36%	45%	40%
21%	32%	23%	21%	30%
35%	34%	38%	33%	28%

Off. Directional Pass Rate (% of Plays which are Passes)

65%	64%	56%	59%	68%
36%	69%	40%	43%	48%
62%	66%	62%	57%	59%

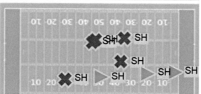

Philadelphia Eagles

Forecast 2016 Wins
7

Past Records
2015: 7-9
2014: 10-6
2013: 10-6

Opponent Strength
Easy — Hard

2016 Schedule & Week by Week Strength of Schedule

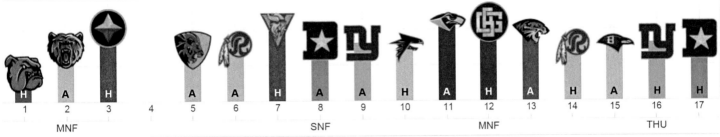

H	H	H		A	A	H	A	A	H	A	H	A	H	A	H	H
1	2	3	4	5	6	7	8	9	10	11	12	13	14	15	16	17

MNF — SNF — MNF — THU

2016 Overview

The Eagles played a game of chicken against themselves and lost. It's hard to imagine that happening, but put yourself in their shoes. You are a professional football team. And a professional football team needs a quarterback. The prior year, you send your QB to the Rams in exchange for Sam Bradford, who can best be described as a below average QB on an above average deal who has not proven to be clutch, accurate deep or sturdy in the pocket. He's better than Nick Foles, but also more expensive. And now his contract is up. You're contemplating signing him to a multi-year deal, but you don't have much confidence in him. Bradford is standing behind door 1. Behind door 2 is a high risk, high reward move of packaging up a bounty of picks to draft North Dakota State product Carson Wentz 2nd overall. Such trades rarely work, but hell, look behind door 1. Why not give it a shot?

Most teams would research the situation, figure out which door to open, and boldly make a choice. The Eagles decided they were not capable of making the decision. They built a third door, and stuck QB Chase Daniel behind that door. The Eagles then decided they still were not capable of making a choice. So instead of opening just one door, and instead of opening two doors, they decided to open ALL the doors. What they got was a mess. Now, they have a below average QB hitting the cap for $12.5M this year and a whopping $22.5M next year. They have a backup QB on a ridiculous 3-year deal that averages $7M per year. And they have a rookie QB from South Dakota State who is making their starting QB extremely jealous and already creating locker room tension.

The fastest way to make the messy quarterback situation disappear is to slap some lipstick on the pig and run the damn football. The Eagles have the 3rd most expensive offensive line in the NFL and the 6th most expensive RB corps. In his three seasons in Kansas City, Doug Pederson spearheaded one of the most balanced and conservative play offenses in the NFL. They attempted an early down deep pass in the first half just over 1 time per game on average, 2nd fewest of any team in the NFL. In total, in the first half they attempted just 97 deep passes in his 48 games. They were the only team below 120 attempts, and the NFL average for the other 31 teams was over 151 deep passes. It's very likely that this same strategy follows Pederson to the Eagles. Coupled with tempo, the 2016 season will look very different on both sides of the ball. In his 3 years in Philadelphia, the Eagles defense led the NFL each season with time on the field. Opponent's had a ton of possession with Kelly's frenetic pace. However, the Chiefs operated their offense with the NFL's 2nd slowest pace in 2015 and in 2014. New OC Frank Reich, from San Diego, saw the Chargers lead the NFL in offensive time of possession the last 3 years combined. Thus, their defense was on the field the least time of possession. Between Pederson and Reich, the plan will be simple. Lower risk, higher completion percentage pass plays and a very balanced run game that the offense can rely on to keep the time of possession on its side. The game will look a lot different to Eagles fans, but it will feel very different to Bradford (if he starts) and to the Eagles defense, which finally might be rested and more focused mentally. That plan works well if the offense can produce. If it can't, the Eagles have options of quarterbacks to turn to. But they've merely spent a lot of capital to defer that decision one more season.

Strength of Schedule In Detail

True Strength of Schedule Rank: 12

Hardest Stretches *(1=Hard, 32=Easy)*
Hardest 3 wk Stretch Rk:	4
Hardest 4 wk Stretch Rk:	7
Hardest 5 wk Stretch Rk:	8

Easiest Stretches *(1=Easy, 32=Hard)*
Easiest 3 wk Stretch Rk:	27
Easiest 4 wk Stretch Rk:	31
Easiest 5 wk Stretch Rk:	30

The Eagles schedule is unique and more difficult than it might seem. They are the only team in the NFL with just one road game in the schedule's first four weeks and last four weeks. But from weeks 5 through 13, they play just three home games and make multiple back-to-back road trips. In addition, Philadelphia is one of the teams most affected by using my proper Strength of Schedule method: using prior season opponent win percentage, the Eagles face the 7th easiest schedule. But that would assume the Cowboys are a 4-win team this year, the Giants are a 6-win team and the Packers lose Jordy Nelson in the preseason again. The reality is the Eagles schedule sees a stretch between weeks 7 through 13 which is the 2nd most difficult of any NFL team. The biggest edge for the Eagles is a close with three home games in four weeks vs the NFC East, but they need to do well enough early on to make those games meaningful.

2015 Play Tendencies

All Pass %	60%
All Pass Rk	16
All Rush %	40%
All Rush Rk	17
1 Score Pass %	58%
1 Score Pass Rk	17
2014 1 Score Pass %	58%
2014 1 Score Pass Rk	13
Pass Increase %	0%
Pass Increase Rk	21
1 Score Rush %	42%
1 Score Rush Rk	16
Up Pass %	47%
Up Pass Rk	21
Up Rush %	53%
Up Rush Rk	12
Down Pass %	68%
Down Pass Rk	16
Down Rush %	32%
Down Rush Rk	17

Although the Eagles were a very uptempo team, they were exceedingly balanced. They ranked 17th in pass frequency in one score games, 16th in pass frequency when trailing and 21st in pass frequency when leading. That pace is likely to change substantially under new HC Doug Peterson, as the Chiefs offense (as well as the Chargers, where OC Frank Reich came from) are both slow tempo.

2015 Offensive Advanced Metrics

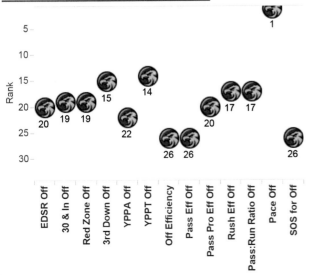

The 2015 Eagles were full of sound and fury, signifying nothing. They operated the fastest paced in the NFL, but did little with it. They were in the bottom half of the NFL in virtually every single offensive metric. Which is hard to do considering they faced the 26th rated schedule, thus only 6 teams had an easier time in 2015 than Philly. Defensively, the Eagles were likewise poor, but were quite bad in two key metrics that a team whose offense is poor can ill afford to be poor in: red zone defense and (when trailing) rush defense. That combination allows opponents to score points effectively, and then prevents the Eagles from getting the other team off the field or stopping the clock in the second half. A third stat which only added to the pain was a 27th rating on 3rd down defense. Opponents could chew up the clock and produce on the ground and the Eagles struggled to stop them.

2015 Defensive Advanced Metrics

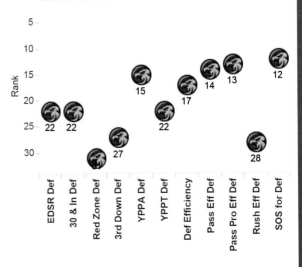

Drafted Players

2016 Draft Grade: #26 (2.4/4)

PERSONNEL & SPENDING

Philadelphia Eagles

Rnd.	Pick #	Pos.	Player	College
1	2	QB	Carson Wentz	North Dakota State
3	79	C	Isaac Seumalo	Oregon State
5	153	RB	Wendell Smallwood	West Virginia
5	164	OT	Halapoulivaati Vaitai	TCU
6	196	CB	Blake Countess	Auburn
7	233	FS	Jalen Mills	LSU
7	240	DE	Alex McCalister	Florida
7	251	ILB	Joe Walker	Oregon

Free Agents/Trades Added

Player (Position)
Brandon Brooks G
Chase Daniel QB
Chris Givens WR
Leodis McKelvin CB
Mike Martin DT
Nigel Bradham LB
Rodney McLeod S
Ron Brooks CB
Rueben Randle WR
Ryan Mueller RB
Ryan Quigley P
Stefen Wisniewski C
Ty Powell LB

Other Signed

Player (Position)
Aziz Shittu DT
Bruce Johnson C
Byron Marshall RB
C.J. Smith CB
Cayleb Jones WR
Cedric O'Neal RB
Connor Wujciak DT
Darrell Greene G
Destiny Vaeao DT
Dillon Gordon TE
Hunter Sharp WR
John DePalma TE
M.J. McFarland TE
Marcus Johnson WR
Myke Tavarres LB
Paul Turner WR
Quentin Gause LB
Ty Powell LB

2015 Players Lost

Transaction	Player (Position)
Cut	Brandon Bair DE
	Brandon Hepburn LB
	Brett Boyko G
	DeMeco Ryans LB
	Freddie Martino WR
	Jerome Couplin S
	Kevin Monangai RB
	Matthew Tucker RB
	McLeod Bethel-Thompson QB
	Quigley, Ryan P
	Riley Cooper WR
	Ross Scheuerman RB
	Ryan Mueller RB
	Seantavius Jones WR
	Tanner Hawkinson T
	Travis Raciti DT
Declared Free Agent	David Molk C
Retired	Thurmond, Walter S

- Sam Bradford has his share of problems. But the question for the 2016 Eagles and new OC Frank Reich/HC Doug Pederson is how can Bradford's positives be accentuated while hiding his deficiencies. That could take some doing. The bigger question would be "why try?" as Bradford's cap hit is extreme and the Eagles traded a ridiculous amount of value to grab Bradford's replacement when they took Carson Wentz #2 overall.
- If they choose to spend the time to design the offense around Bradford's limitations, the first step is utilizing the triangle offense. Not one designed by Phil Jackson, but it's where Bradford feels the most comfortable passing the football. Short left, short right, and deep middle. When throwing in this triangular zone, Bradford completed 70% of passes, 14 TD : 7 INT and a 92 rating. When throwing elsewhere, Bradford completed 53% of passes, 5 TD : 7 INT and a 75 rating, with just 46 first downs on 141 attempts.
- In his career, Bradford is 65% completions, 47 TD : 22 INT and an 85 rating inside the triangle, and 51% completions, 31 TD : 28 INT and a 75 rating outside the triangle.
- Bradford was also terrible inside the red zone in the first half. On early downs, just 29% of Bradford's passes were successful, 2nd worst in the NFL. Meanwhile, the Eagles run game was incredible, with 63% of their run plays grading as successful, 5th best in the NFL. It was very similar to the Chiefs last year, whose early down red zone run game was #1 in the NFL in the first half, while the pass game was 3rd worst. Reich/Pederson need to lean on the run game in those situations.
- The Eagles offense will likely slow it down and focus more on the run, which will have the ability to help a defense which was completely exhausted with Kelly.
- But the Eagles secondary, particularly at CB, is not strong. Vs. the NFC East passing games new DC Jim Schwartz must bring pressure to help.

Lineup & 2016 Cap Hit

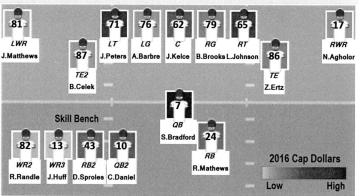

Health Overall & by Unit (2015 v 2014)

2015 Rk	6
2015 AGL	52
Off Rk	10
Def Rk	17
2014 Rk	5
2014 AGL	49

2016 Positional Spending

	All OFF	QB	OL	RB	WR	TE	All DEF	DL	LB	CB	S
2015 Rk	5	9	10	3	25	15	16	29	3	15	11
Rank	7	8	3	6	27	18	23	24	6	25	16
Total	87.8M	22.4M	38.0M	10.6M	10.0M	6.8M	64.5M	15.9M	27.2M	10.4M	11.0M

2016 Offseason Spending

Total Spent	Total Spent Rk	Free Agents #	Free Agents $	Free Agents $ Rk	Waiver #	Waiver $	Waiver $ Rk	Extended #	Sum of Extended $	Sum of Drafted $	Undrafted #	Undrafted $
543M	1	12	116M	6	14	20M	8	9	333M	45M	18	29M

2015 Stats & Fantasy Production

Pos	Player	Ov. Rank	Pos. Rk	Age	Gms	St	Pass Comp	Pass Att	Pass Yds	Pass TD	Pass Int	Rush Att	Rush Yds	Rush YPA	Rush TD	Targ	Recp	Rec Yds	Rec YPC	Rec TDs	Draft King Pts	Fan Duel Pts
QB	Sam Bradford		24	28	14	14	346	532	3,725	19	14	26	39	2							215	209
	Mark Sanchez		46	29	4	2	59	91	616	4	4	6	22	4							41	37
RB	DeMarco Murray	55	18	27	15	8						193	702	4	6	55	44	322	7	1	192	162
	Ryan Mathews		33	28	13	6						107	539	5	6	28	20	146	7	1	134	115
	Darren Sproles*		41	32	16	4						83	317	4	3	83	55	388	7	1	168	134
WR	Jordan Matthews	50	20	23	16	13										126	85	997	12	8	235	188
	Josh Huff		88	24	15	4										42	27	312	12	3	79	63
	Riley Cooper		92	28	16	13										41	21	327	16	2	69	55
	Nelson Agholor		105	22	13	12										44	23	283	12	1	59	44
	Miles Austin		110	31	11	1										31	13	224	17	1	44	35
TE	Zach Ertz	66	10	25	15	6										112	75	853	11	2	174	133
	Brent Celek		27	30	16	13										35	27	398	15	3	88	71

ODDS & TRENDS — Philadelphia Eagles

Avg Line	+1.2	Pred Wins	7	Pred Div Finish	#4

(-) Favorite   Underdog (+)
-7.5   +9.0

2016 Weekly Betting Lines (wks 1-16)

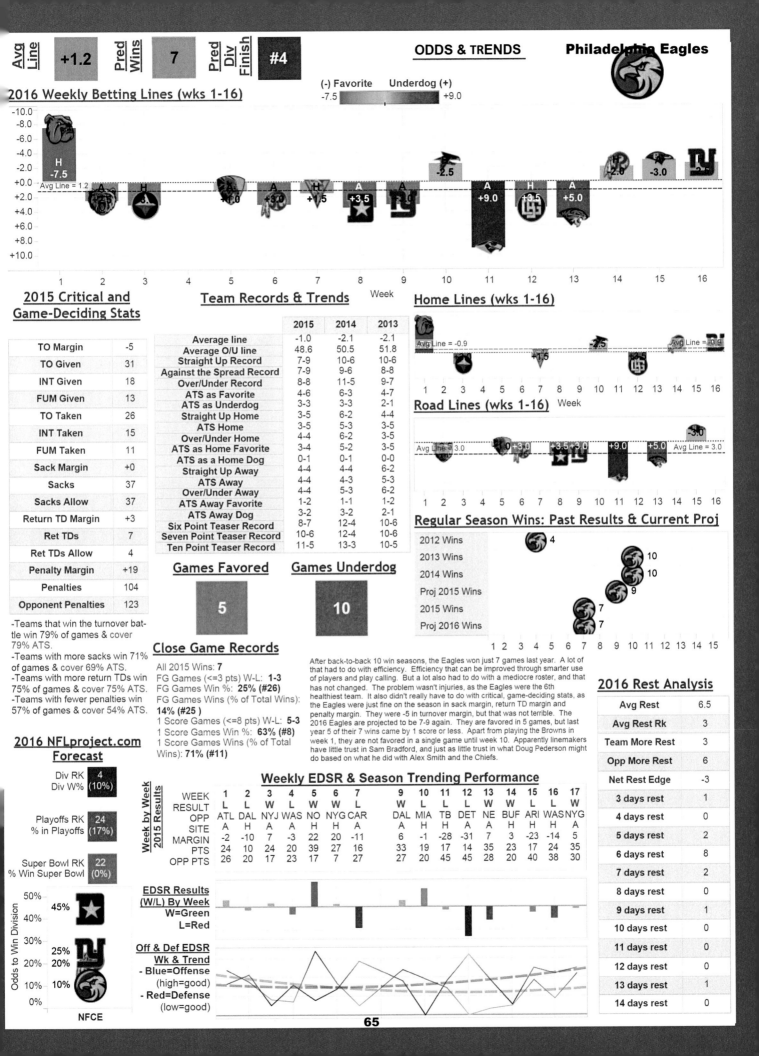

Avg Line = 1.2

Week 1 2 3 4 5 6 7 8 9 10 11 12 13 14 15 16

Week 1: H -7.5
Week 2: A
Week 3: H
Week 5: A +1.0
Week 6: A +3.0
Week 7: H +1.5
Week 8: A +3.5
Week 9: A
Week 10: -2.5
Week 11: A +9.0
Week 12: H +3.5
Week 13: A +5.0
Week 14: -2.0
Week 15: -3.0
Week 16: -2.5

2015 Critical and Game-Deciding Stats

TO Margin	-5
TO Given	31
INT Given	18
FUM Given	13
TO Taken	26
INT Taken	15
FUM Taken	11
Sack Margin	+0
Sacks	37
Sacks Allow	37
Return TD Margin	+3
Ret TDs	7
Ret TDs Allow	4
Penalty Margin	+19
Penalties	104
Opponent Penalties	123

-Teams that win the turnover battle win 79% of games & cover 79% ATS.
-Teams with more sacks win 71% of games & cover 69% ATS.
-Teams with more return TDs win 75% of games & cover 75% ATS.
-Teams with fewer penalties win 57% of games & cover 54% ATS.

2016 NFLproject.com Forecast

Div RK	4	
Div W%	(10%)	
Playoffs RK	24	
% in Playoffs	(17%)	
Super Bowl RK	22	
% Win Super Bowl	(0%)	

Odds to Win Division
45% (star)
25% (NYG)
20% (NYG)
10% (eagle)
NFCE

Team Records & Trends

	2015	2014	2013
Average line	-1.0	-2.1	-2.1
Average O/U line	48.6	50.5	51.8
Straight Up Record	7-9	10-6	10-6
Against the Spread Record	7-9	9-6	8-8
Over/Under Record	8-8	11-5	9-7
ATS as Favorite	4-6	6-3	4-7
ATS as Underdog	3-3	3-3	2-1
Straight Up Home	3-5	6-2	4-4
ATS Home	3-5	5-3	3-5
Over/Under Home	4-4	6-2	3-5
ATS as Home Favorite	3-4	5-2	3-5
ATS as a Home Dog	0-1	0-1	0-0
Straight Up Away	4-4	4-4	6-2
ATS Away	4-4	4-3	5-3
Over/Under Away	4-4	5-3	6-2
ATS Away Favorite	1-2	1-1	1-2
ATS Away Dog	3-2	3-2	2-1
Six Point Teaser Record	8-7	12-4	10-6
Seven Point Teaser Record	10-6	12-4	10-6
Ten Point Teaser Record	11-5	13-3	10-5

Games Favored
5

Games Underdog
10

Close Game Records

All 2015 Wins: **7**
FG Games (<=3 pts) W-L: **1-3**
FG Games Win %: **25% (#26)**
FG Games Wins (% of Total Wins): **14% (#25)**
1 Score Games (<=8 pts) W-L: **5-3**
1 Score Games Win %: **63% (#8)**
1 Score Games Wins (% of Total Wins): **71% (#11)**

Home Lines (wks 1-16)

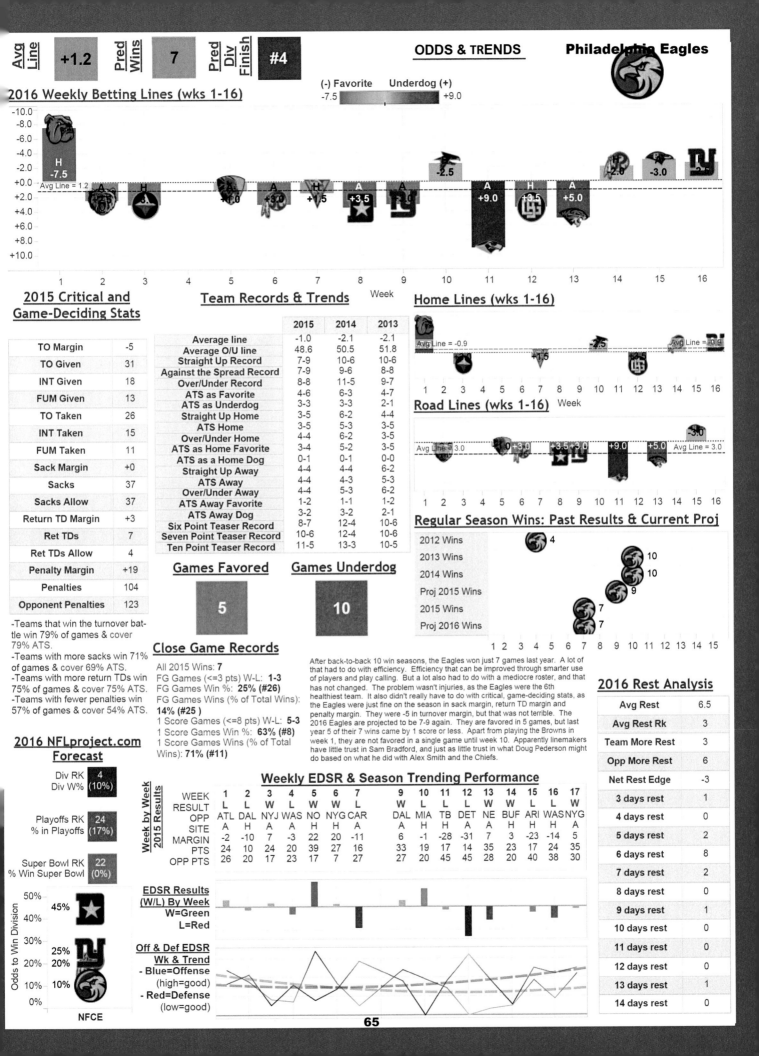

Avg Line = -0.9
Week 1 2 3 4 5 6 7 8 9 10 11 12 13 14 15 16

Road Lines (wks 1-16)   Week

Avg Line = 3.0   +1.0 +3.0   +3.5 +3.0   +9.0   +5.0   Avg Line = 3.0   -3.0
Week 1 2 3 4 5 6 7 8 9 10 11 12 13 14 15 16

Regular Season Wins: Past Results & Current Proj

2012 Wins	4
2013 Wins	10
2014 Wins	10
Proj 2015 Wins	9
2015 Wins	7
Proj 2016 Wins	7

1 2 3 4 5 6 7 8 9 10 11 12 13 14 15

After back-to-back 10 win seasons, the Eagles won just 7 games last year. A lot of that had to do with efficiency. Efficiency that can be improved through smarter use of players and play calling. But a lot also had to do with a mediocre roster, and that has not changed. The problem wasn't injuries, as the Eagles were the 6th healthiest team. It also didn't really have to do with critical, game-deciding stats, as the Eagles were just fine on the season in sack margin, return TD margin and penalty margin. They were -5 in turnover margin, but that was not terrible. The 2016 Eagles are projected to be 7-9 again. They are favored in 5 games, but last year 5 of their 7 wins came by 1 score or less. Apart from playing the Browns in week 1, they are not favored in a single game until week 10. Apparently linemakers have little trust in Sam Bradford, and just as little trust in what Doug Pederson might do based on what he did with Alex Smith and the Chiefs.

2016 Rest Analysis

Avg Rest	6.5
Avg Rest Rk	3
Team More Rest	3
Opp More Rest	6
Net Rest Edge	-3
3 days rest	1
4 days rest	0
5 days rest	2
6 days rest	8
7 days rest	2
8 days rest	0
9 days rest	1
10 days rest	0
11 days rest	0
12 days rest	0
13 days rest	1
14 days rest	0

Weekly EDSR & Season Trending Performance

WEEK	1	2	3	4	5	6	7	9	10	11	12	13	14	15	16	17
RESULT	L	L	W	L	W	W	L	W	L	L	L	W	L	L	L	W
OPP	ATL	DAL	NYJ	WAS	NO	NYG	CAR	DAL	MIA	TB	DET	NE	BUF	ARI	WAS	NYG
SITE	A	H	A	A	H	H	A	A	H	A	H	A	H	H	H	A
MARGIN	-2	-10	7	-3	22	20	-11	6	-1	-28	-31	7	3	-23	-14	5
PTS	24	10	24	20	39	27	16	33	19	17	14	35	23	17	24	35
OPP PTS	26	20	17	23	17	7	27	27	20	45	45	28	20	40	38	30

Week by Week 2015 Results

EDSR Results (W/L) By Week
W=Green
L=Red

Off & Def EDSR Wk & Trend
- Blue=Offense (high=good)
- Red=Defense (low=good)

STATS & VISUALIZATIONS

Philadelphia Eagles

Directional Passer Rating Achieved

Receiver	Short Left	Short Middle	Short Right	Deep Left	Deep Middle	Deep Right
Jordan Matthews	98	54	119	115	104	130
Zach Ertz	78	63	78	112	109	61
Brent Celek	103	17	158	64		118
Josh Huff	135	108	82	89	39	
Nelson Agholor	118	39	72	79	135	39
Riley Cooper	52	58	16	81	95	39
Miles Austin	7	110	118	55	158	18
Trey Burton	87	118	56			
Jonathan Krause	95	83		39		39
Seyi Ajirotutu			83	39	39	

Directional Frequency by Receiver

Receiver	Short Left	Short Middle	Short Right	Deep Left	Deep Middle	Deep Right
Jordan Matthews	28%	38%	29%	15%	23%	30%
Zach Ertz	25%	29%	23%	26%	27%	23%
Brent Celek	7%	6%	11%	13%		3%
Josh Huff	11%	9%	11%	5%	5%	
Nelson Agholor	2%	5%	18%	5%	18%	17%
Riley Cooper	15%	5%	3%	21%	18%	7%
Miles Austin	10%	6%	2%	10%	5%	17%
Trey Burton	1%	1%	1%			
Jonathan Krause	1%	1%		3%		3%
Seyi Ajirotutu			1%	3%	5%	

Defense Passer Rating Allowed

Short Left	Short Middle	Short Right	Deep Left	Deep Middle	Deep Right
100	93	101	71	96	75

Offensive Rush Directional Yds/Carry

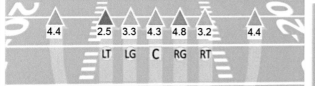

4.4	2.5	3.3	4.3	4.8	3.2	4.4
	LT	LG	C	RG	RT	

Offensive Rush Frequency of Direction

89	38	26	128	27	39	85
	LT	LG	C	RG	RT	

Offensive Explosive Runs by Direction

14	1	1	12	3	3	13
	LT	LG	C	RG	RT	

Defensive Rush Directional Yds/Carry

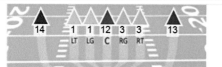

4.9	3.9	7.6	3.7	6.6	4.5	4.8
	LT	LG	C	RG	RT	

Sam Bradford - 1st Down RTG

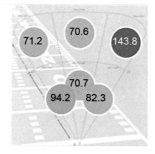

71.2 / 70.6 / 143.8 / 70.7 / 94.2 / 82.3

Sam Bradford - 2nd Down RTG

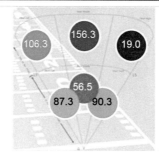

106.3 / 156.3 / 19.0 / 56.5 / 87.3 / 90.3

Sam Bradford - 3rd Down RTG

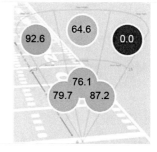

92.6 / 64.6 / 0.0 / 76.1 / 79.7 / 87.2

Sam Bradford - Overall RTG

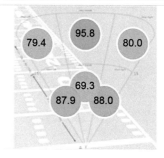

79.4 / 95.8 / 80.0 / 69.3 / 87.9 / 88.0

2nd & Short RUN (1D or not)

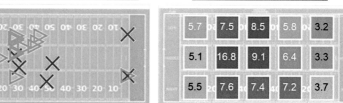

2nd & Short RUN Stats

Run Conv Rk	1D% Run	NFL 1D% Run Avg	Run Freq	NFL Run Freq Avg
17	68%	69%	53%	64%

2nd & Short PASS (1D or not)

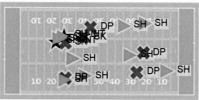

2nd & Short PASS Stats

Pass Conv Rk	1D% Pass	NFL 1D% Pass Avg	Pass Freq	NFL Pass Freq Avg
21	53%	55%	47%	36%

Pass Offense Play Success Rate

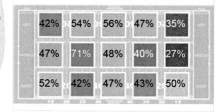

42%	54%	56%	47%	35%
47%	71%	48%	40%	27%
52%	42%	47%	43%	50%

Pass Offense Yds/Play

5.7	7.5	8.5	5.8	3.2
5.1	16.8	9.1	6.4	3.3
5.5	7.6	7.4	7.2	3.7

Off. Directional Tendency (% of Plays Left, Middle or Right)

39%	44%	38%	43%	31%
22%	13%	19%	20%	20%
39%	43%	43%	36%	48%

Off. Directional Pass Rate (% of Plays which are Passes)

64%	66%	63%	83%	50%
54%	26%	38%	46%	37%
74%	64%	71%	70%	55%

2016 College Football Forecast

Last month, the first Vegas bookmakers were hard at work preparing for the 2016 College Football Season. South Point released regular season win totals on all 128 Division 1 FBS teams, while CG Technology updated their National Title and Conference odds for most of the top programs.

Nationally, Alabama (+650), Clemson (+750), Ohio State (+800) and Michigan (+800) are the 4 largest favorites, standing apart from the next tier of teams which includes Oklahoma (+1100), Florida State (+1200), LSU (+1200), Baylor (+1500), Tennessee (+1600) and Notre Dame (+1800). Those programs round out the top 10, and all other programs are +2000 or greater.

Baylor was immediately faded as news of the legal and potentially criminal actions unfolded. Their odds are better than +1800 currently.

Marching through the Power 5 Conferences, let's examine projected success for 2016:

In terms of win totals, in the SEC, Alabama (10), LSU (10) and Tennessee (9.5) are the schools most likely to enjoy success. However, both are in the SEC West and thus, competing with one another before making the title game. That said, both programs are #1 and #2 in overall conference odds (Alabama is +150, LSU is +350) while Tennessee is third at +450, indicating linesmakers belief that the SEC West, at least those top programs) are simply more dominant. LSU is projected to show the most overall improvement, winning 2 more games than 2015. Meanwhile, Florida and Texas A&M are both projected to lose at least 2 more games in 2016 than they did last year.

The SEC could send multiple teams to the playoffs. If Alabama wins the SEC, a one-loss LSU could state its case. Similarly, were Tennessee able to beat Alabama in Tennessee, but drop the SEC title game to the Crimson Tide, they would have a strong case. Can Alabama make 3 consecutive playoff appearances in the 3 years of its existence?

In the ACC, the Clemson Tigers are still projected to be dominant. They have the second best odds to win the National Title, right behind Alabama. They are +140 to win the ACC, with Florida State their only real competition (at +220). Lousiville is third, but is all the way down at +850. Boston College and Georgia Tech are projected to be substantially improved, with each estimated to win 6.5 games this year, more than double their 2015 mark. On the other hand, North Carolina is projected to fall back, dropping to 8.5 wins (2.5 fewer than 2015) but that would still put them in contention in the ACC as well as assuredly landing a good bowl game.

With Clemson and Florida State, the ACC finally has two dominant teams, but unfortunately for them they both reside in the ACC Atlantic, along with the #3 rated Louisville Cardinals. The gap between Pittsburgh and North Carolina may be closer than linesmakers forecast.

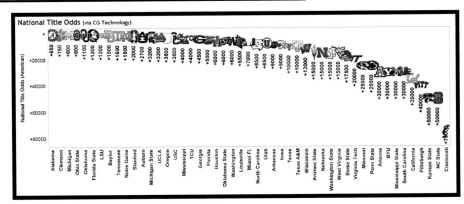

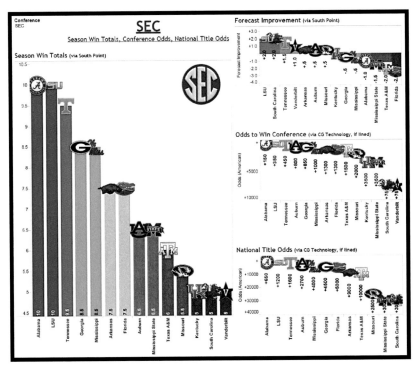

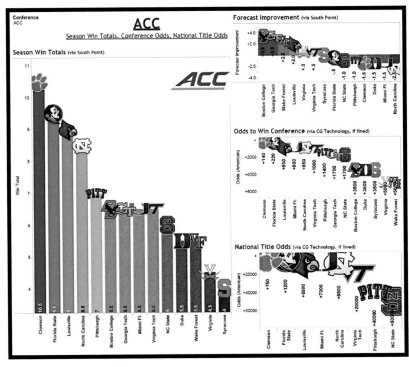

The nation's third most likely champions hail from the Big Ten. Michigan and Ohio State both have identical odds to win the title at +800. They both are between +160 (Ohio State) and +180 (Michigan) to win the Big Ten, with the next closest competition (Michigan State) being +500. It appears South Point is higher on Nebraska than CG Technology, with Nebraska being projected to win 8.5 games in 2016, a massive improvement of 3.5 more wins than 2015. It would be the third most wins in the Big Ten. But CG Technology has them at +900 to win the Big Ten (fifth longest odds) and in terms of the National Title, they are +15000, placing them behind Wisconsin (despite them having better odds to win the Big Ten than Wisconsin).

Per the ESPN Football Power Index, the Big Ten is the only Power 5 conference without a team inside the top 10. Michigan falls at 11, Ohio State at 15 and Nebraska closes out the top 30, coming in at 28. The Wolverines showed tremendous improvement under Jim Harbaugh and have a solid returning class, whereas perineal contenders like Ohio State and Michigan State are reloading to a degree.

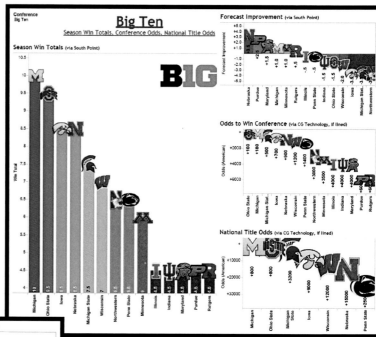

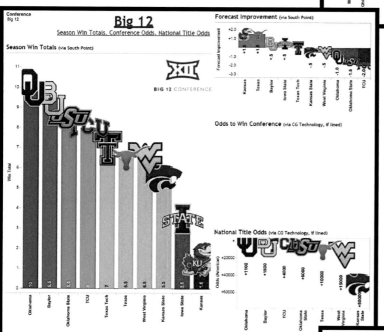

The Big 12 provides the next most likely National Champion, with Oklahoma having the fifth best odds to win the title in 2016. They are projected to win 10 games, most in the Big 12. Kansas pulls up the rear, with 1.5 projected wins, which is 1.5 more wins than they had in 2015. Texas is also projected to show an improvement of 1.5 wins, while TCU is projected to win 8 games, 2 fewer than 2015, and Oklahoma State is projected to show a decline of 1.5 wins as compared to 2015.

Conference favorite Oklahoma must get past Ohio State and Houston prior to starting their Big-12 conference play. Meanwhile, TCU returns just 3 starters on offense from 2015. With the coaching change at Baylor and the scandal for the university, it seems to be a one-horse race in the Big-12 this year, but Oklahoma will need to perform extremely well, early in the season, to set themselves up to be in contention for a shot at the CFP.

Rounding out the Power 5 Conferences, Stanford is +2000 to win the National Title, 11th best in the country. However, they are tied with USC at +280 to win the Pac-12, and USC's title odds are +3500, worse than UCLA (+3200). The team projected to win the most games in the Pac-12, however, is Washington, who South Point is extremely big on. They forecast the Huskies to show a 3 point win improvement as compared to 2015, by far the most in the Pac-12. Meanwhile, CG Technology has Washington at +600 to win the Pac-12, with 4 teams projected with better odds to finish ahead of them. Without Jared Goff, the NFL's #1 overall draft pick last year, Cal is projected to win only 4 games this year, 3 fewer than 2015.

Stanford and Washington may produce an interesting showdown to win the North. But the non-conference schedules for most contenders may see them fall short of the CFP. Stanford takes Kansas State and Notre Dame, USC plays Alabama and Notre Dame while UCLA plays BYU in Utah and Texas A&M.

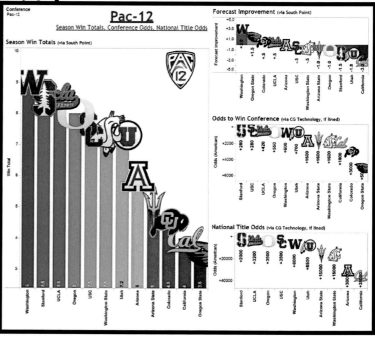

Carolina Panthers

Coaches
Head Coach: **Ron Rivera** (6th yr)
OC: **Mike Shula** (4th yr)
DC: **Sean McDermott** (6th yr)

Past Records
2015: 15-1
2014: 7-8-1
2013: 12-4

Opponent Strength
Easy — Hard

2016 Schedule & Week by Week Strength of Schedule

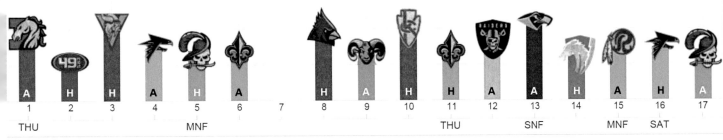

A	H	H	A	A	H	A		H	A	H	H	A	A	H	A	H	A
1	2	3	4	5	6	7		8	9	10	11	12	13	14	15	16	17

THU — MNF — THU — SNF — MNF — SAT

2016 Overview

The 2015 Super Bowl runner-up Panthers played as a wolf in sheep's clothing. Not just to opponents, but to much of the entire nation, and even some in Panther Nation. Essentially, anyone who believed the Panthers were successful only because they had a great defense and were great on the ground. Because the Cam Newton-led Panthers were lethal in the air. What's more, they did it without a cadre of receiving talent. Their best wide receiver was Ted Ginn, a player they, and many other teams cut multiple times. The rest of the wide receiver corps included Jerricho Cotchery, Corey Brown and Devin Funchess. Yet remarkably, Cam Newton finished the season 0.8 rating points shy of a 100 passer rating, with 35 touchdowns and only 10 interceptions. Seven percent of his pass attempts were touchdowns, the best rate of any quarterback last year. In the 15 years since 2000, only 8 QBs ever had a season with a better TD rate than Newton: Peyton Manning (04, 13), Aaron Rodgers (11, 14), Tom Brady (07, 10), Ben Roethlisberger (07) and Tony Romo (14). Not bad company at all.

But let's not lose sight of what is important: that the 2015 Panthers were great only because of their defense. Just ignore the fact that when teams lead at halftime, they win over 75% of the time. Most often, that is because they've used the first half to prove they are the superior team. But there is also something to holding a lead and forcing an opponent to change strategy at halftime. And the 2015 Panthers led at halftime by 9.8 ppg on average. In the last 15 years, the only team to lead by more at halftime on average was the 2007 Patriots (who led by 10.8 ppg on average). So how did the defensive minded Panthers lead by such a huge margin at halftime? Particularly when the offensive minded 07 Patriots were the only other team to lead by such a margin, and the other teams who averaged huge halftime leads included the 2014 Packers, the 2001 Rams and the 2012 Patriots, all teams with ridiculously strong offenses? It must have been with ridiculously strong field position thanks to the defense, right? Or a lot of defensive touchdowns. The Panthers defense scored 3 defensive touchdowns in the first half, while scoring 30 offensive touchdowns. No other team scored 30 offensive first half touchdowns. The NFL average was only 18. Additionally, the Panthers average starting field position was on their own 29 in the first half, which was only 12th best in the NFL.

No team since the 1972 Miami Dolphins lost the Super Bowl and won it the next year, and no team since the 1993 Buffalo Bills even made it back to the title game. However, Ron Rivera can spin the fact that twice in the last 5 years the prior Super Bowl loser made it back to the Conference Championship (2012 Patriots, 2013 49ers). Additionally, the last 8 Super Bowl losers have all won 10+ games the following season, with 3 of the last 4 winning more games than the Super Bowl champion. The Panthers can have another great season because their pieces are so similar with the exception of Josh Norman. They won't have another 15-1 season. But if they get back to the playoffs, it likely will be because the offense (with Kelvin Benjamin this time) was able to keep the efficiency up, the turnovers down and continued to build halftime leads, forcing opponents to adjust against their will.

Strength of Schedule In Detail

True Strength of Schedule Rank: 29

Hardest Stretches (1=Hard, 32=Easy)
Hardest 3 wk Stretch Rk:	25
Hardest 4 wk Stretch Rk:	17
Hardest 5 wk Stretch Rk:	26

Easiest Stretches (1=Easy, 32=Hard)
Easiest 3 wk Stretch Rk:	18
Easiest 4 wk Stretch Rk:	11
Easiest 5 wk Stretch Rk:	14

The season starts off in a very difficult manner, but ends quite manageably. In fact, no team in the NFL has an easier last month of the season than the Panthers. But starting things off is a trip to Denver, and that won't be easy. Playing in Denver in the first couple weeks of the season is as tough as it gets. On the road, at altitude, teams off the long summer with starters who rest much of the preseason struggle: Denver is 27-3 (90%) the first two weeks at home since 1989, by far the best record in the NFL, and since 2000 they are 16-1 (94%). However, Carolina gets extra rest heading into their home opener, and are one of 8 teams this year to only play one back-to-back set of road games (wks 12 & 13 @ OAK and @ SEA). However, given both are on the West coast, it gives the Panthers the ideal option of staying out West between games. Additionally, the Panthers get extra rest (more than 6 days between games) six times this year, the most of any team in the NFL.

2015 Play Tendencies

All Pass %	51%
All Pass Rk	31
All Rush %	49%
All Rush Rk	2
1 Score Pass %	52%
1 Score Pass Rk	28
2014 1 Score Pass %	54%
2014 1 Score Pass Rk	25
Pass Increase %	-2%
Pass Increase Rk	26
1 Score Rush %	48%
1 Score Rush Rk	5
Up Pass %	47%
Up Pass Rk	20
Up Rush %	53%
Up Rush Rk	13
Down Pass %	57%
Down Pass Rk	32
Down Rush %	43%
Down Rush Rk	1

The Panthers ran and ran often. Whether they were up or down the Panthers were a run first team. They ran 2nd most in all situations, 5th most in 1 score games & the most of any team when trailing. In part, that is because they often were not trailing by 14+ points, so even when down, one score would pull them even or give them a lead. Part of that rushing offense came from Cam Newton, who had 132 carries and averaged 4.8 YPC.

2015 Offensive Advanced Metrics

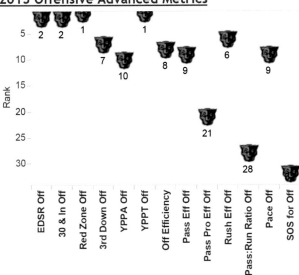

Rank

EDSR Off · 30 & In Off · Red Zone Off · 3rd Down Off · YPPA Off · YPPT Off · Off Efficiency · Pass Eff Off · Pass Pro Eff Off · Rush Eff Off · Pass:Run Ratio Off · Pace Off · SOS for Off

One goal of this publication is to provide information that is absorbed not just from black and white numbers, but visually using relative perspective, because many retain that information better. From thinking back to 2015, the immediate response for the Panthers would be a strong defensive team with an OK offense. That would be very wrong. The Panthers offense was ridiculously balanced, efficient, and strong. It was nearly unstoppable in the red zone, and Newton was magical passing to so many weaker receiving options. However, they did that damage against the NFL's weakest slate of opposing defenses. Defensively, they did go up against weaker offenses (26th) but were at their best against the pass, which really helped them when they were playing in the 2nd half with a lead. The Panthers were #2 in EDSR offense and #3 in EDSR defense. They were the only team inside the top 3 in that key metric.

2015 Defensive Advanced Metrics

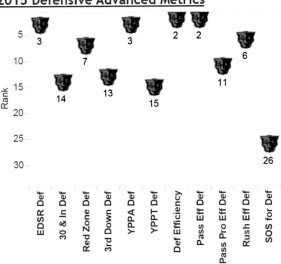

Rank

EDSR Def · 30 & In Def · Red Zone Def · 3rd Down Def · YPPA Def · YPPT Def · Def Efficiency · Pass Eff Def · Pass Pro Eff Def · Rush Eff Def · SOS for Def

Carolina Panthers

| Drafted Players | | **2016 Draft Grade: #32 (2.0/4)** | | | **PERSONNEL & SPENDING** |

Drafted Players

Rnd.	Pick #	Pos.	Player	College
1	30	DT	Vernon Butler	Louisiana Tech
2	62	CB	James Bradberry	Samford
3	77	CB	Daryl Worley	West Virginia
5	141	CB	Zack Sanchez	Oklahoma
7	252	TE	Beau Sandland	Montana State

Free Agents/Trades Added

Player (Position)
Brandon Boykin CB
Charles Johnson DE
Gino Gradkowski C
Paul Soliai NT
Trenton Robinson S

Other Signed

Player (Position)
Andrew Bonnet TE
Braxton Deaver TE
Devon Johnson RB
Jake McGee TE
Jalen Simmons RB
Jared Barber LB
Jared Norris LB
Jenson Stoshak WR
Jeremy Cash LB
Jordan Rigsbee T
Keyarris Garrett WR
Miles Shuler WR
Shaq Richardson CB

2015 Players Lost

Transaction	Player (Position)
Cut	Bonnet, Andrew RB
	Brandon Boykin CB
	Charles Johnson DE
	Dwan Edwards DT
	Jenson Stoshak WR
	McGee, Jake TE
	Nate Chandler T
	Ras-I Dowling S
Declared Free Agent	Brad Nortman P
	Josh Norman CB
Retired	Jared Allen DE

- The Panthers drafted only 5 players, and three were cornerbacks. It could prove to be a really smart move, or a terrible one. Multiple very smart talent evaluators raved about the depth in this CB class, which is why many teams drafted multiple DBs. Chicago, Arizona, Kansas City, Tennessee and San Francisco all drafted 3, the entire AFC North except the Ravens drafted 2 apiece, and the number of other teams which drafted two DBs is massive.
- Obviously without many picks, drafting 3 CBs limits who else you can bring in. The team is also not going to spend a lot in free agency, as GM Dave Gettleman avoids at all costs, and ended up losing CB Josh Norman to the Redskins. Apart from Norman, however, the team didn't lose a lot.
- So the clear plan is simply to rinse and repeat, doing so without Norman. Clearly his loss could mean the secondary is worse in 2016, which means more opponent success. If that is the case, the offense will need to do more, but they will be ready:
- The Panthers get their best WR, Kelvin Benjamin back, who missed the entire 2015 season. It will provide yet another red zone threat and a more reliable threat downfield apart from primarily TE Greg Olsen. His presence will make the run game even better, in addition to the times when Cam Newton keeps the ball and takes on the secondary himself.
- Gettleman worked some serious magic with Charles Johnson. Carolina drafted Johnson and signed him to a 4 year, $2.375M deal. When the deal ended, they broke the bank, paying him $76M over 6 years. His $20M cap number last year did not match his performance, so instead of paying him $15M against the cap this year, the Panthers cut him with 1 year remaining on his contract. But they remarkably were able to re-sign him after cutting him, and only pay him a base salary of $2M, and his cap hit is over $12M less in 2016 than it would have been with his prior deal.

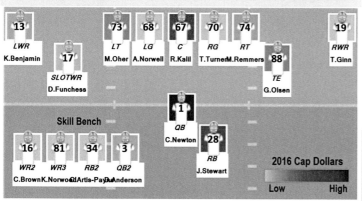

Lineup & 2016 Cap Hit

FS K.Coleman 20
SS T.Boston 33
LB T.Davis 58
LB L.Kuechly 59
RCB B.Benwikere 25
SLOTCB J.Bradberry Rookie
DE K.Ealy 24
DT K.Short 94
DT S.Lotulelei 99
DT 98
DE C.Johnson 95
LCB R.McClain 27
13
LWR K.Benjamin 17
SLOTWR D.Funchess
LT M.Oher 73
LG A.Norwell 68
C R.Kalil 67
RG T.Turner 70
RT M.Remmers 74
TE G.Olsen 88
RWR T.Ginn 19
QB C.Newton 1
RB J.Stewart 28

Skill Bench
WR2 C.Brown 16
WR3 K.Norwood 81
RB2 C.Artis-Payne 34
QB2 D.Anderson 3

2016 Cap Dollars Low — High

Health Overall & by Unit (2015 v 2014)

2015 Rk	4
2015 AGL	51
Off Rk	14
Def Rk	8
2014 Rk	6
2014 AGL	51

2016 Positional Spending

	All OFF	QB	OL	RB	WR	TE	All DEF	DL	LB	CB	S
2015 Rk	9	14	14	2	28	10	18	4	13	31	27
Rank	13	12	19	2	25	9	32	20	17	30	25
Total	81.1M	21.5M	25.5M	11.8M	13.1M	9.2M	50.0M	18.9M	18.9M	5.8M	6.4M

2016 Offseason Spending

Total Spent	Total Spent Rk	Free Agents #	Free Agents $	Free Agents $ Rk	Waiver #	Waiver $	Waiver $ Rk	Extended #	Sum of Extended $	Sum of Drafted $	Undrafted #	Undrafted $
115M	27	7	13M	31	21	13M	17	5	49M	21M	12	19M

2015 Stats & Fantasy Production

Pos	Player	Ov. Rank	Pos. Rk	Age	Gms	St	Pass Comp	Pass Att	Pass Yds	Pass TD	Pass Int	Rush Att	Rush Yds	Rush YPA	Rush TD	Targ	Recp	Rec Yds	Rec YPC	Rec TDs	Draft King Pts	Fan Duel Pts
QB	Cam Newton*+	5	1	26	16	16	296	496	3,837	35	10	132	636	5	10						409	399
RB	Jonathan Stewart*	47	16	28	13	13						242	989	4	6	21	16	99	6	1	168	155
	Mike Tolbert*+		57	30	16	3						62	256	4	1	23	18	154	9	3	89	74
	Cameron Artis-Payne		84	25	7							45	183	4	1	5	5	58	12		38	33
	Fozzy Whittaker		96	26	15	1						25	108	4	1	15	12	64	5		38	29
WR	Ted Ginn	59	26	30	15	13						4	60	15		97	44	739	17	10	187	162
	Devin Funchess		59	21	16	5										63	31	473	15	5	91	91
	Corey Brown	63	24	14	11							6	38	6		54	31	447	14	4	107	88
	Jerricho Cotchery	67	33	14	3							1	16	16		54	39	485	12	3	110	88
TE	Greg Olsen*	18	4	30	16	16										124	77	1,104	14	7	231	189
	Ed Dickson		47	28	16	11										26	17	121	7	2	50	39

70

ODDS & TRENDS — Carolina Panthers

Avg Line	Pred Wins	Pred Div Finish
-5.1	10.5	#1

2016 Weekly Betting Lines (wks 1-16)

(-) Favorite   Underdog (+)
-11.5   +3.0

Avg Line = -5.1

Wk	Site	Line
1	A	+1.5
2	H	-11.5
3	H	-5.5
4	A	-3.5
5	H	-10.0
6	A	-4.5
8		-3.5
9	A	-3.5
10	H	-4.5
11	H	-10.0
12		-3.0
13	A	+3.0
14	H	-10.0
15	A	-3.0
16	H	-8.5

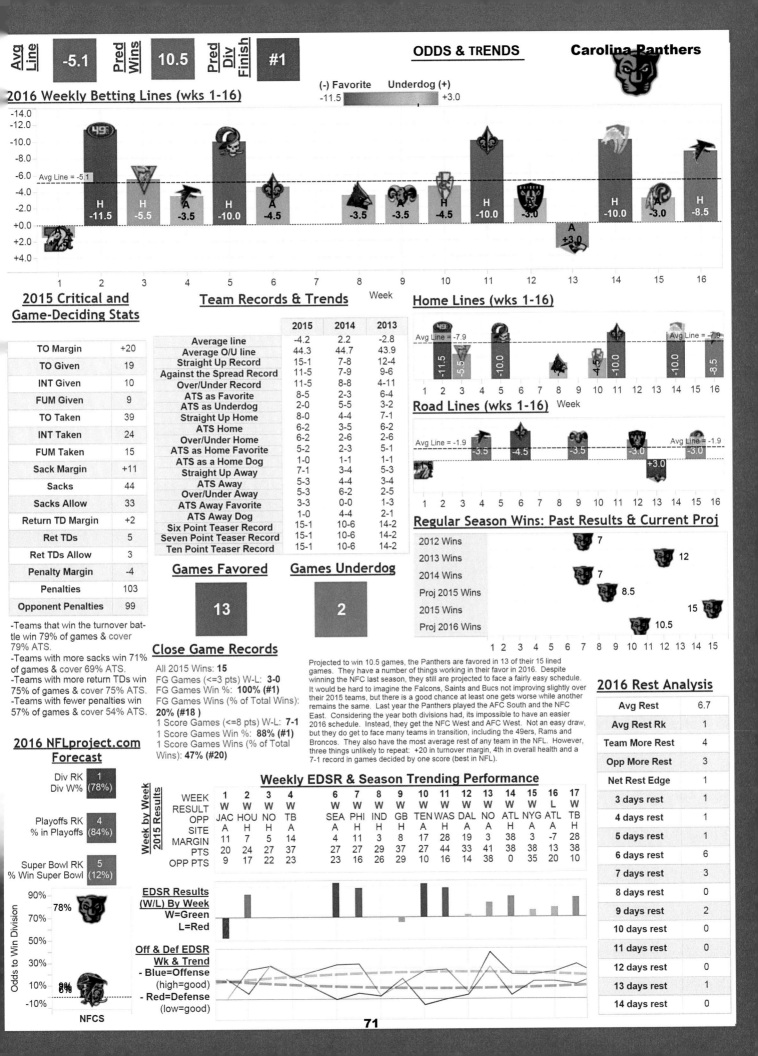

2015 Critical and Game-Deciding Stats

TO Margin	+20
TO Given	19
INT Given	10
FUM Given	9
TO Taken	39
INT Taken	24
FUM Taken	15
Sack Margin	+11
Sacks	44
Sacks Allow	33
Return TD Margin	+2
Ret TDs	5
Ret TDs Allow	3
Penalty Margin	-4
Penalties	103
Opponent Penalties	99

-Teams that win the turnover battle win 79% of games & cover 79% ATS.
-Teams with more sacks win 71% of games & cover 69% ATS.
-Teams with more return TDs win 75% of games & cover 75% ATS.
-Teams with fewer penalties win 57% of games & cover 54% ATS.

2016 NFLproject.com Forecast

Div RK	1	
Div W%		(78%)
Playoffs RK	4	
% in Playoffs		(84%)
Super Bowl RK	5	
% Win Super Bowl		(12%)

Odds to Win Division

78%

8% 8%

NFCS

Team Records & Trends

	2015	2014	2013
Average line	-4.2	2.2	-2.8
Average O/U line	44.3	44.7	43.9
Straight Up Record	15-1	7-8	12-4
Against the Spread Record	11-5	7-9	9-6
Over/Under Record	11-5	8-8	4-11
ATS as Favorite	8-5	2-3	6-4
ATS as Underdog	2-0	5-5	3-2
Straight Up Home	8-0	4-4	7-1
ATS Home	6-2	3-5	6-2
Over/Under Home	6-2	2-6	2-6
ATS as Home Favorite	5-2	2-3	5-1
ATS as a Home Dog	1-0	1-1	1-1
Straight Up Away	7-1	3-4	5-3
ATS Away	5-3	4-4	3-4
Over/Under Away	5-3	6-2	2-5
ATS Away Favorite	3-3	0-0	1-3
ATS Away Dog	1-0	4-4	2-1
Six Point Teaser Record	15-1	10-6	14-2
Seven Point Teaser Record	15-1	10-6	14-2
Ten Point Teaser Record	15-1	10-6	14-2

Games Favored

13

Games Underdog

2

Close Game Records

All 2015 Wins: **15**
FG Games (<=3 pts) W-L: **3-0**
FG Games Wins (% of Total Wins): **20% (#18)**
1 Score Games (<=8 pts) W-L: **7-1**
1 Score Games Win %: **88% (#1)**
1 Score Games Wins (% of Total Wins): **47% (#20)**

Projected to win 10.5 games, the Panthers are favored in 13 of their 15 lined games. They have a number of things working in their favor in 2016. Despite winning the NFC last season, they still are projected to face a fairly easy schedule. It would be hard to imagine the Falcons, Saints and Bucs not improving slightly over their 2015 teams, but there is a good chance at least one gets worse while another remains the same. Last year the Panthers played the AFC South and the NFC East. Considering the year both divisions had, its impossible to have an easier 2016 schedule. Instead, they get the NFC West and AFC West. Not an easy draw, but they do get to face many teams in transition, including the 49ers, Rams and Broncos. They also have the most average rest of any team in the NFL. However, three things unlikely to repeat: +20 in turnover margin, 4th in overall health and a 7-1 record in games decided by one score (best in NFL).

Home Lines (wks 1-16)

Avg Line = -7.9

Wk	Line
2	-11.5
3	-5.5
5	-10.0
8	
10	-4.5
11	-10.0
14	-10.0
16	-8.5

Road Lines (wks 1-16)

Avg Line = -1.9

Wk	Line
4	-3.5
6	-4.5
9	-3.5
12	-3.0
13	+3.0
15	-3.0

Regular Season Wins: Past Results & Current Proj

	Wins
2012 Wins	7
2013 Wins	12
2014 Wins	7
Proj 2015 Wins	8.5
2015 Wins	15
Proj 2016 Wins	10.5

2016 Rest Analysis

Avg Rest	6.7
Avg Rest Rk	1
Team More Rest	4
Opp More Rest	3
Net Rest Edge	1
3 days rest	1
4 days rest	1
5 days rest	1
6 days rest	6
7 days rest	3
8 days rest	0
9 days rest	2
10 days rest	0
11 days rest	0
12 days rest	0
13 days rest	1
14 days rest	0

Weekly EDSR & Season Trending Performance

WEEK	1	2	3	4	6	7	8	9	10	11	12	13	14	15	16	17
RESULT	W	W	W	W	W	W	W	W	W	W	W	W	W	W	L	W
OPP	JAC	HOU	NO	TB	SEA	PHI	IND	GB	TEN	WAS	DAL	NO	ATL	NYG	ATL	TB
SITE	A	A	H	H	A	H	H	H	A	H	A	H	A	H	A	H
MARGIN	11	7	5	14	4	11	3	8	17	28	19	3	38	3	-7	28
PTS	20	24	27	37	27	27	29	37	27	44	33	41	38	38	13	38
OPP PTS	9	17	22	23	23	16	26	29	10	16	14	38	0	35	20	10

EDSR Results (W/L) By Week
W=Green
L=Red

Off & Def EDSR Wk & Trend
- Blue=Offense (high=good)
- Red=Defense (low=good)

Week by Week 2015 Results

STATS & VISUALIZATIONS

Carolina Panthers

Directional Passer Rating Achieved

Receiver	Short Left	Short Middle	Short Right	Deep Left	Deep Middle	Deep Right
Greg Olsen	67	110	110	154	109	117
Ted Ginn	88	119	87	56	28	125
Jerricho Cotchery	95	102	113	109	0	149
Corey Brown	84	93	92	158	127	70
Devin Funchess	112	63	85	47	89	95
Ed Dickson	113	78	92	118		0
Brenton Bersin	118	118	74			
Scott Simonson	108					
Kevin Norwood					0	

Directional Frequency by Receiver

Receiver	Short Left	Short Middle	Short Right	Deep Left	Deep Middle	Deep Right
Greg Olsen	24%	40%	33%	28%	19%	22%
Ted Ginn	27%	11%	13%	41%	29%	16%
Jerricho Cotchery	12%	19%	15%	6%	10%	12%
Corey Brown	9%	4%	19%	11%	16%	35%
Devin Funchess	19%	13%	11%	13%	23%	4%
Ed Dickson	4%	10%	7%	2%		10%
Brenton Bersin	4%	3%	2%			
Scott Simonson	1%					
Kevin Norwood					3%	

Defense Passer Rating Allowed

Short Left	Short Middle	Short Right	Deep Left	Deep Middle	Deep Right
79	62	76	54	74	76

Offensive Rush Directional Yds/Carry

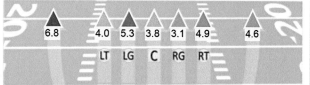

6.8	4.0	5.3	3.8	3.1	4.9	4.6
	LT	LG	C	RG	RT	

Offensive Rush Frequency of Direction

69	65	83	181	64	56	88
	LT	LG	C	RG	RT	

Offensive Explosive Runs by Direction

17	7	7	18	3	11	17
	LT	LG	C	RG	RT	

Defensive Rush Directional Yds/Carry

3.9	3.6	3.5	4.1	3.6	3.7	5.2
	LT	LG	C	RG	RT	

Cam Newton - 1st Down RTG

Cam Newton - 2nd Down RTG

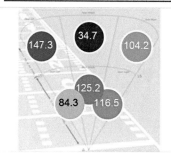

Cam Newton - 3rd Down RTG

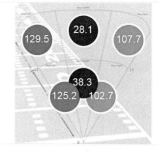

Cam Newton - Overall RTG

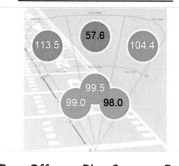

2nd & Short RUN (1D or not)

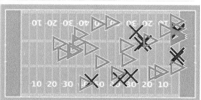

2nd & Short RUN Stats

Run Conv Rk	1D% Run	NFL 1D% Run Avg	Run Freq	NFL Run Freq Avg
15	70%	69%	77%	64%

2nd & Short PASS (1D or not)

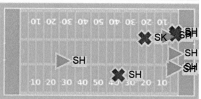

2nd & Short PASS Stats

Pass Conv Rk	1D% Pass	NFL 1D% Pass Avg	Pass Freq	NFL Pass Freq Avg
13	56%	55%	23%	36%

Pass Offense Play Success Rate

58%	47%	60%	48%	54%
57%	50%	61%	55%	37%
37%	44%	60%	42%	61%

Pass Offense Yds/Play

11.5	8.0	8.1	7.4	5.6
12.5	9.2	9.6	9.1	4.4
5.8	8.4	8.9	6.3	5.8

Off. Directional Tendency
(% of Plays Left, Middle or Right)

46%	41%	44%	42%	45%
17%	22%	15%	15%	25%
37%	37%	40%	42%	30%

Off. Directional Pass Rate
(% of Plays which are Passes)

59%	70%	74%	65%	56%
18%	32%	23%	26%	23%
55%	64%	71%	65%	42%

Atlanta Falcons

Coaches
Head Coach: Dan Quinn (2nd yr)
OC: Kyle Shanahan (2nd yr)
DC: Richard Smith (2nd yr)

Forecast
2016 Wins
7

Past Records
2015: 8-8
2014: 6-10
2013: 4-12

Opponent Strength
Easy — Hard

2016 Schedule & Week by Week Strength of Schedule

H	A	H	A	H	A	A	H	A	A		H	H	A	H	A	H
1	2	3	4	5	6	7	8	9	10	11	12	13	14	15	16	17

(MNF at wk 2) (THU at wk 9) (SAT at wk 16)

2016 Overview

Typically teams with significant injuries fall apart late in the season. The Falcons fell apart but still finished 8-8. They didn't fall apart due to injuries however. On the contrary, the team was the 2nd healthiest offense, 5th healthiest defense and 2nd overall after ranking 25th in team health in 2014. Despite their health, the Falcons closed the season 3-8 (after starting 5-0), averaging 16 ppg and winning their 3 games by just 3, 6 and 7 points over the 3-13 Titans, the 5-11 Jaguars and (shockingly) the 15-1 Panthers.

But the reality of their 5-0 start included an overtime win and two wins by 2 and 4 points over the 7-9 Eagles and 6-10 Giants. And the Falcons offense went up against the 3rd easiest schedule of opposing defenses and their defense faced the 6th easiest schedule of opposing offenses. Despite that, many of their metrics (both offensive and defensive) were well below average.

So where do the Falcons turn in 2016? Unfortunately, they turn to the mirror & look for improvement vs a more difficult schedule in a season which should see health regression with more games lost due to injury.

Years ago, the Falcons hitched their wagon to Matt Ryan, who will hit the cap this year for $23.75M, fourth largest hit this season. Landing a legitimate franchise QB is great in their rookie contract, when cap hits are reasonable. Ryan's rookie deal ended in 2012, in the 3rd of 10+ win seasons and trips to the playoffs. Since re-signing with the Falcons, Atlanta hasn't had a winning season and thanks to his cap hit, the Falcons are now spending the 2nd most on the QB position of any team this year.

Re-signing a legitimate franchise QB can work if his performance is equivalent to his pay, such as Ben Roethlisberger or Aaron Rodgers or Tom Brady. But with Matt Ryan no longer being in his rookie deal and performing at a level far below his pay, the Falcons are stretched seriously thin in their ability to build a competitive roster. Particularly when Julio Jones occupies $16M in cap space.

Matt Ryan must improve in 2016 against more difficult defenses for the Falcons to continue the year over year improvement they've posted after a dismal 2013 season. The Julio Jones dominant pass offense, while great for fantasy stats, is far too predictable. Kyle Shanahan was wise to try to employ the run more in 2015 than it was used in 2014, but situationally Shanahan should employ it even more in 2016. For instance, Atlanta converted 25% more often on 2nd and short runs than passes, yet called passes on these plays well above the NFL average.

While they must get Matt Ryan to step up his performance to the level his cap hit necessitates, the pass defense also must improve. And for the Falcons, that starts up front and they largely did nothing to address a glaring weakness which landed them dead last in for 2015: pass rush efficiency. Dan Quinn must get this unit to play substantially better, and unfortunately, they'll have to play better on the road in primetime against the Saints, Bucs and Panthers (with multiple games on short weeks). Atlanta is 0-4 the last 3 years on the road in Primetime, and is 1-10 their last 11.

Strength of Schedule In Detail

True Strength of Schedule Rank: 3

Hardest Stretches *(1=Hard, 32=Easy)*
Hardest 3 wk Stretch Rk:	2
Hardest 4 wk Stretch Rk:	5
Hardest 5 wk Stretch Rk:	3

Easiest Stretches *(1=Easy, 32=Hard)*
Easiest 3 wk Stretch Rk:	31
Easiest 4 wk Stretch Rk:	28
Easiest 5 wk Stretch Rk:	29

Atlanta similarly has three sets of back-to-back road games occurring within the first 10 weeks of the season, and like the Jets, two games on the road involve primetime games (wk 3 @ NO, wk 9 @ TB on Thursday). Absolutely no team has a worse October than the Falcons, who take on the Panthers, Seahawks and Packers from the NFC as well as the Broncos during the month of October. The Falcons will have the option to stay on the West coast for their back-to-backs at Denver and at Seattle, but that falls in as part of the 2nd worst three week stretch this year.

2015 Play Tendencies

All Pass %	61%
All Pass Rk	15
All Rush %	39%
All Rush Rk	18
1 Score Pass %	61%
1 Score Pass Rk	10
2014 1 Score Pass %	64%
2014 1 Score Pass Rk	1
Pass Increase %	-4%
Pass Increase Rk	28
1 Score Rush %	39%
1 Score Rush Rk	23
Up Pass %	49%
Up Pass Rk	15
Up Rush %	51%
Up Rush Rk	18
Down Pass %	67%
Down Pass Rk	21
Down Rush %	33%
Down Rush Rk	12

The 8-8 Falcons passed the ball approximately 60% of play calls in neutral situations, essentially the NFL average, but with Devonta Freeman leading the charge on the ground, Atlanta ran more frequently than they did in 2014. Unlike years past, when trailing, the Falcons didn't go pass-crazy, passing 21st most often. Unfortunately, they were balancing between the 23rd ranked pass offense & the 25th ranked rush offense.

2015 Offensive Advanced Metrics

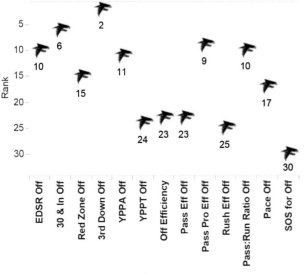

Atlanta was one of the most variant team when it came to EDSR offense vs defense. Considering they were 9th in pass protection efficiency, the fact they were just 23rd in pass efficiency speaks to the predictability of their pass game. Additionally, if it wasn't for the 10th rated EDSR offense coupled with the top rated 3rd down offense & facing the 30th rated opposing defenses, there would have been no way Atlanta would have produced in 2015.

HC Dan Quinn certainly will be focusing on the defense in 2016, as they finished 31st in EDSR last year and 32nd in pass rush efficiency. And keep in mind all of these defensive numbers came against the 27th rated opposing offensive schedule. That schedule will get significantly harder in 2016, given that they will face ARI, GB and SEA instead of the AFC South and the injured/struggling offenses of the NFC East last year.

2015 Defensive Advanced Metrics

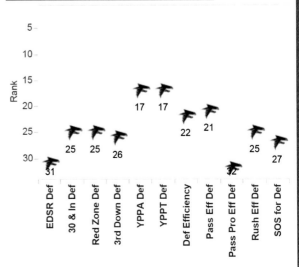

73

Drafted Players   2016 Draft Grade: #31 (2.1/4)   PERSONNEL & SPENDING   Atlanta Falcons

Rnd.	Pick #	Pos.	Player	College
1	17	S	Keanu Neal	Florida
2	52	LB	Deion Jones	LSU
3	81	TE	Austin Hooper	Stanford
4	115	OLB	De'Vondre Campbell	Minnesota
6	195	G	Wes Schweitzer	San Jose State
7	238	WR	Devin Fuller	UCLA

Free Agents/Trades Added

Player (Position)
Alex Mack C
Courtney Upshaw LB
Derrick Shelby DE
LaRoy Reynolds LB
Matt Schaub QB
Mohamed Sanu WR
Sean Weatherspoon LB
Tom Compton T

Other Signed

Player (Position)
Alex Fifita T
Brandon Wilds RB
Brandon Williams DE
Brian Poole S
Chris Mayes NT
Cody Elenz T
Cory Johnson DT
Daje Johnson WR
David Glidden WR
David Mims II CB
David Richards WR
Devonte Johnson CB
Gerald Dixon Jr. DT
Ivan McLennan LB
J.D. McKissic WR
Jake Reed C
Jordan Sefon LB
Josh Dawson DE
Joshua Perkins TE
Malachi Jones WR
Nick Rose K
Shahbaz Ahmed G
Sharrod Neasman S
Torrey Green LB
Will Ratelle RB

2015 Players Lost

Transaction	Player (Position)
Cut	Adam Replogle G
	Alex Fifita T
	Beau Gardner TE
	Collin Mooney RB
	David Richards WR
	Elenz, Cody T
	Gerald Dixon Jr. DT
	Justin Durant LB
	Malachi Jones WR
	Paul Soliai NT
	Roddy White WR
	Travis Howard CB
	William Moore S
Declared Free Agent	Gino Gradkowski C

- Gone is Matt Ryan's oldest, most reliable target of Roddy White. For anyone who watched 2015, there was literally zero production from WRs outside of Roddy White and Julio Jones. In fact, first and 2nd down was basically the Julio Jones show when Matt Ryan dropped back to pass:
- Well over 60% of all passes 15+ yards in the air went to Julio Jones, while 45% of passes within 15 yards of the line of scrimmage went to Julio Jones.
- Matt Ryan struggled tremendously down field, posting a 74 rating on all passes traveling over 15 yards in the air, with 3 TD : 6 INT.
- The Falcons made the (unwise) move to bring in (and overpay) Mohamed Sanu from the Bengals in free agency, but apart from that, nothing was done to provide targets other than drafting TE Austin Hooper in the 3rd round and WR Devin Fuller in the 7th round. And it's not as if they suffered injures to the receiving corps in 2015 and will get players back in 2016: the team was the 2nd healthiest offense of 2015.
- The offense also saw by far the healthiest offensive line of any team last season, which helped provide the protection for Ryan, so its impossible for that health to be better in 2016 thus the protection isn't likely to be substantially improved. Rather, its more likely to regress and Ryan will be under more pressure.
- In the first 5 rounds of the draft, the Falcons took 3 defensive players and 1 offensive player (Austin Hooper).
- Atlanta also brought in C Alex Mack (huge upgrade, as his $45M deal suggests) and T Tom Compton, so the team is focused on keeping Matt Ryan upright & letting him chuck the ball to Julio Jones while sprinkling in targets to Sanu and his young draft picks.
- Atlanta is spending the 2nd most of any team to the QB position in 2016, and the 3rd most to the WR position. Meanwhile, their defense amounts to the 2nd least paid in the NFL as ATL tries to balance the cap around Matt Ryan's huge contract.

Lineup & 2016 Cap Hit

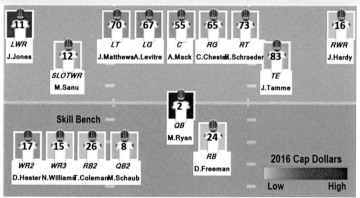

2016 Cap Dollars — Low → High

Health Overall & by Unit (2015 v 2014)

2015 Rk	2
2015 AGL	29
Off Rk	2
Def Rk	5
2014 Rk	25
2014 AGL	94

2016 Positional Spending

	All OFF	QB	OL	RB	WR	TE	All DEF	DL	LB	CB	S
2015 Rk	12	5	28	30	3	29	30	12	32	27	19
Rank	5	2	17	32	3	21	31	10	29	27	29
Total	88.0M	26.8M	25.0M	2.9M	27.5M	5.9M	49.4M	22.3M	13.0M	7.9M	6.3M

2016 Offseason Spending

Total Spent	Total Spent Rk	Free Agents #	Free Agents $	Free Agents $ Rk	Waiver #	Waiver $	Waiver $ Rk	Extended #	Sum of Extended $	Sum of Drafted $	Undrafted #	Undrafted $
192M	15	15	117M	5	7	8M	24	0	0M	26M	25	41M

2015 Stats & Fantasy Production

Pos	Player	Ov. Rank	Pos. Rk	Age	Gms	St	Pass Comp	Pass Att	Pass Yds	Pass TD	Pass Int	Rush Att	Rush Yds	Rush YPA	Rush TD	Targ	Recp	Rec Yds	Rec YPC	Rec TDs	Draft King Pts	Fan Duel Pts
QB	Matt Ryan		19	30	16	16	407	614	4,591	21	16	37	63	2							256	248
RB	Devonta Freeman*	2	1	23	15	13						265	1,056	4	11	97	73	578	8	3	324	280
	Tevin Coleman		76	22	12	3						87	392	5	1	11	2	14	7		49	42
	Patrick DiMarco*		97	26	16	8						1				17	13	110	8	2	39	30
	Terron Ward		98	23	13							29	95	3	1	13	9	73	8		32	27
WR	Julio Jones*+	3	2	26	16	16										203	136	1,871	14	8	379	307
	Roddy White		82	34	16	16										70	43	506	12	1	103	78
	Nick Williams		112	25	14											25	17	159	9	2	48	36
	Justin Hardy		132	24	9	1										36	21	194	9		43	30
TE	Jacob Tamme		18	30	15	8										81	59	657	11	1	134	101

Avg Line	+2.4	Pred Wins	7	Pred Div Finish	#2

ODDS & TRENDS

Atlanta Falcons

2016 Weekly Betting Lines (wks 1-16)

(-) Favorite   Underdog (+)
-5.0 ... +10.0

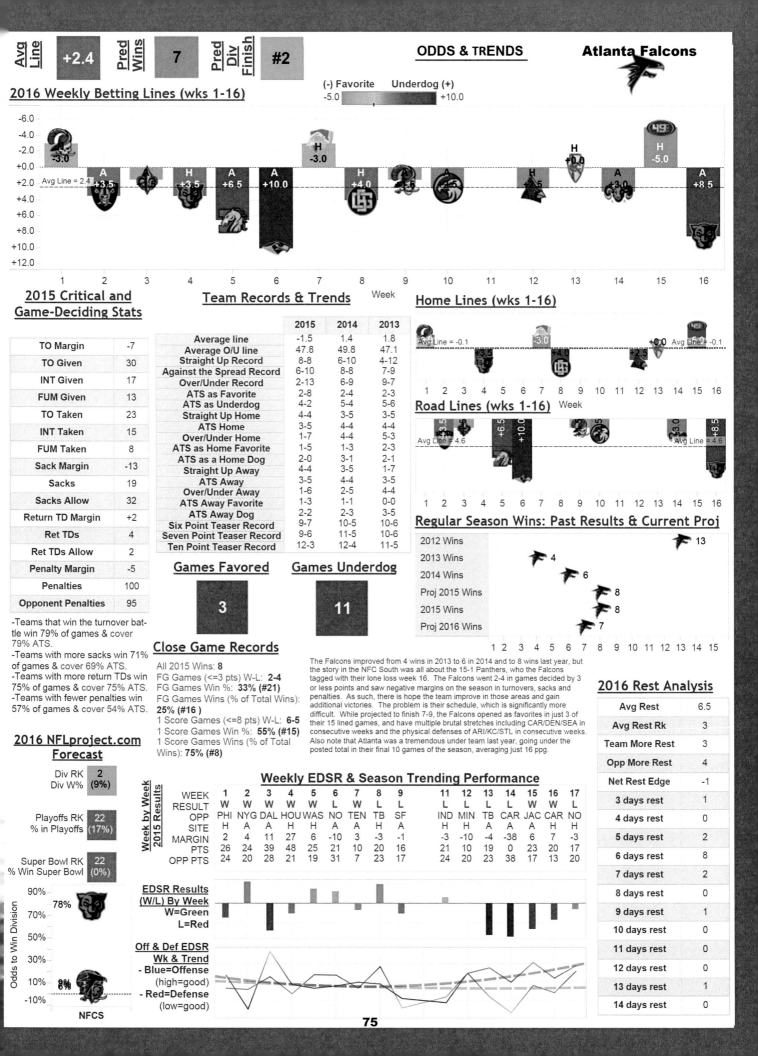

Week: 1 2 3 4 5 6 7 8 9 10 11 12 13 14 15 16

2015 Critical and Game-Deciding Stats

TO Margin	-7
TO Given	30
INT Given	17
FUM Given	13
TO Taken	23
INT Taken	15
FUM Taken	8
Sack Margin	-13
Sacks	19
Sacks Allow	32
Return TD Margin	+2
Ret TDs	4
Ret TDs Allow	2
Penalty Margin	-5
Penalties	100
Opponent Penalties	95

-Teams that win the turnover battle win 79% of games & cover 79% ATS.
-Teams with more sacks win 71% of games & cover 69% ATS.
-Teams with more return TDs win 75% of games & cover 75% ATS.
-Teams with fewer penalties win 57% of games & cover 54% ATS.

2016 NFLproject.com Forecast

Div RK	2
Div W%	(9%)

Playoffs RK	22
% in Playoffs	(17%)

Super Bowl RK	22
% Win Super Bowl	(0%)

Odds to Win Division
90%
78%
70%
50%
30%
10% 8% 8%
-10%
NFCS

Team Records & Trends

	2015	2014	2013
Average line	-1.5	1.4	1.8
Average O/U line	47.8	49.8	47.1
Straight Up Record	8-8	6-10	4-12
Against the Spread Record	6-10	8-8	7-9
Over/Under Record	2-13	6-9	9-7
ATS as Favorite	2-8	2-4	2-3
ATS as Underdog	4-2	5-4	5-6
Straight Up Home	4-4	3-5	3-5
ATS Home	3-5	4-4	4-4
Over/Under Home	1-7	4-4	5-3
ATS as Home Favorite	1-5	1-3	2-3
ATS as a Home Dog	2-0	3-1	2-1
Straight Up Away	4-4	3-5	1-7
ATS Away	3-5	4-4	3-5
Over/Under Away	1-6	2-5	4-4
ATS Away Favorite	1-3	1-1	0-0
ATS Away Dog	2-2	2-3	3-5
Six Point Teaser Record	9-7	10-5	10-6
Seven Point Teaser Record	9-6	11-5	10-6
Ten Point Teaser Record	12-3	12-4	11-5

Games Favored

3

Games Underdog

11

Close Game Records

All 2015 Wins: 8
FG Games (<=3 pts) W-L: 2-4
FG Games Win %: 33% (#21)
FG Games Wins (% of Total Wins): 25% (#16)
1 Score Games (<=8 pts) W-L: 6-5
1 Score Games Win %: 55% (#15)
1 Score Games Wins (% of Total Wins): 75% (#8)

Home Lines (wks 1-16)

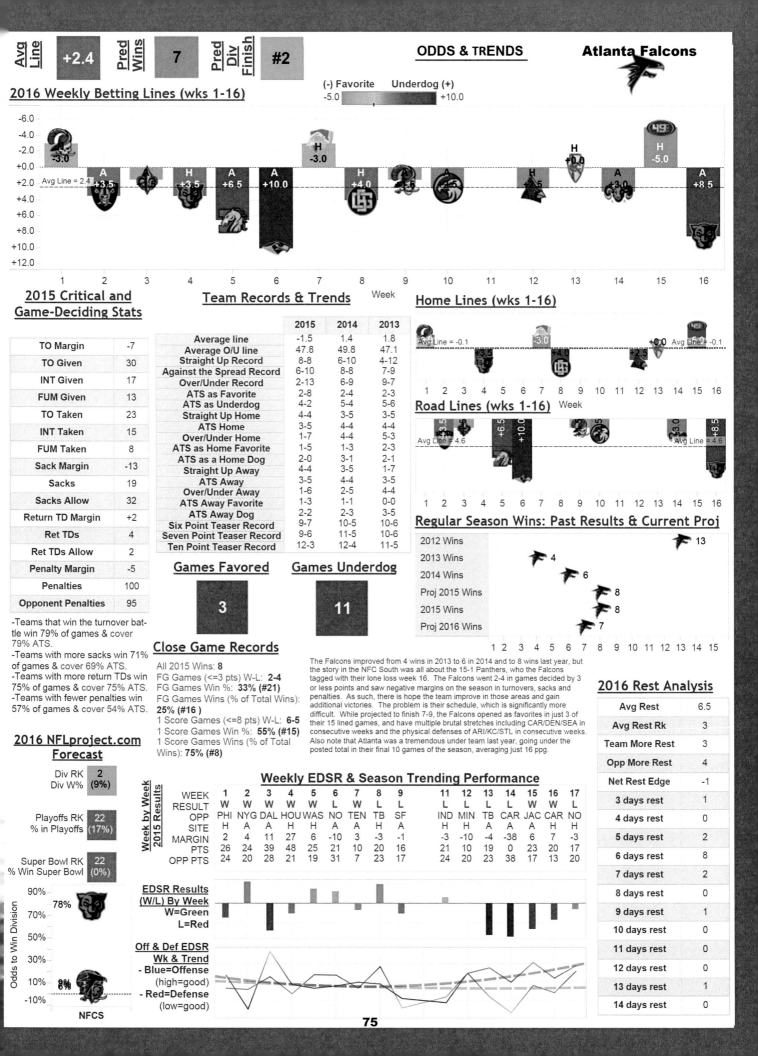

Avg Line = -0.1
1 2 3 4 5 6 7 8 9 10 11 12 13 14 15 16

Road Lines (wks 1-16) Week

Avg Line = 4.6
1 2 3 4 5 6 7 8 9 10 11 12 13 14 15 16

Regular Season Wins: Past Results & Current Proj

2012 Wins	13
2013 Wins	4
2014 Wins	6
Proj 2015 Wins	8
2015 Wins	8
Proj 2016 Wins	7

1 2 3 4 5 6 7 8 9 10 11 12 13 14 15

The Falcons improved from 4 wins in 2013 to 6 in 2014 and to 8 wins last year, but the story in the NFC South was all about the 15-1 Panthers, who the Falcons tagged with their lone loss week 16. The Falcons went 2-4 in games decided by 3 or less points and saw negative margins on the season in turnovers, sacks and penalties. As such, there is hope the team improve in those areas and gain additional victories. The problem is their schedule, which is significantly more difficult. While projected to finish 7-9, the Falcons opened as favorites in just 3 of their 15 lined games, and have multiple brutal stretches including CAR/DEN/SEA in consecutive weeks and the physical defenses of ARI/KC/STL in consecutive weeks. Also note that Atlanta was a tremendous under team last year, going under the posted total in their final 10 games of the season, averaging just 16 ppg.

2016 Rest Analysis

Avg Rest	6.5
Avg Rest Rk	3
Team More Rest	3
Opp More Rest	4
Net Rest Edge	-1
3 days rest	1
4 days rest	0
5 days rest	2
6 days rest	8
7 days rest	2
8 days rest	0
9 days rest	1
10 days rest	0
11 days rest	0
12 days rest	0
13 days rest	1
14 days rest	0

Weekly EDSR & Season Trending Performance

WEEK	1	2	3	4	5	6	7	8	9		11	12	13	14	15	16	17
RESULT	W	W	W	W	W	L	W	L	L		L	L	L	L	W	W	L
OPP	PHI	NYG	DAL	HOU	WAS	NO	TEN	TB	SF		IND	MIN	TB	CAR	JAC	CAR	NO
SITE	H	A	A	A	H	A	H	A	H		H	H	A	A	H	A	H
MARGIN	2	4	11	27	6	-10	3	-3	-1		-3	-10	-4	-38	6	7	-3
PTS	26	24	39	48	25	21	10	20	16		21	10	19	0	23	20	17
OPP PTS	24	20	28	21	19	31	7	23	17		24	20	23	38	17	13	20

Week by Week 2015 Results

EDSR Results (W/L) By Week
W=Green
L=Red

Off & Def EDSR Wk & Trend
- Blue=Offense (high=good)
- Red=Defense (low=good)

75

STATS & VISUALIZATIONS

Atlanta Falcons

Directional Passer Rating Achieved

Receiver	Short Left	Short Middle	Short Right	Deep Left	Deep Middle	Deep Right
Julio Jones	103	86	102	108	80	158
Jacob Tamme	73	62	96	95	118	118
Roddy White	93	74	82	59	15	39
Leonard Hankerson	110	91	113	54	87	39
Justin Hardy	90	65	98		0	0
Nick Williams	97	60	133		0	39
Levine Toilolo	56	59	87	39		
Tony Moeaki	112	39	149			
Eric Weems	112					

Directional Frequency by Receiver

Receiver	Short Left	Short Middle	Short Right	Deep Left	Deep Middle	Deep Right
Julio Jones	43%	36%	41%	54%	57%	46%
Jacob Tamme	21%	19%	15%	11%	7%	8%
Roddy White	11%	15%	14%	24%	21%	8%
Leonard Hankerson	10%	12%	8%	8%	7%	8%
Justin Hardy	5%	12%	7%		4%	23%
Nick Williams	6%	2%	9%		4%	8%
Levine Toilolo	1%	3%	4%	3%		
Tony Moeaki	1%	1%	2%			
Eric Weems	1%					

Defense Passer Rating Allowed

Short Left	Short Middle	Short Right	Deep Left	Deep Middle	Deep Right
91	78	83	59	111	66

Offensive Rush Directional Yds/Carry

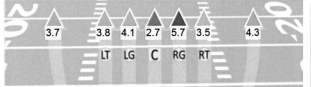
3.7 | 3.8 | 4.1 | 2.7 | 5.7 | 3.5 | 4.3
LT | LG | C | RG | RT

Offensive Rush Frequency of Direction

95 | 48 | 39 | 46 | 49 | 36 | 93

Offensive Explosive Runs by Direction

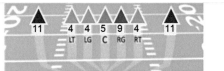
11 | 4 | 4 | 5 | 9 | 4 | 11
LT | LG | C | RG | RT

Defensive Rush Directional Yds/Carry

6.4 | 3.5 | 4.5 | 5.3 | 3.1 | 3.7 | 3.6
LT | LG | C | RG | RT

Matt Ryan - 1st Down RTG
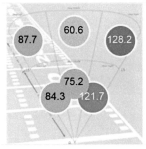

Matt Ryan - 3rd Down RTG
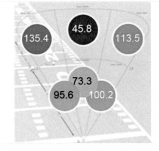

Matt Ryan - 2nd Down RTG
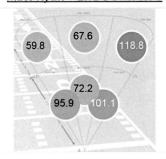

Matt Ryan - Overall RTG
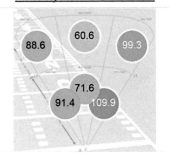

2nd & Short RUN (1D or not)
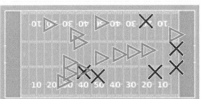

2nd & Short RUN Stats

Run Conv Rk	1D% Run	NFL 1D% Run Avg	Run Freq	NFL Run Freq Avg
17	68%	69%	58%	64%

2nd & Short PASS (1D or not)
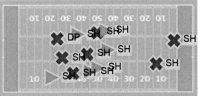

2nd & Short PASS Stats

Pass Conv Rk	1D% Pass	NFL 1D% Pass Avg	Pass Freq	NFL Pass Freq Avg
26	43%	55%	42%	36%

Pass Offense Play Success Rate

Pass Offense Yds/Play
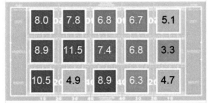

Off. Directional Tendency (% of Plays Left, Middle or Right)
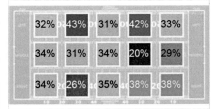

Off. Directional Pass Rate (% of Plays which are Passes)
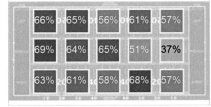

Tampa Bay Buccaneers

Coaches

Head Coach: Dirk Koetter (TB OC) (1st yr)
OC: Todd Monken (U. So. Miss HC) (1st yr)
DC: Mike Smith (ATL HC 2014) (1st yr)

Forecast 2016 Wins

7

Past Records

2015: 6-10
2014: 2-14
2013: 4-12

Opponent Strength
Easy — Hard

2016 Schedule & Week by Week Strength of Schedule

A	A	H	H	A		A	H	H	H	A	A	A	H	A	A	H
1	2	3	4	5	6	7	8	9	10	11	12	13	14	15	16	17

MNF (under 5) · THU (under 9) · SAT (under 15)

2016 Overview

The Buccaneers are one of the up and coming teams led by a young QB who is hoping to turn the fortunes of Tampa Bay around and up, out of the NFC South dungeon that they've occupied for the last 5 consecutive seasons. They gave Lovie Smith 2 years, equivalent to the time they gave Greg Schiano before him, and moved on to Dirk Koetter, their offensive coordinator from 2015.

Many recent NFL success stories have come with a young QB, on his inexpensive rookie deal, leading a balanced team to playoff success. Sure enough, the Buccaneers are not allocating much cap at all to their QB position in 2015 (26th most) so they can spend elsewhere. The NFL is a league where you can't simply buy performance. You can try, as Dan Snyder did for years in Washington, but you must build a team which plays like a team, with pieces that compliment one another and can cover up weaknesses for one another. It won't be shocking to Bucs fans to know that the most expensive 4 defenses in 2016 are the Jets, Jaguars, Seahawks and Broncos. The Jaguars are the team that stands out the most, but they made massive splashes in free agency on a huge scale, and needed to spend to exceed the salary cap floor. But it might be shocking for Bucs fans to know that before the Texans, who check in at #6 most expensive with their solid defense, are the #5 ranked Bucs.

It is a big jump from 2015, when they were just the 23rd most expensive defense. The Bucs defense has a lot of improving to do to live up to that type of price tag. Another positional unit with a lot of work to do is the wide receiver position. Most Tampa Bay fans know how solid Mike Evans has been for the Bucs. But apart from Evans, the Bucs have an oft-injured Vincent Jackson and little else. However, just ahead of the Packers, Cowboys and Steelers are the Bucs and their 8th most expensive wide receiver corps. The Buccaneers are also allocating the 5th most to the RB position in 2016.

In 2015, the Bucs had the 26th most expensive offense and the 23rd most expensive defense. They are spending significantly more relative to the NFL average and have moved up into the upper echelon. They are spending almost $160M cap dollars in 2016, the 4th most in the NFL behind only the Cardinals, Redskins and Packers, with the Vikings checking in 5th. The Bucs are spending like the up and coming team many believe they are. But it must translate onto the field.

If their 2015 games ended after 3 quarters, the Bucs would have been 7-9. They won 6 games, and 5 of the 6 wins were by one score or less. Their defense must play better in the 4th quarter: in one-score games they allowed 34% of all 4th quarter plays to result in a 1st down, 3rd worst in the NFL. Offensively, Jameis Winston's 4th quarter passer rating in one-score games of 78.6 was well below average. But the Bucs were tremendous on the ground last year. Between the 20s, the Bucs run game was the single most efficient run game in the NFL, with over 51% of their run plays being graded as successful plays. Their play calling was also strong, allowing the run game to play a large role in their offense, and situationally they were incredible: 77% of 2nd & short plays resulted in a first down, 4th best in the NFL, including 91% when the game was with one-score (NFL avg = 64%).

Strength of Schedule In Detail

True Strength of Schedule Rank: 6

Hardest Stretches (1=Hard, 32=Easy)
Hardest 3 wk Stretch Rk: **17**
Hardest 4 wk Stretch Rk: **10**
Hardest 5 wk Stretch Rk: **12**

Easiest Stretches (1=Easy, 32=Hard)
Easiest 3 wk Stretch Rk: **21**
Easiest 4 wk Stretch Rk: **14**
Easiest 5 wk Stretch Rk: **23**

Playing the AFC West and NFC West automatically gives the Buccaneers a tough draw, and because of their 4th place finish in the NFC South last year, they draw the Cowboys and Bears, both of which are poised to compensate for those poor 2015 seasons. The reality for Tampa Bay is their first 5 weeks (before their week 6 bye) is the 3rd most difficult start any team has this year, with games against the Cardinals, Broncos and Panthers. But from weeks 7 onward, their schedule is actually well easier than average.

2015 Play Tendencies

All Pass %	55%
All Pass Rk	24
All Rush %	45%
All Rush Rk	9
1 Score Pass %	53%
1 Score Pass Rk	26
2014 1 Score Pass %	57%
2014 1 Score Pass Rk	17
Pass Increase %	-4%
Pass Increase Rk	30
1 Score Rush %	47%
1 Score Rush Rk	7
Up Pass %	45%
Up Pass Rk	27
Up Rush %	55%
Up Rush Rk	6
Down Pass %	62%
Down Pass Rk	28
Down Rush %	38%
Down Rush Rk	5

The Bucs were a run heavy team, as to be expected when working in a rookie QB. They passed the ball 6% less often in one score games as compared to 2014, which was the 4th largest move toward the run in play calling of any team last year. Even when they trailed in games, the still only called 62% pass plays, 5th fewest in the NFL. It will be interesting to see what Dirk Koetter and Todd Monken try with Jameis Winston now in his 2nd year.

2015 Offensive Advanced Metrics

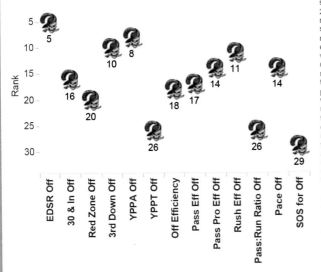

One thing to factor in when looing at Tampa was their schedule was extremely easy in 2015. So in some cases, the non-schedule adjusted metrics should be framed with that in mind. However, what was extremely impressive offensively was their 5th rated EDSR. Coupled with a solid 3rd down ranking, the team actually had the 13th most red zone attempts per game last year. But the team was not as strong in conversion rate, and coupled with 28 turnovers, as not as consistent as they needed to be in 2015. However, defensively the Bucs struggled immensely against a very easy schedule (30th rated). In early downs, 3rd downs and inside the red zone, they were one of the worst in the NFL. Defensively, from a pass rush and a run defense efficiency, they were strong, but in the key areas that account for preventing or allowing points, their defense fell short often. In the 1st through 3rd quarter, the Bucs allowed 48% conversions on 3rd down, worst in the NFL.

2015 Defensive Advanced Metrics

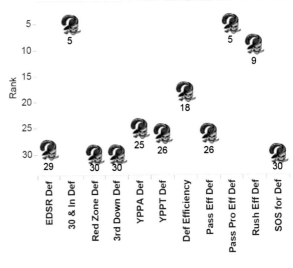

Drafted Players — 2016 Draft Grade: #27 (2.3/4)

Rnd.	Pick #	Pos.	Player	College
1	11	CB	Vernon Hargreaves	Florida
2	39	OLB	Noah Spence	Eastern Kentucky
2	59	K	Roberto Aguayo	Florida State
4	108	CB	Ryan Smith	North Carolina Central
5	148	OT	Caleb Benenoch	UCLA
6	183	OLB	Devante Bond	Oklahoma
6	197	FB	Dan Vitale	Northwestern

PERSONNEL & SPENDING

Free Agents/Trades Added

Player (Position)

Bryan Anger P

Daryl Smith LB

J.R. Sweezy G

Josh Robinson CB

Robert Ayers Jr. DE

Other Signed

Player (Position)

A.J. Francis DT
Alan Cross RB
Andre Davis WR
Anthony Kelly WR
Cassanova McKinzy LB
Channing Ward DE
DaVonte Lambert DT
Dez Stewart WR
Dominique Robertson G
Elijah Shumate S
Freddie Martino WR
Isaiah Johnson S
Jontavius Morris DT
Kelby Johnson T
Kivon Cartwright TE
Leonard Wester T
Luke Rhodes LB
Micah Awe LB
Peyton Barber RB
Russell Hansbrough RB
Taylor Fallin T
Tim Brown RB
Traveon Henry S
Travis Britz DT
Tyson Coleman LB

2015 Players Lost

Transaction	Player (Position)
Cut	Andre Davis WR
	Antoine Everett G
	Bruce Carter LB
	C.J. Roberts CB
	Connor Barth K
	Darius Eubanks LB
	Davon Coleman DT
	Derrick Lott DT
	Dez Stewart WR
	Gerod Holliman S
	Jermauria Rasco LB
	Jontavius Morris DT
	Kimario McFadden S
	Martin Ifedi DE
	Murray, Patrick K
	Tim Brown RB
	Traveon Henry S
	Tyson Coleman LB
Declared Free Agent	Bobby Rainey RB
Retired	Logan Mankins G
	Lowdermilk, John S

- Unfortunately the Bucs have the chance for their 2016 draft to be remembered for trading up into the 2nd round to draft a kicker. If Roberto Aguayo is a lights out kicker and deadly accurate from 48-56 yards, most skeptics will not carry the negative sentiment too far down the road. The issue always gets back to opportunity cost, and while Aguayo could be a good kicker, did the Bucs need to trade picks to move up to the 2nd round to draft him? Obviously its easy to argue that Aguayo could have more impact for the Bucs this year than the 11th overall selection of CB Vernon Hargreaves, but that doesn't mean you draft a kicker in the first round, so suggesting that he'll help the Bucs as much as much if not more than any other player they could have taken at 59 is an inefficient manner to study the marketplace.

- While some might look at the general advanced metrics and see the Bucs at 18th on overall defensive efficiency, 5th in pass rush and 9th in run defense, the more custom metrics I utilize showed they really needed help defensively. As such, they did not draft an offensive player until the 5th round, using 3 of their first 4 picks on the defensive side of the ball. In addition, the Bucs brought in help via free agency through DE Robert Ayers, LB Daryl Smith and CB Brent Grimes.

- Unfortunately, they didn't help their young QB much this offseason. The offensive line still needs serious work despite signing the veteran J.R. Sweezy, but he is there to replace the retired Logan Mankins, hence a piece to upgrade the 2015 line.

- The Bucs also have little to utilize in the passing game apart from the reliable Mike Evans. The Bucs two other best receivers from 2015 (Vincent Jackson and Austin Seferian-Jenkins) missed 15 games between them. And there is not much depth beyond that.

- On 3rd down, when Winston passed the ball 15+ yards downfield, his 10/28 for 225 yds, 0 TDs and 2 Ints equated to a 36 RTG, the NFL's worst.

Lineup & 2016 Cap Hit

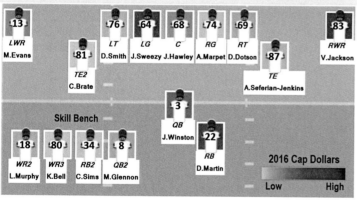

FS — C.Conte 23
SS — B.McDougald 30
LB — L.David 54
LB — K.Alexander 58
RCB — V.Hargreaves Rookie 28
SLOTCB — A.Verner 21
DE — R.Ayers 91
DT — C.McDonald 98
DT — G.McCoy 93
DE — N.Spence Rookie 57
LCB — B.Grimes 21

LWR — M.Evans 13
LT — D.Smith 76
LG — J.Sweezy 64
C — J.Hawley 68
RG — A.Marpet 74
RT — D.Dotson 69
RWR — V.Jackson 83
TE2 — C.Brate 81
TE — A.Seferian-Jenkins 87

QB — J.Winston 3
RB — D.Martin 22

Skill Bench
WR2 — L.Murphy 18
WR3 — K.Bell 80
RB2 — C.Sims 34
QB2 — M.Glennon 8

2016 Cap Dollars — Low / High

Health Overall & by Unit (2015 v 2014)

2015 Rk	22
2015 AGL	75
Off Rk	21
Def Rk	20
2014 Rk	23
2014 AGL	87

2016 Positional Spending

	All OFF	QB	OL	RB	WR	TE	All DEF	DL	LB	CB	S
2015 Rk	26	26	18	16	7	27	23	6	25	24	31
Rank	14	26	12	4	8	19	5	5	19	13	21
Total	76.1M	8.8M	28.1M	10.9M	22.4M	5.8M	83.8M	34.0M	17.2M	23.9M	8.7M

2016 Offseason Spending

Total Spent	Total Spent Rk	Free Agents #	Free Agents $	Free Agents $ Rk	Waiver #	Waiver $	Waiver $ Rk	Extended #	Sum of Extended $	Sum of Drafted $	Undrafted #	Undrafted $
199M	13	8	75M	10	15	16M	11	1	36M	35M	23	37M

2015 Stats & Fantasy Production

Pos	Player	Ov. Rank	Pos. Rk	Age	Gms	St	Pass Comp	Pass Att	Pass Yds	Pass TD	Pass Int	Rush Att	Rush Yds	Rush YPA	Rush TD	Targ	Recp	Rec Yds	Rec YPC	Rec TDs	Draft King Pts	Fan Duel Pts
QB	Jameis Winston*		13	21	16	16	312	535	4,042	22	15	53	210	4	6						296	288
RB	Doug Martin*+	11	3	26	16	16						288	1,402	5	6	44	33	271	8	1	243	216
RB	Charles Sims	68	22	25	16							107	529	5		70	51	561	11	4	188	155
WR	Mike Evans	63	27	22	15	14										148	74	1,206	16	3	215	174
WR	Vincent Jackson	62	32	10	9											62	33	543	16	3	110	91
WR	Adam Humphries	103	22	13												40	27	260	10	1	62	46
TE	Austin Seferian-Jenk..	28	23	7	3											39	21	338	16	4	82	68
TE	Cameron Brate	35	24	14	4											30	23	288	13	3	73	58

Avg Line	+2.6	Pred Wins	7	Pred Div Finish	#3

2016 Weekly Betting Lines (wks 1-16)

(-) Favorite   Underdog (+)
-3.0   +10.0

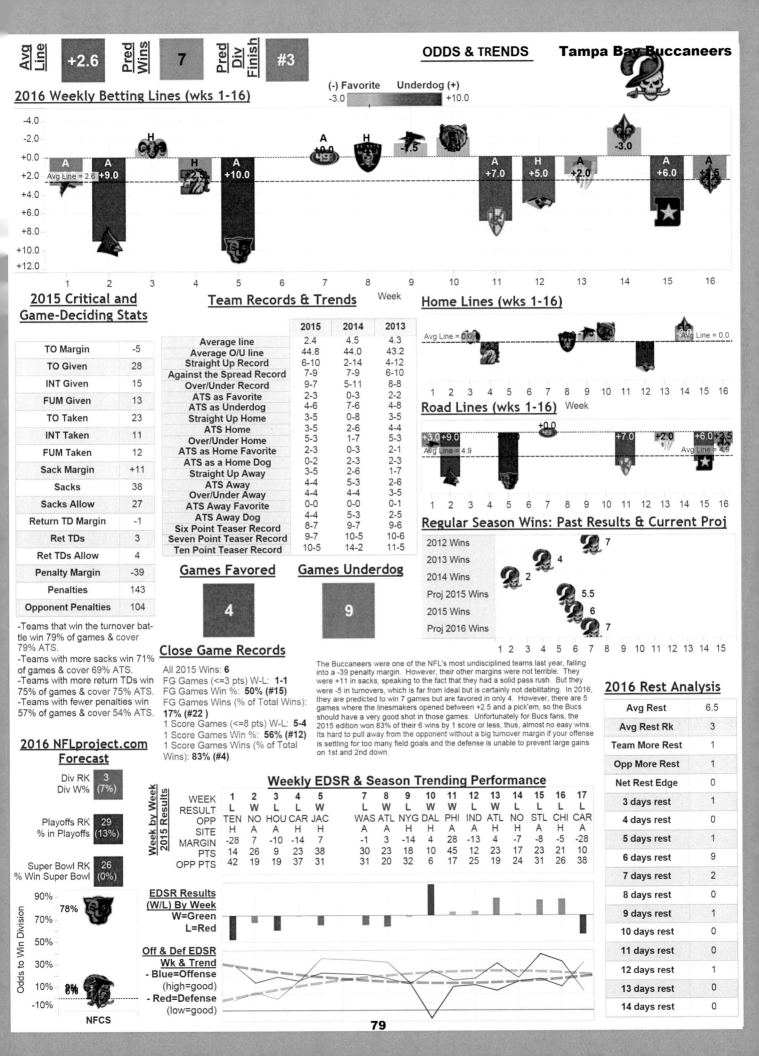

2015 Critical and Game-Deciding Stats

TO Margin	-5
TO Given	28
INT Given	15
FUM Given	13
TO Taken	23
INT Taken	11
FUM Taken	12
Sack Margin	+11
Sacks	38
Sacks Allow	27
Return TD Margin	-1
Ret TDs	3
Ret TDs Allow	4
Penalty Margin	-39
Penalties	143
Opponent Penalties	104

-Teams that win the turnover battle win 79% of games & cover 79% ATS.
-Teams with more sacks win 71% of games & cover 69% ATS.
-Teams with more return TDs win 75% of games & cover 75% ATS.
-Teams with fewer penalties win 57% of games & cover 54% ATS.

2016 NFLproject.com Forecast

Div RK	3
Div W%	(7%)
Playoffs RK	29
% in Playoffs	(13%)
Super Bowl RK	26
% Win Super Bowl	(0%)

Odds to Win Division
78%
8%
6%
NFCS

Team Records & Trends

	2015	2014	2013
Average line	2.4	4.5	4.3
Average O/U line	44.8	44.0	43.2
Straight Up Record	6-10	2-14	4-12
Against the Spread Record	7-9	7-9	6-10
Over/Under Record	9-7	5-11	8-8
ATS as Favorite	2-3	0-3	2-2
ATS as Underdog	4-6	7-6	4-8
Straight Up Home	3-5	0-8	3-5
ATS Home	3-5	2-6	4-4
Over/Under Home	5-3	1-7	5-3
ATS as Home Favorite	2-3	0-3	2-1
ATS as a Home Dog	0-2	2-3	2-3
Straight Up Away	3-5	2-6	1-7
ATS Away	4-4	5-3	2-6
Over/Under Away	4-4	4-4	3-5
ATS Away Favorite	0-0	0-0	0-1
ATS Away Dog	4-4	5-3	2-5
Six Point Teaser Record	8-7	9-7	9-6
Seven Point Teaser Record	9-7	10-5	10-6
Ten Point Teaser Record	10-5	14-2	11-5

Games Favored
4

Games Underdog
9

Close Game Records

All 2015 Wins: 6
FG Games (<=3 pts) W-L: 1-1
FG Games Win %: 50% (#15)
FG Games Wins (% of Total Wins): 17% (#22)
1 Score Games (<=8 pts) W-L: 5-4
1 Score Games Win %: 56% (#12)
1 Score Games Wins (% of Total Wins): 83% (#4)

Home Lines (wks 1-16)

Avg Line = 0.0

Road Lines (wks 1-16)

Avg Line = 4.9
Avg Line = 4.9

Regular Season Wins: Past Results & Current Proj

2012 Wins	7
2013 Wins	4
2014 Wins	2
Proj 2015 Wins	5.5
2015 Wins	6
Proj 2016 Wins	7

The Buccaneers were one of the NFL's most undisciplined teams last year, falling into a -39 penalty margin. However, their other margins were not terrible. They were +11 in sacks, speaking to the fact that they had a solid pass rush. But they were -5 in turnovers, which is far from ideal but is certainly not debilitating. In 2016, they are predicted to win 7 games but are favored in only 4. However, there are 5 games where the linesmakers opened between +2.5 and a pick'em, so the Bucs should have a very good shot in those games. Unfortunately for Bucs fans, the 2015 edition won 83% of their 6 wins by 1 score or less, thus, almost no easy wins. Its hard to pull away from the opponent without a big turnover margin if your offense is settling for too many field goals and the defense is unable to prevent large gains on 1st and 2nd down.

2016 Rest Analysis

Avg Rest	6.5
Avg Rest Rk	3
Team More Rest	1
Opp More Rest	1
Net Rest Edge	0
3 days rest	1
4 days rest	0
5 days rest	1
6 days rest	9
7 days rest	2
8 days rest	0
9 days rest	1
10 days rest	0
11 days rest	0
12 days rest	1
13 days rest	0
14 days rest	0

Weekly EDSR & Season Trending Performance

WEEK	1	2	3	4	5		7	8	9	10	11	12	13	14	15	16	17
RESULT	L	W	L	L	W		L	W	L	W	W	L	W	L	L	L	L
OPP	TEN	NO	HOU	CAR	JAC		WAS	ATL	NYG	DAL	PHI	IND	ATL	NO	STL	CHI	CAR
SITE	A	H	A	A	H		A	H	H	A	H	A	A	H	A	H	A
MARGIN	-28	7	-10	-14	7		-1	3	-14	4	28	-13	4	-7	-8	-5	-28
PTS	14	26	9	23	38		30	23	18	10	45	12	23	17	23	21	10
OPP PTS	42	19	19	37	31		31	20	32	6	17	25	19	24	31	26	38

Week by Week 2015 Results

EDSR Results (W/L) By Week
W=Green
L=Red

Off & Def EDSR Wk & Trend
- Blue=Offense (high=good)
- Red=Defense (low=good)

79

STATS & VISUALIZATIONS Tampa Bay Buccaneers

Directional Passer Rating Achieved

Receiver	Short Left	Short Middle	Short Right	Deep Left	Deep Middle	Deep Right
Mike Evans	63	73	62	87	91	61
Vincent Jackson	111	143	73	42	56	47
Adam Humphries	47	38	113	77	118	27
Cameron Brate	129	39	52	116	158	118
Austin Seferian-Jen..	140	149	45	59	95	149
Brandon Myers	102		40		39	
Donteea Dye	85	118	49	39	52	39
Louis Murphy	60	70	60	118		109
Luke Stocker	67	109	95			
Russell Shepard	81		91	39	118	39

Directional Frequency by Receiver

Receiver	Short Left	Short Middle	Short Right	Deep Left	Deep Middle	Deep Right
Mike Evans	26%	36%	36%	55%	36%	43%
Vincent Jackson	14%	23%	11%	14%	12%	23%
Adam Humphries	13%	11%	11%	4%	4%	7%
Cameron Brate	8%	7%	8%	8%	8%	5%
Austin Seferian-Jenki..	9%	11%	11%	6%	16%	7%
Brandon Myers	7%		6%		8%	
Donteea Dye	10%	2%	9%	2%	12%	7%
Louis Murphy	6%	5%	3%	4%		7%
Luke Stocker	5%	5%	4%			
Russell Shepard	3%		1%	6%	4%	2%

Defense Passer Rating Allowed

Short Left	Short Middle	Short Right	Deep Left	Deep Middle	Deep Right
109	99	114	88	80	99

Offensive Rush Directional Yds/Carry

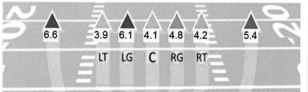

	LT	LG	C	RG	RT	
6.6	3.9	6.1	4.1	4.8	4.2	5.4

Offensive Rush Frequency of Direction

	LT	LG	C	RG	RT	
51	55	50	98	76	57	57

Offensive Explosive Runs by Direction

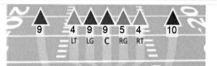

	LT	LG	C	RG	RT	
9	4	9	9	5	4	10

Defensive Rush Directional Yds/Carry

	LT	LG	C	RG	RT	
3.3	3.8	3.9	3.4	3.9	3.6	3.9

Jameis Winston - 1st Down RTG

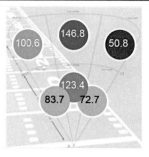

Jameis Winston - 3rd Down RTG

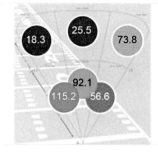

Jameis Winston - 2nd Down RTG

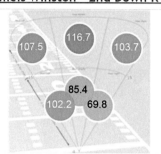

Jameis Winston - Overall RTG

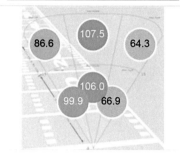

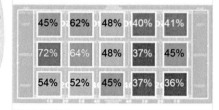

2nd & Short RUN (1D or not)

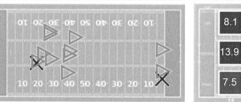

2nd & Short RUN Stats

Run Conv Rk	1D% Run	NFL 1D% Run Avg	Run Freq	NFL Run Freq Avg
5	85%	69%	59%	64%

2nd & Short PASS (1D or not)

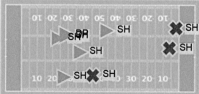

2nd & Short PASS Stats

Pass Conv Rk	1D% Pass	NFL 1D% Pass Avg	Pass Freq	NFL Pass Freq Avg
4	67%	55%	41%	36%

Pass Offense Play Success Rate

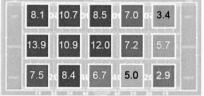

45%	62%	48%	40%	41%
72%	64%	48%	37%	45%
54%	52%	45%	37%	36%

Pass Offense Yds/Play

8.1	10.7	8.5	7.0	3.4
13.9	10.9	12.0	7.2	5.7
7.5	8.4	6.7	5.0	2.9

Off. Directional Tendency (% of Plays Left, Middle or Right)

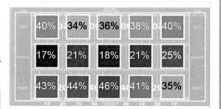

40%	34%	36%	38%	40%
17%	21%	18%	21%	25%
43%	44%	46%	41%	35%

Off. Directional Pass Rate (% of Plays which are Passes)

68%	54%	63%	74%	74%
29%	31%	31%	35%	36%
71%	70%	65%	66%	57%

New Orleans Saints

Coaches

Head Coach: Sean Payton (11th yr)
OC: Pete Carmichael (8th yr)
DC: Dennis Allen (2nd yr)

Forecast 2016 Wins

7

Past Records

2015: 7-9
2014: 7-9
2013: 11-5

Opponent Strength
Easy — Hard

2016 Schedule & Week by Week Strength of Schedule

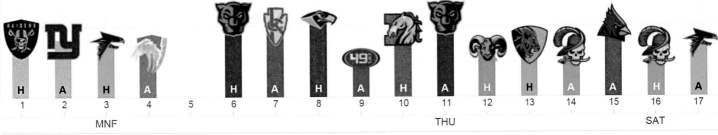

H	A	H	A		H	A	H	A	H	A	H	H	A	H	H	A
1	2	3	4	5	6	7	8	9	10	11	12	13	14	15	16	17

MNF (week 3), THU (week 11), SAT (week 16)

2016 Overview

One year after the San Diego Chargers franchised Drew Brees in 2005, the Saints signed him to a 6 year, $60M deal. He'll make half of that this season alone, thanks to his $30M cap hit. Brees played out that contract, which never hit the cap for more than $12.5M, and in 2012 signed a record breaking 5 year, $100M deal, which hit the cap for $17M in 2013, $18M in 2014, $24M last year and $30M this year. In his first deal Brees led the Saints to 4 winning seasons, 4 playoff appearances, won 1 Super Bowl and posted only 1 losing season. Collectively, they won 65% of their games, posting a 62-34 record. However, since signing his blockbuster $100M deal, the Saints are 32-32, including 1-1 in the playoffs. They have posted 3 losing seasons and just 1 winning season.

NFL teams don't have to have a quarterback to win games, but he doesn't have to be a veteran, nor does he have to be paid a ridiculous sum. In fact, often its completely counterproductive to have one of that ilk: the Bears are 11-21 after signing Jay Cutler to a 7 year, $126.7M deal. The Falcons are 18-30 after signing Matt Ryan to a 5 year, $103.75M deal. The Ravens are 23-25 after signing Joe Flacco to a 6 year, $120.6M deal. The Patriots figured out the QB game, signing Tom Brady repeatedly to deals where the cap hit does not exceed $15M. In fact, despite being one of if not the best QB for over a decade, and winning multiple Super Bowl rights, Brady has hit the cap for $15M only once in his 16 seasons. That is remarkable. Tom Brady will hit the cap for the next two years combined for less than what Drew Brees will hit it in 2016. Brady hits the 2016 cap for $14M (same as his 2017 number), which is 17th in the NFL, behind the likes of Colin Kaepernick, Jay Cutler and Alex Smith.

To win it all, a team needs much more than just a quarterback. It takes a full 53-man squad, full of capable starters as well depth to compensate for injuries, plus a sound strategy and game plan. But the facts are the facts: from 2003 through 2013 (11 seasons) no QB on anything but his rookie deal or his 2nd deal won the Super Bowl and none had a cap hit that season in excess of $14.1M, with the average being $7.3M. There were a number of great QBs in those years, who went on to make a lot more money and hit the cap for much larger numbers, including Peyton Manning, Ben Roethlisberger, Eli Manning, Aaron Rodgers and of course, Tom Brady and Drew Brees, in addition to Joe Flacco and the young Russell Wilson in 2013 who hit the cap for only $681K. The only QB to hit the salary cap for $15M or more the year he won the Super Bowl was Peyton Manning last year, and oddly, Peyton played at a level far below a $17.5M cap figure. While the cap itself is rising and ultimately more QBs will win the Super Bowl hitting the cap at $15M, the research simply shows how difficult that is. In 2016, 8 QBs hit the cap for $20M+, with Brees the only one hitting it for $30M. The lesson here is that while a great QB can win games, you need a great team to win it all. And it's extremely hard to build a great team with nearly 20% of your total cap allocated to one player. As such, the unfortunate truth for the Saints is that they must have Drew Brees play off the charts. For many teams, a season of off the charts performance from the QB position would ensure the team wins the division and heads (deep) into the playoffs. But that won't be the case for the Saints. Due to their roster constraints, it guarantees nothing even if Brees is magical. The team, particularly the defense, must play a lot better than they did in 2015 to even have a chance.

Strength of Schedule In Detail

True Strength of Schedule Rank: 7

Hardest Stretches (1=Hard, 32=Easy)
Hardest 3 wk Stretch Rk:	1
Hardest 4 wk Stretch Rk:	11
Hardest 5 wk Stretch Rk:	6

Easiest Stretches (1=Easy, 32=Hard)
Easiest 3 wk Stretch Rk:	19
Easiest 4 wk Stretch Rk:	27
Easiest 5 wk Stretch Rk:	22

The Saints are one of eight teams with only one back-to-back road game stretch, but it comes weeks 14 and 15, and leaves them closing the season with 3 of 4 games on the road, one of only four teams to do so. New Orleans has an easier start (weeks 1-4) and finish (weeks 12-17), but the 6 week stretch from weeks 6 through 11 is by far the most brutal of any team this year. They face the Panthers twice, the Seahawks, Broncos and Chiefs during that span. And New Orleans has an incredible home field edge, but hosts just one primetime game in 2016 (wk 3 vs ATL).

2015 Play Tendencies

All Pass %	64%
All Pass Rk	6
All Rush %	36%
All Rush Rk	27
1 Score Pass %	69%
1 Score Pass Rk	1
2014 1 Score Pass %	63%
2014 1 Score Pass Rk	4
Pass Increase %	6%
Pass Increase Rk	6
1 Score Rush %	31%
1 Score Rush Rk	32
Up Pass %	56%
Up Pass Rk	6
Up Rush %	44%
Up Rush Rk	27
Down Pass %	70%
Down Pass Rk	10
Down Rush %	30%
Down Rush Rk	23

The Saints were the most pass heavy team in the NFL, and their rate of passing in one-score games increased from 2014 to 2015 by an additional 6% even though they were the 4th most pass-heavy team in 2014. The NFL average for pass rate in one-score games last year was 58%, so for the Saints to be over 10% above that average was certainly huge. The 2nd ranked team was at 65%. Despite passing so often, the Saints still were top 7 in passing efficiency. Their rush efficiency ranked 15th.

2015 Offensive Advanced Metrics

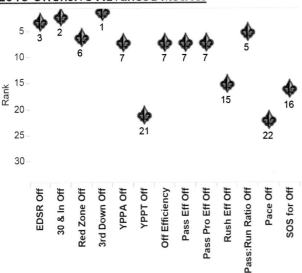

Rank (EDSR Off: 3, 30 & In Off: 2, Red Zone Off: 6, 3rd Down Off: 1, YPPA Off: 7, YPPT Off: 21, Off Efficiency: 7, Pass Eff Off: 7, Pass Pro Eff Off: 7, Rush Eff Off: 15, Pass:Run Ratio Off: 5, Pace Off: 22, SOS for Off: 16)

What do you get when you have an all-time horrible defense, ranking dead last in almost every single key advanced metric, and an offense led by Sean Payton and Drew Brees? You get the 2015 New Orleans Saints, who were very strong offensively, top 10 across the board for most metrics, but that firepower could not overcome the miserable defense. And the team finished 7-9. The worst part of the defensive performance was that it came against the 29th rated schedule of opposing offenses. The Saints did suffer more than their share of injures defensively to help facilitate the bad ranking, but there was more wrong with the defense than simply the injuries. It is simply not an overly talented group and they must get significantly better performance in 2016 if the team hopes to avoid a 3rd straight losing season.

2015 Defensive Advanced Metrics

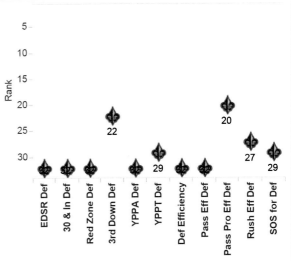

Rank (EDSR Def: 32, 30 & In Def: 32, Red Zone Def: 32, 3rd Down Def: 22, YPPA Def: 32, YPPT Def: 29, Def Efficiency: 32, Pass Eff Def: 32, Pass Pro Eff Def: 20, Rush Eff Def: 27, SOS for Def: 29)

Drafted Players

2016 Draft Grade: #13 (3.1/4)

Rnd.	Pick #	Pos.	Player	College
1	12	DT	Sheldon Rankins	Louisville
2	47	WR	Michael Thomas	Ohio State
2	61	S	Vonn Bell	Ohio State
4	120	DT	David Onyemata	Manitoba
7	237	RB	Daniel Lasco	California

PERSONNEL & SPENDING

New Orleans Saints

Free Agents/Trades Added

Player (Position)

Coby Fleener TE
Craig Robertson LB
James Laurinaitis LB
Nate Stupar LB
Nick Fairley DT

Other Signed

Player (Position)

Avery Young T
Chris Highland TE
D.J. Pettway DE
De'Vante Harris S
Dillon Lee LB
Dominique Tovell LB
Jack Allen C
Jake Lampman WR
Jared Dangerfield WR
Jeff Schoettmer LB
Jimmy Pruitt CB
Jordan Williams-Lambert WR
Joseph Cheek G
Ken Crawley CB
Landon Turner G
Marcus Henry C
Mike Caputo S
Mitchell Loewen DE
Ryker Mathews G
Sione Houma RB
Tommylee Lewis WR
Tony Steward LB
Trae Elston S
Tyrus Thompson T

2015 Players Lost

Transaction	Player (Position)
Cut	Brandon Browner CB
	Bryan Witzmann T
	David Hawthorne LB
	Griffin Neal QB
	Highland, Chris TE
	Jahri Evans G
	Josh Scobee K
	Marques Colston WR
	Mike Caputo S
	Phillip Hunt DE
	Ramon Humber LB
	Seantavius Jones WR
	Shane Wynn WR
	Tavaris Barnes DE
	Toben Opurum RB
	Vick Ballard RB
	Vinnie Sunseri S
Declared Free Agent	Benjamin Watson TE
	Khiry Robinson RB

- There are a lot of upsides about having a veteran QB with the intelligence, skill and leadership of Drew Brees. Unfortunately, the downsides can cripple a team. Brees hits the cap at $30M this year, the most of any player by a margin. The problem is Brees is still extremely capable, has not largely fallen back despite being 37 years old now, and is an icon in New Orleans. Surely the Saints front office believes there is little alternative but to keep Brees in New Orleans as long as he plays at this level. However, why they were unable to do so prior to the $30M cap hit is odd. And it makes you wonder how low the offer was or how much Brees was resistant to taking anything but a ridiculous extension.

- In 2016, in addition to the most expensive QB cap hit, the Saints are spending the 8th most at the RB position, which seems extremely odd and unnecessary considering how often they pass the football. But with both CJ Spiller and Mark Ingram on board, in addition to Tim Hightower, the Saints have a lot of veteran ball carriers on the roster, and they aren't cheap.

- Oddly, despite so much tied up at RB, considering they are the NFL's most pass-heavy team, the roster has the least amount tied up on the wide receiver position of any team. A 22 year old Brandin Cooks led the team in receptions last season, and playing alongside him is slotted the Ohio State rookie Michael Thomas, with 23 year old Willie Snead filling in at WR #3.

- The Saints lost WR Marques Colston and TE Benjamin Watson this past offseason, and to replace that veteran receiving talent, the bought TE Coby Fleener, but they signed him to an incredible deal. Fleener received $36M over 5 years. There is no doubt from a fantasy perspective Fleener instantly becomes a coveted TE due to his expected usage, but from a roster construction perspective and the holes on defense, it was not the most "roster sound" decision.

Lineup & 2016 Cap Hit

FS J.Byrd 31
SS K.Vaccaro 32
LB J.Laurinaitis 55
LB S.Anthony 50
RCB K.Lewis 21
SLOTCB D.Swann 38
DE B.Richardson 78
DT N.Fairley 98
DT S.Rankins *Rookie* 99
DE C.Jordan 94
LCB D.Breaux 40

LWR B.Cooks 10
LT T.Armstead 72
LG T.Lelito 68
C M.Unger 60
RG A.Peat 75
RT Z.Strief 64
RWR W.Snead 83
SLOTWR M.Thomas 31
TE C.Fleener 80
QB D.Brees 9
RB M.Ingram 22

Skill Bench
WR2 B.Coleman 16
WR3 R.Harris 14
RB2 T.Hightower 34
QB2 L.McCown 7

2016 Cap Dollars
Low — High

Health Overall & by Unit (2015 v 2014)

2015 Rk	8
2015 AGL	56
Off Rk	3
Def Rk	23
2014 Rk	9
2014 AGL	58

2016 Positional Spending

	All OFF	QB	OL	RB	WR	TE	All DEF	DL	LB	CB	S
2015 Rk	15	1	23	12	26	26	32	30	28	21	10
Rank	11	1	23	7	32	16	28	28	27	19	2
Total	79.7M	32.0M	22.0M	10.6M	8.0M	7.1M	56.6M	14.3M	13.7M	11.9M	16.7M

2016 Offseason Spending

Total Spent	Total Spent Rk	Free Agents #	Free Agents $	Free Agents $ Rk	Waiver #	Waiver $	Waiver $ Rk	Extended #	Sum of Extended $	Sum of Drafted $	Undrafted #	Undrafted $
214M	10	14	66M	14	17	14M	13	3	71M	27M	22	36M

2015 Stats & Fantasy Production

Pos	Player	Ov. Rank	Pos. Rk	Age	Gms	St	Pass Comp	Pass Att	Pass Yds	Pass TD	Pass Int	Rush Att	Rush Yds	Rush YPA	Rush TD	Targ	Recp	Rec Yds	Rec YPC	Rec TDs	Draft King Pts	Fan Duel Pts
QB	Drew Brees	51	6	36	15	15	428	627	4,870	32	11	24	14	1	1						320	315
RB	Mark Ingram	43	15	26	12	10						166	769	5	6	60	50	405	8		210	178
	Tim Hightower		54	29	8	3						96	375	4	4	13	12	129	11		92	80
	Khiry Robinson		67	26	8							56	180	3	4	20	17	115	7		77	62
	C.J. Spiller		71	28	13	2						36	112	3			44	34	239	7	2	87	64
WR	Brandin Cooks	30	12	22	16	13						8	18	2		129	84	1,138	14	9	257	212
	Willie Snead		35	23	15	9										101	69	984	14	3	187	149
	Marques Colston		57	32	13	5										67	45	520	12	4	124	99
	Brandon Coleman		81	23	16	3										49	30	454	15	2	90	72
TE	Ben Watson	44	8	35	16	16										110	74	825	11	6	195	154
	Josh Hill		48	25	16	7										30	16	120	8	2	43	32

Avg Line	+2.7	Pred Wins	7	Pred Div Finish	#4

2016 Weekly Betting Lines (wks 1-16)

(-) Favorite   Underdog (+)
-2.5   +10.0

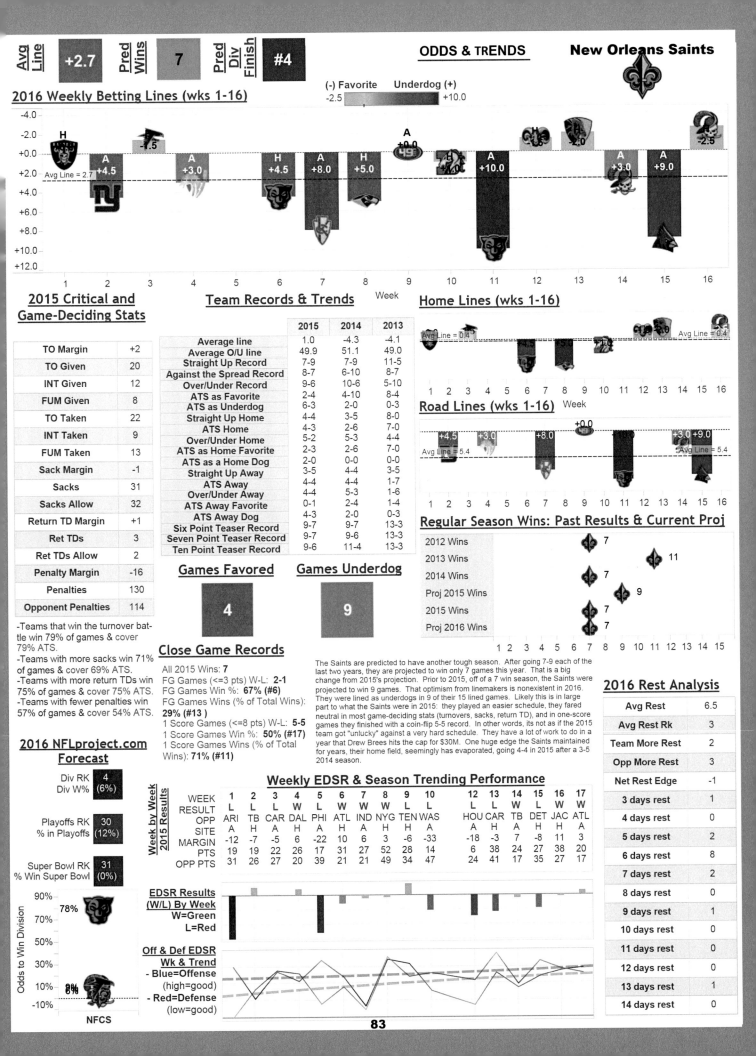

Avg Line = 2.7

Week

2015 Critical and Game-Deciding Stats

TO Margin	+2
TO Given	20
INT Given	12
FUM Given	8
TO Taken	22
INT Taken	9
FUM Taken	13
Sack Margin	-1
Sacks	31
Sacks Allow	32
Return TD Margin	+1
Ret TDs	3
Ret TDs Allow	2
Penalty Margin	-16
Penalties	130
Opponent Penalties	114

-Teams that win the turnover battle win 79% of games & cover 79% ATS.
-Teams with more sacks win 71% of games & cover 69% ATS.
-Teams with more return TDs win 75% of games & cover 75% ATS.
-Teams with fewer penalties win 57% of games & cover 54% ATS.

2016 NFLproject.com Forecast

Div RK	4
Div W%	(6%)
Playoffs RK	30
% in Playoffs	(12%)
Super Bowl RK	31
% Win Super Bowl	(0%)

Odds to Win Division

78%

8%
8%

NFCS

Team Records & Trends

	2015	2014	2013
Average line	1.0	-4.3	-4.1
Average O/U line	49.9	51.1	49.0
Straight Up Record	7-9	7-9	11-5
Against the Spread Record	8-7	6-10	8-7
Over/Under Record	9-6	10-6	5-10
ATS as Favorite	2-4	4-10	8-4
ATS as Underdog	6-3	2-0	0-3
Straight Up Home	4-4	3-5	8-0
ATS Home	4-3	2-6	7-0
Over/Under Home	5-2	5-3	4-4
ATS as Home Favorite	2-3	2-6	7-0
ATS as a Home Dog	2-0	0-0	0-0
Straight Up Away	3-5	4-4	3-5
ATS Away	4-4	4-4	1-7
Over/Under Away	4-4	5-3	1-6
ATS Away Favorite	0-1	2-4	1-4
ATS Away Dog	4-3	2-0	0-3
Six Point Teaser Record	9-7	9-7	13-3
Seven Point Teaser Record	9-7	9-6	13-3
Ten Point Teaser Record	9-6	11-4	13-3

Games Favored

4

Games Underdog

9

Close Game Records

All 2015 Wins: 7
FG Games (<=3 pts) W-L: **2-1**
FG Games Win %: **67% (#6)**
FG Games Wins (% of Total Wins): **29% (#13)**
1 Score Games (<=8 pts) W-L: **5-5**
1 Score Games Win %: **50% (#17)**
1 Score Games Wins (% of Total Wins): 71% (#11)

The Saints are predicted to have another tough season. After going 7-9 each of the last two years, they are projected to win only 7 games this year. That is a big change from 2015's projection. Prior to 2015, off of a 7 win season, the Saints were projected to win 9 games. That optimism from linemakers is nonexistent in 2016. They were lined as underdogs in 9 of their 15 lined games. Likely this is in large part to what the Saints were in 2015: they played an easier schedule, they fared neutral in most game-deciding stats (turnovers, sacks, return TD), and in one-score games they finished with a coin-flip 5-5 record. In other words, its not as if the 2015 team got "unlucky" against a very hard schedule. They have a lot of work to do in a year that Drew Brees hits the cap for $30M. One huge edge the Saints maintained for years, their home field, seemingly has evaporated, going 4-4 in 2015 after a 3-5 2014 season.

Home Lines (wks 1-16)

Avg Line = 0.4

Week

Road Lines (wks 1-16)

Avg Line = 5.4   Avg Line = 5.4

Regular Season Wins: Past Results & Current Proj

2012 Wins	7
2013 Wins	11
2014 Wins	7
Proj 2015 Wins	9
2015 Wins	7
Proj 2016 Wins	7

1 2 3 4 5 6 7 8 9 10 11 12 13 14 15

2016 Rest Analysis

Avg Rest	6.5
Avg Rest Rk	3
Team More Rest	2
Opp More Rest	3
Net Rest Edge	-1
3 days rest	1
4 days rest	0
5 days rest	2
6 days rest	8
7 days rest	2
8 days rest	0
9 days rest	1
10 days rest	0
11 days rest	0
12 days rest	0
13 days rest	1
14 days rest	0

Weekly EDSR & Season Trending Performance

WEEK	1	2	3	4	5	6	7	8	9	10		12	13	14	15	16	17
RESULT	L	L	L	W	L	W	W	W	L	L		L	L	W	L	W	W
OPP	ARI	TB	CAR	DAL	PHI	ATL	IND	NYG	TEN	WAS		HOU	CAR	TB	DET	JAC	ATL
SITE	A	H	A	H	A	H	A	H	H	A		A	H	A	H	H	A
MARGIN	-12	-7	-5	6	-22	10	6	3	-6	-33		-18	-3	7	-8	11	3
PTS	19	19	22	26	17	31	27	52	28	14		6	38	24	27	38	20
OPP PTS	31	26	27	20	39	21	21	49	34	47		24	41	17	35	27	17

Week by Week 2015 Results

EDSR Results (W/L) By Week
W=Green
L=Red

Off & Def EDSR Wk & Trend
- Blue=Offense (high=good)
- Red=Defense (low=good)

All visualizations courtesy of SharpFootballStats.com. See Table of Contents for definition of stats & coding used. See SharpFootballStats.com for interactive visualizations which break data into more segments, allow customization & user download. Updated weekly throughout the 2016 NFL season.

Directional Passer Rating Achieved

Receiver	Short Left	Short Middle	Short Right	Deep Left	Deep Middle	Deep Right
Brandin Cooks	103	99	94	116	85	19
Ben Watson	103	112	97	54	64	118
Willie Snead	106	61	102	109	118	135
Marques Colston	105	132	87	39	0	109
Brandon Coleman	99	72	92	84	89	110
Josh Hill	125	59	90	39	39	
Michael Hoomanawa..	87	39	109		118	118
T.J. Graham	79		79			
Seantavius Jones			39			

Directional Frequency by Receiver

Receiver	Short Left	Short Middle	Short Right	Deep Left	Deep Middle	Deep Right
Brandin Cooks	25%	17%	20%	42%	31%	34%
Ben Watson	22%	31%	20%	12%	34%	10%
Willie Snead	26%	15%	20%	23%	7%	20%
Marques Colston	13%	23%	13%	2%	14%	7%
Brandon Coleman	8%	3%	9%	17%	7%	24%
Josh Hill	4%	8%	10%	4%	3%	
Michael Hoomanawa..	2%	1%	6%		3%	5%
T.J. Graham	1%		1%			
Seantavius Jones			1%			

Defense Passer Rating Allowed

Short Left	Short Middle	Short Right	Deep Left	Deep Middle	Deep Right
103	134	114	127	102	96

Offensive Rush Directional Yds/Carry

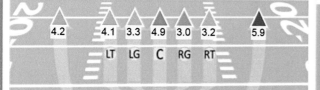

	LT	LG	C	RG	RT	
4.2	4.1	3.3	4.9	3.0	3.2	5.9

Offensive Rush Frequency of Direction

	LT	LG	C	RG	RT	
50	43	63	49	77	53	46

Offensive Explosive Runs by Direction

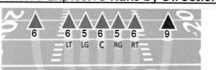

	LT	LG	C	RG	RT	
6	6	5	6	5	6	9

Defensive Rush Directional Yds/Carry

	LT	LG	C	RG	RT	
6.6	5.7	4.4	3.6	3.8	6.5	5.5

Drew Brees - 1st Down RTG

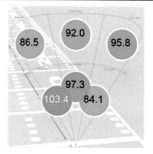

86.5 | 92.0 | 95.8
97.3
103.4 | 84.1

Drew Brees - 2nd Down RTG

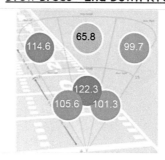

114.6 | 65.8 | 99.7
122.3
105.6 | 101.3

Drew Brees - 3rd Down RTG

92.0 | 22.9 | 118.3
82.9
91.6 | 100.5

Drew Brees - Overall RTG

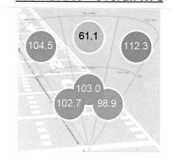

104.5 | 61.1 | 112.3
103.0
102.7 | 98.9

2nd & Short RUN (1D or not)

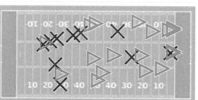

2nd & Short RUN Stats

Run Conv Rk	1D% Run	NFL 1D% Run Avg	Run Freq	NFL Run Freq Avg
22	64%	69%	74%	64%

2nd & Short PASS (1D or not)

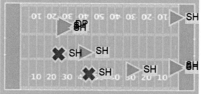

2nd & Short PASS Stats

Pass Conv Rk	1D% Pass	NFL 1D% Pass Avg	Pass Freq	NFL Pass Freq Avg
2	80%	55%	26%	36%

Pass Offense Play Success Rate

54%	57%	64%	47%	50%
50%	44%	60%	45%	39%
46%	54%	48%	50%	42%

Pass Offense Yds/Play

6.3	8.8	11.3	8.5	4.3
8.1	7.8	11.5	6.2	4.7
8.1	7.6	7.3	6.9	3.8

Off. Directional Tendency (% of Plays Left, Middle or Right)

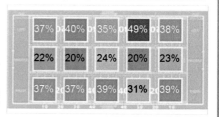

37%	40%	35%	49%	38%
22%	20%	24%	20%	23%
37%	37%	39%	31%	39%

Off. Directional Pass Rate (% of Plays which are Passes)

83%	74%	67%	71%	79%
46%	48%	52%	41%	28%
77%	76%	69%	65%	63%

Pittsburgh Steelers

Coaches

Head Coach: Mike Tomlin (10th yr)
OC: Todd Haley (5th yr)
DC: Keith Butler (2nd yr)

Forecast
2016 Wins

10.5

Past
Records

2015: 10-6
2014: 11-5
2013: 8-8

Opponent Strength
Easy   Hard

2016 Schedule & Week by Week Strength of Schedule

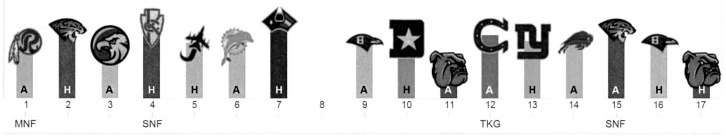

A	H	H	H	H	A	H		A	H	A	A	H	A	A	H	H
1	2	3	4	5	6	7	8	9	10	11	12	13	14	15	16	17

MNF   SNF   TKG   SNF

2016 Overview

To live and die by the deep ball in Pittsburgh. What a time to be alive. The old smashmouth team from Three Rivers Stadium, known for the Steel Curtain and a blue collar run game took that strategy, and reversed the process. Back to the foundry, the steel was melted in a furnace into molten metal. Elsewhere, the Rooneys tinkered away to make a mold of Ben Roethlisberger. The mold was shipped to the foundry, filled with the molten metal, and the Steelers became a team that is completely Ben Roethlisberger, through and through. Watching the Steelers offense, at times, is as if OC Todd Haley doesn't have a plan - he has Ben.

Last season, no quarterback attempted more deep passes than Ben Roethlisberger, who averaged over 9 passes traveling 15+ yards in the air per game. It was more than Blake Bortles, who was always trailing, and it was more than Carson Palmer, whose deep offense under Bruce Arians was known league-wide. But here comes the surprise: 23 quarterbacks attempted over 75 passes 15+ yards in the air last year. Ben Roethlisberger ranked just 20th in passer rating, recording a rating of 70 on these passes. The only players worse? Marcus Mariota, Ryan Fitzpatrick and Teddy Bridgewater. On these passes, Roethlisberger threw 11 INTs to only 6 TDs. So while the Steelers attempted a lot of deep shots, whatever huge chunks they gained were the result of volume rather than efficiency.

Unfortunately for the Steelers, their defense was quite susceptible to the deep pass as well. This number is astonishing, but when opponents attempted a pass 15+ yards in the air, it gained a first down over 49% of the time. That number was the worst in the NFL, and clearly way above the league average. And that considers the fact that the Steelers played these QBs last year: Nick Foles, Charlie Whitehurst, Austin Davis, Matt Hasselbeck, Ryan Mallett, Johnny Manziel, Alex Smith and Colin Kaepernick. That is one motley list. Clearly the Steelers like the thought of the deep ball. A lot of teams like the thought of the deep ball. What more NFL teams need to realize is its impact on game outcomes. Gaining yardage in huge chunks, even if the drive does not result in points, has tremendous impact on games. The last 2 years, when the Steelers have at least one drive which gains over 40 yards in no more than 3 plays, they are 10-2 in those games. For the few teams who understand the worth of chunk plays, most don't know when to take them. Many teams still think going deep on 2nd and short is the best time to go deep. Eli Manning attempted this play 6 times last year, and recorded just 1 completion. The last 3 years, the average rating is just 71 on these attempts, with almost as many interceptions (12) as touchdowns (14).

The Steelers need to figure out how to optimize the deep ball on offense, and defend it on defense. And quickly. That is because arguably their 2 most important skill players are about to see their contracts expire. Le'Veon Bell's rookie deal ends after 2016 & his cap hit will be a huge jump from his current $1M annually. Antonio Brown's deal expires after 2017, but he is already hitting the cap for $12M this year (after hits of $4.5 and $7M the last two years). The defense clearly isn't leading this team any longer. It's Roethlisberger's team. And for the 34 year old QB as well as his extremely talented co-stars on this offense, they may be on the verge of seeing their window close.

Strength of Schedule In Detail

True Strength of Schedule Rank: 30

Hardest Stretches (1=Hard, 32=Easy)
Hardest 3 wk Stretch Rk:	26
Hardest 4 wk Stretch Rk:	22
Hardest 5 wk Stretch Rk:	22

Easiest Stretches (1=Easy, 32=Hard)
Easiest 3 wk Stretch Rk:	15
Easiest 4 wk Stretch Rk:	20
Easiest 5 wk Stretch Rk:	18

For a team coming off a 2nd place finish in the AFC North, the Steelers should feel fortunate to have such a tremendous schedule. They do have back-to-back road trips after week 11 of the season, with the 2nd of each being in primetime. But they literally are not covering much ground in these road trips (@ CLE then @ IND wks 11-12, and @ BUF and @ CIN wks 14-15). The fact that they get to face the Browns twice significantly helps their schedule. Also helping their schedule is the fact that the most difficult non-division teams they face (NE, KC, and DAL) will all play in Pittsburgh. The Giants game at home week 13 will be their lone home game in a 5 week span, as it's the only home game from November 14th through Christmas (December 25th).

2015 Play Tendencies

All Pass %	62%
All Pass Rk	12
All Rush %	38%
All Rush Rk	21
1 Score Pass %	61%
1 Score Pass Rk	8
2014 1 Score Pass %	58%
2014 1 Score Pass Rk	15
Pass Increase %	4%
Pass Increase Rk	10
1 Score Rush %	39%
1 Score Rush Rk	25
Up Pass %	59%
Up Pass Rk	3
Up Rush %	41%
Up Rush Rk	30
Down Pass %	64%
Down Pass Rk	25
Down Rush %	36%
Down Rush Rk	8

The Steelers were the most pass happy team in the NFL if you exclude games stated by Vick and Jones. In part that is because the team lost starting RB Le'Veon Bell early, and had no depth behind DeAngelo Williams. But they still were slightly more pass-happy than average in 2014 as well. With Ben Roethlisberger at the helm, the Steelers will likely continue to be slightly more pass heavy than average.

2015 Offensive Advanced Metrics

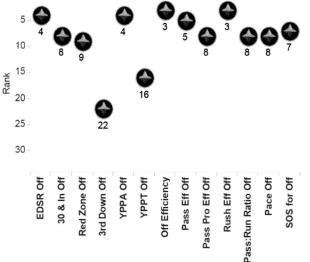

The Steelers' 2015 season was more impressive than it looks on the surface when you put it into the context that they had 5 totals QB starts from the likes of Michael Vick and Landry Jones, and Le'Veon Bell started only 6 games. Despite that, the Steelers finished an insanely high level across most offensive metrics. Factoring out the games started by Vick and Jones, the numbers are more tremendous. They recorded double the EDSR offensive efficiency when Ben Roethlisberger started and finished games. Defensively the Steelers had their share of issues last season. In taking over for Dick LeBeau, DC Keith Butler struggled initially, failing to even get his defense lined up over Rob Gronkowski in week 1. But eventually, the defense played much better, allowing more than 23 points just once through their final 7 games. Over the course of the entire season, they allowed more than 23 points (the NFL average ppg) in just 4 out of 18 games.

2015 Defensive Advanced Metrics

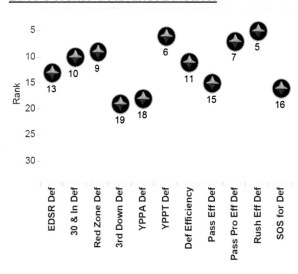

Drafted Players

Rnd.	Pick #	Pos.	Player	College
1	25	CB	Artie Burns	Miami (FL)
2	58	S	Sean Davis	Maryland
3	89	DT	Javon Hargrave	South Carolina State
4	123	OT	Jerald Hawkins	LSU
6	220	OLB	Travis Feeney	Washington
7	229	WR	Demarcus Ayers	Houston
7	246	OLB	Tyler Matakevich	Temple

Free Agents/Trades Added

Player (Position)
David Johnson TE
Ladarius Green TE
Ricardo Mathews DE
Ryan Harris T
Steven Johnson LB

Other Signed

Player (Position)
Brandon Brown-Dukes RB
Cameron Stingily RB
Canaan Severin WR
Christian Powell RB
David Johnson TE
David Reeves TE
Devaunte Sigler DE
Donald Washington CB
Giorgio Newberry DT
Jay Rome TE
Johnny Maxey DE
Marcus Tucker WR
Quinton Schooley C
Tyriq McCord LB
Will Monday P

2015 Players Lost

Transaction	Player (Position)
Cut	Abou Toure RB
	Christian Powell RB
	Cortez Allen CB
	David Nelson WR
	David Reeves TE
	Isaiah Frey CB
	Kelvin Palmer T
	Micah Hatchie T
	Mike Adams T
	Mitchell Van Dyk T
	Rajion Neal RB
	Rob Blanchflower TE
	Tobais Palmer WR
	Ty Long K
Declared Free Agent	Antwon Blake CB
	Kelvin Beachum T
	Sean Spence LB
	Steve McLendon NT
Retired	Heath Miller TE

- The Steelers made two moves in free agency to help their offense. They signed TE Ladarius Green (formerly of San Diego) and T Ryan Harris
- Ladarius Green is faster, taller & longer than Heath Miller. And when Antonio Gates missed games, Philip Rivers recorded a 132 rating when passing to Green. Green is one TE in a line of several added by solid, intelligent teams this past offseason. This includes the Packers signing Jared Cook, the Patriots signing Martellus Bennett and the Redskins re-signing Jordan Reed. Redskins GM Scot McCloughan was previously GM in Seattle. Seattle locked up Jimmy Graham last year. Add to that list the Baltimore Ravens adding Benjamin Watson. Between those teams and their GMs, you literally have the some of the best of the best in the NFL. Personnel guys who "get it". Bill Belichick, Scot McCloughan, Ted Thompson, Kevin Colbert, Ozzie Newsome, John Schneider. And they "got" tight ends either this year or last year. And these are not teams accustomed to outbidding or overspending. But perhaps they see the market for solid tight ends is undervalued right now, and these elite difference makers are well worth it. Time will tell. But when so many of the very best have made the similar moves after coming to similar conclusions, it's wise to take heed.
- Pittsburgh attempted to address their defensive issues early in the draft, going defense with each pick in rounds 1-3, starting with the the secondary.
- Predicting a lot of fantasy value for the Steelers in 2016 plays right into the way this team is built. They will field the 3rd most expensive offense in the NFL (up from 18th in 2015). And that is before paying Le'Veon Bell, which they inevitably will need to do at some point before next March, as Bell enters his final season of his rookie deal. Affording Roethlisberger, Bell and Antonio Brown will be extremely difficult. They will need to stay young on defense, and hope the offense does enough to carry the day every Sunday afternoon.

Lineup & 2016 Cap Hit

FS M.Mitchell 23
SS S.Davis Rookie 28
LB R.Shazier 50
LB L.Timmons 94
RCB R.Cockrell 31
SLOTCB W.Gay 22
OLB J.Harrison 92
DE C.Heyward 97
DE S.Tuitt 91
OLB B.Dupree 48
LCB A.Burns Rookie 25
LWR A.Brown 84
LT A.Villanueva 78
LG R.Foster 73
C M.Pouncey 53
RG D.DeCastro 66
RT M.Gilbert 77
RWR S.Coates 14
SLOTWR M.Wheaton 11
TE L.Green 80
QB B.Roethlisberger 7
RB L.Bell 26

Skill Bench

WR2 D.Heyward-Bey 88
WR3 Dy Ayers Rookie 82
RB2 D.Williams 34
QB2 B.Gradkowski 5

2016 Cap Dollars: Low — High

Health Overall & by Unit (2015 v 2014)

2015 Rk	19
2015 AGL	67
Off Rk	23
Def Rk	9
2014 Rk	4
2014 AGL	43

2016 Positional Spending

	All OFF	QB	OL	RB	WR	TE	All DEF	DL	LB	CB	S
2015 Rk	18	4	20	22	22	16	21	22	9	17	25
Rank	1	3	4	21	11	22	24	25	4	32	13
Total	92.9M	25.9M	33.5M	6.1M	21.3M	6.1M	66.1M	17.2M	32.1M	5.4M	11.5M

2016 Offseason Spending

Total Spent	Total Spent Rk	Free Agents #	Free Agents $	Free Agents $ Rk	Waiver #	Waiver $	Waiver $ Rk	Extended #	Sum of Extended $	Sum of Drafted $	Undrafted #	Undrafted $
112M	28	7	28M	26	26	19M	9	3	18M	27M	13	20M

2015 Stats & Fantasy Production

Pos	Player	Ov. Rank	Pos. Rk	Age	Gms	St	Pass Comp	Pass Att	Pass Yds	Pass TD	Pass Int	Rush Att	Rush Yds	Rush YPA	Rush TD	Targ	Recp	Rec Yds	Rec YPC	Rec TDs	Draft King Pts	Fan Duel Pts
QB	Ben Roethlisberger*		20	33	12	11	319	469	3,938	21	16	15	29	2				-3			231	228
	Michael Vick		47	35	5	3	40	66	371	2	1	20	99	5							35	32
	Landry Jones		49	26	7	2	32	55	513	3	4	5	-5	-1							30	26
RB	DeAngelo Williams	14	4	32	16	10						200	907	5	11	47	40	367	9		239	211
	Le'Veon Bell		46	23	6	6						113	556	5	3	26	24	136	6		117	99
WR	Antonio Brown*+	1	1	27	16	16						3	28	9		193	136	1,834	13	10	393	320
	Martavis Bryant		34	24	11	5						5	37	7	1	92	50	765	15	6	174	145
	Markus Wheaton		40	24	16	8										79	44	749	17	5	154	129
	Darrius Heyward-Bey		90	28	16	4										39	21	314	15	2	67	54
TE	Heath Miller		23	33	15	15						1	2	2		81	60	535	9	2	131	98

Avg Line	-4.0	Pred Wins	10.5	Pred Div Finish	#1

ODDS & TRENDS

Pittsburgh Steelers

2016 Weekly Betting Lines (wks 1-16)

(-) Favorite   Underdog (+)
-8.5   +0.0

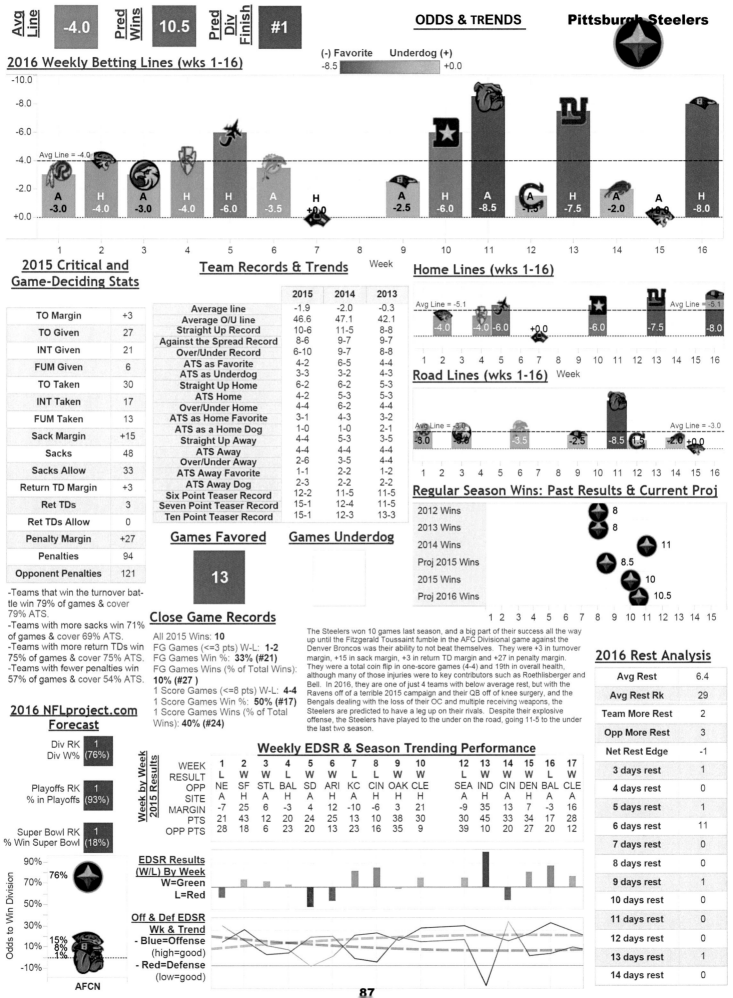

Week	1	2	3	4	5	6	7	8	9	10	11	12	13	14	15	16
Site	A	H	A	H	H	A	H		A	H	A	C	H	A	A	H
Line	-3.0	-4.0	-3.0	-4.0	-6.0	-3.5	+0.0		-2.5	-6.0	-8.5	-1.5	-7.5	-2.0	+0.0	-8.0

2015 Critical and Game-Deciding Stats

TO Margin	+3
TO Given	27
INT Given	21
FUM Given	6
TO Taken	30
INT Taken	17
FUM Taken	13
Sack Margin	+15
Sacks	48
Sacks Allow	33
Return TD Margin	+3
Ret TDs	3
Ret TDs Allow	0
Penalty Margin	+27
Penalties	94
Opponent Penalties	121

-Teams that win the turnover battle win 79% of games & cover 79% ATS.
-Teams with more sacks win 71% of games & cover 69% ATS.
-Teams with more return TDs win 75% of games & cover 75% ATS.
-Teams with fewer penalties win 57% of games & cover 54% ATS.

2016 NFLproject.com Forecast

Div RK	1
Div W%	(76%)

Playoffs RK	1
% in Playoffs	(93%)

Super Bowl RK	1
% Win Super Bowl	(18%)

Odds to Win Division
90%
70%
50%
30%
76%
10%   15%
8%
1%
-10%

AFCN

Team Records & Trends

	2015	2014	2013
Average line	-1.9	-2.0	-0.3
Average O/U line	46.6	47.1	42.1
Straight Up Record	10-6	11-5	8-8
Against the Spread Record	8-6	9-7	9-7
Over/Under Record	6-10	9-7	8-8
ATS as Favorite	4-2	6-5	4-4
ATS as Underdog	3-3	3-2	4-3
Straight Up Home	6-2	6-2	5-3
ATS Home	4-2	5-3	5-3
Over/Under Home	4-4	6-2	4-4
ATS as Home Favorite	3-1	4-3	3-2
ATS as a Home Dog	1-0	1-0	2-1
Straight Up Away	4-4	5-3	3-5
ATS Away	4-4	4-4	4-4
Over/Under Away	2-6	3-5	4-4
ATS Away Favorite	1-1	2-2	1-2
ATS Away Dog	2-3	2-2	2-2
Six Point Teaser Record	12-2	11-5	11-5
Seven Point Teaser Record	15-1	12-4	11-5
Ten Point Teaser Record	15-1	12-3	13-3

Games Favored

13

Games Underdog

Close Game Records

All 2015 Wins: **10**
FG Games (<=3 pts) W-L: **1-2**
FG Games Win %: **33% (#21)**
FG Games Wins (% of Total Wins): **10% (#27)**
1 Score Games (<=8 pts) W-L: **4-4**
1 Score Games Win %: **50% (#17)**
1 Score Games Wins (% of Total Wins): **40% (#24)**

Home Lines (wks 1-16)

Avg Line = -5.1   Avg Line = -5.1

| | -4.0 | -4.0 | -6.0 | +0.0 | -6.0 | -7.5 | -8.0 |

| 1 | 2 | 3 | 4 | 5 | 6 | 7 | 8 | 9 | 10 | 11 | 12 | 13 | 14 | 15 | 16 |

Road Lines (wks 1-16)   Week

Avg Line = -3.0   Avg Line = -3.0

| -3.0 | -3.0 | -3.5 | -2.5 | -8.5 | 1.5 | -2.0 | +0.0 |

| 1 | 2 | 3 | 4 | 5 | 6 | 7 | 8 | 9 | 10 | 11 | 12 | 13 | 14 | 15 | 16 |

Regular Season Wins: Past Results & Current Proj

2012 Wins	8
2013 Wins	8
2014 Wins	11
Proj 2015 Wins	8.5
2015 Wins	10
Proj 2016 Wins	10.5

| 1 | 2 | 3 | 4 | 5 | 6 | 7 | 8 | 9 | 10 | 11 | 12 | 13 | 14 | 15 |

The Steelers won 10 games last season, and a big part of their success all the way up until the Fitzgerald Toussaint fumble in the AFC Divisional game against the Denver Broncos was their ability to not beat themselves. They were +3 in turnover margin, +15 in sack margin, +3 in return TD margin and +27 in penalty margin. They were a total coin flip in one-score games (4-4) and 19th in overall health, although many of those injuries were to key contributors such as Roethlisberger and Bell. In 2016, they are one of just 4 teams with below average rest, but with the Ravens off of a terrible 2015 campaign and their QB off of knee surgery, and the Bengals dealing with the loss of their OC and multiple receiving weapons, the Steelers are predicted to have a leg up on their rivals. Despite their explosive offense, the Steelers have played to the under on the road, going 11-5 to the under the last two season.

2016 Rest Analysis

Avg Rest	6.4
Avg Rest Rk	29
Team More Rest	2
Opp More Rest	3
Net Rest Edge	-1
3 days rest	1
4 days rest	0
5 days rest	1
6 days rest	11
7 days rest	0
8 days rest	0
9 days rest	1
10 days rest	0
11 days rest	0
12 days rest	0
13 days rest	1
14 days rest	0

Weekly EDSR & Season Trending Performance

Week by Week 2015 Results	WEEK	1	2	3	4	5	6	7	8	9	10		12	13	14	15	16	17
	RESULT	L	W	W	L	W	W	L	L	W	W		L	W	W	W	L	W
	OPP	NE	SF	STL	BAL	SD	ARI	KC	CIN	OAK	CLE		SEA	IND	CIN	DEN	BAL	CLE
	SITE	A	H	A	H	A	H	A	H	A	H		A	H	A	H	A	A
	MARGIN	-7	25	6	-3	4	12	-10	-6	3	21		-9	35	13	7	-3	16
	PTS	21	43	12	20	24	25	13	10	38	30		30	45	33	34	17	28
	OPP PTS	28	18	6	23	20	13	23	16	35	9		39	10	20	27	20	12

EDSR Results (W/L) By Week
W=Green
L=Red

Off & Def EDSR Wk & Trend
- Blue=Offense (high=good)
- Red=Defense (low=good)

STATS & VISUALIZATIONS

Pittsburgh Steelers

Directional Passer Rating Achieved

Receiver	Short Left	Short Middle	Short Right	Deep Left	Deep Middle	Deep Right
Antonio Brown	123	84	113	68	59	75
Martavis Bryant	72	63	108	75	109	102
Heath Miller	101	90	75	118	116	39
Markus Wheaton	83	75	70	66	106	99
Darrius Heyward-Bey	133	77	83	29	156	0
Jesse James		153	77	39		
Matt Spaeth	39	87	79			
Sammie Coates		93	118		39	
Tyler Murphy	118					

Directional Frequency by Receiver

Receiver	Short Left	Short Middle	Short Right	Deep Left	Deep Middle	Deep Right
Antonio Brown	42%	26%	36%	38%	41%	38%
Martavis Bryant	18%	13%	25%	20%	9%	32%
Heath Miller	13%	34%	15%	3%	12%	2%
Markus Wheaton	18%	15%	13%	18%	24%	18%
Darrius Heyward-Bey	7%	3%	6%	17%	12%	10%
Jesse James		5%	2%	3%		
Matt Spaeth	1%	2%	1%			
Sammie Coates		2%	1%		3%	
Tyler Murphy	1%					

Defense Passer Rating Allowed

Short Left	Short Middle	Short Right	Deep Left	Deep Middle	Deep Right
84	95	88	106	91	84

Offensive Rush Directional Yds/Carry

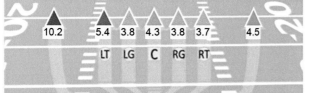

10.2   5.4   3.8   4.3   3.8   3.7   4.5

LT   LG   C   RG   RT

Offensive Rush Frequency of Direction

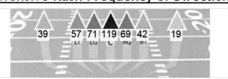

39   57   71   119   69   42   19

LT LG C RG RT

Offensive Explosive Runs by Direction

11   9   6   14   5   4   3

LT   LG   C   RG   RT

Defensive Rush Directional Yds/Carry

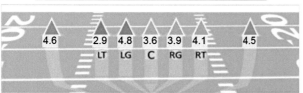

4.6   2.9   4.8   3.6   3.9   4.1   4.5

LT   LG   C   RG   RT

Ben Roethlisberger - 1st Down RTG

50.3   95.8   115.3
86.8   115.4   103.5

Ben Roethlisberger - 2nd Down RTG

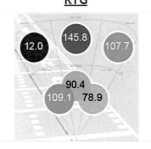

12.0   145.8   107.7
109.1   90.4   78.9

2nd & Short RUN (1D or not)

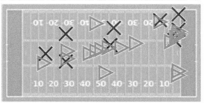

2nd & Short RUN Stats

Run Conv Rk	1D% Run	NFL 1D% Run Avg	Run Freq	NFL Run Freq Avg
21	67%	69%	57%	64%

2nd & Short PASS (1D or not)

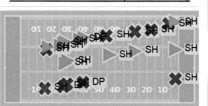

2nd & Short PASS Stats

Pass Conv Rk	1D% Pass	NFL 1D% Pass Avg	Pass Freq	NFL Pass Freq Avg
16	55%	55%	43%	36%

Ben Roethlisberger - 3rd Down RTG

67.3   87.5   78.0
112.4   76.6   116.0

Ben Roethlisberger - Overall RTG

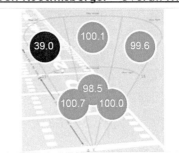

39.0   100.1   99.6
100.7   98.5   100.0

Pass Offense Play Success Rate

39%	52%	51%	45%	41%
57%	64%	58%	60%	38%
57%	49%	55%	31%	49%

Pass Offense Yds/Play

6.7	10.6	9.4	6.0	3.1
12.6	12.0	8.0	7.7	4.3
8.2	10.5	8.2	5.4	4.0

Off. Directional Tendency (% of Plays Left, Middle or Right)

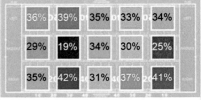

36%	39%	35%	33%	34%
29%	19%	34%	30%	25%
35%	42%	31%	37%	41%

Off. Directional Pass Rate (% of Plays which are Passes)

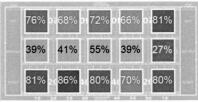

76%	68%	72%	66%	81%
39%	41%	55%	39%	27%
81%	86%	80%	70%	80%

Cincinnati Bengals

Coaches

Head Coach: Marvin Lewis (14th yr)
OC: Ken Zampese (CIN QB) (1st yr)
DC: Paul Guenther (3rd yr)

Forecast 2016 Wins
9.5

Past Records
2015: 12-4
2014: 10-5-1
2013: 11-5

Opponent Strength
Easy — Hard

2016 Schedule & Week by Week Strength of Schedule

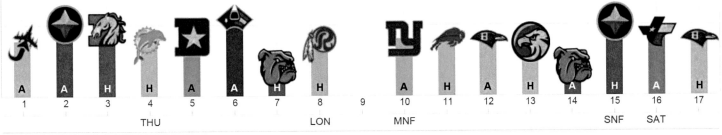

A	A	H	H	A	A	H	H		A	H	A	H	A	H	A	H
1	2	3	4	5	6	7	8	9	10	11	12	13	14	15	16	17

THU   LON   MNF   SNF   SAT

2016 Overview

How you feel about the Bengals says a lot about how you look at life, particularly if you are a fan. Do you celebrate the little victories and moments of joy, or is it all about the big prize and a journey that doesn't accomplish the ultimate goal is a failed journey? The Bengals moved from a 4-win team in 2008 and 2010 to a team that won 9 games in 2011 and double digit wins the last 4 years, recording 12 wins in 2015, tied for the most in franchise history. Despite winning 12 games, the Bengals did not receive a first round bye, which unfortunately meant an appearance in yet another Wild Card game. And for the 5th consecutive year, they lost in the Wild Card round.

Thanks to an easier schedule and a very well-rounded roster, the Bengals should once again be more than competitive during the regular season. The NFL playoffs are a tournament that you hope to make, ideally with a first round bye and home games until the Super Bowl. And only two teams out of 32 are that fortunate each year. In the ultra competitive AFC North, making the playoffs 5 straight years is an achievement. The Steelers haven't done it since 1993-1997. The Ravens did it once, from 2008-2012, and capped it off by winning the Super Bowl. But they've missed the playoffs two out of the last 3 years.

What do the Bengals need to do to have more success in the playoffs? They lost 3 of the 5 playoff games with -2 or worse turnover margins. Playoff teams -2 or worse in turnover margin are 6-47 (11%) the last 10 years, so the turnovers alone likely cost them those three games. The other two years (2012, 2014) they trailed by just 2 or 3 points at halftime before coming out flat in the 3rd quarter, and scored 2 FGs combined in both games' second halves.

But the 2015, and now the 2016 Bengals, are as strong a group from top to bottom that the Bengals have assembled. They don't need to really do anything differently in 2016 to see more success or give themselves better chances. Perhaps the vet Karlos Dansby will provide composure to an emotional defense. But what the Bengals need to do is to maintain their 2015 level of performance. I'm confident the passing game will be OK without Jones and Sanu. My questions center around the strategy & play calling of new OC Ken Zampese. For example, the Bengals were the NFL's best in a situation that needs to be appreciated more: 2nd and short. They converted 82% of snaps into first downs, the best in the NFL (avg was 64%). They smartly ran well above the NFL avg, and with sparse passing, converted at a ridiculous clip. How will Zampese approach these play calls? Will he pass more overall? Will he take more deep shots? Will the Bengals be faced with more 3rd downs as a result? They were 54% run in the red zone, while the NFL average was 56% pass. Will Zampese change this formula? Overall, Cincinnati fans should feel good about the roster talent. The team survived the loss of Mike Zimmer 3 years ago. Will they survive the loss of Hue Jackson? If so, 2016 should be a successful season so long as the roster can handle the injuries. Their ability to win in the postseason will again hinge on execution & play calling in their most pivotal game of the season.

Strength of Schedule In Detail

True Strength of Schedule Rank: 27

Hardest Stretches *(1=Hard, 32=Easy)*
Hardest 3 wk Stretch Rk:	22
Hardest 4 wk Stretch Rk:	17
Hardest 5 wk Stretch Rk:	7

Easiest Stretches *(1=Easy, 32=Hard)*
Easiest 3 wk Stretch Rk:	6
Easiest 4 wk Stretch Rk:	10
Easiest 5 wk Stretch Rk:	9

The defending AFC North Champion Bengals have a bye at the exact midpoint of the season, but they lose a home game to London (vs WAS) immediately prior to the bye. The Bengals have to be ready to roll out of the preseason, as they are one of four teams to pay two straight road games to start the season. And, their schedule from weeks 1-6 is actually the 3rd most difficult in the NFL, facing the division rival Steelers week 2, as well as the Broncos, Cowboys and Patriots over the following four games. However, after the game in New England week 6, the Bengals face the NFL's easiest schedule (by a large gap) from weeks 7 through 14. They do not play a single team expected to fare better than 8-8 during that span, and get the Browns twice. It should put the Bengals into a perfect position (record-wise and rest-wise) to take on the Steelers, Texans and Ravens to close the season, with both divisional contests coming in Cincinnati.

2015 Play Tendencies

All Pass %	53%
All Pass Rk	27
All Rush %	47%
All Rush Rk	6
1 Score Pass %	53%
1 Score Pass Rk	25
2014 1 Score Pass %	51%
2014 1 Score Pass Rk	28
Pass Increase %	2%
Pass Increase Rk	12
1 Score Rush %	47%
1 Score Rush Rk	8
Up Pass %	46%
Up Pass Rk	23
Up Rush %	54%
Up Rush Rk	10
Down Pass %	73%
Down Pass Rk	2
Down Rush %	27%
Down Rush Rk	31

The Bengals have been a sneaky run team the last couple years under Hue Jackson. With Jay Gruden in 2012-2013, the Bengals passed the ball 59% of play calls in 1 score games. But the last 2 years with Hue at the helm, they passed the ball only 52%. That is a MASSIVE swing. Only SEA, DAL and NYJ were more run-based. With Hue Jackson (their former RB coach) gone, Ken Zampese (their former QB coach) takes over. Will he stay run heavy?

2015 Offensive Advanced Metrics

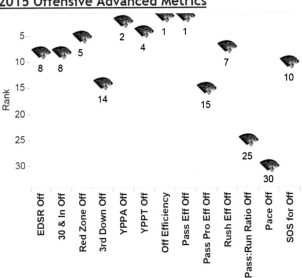

For years the Bengals have been one of the most consistent teams in the NFL on both sides of the ball. Unfortunately that hasn't translated into any type of playoff success, but 2015 was another year where this team ranked top 17 in literally every single metric offensively or defensively, with the vast majority being top 10. One of the lone down points was 3rd down offense & defense (17th). They had the NFL's most efficient pass offense in 2015 & were tremendous inside the red zone. Part of their success came because they ran the ball 2nd most of any team in the red zone (behind CAR) and red zone rushing is some of the most efficient rushing a team can have. Gio Bernard led the way with 22 red zone carries, but his 6 YPA was significantly more than Jeremy Hill's 2.4 YPA. AJ Green and Tyler Eifert led the passing targets, but Marvin Jones' and Mohamed Sanu's 14 targets will get redistributed.

2015 Defensive Advanced Metrics

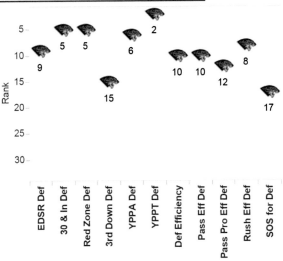

Drafted Players 2016 Draft Grade: **#4** (3.4/4)

Rnd.	Pick #	Pos.	Player	College
1	24	CB	William Jackson	Houston
2	55	WR	Tyler Boyd	Pittsburgh
3	87	ILB	Nick Vigil	Utah State
4	122	DT	Andrew Billings	Baylor
5	161	G	Christian Westerman	Arizona State
6	199	WR	Cody Core	Ole Miss
7	245	S	Clayton Fejedelem	Illinois

PERSONNEL & SPENDING

Cincinnati Bengals

Free Agents/Trades Added

Player (Position)

Karlos Dansby LB

Taylor Mays S

Vincent Rey LB

2015 Players Lost

Transaction	Player (Position)
Cut	A.J. Hawk LB
	Brown, Jonathan K
	Darryl Baldwin T
	Matt Johnson QB
Declared Free Agent	Leon Hall CB
	Marvin Jones WR
	Mohamed Sanu WR
	Reggie Nelson S

Other Signed

Player (Position)

Aaron Epps T
Alex Cooper G
Alex Erickson WR
Alex Redmond G
Alonzo Russell WR
Antwane Grant WR
Corey Tindal CB
Darien Harris LB
Darius Hillary CB
David Dean DT
Dy'Shawn Mobley RB
Gionni Paul LB
Joe Licata QB
John Weidenaar T
Jonathan Brown K
Matt Johnson QB
Ryan Brown DE
Tra Carson RB
Trip Thurman G

- The personnel story in Cincinnati is fascinating this year, primarily because the new signal caller and his background. Previous OC Hue Jackson was a former running backs coach. He significantly increased the run frequency for the Bengals in his 2 years as coordinator. But he was hired to be the Browns HC. The new OC is Ken Zampese, who has been the Bengals QB coach since 2003. He molded the rookie Andy Dalton and has seen Dalton develop to his current level.
- If Zampese wants to pass more, he'll have to do it to new #2 and #3 WRs, as both Marvin Jones and Mohamed Sanu left in free agency. But that is to the benefit of the Bengals. Because the Lions and Falcons significantly overpaid for players who excelled in their roles with the opportunity to run routes while AJ Green is taking the focus of the secondary, and run routes for a team who suddenly became surprisingly run-dominant in play calls, forcing the defense to respect the run more often. The Bengals were wise to not attempt to outbid those teams.
- The Bengals also resisted temptation to sign a high priced WR. Instead CIN will let the 55th overall pick Tyler Boyd and signed Brandon LaFell to a 1-year deal for just $2.5M. Both will be in similar, favorable situations that made Jones and Sanu rich.
- The Bengals retained CB Adam Jones & S George Iloka, two key cogs in the secondary, but did lose S Reggie Nelson & CB Leon Hall. An underrated move in free agency was signing LB Karlos Dansby. Dansby was one of the old-regime Browns splash signings in 2014, for 4 yrs / $24M. The Bengals signed him to just a 1 yr deal for only $2M. Dansby's leadership & price tag, coupled with his ability to play in coverage, makes this a wise move.
- The Bengals nabbed CB William Jackson III right before the Steelers took a CB, & added Pitt product Tyler Boyd & DT Andrew Billings (after a huge slide) before another PIT selection made an impression vs their rival.

Lineup & 2016 Cap Hit

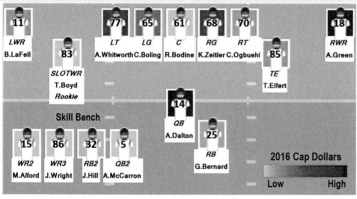

2016 Cap Dollars — Low ... High

Health Overall & by Unit (2015 v 2014)

2015 Rk	1
2015 AGL	28
Off Rk	1
Def Rk	6
2014 Rk	16
2014 AGL	72

2016 Positional Spending

	All OFF	QB	OL	RB	WR	TE	All DEF	DL	LB	CB	S
2015 Rk	13	19	7	20	6	25	5	8	11	8	18
Rank	18	21	13	12	13	25	11	9	18	15	22
Total	79.2M	14.7M	28.6M	8.9M	21.1M	5.9M	79.4M	32.2M	18.8M	20.1M	8.2M

2016 Offseason Spending

Total Spent	Total Spent Rk	Free Agents #	Free Agents $	Free Agents $ Rk	Waiver #	Waiver $	Waiver $ Rk	Extended #	Sum of Extended $	Sum of Drafted $	Undrafted #	Undrafted $
177M	18	7	39M	22	15	13M	15	4	67M	27M	19	31M

2015 Stats & Fantasy Production

Pos	Player	Ov. Rank	Pos. Rk	Age	Gms	St	Pass Comp	Pass Att	Pass Yds	Pass TD	Pass Int	Rush Att	Rush Yds	Rush YPA	Rush TD	Targ	Recp	Rec Yds	Rec YPC	Rec TDs	Draft King Pts	Fan Duel Pts
QB	Andy Dalton		18	28	13	13	255	386	3,250	25	7	57	142	2	3						259	251
	A.J. McCarron		39	25	7	3	79	119	854	6	2	14	31	2							61	57
RB	Jeremy Hill	39	13	23	16	15						223	794	4	11	19	15	79	5	1	176	163
	Giovani Bernard	65	21	24	16	1						154	730	5	2	66	49	472	10		187	157
WR	A.J. Green*	17	8	27	16	16										132	86	1,297	15	10	278	231
	Marvin Jones		39	25	16	13						5	33	7		103	65	816	13	4	177	141
	Mohamed Sanu		77	26	16	4						10	71	7	2	49	33	394	12		95	75
TE	Tyler Eifert*	23	6	25	13	12										74	52	615	12	13	195	166

ODDS & TRENDS — Cincinnati Bengals

Avg Line	Pred Wins	Pred Div Finish
-2.7	9.5	#2

2016 Weekly Betting Lines (wks 1-16)

(-) Favorite   Underdog (+)
-11.5   +4.0

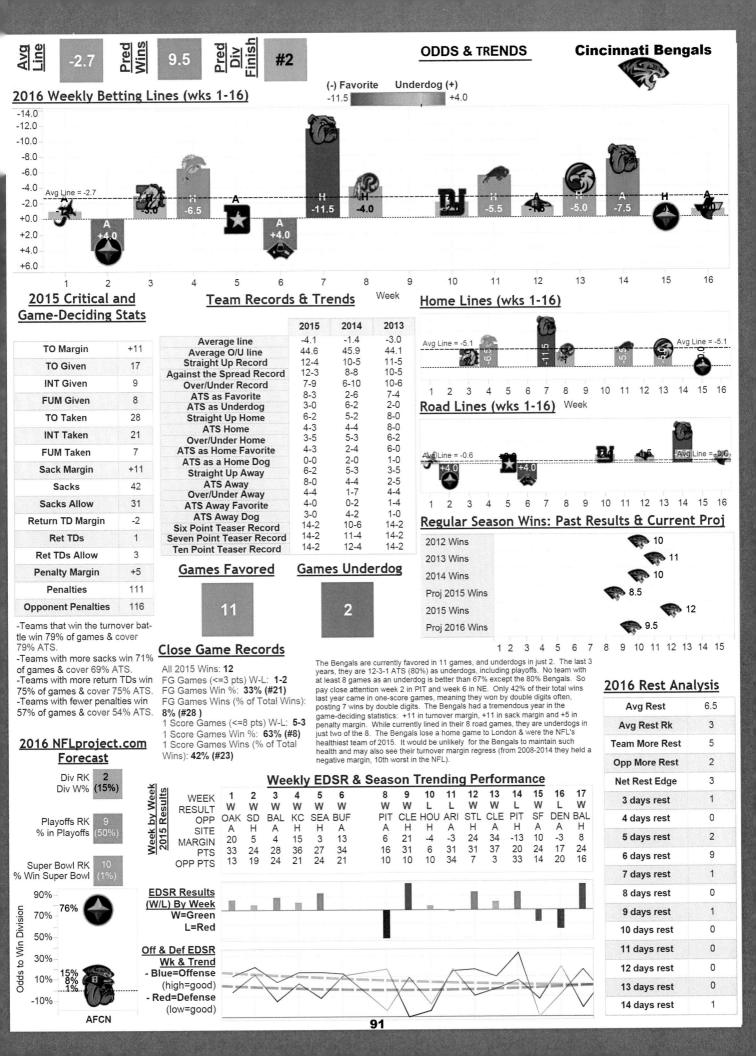

Avg Line = -2.7

Weeks 1–16

2015 Critical and Game-Deciding Stats

TO Margin	+11
TO Given	17
INT Given	9
FUM Given	8
TO Taken	28
INT Taken	21
FUM Taken	7
Sack Margin	+11
Sacks	42
Sacks Allow	31
Return TD Margin	-2
Ret TDs	1
Ret TDs Allow	3
Penalty Margin	+5
Penalties	111
Opponent Penalties	116

-Teams that win the turnover battle win 79% of games & cover 79% ATS.
-Teams with more sacks win 71% of games & cover 69% ATS.
-Teams with more return TDs win 75% of games & cover 75% ATS.
-Teams with fewer penalties win 57% of games & cover 54% ATS.

2016 NFLproject.com Forecast

Div RK	2
Div W%	(15%)
Playoffs RK	9
% in Playoffs	(50%)
Super Bowl RK	10
% Win Super Bowl	(1%)

Odds to Win Division

76%
15%
8%
1%

AFCN

Team Records & Trends

	2015	2014	2013
Average line	-4.1	-1.4	-3.0
Average O/U line	44.6	45.9	44.1
Straight Up Record	12-4	10-5	11-5
Against the Spread Record	12-3	8-8	10-5
Over/Under Record	7-9	6-10	10-6
ATS as Favorite	8-3	2-6	7-4
ATS as Underdog	3-0	6-2	2-0
Straight Up Home	6-2	5-2	8-0
ATS Home	4-3	4-4	8-0
Over/Under Home	3-5	5-3	6-2
ATS as Home Favorite	4-3	2-4	6-0
ATS as a Home Dog	0-0	2-0	1-0
Straight Up Away	6-2	5-3	3-5
ATS Away	8-0	4-4	2-5
Over/Under Away	4-4	1-7	4-4
ATS Away Favorite	4-0	0-2	1-4
ATS Away Dog	3-0	4-2	1-0
Six Point Teaser Record	14-2	10-6	14-2
Seven Point Teaser Record	14-2	11-4	14-2
Ten Point Teaser Record	14-2	12-4	14-2

Games Favored: 11

Games Underdog: 2

Close Game Records

All 2015 Wins: 12
FG Games (<=3 pts) W-L: 1-2
FG Games Win %: 33% (#21)
FG Games Wins (% of Total Wins): 8% (#28)
1 Score Games (<=8 pts) W-L: 5-3
1 Score Games Win %: 63% (#8)
1 Score Games Wins (% of Total Wins): 42% (#23)

The Bengals are currently favored in 11 games, and underdogs in just 2. The last 3 years, they are 12-3-1 ATS (80%) as underdogs, including playoffs. No team with at least 8 games as an underdog is better than 67% except the 80% Bengals. So pay close attention week 2 in PIT and week 6 in NE. Only 42% of their total wins last year came in one-score games, meaning they won by double digits often, posting 7 wins by double digits. The Bengals had a tremendous year in the game-deciding statistics: +11 in turnover margin, +11 in sack margin and +5 in penalty margin. While currently lined in their 8 road games, they are underdogs in just two of the 8. The Bengals lose a home game to London & were the NFL's healthiest team of 2015. It would be unlikely for the Bengals to maintain such health and may also see their turnover margin regress (from 2008-2014 they held a negative margin, 10th worst in the NFL).

Home Lines (wks 1-16)

Avg Line = -5.1

Road Lines (wks 1-16)   Week

Avg Line = -0.6

Regular Season Wins: Past Results & Current Proj

2012 Wins	10
2013 Wins	11
2014 Wins	10
Proj 2015 Wins	8.5
2015 Wins	12
Proj 2016 Wins	9.5

2016 Rest Analysis

Avg Rest	6.5
Avg Rest Rk	3
Team More Rest	5
Opp More Rest	2
Net Rest Edge	3
3 days rest	1
4 days rest	0
5 days rest	2
6 days rest	9
7 days rest	1
8 days rest	0
9 days rest	1
10 days rest	0
11 days rest	0
12 days rest	0
13 days rest	0
14 days rest	1

Weekly EDSR & Season Trending Performance

WEEK	1	2	3	4	5	6	8	9	10	11	12	13	14	15	16	17
RESULT	W	W	W	W	W	W	W	W	L	L	W	L	W	L	W	W
OPP	OAK	SD	BAL	KC	SEA	BUF	PIT	CLE	HOU	ARI	STL	CLE	PIT	SF	DEN	BAL
SITE	A	H	A	H	H	A	A	H	A	H	A	H	A	H	A	H
MARGIN	20	5	4	15	3	13	6	21	-4	-3	24	34	-13	10	-3	8
PTS	33	24	28	36	27	34	16	31	6	31	31	37	20	24	17	24
OPP PTS	13	19	24	21	24	21	10	10	10	34	7	3	33	14	20	16

Week by Week 2015 Results

EDSR Results (W/L) By Week
W=Green
L=Red

Off & Def EDSR Wk & Trend
- Blue=Offense (high=good)
- Red=Defense (low=good)

STATS & VISUALIZATIONS

Cincinnati Bengals

Directional Passer Rating Achieved

Receiver	Short Left	Short Middle	Short Right	Deep Left	Deep Middle	Deep Right
A.J. Green	109	102	100	129	149	68
Marvin Jones	90	114	80	31	113	52
Tyler Eifert	116	129	128	158	104	149
Mohamed Sanu	53	69	89	91	118	0
Tyler Kroft	85	93	107	158		39
Ryan Hewitt	95	118	61	39	118	
Brandon Tate	83		39			158
C.J. Uzomah				83		
Mario Alford	118					

Directional Frequency by Receiver

Receiver	Short Left	Short Middle	Short Right	Deep Left	Deep Middle	Deep Right
A.J. Green	33%	19%	31%	48%	23%	55%
Marvin Jones	25%	13%	30%	32%	27%	31%
Tyler Eifert	16%	42%	19%	11%	19%	7%
Mohamed Sanu	16%	17%	12%	5%	23%	2%
Tyler Kroft	6%	6%	3%	2%		2%
Ryan Hewitt	1%	3%	4%	2%	8%	
Brandon Tate	1%		1%			2%
C.J. Uzomah				1%		
Mario Alford	1%					

Defense Passer Rating Allowed

Short Left	Short Middle	Short Right	Deep Left	Deep Middle	Deep Right
89	78	93	42	33	73

Offensive Rush Directional Yds/Carry

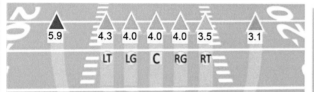

5.9 | 4.3 | 4.0 | 4.0 | 4.0 | 3.5 | 3.1
LT | LG | C | RG | RT

Offensive Rush Frequency of Direction

38 | 50 | 74 | 118 | 97 | 63 | 34
LT | LG | C | RG | RT

Offensive Explosive Runs by Direction

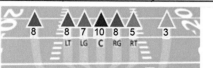

8 | 8 | 7 | 10 | 8 | 5 | 3
LT | LG | C | RG | RT

Defensive Rush Directional Yds/Carry

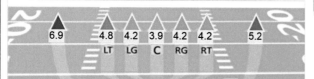

6.9 | 4.8 | 4.2 | 3.9 | 4.2 | 4.2 | 5.2
LT | LG | C | RG | RT

Andy Dalton - 1st Down RTG

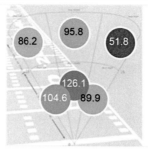

Andy Dalton - 2nd Down RTG

Andy Dalton - 3rd Down RTG

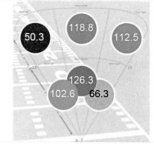

Andy Dalton - Overall RTG

2nd & Short RUN (1D or not)

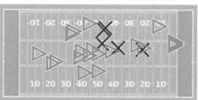

2nd & Short RUN Stats

Run Conv Rk	1D% Run	NFL 1D% Run Avg	Run Freq	NFL Run Freq Avg
8	79%	69%	73%	64%

2nd & Short PASS (1D or not)

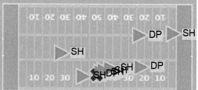

2nd & Short PASS Stats

Pass Conv Rk	1D% Pass	NFL 1D% Pass Avg	Pass Freq	NFL Pass Freq Avg
1	89%	55%	27%	36%

Pass Offense Play Success Rate

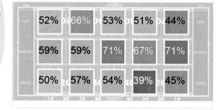

52%	66%	53%	51%	44%
59%	59%	71%	67%	71%
50%	57%	54%	39%	45%

Pass Offense Yds/Play

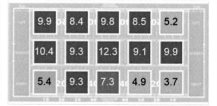

9.9	8.4	9.8	8.5	5.2
10.4	9.3	12.3	9.1	9.9
5.4	9.3	7.3	4.9	3.7

Off. Directional Tendency (% of Plays Left, Middle or Right)

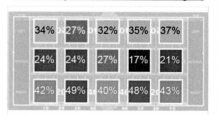

34%	27%	32%	35%	37%
24%	24%	27%	17%	21%
42%	49%	40%	48%	43%

Off. Directional Pass Rate (% of Plays which are Passes)

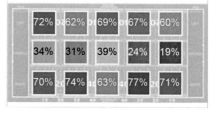

72%	62%	69%	67%	60%
34%	31%	39%	24%	19%
70%	74%	63%	77%	71%

Baltimore Ravens

Coaches

Head Coach: John Harbaugh (9th yr)
OC: Marc Trestman (2nd yr)
DC: Dean Pees (5th yr)

Forecast 2016 Wins

8

Past Records

2015: 5-11
2014: 10-6
2013: 8-8

Opponent Strength
Easy   Hard

2016 Schedule & Week by Week Strength of Schedule

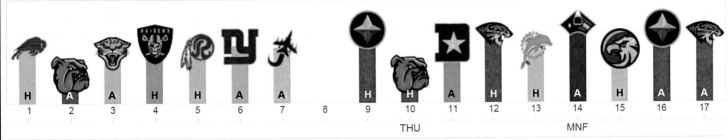

H	A	A	H	H	A	A		H	H	A	H	H	A	H	A	A
1	2	3	4	5	6	7	8	9	10	11	12	13	14	15	16	17

THU   MNF

2016 Overview

When a proud organization sees their team finish in 3rd place in the division for 3 consecutive seasons after making the playoffs for 5 straight years and winning a Super Bowl in that final year, what do they do? Some would panic. Some would make desperate moves. The Ravens and John Harbaugh went back to the basics, with a couple of small tweaks. They added an intelligent, physical safety at the start of free agency, signing the 31 year old Eric Weddle to a 4 year, $26M deal and likely locking him up for whatever productive years he has left in the NFL. Then, they retooled in the draft, selecting physical players who are capable of either protecting the passer (6th overall selecting Ronnie Stanley, OT) or rush the passer (42nd overall selection Kamalei Correa, LB & 70th overall selection Bronson Kaufusi, DE). Then, the Ravens made a few less-Raven moves, such as adding WR Mike Wallace via free agency, along with TE Benjamin Watson who was obviously at a "buy high" after his 2015 season in New Orleans. However, they signed very Raven-friendly contracts.

The optimism returned for many in the organization and those that support it following these moves. In reality, despite three straight third place finishes in the AFC North and a 5-11 campaign in 2015, it should never have left. The Ravens are 12-17 the last 3 years in games decided by one score with Joe Flacco at QB, including 3-7 last year. The last 3 years, no team has lost more games decided by one score than the Ravens. No team has played in more games decided by one score, either. With Joe Flacco at the helm, the Ravens have lost just 5 games the last 3 years by more than one score, meaning that 77% of their losses have come by one score, the second highest rate behind only Seattle. If the Ravens can change their style in 2016 to perform better, both offensively and defensively, in late, close games, it could produce a windfall of added wins.

There are many other reasons to be optimistic looking only at the 2016 season: no team suffered more injuries offensively, and overall the Ravens went from the 7th healthiest team in 2014 to the 3rd most injured team in 2015. If the injuries regress, it will bode well for the 2016 season. Then you have the fact that the 2015 Ravens were unable to get takeaways. As a result, they lost the turnover battle in 11 of their 16 games, the most of any team in the NFL. No commonly used, traditional statistic has more of a correlation to wins or losses than turnover margin. Historically teams that lose the turnover battle lose 79% of games. The 2015 Ravens lost 82% of the 11 games they lost the turnover battle. That has not been the Ravens tendency in recent or longer term history, and is likely to regress in 2016. The Ravens were also -19 in season penalty margin and allowed 5 return TDs. Finally, they played an extremely difficult schedule: 8th hardest offensively, 5th hardest defensively, with games against the difficult NFC West and AFC West. In 2016, they face a far easier slate. While all of those things are positives, there are a few black clouds. The Ravens are paying Joe Flacco more on average than any other player in the NFL. Even after renegotiating his contract this year, Flacco's 2017 cap hit of $24.55M is 2nd most of any player. It is very hard to build a sound roster when allocating so much cap space to the QB position. The short term forecast in Baltimore looks optimistic. The longer term forecast is less so, unless Flacco eventually can play up to the level of his pay.

Strength of Schedule In Detail

True Strength of Schedule Rank: 26

Hardest Stretches *(1=Hard, 32=Easy)*

Hardest 3 wk Stretch Rk:	14
Hardest 4 wk Stretch Rk:	8
Hardest 5 wk Stretch Rk:	9

Easiest Stretches *(1=Easy, 32=Hard)*

Easiest 3 wk Stretch Rk:	5
Easiest 4 wk Stretch Rk:	7
Easiest 5 wk Stretch Rk:	6

Baltimore does have three sets of back-to-back road games, tied for most in the NFL. Their early schedule, through week 8's bye, is substantially easier than their late schedule. In fact, they have the NFL's easiest schedule over the first 8 games. But from week 9 onward, their schedule is actually the 5th toughest, though that primarily is due to simply being in the AFC North, as they face the Steelers and Bengals twice apiece in that span of 9 games. The Ravens also are one of four teams to close with three road games of their last four, and they are not easy spots (@ NE, @ PIT, @ CIN).

2015 Play Tendencies

All Pass %	65%
All Pass Rk	3
All Rush %	35%
All Rush Rk	30
1 Score Pass %	63%
1 Score Pass Rk	7
2014 1 Score Pass %	56%
2014 1 Score Pass Rk	22
Pass Increase %	7%
Pass Increase Rk	4
1 Score Rush %	38%
1 Score Rush Rk	26
Up Pass %	59%
Up Pass Rk	4
Up Rush %	41%
Up Rush Rk	29
Down Pass %	68%
Down Pass Rk	13
Down Rush %	32%
Down Rush Rk	20

In Marc Trestman's 1st year as offensive coordinator, things went about as well as they did in Chicago in his last season. However, one thing Trestman brought was a pass heavy offense. The Ravens moved from 56% pass in one-score games in 2014 (22nd) to 63% in 2015, a 7% increase, 4th largest of any team last year. Even with a lead last year, the Ravens still passed 59% of play calls, 4th most often.

2015 Offensive Advanced Metrics

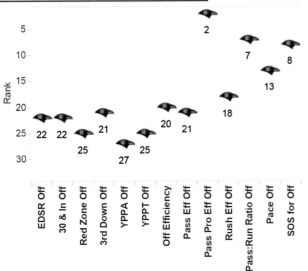

Given his salary as well as his coach's continued praise as being elite, Joe Flacco has not lived up to the Super Bowl season which he parlayed into a massive contract. The Ravens passing offense was 27th in yds/pass and 21st in passing efficiency. While Flacco did not play but 10 games last year, Matt Schaub had identical yds/pass numbers, which were only marginally better than Jimmy Clausen in his 2 starts. The Ravens offense was extremely inefficient on early downs, as well as on 3rd down and inside the red zone, so a lot of improvement is needed in 2016. Defensively the team was extremely bad in two key areas: pass efficiency and yds/point allowed. The defense did not force nearly enough takeaways (6 interceptions all season). Things would have been significantly worse had the Ravens not finished 8th in red zone defense.

2015 Defensive Advanced Metrics

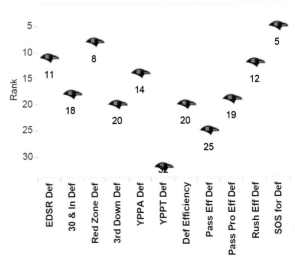

Drafted Players

2016 Draft Grade: #3 (3.6/4)

Rnd.	Pick #	Pos.	Player	College
1	6	OT	Ronnie Stanley	Notre Dame
2	42	LB	Kamalei Correa	Boise State
3	70	DE	Bronson Kaufusi	BYU
4	104	CB	Tavon Young	Temple
4	107	WR	Chris Moore	Cincinnati
4	130	OT	Alex Lewis	Nebraska
4	132	DT	Willie Henry	Michigan
4	134	RB	Kenneth Dixon	Louisiana Tech
5	146	DE	Matt Judon	Grand Valley State
6	182	RB	Keenan Reynolds	Navy
6	209	CB	Maurice Canady	Virginia

Free Agents/Trades Added

Player (Position)
- Benjamin Watson TE
- Eric Weddle S
- Jerraud Powers CB
- Josh Johnson QB
- Mike Wallace WR
- Vladimir Ducasse G

Other Signed

Player (Position)
- Anthony Fabiano C
- Cavellis Luckett LB
- Jarell Broxton G
- Jerraud Powers CB
- Josh Johnson QB
- Mario Ojemudia LB
- Matt Skura C
- Michael Pierce DT
- Patrick Onwuasor LB
- Sam Brown S
- Stephane Nembot T
- Trevon Coley DT
- Victor Ochi LB
- Vladimir Ducasse G
- Wil Lutz K

2015 Players Lost

Transaction	Player (Position)
Cut	Daryl Smith LB
	Harold Spears TE
	Jermaine Whitehead S
	Marlon Brown WR
	Nick Perry S
	Will Hill III S
Deceased	Tray Walker CB
Declared Free Agent	Chris Canty DE
	Chris Givens WR
	Courtney Upshaw LB
	Kelechi Osemele G
	Matt Schaub QB

- In Baltimore, the team is built firmly around the quarterback. It seems as if their constant goal is to provide Joe Flacco with enough pieces to make it work. That strategy made a lot of sense when Flacco was a younger player. But now that he is commanding an avg salary of $22M, the most of any QB in the NFL, it seems a bit backwards.

- This past offseason, the team went out in free agency and signed the veteran Mike Wallace and Benjamin Watson to pair with another free agent acquisition, Steve Smith, to form Flacco's receiving corps. They also drafted OT Ronnie Stanley to fortify his protection, selecting Stanley 6th overall. The only positive was that Mike Wallace, while he signed a 2 yr, $11.5M deal, has the 2017 season as a club option, and that is where an $8M cap hit comes into play.

- The shocking part about Ozzie Newsome, and how strong he is drafting and building his roster the right way, is how bad he's been when it comes to receivers. In trying to pair a drafted receiver to work with Joe Flacco, only 1 receiver since 2008 (when Flacco was drafted) has more than 75 receptions. And that was Torrey Smith, who left Baltimore after his rookie deal and signed in San Francisco. Other players like Mark Clayton, Tandon Doss, Demetrius Williams, Michael Campanaro, David Reed, Darren Waller, Yamon Figurs, Justin Harper, Marcus Smith and Tommy Streeter were all drafted by Newsome, played with Flacco, and amounted to nothing.

- The addition of S Eric Weddle in free agency was a power move by Newsome. Baltimore has needed a player like Weddle up the middle for several years now. His intelligence is one of the elements that gets underestimated when examining him. But his ability to diagnose plays, QB the defense and has been extremely reliable. From 2010 through 2014 (5 years) he started all 16 games every single season for the Chargers. Last year he missed 3 starts, his first missed since 2009.

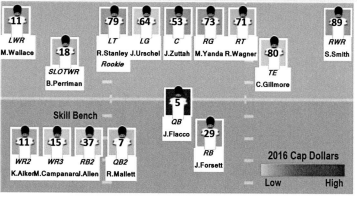

Lineup & 2016 Cap Hit

FS E.Weddle 32
SS L.Webb 21
LB Z.Orr 54
LB C.Mosley 57
RCB J.Smith 22
SLOTCB M.Elam 26
OLB T.Suggs 55
DE L.Guy 67
DE T.Jernigan 97
OLB E.Dumervil 58
LCB S.Wright 35

LWR M.Wallace 11
LT R.Stanley (Rookie) 79
LG J.Urschel 64
C J.Zuttah 53
RG M.Yanda 73
RT R.Wagner 71
RWR S.Smith 89
SLOTWR B.Perriman 18
TE C.Gillmore 80
QB J.Flacco 5
RB J.Forsett 29

Skill Bench
WR2 K.Aiken 11
WR3 M.Campanaro 15
RB2 J.Allen 37
QB2 R.Mallett 7

2016 Cap Dollars — Low / High

Health Overall & by Unit (2015 v 2014)

2015 Rk	30
2015 AGL	96
Off Rk	32
Def Rk	12
2014 Rk	7
2014 AGL	53

2016 Positional Spending

	All OFF	QB	OL	RB	WR	TE	All DEF	DL	LB	CB	S
2015 Rk	19	12	17	27	23	7	24	31	7	10	16
Rank	9	5	22	17	16	13	25	32	15	11	14
Total	85.0M	25.1M	28.1M	7.3M	16.1M	8.4M	67.2M	8.1M	25.5M	23.9M	9.7M

2016 Offseason Spending

Total Spent	Total Spent Rk	Free Agents #	Free Agents $	Free Agents $ Rk	Waiver #	Waiver $	Waiver $ Rk	Extended #	Sum of Extended $	Sum of Drafted $	Undrafted #	Undrafted $
216M	8	9	50M	19	13	10M	23	4	89M	51M	12	19M

2015 Stats & Fantasy Production

Pos	Player	Ov. Rank	Pos. Rk	Age	Gms	St	Pass Comp	Pass Att	Pass Yds	Pass TD	Pass Int	Rush Att	Rush Yds	Rush YPA	Rush TD	Targ	Recp	Rec Yds	Rec YPC	Rec TDs	Draft King Pts	Fan Duel Pts
QB	Joe Flacco		26	30	10	10	266	413	2,791	14	12	13	23	2	3						177	172
	Matt Schaub		48	34	2	2	52	80	540	3	4	4	10	3							34	31
RB	Javorius Allen		36	24	16	6						137	514	4	1	62	45	353	8	2	154	123
	Justin Forsett		42	30	10	10						151	641	4	2	41	31	153	5		128	107
	Kyle Juszczyk		64	24	16	11						2	3	2		56	41	321	8	4	100	77
WR	Kamar Aiken	77	30	26	16	14										127	75	944	13	5	201	160
	Steve Smith		52	36	7	7										73	46	670	15	3	134	108
	Jeremy Butler		99	24	8											44	31	363	12		70	52
TE	Crockett Gillmore		24	24	10	10										47	33	412	12	4	101	82
	Maxx Williams		43	21	14	7										48	32	268	8	1	68	49
	Nick Boyle		59	22	11	2										23	18	153	9		38	26

Avg Line	+0.9	Pred Wins	8	Pred Div Finish	#3

2016 Weekly Betting Lines (wks 1-16)

(-) Favorite   Underdog (+)
-8.5 ___ +9.0

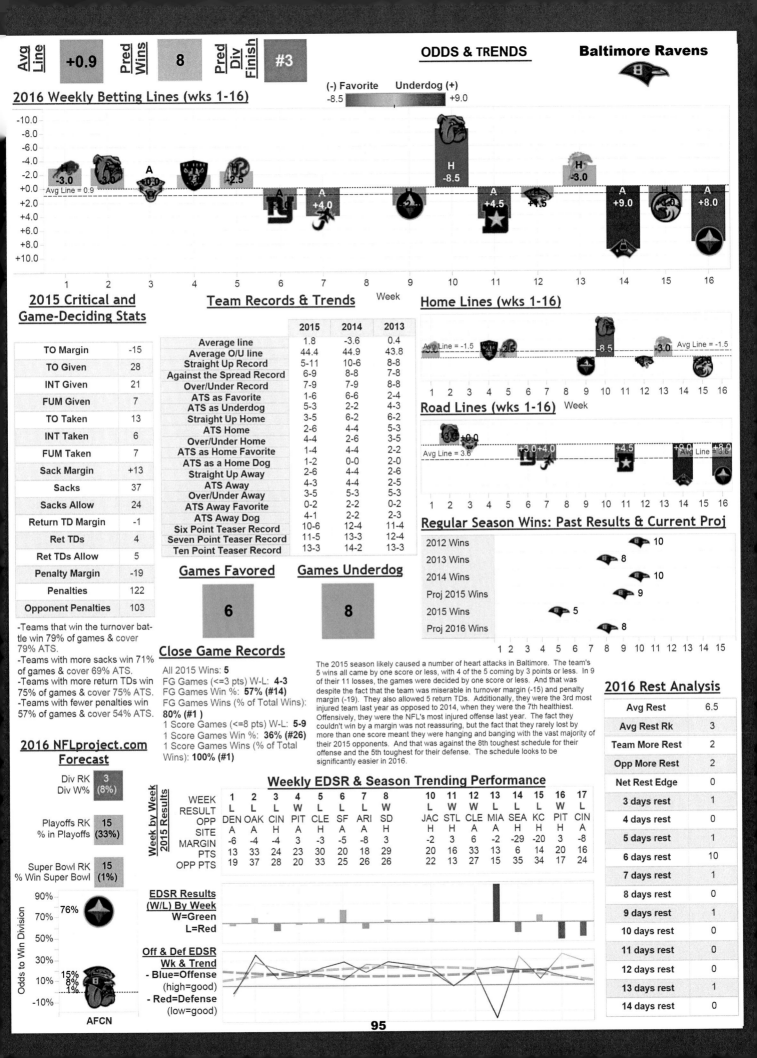

2015 Critical and Game-Deciding Stats

TO Margin	-15
TO Given	28
INT Given	21
FUM Given	7
TO Taken	13
INT Taken	6
FUM Taken	7
Sack Margin	+13
Sacks	37
Sacks Allow	24
Return TD Margin	-1
Ret TDs	4
Ret TDs Allow	5
Penalty Margin	-19
Penalties	122
Opponent Penalties	103

-Teams that win the turnover battle win 79% of games & cover 79% ATS.
-Teams with more sacks win 71% of games & cover 69% ATS.
-Teams with more return TDs win 75% of games & cover 75% ATS.
-Teams with fewer penalties win 57% of games & cover 54% ATS.

2016 NFLproject.com Forecast

Div RK	3
Div W%	(8%)

Playoffs RK	15
% in Playoffs	(33%)

Super Bowl RK	15
% Win Super Bowl	(1%)

Odds to Win Division
90% / 70% / 50% / 30% / 10% / -10%
76%
15%
8%
1%
AFCN

Team Records & Trends

	2015	2014	2013
Average line	1.8	-3.6	0.4
Average O/U line	44.4	44.9	43.8
Straight Up Record	5-11	10-6	8-8
Against the Spread Record	6-9	8-8	7-8
Over/Under Record	7-9	7-9	8-8
ATS as Favorite	1-6	6-6	2-4
ATS as Underdog	5-3	2-2	4-3
Straight Up Home	3-5	6-2	6-2
ATS Home	2-6	4-4	5-3
Over/Under Home	4-4	2-6	3-5
ATS as Home Favorite	1-4	4-4	2-2
ATS as a Home Dog	1-2	0-0	2-0
Straight Up Away	2-6	4-4	2-6
ATS Away	4-3	4-4	2-5
Over/Under Away	3-5	5-3	5-3
ATS Away Favorite	0-2	2-2	0-2
ATS Away Dog	4-1	2-2	2-3
Six Point Teaser Record	10-6	12-4	11-4
Seven Point Teaser Record	11-5	13-3	12-4
Ten Point Teaser Record	13-3	14-2	13-3

Games Favored
6

Games Underdog
8

Close Game Records

All 2015 Wins: 5
FG Games (<=3 pts) W-L: **4-3**
FG Games Win %: **57% (#14)**
FG Games Wins (% of Total Wins): **80% (#1)**
1 Score Games (<=8 pts) W-L: **5-9**
1 Score Games Win %: **36% (#26)**
1 Score Games Wins (% of Total Wins): **100% (#1)**

The 2015 season likely caused a number of heart attacks in Baltimore. The team's 5 wins all came by one score or less, with 4 of the 5 coming by 3 points or less. In 9 of their 11 losses, the games were decided by one score or less. And that was despite the fact that the team was miserable in turnover margin (-15) and penalty margin (-19). They also allowed 5 return TDs. Additionally, they were the 3rd most injured team last year as opposed to 2014, when they were the 7th healthiest. Offensively, they were the NFL's most injured offense last year. The fact that they couldn't win by a margin was not reassuring, but the fact that they rarely lost by more than one score meant they were hanging and banging with the vast majority of their 2015 opponents. And that was against the 8th toughest schedule for their offense and the 5th toughest for their defense. The schedule looks to be significantly easier in 2016.

Home Lines (wks 1-16)
Avg Line = -1.5

Road Lines (wks 1-16)
Avg Line = 3.6

Regular Season Wins: Past Results & Current Proj

2012 Wins	10
2013 Wins	8
2014 Wins	10
Proj 2015 Wins	9
2015 Wins	5
Proj 2016 Wins	8

2016 Rest Analysis

Avg Rest	6.5
Avg Rest Rk	3
Team More Rest	2
Opp More Rest	2
Net Rest Edge	0
3 days rest	1
4 days rest	0
5 days rest	1
6 days rest	10
7 days rest	1
8 days rest	0
9 days rest	1
10 days rest	0
11 days rest	0
12 days rest	0
13 days rest	1
14 days rest	0

Weekly EDSR & Season Trending Performance

WEEK	1	2	3	4	5	6	7	8	10	11	12	13	14	15	16	17
RESULT	L	L	L	W	L	L	L	W	L	W	W	L	L	L	W	L
OPP	DEN	OAK	CIN	PIT	CLE	SF	ARI	SD	JAC	STL	CLE	MIA	SEA	KC	PIT	CIN
SITE	H	A	H	A	H	A	A	H	H	H	A	A	H	A	H	A
MARGIN	-6	-4	-4	3	-3	-5	-8	3	-2	3	6	-2	-29	-20	3	-8
PTS	13	33	24	23	30	20	18	29	20	16	33	13	6	14	20	16
OPP PTS	19	37	28	20	33	25	26	26	22	13	27	15	35	34	17	24

EDSR Results (W/L) By Week
W=Green
L=Red

Off & Def EDSR Wk & Trend
- Blue=Offense (high=good)
- Red=Defense (low=good)

Baltimore Ravens

Directional Passer Rating Achieved

Receiver	Short Left	Short Middle	Short Right	Deep Left	Deep Middle	Deep Right
Kamar Aiken	106	62	62	107	47	69
Steve Smith	58	107	75	101	118	129
Crockett Gillmore	144	118	82		23	109
Maxx Williams	78	81	58	39	95	98
Jeremy Butler	60	106	101	118	118	33
Chris Givens	14	86	39	95	39	50
Nick Boyle	103	90	85		39	118
Marlon Brown	68	71	39	39	39	109
Chris Matthews	56	136	54	87		39
Jeremy Ross	92	39	102	39		39
Daniel Brown	83	39	0	118	118	39
Mike Campanaro	97	85	79			
Darren Waller			82	39		39

Directional Frequency by Receiver

Receiver	Short Left	Short Middle	Short Right	Deep Left	Deep Middle	Deep Right
Kamar Aiken	29%	18%	22%	37%	21%	31%
Steve Smith	14%	10%	18%	16%	11%	17%
Crockett Gillmore	5%	17%	10%		32%	5%
Maxx Williams	10%	14%	10%	2%	11%	5%
Jeremy Butler	11%	9%	8%	5%	5%	10%
Chris Givens	12%	6%	8%	23%	5%	12%
Nick Boyle	3%	9%	6%		5%	2%
Marlon Brown	6%	8%	6%	2%	5%	5%
Chris Matthews	2%	6%	2%	5%		5%
Jeremy Ross	3%	1%	5%	2%		2%
Daniel Brown	3%	1%	1%	2%	5%	3%
Mike Campanaro	2%	3%	1%			
Darren Waller				2%	5%	2%

Defense Passer Rating Allowed

Short Left	Short Middle	Short Right	Deep Left	Deep Middle	Deep Right
92	101	98	85	120	115

Offensive Rush Directional Yds/Carry

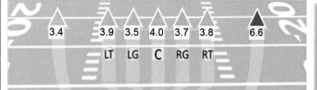

3.4 | 3.9 | 3.5 | 4.0 | 3.7 | 3.8 | 6.6
LT | LG | C | RG | RT

Offensive Rush Frequency of Direction

14 | 60 | 85 | 74 | 59 | 73 | 16
LT | LG | C | RG | RT

Offensive Explosive Runs by Direction

1 | 6 | 7 | 8 | 4 | 8 | 4
LT | LG | C | RG | RT

Defensive Rush Directional Yds/Carry

6.0 | 4.9 | 3.9 | 4.3 | 3.4 | 3.6 | 4.3
LT | LG | C | RG | RT

Joe Flacco - 1st Down RTG

27.4 | 10.8 | 107.7
87.6 | 112.9 | 82.9

Joe Flacco - 2nd Down RTG

135.4 | 72.9 | 82.1
104.9 | 74.7 | 75.1

Joe Flacco - 3rd Down RTG

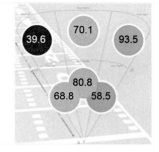

39.6 | 70.1 | 93.5
68.8 | 80.8 | 58.5

Joe Flacco - Overall RTG

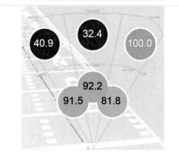

40.9 | 32.4 | 100.0
91.5 | 92.2 | 81.8

2nd & Short RUN (1D or not)

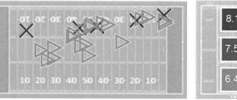

2nd & Short RUN Stats

Run Conv Rk	1D% Run	NFL 1D% Run Avg	Run Freq	NFL Run Freq Avg
6	84%	69%	74%	64%

2nd & Short PASS (1D or not)

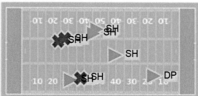

2nd & Short PASS Stats

Pass Conv Rk	1D% Pass	NFL 1D% Pass Avg	Pass Freq	NFL Pass Freq Avg
13	56%	55%	26%	36%

Pass Offense Play Success Rate

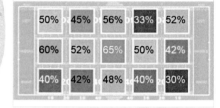

50%	45%	56%	33%	52%
60%	52%	65%	50%	42%
40%	42%	48%	40%	30%

Pass Offense Yds/Play

8.1	6.8	8.5	5.3	4.1
7.5	6.5	7.8	6.8	4.9
6.4	6.8	8.0	6.3	2.7

Off. Directional Tendency (% of Plays Left, Middle or Right)

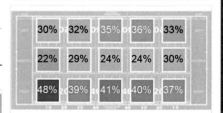

30%	32%	35%	36%	33%
22%	29%	24%	24%	30%
48%	39%	41%	40%	37%

Off. Directional Pass Rate (% of Plays which are Passes)

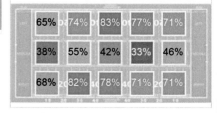

65%	74%	83%	77%	71%
38%	55%	42%	33%	46%
68%	82%	78%	71%	71%

Cleveland Browns

Coaches

Head Coach: Hue Jackson (CIN OC) (1st yr)
OC: (Hue Jackson will call plays) (1st yr)
DC: Ray Horton (TEN DC) (1st yr)

Forecast 2016 Wins

4.5

Past Records

2015: 3-13
2014: 7-9
2013: 4-12

Opponent Strength
Easy — Hard

2016 Schedule & Week by Week Strength of Schedule

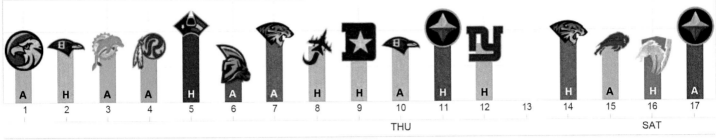

A	H	A	A	H	A	A	H	H	A	H	H		H	A	H	A
1	2	3	4	5	6	7	8	9	10	11	12	13	14	15	16	17

THU   SAT

2016 Overview

During Mike Pettine tenure as Browns coach in 2014 and 2015, the Browns tried a few strategies when it came to team building. They traded up in the draft to land Justin Gilbert, Johnny Manziel and Terrance West. They spent $90M in 2014's free agency and $69M in 2015, landing players like Dwayne Bowe, Tramon Williams and Ben Tate. And they spent heavily on defense, occupying the 8th most cap space on defense in 2014 and the 3rd most in 2015. As it turns out, trading up in the draft, overpaying players in free agency and trying to spend haphazardly to put together a patchwork defense are not winning formulas.

The Browns turned the corner in 2016. They let free agents walk and will recoup compensatory picks. The repeatedly traded down in the draft to gain a ton of talent. They refused to spend in free agency, with only $32M spent, roughly one third of 2014's spree and one half of 2015's expenditures. They brought on a new coach and a new management team, and are focused on the future rather than winning now. And its a smart move.

This year, a 34 year old Ben Roethlisberger will hit the cap at roughly $24M, as he will do 3 of the next 4 years. A 31 year old Joe Flacco will hit the cap for $23M this year and up to $28M over the next 4 years. A 28 year old Andy Dalton hits the cap for $13M this year and up to $18M in the next 4 years. Its hard to win in the NFL, and its even more difficult without a quarterback. But as these old AFC North QBs get older and more expensive, it will progressively become easier for the Browns to build a balanced roster focused around a young, cheap QB on a 5-year deal. With the Browns current roster, in order to win, a QB will be called upon to do a lot. They just don't have the surrounding talent. So you can imagine the pressure on a high-drafted rookie QB. Instead, the Browns will try to build out the roster so when the right QB is available the team will be capable of winning with very little being required of him. In the AFC North, both Ben Roethlisberger (2005) and Joe Flacco (2012) won the Super Bowl in their rookie deal, when the team had veteran leadership and played solid defense.

If the Browns are building for the future through the draft, where does that leave the 2016 team? As underdogs in all 15 of their lined games, with expectations to win just 4.5 games, and in need of more than just lucky bounces to win games. Case in point: the last two years, even when winning the turnover battle, the Browns have won just 4 of 10 games (40%). The NFL average is winning almost 80% of these games.

In the immediate future, Hue Jackson and Robert Griffin III will have to try to scheme and execute their way above the talent along the line, which was more talented and more expensive in 2015 but still allowed 53 sacks and ranked 29th in run blocking efficiency. Hue Jackson must focus the Browns, offensively and defensively, to focus on the little things each week, improve and execute, and not worry about the big picture right now. Cauterization does not smell pleasant, but the Browns were hemorrhaging. If fans can put up with the smell on seven Sundays and one Saturday this year, their team will be better for it in the future.

Strength of Schedule In Detail

True Strength of Schedule Rank: 13

Hardest Stretches *(1=Hard, 32=Easy)*
Hardest 3 wk Stretch Rk: **31**
Hardest 4 wk Stretch Rk: **31**
Hardest 5 wk Stretch Rk: **18**

Easiest Stretches *(1=Easy, 32=Hard)*
Easiest 3 wk Stretch Rk: **30**
Easiest 4 wk Stretch Rk: **26**
Easiest 5 wk Stretch Rk: **24**

The Browns start off as one of five teams to play three road games in the first four weeks. For better teams, the consolation is their opponents during this stretch are some of the easiest on their schedule, but we know better than to make that assumption for the Browns, as they will be underdogs in all 4 games. A road game in Tennessee week 6 looks like the best opportunity to project success for the Browns. Cleveland fans won't find any irony in the fact their team has the unlucky 13th hardest schedule.

2015 Play Tendencies

All Pass %	64%
All Pass Rk	7
All Rush %	36%
All Rush Rk	26
1 Score Pass %	64%
1 Score Pass Rk	3
2014 1 Score Pass %	54%
2014 1 Score Pass Rk	26
Pass Increase %	10%
Pass Increase Rk	2
1 Score Rush %	36%
1 Score Rush Rk	30
Up Pass %	46%
Up Pass Rk	22
Up Rush %	54%
Up Rush Rk	11
Down Pass %	68%
Down Pass Rk	14
Down Rush %	32%
Down Rush Rk	19

Typically for teams unsettled at the QB position, a run heavy attack is advised. However, despite 8 starts from Josh McCown, 6 from Johnny Manziel and 2 from Austin Davis, the Browns passed the ball on 64% of plays when the game was within 1 score(3rd most), a massive 9% increase from 2015 when they passed the ball on 54% of those plays (26th most). Coupled with bad QB play & virtually no quality WRs, this play calling only exacerbated their problems.

2015 Offensive Advanced Metrics

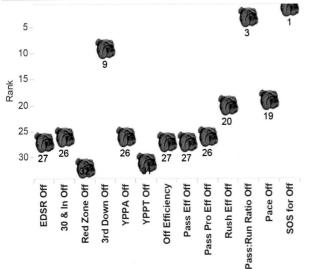

If there is one thing positive to say about the Browns terrible metrics, its that at least they were terrible against a great schedule. Their offense played the #1 schedule of opposing defenses last year, and their defense played the #3 schedule of opposing offenses. The results in those games were not very good, as their 3-13 record indicates. Making matters much worse for the Browns offense was that while they made an average number of trips into the red zone per game (3), they converted on just 38% of those trips, significantly below the NFL's average. While converting better would not have been the difference to somehow turn the Browns into a playoff contender, it would have made a big difference to give them a handful of more wins, as they went just 1-5 in games decided by 1 score or less. A 17% win rate was the worst in the NFL last year.

2015 Defensive Advanced Metrics

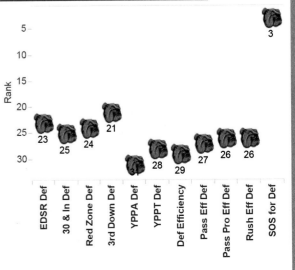

Drafted Players

2016 Draft Grade: #29 (2.2/4)

PERSONNEL & SPENDING

Cleveland Browns

Rnd.	Pick #	Pos.	Player	College
1	15	WR	Corey Coleman	Baylor
2	32	DE	Emmanuel Ogbah	Oklahoma State
3	65	DE	Carl Nassib	Penn State
3	76	OT	Shon Coleman	Auburn
	93	QB	Cody Kessler	USC
	99	OLB	Joe Schobert	Wisconsin
4	114	WR	Ricardo Louis	Auburn
	129	S	Derrick Kindred	TCU
	138	WR	Seth DeValve	Princeton
	154	WR	Jordan Payton	UCLA
5	168	OT	Spencer Drango	Baylor
	172	WR	Rashard Higgins	Colorado State
	173	CB	Trey Caldwell	Louisiana-Monroe
7	250	LB	Scooby Wright III	Arizona

Lineup & 2016 Cap Hit

FS J.Poyer -33-
SS I.Campbell -30-
LB C.Kirksey -58-
LB D.Davis -56-
RCB T.Williams -22-
SLOTCB K.Williams -36-
OLB E.Ogbah Rookie -90-
DE D.Bryant -92-
DT D.Shelton -71-
OLB P.Kruger -99-
LCB J.Haden -23-

-19-
LWR C.Coleman Rookie
-16-
SLOTWR A.Hawkins
-73- LT J.Thomas
-75- LG J.Bitonio
-74- C C.Erving
-77- RG J.Greco
-78- RT A.Bailey
-82- TE G.Barnidge
-18- RWR T.Gabriel

Skill Bench
-80- WR2 R.Louis Rookie
-84- WR3 J.Payton Rookie
-34- RB2 I.Crowell
-13- QB2 J.McCown
-10- QB R.Griffin
-29- RB D.Johnson

2016 Cap Dollars
Low — High

Free Agents/Trades Added

Player (Position)

Alvin Bailey G

Demario Davis LB

Jamar Taylor CB

Justin Tuggle LB

Robert Griffin III QB

Other Signed

Player (Position)

A.J. Stamps S
Brad Craddock K
Dominique Alexander LB
Eric Patterson CB
J.P. Holtz TE
Kenya Dennis S
Kyle Rose DT
Mike Matthews C
Mikell Everette S
Nile Lawrence-Stample DT
Patrick Skov RB
Tracy Howard S

Health Overall & by Unit (2015 v 2014)

2015 Rk	21
2015 AGL	71
Off Rk	18
Def Rk	21
2014 Rk	14
2014 AGL	67

2015 Players Lost

Transaction	Player (Position)
Cut	Brad Craddock K
	Chase Ford TE
	Donte Whitner S
	Dwayne Bowe WR
	Hartline, Brian WR
	Ifo Ekpre-Olomu CB
	Jim Dray TE
	Johnny Manziel QB
	Karlos Dansby LB
	Kenya Dennis S
	Randy Starks DT
	Saalim Hakim WR
	Scott Solomon LB
Declared Free Agent	Alex Mack C
	Mitchell Schwartz T
	Tashaun Gipson S
	Travis Benjamin WR
Retired	Oberkrom, Jaden K

- The Browns new management made some intelligent moves in the draft to acquire new talent. As such, it's hard to "grade" how well they performed, because so much of what they did will be tied to how future picks pan out, and those players are still in college right now. But generally speaking, I disagree with the 29th rated draft which was the collective grade assigned by the "experts" to the Browns.
- Cleveland let a number of free agents walk, and will add numerous compensatory picks in future drafts, and those picks (unlike in years past) are able to be traded. Additionally, their moves down the board effectively netted them the value of a 1st overall draft pick.
- They still drafted a ton of young talent. WR Corey Coleman from Baylor should be exactly the type of receiver that a QB like Robert Griffin III needs and can use. They are both from the same system at Baylor, and Coleman should catch on quickly.
- While some teams went with a volume approach at CB, which was said to be the best, deepest class in memory, the Browns went with a high volume approach at WR: They drafted 5 WRs in the first 5 rounds of the draft. We know Cleveland had no one at receiver last year. In terms of catches, their #1 receiver was TE Gary Barnidge, and #3 was RB Duke Johnson.
- Cleveland gutted their roster at offensive line, linebacker and safety this past offseason. Their offensive line went form 6th most expensive to 21st, their linebackers went from 5th most to 16th and their safeties went from 7th most expensive to 28th. They currently have the NFL's cheapest offense and 18th most expensive defense.
- To tell you how horrible things were in Cleveland last year: they had the 3rd most expensive defense in the NFL from a cap hit perspective. LB, CB and S were all inside the top 7. And yet the defense ranked 29th in total efficiency and was virtually bottom 10 in all major metrics.

2016 Positional Spending

	All OFF	QB	OL	RB	WR	TE	All DEF	DL	LB	CB	S
2015 Rk	22	23	6	31	12	20	3	21	5	3	7
Rank	32	24	21	30	26	23	18	23	16	3	28
Total	54.2M	12.8M	23.5M	2.9M	9.4M	5.6M	73.6M	16.9M	22.8M	28.3M	5.6M

2016 Offseason Spending

Total Spent	Total Spent Rk	Free Agents #	Free Agents $	Free Agents $ Rk	Waiver #	Waiver $	Waiver $ Rk	Extended #	Sum of Extended $	Sum of Drafted $	Undrafted #	Undrafted $
105M	31	6	32M	24	13	8M	27	0	0M	49M	10	16M

2015 Stats & Fantasy Production

Pos	Player	Ov. Rank	Pos. Rk	Age	Gms	St	Pass Comp	Pass Att	Pass Yds	Pass TD	Pass Int	Rush Att	Rush Yds	Rush YPA	Rush TD	Targ	Recp	Rec Yds	Rec YPC	Rec TDs	Draft King Pts	Fan Duel Pts
QB	Josh McCown		27	36	8	8	186	292	2,109	12	4	20	98	5	1						141	132
	Johnny Manziel		34	23	10	6	129	223	1,500	7	5	37	230	6							109	100
RB	Isaiah Crowell		28	22	16	9						185	706	4	4	22	19	182	10	1	144	128
	Duke Johnson		34	22	16	7						104	379	4		74	61	534	9	2	170	134
WR	Travis Benjamin	71	28	26	16	15						4	12	3		125	68	966	14	5	203	164
	Brian Hartline		72	29	12	4										77	46	523	11	2	113	87
	Andrew Hawkins		113	29	8	8										43	27	276	10		59	41
	Taylor Gabriel		122	24	13	4										48	28	241	9		56	38
TE	Gary Barnidge*	12	2	30	16	13										125	79	1,043	13	9	240	198

ODDS & TRENDS — Cleveland Browns

Avg Line	+6.4	Pred Wins	4.5	Pred Div Finish	#4

2016 Weekly Betting Lines (wks 1-16)

(-) Favorite   Underdog (+)
+0.0 ———————— +11.5

Week	1	2	3	4	5	6	7	8	9	10	11	12	13	14	15	16
Site	A	H	A	A	H	A	H	H	H	A	H	H		H	A	H
Line	+7.5	+3.0	+7.0	+7.5	+7.0	+3.5	+11.5	+5.0	+5.0	+8.5	+8.5	+3.5		+7.5	+9.0	+2.0

Avg Line = 6.4

2015 Critical and Game-Deciding Stats

TO Margin	-9
TO Given	30
INT Given	12
FUM Given	18
TO Taken	21
INT Taken	11
FUM Taken	10
Sack Margin	-24
Sacks	29
Sacks Allow	53
Return TD Margin	-1
Ret TDs	3
Ret TDs Allow	4
Penalty Margin	-12
Penalties	120
Opponent Penalties	108

-Teams that win the turnover battle win 79% of games & cover 79% ATS.
-Teams with more sacks win 71% of games & cover 69% ATS.
-Teams with more return TDs win 75% of games & cover 75% ATS.
-Teams with fewer penalties win 57% of games & cover 54% ATS.

2016 NFLproject.com Forecast

Div RK	4	
Div W%		(1%)
Playoffs RK	32	
% in Playoffs		(4%)
Super Bowl RK	32	
% Win Super Bowl		(0%)

Odds to Win Division

90%
76%
70%
50%
30%
15%
10% 8%
1%
-10%

AFCN

Team Records & Trends

	2015	2014	2013
Average line	5.5	1.2	3.1
Average O/U line	43.3	44.3	42.3
Straight Up Record	3-13	7-9	4-12
Against the Spread Record	6-10	10-6	6-10
Over/Under Record	7-8	5-11	9-7
ATS as Favorite	1-2	2-4	1-3
ATS as Underdog	4-8	7-2	5-6
Straight Up Home	2-6	4-4	3-5
ATS Home	3-5	4-4	3-5
Over/Under Home	4-3	2-6	5-3
ATS as Home Favorite	1-2	2-3	1-3
ATS as a Home Dog	1-3	2-1	2-1
Straight Up Away	1-7	3-5	1-7
ATS Away	3-5	6-2	3-5
Over/Under Away	3-5	4-4	4-4
ATS Away Favorite	0-0	0-1	0-0
ATS Away Dog	3-5	5-1	3-5
Six Point Teaser Record	8-8	12-4	8-8
Seven Point Teaser Record	8-8	12-4	8-7
Ten Point Teaser Record	11-5	12-4	11-5

Games Favored

Games Underdog
15

Close Game Records

All 2015 Wins: 3
FG Games (<=3 pts) W-L: 1-2
FG Games Win %: 33% (#21)
FG Games Wins (% of Total Wins): 33% (#8)
1 Score Games (<=8 pts) W-L: 1-5
1 Score Games Win %: 17% (#32)
1 Score Games Wins (% of Total Wins): 33% (#29)

Home Lines (wks 1-16)

	+3.0	+7.0	+5.0	+5.0	+8.5	+3.5	+7.5	+2.0

Avg Line = 5.2

Week: 1 2 3 4 5 6 7 8 9 10 11 12 13 14 15 16

Road Lines (wks 1-16)   Week

+7.5	+7.0	+7.5	+3.5	+11.5	+8.5	+9.0

Avg Line = 7.8

1 2 3 4 5 6 7 8 9 10 11 12 13 14 15 16

Regular Season Wins: Past Results & Current Proj

2012 Wins	5
2013 Wins	4
2014 Wins	7
Proj 2015 Wins	6
2015 Wins	3
Proj 2016 Wins	4.5

1 2 3 4 5 6 7 8 9 10 11 12 13 14 15

This Browns page has a lot of red on it. Which is obviously not a good thing. They are not favored in a single game, and their best line is +2 at home to the Chargers in week 16. We know the Browns were a bad team in 2015. Bad teams put up bad stats. Bad teams are usually bad in the most critical stats. Such as having negative turnover margins, sack margins and penalty margins. They also are bad in crunch time, which led to the Browns 1-5 (17%) record in games decide by 1 score, the NFL's worst record last year. In many cases, having such terrible numbers in those key metrics is not repeatable. Therefore, things should be predicted to improve for a team the following year. But let's examine the sack numbers: The Browns were a ridiculous -24, getting sacked 53 times and recording 29. Has their protection improved significantly? Do they have a QB who can avoid sacks better? How about their own pass rush? Unfortunately, there still isn't much to feel great about for 2016.

2016 Rest Analysis

Avg Rest	6.5
Avg Rest Rk	3
Team More Rest	3
Opp More Rest	0
Net Rest Edge	3
3 days rest	1
4 days rest	0
5 days rest	1
6 days rest	10
7 days rest	1
8 days rest	0
9 days rest	1
10 days rest	0
11 days rest	0
12 days rest	0
13 days rest	1
14 days rest	0

Weekly EDSR & Season Trending Performance

Week by Week 2015 Results

WEEK	1	2	3	4	5	6	7	8	9	10		12	13	14	15	16	17
RESULT	L	W	L	L	W	L	L	L	L	L		L	L	W	L	L	L
OPP	NYJ	TEN	OAK	SD	BAL	DEN	STL	ARI	CIN	PIT		BAL	CIN	SF	SEA	KC	PIT
SITE	A	H	A	A	H	A	H	A	H	A		H	H	H	A	A	H
MARGIN	-21	14	-7	-3	3	-3	-18	-14	-21	-21		-6	-34	14	-17	-4	-16
PTS	10	28	20	27	33	23	6	20	10	9		27	3	24	13	13	12
OPP PTS	31	14	27	30	30	26	24	34	31	30		33	37	10	30	17	28

EDSR Results (W/L) By Week
W=Green
L=Red

Off & Def EDSR Wk & Trend
- Blue=Offense (high=good)
- Red=Defense (low=good)

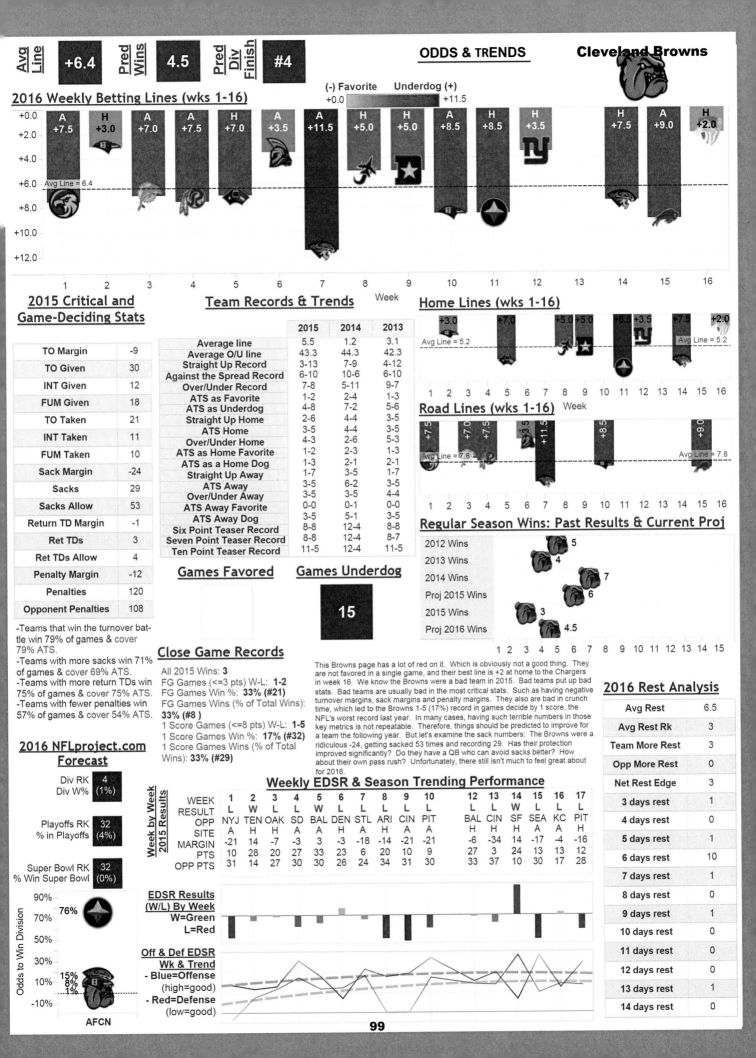

99

STATS & VISUALIZATIONS

Cleveland Browns

Directional Passer Rating Achieved

Receiver	Short Left	Short Middle	Short Right	Deep Left	Deep Middle	Deep Right
Gary Barnidge	66	107	115	106	109	122
Travis Benjamin	60	73	78	127	125	19
Brian Hartline	60	141	45	95	0	45
Taylor Gabriel	72	47	90	0	79	85
Andrew Hawkins	70	98	47	118	39	118
Darius Jennings	89	61	72			118
Marlon Moore	104	118	73			
Jim Dray	118	64	42	39		
Dwayne Bowe	95	95	63	0	39	39
E.J. Bibbs	39		95			
Rob Housler	39	91	39			
Terrelle Pryor	39	39	39	95		

Directional Frequency by Receiver

Receiver	Short Left	Short Middle	Short Right	Deep Left	Deep Middle	Deep Right
Gary Barnidge	26%	32%	24%	20%	15%	23%
Travis Benjamin	18%	15%	29%	43%	40%	42%
Brian Hartline	15%	20%	16%	15%	10%	13%
Taylor Gabriel	16%	5%	7%	8%	20%	6%
Andrew Hawkins	10%	11%	9%	3%	10%	3%
Darius Jennings	6%	7%	3%			3%
Marlon Moore	1%	3%	3%			
Jim Dray	1%	4%	6%	5%		
Dwayne Bowe	2%	1%	2%	3%	5%	10%
E.J. Bibbs	1%		1%			
Rob Housler	1%	1%	1%			
Terrelle Pryor	2%	1%	1%	5%		

Defense Passer Rating Allowed

Short Left	Short Middle	Short Right	Deep Left	Deep Middle	Deep Right
105	109	89	94	115	129

Offensive Rush Directional Yds/Carry

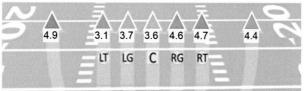

4.9 3.1 3.7 3.6 4.6 4.7 4.4
LT LG C RG RT

Offensive Rush Frequency of Direction

33 28 72 74 84 45 37
LT LG C RG RT

Offensive Explosive Runs by Direction

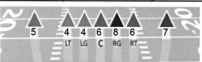

5 4 4 6 8 6 7
LT LG C RG RT

Defensive Rush Directional Yds/Carry

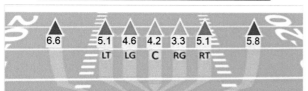

6.6 5.1 4.6 4.2 3.3 5.1 5.8
LT LG C RG RT

Josh McCown - 1st Down RTG

39.6 89.9 118.8
89.6
85.8 74.6

Josh McCown - 2nd Down RTG

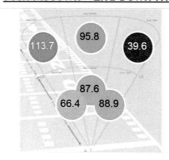

113.7 95.8 39.6
87.6
66.4 88.9

Josh McCown - 3rd Down RTG

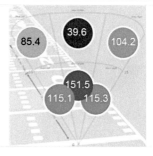

85.4 39.6 104.2
151.5
115.1 115.3

Josh McCown - Overall RTG

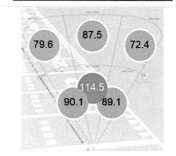

79.6 87.5 72.4
114.5
90.1 89.1

2nd & Short RUN (1D or not)

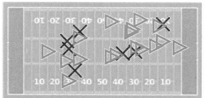

2nd & Short RUN Stats

Run Conv Rk	1D% Run	NFL 1D% Run Avg	Run Freq	NFL Run Freq Avg
13	71%	69%	71%	64%

2nd & Short PASS (1D or not)

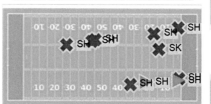

2nd & Short PASS Stats

Pass Conv Rk	1D% Pass	NFL 1D% Pass Avg	Pass Freq	NFL Pass Freq Avg
32	20%	55%	29%	36%

Pass Offense Play Success Rate

39%	48%	46%	47%	36%
52%	51%	65%	40%	28%
59%	49%	40%	54%	28%

Pass Offense Yds/Play

6.1	7.5	8.6	6.6	2.5
8.1	10.4	11.4	6.7	3.2
8.4	6.8	5.8	6.7	2.9

Off. Directional Tendency (% of Plays Left, Middle or Right)

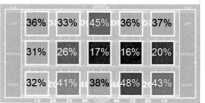

36%	33%	45%	36%	37%
31%	26%	17%	16%	20%
32%	41%	38%	48%	43%

Off. Directional Pass Rate (% of Plays which are Passes)

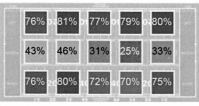

76%	81%	77%	79%	80%
43%	46%	31%	25%	33%
76%	80%	72%	70%	75%

New England Patriots

Coaches

Head Coach: Bill Belichick (17th yr)
OC: Josh McDaniels (5th yr)
DC: Matt Patrica (5th yr)

Forecast 2016 Wins

10.5

Past Records

2015: 12-4
2014: 12-4
2013: 12-4

Opponent Strength
Easy — Hard

2016 Schedule & Week by Week Strength of Schedule

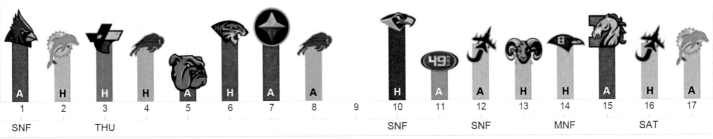

A	H	H	H	H	A	A	A		H	A	A	H	H	A	H	A
1	2	3	4	5	6	7	8	9	10	11	12	13	14	15	16	17

SNF — THU — SNF — SNF — MNF — SAT

2016 Overview

The easy answer as to why the Patriots are so great, and have won 4 Super Bowls since 2002 while no other team has won more than 2 (Steelers, Giants) is the combination of Tom Brady and Bill Belichick. But if that's clearly not the reason. The reason may very well be the least discussed ingredient for the Patriots' success. The reason is the combination of Tom Brady and his insane low cap hit for well over a decade, and Bill Belichick.

There are only 20 starting quarterbacks on veteran deals in the NFL which did not see a replacement drafted this year. Tom Brady is arguably the best of that group based on his reputation and accomplishments. Thus, no one would be shocked if his contract was the largest of that group. But that is not the case. Salary cap is the ultimate equalizer in the NFL. And the Patriots know how to make it work in their favor. Of those 20 veteran starting quarterbacks, Tom Brady's 2016 cap hit is not the most, or 2nd, or 3rd. It is not 5th or 10th or even 15th. Tom Brady's 2016 cap hit is $14M, ranking 17th out of 20. Quarterbacks directly above him who take up more of their team's cap are Colin Kaepernick, Jay Cutler and Alex Smith. This year is not a low-cap aberration. From 2011-2017, Brady did not (and will not) hit the cap for anything above $14.8M. Brady's cap hit for 2017 is $14M, as it was in 2015 and 2016. For comparison, this year Drew Brees hits the cap for $30M. The 2nd & 3rd highest hits are Eli Manning ($24M) and Ben Roethlisberger ($23.95M). Conveniently the only other QBs to lead their team to 2 Super Bowls since 2002. The 3 quarterbacks directly below Brady's $14M are not there by much & will all rocket past Brady in 2017. Ryan Tannehill will hit the cap for $20.3M, Brock Osweiler for $19M & Andy Dalton for $15.7M. Somehow the Patriots have figured out a way to pay the quarterback who deserves to be paid the most based on achievement, the least amount based on cap space. Brady has signed deal after deal after deal the last few years, each of which get ripped to shreds with at least 2 years remaining on the deal. He signed a 5 year deal in 2010, a 5 year deal in 2013, a 3 year deal in 2015 and a 4 year deal the very next year, in March of 2016.

By figuring a way around the salary cap for the player who deserves to hit it the most, the Patriots have significant cap space to sign other players to contribute. As great as the Tom Brady/Bill Belichick duo is, they have won their 4 Super Bowls by margins of 3, 3, 3 & 4 points. Every run has taken a full team effort. Every single season, the depth of talent and coaching ability is on display in New England. And they would not have the breadth nor depth of talent if they had Tom Brady hitting the cap at the level most other veterans do, not to mention the level his achievements should earn him - far an above the other 19 veteran quarterbacks in this group. That added cap space in part helped the Patriots bring in TE Martellus Bennett to provide what could be a "never-sub" lineup of skill players that can play uptempo, with a multitude of run or pass plays at their disposal & wear a defense into the ground. It also helped them bring in Chris Long, Terrance Knighton & Nate Washington in free agency. When the majority of the NFL doesn't understand the value of draft picks or the comp pick system & your team has mastered both, with one of the best tactician coaches in the NFL, and you are able to get the most deserving QB for year after year at a fraction of the cap hit you should be paying, it is no wonder the Patriots have won 10+ games in 13 straight seasons, the only team in the NFL salary cap era with such sustained success.

Strength of Schedule In Detail

True Strength of Schedule Rank: 23

Hardest Stretches *(1=Hard, 32=Easy)*
Hardest 3 wk Stretch Rk:	20
Hardest 4 wk Stretch Rk:	32
Hardest 5 wk Stretch Rk:	32

Easiest Stretches *(1=Easy, 32=Hard)*
Easiest 3 wk Stretch Rk:	11
Easiest 4 wk Stretch Rk:	12
Easiest 5 wk Stretch Rk:	20

The Patriots are another team whose Strength of Schedule is more difficult than it appears, but is offset by a couple of very easy opponents (@ CLE, @ SF). Fortunately, both of their easy teams are on the road, which means they have more home games against difficult competition where the home field advantage stands to benefit New England more. After that difficult game week 1 in Arizona, the Patriots play three straight home games, then travel to Cleveland, before hosting the Bengals in week 6. The Patriots will enjoy their bye week immediately prior to hosting Seattle in primetime week 10, and after that, the most difficult game they face is week 15 in Denver. From week 11 onward, the Patriots actually play the 3rd easiest schedule in the NFL.

2015 Play Tendencies

All Pass %	64%
All Pass Rk	8
All Rush %	36%
All Rush Rk	25
1 Score Pass %	64%
1 Score Pass Rk	5
2014 1 Score Pass %	61%
2014 1 Score Pass Rk	7
Pass Increase %	3%
Pass Increase Rk	11
1 Score Rush %	36%
1 Score Rush Rk	28
Up Pass %	60%
Up Pass Rk	2
Up Rush %	40%
Up Rush Rk	31
Down Pass %	69%
Down Pass Rk	12
Down Rush %	31%
Down Rush Rk	21

The Patriots passed the ball more frequently in 2015 than they did in 2016, but that was in large part due to injuries and lack of production on the ground. But the interesting angle regarding the Patriots is their tendency to go to the offensive left with the vast majority of their play calls. For instance, between the 40s, almost 50% of play calls are to the left. Tom Brady's passing numbers are significantly better when throwing short left instead of right.

2015 Offensive Advanced Metrics

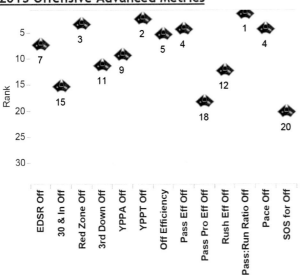

Considering their injury struggles, the Patriots once again were tremendous in their ability to overcome obstacles and still produce. The team struggled through the injuries so overall production was not as it could have been, but it was far better than what would happen to other teams given similar injuries. The team was still the 4th most efficient pass offense & the 3rd best inside the red zone. Defensively their numbers are quite strong but the strength of competition should be noted. The Patriots played the NFL's easiest schedule of opposing offenses in the AFC South & NFC East. Defensively, they were top 5 in EDSR and 2nd best in rushing the passer, though in 2016 they will have to achieve that feat without Chandler Jones. The defense would have produced an even better result had they performed better in the red zone. But in their last 3 games (of which 2 were losses) they allowed just 20 points in each game. Their offense could not get the job done.

2015 Defensive Advanced Metrics

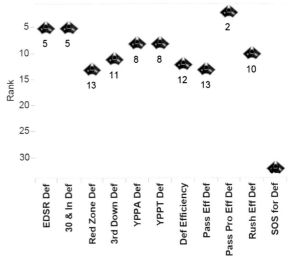

Drafted Players   2016 Draft Grade: #30 (2.2/4)

Rnd.	Pick #	Pos.	Player	College
2	60	CB	Cyrus Jones	Alabama
	78	G	Joe Thuney	North Carolina State
3	91	QB	Jacoby Brissett	North Carolina State
	96	DT	Vincent Valentine	Nebraska
4	112	WR	Malcolm Mitchell	Georgia
	208	SS	Kamu Grugier-Hill	Eastern Illinois
6	214	ILB	Elandon Roberts	Houston
	221	G	Ted Karras III	Illinois
7	225	WR	Devin Lucien	Arizona State

Free Agents/Trades Added

Player (Position)
Chris Long DE
Clay Harbor TE
Donald Brown RB
E.J. Biggers CB
Frank Kearse DT
Jonathan Cooper G
Markus Kuhn DT
Martellus Bennett TE
Nate Washington WR
Shea McClellin LB
Terrance Knighton NT

Other Signed

Player (Position)
Anthony Johnson DT
Bryce Williams TE
C.J. Johnson LB
Cre'von LeBlanc CB
D.J. Foster RB
Joey Iosefa RB
Jonathan Jones CB
Steven Scheu TE
V'Angelo Bentley CB
Woodrow Hamilton DT

2015 Players Lost

Transaction	Player (Position)
Cut	Brandon LaFell WR
	Chris Jones DT
	Dane Fletcher LB
	Darius Fleming LB
	Dominique Easley DT
	Ishmaa'ily Kitchen NT
	James Vaughters LB
	Joey Iosefa RB
	Leonard Johnson CB
	Rashaan Melvin CB
	Scott Chandler TE
	Tony Steward LB
	Tyler Gaffney RB
Declared Free Agent	Akiem Hicks DT
Retired	Jerod Mayo LB

- The Patriots continue to make a majority of correct decisions and it's what allows the team to stay so competitive, year in and year out, despite inevitable injuries.
- Tom Brady is again suspended for the first 4 games of the season. Given the legal team he has assembled, I'll believe it when I see it. They have 3 straight home games in weeks 2-4, including the huge edge gained by hosting a Thursday night game.
- Trading away Chandler Jones was smart. The reality is they likely would not have re-signed him after this year, and with the two draft picks they received in return (as well as G Jonathan Cooper) they will be in a better position in 2017 and 2018 than they would otherwise be.
- They added another stud TE in Martellus Bennett to build the offense to be more multiple than it has been since Aaron Hernandez. Getting Bennett on the field simultaneously with Rob Gronkowski presents two ridiculous mismatches for any defense. The unit can run uptempo without substituting and completely wear defenses down.
- They also will receive the return of O-Line coach Dante Scarnecchia, who they were without the past two years.
- Other lower cost, veteran free agents they added included Nate Washington and on defense, DE Chris Long and DT Terrance Knighton. They improved their secondary and perhaps their return game in one pick, selecting CB Cyrus Jones out of Alabama. If his presence improves field position even further for the highly efficient Patriots, it could be a very special season in New England.
- Without Chandler Jones and Jerod Mayo on defense, the Patriots are reminiscent of the teams in the 2010-2013 period. This Patriots team has the 3rd most expensive offense but the 26th most expensive defense. They field the most expensive TE group and the 7th most expensive WR group. And thanks to Brady's cap friendly contract, they have just the 20th most expensive QB corps.

Lineup & 2016 Cap Hit

FS D.McCourty 32
SS P.Chung 23
LB J.Collins 91
LB D.Hightower 54
RCB L.Ryan 26
SLOTCB C.Jones Rookie 24
DE R.Ninkovich 50
DT M.Brown 90
DT T.Knighton 98
DE J.Sheard 93
LCB M.Butler 21

LWR C.Hogan 15
LT N.Solder 83
LG S.Mason 77
C B.Stork 69
RG J.Cooper 66
RT S.Vollmer 61 76
TE2 M.Bennett
TE R.Gronkowski 87
RWR J.Edelman 11
QB T.Brady 12
RB D.Lewis 33

Skill Bench
WR2 D.Amendola 80
WR3 K.Martin 82
RB2 L.Blount 29
QB2 J.Garoppolo 10

2016 Cap Dollars Low High

Health Overall & by Unit (2015 v 2014)

2015 Rk	29
2015 AGL	93
Off Rk	29
Def Rk	19
2014 Rk	12
2014 AGL	62

2016 Positional Spending

	All OFF	QB	OL	RB	WR	TE	All DEF	DL	LB	CB	S
2015 Rk	6	16	16	19	9	3	28	20	15	32	8
Rank	3	20	9	20	7	1	26	21	11	31	4
Total	87.6M	15.4M	30.5M	6.4M	19.7M	15.5M	64.4M	18.9M	22.3M	6.7M	16.5M

2016 Offseason Spending

Total Spent	Total Spent Rk	Free Agents #	Free Agents $	Free Agents $ Rk	Waiver #	Waiver $	Waiver $ Rk	Extended #	Sum of Extended $	Sum of Drafted $	Undrafted #	Undrafted $
137M	24	15	39M	23	14	7M	30	4	52M	26M	8	13M

2015 Stats & Fantasy Production

Pos	Player	Ov. Rank	Pos. Rk	Age	Gms	St	Pass Comp	Pass Att	Pass Yds	Pass TD	Pass Int	Rush Att	Rush Yds	Rush YPA	Rush TD	Targ	Recp	Rec Yds	Rec YPC	Rec TDs	Draft King Pts	Fan Duel Pts
QB	Tom Brady*	22	3	38	16	16	402	624	4,770	36	7	34	53	2	3	1	1	36	36		357	351
RB	LeGarrette Blount		29	29	12	6						165	703	4	6	7	6	43	7	1	126	120
	Dion Lewis		49	25	7	6						49	234	5	2	50	36	388	11	2	127	102
	James White		50	23	14	1						22	56	3	2	54	40	410	10	4	126	103
	Brandon Bolden		69	25	15	2						63	207	3		30	19	180	9	2	76	60
WR	Julian Edelman		37	29	9	9						3	23	8		88	61	692	11	7	177	142
	Danny Amendola		53	30	14	7	1	1	36			2	11	6		87	65	648	10	3	152	116
	Brandon LaFell		85	29	11	7						2	9	5		74	37	515	14		92	71
	Keshawn Martin		98	25	9	8						1	6	6		37	24	269	11	2	66	50
TE	Rob Gronkowski*+	9	1	26	15	15										120	72	1,176	16	11	259	220
	Scott Chandler		32	30	15	4										42	23	259	11	4	76	61

New England Patriots

Avg Line	-4.9	Pred Wins	10.5	Pred Div Finish	#1

2016 Weekly Betting Lines (wks 1-16)

(-) Favorite   Underdog (+)
-9.5 ———— +1.0

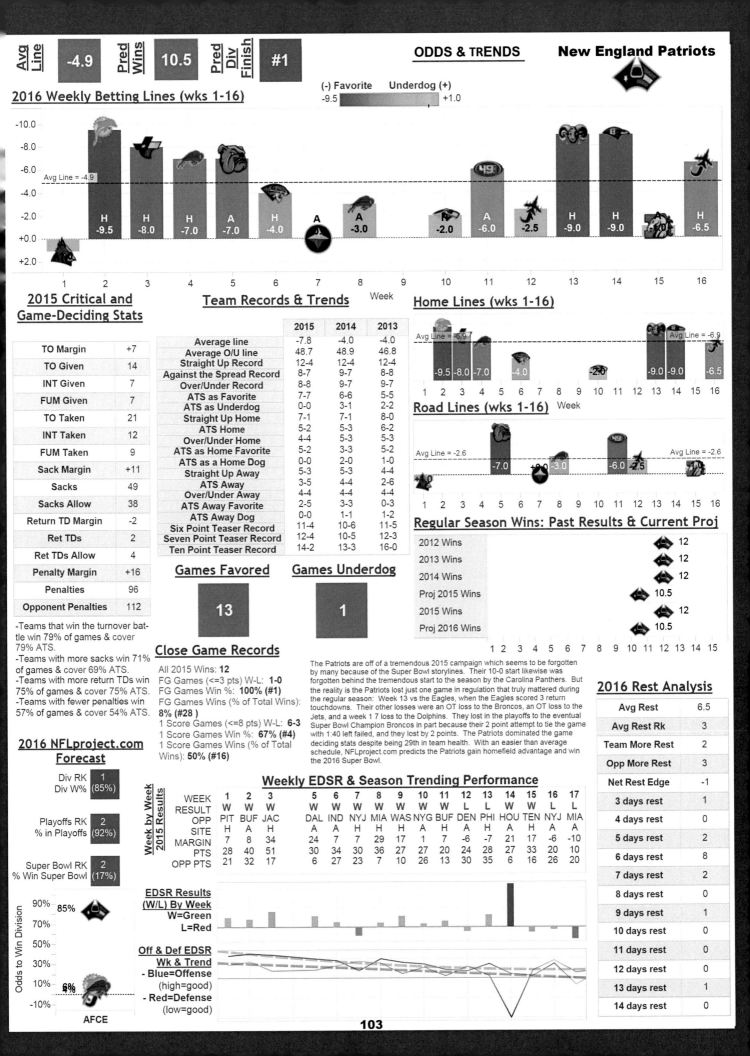

Week	1	2	3	4	5	6	7	8	9	10	11	12	13	14	15	16
Site		H	H	H	A	H	A	A		H	A		H	H		H
Line		-9.5	-8.0	-7.0	-7.0	-4.0		-3.0		-2.0	-6.0	-2.5	-9.0	-9.0		-6.5

Avg Line = -4.9

2015 Critical and Game-Deciding Stats

TO Margin	+7
TO Given	14
INT Given	7
FUM Given	7
TO Taken	21
INT Taken	12
FUM Taken	9
Sack Margin	+11
Sacks	49
Sacks Allow	38
Return TD Margin	-2
Ret TDs	2
Ret TDs Allow	4
Penalty Margin	+16
Penalties	96
Opponent Penalties	112

-Teams that win the turnover battle win 79% of games & cover 79% ATS.
-Teams with more sacks win 71% of games & cover 69% ATS.
-Teams with more return TDs win 75% of games & cover 75% ATS.
-Teams with fewer penalties win 57% of games & cover 54% ATS.

2016 NFLproject.com Forecast

Div RK	1
Div W%	(85%)
Playoffs RK	2
% in Playoffs	(92%)
Super Bowl RK	2
% Win Super Bowl	(17%)

Odds to Win Division
90% — 85%
70%
50%
30%
10% — 6%
-10%
AFCE

Team Records & Trends

	2015	2014	2013
Average line	-7.8	-4.0	-4.0
Average O/U line	48.7	48.9	46.8
Straight Up Record	12-4	12-4	12-4
Against the Spread Record	8-7	9-7	8-8
Over/Under Record	8-8	9-7	9-7
ATS as Favorite	7-7	6-6	5-5
ATS as Underdog	0-0	3-1	2-2
Straight Up Home	7-1	7-1	8-0
ATS Home	5-2	5-3	6-2
Over/Under Home	4-4	5-3	5-3
ATS as Home Favorite	5-2	3-3	5-2
ATS as a Home Dog	0-0	2-0	1-0
Straight Up Away	5-3	5-3	4-4
ATS Away	3-5	4-4	2-6
Over/Under Away	4-4	4-4	4-4
ATS Away Favorite	2-5	3-3	0-3
ATS Away Dog	0-0	1-1	1-2
Six Point Teaser Record	11-4	10-6	11-5
Seven Point Teaser Record	12-4	10-5	12-3
Ten Point Teaser Record	14-2	13-3	16-0

Games Favored: 13
Games Underdog: 1

Close Game Records

All 2015 Wins: 12
FG Games (<=3 pts) W-L: 1-0
FG Games Win %: 100% (#1)
FG Games Wins (% of Total Wins): 8% (#28)
1 Score Games (<=8 pts) W-L: 6-3
1 Score Games Win %: 67% (#4)
1 Score Games Wins (% of Total Wins): 50% (#16)

Home Lines (wks 1-16)

Avg Line = -6.9

1	2	3	4	5	6	7	8	9	10	11	12	13	14	15	16
	-9.5	-8.0	-7.0		-4.0				-2.0			-9.0	-9.0		-6.5

Road Lines (wks 1-16) Week

Avg Line = -2.6

1	2	3	4	5	6	7	8	9	10	11	12	13	14	15	16
+1.0				-7.0		+0.0	-3.0			-6.0	-2.5			-1.0	

Regular Season Wins: Past Results & Current Proj

2012 Wins	12
2013 Wins	12
2014 Wins	12
Proj 2015 Wins	10.5
2015 Wins	12
Proj 2016 Wins	10.5

The Patriots are off of a tremendous 2015 campaign which seems to be forgotten by many because of the Super Bowl storylines. Their 10-0 start likewise was forgotten behind the tremendous start to the season by the Carolina Panthers. But the reality is the Patriots lost just one game in regulation that truly mattered during the regular season: Week 13 vs the Eagles, when the Eagles scored 3 return touchdowns. Their other losses were an OT loss to the Broncos, an OT loss to the Jets, and a week 1 7 loss to the Dolphins. They lost in the playoffs to the eventual Super Bowl Champion Broncos in part because their 2 point attempt to tie the game with 1:40 left failed, and they lost by 2 points. The Patriots dominated the game deciding stats despite being 29th in team health. With an easier than average schedule, NFLproject.com predicts the Patriots gain homefield advantage and win the 2016 Super Bowl.

2016 Rest Analysis

Avg Rest	6.5
Avg Rest Rk	3
Team More Rest	2
Opp More Rest	3
Net Rest Edge	-1
3 days rest	1
4 days rest	0
5 days rest	2
6 days rest	8
7 days rest	2
8 days rest	0
9 days rest	1
10 days rest	0
11 days rest	0
12 days rest	0
13 days rest	1
14 days rest	0

Weekly EDSR & Season Trending Performance

Week by Week 2015 Results

WEEK	1	2	3		5	6	7	8	9	10	11	12	13	14	15	16	17
RESULT	W	W	W		W	W	W	W	W	W	L	L	L	W	W	L	L
OPP	PIT	BUF	JAC		DAL	IND	NYJ	MIA	WAS	NYG	BUF	DEN	PHI	HOU	TEN	NYJ	MIA
SITE	H	A	H		A	H	H	H	A	H	A	H	A	H	A	A	A
MARGIN	7	8	34		24	7	7	29	17	1	7	-6	-7	21	17	-6	-10
PTS	28	40	51		30	34	30	36	27	27	20	24	28	27	33	20	10
OPP PTS	21	32	17		6	27	23	7	10	26	13	30	35	6	16	26	20

EDSR Results (W/L) By Week
W=Green
L=Red

Off & Def EDSR Wk & Trend
- Blue=Offense (high=good)
- Red=Defense (low=good)

STATS & VISUALIZATIONS New England Patriots

Directional Passer Rating Achieved

Receiver	Short Left	Short Middle	Short Right	Deep Left	Deep Middle	Deep Right
Rob Gronkowski	145	153	54	20	155	77
Julian Edelman	113	107	75	158	54	39
Danny Amendola	96	106	89	116		56
Brandon LaFell	53	72	87	100	64	13
Keshawn Martin	125	91	42	71	106	95
Scott Chandler	125	109	86	95	109	52
Aaron Dobson	84	118	56	118	39	39
Michael Williams	39	106	42			
Asante Cleveland	79					
Chris Harper	91		39		0	
Matthew Slater						39

Directional Frequency by Receiver

Receiver	Short Left	Short Middle	Short Right	Deep Left	Deep Middle	Deep Right
Rob Gronkowski	20%	23%	33%	27%	29%	38%
Julian Edelman	20%	27%	26%	6%	23%	5%
Danny Amendola	17%	28%	16%	12%		14%
Brandon LaFell	19%	9%	7%	27%	26%	14%
Keshawn Martin	10%	3%	5%	15%	10%	11%
Scott Chandler	6%	7%	9%	6%	10%	14%
Aaron Dobson	8%	1%	2%	3%	3%	3%
Michael Williams	1%	2%	2%			
Asante Cleveland	1%					
Chris Harper	1%		1%	3%		
Matthew Slater						3%

Defense Passer Rating Allowed

Short Left	Short Middle	Short Right	Deep Left	Deep Middle	Deep Right
101	92	85	75	46	76

Offensive Rush Directional Yds/Carry

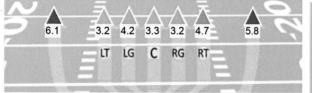

6.1	3.2	4.2	3.3	3.2	4.7	5.8
	LT	LG	C	RG	RT	

Offensive Rush Frequency of Direction

32	45	54	127	66	49	17
	LT	LG	C	RG	RT	

Offensive Explosive Runs by Direction

9	3	9	6	3	8	5
	LT	LG	C	RG	RT	

Defensive Rush Directional Yds/Carry

4.7	4.6	4.3	3.8	3.5	4.3	3.7
	LT	LG	C	RG	RT	

Tom Brady - 1st Down RTG

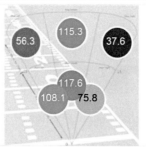

Tom Brady - 3rd Down RTG

Tom Brady - 2nd Down RTG

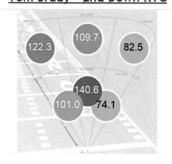

Tom Brady - Overall RTG

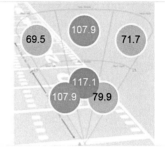

2nd & Short RUN (1D or not)

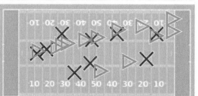

2nd & Short RUN Stats

Run Conv Rk	1D% Run	NFL 1D% Run Avg	Run Freq	NFL Run Freq Avg
29	55%	69%	50%	64%

2nd & Short PASS (1D or not)

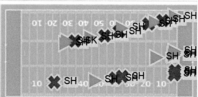

2nd & Short PASS Stats

Pass Conv Rk	1D% Pass	NFL 1D% Pass Avg	Pass Freq	NFL Pass Freq Avg
22	50%	55%	50%	36%

Pass Offense Play Success Rate

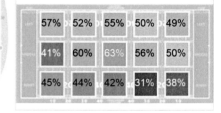

57%	52%	55%	50%	49%
41%	60%	63%	56%	50%
45%	44%	42%	31%	38%

Pass Offense Yds/Play

8.0	7.6	9.0	6.7	4.3
5.3	13.0	13.9	9.3	4.8
6.7	7.9	5.3	4.3	3.9

Off. Directional Tendency (% of Plays Left, Middle or Right)

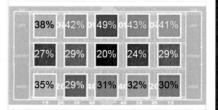

38%	42%	49%	43%	41%
27%	29%	20%	24%	29%
35%	29%	31%	32%	30%

Off. Directional Pass Rate (% of Plays which are Passes)

82%	80%	82%	77%	80%
49%	44%	40%	43%	38%
82%	77%	77%	83%	67%

Miami Dolphins

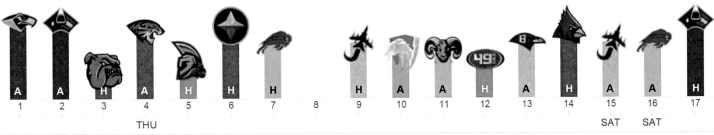

Coaches

Head Coach: Adam Gase (CHI OC) (1st yr)
OC: Clyde Christensen (IND QB) (1st yr)
DC: Vance Joseph (CIN DB) (1st yr)

<u>Forecast</u>
<u>2016 Wins</u>

7

<u>Past</u>
<u>Records</u>

2015: 6-10
2014: 8-8
2013: 8-8

Opponent Strength
Easy   Hard

2016 Schedule & Week by Week Strength of Schedule

A	A	H	H	H	H	H		H	A	A	H	A	H	A	A	H
1	2	3	4	5	6	7	8	9	10	11	12	13	14	15	16	17

THU   SAT   SAT

2016 Overview

Any conversation about the Miami Dolphins must start with owner Stephen Ross, who bought the team from Wayne Huizenga in 2009. Ross is willing to spend the money, but as often happens to men without experience, they can get taken for their money quite easily. In his 7 years the Dolphins have never had a winning season and zero trips to the playoffs. Ross kept GM Jeff Ireland, a holdover from the last year of Huizenga, on through 2013. Ireland did far better in the draft than he did in free agency, but will largely be remembered for his overspending in free agency and the Jonathan Martin case which appeared to finally give Ross the urge to part ways with Ireland. Lost in the mix was the fact that Ireland's hit rate in the draft was well above average. His worst move was trading up to draft DE Dion Jordan 3rd overall in 2013, but that was his lone first round miss (Ryan Tannehill, Mike Pouncey, Jared Odrick and Vontae Davis). He hit on DB Sean Smith & LB Koa Misi in the 2nd round, and he drafted 8 players in rounds 3-7 who started over 35 games, including Reshad Jones, Charles Clay, Lamar Miller and Olivier Vernon. The NFL average during that 5 year span was less than half that number (3.8). Teams #2 and #3 hit on 6 players. Ireland's 8 late round hits was by far the best.

Another of Ireland's failings was selecting the right head coach. Ross and Ireland stuck with Tony Sparano for two straight back to back 7-9 seasons. But finally after starting 4-9 in 2011, they fired Sparano and promoted Todd Bowles. Bowles went 2-1 (the only Miami coach with a winning record in the Ross era), but was not hired as head coach in 2012. The team instead turned to Joe Philbin. Three straight non-winning seasons and a 1-3 start to his 4th, Philbin was fired and Dan Campbell replaced him. Over that course, Bowles was named Assistant Coach of the Year in 2014 in Arizona & landed as the head coach of the Dolphins rival: the Jets. Bowles went 10-6 last year, sweeping the Dolphins by scores of 27-14 & 38-20.

Ross replaced Ireland with Dennis Hickey, who lasted just two years. Hickey should be best remembered for letting a number of the players that Ireland hit on walk, while signing even more high priced players in free agency: signing LT Branden Albert, DT Ndamukong Suh & watching TE Charles Clay, DE Jared Odrick and FS Chris Clemons walk. His hit rate on later round picks was very poor, and his strongest draft selections may turn out to be WRs in the top 2 rounds (Jarvis Landry, DeVante Parker). Ross fired Hickey, and replaced him this past January with Chris Grier, an internal hire from the scouting department. More solid Ireland draft picks left this past spring (RB Miller, DE Vernon) and some of the early personnel moves have been puzzling at best, including repeated trades up in the draft, trading for a underperforming CB with a bad contract (Byron Maxwell), and re-signing a 34 year old DE off a torn Achilles (Cameron Wake). It's likely that with a new head coach at the helm, that Ross will be more patient with the Gase/Grier combo and allow them time to build the team. The focus must shift away from free agency. They must avoid the impulse to trade up to go 11-5 immediately. It is in Miami's best interest to think long term, particularly with a 39 year old (this August) Tom Brady in New England. On the field, Miami must return efficiency and balance to the offensive side of the ball. They have to start games better, as their first half plays/drive and time/drive was 2nd worst in the NFL last year. But it is hard to envision the Dolphins having much success on the field unless their off field strategy changes drastically.

Strength of Schedule In Detail

True Strength of Schedule Rank: 16

Hardest Stretches *(1=Hard, 32=Easy)*
Hardest 3 wk Stretch Rk: 28
Hardest 4 wk Stretch Rk: 12
Hardest 5 wk Stretch Rk: 13

Easiest Stretches *(1=Easy, 32=Hard)*
Easiest 3 wk Stretch Rk: 3
Easiest 4 wk Stretch Rk: 3
Easiest 5 wk Stretch Rk: 4

Miami has the 5th most difficult first month of the year, made more difficult with a very rare back-to-back road trip to start the season. And that road trip won't be easy – from Miami across to Seattle, representing the longest trip possible in the NFL, followed by a trip up the East coast to New England. When four of a team's first six games include the Steelers, Bengals and afore mentioned Seahawks and Patriots, it's a brutal start. Only made easier by home games against the Browns and Titans. Miami also has the 2nd hardest last month of the year (vs ARI, @ NYJ, @ BUF, vs NE).

2015 Play Tendencies

All Pass %	64%
All Pass Rk	4
All Rush %	36%
All Rush Rk	29
1 Score Pass %	61%
1 Score Pass Rk	9
2014 1 Score Pass %	62%
2014 1 Score Pass Rk	5
Pass Increase %	-1%
Pass Increase Rk	23
1 Score Rush %	39%
1 Score Rush Rk	24
Up Pass %	44%
Up Pass Rk	29
Up Rush %	56%
Up Rush Rk	4
Down Pass %	72%
Down Pass Rk	4
Down Rush %	28%
Down Rush Rk	29

The Dolphins shifted from a top 5 pass team in neutral situations in 2015 to 9th in 2016, but they decreased by just 1% in pass frequency. However, they were a very predictable team when it came to style: when trailing they ran the ball just 28% of the time, 4th least. When winning, they ran the ball 56% of the time, 4th most often. Defenses had a great idea as to what they were going to see based on the scoreboard, which is never ideal for an offense.

2015 Offensive Advanced Metrics

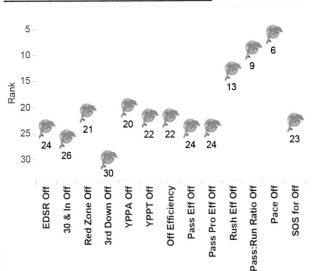

Against an easier than average schedule last year, the Dolphins were completely underwhelming in posting a 6-10 record, which resulted in Joe Philbin getting fired and Adam Gase hired this offseason. Offensively, the best thing going for the Dolphins from an efficiency perspective was their run game, but they were extremely pass heavy. They were at their worst on 3rd down, on early downs, and when passing. They ranked bottom 10 in all of these key metrics. Defensively, they were not great and struggled in particular to stop the pass, ranking bottom 5 in pass defense. Miami's up tempo offense coupled with their terrible record on 3rd downs put the defense in plenty of bad situations with little rest. I expect to see a more composed Dolphins offense from a pace perspective in 2016 under Adam Gase. Balance and slower tempo should reduce stress on Ryan Tannehill (similar to Gase's approach with Jay Cutler) while giving the defense time to regroup.

2015 Defensive Advanced Metrics

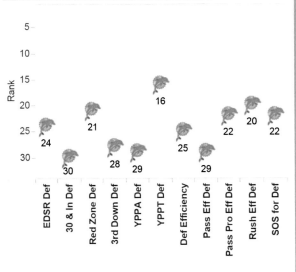

Drafted Players

2016 Draft Grade: #23 (2.6/4)

Rnd.	Pick #	Pos.	Player	College
1	13	OT	Laremy Tunsil	Ole Miss
2	38	CB	Xavien Howard	Baylor
3	73	RB	Kenyan Drake	Alabama
3	86	WR	Leonte Carroo	Rutgers
6	186	WR	Jakeem Grant	Texas Tech
6	204	SS	Jordan Lucas	Penn State
7	223	QB	Brandon Doughty	Western Kentucky
7	231	TE	Thomas Duarte	UCLA

PERSONNEL & SPENDING

Miami Dolphins

Free Agents/Trades Added

Player (Position)

Andre Branch DE
Byron Maxwell CB
Isa Abdul-Quddus S
Jason Jones DE
Jermon Bushrod T
Kiko Alonso LB
Mario Williams DE
MarQueis Gray TE
Sam Young T

Other Signed

Player (Position)

A.J. Hendy S
Akil Blount LB
Brandon Shippen WR
Farrington Huguenin DE
Gabe Hughes TE
James Burgess LB
Jason Jones DE
Lafayette Pitts CB
Marshall Koehn K
Rashawn Scott WR
Ruben Carter C
Ryan DiSalvo LB
Tyler Gray LB

2015 Players Lost

Transaction	Player (Position)
Cut	Brent Grimes CB
	Brice McCain CB
	Christion Jones WR
	Damarr Aultman CB
	Damontre Moore DE
	Dax Swanson CB
	Greg Jennings WR
	Jahwan Edwards RB
	Jason Fox T
	Quinton Coples DE
	Robert Herron WR
	Robert Thomas DT
	Terrell Manning LB
	Tyler Davis WR
Declared Free Agent	Derrick Shelby DE
	Lamar Miller RB
	Olivier Vernon DE

- Spending in free agency is negatively correlated with winning games, and it has been that way for years. And for several years now, the Dolphins were the NFL's most egregious offender and it wasn't particularly close. Not only did it hurt their ability to build a roster with so much cap tied into high priced free agents, but it prevented them from re-signing their own players. Players who went elsewhere only because of the success they had in Miami's system. These included CB Sean Smith, LB Karlos Dansby, TE Charles Clay, DE Olivier Vernon and RB Lamar Miller, among others.
- The left side of the offensive line should be strong, and for this year will have LT Branden Albert and LG Laremy Tunsil to the left of C Mike Pouncey.
- The Dolphins made the move to acquire Mario Williams once Olivier Vernon was lost to the Giants. Miami could have made a move prior to Vernon's deal expiring, but the Dolphins simply did not have the cap space to make that move. Their defensive line is now weaker as a result.
- Due to huge contracts along the line including Williams, the Dolphins are spending the 2nd most on the defensive line of any team. However, the Dolphins have the least expensive LB corps in the NFL, and their RB and WR corps each rank as the 2nd least expensive in the NFL. The Dolphins tried to acquire RB C.J. Anderson from the Broncos, but Denver matched the deal, and RB Lamar Miller left for Houston.
- The Dolphins let CB Brent Grimes leave to Tampa and replaced him with CB Byron Maxwell in a trade, who has struggled outside Seattle. The Dolphins defense (29th vs pass, in part due to Grimes) may not be improved by much with Maxwell. Meanwhile, had the Dolphins just stuck with CB Sean Smith in 2013, instead of allowing him to leave for the Chiefs while signing that offseason WR Mike Wallace ($60M), Dannell Ellerbe ($35M), Philip Wheeler ($26M) and Grimes (1 yr, $5.5M), they would have been much more stable at CB and never needed to give up picks to trade for Maxwell.

Lineup & 2016 Cap Hit

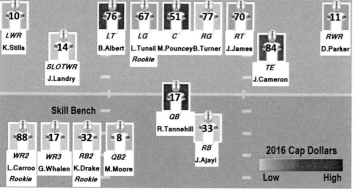

Health Overall & by Unit (2015 v 2014)

2015 Rk	15
2015 AGL	63
Off Rk	7
Def Rk	24
2014 Rk	21
2014 AGL	80

2016 Positional Spending

	All OFF	QB	OL	RB	WR	TE	All DEF	DL	LB	CB	S
2015 Rk	30	24	11	28	30	14	12	5	31	14	12
Rank	24	22	6	31	31	6	15	2	32	23	9
Total	72.5M	14.6M	34.2M	2.9M	8.8M	12.0M	78.1M	40.4M	11.2M	14.0M	12.5M

2016 Offseason Spending

Total Spent	Total Spent Rk	Free Agents #	Free Agents $	Free Agents $ Rk	Waiver #	Waiver $	Waiver $ Rk	Extended #	Sum of Extended $	Sum of Drafted $	Undrafted #	Undrafted $
122M	26	13	28M	25	23	28M	3	1	15M	31M	12	19M

2015 Stats & Fantasy Production

Pos	Player	Ov. Rank	Pos. Rk	Age	Gms	St	Pass Comp	Pass Att	Pass Yds	Pass TD	Pass Int	Rush Att	Rush Yds	Rush YPA	Rush TD	Targ	Recp	Rec Yds	Rec YPC	Rec TDs	Draft King Pts	Fan Duel Pts
QB	Ryan Tannehill		17	27	16	16	363	586	4,208	24	12	32	141	4	1	1	1	9	9		277	268
RB	Lamar Miller	20	6	24	16	16						194	872	4	8	57	47	397	8	2	239	208
	Jay Ajayi		79	22	9							49	187	4	1	11	7	90	13		46	39
	Damien Williams		95	23	16							16	59	4		28	21	142	7	1	49	35
WR	Jarvis Landry*	37	15	23	16	14	1	1			9	18	113	6	1	166	110	1,157	11	4	281	220
	Rishard Matthews		49	26	11	11						1	4	4		61	43	662	15	4	137	112
	DeVante Parker		66	22	15	4										50	26	494	19	3	96	80
	Kenny Stills		73	23	16	8										63	27	440	16	3	92	76
	Greg Jennings		117	32	16	5										36	19	208	11	1	49	36
TE	Jordan Cameron		29	27	16	16										70	35	386	11	3	95	74
	Dion Sims		61	24	13	4										25	18	127	7	1	39	26

Miami Dolphins — ODDS & TRENDS

Avg Line	Pred Wins	Pred Div Finish
+1.8	7	#4

2016 Weekly Betting Lines (wks 1-16)

(-) Favorite   Underdog (+)
-7.0 ———— +9.5

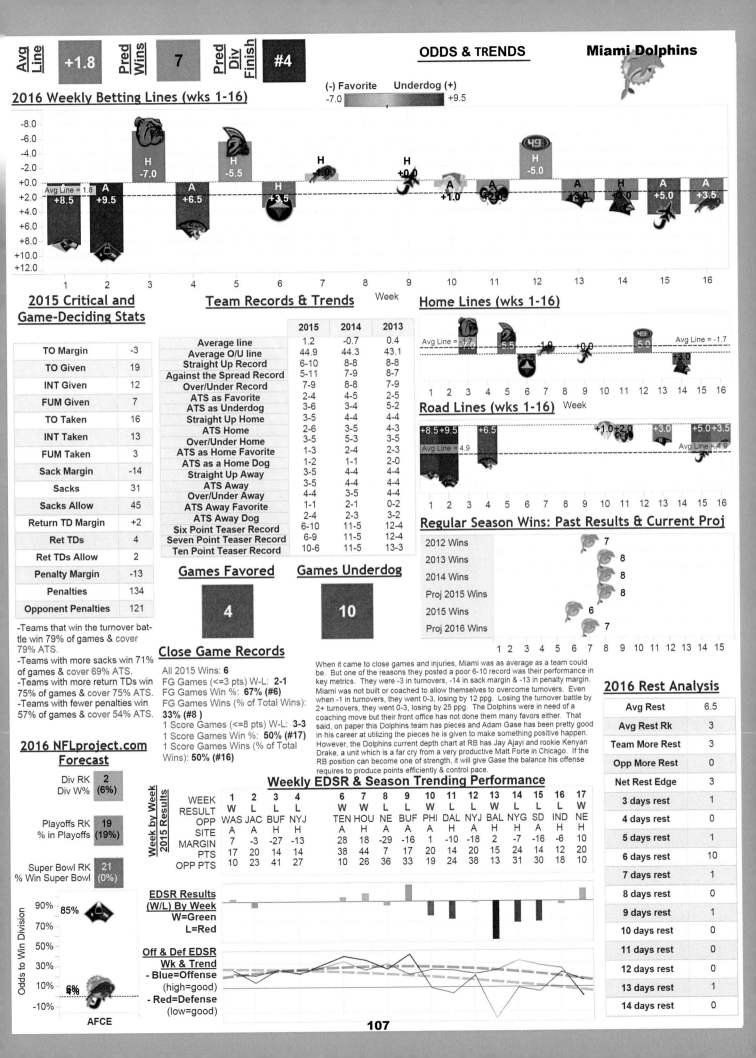

Avg Line = 1.8

Weekly lines (by week):
- Wk1: A +8.5
- Wk2: A +9.5
- Wk3: H -7.0
- Wk4: A +6.5
- Wk5: H -5.5
- Wk6: H +3.5
- Wk7: H -1.0
- Wk8: H +0.0
- Wk9: A +1.0
- Wk10: +2.0
- Wk11: A +3.0
- Wk12: H -5.0
- Wk13: H +3.0
- Wk14: A +5.0
- Wk15: A +5.0
- Wk16: A +3.5

2015 Critical and Game-Deciding Stats

TO Margin	-3
TO Given	19
INT Given	12
FUM Given	7
TO Taken	16
INT Taken	13
FUM Taken	3
Sack Margin	-14
Sacks	31
Sacks Allow	45
Return TD Margin	+2
Ret TDs	4
Ret TDs Allow	2
Penalty Margin	-13
Penalties	134
Opponent Penalties	121

-Teams that win the turnover battle win 79% of games & cover 79% ATS.
-Teams with more sacks win 71% of games & cover 69% ATS.
-Teams with more return TDs win 75% of games & cover 75% ATS.
-Teams with fewer penalties win 57% of games & cover 54% ATS.

2016 NFLproject.com Forecast

Div RK	2
Div W%	(6%)
Playoffs RK	19
% in Playoffs	(19%)
Super Bowl RK	21
% Win Super Bowl	(0%)

Odds to Win Division:
- 85%
- 6%

AFCE

Team Records & Trends

	2015	2014	2013
Average line	1.2	-0.7	0.4
Average O/U line	44.9	44.3	43.1
Straight Up Record	6-10	8-8	8-8
Against the Spread Record	5-11	7-9	8-7
Over/Under Record	7-9	8-8	7-9
ATS as Favorite	2-4	4-5	2-5
ATS as Underdog	3-6	3-4	5-2
Straight Up Home	3-5	4-4	4-4
ATS Home	2-6	3-5	4-3
Over/Under Home	3-5	5-3	3-5
ATS as Home Favorite	1-3	2-4	2-3
ATS as a Home Dog	1-2	1-1	2-0
Straight Up Away	3-5	4-4	4-4
ATS Away	3-5	4-4	4-4
Over/Under Away	4-4	3-5	4-4
ATS Away Favorite	1-1	2-1	0-2
ATS Away Dog	2-4	2-3	3-2
Six Point Teaser Record	6-10	11-5	12-4
Seven Point Teaser Record	6-9	11-5	12-4
Ten Point Teaser Record	10-6	11-5	13-3

Games Favored
4

Games Underdog
10

Close Game Records

All 2015 Wins: 6
FG Games (<=3 pts) W-L: 2-1
FG Games Win %: 67% (#6)
FG Games Wins (% of Total Wins): 33% (#8)
1 Score Games (<=8 pts) W-L: 3-3
1 Score Games Win %: 50% (#17)
1 Score Games Wins (% of Total Wins): 50% (#16)

Home Lines (wks 1-16)

Avg Line = -1.7

Home lines: -7.0, -5.5, -1.0, +3.5, +0.0, -5.0, +3.0

Road Lines (wks 1-16)

Avg Line = 4.9

Road lines: +8.5 +9.5, +6.5, +1.0 +2.0, +3.0, +5.0 +3.5

Regular Season Wins: Past Results & Current Proj

2012 Wins	7
2013 Wins	8
2014 Wins	8
Proj 2015 Wins	8
2015 Wins	6
Proj 2016 Wins	7

When it came to close games and injuries, Miami was as average as a team could be. But one of the reasons they posted a poor 6-10 record was their performance in key metrics. They were -3 in turnovers, -14 in sack margin & -13 in penalty margin. Miami was not built or coached to allow themselves to overcome turnovers. Even when -1 in turnovers, they went 0-3, losing by 12 ppg. Losing the turnover battle by 2+ turnovers, they went 0-3, losing by 25 ppg. The Dolphins were in need of a coaching move but their front office has not done them many favors either. That said, on paper this Dolphins team has pieces and Adam Gase has been pretty good in his career at utilizing the pieces he is given to make something positive happen. However, the Dolphins current depth chart at RB has Jay Ajayi and rookie Kenyan Drake, a unit which is a far cry from a very productive Matt Forte in Chicago. If the RB position can become one of strength, it will give Gase the balance his offense requires to produce points efficiently & control pace.

2016 Rest Analysis

Avg Rest	6.5
Avg Rest Rk	3
Team More Rest	3
Opp More Rest	0
Net Rest Edge	3
3 days rest	1
4 days rest	0
5 days rest	1
6 days rest	10
7 days rest	1
8 days rest	0
9 days rest	1
10 days rest	0
11 days rest	0
12 days rest	0
13 days rest	1
14 days rest	0

Weekly EDSR & Season Trending Performance

Week by Week 2015 Results

WEEK	1	2	3	4		6	7	8	9	10	11	12	13	14	15	16	17
RESULT	W	L	L	L		W	W	L	L	W	L	L	W	L	L	L	W
OPP	WAS	JAC	BUF	NYJ		TEN	HOU	NE	BUF	PHI	DAL	NYJ	BAL	NYG	SD	IND	NE
SITE	A	A	H	H		A	H	A	A	H	A	H	A	H	H	H	H
MARGIN	7	-3	-27	-13		28	18	-29	-16	1	-10	-18	2	-7	-16	-6	10
PTS	17	20	14	14		38	44	7	17	20	14	20	15	24	14	12	20
OPP PTS	10	23	41	27		10	26	36	33	19	24	38	13	31	30	18	10

EDSR Results (W/L) By Week
W=Green
L=Red

Off & Def EDSR Wk & Trend
- Blue=Offense (high=good)
- Red=Defense (low=good)

STATS & VISUALIZATIONS

Miami Dolphins

Directional Passer Rating Achieved

Receiver	Short Left	Short Middle	Short Right	Deep Left	Deep Middle	Deep Right
Jarvis Landry	103	80	85	53	104	80
Rishard Matthews	132	78	104	63	102	135
Jordan Cameron	81	45	95	17	65	12
Kenny Stills	49	89	64	74	61	86
DeVante Parker	103	94	55	95	156	81
Greg Jennings	85	51	97	118		39
Dion Sims	82	95	119	89	39	39
Jake Stoneburner	139	149	100			
Matt Hazel		39				

Directional Frequency by Receiver

Receiver	Short Left	Short Middle	Short Right	Deep Left	Deep Middle	Deep Right
Jarvis Landry	37%	49%	35%	33%	24%	15%
Rishard Matthews	10%	9%	17%	8%	24%	11%
Jordan Cameron	12%	13%	18%	10%	14%	17%
Kenny Stills	14%	5%	7%	31%	14%	30%
DeVante Parker	12%	9%	9%	10%	19%	11%
Greg Jennings	8%	9%	7%	3%		11%
Dion Sims	6%	1%	7%	5%	5%	4%
Jake Stoneburner	1%	4%	1%			
Matt Hazel		1%				

Defense Passer Rating Allowed

Short Left	Short Middle	Short Right	Deep Left	Deep Middle	Deep Right
88	110	87	114	128	45

Offensive Rush Directional Yds/Carry

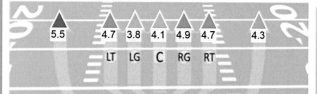

5.5	4.7	3.8	4.1	4.9	4.7	4.3
	LT	LG	C	RG	RT	

Offensive Rush Frequency of Direction

44	26	32	80	43	53	55
	LT	LG	C	RG	RT	

Offensive Explosive Runs by Direction

10	4	2	7	4	6	8
	LT	LG	C	RG	RT	

Defensive Rush Directional Yds/Carry

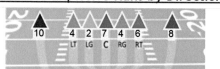

3.4	4.6	4.8	4.1	3.4	3.4	6.2
	LT	LG	C	RG	RT	

Ryan Tannehill - 1st Down RTG

80.4 129.2 92.8
84.1
107.8 80.6

Ryan Tannehill - 2nd Down RTG

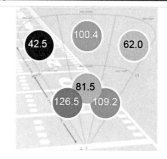

42.5 100.4 62.0
81.5
126.5 109.2

2nd & Short RUN (1D or not)

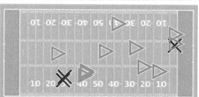

2nd & Short RUN Stats

Run Conv Rk	1D% Run	NFL 1D% Run Avg	Run Freq	NFL Run Freq Avg
9	79%	69%	50%	64%

2nd & Short PASS (1D or not)

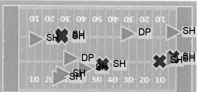

2nd & Short PASS Stats

Pass Conv Rk	1D% Pass	NFL 1D% Pass Avg	Pass Freq	NFL Pass Freq Avg
11	57%	55%	50%	36%

Ryan Tannehill - 3rd Down RTG

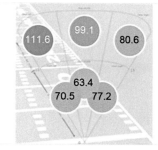

111.6 99.1 80.6
63.4
70.5 77.2

Ryan Tannehill - Overall RTG

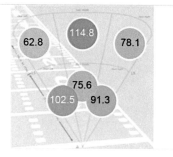

62.8 114.8 78.1
75.6
102.5 91.3

Pass Offense Play Success Rate

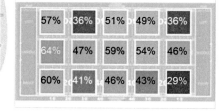

57%	36%	51%	49%	36%
64%	47%	59%	54%	46%
60%	41%	46%	43%	29%

Pass Offense Yds/Play

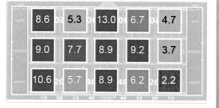

8.6	5.3	13.0	6.7	4.7
9.0	7.7	8.9	9.2	3.7
10.6	5.7	8.9	6.2	2.2

Off. Directional Tendency
(% of Plays Left, Middle or Right)

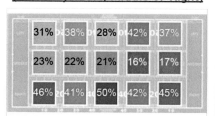

31%	38%	28%	42%	37%
23%	22%	21%	16%	17%
46%	41%	50%	42%	45%

Off. Directional Pass Rate
(% of Plays which are Passes)

59%	79%	80%	80%	72%
39%	50%	44%	42%	35%
71%	69%	68%	70%	79%

Buffalo Bills

Coaches
Head Coach: Rex Ryan (2nd yr)
OC: Greg Roman (2nd yr)
DC: Dennis Thurman (2nd yr)

Forecast 2016 Wins
8

Past Records
2015: 8-8
2014: 9-7
2013: 6-10

Opponent Strength
Easy — Hard

2016 Schedule & Week by Week Strength of Schedule

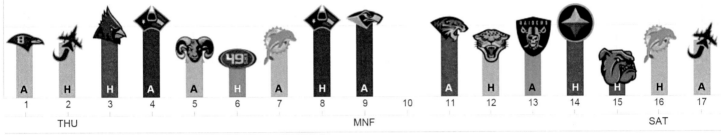

A	H	H	A	A	H	A	H	A		A	H	A	H	H	H	A
1	2	3	4	5	6	7	8	9	10	11	12	13	14	15	16	17

THU   MNF   SAT

2016 Overview

Rex Ryan is known for making big splashes. One year after being named defensive coordinator in Baltimore, he led the defense to the #1 overall ranking and the team went 13-3, the most wins in franchise history. The year he was named head coach for the New York Jets, he led the defense to the #1 overall ranking and the team to the first of back to back playoff trips to the Conference Championships, something never done before in Jets history.

However, his first year in Buffalo saw the Bills defense move from #2 overall down to #24 in total efficiency and the team won fewer games (8) then they won the prior season. There was no big splash in Buffalo. At least not yet. Rex Ryan has another shot, and the team put all their eggs in one basket this past offseason. They let the overpaid Mario Williams walk, and went defense with their first 3 draft picks, trading up to obtain Alabama's Reggie Ragland, and drafting from other strong football programs like Ohio State (Adolphus Washington) and Clemson (Shaq Lawson). They let two other defensive starters go, in Nigel Bradham and Bacarri Rambo, and signed a bevy of lower paid free agent defenders.

When the dust settled, Rex Ryan saw his defense get younger & cheaper (moving from 2nd most paid to 14th). And hope that the defense, which was the 5th most "injured" unit in 2015, has better luck in the health department. Rex Ryan needs his defense to pressure the quarterback to be successful. It's not a mystery. It's not a secret winning formula that Rex cooked up. It's common sense, considering that pass efficiency contributes over 4 times more to wins than does rush efficiency, that lowering the opposing quarterback's efficiency via a formidable pass rush will go a long way. Unfortunately, the Bills pass rush dropped from #1 in efficiency in 2014 (pre-Rex) to #31 in efficiency in 2015, as their adjusted sack rate dropped from 8.8% down to 3.8%. Rex Ryan must get the pass rush back on track in 2016. That may be easier said than done given the slate of non-divisional quarterbacks they will face:

In 2015, the Bills played 7 games against QBs who were not their team's starter the prior year: Kellen Moore, Marcus Mariota (R), Brian Hoyer, Kirk Cousins, Sam Bradford & Ryan Fitzpatrick (2x). In 2016, assuming Fitzpatrick is back in New York, that number likely drops to just 2: STL & CLE.

If the defense improves, the offense likewise must get better, and the answer may be simple: let Tyrod Taylor pass into more favorable situations. The team ran the ball 61% of the time on 1st down, almost 10% above avg, despite Tyrod Taylor posting a 112 RTG (5th best) with a 5 TD : 1 INT ratio. On early down passing, Taylor's 104 rating was 8th best in the NFL. But importantly for Rex and his philosophy, Taylor had the fewest negative plays of any QB in that top 8: he threw just 1 INT and took only 13 sacks, least of any QB in the top 8 for both stats. Yet the Bills went 57% run on 1st/2nd down, almost 10% above NFL average, and by far the most run heavy in the NFL. If they trusted Taylor more to pass on the early downs while avoiding negative plays, it would increase the run efficiency even more, and would allow Buffalo to avoid more 3rd downs.

Strength of Schedule In Detail

True Strength of Schedule Rank: 9

Hardest Stretches *(1=Hard, 32=Easy)*
Hardest 3 wk Stretch Rk: **10**
Hardest 4 wk Stretch Rk: **13**
Hardest 5 wk Stretch Rk: **19**

Easiest Stretches *(1=Easy, 32=Hard)*
Easiest 3 wk Stretch Rk: **4**
Easiest 4 wk Stretch Rk: **23**
Easiest 5 wk Stretch Rk: **17**

Buffalo's schedule will always feature the Patriots twice, a team they are 3-27 (10%) against in their last 30 games. But in 2016, Buffalo also must face the Seahawks, Cardinals, Steelers and Bengals. Buffalo has both the 49ers and Browns at home, giving them a couple of games they should be able to beat. Pay close attention to their game in Seattle week 9, which is on Monday night. Circadian biorhythms will provide a significant edge to the Seahawks in that game.

2015 Play Tendencies

All Pass %	50%
All Pass Rk	32
All Rush %	50%
All Rush Rk	1
1 Score Pass %	52%
1 Score Pass Rk	29
2014 1 Score Pass %	59%
2014 1 Score Pass Rk	10
Pass Increase %	-8%
Pass Increase Rk	31
1 Score Rush %	48%
1 Score Rush Rk	4
Up Pass %	39%
Up Pass Rk	32
Up Rush %	61%
Up Rush Rk	1
Down Pass %	58%
Down Pass Rk	31
Down Rush %	42%
Down Rush Rk	2

BUF was the most run heavy team, and in one score games, they barely passed the ball 52% of the time. Even when they were trailing, when some teams are calling pass plays well over 70% of the time, the Bills were only at 58%. With a lead, they were far too predictable, calling run plays 61% of the time, most in the NFL. With a 2nd half lead, they gained just 3.3 YPC, well below avg, and ran 71% of the time, well above avg.

2015 Offensive Advanced Metrics

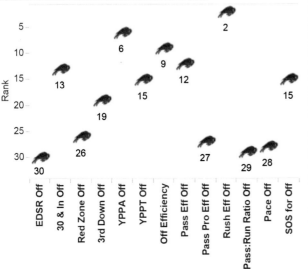

Rex Ryan stepped in the door and promptly changed the defense. In turn, the pass rush dropped from #1 to #31 and the defense was not nearly as efficient as in years past. The Bills were middle of the pack in most areas, but were terrible against the run (30th) and on 3rd down. That's a deadly combination, and was a driving reason the Bills went 3-5 in games decided by one score - they couldn't get the other team's offense off the field. They went 1-7 when trailing at halftime, simply incapable of rallying. Offensively, the Bills could have performed substantially better if they were only slightly better from an EDSR and red zone standpoint. But the Bills had Tyrod Taylor operate at an extremely slow pace and called a ridiculous number of run plays. They rode the run efficiency as far as it could take them, but a few small changes could make a big difference in their 2016 results.

2015 Defensive Advanced Metrics

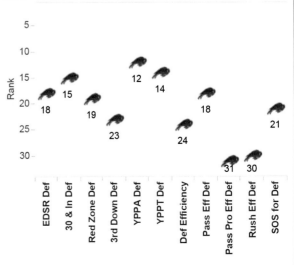

109

Drafted Players   2016 Draft Grade: #11 (3.1/4)

Rnd.	Pick #	Pos.	Player	College
1	19	DE	Shaq Lawson	Clemson
2	41	ILB	Reggie Ragland	Alabama
3	80	DT	Adolphus Washington	Ohio State
4	139	QB	Cardale Jones	Ohio State
5	156	RB	Jonathan Williams	Arkansas
6	192	WR	Kolby Listenbee	TCU
6	218	CB	Kevon Seymour	USC

Free Agents/Trades Added

Player (Position)

Colt Anderson S
Corey White CB
Fernando Velasco C
Lorenzo Alexander LB
Robert Blanton S
Sterling Moore CB
Zach Brown LB

Other Signed

Player (Position)

Bryson Albright LB
Claudell Louis DE
Davonte Allen WR
Eric Striker LB
Gary Chambers WR
Glenn Gronkowski RB
Jamison Lalk G
Julian Whigham CB
Justin Zimmer DT
Keith Lumpkin T
Marquis Lucas T
Marshall Morgan K
Reid Ferguson C
Robert Kugler C

2015 Players Lost

Transaction	Player (Position)
Cut	Boobie Dixon RB
	Bud Noel CB
	Cam Thomas CB
	Jacob Maxwell TE
	Jarius Wynn DE
	Kraig Urbik G
	Leodis McKelvin CB
	Mario Williams DE
	Ronald Patrick C
	Tony Steward LB
	Tyson Chandler T
Declared Free Agent	Nigel Bradham LB
	Percy Harvin WR
	Ron Brooks CB
Retired	AJ Tarpley LB
	Percy Harvin WR

- Rex Ryan wanted more talent for his defense, and he got it this offseason, primarily via the draft. Adding talent from marquee programs like Alabama, Ohio State & Clemson, the Bills added DE Shaq Lawson, ILB Reggie Ragland & DT Adolphus Washington. But then, following offseason practices, Shaq Lawson reinjured his shoulder, requiring surgery. Early projections include everything from missing most of his rookie season to missing the season in its entirety.
- Then it was announced that Bills #1 WR Sammy Watkins received surgery to repair a broken bone in his foot, and reportedly may miss training camp and the preseason.
- The Bills made the smart move of releasing DE Mario Williams. Largely due to his release, the Bills moved from the 2nd most expensive defense in 2015 to the 14th in 2016. That enabled them to spend more offensively, and in particular, along the offensive line, which went from the 27th to top 10.
- That same offensive line, which helped to build the 2nd rated run offense but was 27th in pass protection, retained Richie Incognito & Cordy Glenn.
- BUF did little to address the weaponry for starting QB Tyrod Taylor. They drafted a WR in the 6th round, lost Chris Hogan via Free Agency to the Patriots, may be without Sammy Watkins in the early part of the preseason, and Taylor will have to live with it. As such, the top 10 paid backfield will likely be called upon again in what may continue to be an extremely balanced (detrimentally so) attack strategy.
- However, if the Bills defense can bounce back and improve in its metrics, they may be poised to win the old fashioned way, via defense & a ground attack.
- The Bills passing offense is likely to focus on Charles Clay, particularly if Watkins is not 100% at the start of the season: when Watkins missed action last yr and Taylor had at least 20 attempts, Clay averaged: 7 catches, 97 yds, 0.5 TDs.

Lineup & 2016 Cap Hit

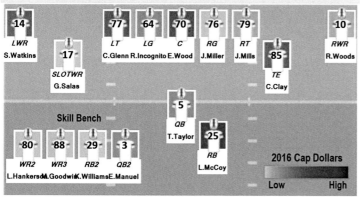

Health Overall & by Unit (2015 v 2014)

2015 Rk	25
2015 AGL	81
Off Rk	19
Def Rk	28
2014 Rk	10
2014 AGL	59

2016 Positional Spending

	All OFF	QB	OL	RB	WR	TE	All DEF	DL	LB	CB	S
2015 Rk	31	31	27	8	17	17	2	2	21	9	24
Rank	20	29	7	11	21	12	14	11	21	6	20
Total	63.0M	6.4M	23.7M	9.8M	14.7M	8.4M	78.1M	28.2M	18.0M	22.0M	9.9M

2016 Offseason Spending

Total Spent	Total Spent Rk	Free Agents #	Free Agents $	Free Agents $ Rk	Waiver #	Waiver $	Waiver $ Rk	Extended #	Sum of Extended $	Sum of Drafted $	Undrafted #	Undrafted $
150M	22	12	10M	32	15	26M	4	2	76M	30M	14	23M

2015 Stats & Fantasy Production

Pos	Player	Ov. Rank	Pos. Rk	Age	Gms	St	Pass Comp	Pass Att	Pass Yds	Pass TD	Pass Int	Rush Att	Rush Yds	Rush YPA	Rush TD	Targ	Recp	Rec Yds	Rec YPC	Rec TDs	Draft King Pts	Fan Duel Pts
QB	Tyrod Taylor*		14	26	14	14	242	380	3,035	20	6	104	568	5	4	1	1	4	4		285	277
	EJ Manuel		43	25	7	2	52	84	561	3	3	17	64	4	1						46	42
RB	LeSean McCoy*	48	17	27	12	12						203	895	4	3	50	32	292	9	2	187	163
	Karlos Williams		31	22	11	3						93	517	6	7	14	11	96	9	2	128	119
	Mike Gillislee		74	25	5	1						47	267	6	3	7	6	29	5		56	49
WR	Sammy Watkins	38	16	22	13	13						1	1	1		96	60	1,047	17	9	222	189
	Robert Woods		65	23	14	9						1				80	47	552	12	3	122	95
	Chris Hogan		80	27	16	4	1	1	1	4		1	4	4		59	36	450	13	2	97	76
	Percy Harvin		100	27	5	5						5	31	6		30	19	218	11	1	53	40
TE	Charles Clay		20	26	13	13										77	51	528	10	3	125	96

ODDS & TRENDS

Buffalo Bills

Avg Line	Pred Wins	Pred Div Finish
+0.7	8	#2

2016 Weekly Betting Lines (wks 1-16)

(-) Favorite   Underdog (+)
-9.0 .... +10.0

Avg Line = 0.7

Week lines: A -2.0(wk1), N(wk2), A +7.0(wk4), A +1.0(wk5), H -7.0(wk6), A +1.0(wk7), H(wk8), A +10.0(wk9), A +5.5(wk11), H -5.0(wk12), (wk13), H -9.0(wk15), H -3.5(wk16)

Weeks: 1 2 3 4 5 6 7 8 9 10 11 12 13 14 15 16

2015 Critical and Game-Deciding Stats

TO Margin	+6
TO Given	19
INT Given	9
FUM Given	10
TO Taken	25
INT Taken	17
FUM Taken	8
Sack Margin	-21
Sacks	21
Sacks Allow	42
Return TD Margin	+1
Ret TDs	3
Ret TDs Allow	2
Penalty Margin	-30
Penalties	143
Opponent Penalties	113

-Teams that win the turnover battle win 79% of games & cover 79% ATS.
-Teams with more sacks win 71% of games & cover 69% ATS.
-Teams with more return TDs win 75% of games & cover 75% ATS.
-Teams with fewer penalties win 57% of games & cover 54% ATS.

2016 NFLproject.com Forecast

Div RK	3
Div W%	(6%)
Playoffs RK	21
% in Playoffs	(17%)
Super Bowl RK	28
% Win Super Bowl	(0%)

Odds to Win Division
90% — 85%
70%
50%
30%
10% — 6%
-10%
AFCE

Team Records & Trends

	2015	2014	2013
Average line	-0.2	1.4	3.7
Average O/U line	43.7	43.6	43.8
Straight Up Record	8-8	9-7	6-10
Against the Spread Record	7-8	9-7	8-8
Over/Under Record	8-8	3-13	10-6
ATS as Favorite	3-4	3-3	1-1
ATS as Underdog	4-3	6-3	7-7
Straight Up Home	5-3	5-3	4-4
ATS Home	5-3	4-4	6-2
Over/Under Home	4-4	1-7	4-4
ATS as Home Favorite	3-1	3-2	0-1
ATS as a Home Dog	2-1	1-1	6-1
Straight Up Away	3-5	4-4	2-6
ATS Away	2-5	5-3	2-6
Over/Under Away	4-4	2-6	6-2
ATS Away Favorite	0-3	0-1	1-0
ATS Away Dog	2-2	5-2	1-6
Six Point Teaser Record	11-5	12-4	10-5
Seven Point Teaser Record	12-4	12-4	12-3
Ten Point Teaser Record	13-2	14-2	14-1

Games Favored

5

Games Underdog

10

Close Game Records

All 2015 Wins: 8
FG Games (<=3 pts) W-L: **1-2**
FG Games Win %: **33% (#21)**
FG Games Wins (% of Total Wins): **13% (#26)**
1 Score Games (<=8 pts) W-L: **3-5**
1 Score Games Win %: **38% (#25)**
1 Score Games Wins (% of Total Wins): **38% (#27)**

Home Lines (wks 1-16)

Avg Line = -2.4

Lines: (wk3) +1.5, (wk6) -7.0, (wk8) +3.0, (wk12) -5.0, (wk14) -2.4, (wk15) -9.0, (wk16) -3.5

Avg Line = -2.4

Weeks: 1 2 3 4 5 6 7 8 9 10 11 12 13 14 15 16

Road Lines (wks 1-16)

Avg Line = 4.1

Lines: +3.0(wk1), +7.0(wk4), +1.0(wk5), +1.0(wk7), +10.0(wk9), +5.5(wk11)

Avg Line = 4.1

Weeks: 1 2 3 4 5 6 7 8 9 10 11 12 13 14 15 16

Regular Season Wins: Past Results & Current Proj

2012 Wins	6
2013 Wins	6
2014 Wins	9
Proj 2015 Wins	8.5
2015 Wins	8
Proj 2016 Wins	8

1 2 3 4 5 6 7 8 9 10 11 12 13 14 15

The Bills are projected to win 8 games, the same total as 2015, but it will be important to start fast. A game in Baltimore will be familiar for Rex Ryan, and he follows that up with hosting the Jets on a short week. Toss in the Patriots week 4, and the season starts extremely emotionally for Rex. The schedule is difficult, but is offset by hosting some very bad teams (SF and CLE). Despite winning the turnover battle by a +6 margin, the Bills were absolutely embarrassed in sack margin (-21) and penalty margin (-30). Both were 3rd worst in the NFL last year. Buffalo has historically been a terrible road favorite, and were 0-3 in that role last year, but may not be a road favorite at all this season. It will be very hard for the Bills to make the playoffs as a Wild Card team - the AFC East hasn't landed a Wild Card playoff team since 2010.

2016 Rest Analysis

Avg Rest	6.5
Avg Rest Rk	3
Team More Rest	2
Opp More Rest	3
Net Rest Edge	-1
3 days rest	1
4 days rest	0
5 days rest	1
6 days rest	9
7 days rest	2
8 days rest	0
9 days rest	1
10 days rest	0
11 days rest	0
12 days rest	1
13 days rest	0
14 days rest	0

Weekly EDSR & Season Trending Performance

WEEK	1	2	3	4	5	6	7	9	10	11	12	13	14	15	16	17
RESULT	W	L	W	L	W	L	L	W	W	L	L	W	L	L	W	W
OPP	IND	NE	MIA	NYG	TEN	CIN	JAC	MIA	NYJ	NE	KC	HOU	PHI	WAS	DAL	NYJ
SITE	H	H	A	H	A	H	A	H	A	A	A	H	A	H	H	H
MARGIN	13	-8	27	-14	1	-13	-3	16	5	-7	-8	9	-3	-10	10	5
PTS	27	32	41	10	14	21	31	33	22	13	22	30	20	25	16	22
OPP PTS	14	40	14	24	13	34	34	17	17	20	30	21	23	35	6	17

(Week by Week 2015 Results)

EDSR Results (W/L) By Week
W=Green
L=Red

Off & Def EDSR
Wk & Trend
- Blue=Offense (high=good)
- Red=Defense (low=good)

111

STATS & VISUALIZATIONS

Buffalo Bills

Directional Passer Rating Achieved

Receiver	Short Left	Short Middle	Short Right	Deep Left	Deep Middle	Deep Right
Sammy Watkins	110	56	93	139	39	98
Charles Clay	110	61	92	39	149	8
Robert Woods	81	72	78	39	118	87
Chris Hogan	78	100	84	63	39	54
Percy Harvin	95		89	39		135
Chris Gragg	82	99	48	83	39	118
Greg Salas	107			39		
Marquise Goodwin	116					
Marcus Easley				39		135
MarQueis Gray		79				
Matthew Mulligan	79					
Nick O'Leary			39	95		

Directional Frequency by Receiver

Receiver	Short Left	Short Middle	Short Right	Deep Left	Deep Middle	Deep Right
Sammy Watkins	27%	17%	15%	43%	40%	34%
Charles Clay	19%	25%	25%	19%	30%	9%
Robert Woods	16%	19%	32%	6%	10%	23%
Chris Hogan	12%	19%	15%	17%	10%	23%
Percy Harvin	14%		6%	9%		4%
Chris Gragg	4%	14%	5%	4%	10%	2%
Greg Salas	4%			2%		
Marquise Goodwin	2%					
Marcus Easley				1%		4%
MarQueis Gray		3%				
Matthew Mulligan	1%					
Nick O'Leary			3%	2%		

Defense Passer Rating Allowed

Short Left	Short Middle	Short Right	Deep Left	Deep Middle	Deep Right
77	109	82	54	105	54

Offensive Rush Directional Yds/Carry

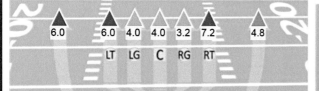

Offensive Rush Frequency of Direction

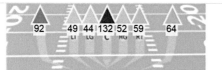

Offensive Explosive Runs by Direction

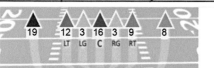

Defensive Rush Directional Yds/Carry

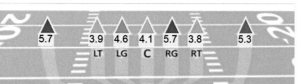

Tyrod Taylor - 1st Down RTG

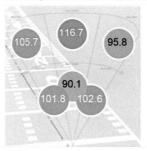

Tyrod Taylor - 2nd Down RTG

Tyrod Taylor - 3rd Down RTG

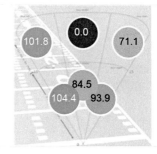

Tyrod Taylor - Overall RTG

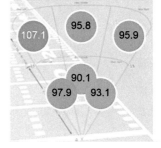

2nd & Short RUN (1D or not)

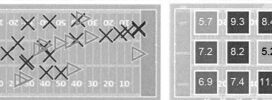

2nd & Short RUN Stats

Run Conv Rk	1D% Run	NFL 1D% Run Avg	Run Freq	NFL Run Freq Avg
31	41%	69%	77%	64%

2nd & Short PASS (1D or not)

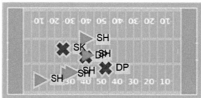

2nd & Short PASS Stats

Pass Conv Rk	1D% Pass	NFL 1D% Pass Avg	Pass Freq	NFL Pass Freq Avg
6	63%	55%	23%	36%

Pass Offense Play Success Rate

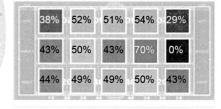

Pass Offense Yds/Play

Off. Directional Tendency (% of Plays Left, Middle or Right)

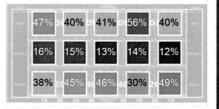

Off. Directional Pass Rate (% of Plays which are Passes)

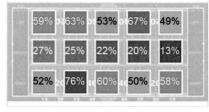

New York Jets

Coaches
Head Coach: Todd Bowles (2nd yr)
OC: Chan Gailey (2nd yr)
DC: Kacy Rodgers (2nd yr)

Forecast 2016 Wins
8

Past Records
2015: 10-6
2014: 4-12
2013: 8-8

Opponent Strength
Easy — Hard

2016 Schedule & Week by Week Strength of Schedule

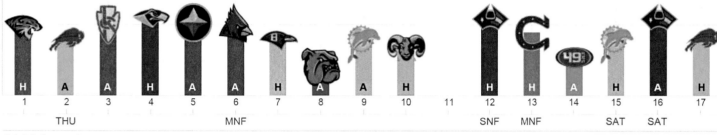

H	A	A	H	A	A	A	H	A	H		H	H	A	H	A	H
1	2	3	4	5	6	7	8	9	10	11	12	13	14	15	16	17
	THU				MNF						SNF	MNF		SAT	SAT	

2016 Overview

After securing their first winning season since the Mark Sanchez/Rex Ryan honeymoon seasons in 2009 and 2010, the Jets seem like they are back on track. But how much of their season last year was simply a result of one of the easiest schedules the NFL offered? Of their 16 games, 6 saw them win by more than 1 score: Twice vs the last place Dolphins, once vs the last place Browns, once vs the last place Titans, once vs the 8-8 Colts, and once vs the Redskins. The Jets went 3-1 vs both the AFC South and the NFC East, two of the worst divisions in football last season. They flipped coins in their other 8 games, going 4-4.

It is pretty obvious they were better with Ryan Fitzpatrick under center than other quarterbacks they've used. From 2013 to 2014, the motley crew consisted of Geno Smith, Michael Vick and Matt Simms. So when Fitzpatrick threw 2 TDs for every 1 INT, fans were sacrificing on his altar. But the sad part is that Fitzpatrick's interception rate ranked 35th in the NFL last year among qualifying quarterbacks. And that was one of the best things Fitzpatrick had going for him. Flip to the Jets' Stats & Visualizations page from Sharp Football Stats, and you'll see how terrible Fitzpatrick was on first down doing anything other than throwing it short. Look at the Directional Frequency visualization, and you'll see he almost entirely locked in to Brandon Marshall and Eric Decker. His ratings were terrible to virtually every other target.

Let's assume Fitzpatrick returns to the Jets and they don't have to give up their season with Geno Smith under center. Instead of facing the weak AFC South and NFC East, they must take on the tough AFC North and NFC West. They also must play two teams who have legitimate shots to win their divisions this year, but just missed out last year, finishing 2nd (like the Jets), in the Chiefs and Colts. It's the hardest schedule through the first 7 weeks.

There is every reason to believe Fitzpatrick won't see the same offensive success against those defenses, nor will the Jets find it as easy to play against Ben Roethlisberger, Carson Palmer, Russell Wilson and Andy Dalton as they did playing against Marcus Mariota, Johnny Manziel, Kellen Moore, T.J. Yates and Sam Bradford last year. So what can the Jets improve upon to help them perform more efficiently in 2016?

For starters, they need to improve on 2nd and short. Particularly when running. They ranked 30th in 2nd and short conversion rate. Matt Forte helped spearhead the #2 ranked Bears rush offense in short yardage last season. Picture this: the Bears converted 90% of their 2nd and short rushes into first downs, and they weren't playing game theory and passing a ton to increase their run odds - they ran the ball 79% of those play calls. OC Chan Gailey must find out how Forte ran well on short yardage and replicate it in New York. Second, Chan Gailey must be more aggressive earlier in the game. Just 41% of the Jets' first half offensive plays were graded as successful, 31st in the NFL. In the 2nd half, that rate increased to 49% and ranked 9th. In particular, while passing on 1st down in the first half was generally successful, with the average team recording 55% success rate, the Jets ranked 29th. And on 1st and 2nd down in the first half, they ranked dead last in successful play rate. These are easy things to focus on and would tremendously help efficiency.

Strength of Schedule In Detail

True Strength of Schedule Rank: 2

Hardest Stretches *(1=Hard, 32=Easy)*
Hardest 3 wk Stretch Rk:	3
Hardest 4 wk Stretch Rk:	1
Hardest 5 wk Stretch Rk:	1

Easiest Stretches *(1=Easy, 32=Hard)*
Easiest 3 wk Stretch Rk:	2
Easiest 4 wk Stretch Rk:	2
Easiest 5 wk Stretch Rk:	12

New York is in store for a roller coaster 2016. They face the NFL's most difficult first month (vs CIN, @ BUF, @ KC, vs SEA) and that stretch continues through weeks 5 and 6 against the Steelers and Cardinals, both on the road in back to back weeks. Looking at the Jets first 7 weeks, there is a huge gap in opponent strength between them and any other team in the league. If they can somehow survive until week 8, they face the 2nd easiest 3 game stretch heading into their bye, and then find themselves hosting two annual playoff contenders in primetime (consecutively): the Patriots and Colts. Their schedule is back-heavy with division opponents, making it even more difficult to prepare for the very strong non-division opponents they will face to start the season. Lastly, not only do the Jets face three sets of back-to-back road games, all trips occur in the first 9 weeks of the year, and two involve primetime road games (wk 2 @ BUF on Thursday, wk 6 @ ARI)

2015 Play Tendencies

All Pass %	58%
All Pass Rk	19
All Rush %	42%
All Rush Rk	14
1 Score Pass %	58%
1 Score Pass Rk	19
2014 1 Score Pass %	48%
2014 1 Score Pass Rk	31
Pass Increase %	10%
Pass Increase Rk	3
1 Score Rush %	42%
1 Score Rush Rk	14
Up Pass %	48%
Up Pass Rk	17
Up Rush %	52%
Up Rush Rk	16
Down Pass %	71%
Down Pass Rk	7
Down Rush %	29%
Down Rush Rk	26

Ryan Fitzpatrick was not as good as many surface level, old-school stats think he was last year. But he still was much better than Geno Smith and prior QBs. Which is why the Jets allowed him to pass the ball 10% more often in one-score games, the 3rd greatest increase of any team last year vs. the prior year. They still were slightly below average, but they went from completely run dominant if the game was close at all to a team much more willing to pass.

2015 Offensive Advanced Metrics

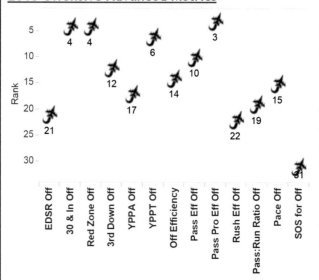

So much was made about the Jets offensive resurgence last season. But the reality is, the Jets were a good but not great offensively. They just happened to be extremely good in the red zone against bad defenses (31st). They were below average in EDSR and yds/pass, and just 14th in overall efficiency on offense. On the surface, Ryan Fitzpatrick's cumulative numbers may look impressive, but there was a reason the team was hesitant to re-sign him. His defense game him plenty of opportunities in solid field position against poor opponents, and offensively the Jets were far from incredible despite weak opposition. The defense performed great, which should be expected when facing the 28th rated schedule of opponents. But they were top 5 in virtually all key metrics. They must improve their pass rush efficiency a bit more in 2016, but apart from that, this defense really helped Fitzpatrick and the offense a lot.

2015 Defensive Advanced Metrics

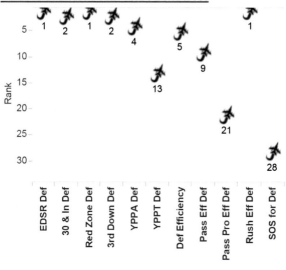

Drafted Players

PERSONNEL & SPENDING

New York Jets

Rnd.	Pick #	Pos.	Player	College
1	20	OLB	Darron Lee	Ohio State
2	51	QB	Christian Hackenberg	Penn State
3	83	OLB	Jordan Jenkins	Georgia
4	118	CB	Juston Burris	North Carolina State
5	158	OT	Brandon Shell	South Carolina
7	235	P	Lac Edwards	Sam Houston State
	241	WR	Charone Peake	Clemson

Free Agents/Trades Added

Player (Position)

Darryl Morris CB
Jarvis Jenkins DE
Jeremy Ross WR
Khiry Robinson RB
Matt Forte RB
Ryan Clady T
Steve McLendon NT

Other Signed

Player (Position)

Bryson Keeton CB
Claude Pelon DE
Doug Middleton S
Helva Matungulu DE
Jalin Marshall WR
Jason Vander Laan TE
Julien Obioha DE
Kyle Friend C
Lawrence Thomas DE
Quenton Bundrage WR
Robby Anderson WR
Ross Martin K
Tarow Barney DT
Tom Hackett P

2015 Players Lost

Transaction	Player (Position)
Cut	Adrien Robinson TE
	Antonio Cromartie CB
	Cunningham, Jerome TE
	Dri Archer RB
	Jeff Cumberland TE
	Jeremy Kerley WR
	Joe Anderson WR
	Kyle Brindza K
	Sean Hickey T
Declared Free Agent	Antonio Allen S
	Chris Ivory RB
	Damon Harrison NT
	Darrin Walls CB
	Stevan Ridley RB
Retired	D'Brickashaw Ferguson T

- The most expensive defense in the NFL this year got younger in the draft. Despite the strength of the defense from 2015, the Jets went defense with 3 of their first 4 draft picks. They currently have the most expensive defense in the NFL, featuring the 6th most expensive line and the most expensive CB despite cutting Antonio Cromartie.
- Ryan Fitzpatrick wanted more money, but here are some interesting facts and reasons why the Jets were smart to avoid forking over a larger sum. Early down efficiency is massive, and Fitzpatrick's 1st down passer rating in the 2nd half was 67, the worst in the NFL. Late performance is also key, and Fitzpatrick had the 2nd worst 4th quarter passer rating in the NFL. If trailing by any amount, it dipped to 55, with 8 INTs to only 4 TDs. This is a big concern because the Jets faced the 2nd easiest schedule of opposing defenses.
- It's hard to imagine Christian Hackenberg will be the answer for the Jets long term. Ideally, the Jets can sign Fitzpatrick to a team friendly deal that allows them to cut him before his cap hits get too large.
- The Jets did well to replace the retiring D'Brickashaw Ferguson with LT Ryan Clady, and Matt Forte will be an excellent safety valve for Fitzpatrick.
- Virtually no team has relied more on their defense to win games than teams led by Fitzpatrick: The last 4 years, Fitzpatrick has led his team to a 2-24 (7.7%) record when the defense allows over 20 points. Last year, the Jets went 1-6 when the opponent scored over 20 points.
- Additionally, Fitzpatrick has led his team to a 30-2 (94%) record when his defense holds opponents to less than 17 points. But NFL teams score 23 ppg on average. And Fitzpatrick's teams are 16-61 (21%) when the opponent scores 17+ points. It's one of the worst rates for any quarterback.
- With Brandon Marshall, Eric Decker and Matt Forte, the Jets have a very nice group of skill players which should improve the numbers of any QB attempting passes.

Lineup & 2016 Cap Hit

FS M.Gilchrist 21
SS C.Pryor 25
LB E.Henderson 58
LB D.Harris 52
RCB M.Williams 20
SLOTCB B.Skrine 41
DE S.Richardson 91
DT L.Williams 62
DE M.Wilkerson 96
OLB L.Mauldin 55
LCB D.Revis 24
LWR D.Smith 19
LT R.Clady 78
LG J.Carpenter 77
C N.Mangold 74
RG B.Winters 67
RT B.Giacomini 68
RWR B.Marshall 15
SLOTWR E.Decker 87
TE J.Amaro 88
QB R.Fitzpatrick 14
RB M.Forte 22

Skill Bench
WR2 Q.Enunwa 81
WR3 K.Thompkins 10
RB2 B.Powell 29
QB2 G.Smith 7

2016 Cap Dollars
Low — High

Health Overall & by Unit (2015 v 2014)

2015 Rk	13
2015 AGL	62
Off Rk	24
Def Rk	1
2014 Rk	2
2014 AGL	42

2016 Positional Spending

	All OFF	QB	OL	RB	WR	TE	All DEF	DL	LB	CB	S
2015 Rk	3	29	1	10	5	23	4	19	18	1	14
Rank	19	32	8	15	6	29	1	6	25	1	19
Total	69.1M	3.1M	29.6M	8.0M	24.5M	4.0M	89.2M	32.2M	14.6M	32.4M	10.0M

2016 Offseason Spending

Total Spent	Total Spent Rk	Free Agents #	Free Agents $	Free Agents $ Rk	Waiver #	Waiver $	Waiver $ Rk	Extended #	Sum of Extended $	Sum of Drafted $	Undrafted #	Undrafted $
109M	30	14	51M	18	22	33M	2	0	0M	18M	15	23M

2015 Stats & Fantasy Production

Pos	Player	Ov. Rank	Pos. Rk	Age	Gms	St	Pass Comp	Pass Att	Pass Yds	Pass TD	Pass Int	Rush Att	Rush Yds	Rush YPA	Rush TD	Targ	Recp	Rec Yds	Rec YPC	Rec TDs	Draft King Pts	Fan Duel Pts
QB	Ryan Fitzpatrick	78	12	33	16	16	335	562	3,905	31	15	60	270	5	2						308	300
RB	Chris Ivory*	25	9	27	15	14						247	1,070	4	7	37	30	217	7	1	211	188
	Bilal Powell		45	27	11	2						70	313	4	1	63	47	388	8	2	141	112
	Zac Stacy		101	24	8							31	89	3	1	12	9	65	7		30	26
WR	Brandon Marshall*	6	3	31	16	16										173	109	1,502	14	14	344	285
	Eric Decker	28	10	28	15	13										132	80	1,027	13	12	257	213
	Quincy Enunwa	106	23	12	6											46	22	315	14		57	43
	Jeremy Kerley	115	27	16	1											26	16	152	10	2	46	35
	Kenbrell Thompkins	136	27	7	2											33	17	165	10		37	25

ODDS & TRENDS
New York Jets

Avg Line	+0.5	Pred Wins	8	Pred Div Finish	#2

(-) Favorite   Underdog (+)
-5.0   +6.5

2016 Weekly Betting Lines (wks 1-16)

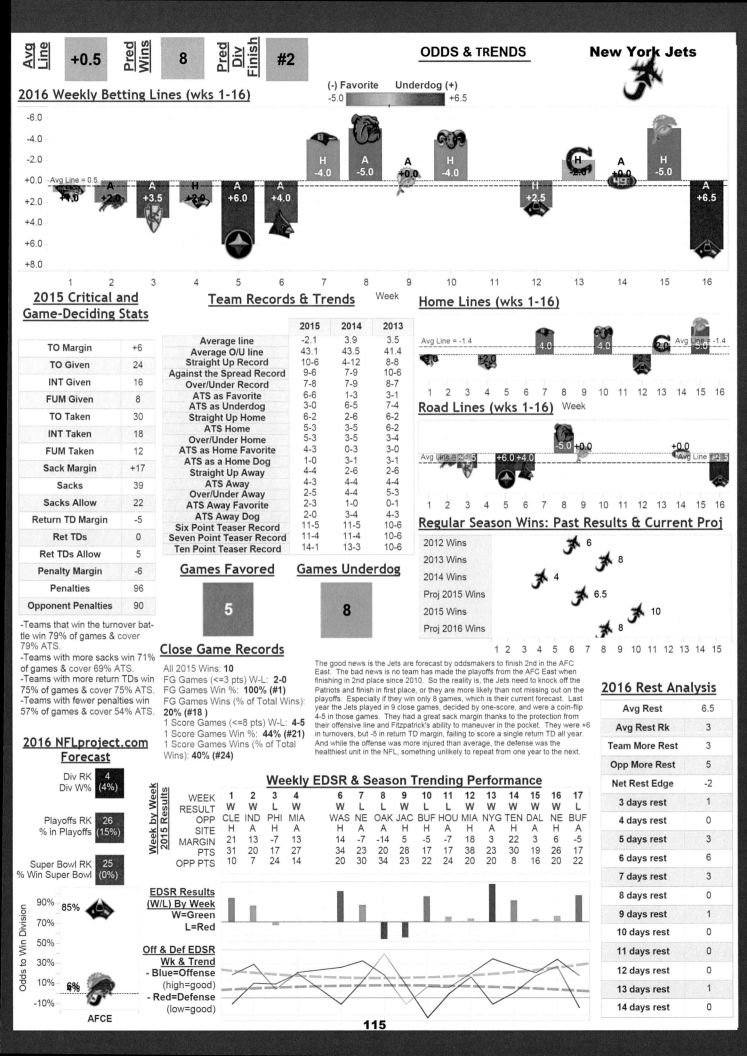

Week

	2015	2014	2013
Average line	-2.1	3.9	3.5
Average O/U line	43.1	43.5	41.4
Straight Up Record	10-6	4-12	8-8
Against the Spread Record	9-6	7-9	10-6
Over/Under Record	7-8	7-9	8-7
ATS as Favorite	6-6	1-3	3-1
ATS as Underdog	3-0	6-5	7-4
Straight Up Home	6-2	2-6	6-2
ATS Home	5-3	3-5	6-2
Over/Under Home	5-3	3-5	3-4
ATS as Home Favorite	4-3	0-3	3-0
ATS as a Home Dog	1-0	3-1	3-1
Straight Up Away	4-4	2-6	2-6
ATS Away	4-3	4-4	4-4
Over/Under Away	2-5	4-4	5-3
ATS Away Favorite	2-3	1-0	0-1
ATS Away Dog	2-0	3-4	4-3
Six Point Teaser Record	11-5	11-5	10-6
Seven Point Teaser Record	11-4	11-4	10-6
Ten Point Teaser Record	14-1	13-3	10-6

Team Records & Trends

2015 Critical and Game-Deciding Stats

TO Margin	+6
TO Given	24
INT Given	16
FUM Given	8
TO Taken	30
INT Taken	18
FUM Taken	12
Sack Margin	+17
Sacks	39
Sacks Allow	22
Return TD Margin	-5
Ret TDs	0
Ret TDs Allow	5
Penalty Margin	-6
Penalties	96
Opponent Penalties	90

-Teams that win the turnover battle win 79% of games & cover 79% ATS.
-Teams with more sacks win 71% of games & cover 69% ATS.
-Teams with more return TDs win 75% of games & cover 75% ATS.
-Teams with fewer penalties win 57% of games & cover 54% ATS.

Home Lines (wks 1-16)

Avg Line = -1.4   Avg Line = -1.4

Road Lines (wks 1-16)   Week

Avg Line = 2.5   Avg Line = 2.5

Regular Season Wins: Past Results & Current Proj

2012 Wins	6
2013 Wins	8
2014 Wins	4
Proj 2015 Wins	6.5
2015 Wins	10
Proj 2016 Wins	8

Games Favored
5

Games Underdog
8

Close Game Records

All 2015 Wins: **10**
FG Games (<=3 pts) W-L: **2-0**
FG Games Win %: **100% (#1)**
FG Games Wins (% of Total Wins): **20% (#18)**
1 Score Games (<=8 pts) W-L: **4-5**
1 Score Games Win %: **44% (#21)**
1 Score Games Wins (% of Total Wins): **40% (#24)**

The good news is the Jets are forecast by oddsmakers to finish 2nd in the AFC East. The bad news is no team has made the playoffs from the AFC East when finishing in 2nd place since 2010. So the reality is, the Jets need to knock off the Patriots and finish in first place, or they are more likely than not missing out on the playoffs. Especially if they win only 8 games, which is their current forecast. Last year the Jets played in 9 close games, decided by one-score, and were a coin-flip 4-5 in those games. They had a great sack margin thanks to the protection from their offensive line and Fitzpatrick's ability to maneuver in the pocket. They were +6 in turnovers, but -5 in return TD margin, failing to score a single return TD all year. And while the offense was more injured than average, the defense was the healthiest unit in the NFL, something unlikely to repeat from one year to the next.

2016 NFLproject.com Forecast

Div RK	4
Div W%	(4%)
Playoffs RK	26
% in Playoffs	(15%)
Super Bowl RK	25
% Win Super Bowl	(0%)

Odds to Win Division
90% — 85%
70%
50%
30%
10% — 6%
-10%
AFCE

2016 Rest Analysis

Avg Rest	6.5
Avg Rest Rk	3
Team More Rest	3
Opp More Rest	5
Net Rest Edge	-2
3 days rest	1
4 days rest	0
5 days rest	3
6 days rest	6
7 days rest	3
8 days rest	0
9 days rest	1
10 days rest	0
11 days rest	0
12 days rest	0
13 days rest	1
14 days rest	0

Weekly EDSR & Season Trending Performance

WEEK	1	2	3	4		6	7	8	9	10	11	12	13	14	15	16	17
RESULT	W	W	L	W		W	L	L	W	L	L	W	W	W	W	W	L
OPP	CLE	IND	PHI	MIA		WAS	NE	OAK	JAC	BUF	HOU	MIA	NYG	TEN	DAL	NE	BUF
SITE	H	A	H	A		H	A	A	H	A	H	A	H	A	H	A	A
MARGIN	21	13	-7	13		14	-7	-14	5	-5	-7	18	3	22	3	6	-5
PTS	31	20	17	27		34	23	20	28	17	17	38	23	30	19	26	17
OPP PTS	10	7	24	14		20	30	34	23	22	24	20	20	8	16	20	22

Week by Week 2015 Results

EDSR Results (W/L) By Week
W=Green
L=Red

Off & Def EDSR Wk & Trend
- Blue=Offense (high=good)
- Red=Defense (low=good)

STATS & VISUALIZATIONS

New York Jets

Directional Passer Rating Achieved

Receiver	Short Left	Short Middle	Short Right	Deep Left	Deep Middle	Deep Right
Brandon Marshall	125	84	92	85	61	94
Eric Decker	106	139	75	25	100	145
Quincy Enunwa	88	60	72	95	56	56
Kenbrell Thompkins	94	77	16	39	81	13
Jeremy Kerley	85	109	116		39	
Devin Smith	90	42	95	0	91	0
Chris Owusu	93	83	42	39	87	95
Jeff Cumberland	39	58	65	95	39	39
Kellen Davis	39	42	87			39

Directional Frequency by Receiver

Receiver	Short Left	Short Middle	Short Right	Deep Left	Deep Middle	Deep Right
Brandon Marshall	43%	17%	45%	46%	21%	30%
Eric Decker	28%	39%	21%	23%	36%	23%
Quincy Enunwa	8%	12%	10%	4%	18%	9%
Kenbrell Thompkins	6%	10%	5%	4%	8%	16%
Jeremy Kerley	6%	11%	6%		3%	
Devin Smith	2%	4%	3%	16%	8%	14%
Chris Owusu	2%	1%	2%	5%	5%	5%
Jeff Cumberland	3%	2%	3%	4%	3%	2%
Kellen Davis	2%	4%	4%			2%

Defense Passer Rating Allowed

Short Left	Short Middle	Short Right	Deep Left	Deep Middle	Deep Right
73	102	75	63	84	51

Offensive Rush Directional Yds/Carry

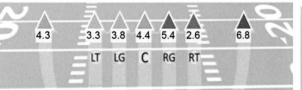

	LT	LG	C	RG	RT	
4.3	3.3	3.8	4.4	5.4	2.6	6.8

Offensive Rush Frequency of Direction

	LT	LG	C	RG	RT	
40	36	50	149	39	69	52

Offensive Explosive Runs by Direction

	LT	LG	C	RG	RT	
7	2	6	21	5	3	12

Defensive Rush Directional Yds/Carry

	LT	LG	C	RG	RT	
4.7	3.2	3.4	3.4	1.9	4.1	4.9

Ryan Fitzpatrick - 1st Down RTG

Ryan Fitzpatrick - 2nd Down RTG

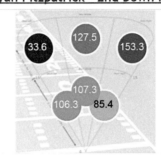

Ryan Fitzpatrick - 3rd Down RTG

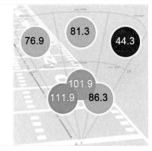

Ryan Fitzpatrick - Overall RTG

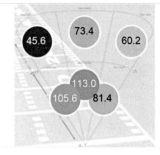

2nd & Short RUN (1D or not)

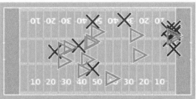

2nd & Short RUN Stats

Run Conv Rk	1D% Run	NFL 1D% Run Avg	Run Freq	NFL Run Freq Avg
30	54%	69%	69%	64%

2nd & Short PASS (1D or not)

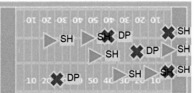

2nd & Short PASS Stats

Pass Conv Rk	1D% Pass	NFL 1D% Pass Avg	Pass Freq	NFL Pass Freq Avg
17	55%	55%	31%	36%

Pass Offense Play Success Rate

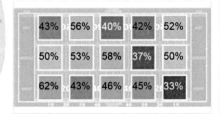

43%	56%	40%	42%	52%
50%	53%	58%	37%	50%
62%	43%	46%	45%	33%

Pass Offense Yds/Play

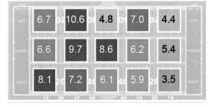

6.7	10.6	4.8	7.0	4.4
6.6	9.7	8.6	6.2	5.4
8.1	7.2	6.1	5.9	3.5

Off. Directional Tendency (% of Plays Left, Middle or Right)

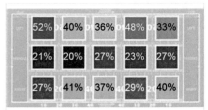

52%	40%	36%	48%	33%
21%	20%	27%	23%	27%
27%	41%	37%	29%	40%

Off. Directional Pass Rate (% of Plays which are Passes)

73%	84%	74%	78%	69%
33%	32%	47%	35%	38%
48%	67%	64%	67%	69%

Kansas City Chiefs

Coaches

Head Coach: Andy Reid (4th yr)
OC: Brad Childress (KC OFF Consultant (1st yr)
DC: Bob Sutton (4th yr)

Forecast
2016 Wins
9.5

Past
Records
2015: 11-5
2014: 9-7
2013: 11-5

Opponent Strength
Easy — Hard

2016 Schedule & Week by Week Strength of Schedule

H	A	A	A		A		A		A		A		H	H	H	A
1	2	3	4	5	6	7	8	9	10	11	12	13	14	15	16	17

SNF (under 4), THU (under 14), SNF (under 16)

2016 Overview

Watching the Chiefs under Andy Reid is like watching a kindergarten bully try to reign in a neighborhood swimming pool. He can dominate in the shallow end, where he doesn't need to take risks or go outside of his comfort zone, terrorizing his peers and stealing their dive toys. But when he tries to navigate into deeper waters, he realizes he can't swim. And soon others realize it as well, and then he gets back everything he dished out (and then some) by those who can swim.

Reid has built the perfect low ceiling, high floor team. One that is extremely efficient in dispatching the poorly built units that are littered around the NFL. But put him up against a better team, particularly in a game that matters, and he rarely perseveres. The last 2 seasons, here are the teams that Reid has defeated by 7 or more points without being at least +2 in turnover margin (teams +2 in turnover margin historically win 88% of their games): STL (2014), MIA (2014), OAK (2014), NYJ (2014), OAK (2015). That is it. The QBs in those games were Austin Davis, Ryan Tannehill, Derek Carr and Michael Vick. The records for those teams were: 3-13, 4-12, 6-10, 7-9 and 8-8.

But the Chiefs are a stubborn bunch. An outsider's view would see a team in need of some type of offensive spark to get over the hump. One of the biggest ways to put up points, to open up an offense and to compete with better opponents is through big chunk plays in the passing game. Think Carson Palmer and the Cardinals, or Ben Roethlisberger and the Steelers. Smith threw 15 or more yards in the air at the smallest rate of any quarterback in the NFL last year. The move to help that aspect this offseason? WR Rod Streeter, an undrafted free agent out of Temple who couldn't crack the lineup on the 8-8 Raiders last season. In the draft, the Chiefs used 3 of their first 4 picks on the defensive side of the ball, and didn't select a WR until the 126th overall pick, which they used on a player who was suspended four times in college.

It appears the Chiefs have no interest in trying to solve their inability to defeat teams that have offenses capable of scoring on the Chiefs defense. They are simply playing the odds: they won't face many superb offenses in a given year, and they will be able to beat the average to poor teams on their schedule with their defense and efficient run game. It's the recipe to give them 9 wins and a shot at the playoffs. And at that point, they'll roll the dice that their opponent will be a poor offense (like Houston last year). And if not, perhaps their opponent will have a bad game. Because under Andy Reid, from week 11 onward & including the playoffs, the Chiefs are 1-8 when playing a team with a winning record that averages 23+ ppg. The games are almost all close at half, but the KC offense which averages 14 first half points is particularly conservative and anemic in the 3rd quarter, averaging less than a FG and totaling less than 8 in the 2nd half.

If the Chiefs want to maximize their chances, stop targeting Albert Wilson on early downs in KC territory (3 ints), run Smith more on 3rd down in KC territory (78% first downs) rather than have him pass short of sticks (39% first downs) & improve on 3rd down in red zone (17% first downs). Reid must design opportunities for the offense to get chunk plays & focus more on a few key areas which easily increase offensive efficiency if the Chiefs want to do something more than see another winning season end with an early playoff exit.

Strength of Schedule In Detail

True Strength of Schedule Rank: 25

Hardest Stretches *(1=Hard, 32=Easy)*
Hardest 3 wk Stretch Rk: **23**
Hardest 4 wk Stretch Rk: **29**
Hardest 5 wk Stretch Rk: **22**

Easiest Stretches *(1=Easy, 32=Hard)*
Easiest 3 wk Stretch Rk: **21**
Easiest 4 wk Stretch Rk: **24**
Easiest 5 wk Stretch Rk: **16**

Kansas City has a lot to like with their schedule. They play easiest slate of any team in the NFL from week 13 to the end of the season (@ ATL, vs OAK, vs TEN, vs DEN, @ SD), they have a 3-game home stand to close the month of December, and they host a Thursday night game (games on Thursday are far more difficult for the team traveling). The only qualms the Chiefs might have are that they have a fairly early bye week (wk 5) and their most difficult games are on the road. If you look at their schedule prior to hosting Denver week 16, their most difficult opponents are all on the road (@ HOU, @ PIT, @ IND, @ CAR, @ DEN). Their home schedule during that span (vs SD, vs NYJ, vs NO, vs JAC, vs TB) is significantly easier.

2015 Play Tendencies

All Pass %	54%
All Pass Rk	26
All Rush %	46%
All Rush Rk	7
1 Score Pass %	57%
1 Score Pass Rk	21
2014 1 Score Pass %	56%
2014 1 Score Pass Rk	20
Pass Increase %	0%
Pass Increase Rk	20
1 Score Rush %	43%
1 Score Rush Rk	12
Up Pass %	49%
Up Pass Rk	14
Up Rush %	51%
Up Rush Rk	19
Down Pass %	66%
Down Pass Rk	23
Down Rush %	34%
Down Rush Rk	10

When Alex Smith is quarterback and a team has literally nothing at receiver apart from Jeremy Maclin, the best offense is a handoff, and that is exactly what Andy Reid's offense has become in Kansas City. Only 6 teams ran the ball more frequently than the Chiefs, and it's the second year in a row the Chiefs have called pass in a one-score game just 56% of the time. The benefit for the Chiefs is that the run sets up the pass.

2015 Offensive Advanced Metrics

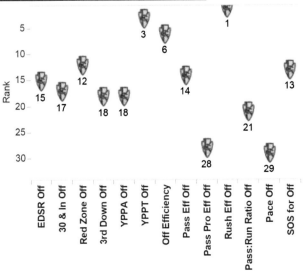

The Chiefs are one of the teams whose defense has been so strong for so long that the offense needs only to be mediocre and avoid turnovers to see success. And as seen, the offense is fairly consistently mediocre. Running a slower tempo and a more run heavy offense, the Chiefs used their #1 rushing offense to rank 6th overall in offensive efficiency. There were essentially average in most key stats, such as EDSR and red zone efficiency. However, the fact that they threw just 7 interceptions all year while taking 22 gave them great field position and led them to quick points, rather than letting their opponent get them, and that translated into very solid yds/point numbers. Defensively, this was a team without many glaring weaknesses, and one that was extremely good against the pass. They are going to be without pass rusher Justin Houston (ACL) and CB Sean Smith (OAK) to start the season, and Houston potentially for the entire season.

2015 Defensive Advanced Metrics

(Ranks by category: EDSR Def 12, 30 & In Def 5, Red Zone Def, 3rd Down Def 5, YPPA Def 10, YPPT Def 1, Def Efficiency 6, Pass Eff Def 5, Pass Pro Eff Def 4, Rush Eff Def 11, SOS for Def 14)

Drafted Players   2016 Draft Grade: #20 (2.7/4)

PERSONNEL & SPENDING — Kansas City Chiefs

Rnd.	Pick #	Pos.	Player	College
2	37	DT	Chris Jones	Mississippi State
3	74	CB	Keivarae Russell	Notre Dame
	105	G	Parker Ehinger	Cincinnati
4	106	CB	Eric Murray	Minnesota
	126	WR	Demarcus Robinson	Florida
5	162	QB	Kevin Hogan	Stanford
	165	WR	Tyreek Hill	West Alabama
6	178	CB	D. J. White	Georgia Tech
	203	OLB	Dadi Lhomme Nicolas	Virginia Tech

Free Agents/Trades Added

Player (Position)

Andy Mulumba LB

Frank Zombo LB

Mitchell Schwartz T

Rod Streater WR

Other Signed

Player (Position)

Ben Clarke C

Drew Nowak G

Garrick Mayweather G

Jake Bernstein G

Mitch Mathews WR

Shak Randolph CB

Terrance Smith LB

Tre Jones CB

Vernon Harris CB

Zach Sterup G

2015 Players Lost

Transaction	Player (Position)
Cut	Ben Clarke C
	Ben Grubbs G
	Cameron Gordon LB
	Jake Bernstein G
	Jimmy Wilson S
	Jordan Kovacs S
	Laurence Gibson T
	Michael Liedtke G
	Paul Fanaika G
	Tautvydas Kieras LB
Declared Free Agent	Donald Stephenson T
	Husain Abdullah S
	Jeff Allen G
	Mike DeVito DE
	Sean Smith CB
	Tyvon Branch S
Retired	Husain Abdullah S

- On the surface, the Chiefs seem well rounded and without many holes. And while compared to some teams that may be true, they have weakness that get exposed vs solid teams and it bites them.
- When facing great offenses, capable of putting up points, the Chiefs struggle to keep pace. The best they faced last year, the Patriots, Bengals and Packers, went 3-0 against KC, and won each game by at least 7 points. The Chiefs didn't have a problem dispatching weaker offenses, but the last two years, they are 0-6 against teams who were averaging over 27 ppg at the time of their meeting, losing games by an avg final score of 30-19.
- When they have to drop back to pass more often, the issues with the offensive line get exposed. They had one of the worst pass blocking units in the NFL last year (ranked 28th), and their offensive guards are not very strong. If the line does enough to block, they simply don't have the receivers to make plays down field, so their style is not geared toward producing chunk plays through the air.
- Alex Smith threw just 61 passes that went 15 or more yards in the air last year. It was 28th most in the NFL last year. However, considering he started all 16 games and a number of players started less, his deep pass frequency was even less often. Smith threw just 3.8 passes that went 15+ yards in the air per game. It was the least frequent of any player to start at least 4 games.
- Almost 40% of his completions came in just 4 games, when his team was trailing by more than 1 score. When playing with a lead of any kind, Alex Smith completed just 9 of 30 attempts for a 51 rating. There is virtually no risk taking with a lead of any kind.
- Losing Justin Houston and Sean Smith means the Chiefs will have to offset their absence, which is not easy to do given the caliber of both players. They will regain the services of Jamaal Charles (71 att, 4 TDs). However, in his 5 games, his carry totals were: 16, 21, 11, 11 & 12.

Lineup & 2016 Cap Hit

Health Overall & by Unit (2015 v 2014)

2015 Rk	7
2015 AGL	55
Off Rk	13
Def Rk	18
2014 Rk	26
2014 AGL	99

2016 Positional Spending

	All OFF	QB	OL	RB	WR	TE	All DEF	DL	LB	CB	S
2015 Rk	23	3	26	7	32	31	17	26	8	19	3
Rank	25	15	29	8	17	24	8	17	1	28	3
Total	74.5M	19.6M	17.3M	10.3M	21.9M	5.4M	80.7M	19.3M	37.9M	7.9M	15.6M

2016 Offseason Spending

Total Spent	Total Spent Rk	Free Agents #	Free Agents $	Free Agents $ Rk	Waiver #	Waiver $	Waiver $ Rk	Extended #	Sum of Extended $	Sum of Drafted $	Undrafted #	Undrafted $
207M	12	10	71M	11	19	20M	7	5	81M	29M	12	16M

2015 Stats & Fantasy Production

Pos	Player	Ov. Rank	Pos. Rk	Age	Gms	St	Pass Comp	Pass Att	Pass Yds	Pass TD	Pass Int	Rush Att	Rush Yds	Rush YPA	Rush TD	Targ	Recp	Rec Yds	Rec YPC	Rec TDs	Draft King Pts	Fan Duel Pts
QB	Alex Smith		16	31	16	16	307	470	3,486	20	7	84	498	6	2						280	274
RB	Charcandrick West		32	24	15	9						160	634	4	4	34	20	214	11	1	140	123
	Jamaal Charles		51	29	5	5						71	364	5	4	29	21	177	8	1	109	91
	Spencer Ware		52	24	11	2						72	403	6	6	6	6	5	1		86	80
WR	Jeremy Maclin	41	17	27	15	15						3	14	5		124	87	1,088	13	8	247	200
	Albert Wilson		76	23	14	12						5	26	5		57	35	451	13	2	98	77
	De'Anthony Thomas		114	22	10	1						9	34	4	1	25	17	140	8	1	48	36
	Chris Conley		118	23	16	5										31	17	199	12	1	46	34
TE	Travis Kelce*	42	7	26	16	16										103	72	875	12	5	195	154

118

Avg Line	Pred Wins	Pred Div Finish
-2.3	9.5	#1

2016 Weekly Betting Lines (wks 1-16)

(-) Favorite   Underdog (+)
-9.0   +4.5

Avg Line = -2.3

Week 1: H -7.0, Week 2: A +1.0, Week 3: H -3.5, Week 4: A +4.0, Week 6: A, Week 7: H -8.0, Week 8: +1.0, Week 9: H -7.0, Week 10: A +4.5, Week 11: H -7.0, Week 12: A +3.0, Week 13: A +1.0, Week 14: H -4.5, Week 15: H -9.0, Week 16: H -1.5

Weeks: 1 2 3 4 5 6 7 8 9 10 11 12 13 14 15 16 — Week

2015 Critical and Game-Deciding Stats

TO Margin	+14
TO Given	15
INT Given	7
FUM Given	8
TO Taken	29
INT Taken	22
FUM Taken	7
Sack Margin	+2
Sacks	47
Sacks Allow	45
Return TD Margin	+4
Ret TDs	6
Ret TDs Allow	2
Penalty Margin	+6
Penalties	104
Opponent Penalties	110

-Teams that win the turnover battle win 79% of games & cover 79% ATS.
-Teams with more sacks win 71% of games & cover 69% ATS.
-Teams with more return TDs win 75% of games & cover 75% ATS.
-Teams with fewer penalties win 57% of games & cover 54% ATS.

2016 NFLproject.com Forecast

Div RK	1
Div W%	(36%)
Playoffs RK	10
% in Playoffs	(48%)
Super Bowl RK	9
% Win Super Bowl	(1%)

Odds to Win Division:
- 36%
- 33%
- 20%
- 11%

AFCW

Team Records & Trends

	2015	2014	2013
Average line	-3.1	-0.6	-2.1
Average O/U line	43.7	44.2	43.9
Straight Up Record	11-5	9-7	11-5
Against the Spread Record	8-8	11-5	9-7
Over/Under Record	8-7	5-11	7-9
ATS as Favorite	6-5	5-3	7-5
ATS as Underdog	1-3	5-2	2-2
Straight Up Home	6-2	6-2	5-3
ATS Home	3-5	6-2	2-6
Over/Under Home	3-5	3-5	3-5
ATS as Home Favorite	3-5	5-1	2-5
ATS as a Home Dog	0-0	1-1	0-1
Straight Up Away	5-3	3-5	6-2
ATS Away	5-3	5-3	7-1
Over/Under Away	5-2	2-6	4-4
ATS Away Favorite	3-0	0-2	5-0
ATS Away Dog	1-3	4-1	2-1
Six Point Teaser Record	12-4	13-3	14-2
Seven Point Teaser Record	12-4	13-3	14-1
Ten Point Teaser Record	13-1	13-3	15-1

Games Favored
8

Games Underdog
4

Close Game Records

All 2015 Wins: **11**
FG Games (<=3 pts) W-L: **0-1**
FG Games Win %: **0% (#30)**
FG Games Wins (% of Total Wins): **0% (#30)**
1 Score Games (<=8 pts) W-L: **5-3**
1 Score Games Win %: **63% (#8)**
1 Score Games Wins (% of Total Wins): **45% (#21)**

Home Lines (wks 1-16)

Avg Line = -5.9

Week 1: -7.0, Week 3: -3.5, Week 7: -8.0, Week 9: -7.0, Week 11: -7.0, Week 14: -4.5, Week 15: -9.0, Week 16: -1.5

Weeks: 1 2 3 4 5 6 7 8 9 10 11 12 13 14 15 16 — Week

Road Lines (wks 1-16)

Avg Line = 1.8

Week 4: +4.0, Week 10: +4.5, Week 12: +3.0

Weeks: 1 2 3 4 5 6 7 8 9 10 11 12 13 14 15 16

Regular Season Wins: Past Results & Current Proj

	Wins
2012 Wins	2
2013 Wins	11
2014 Wins	9
Proj 2015 Wins	8.5
2015 Wins	11
Proj 2016 Wins	9.5

1 2 3 4 5 6 7 8 9 10 11 12 13 14 15

Your 2016 AFC West Division Champions, the Kansas City Chiefs. If that sounds strange, its because in the last 12 years, it has happened only once, in Todd Haley's 2nd seasons back in 2010. After three consecutive 2nd place finishes under Andy Reid, the departure of Peyton Manning has linemakers predicting the Chiefs win the West. Kansas City won 11 games last year by being fundamentally sound with a defense not often seen in the NFL. The team won all they key stat categories: +14 in turnovers, +2 in sacks, +4 in return TDs and +6 in penalties. They went 5-3 in one-score games, and were the 7th healthiest. It will be hard to replicate success in each of those areas in 2016, however, thanks to playing the AFC South and the NFC South, the Chiefs face a significantly easier schedule in 2016. Despite the somewhat anemic and boring offense, the Chiefs won 7 of their final 12 games by double digits.

Weekly EDSR & Season Trending Performance

WEEK	1	2	3	4	5	6	7	8	10	11	12	13	14	15	16	17
RESULT	W	L	L	L	L	L	W	W	W	W	W	W	W	W	W	W
OPP	HOU	DEN	GB	CIN	CHI	MIN	PIT	DET	DEN	SD	BUF	OAK	SD	BAL	CLE	OAK
SITE	A	H	A	H	H	A	H	H	A	A	H	A	H	A	H	H
MARGIN	7	-7	-10	-15	-1	-6	10	35	16	30	8	14	7	20	4	6
PTS	27	24	28	21	17	10	23	45	29	33	30	34	10	34	17	23
OPP PTS	20	31	38	36	18	16	13	10	13	3	22	20	3	14	13	17

Week by Week 2015 Results

EDSR Results (W/L) By Week
W=Green
L=Red

Off & Def EDSR Wk & Trend
- Blue=Offense (high=good)
- Red=Defense (low=good)

2016 Rest Analysis

Avg Rest	6.5
Avg Rest Rk	3
Team More Rest	2
Opp More Rest	4
Net Rest Edge	-2
3 days rest	1
4 days rest	0
5 days rest	0
6 days rest	12
7 days rest	0
8 days rest	0
9 days rest	1
10 days rest	0
11 days rest	0
12 days rest	0
13 days rest	1
14 days rest	0

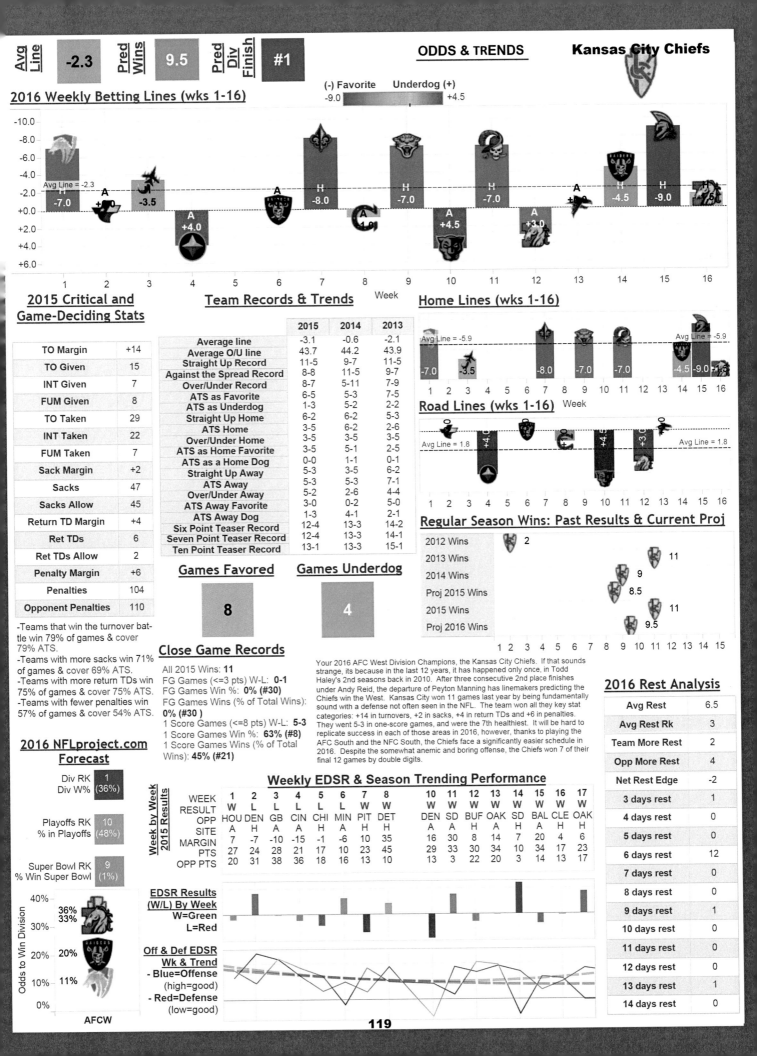

Directional Passer Rating Achieved

Receiver	Short Left	Short Middle	Short Right	Deep Left	Deep Middle	Deep Right
Jeremy Maclin	93	123	94	57	158	69
Travis Kelce	122	114	88	81	104	79
Albert Wilson	111	95	75	50	90	0
Chris Conley	83	133	77	77	77	77
Jason Avant	92	78	77	118	39	118
Demetrius Harris	91	121	101			39
James O'Shaughnes..	93	110	109			39
Frankie Hammond	79		79			
Brian Parker			56			

Directional Frequency by Receiver

Receiver	Short Left	Short Middle	Short Right	Deep Left	Deep Middle	Deep Right
Jeremy Maclin	26%	31%	31%	33%	38%	42%
Travis Kelce	26%	40%	32%	11%	24%	8%
Albert Wilson	25%	8%	12%	30%	19%	31%
Chris Conley	13%	2%	10%	22%	10%	8%
Jason Avant	5%	10%	7%	4%	10%	4%
Demetrius Harris	1%	6%	3%			4%
James O'Shaughnes..	3%	2%	2%			4%
Frankie Hammond	1%		1%			
Brian Parker			1%			

Defense Passer Rating Allowed

Short Left	Short Middle	Short Right	Deep Left	Deep Middle	Deep Right
83	81	73	97	53	47

Offensive Rush Directional Yds/Carry

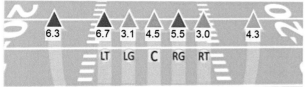

	6.3		6.7	3.1	4.5	5.5	3.0		4.3	
			LT	LG	C	RG	RT			

Offensive Rush Frequency of Direction

	69		29	52	191	61	32		56	
			LT	LG	C	RG	RT			

Offensive Explosive Runs by Direction

	18		6	2	19	9	1		5	
			LT	LG	C	RG	RT			

Defensive Rush Directional Yds/Carry

	7.1		3.2	3.7	3.7	4.3	4.9		3.8	
			LT	LG	C	RG	RT			

Alex Smith - 1st Down RTG

81.5 · 101.8 · 61.9 · 122.1 · 110.8 · 83.1

Alex Smith - 3rd Down RTG

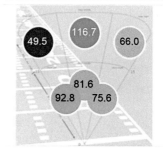

49.5 · 116.7 · 66.0 · 81.6 · 92.8 · 75.6

Alex Smith - 2nd Down RTG

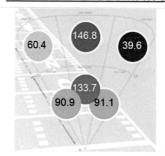

60.4 · 146.8 · 39.6 · 133.7 · 90.9 · 91.1

Alex Smith - Overall RTG

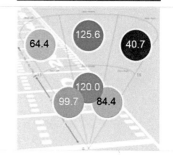

64.4 · 125.6 · 40.7 · 120.0 · 99.7 · 84.4

2nd & Short RUN (1D or not)

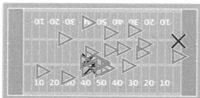

2nd & Short RUN Stats

Run Conv Rk	1D% Run	NFL 1D% Run Avg	Run Freq	NFL Run Freq Avg
3	86%	69%	60%	64%

2nd & Short PASS (1D or not)

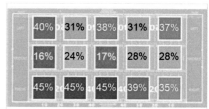

2nd & Short PASS Stats

Pass Conv Rk	1D% Pass	NFL 1D% Pass Avg	Pass Freq	NFL Pass Freq Avg
11	57%	55%	40%	36%

Pass Offense Play Success Rate

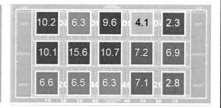

55%	55%	48%	29%	25%
69%	76%	59%	54%	57%
46%	49%	42%	51%	31%

Pass Offense Yds/Play

10.2	6.3	9.6	4.1	2.3
10.1	15.6	10.7	7.2	6.9
6.6	6.5	6.3	7.1	2.8

Off. Directional Tendency (% of Plays Left, Middle or Right)

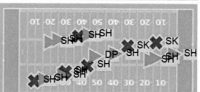

40%	31%	38%	31%	37%
16%	24%	17%	28%	28%
45%	45%	45%	39%	35%

Off. Directional Pass Rate (% of Plays which are Passes)

85%	60%	64%	57%	70%
21%	36%	23%	28%	32%
74%	71%	67%	78%	74%

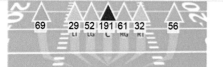
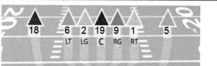

Denver Broncos

Coaches

Head Coach: Gary Kubiak (2nd yr)
OC: Rick Dennison (2nd yr)
DC: Wade Phillips (2nd yr)

Forecast 2016 Wins

9.5

Past Records

2015: 12-4
2014: 12-4
2013: 13-3

Opponent Strength
Easy — Hard

2016 Schedule & Week by Week Strength of Schedule

| 1 H THU | 2 H | 3 A | 4 A | 5 H | 6 A THU | 7 H MNF | 8 H | 9 A | 10 A | 11 | 12 H | 13 A | 14 A | 15 H | 16 A | 17 H |

SNF

SNF

2016 Overview

What an awesome rollercoaster ride John Elway has taken the Broncos faithful on the past 5 years since becoming GM. In 2011, his first year as GM, he inherited a team which (the prior year) traded up to draft Tim Tebow in the first round. Denver had won 7, 8, 8 and 4 games in the prior 4 seasons. Elway's first draft was legendary, getting Von Miller, Rahim Moore, Orlando Franklin, Julius Thomas among others. That 2011 team won ugly, led by Tim Tebow's 11 starts, but they won the division and upset the Steelers in the playoffs. In 2012, Elway nabbed Peyton Manning and the Broncos never looked back, winning the AFC West every single season Elway has been GM.

After the Super Bowl, a key decision created controversy. Instead of agreeing to tie up salary cap hits of $12M, $19M, $21M and $20M the next 4 years to QB Brock Osweiler, Elway let him loose to Houston and brought in Mark Sanchez for just $3.75M. He also drafted 6'7", 244 pound QB Paxton Lynch. What makes the move controversial is not that it's unintelligent. But that it's rare. Far too many NFL owners, GMs and coaches are scared. They hate negative press. They fear little black rain clouds. That fear creates irrational decisions. Decisions organizations regret. Decisions which hamstring the franchise & are impediments to winning.

Most often, Super Bowl Champions take a step back the following season. One reason teams fall off is because major contributors in their final year become free agents. Their now inflated price tag makes it cost prohibitive to re-sign. Denver saw players like DE Malik Jackson, LB Danny Trevathan, G Evan Mathis, OT Ryan Harris and Osweiler leave. With so many pieces leaving in free agency, and Elway looking beyond the 2016 season with his QB situation, what can and will Denver do to try to replicate success in 2016?

The defense is still in great hands with Wade Phillips. The difference Phillips made in his 1st year compared to what Jack Del Rio did in Manning's first 3 years was impressive. The secondary is intact and Wade still has ridiculous edge talent in Von Miller & Demarcus Ware. They are much less proven up the middle which will be a challenge for Phillips. Offensively the Broncos only returning starter along the offensive line is C Matt Paradis, a 6th-round pick from 2014. If it's Mark Sanchez under center week 1, he'll still have Demaryius Thomas, Emmanuel Sanders and C.J. Anderson. That is a lot of change for any team to deal with, even if it was a veteran Peyton Manning under center.

But we've seen many teams win it all with similar formulas. Defense, a ground game, and acceptable but at times brilliant QB play. Denver did it last year. Seattle, Pittsburgh and Baltimore (pre-Flacco money) have all done it in the last 8 years. Teams that haven't done it include Chicago (11-21 post-Cutler money), Atlanta (18-30 post Ryan money) and Detroit (25-23 post-Stafford money). Add teams who paid their QBs big after the Super Bowl, like New Orleans (32-32 post-Brees money) and Baltimore (23-25 post-Flacco money) and its apparent that overspending to re-sign a QB is not the formula to win hardware, nor does it even guarantee a .500 record. Elway's decision to let Osweiler leave was controversial, rare and brilliant.

Strength of Schedule In Detail

True Strength of Schedule Rank: 11

Hardest Stretches *(1=Hard, 32=Easy)*
Hardest 3 wk Stretch Rk: **9**
Hardest 4 wk Stretch Rk: **17**
Hardest 5 wk Stretch Rk: **19**

Easiest Stretches *(1=Easy, 32=Hard)*
Easiest 3 wk Stretch Rk: **16**
Easiest 4 wk Stretch Rk: **16**
Easiest 5 wk Stretch Rk: **10**

Denver starts its title defense with the 4th most difficult September of any team, featuring three straight games against the Panthers, Colts and Bengals. But from weeks 4 through 14, the Broncos play only two teams projected to have a winning record in 2016 (HOU, KC) and both are in Denver. In fact, over this span the Broncos will actually face the easiest schedule of any team in the NFL. They close with home games against the Patriots and Raiders and a trip to the Chiefs. Should they see early success against strong opposition, their schedule's weak middle sets up a very strong season in defense of the Lombardi.

2015 Play Tendencies

All Pass %	61%
All Pass Rk	14
All Rush %	39%
All Rush Rk	19
1 Score Pass %	63%
1 Score Pass Rk	6
2014 1 Score Pass %	58%
2014 1 Score Pass Rk	16
Pass Increase %	5%
Pass Increase Rk	7
1 Score Rush %	37%
1 Score Rush Rk	27
Up Pass %	53%
Up Pass Rk	8
Up Rush %	47%
Up Rush Rk	25
Down Pass %	71%
Down Pass Rk	5
Down Rush %	29%
Down Rush Rk	28

Despite how bad the overall performance was from the passing attack, the Broncos still passed the ball in one score games 63% of the time, 6th most in the NFL. And that was actually a 5% increase over 2014. Denver averaged 4.2 YPC on the ground with 5 fumbles. The pass attack only averaged 6.2 YPA and had 23 interceptions, 8 fumbles and took 39 sacks. I would be shocked if Denver didn't run more frequently in 2016.

2015 Offensive Advanced Metrics

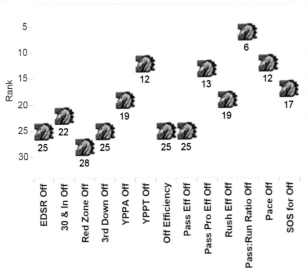

One look and its obvious what won the 2015 Denver Broncos the Super Bowl. Ironically, in his least helpful season in the NFL, Peyton Manning won a Super Bowl. His offense ranked 25th in passing efficiency, 25th in passing efficiency, 25th in EDSR and 28th inside the red zone. On passes 15+ yards in the air, Denver converted first downs just 32% of attempts, 2nd worst in the NFL. Despite a league average 3rd down offense and few big plays made, the Broncos offense achieved by sheer volume of opportunity because of their defense. It was a juggernaut, of a defense, finishing 2nd in EDSR, and holding opponents to an average of only 2:30 per drive, 5th best in the NFL. That enabled the defense to continue to recycle the ball back to the offense, play field position, and eventually put up enough points to squeak by the opponent. And that they did, going a whopping 9-3 (75%) in games decided by 1 score.

2015 Defensive Advanced Metrics

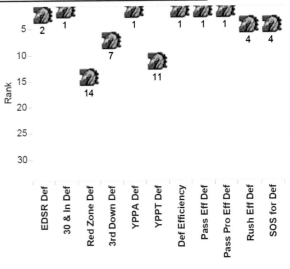

Drafted Players

2016 Draft Grade: #16 (3.0/4)

Rnd.	Pick #	Pos.	Player	College
1	26	QB	Paxton Lynch	Memphis
2	63	DT	Adam Gotsis	Georgia Tech
3	98	S	Justin Simmons	Boston College
4	136	RB	Devontae Booker	Utah
5	144	G	Connor McGovern	Missouri
6	176	FB	Andy Janovich	Nebraska
6	219	S	Will Parks	Arizona
7	228	P	Riley Dixon	Syracuse

PERSONNEL & SPENDING

Free Agents/Trades Added

Player (Position)
- Brandian Ross S
- Casey Kreiter C
- Connor McGovern G
- Dekoda Watson LB
- Donald Stephenson T
- Garrett Graham TE
- Jared Crick DE
- Mark Sanchez QB
- Russell Okung T

Other Signed

Player (Position)

Aaron Neary G
Anthony Norris TE
Antonio Glover S
Bralon Addison WR
Calvin Heurtelou DT
Connor McGovern G
David Moala DT
Dekoda Watson LB
Durron Neal WR
Dwayne Norman LB
Eddie Yarbrough DE
Frank Shannon LB
Henry Krieger-Coble TE
John Tidwell CB
Justin Murray T
Kalif Raymond WR
Kyle Kragen LB
Kyle Peko DT
Lars Hanson T
Mose Frazier WR
Nathan Theus LB
Sadat Sulleyman G
Shaneil Jenkins DE
Vontarrius Dora LB

2015 Players Lost

Transaction	Player (Position)
Cut	Louis Vasquez G
	Owen Daniels TE
	Ryan Murphy S
Declared Free Agent	Andre Caldwell WR
	Brock Osweiler QB
	Danny Trevathan LB
	David Bruton Jr. S
	Evan Mathis G
	Malik Jackson DT
	Omar Bolden S
	Ronnie Hillman RB
	Ryan Harris T
	Tyler Polumbus T
Retired	Peyton Manning QB

- Denver's roster change is a fascinating one. Last year they had the NFL's most expensive offense, and it ranked 25th in efficiency. Last year they had the 15th most expensive defense which ranked #1 in efficiency. This year, Denver's offense is the 5th cheapest, with massive costs cut along the offensive line and at the QB position. Also, the tight end position is 5th cheapest, a significant drop from 2015. Their RB position, however, is up from 29th in 2015 to 6th in 2016, with CJ Anderson ($6M) and Ronnie Hillman ($2M) increasing their cap hits substantially from 2015 ($589K and $943K respectively).

- While the Broncos were the best defense in the NFL in 2015, they will almost be the most expensive in 2016, falling behind only the Jets, Jaguars and Seahawks. The cost increased the most at CB, where they went from 16th most expensive now up to 5th in 2016.

- I absolutely love what John Elway did with the QB position this past offseason because it's so rarely done, but it was the right move for certain. It was the right move regardless of whether or not Denver's QBs perform well this year or not:

* Elway saw Brock Osweiler for 4 years in Denver. He was groomed for this position. He was drafted weeks after Peyton Manning signed as a free agent back in 2012. While they both were on the roster, Brock was hitting the cap between $640K and $1.1M per year while Peyton hit at $17.5M almost every year.

* Elway wanted Brock to stay in Denver for his 2nd contract, but he wasn't about to overpay or mortgage his ability to build a roster to sign a player he didn't believe was worth the price tag.

* In Houston, Brock will hit the cap for $12M this year, but approximately $20M from 2017-2019.

* Elway stuck to his guns when most GMs would have tucked tail and caved. The fear of "losing" your groomed QB is all too real. We've seen it time and time again, and we've seen a great many of those teams unable to see success after apportioning too much to undeserving QBs.

Lineup & 2016 Cap Hit

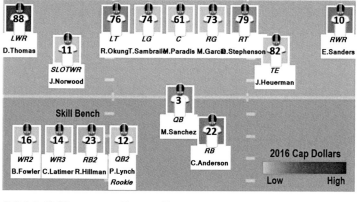

Health Overall & by Unit (2015 v 2014)

2015 Rk	10
2015 AGL	57
Off Rk	22
Def Rk	2
2014 Rk	1
2014 AGL	37

2016 Positional Spending

	All OFF	QB	OL	RB	WR	TE	All DEF	DL	LB	CB	S
2015 Rk	1	7	8	29	4	11	15	27	4	16	9
Rank	28	28	27	5	5	26	3	13	14	5	15
Total	66.8M	6.8M	17.3M	10.8M	27.1M	4.7M	84.3M	26.0M	22.9M	24.3M	11.1M

2016 Offseason Spending

Total Spent	Total Spent Rk	Free Agents #	Free Agents $	Free Agents $ Rk	Waiver #	Waiver $	Waiver $ Rk	Extended #	Sum of Extended $	Sum of Drafted $	Undrafted #	Undrafted $
243M	6	9	77M	9	21	15M	12	3	87M	29M	22	36M

2015 Stats & Fantasy Production

Pos	Player	Ov. Rank	Pos. Rk	Age	Gms	St	Pass Comp	Pass Att	Pass Yds	Pass TD	Pass Int	Rush Att	Rush Yds	Rush YPA	Rush TD	Targ	Recp	Rec Yds	Rec YPC	Rec TDs	Draft King Pts	Fan Duel Pts
QB	Brock Osweiler		30	25	8	7	170	275	1,967	10	6	21	61	3	1						127	123
	Peyton Manning		33	39	10	9	198	331	2,249	9	17	6	-6	-1							111	108
RB	Ronnie Hillman	61	19	24	16	11						207	863	4	7	35	24	111	5		168	149
	C.J. Anderson		30	24	15	5						152	720	5	5	36	25	183	7		149	129
WR	Demaryius Thomas	32	13	28	16	16										177	105	1,304	12	6	272	215
	Emmanuel Sanders	46	18	28	15	15						3	29	10		136	76	1,135	15	6	229	186
	Bennie Fowler		126	24	16	1										25	16	203	13		39	28
	Jordan Norwood		128	29	11	5										32	22	207	9		46	32
TE	Owen Daniels		21	33	16	16										77	46	517	11	3	119	93
	Virgil Green		50	27	16	5										15	12	173	14	1	38	29

Avg Line	Pred Wins	Pred Div Finish
-2.7	9.5	#1

2016 Weekly Betting Lines (wks 1-16)

(-) Favorite   Underdog (+)
-7.0   +3.0

Avg Line = -2.7

Week																
	1	2	3	4	5	6	7	8	9	10	11	12	13	14	15	16

H -5.0, A +3.0, A -2.5, H -6.5, A -3.0, H -6.5, H -7.0, H, A, H -3.0, A -3.5, A -5.5, H, A +1.5

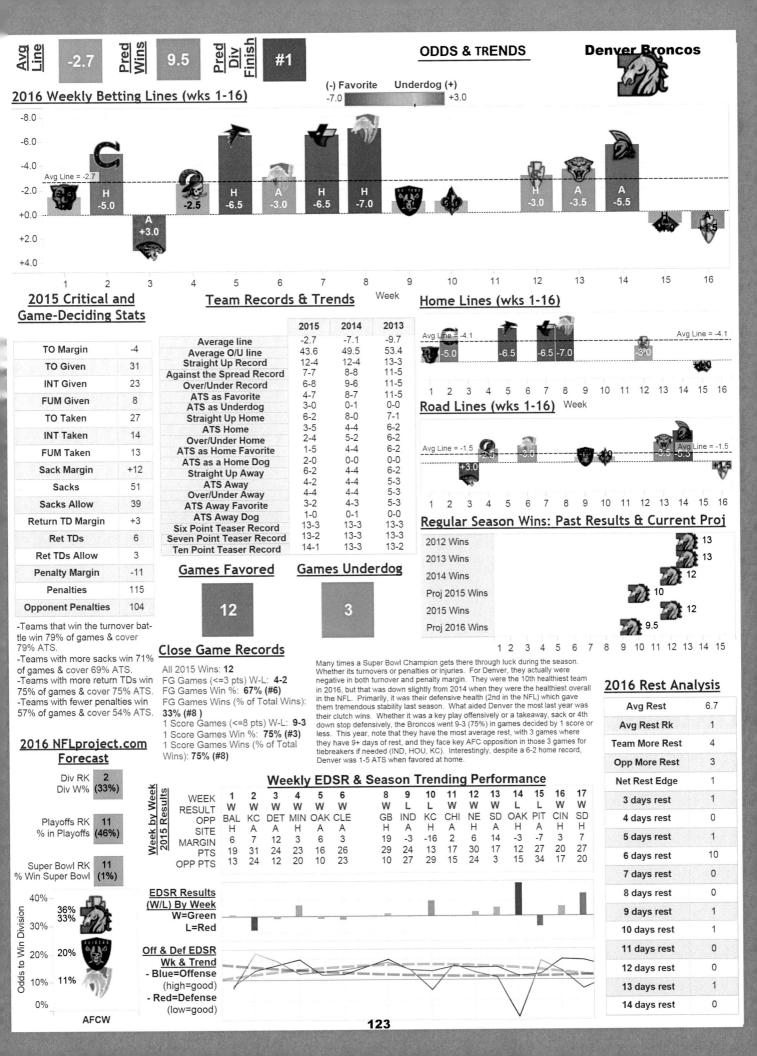

2015 Critical and Game-Deciding Stats

TO Margin	-4
TO Given	31
INT Given	23
FUM Given	8
TO Taken	27
INT Taken	14
FUM Taken	13
Sack Margin	+12
Sacks	51
Sacks Allow	39
Return TD Margin	+3
Ret TDs	6
Ret TDs Allow	3
Penalty Margin	-11
Penalties	115
Opponent Penalties	104

-Teams that win the turnover battle win 79% of games & cover 79% ATS.
-Teams with more sacks win 71% of games & cover 69% ATS.
-Teams with more return TDs win 75% of games & cover 75% ATS.
-Teams with fewer penalties win 57% of games & cover 54% ATS.

2016 NFLproject.com Forecast

Div RK	2
Div W%	(33%)
Playoffs RK	11
% in Playoffs	(46%)
Super Bowl RK	11
% Win Super Bowl	(1%)

Odds to Win Division
36%
33%
20%
11%
AFCW

Team Records & Trends

	2015	2014	2013
Average line	-2.7	-7.1	-9.7
Average O/U line	43.6	49.5	53.4
Straight Up Record	12-4	12-4	13-3
Against the Spread Record	7-7	8-8	11-5
Over/Under Record	6-8	9-6	11-5
ATS as Favorite	4-7	8-7	11-5
ATS as Underdog	3-0	0-1	0-0
Straight Up Home	6-2	8-0	7-1
ATS Home	3-5	4-4	6-2
Over/Under Home	2-4	5-2	6-2
ATS as Home Favorite	1-5	4-4	6-2
ATS as a Home Dog	2-0	0-0	0-0
Straight Up Away	6-2	4-4	6-2
ATS Away	4-2	4-4	5-3
Over/Under Away	4-4	4-4	5-3
ATS Away Favorite	3-2	4-3	5-3
ATS Away Dog	1-0	0-1	0-0
Six Point Teaser Record	13-3	13-3	13-3
Seven Point Teaser Record	13-2	13-3	13-3
Ten Point Teaser Record	14-1	13-3	13-2

Games Favored

12

Games Underdog

3

Close Game Records

All 2015 Wins: **12**
FG Games (<=3 pts) W-L: **4-2**
FG Games Win %: **67% (#6)**
FG Games Wins (% of Total Wins): **33% (#8)**
1 Score Games (<=8 pts) W-L: **9-3**
1 Score Games Win %: **75% (#3)**
1 Score Games Wins (% of Total Wins): **75% (#8)**

Home Lines (wks 1-16)

Avg Line = -4.1

-5.0, -6.5, -6.5 -7.0, -3.0

Week																
1	2	3	4	5	6	7	8	9	10	11	12	13	14	15	16	

Road Lines (wks 1-16) Week

Avg Line = -1.5

+3.0, -2.5, -3.0, -3.5 -5.5, +1.5

1	2	3	4	5	6	7	8	9	10	11	12	13	14	15	16

Regular Season Wins: Past Results & Current Proj

2012 Wins	13
2013 Wins	13
2014 Wins	12
Proj 2015 Wins	10
2015 Wins	12
Proj 2016 Wins	9.5

1 2 3 4 5 6 7 8 9 10 11 12 13 14 15

Many times a Super Bowl Champion gets there through luck during the season. Whether its turnovers or penalties or injuries. For Denver, they actually were negative in both turnover and penalty margin. They were the 10th healthiest team in 2016, but that was down slightly from 2014 when they were the healthiest overall in the NFL. Primarily, it was their defensive health (2nd in the NFL) which gave them tremendous stability last season. What aided Denver the most last year was their clutch wins. Whether it was a key play offensively or a takeaway, sack or 4th down stop defensively, the Broncos went 9-3 (75%) in games decided by 1 score or less. This year, note that they have the most average rest, with 3 games where they have 9+ days of rest, and they face key AFC opposition in those 3 games for tiebreakers if needed (IND, HOU, KC). Interestingly, despite a 6-2 home record, Denver was 1-5 ATS when favored at home.

2016 Rest Analysis

Avg Rest	6.7
Avg Rest Rk	1
Team More Rest	4
Opp More Rest	3
Net Rest Edge	1
3 days rest	1
4 days rest	0
5 days rest	1
6 days rest	10
7 days rest	0
8 days rest	0
9 days rest	1
10 days rest	1
11 days rest	0
12 days rest	0
13 days rest	1
14 days rest	0

Weekly EDSR & Season Trending Performance

WEEK	1	2	3	4	5	6		8	9	10	11	12	13	14	15	16	17
RESULT	W	W	W	W	W	W		W	L	L	W	W	W	L	L	W	W
OPP	BAL	KC	DET	MIN	OAK	CLE		GB	IND	KC	CHI	NE	SD	OAK	PIT	CIN	SD
SITE	H	A	H	A	H	A		H	A	H	A	H	A	H	A	H	H
MARGIN	6	7	12	3	6	3		19	-3	-16	2	6	14	-3	-7	3	7
PTS	19	31	24	23	16	26		29	24	13	17	30	17	12	27	20	27
OPP PTS	13	24	12	20	10	23		10	27	29	15	24	3	15	34	17	20

2015 Results (Week by Week)

EDSR Results (W/L) By Week
W=Green
L=Red

Off & Def EDSR Wk & Trend
- Blue=Offense (high=good)
- Red=Defense (low=good)

STATS & VISUALIZATIONS

Denver Broncos

Directional Passer Rating Achieved

Receiver	Short Left	Short Middle	Short Right	Deep Left	Deep Middle	Deep Right
Demaryius Thomas	85	86	78	51	47	42
Emmanuel Sanders	71	75	94	69	102	104
Owen Daniels	94	47	117	39	74	95
Jordan Norwood	61	31	87	39	95	39
Vernon Davis	95	94	104	39	118	39
Bennie Fowler	89	109	65		95	39
Virgil Green	57	158	118			
Andre Caldwell	77	115	25	39	39	50
Cody Latimer	75	122	100			0

Directional Frequency by Receiver

Receiver	Short Left	Short Middle	Short Right	Deep Left	Deep Middle	Deep Right
Demaryius Thomas	32%	30%	35%	44%	26%	29%
Emmanuel Sanders	25%	17%	24%	44%	32%	43%
Owen Daniels	13%	22%	14%	2%	16%	7%
Jordan Norwood	8%	8%	5%	2%	13%	3%
Vernon Davis	6%	5%	3%	4%	3%	3%
Bennie Fowler	5%	7%	5%		6%	3%
Virgil Green	4%	2%	5%			
Andre Caldwell	4%	5%	3%	4%	3%	7%
Cody Latimer	2%	4%	3%			3%

Defense Passer Rating Allowed

Short Left	Short Middle	Short Right	Deep Left	Deep Middle	Deep Right
85	80	76	60	74	75

Offensive Rush Directional Yds/Carry

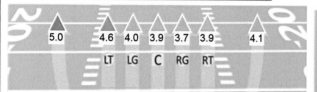

5.0	4.6	4.0	3.9	3.7	3.9	4.1
	LT	LG	C	RG	RT	

Offensive Rush Frequency of Direction

51	79	59	121	59	88	34
	LT	LG	C	RG	RT	

Offensive Explosive Runs by Direction

6	12	6	9	4	11	5
	LT	LG	C	RG	RT	

Defensive Rush Directional Yds/Carry

6.4	4.0	2.7	3.5	2.8	2.3	4.4
	LT	LG	C	RG	RT	

Peyton Manning - 1st Down RTG

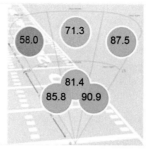

Peyton Manning - 2nd Down RTG

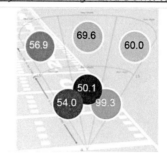

Peyton Manning - 3rd Down RTG

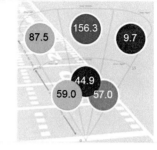

Peyton Manning - Overall RTG

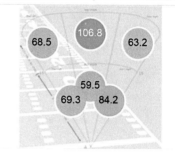

2nd & Short RUN (1D or not)

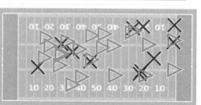

2nd & Short RUN Stats

Run Conv Rk	1D% Run	NFL 1D% Run Avg	Run Freq	NFL Run Freq Avg
12	74%	69%	77%	64%

2nd & Short PASS (1D or not)

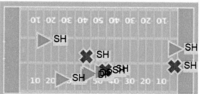

2nd & Short PASS Stats

Pass Conv Rk	1D% Pass	NFL 1D% Pass Avg	Pass Freq	NFL Pass Freq Avg
6	63%	55%	23%	36%

Pass Offense Play Success Rate

40%	50%	44%	43%	39%
45%	49%	54%	53%	46%
47%	45%	47%	42%	26%

Pass Offense Yds/Play

5.6	6.4	8.0	4.8	3.3
6.9	9.0	8.5	8.7	4.0
7.3	8.5	8.0	5.8	3.2

Off. Directional Tendency
(% of Plays Left, Middle or Right)

39%	34%	42%	42%	39%
19%	28%	28%	28%	33%
42%	36%	30%	30%	27%

Off. Directional Pass Rate
(% of Plays which are Passes)

73%	67%	63%	65%	73%
35%	49%	47%	47%	38%
80%	70%	58%	56%	58%

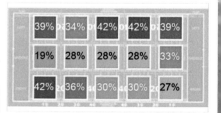

124

Oakland Raiders

Coaches

Head Coach: Jack Del Rio (2nd yr)
OC: Bill Musgrave (2nd yr)
DC: Ken Norton Jr. (2nd yr)

Forecast 2016 Wins

8

Past Records

2015: 7-9
2014: 3-13
2013: 4-12

Opponent Strength
Easy — Hard

2016 Schedule & Week by Week Strength of Schedule

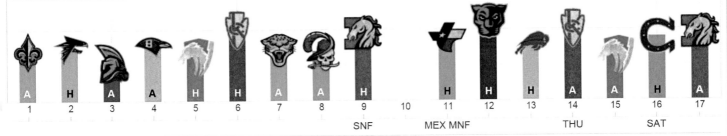

A	H	A	A	H	H	A	A	H		H	H	H	A	A	H	A
1	2	3	4	5	6	7	8	9	10	11	12	13	14	15	16	17

SNF   MEX MNF   THU   SAT

2016 Overview

Much like the Jaguars, another team with a young, budding QB on his rookie deal, the Oakland Raiders spent this offseason to help the defense. But this team has a lot of work to do in order to meet now hopeful expectations. They must play better down the stretch. If games ended after 3 quarters last year the Raiders would have been 8-7 with one tie. They trailed by more than 6 points entering the 4th quarter just twice all season, both to playoff teams (CIN & KC). But with a lack of discipline, bad penalties and 10 fourth quarter turnovers (tied for the 4th most in the NFL), the Raiders did not end games very strongly. In fact, in one score games in the 4th quarter, the Raiders committed 8 turnovers, tied for the most in the NFL last year. On the opposite end of the spectrum sat teams like NE, SEA and CAR, with two or fewer turnovers in those situations. Teams that win the turnover battle win 79% of games, and a lack of focus in a 1-score game in the 4th quarter can be the difference between a win, a loss and a playoff berth.

But the Raiders have a key positional piece going for them this year, and that's the contract of QB Derek Carr. The 2nd round pick from 2014 is slated to hit the cap for just $1.45M this year & $1.7M next year. After that, if his performance improves, the Raiders will be tying up cap hits of over $10M annually. But for now, they are spending the 2nd least at the position. That has enabled them to build the 2nd most expensive offensive line, the 5th most expensive safeties in the secondary, and the 10th most expensive LB corps.

A very weak secondary from 2015 with the exception of the now retired Charles Woodson suddenly has S Reggie Nelson and CB Sean Smith, in addition to the 14th overall selection S Karl Joseph from West Virginia. They also added pass rush help in the form of LB Bruce Irvin. With the secondary hopefully forcing opposing QBs to hold onto the football longer, it will make the pass rush from Khalil Mack and Bruce Irvin that much more dangerous.

Offensively, the team must improve in the run game, as well as with situational play calling. In the red zone, despite a strong overall conversion rate, the rate tailed off late in the season, and they converted just 33% of trips into TDs the last 3 weeks of the season. Part of the issue became predictability, which opponents may have picked up on. While overall the Raiders were 55% pass and 45% rush in the red zone, they ran over 50% of all their plays to the right side of the offense, and 84% of those plays were passes. However, they had a miserable 35% play success rate on those plays. Specifically, when passing to his right in the red zone (which was their dominant directional tendency and play type), Carr was just 11/28 (39%) with a 72 rating and 2.8 YPA. Oakland must become less predictable inside the red zone with directional play calling. They ran the ball up the middle 72% of all plays, but when passing up the middle they gained 6.4 YPA, by far the best of any directional pass in the red zone, and Carr recorded a 115 rating. Yet they used it far too infrequently.

This team could make some great strides in 2016 and 2017 with Carr so inexpensive, but they must play smarter in the 4th quarter and make better decisions from a play calling perspective.

Strength of Schedule In Detail

True Strength of Schedule Rank: 18

Hardest Stretches (1=Hard, 32=Easy)
Hardest 3 wk Stretch Rk: 12
Hardest 4 wk Stretch Rk: 9
Hardest 5 wk Stretch Rk: 17

Easiest Stretches (1=Easy, 32=Hard)
Easiest 3 wk Stretch Rk: 8
Easiest 4 wk Stretch Rk: 6
Easiest 5 wk Stretch Rk: 3

Oakland's start features the 5th easiest in the NFL (@ NO, vs ATL, @ TEN, @ BAL) and adding their week 5 game vs the Chargers, Oakland has the single easiest first games in the NFL. The problem for Oakland is their early starts during those games, and losing a home game to Mexico. Oakland plays five games at 10 AM for their body clock, including three in the first four games of the season. It's the most "early starts" for any Pacific-based team. They lose their week 11 home game vs the Texans on Monday night to Mexico. And to close the year, from week 9 onward, the Raiders play the 2nd most difficult schedule in the NFL.

2015 Play Tendencies

All Pass %	63%
All Pass Rk	9
All Rush %	37%
All Rush Rk	24
1 Score Pass %	59%
1 Score Pass Rk	13
2014 1 Score Pass %	59%
2014 1 Score Pass Rk	9
Pass Increase %	0%
Pass Increase Rk	22
1 Score Rush %	41%
1 Score Rush Rk	20
Up Pass %	53%
Up Pass Rk	9
Up Rush %	47%
Up Rush Rk	24
Down Pass %	70%
Down Pass Rk	11
Down Rush %	30%
Down Rush Rk	22

In one score games, the Raiders passed 13th most often and overall their pass numbers were not too extreme. With the 4th rated pass protection leading to the 11th rated passing offense, and a 24th rated run offense, it's only natural the Raiders would try to pass a bit more than average, but they did a good job of not getting too carried away and overly aggressive with the pass offense regardless of situation.

2015 Offensive Advanced Metrics

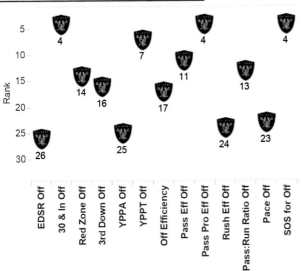

Despite improving from 3 wins to 7 wins, the Raiders were all over the map in terms of their efficiency. Particularly on offense, where they were top 5 in pass protection & were one of the best 30 & In teams, converting TDs on a large % of drives which start from average field position. But they did not run particularly efficiently behind their strong line, and were very inefficient on both the early downs as well as on 3rd down. Defensively they were middle of the pack in most areas. Not particularly strong anywhere, but not terrible either. Fortunately, they posted such numbers against the 8th rated opposing offenses, so it was not as if they played a terrible schedule of opposing offenses. Considering that 6 of their 7 wins (86%) came on games decided by one score, with an overall 6-5 record in these games, a slight improvement in some efficiency metrics would likely have resulted in a winning season for the Raiders.

2015 Defensive Advanced Metrics

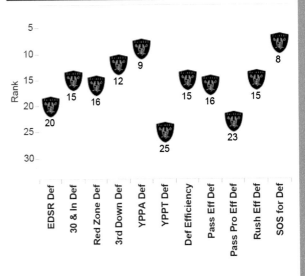

Drafted Players   2016 Draft Grade: #9 (3.1/4)

Rnd.	Pick #	Pos.	Player	College
1	14	S	Karl Joseph	West Virginia
2	44	DE	Jihad Ward	Illinois
3	75	DE	Shilique Calhoun	Michigan State
4	100	QB	Connor Cook	Michigan State
5	143	RB	DeAndre Washington	Texas Tech
6	194	LB	Cory James	Colorado State
7	234	G	Vadal Alexander	LSU

PERSONNEL & SPENDING   Oakland Raiders

Free Agents/Trades Added

Player (Position)

Bruce Irvin LB

Brynden Trawick S

Daren Bates LB

Kelechi Osemele G

Reggie Nelson S

Sean Smith CB

Other Signed

Player (Position)

Antonio Hamilton CB
Branden Jackson DE
Chris Edwards S
Damontre Moore DE
Darius Latham DT
Denver Kirkland G
Drew Iddings DE
Greg Townsend Jr. DE
Jalen Richard RB
James Cowser LB
Jaydon Mickens WR
Joe Hansley WR
Johnny Holton WR
K.J. Brent WR
Kenneth Durden CB
Kyrie Wilson LB
Max McCaffrey WR
Oni Omoile G
Ross Burbank C
Ryan O'Malley TE
Terran Vaughn G
Tony McRae CB
Torian White T

2015 Players Lost

Transaction	Player (Position)
Cut	Curtis Lofton LB
	Debose, Andre WR
	Gilbert, Garrett QB
	Herron, Robert WR
	Nate Allen S
	Shelby Harris DE
	Tevin McDonald S
	Tony McRae CB
Declared Free Agent	J'Marcus Webb G
Retired	Charles Woodson S
	Justin Tuck DE

- The Raiders are a young team that is looking to take the AFC West but isn't good enough or consistent to overlook any opponent. They are talented at key positions, however. Offensively, it starts up front with one of the NFL's best offensive lines which already recorded tremendous pass protection for Derek Carr last year. But they must improve in run blocking to help out a rushing offense that didn't add any pieces aside from a 5th round draft pick (who will be likely used as a receiving back), and was not very good in 2015.
- Latavius Murray averaged exactly 4 YPC last year against some porous run defenses that should have been exploited for more yardage. One area to utilize the run game is situationally, and despite a poor overall ranking, the Raiders excelled on the ground in certain situations. When running the football on 2nd and short, the Raiders converted 86% of runs into first down, the 3rd best rate in the NFL. Compare that to when they passed on 2nd and short and converted only 33% into first down (the 3rd worst rate in the NFL).
- They likewise were tremendous on 3rd and short, converting 80% info first down (3rd best in the NFL). Yet when they passed, they converted on only 53%.
- Combining short yardage runs on 2nd or 3rd down, the Raiders converted 82% (#1 in the NFL) of runs vs an avg 69%, but converted just 48% of passes. Yet for some reason, they still went 40% pass on these play calls which is the NFL average. The Raiders, behind that solid offensive line, was the NFL's best short yardage run team and needs to utilize that weapon more frequently in 2016.
- The Raiders are still on Carr's rookie deal, and thus are spending the 2nd least at the QB position of any team this year. If he outperforms his deal, the team has spent elsewhere on enough talent to create some noise in the AFC West and beyond.

Lineup & 2016 Cap Hit

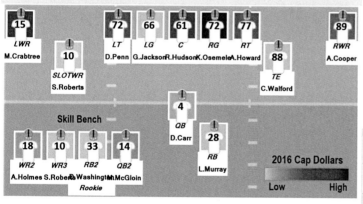

Health Overall & by Unit (2015 v 2014)

2015 Rk	11
2015 AGL	58
Off Rk	8
Def Rk	22
2014 Rk	29
2014 AGL	104

2016 Positional Spending

	All OFF	QB	OL	RB	WR	TE	All DEF	DL	LB	CB	S
2015 Rk	25	32	2	21	18	22	20	17	14	30	2
Rank	17	31	2	22	14	20	19	29	10	20	5
Total	77.8M	5.1M	39.8M	5.3M	21.5M	6.2M	74.9M	14.8M	24.3M	18.0M	17.8M

2016 Offseason Spending

Total Spent	Total Spent Rk	Free Agents #	Free Agents $	Free Agents $ Rk	Waiver #	Waiver $	Waiver $ Rk	Extended #	Sum of Extended $	Sum of Drafted $	Undrafted #	Undrafted $
258M	4	11	170M	3	8	8M	26	1	17M	28M	23	36M

2015 Stats & Fantasy Production

Pos	Player	Ov. Rank	Pos. Rk	Age	Gms	St	Pass Comp	Pass Att	Pass Yds	Pass TD	Pass Int	Rush Att	Rush Yds	Rush YPA	Rush TD	Targ	Recp	Rec Yds	Rec YPC	Rec TDs	Draft King Pts	Fan Duel Pts
QB	Derek Carr*		15	24	16	16	350	573	3,987	32	13	33	138	4							291	282
RB	Latavius Murray*	31	10	25	16	16						266	1,066	4	6	53	41	232	6		212	184
	Marcel Reece	70	30	30	15	7						10	36	4		37	30	269	9	3	82	64
	Jamize Olawale	91	26	26	14	3						24	110	5	1	11	9	84	9		37	30
	Taiwan Jones	99	27	27	12							16	74	5		9	7	106	15	1	33	26
WR	Michael Crabtree	49	19	28	16	15										146	85	922	11	9	234	189
	Amari Cooper*	57	24	21	16	15						3	-3	-1		130	72	1,070	15	6	217	177
	Seth Roberts	55	24	24	16	5										55	32	480	15	5	115	96
	Andre Holmes	93	27	27	16	1										33	14	201	14	4	61	51
TE	Clive Walford	30	24	24	16	2										50	28	329	12	3	82	65
	Mychal Rivera	42	25	25	16											46	32	280	9	1	69	50

ODDS & TRENDS

Oakland Raiders

Avg Line	Pred Wins	Pred Div Finish
-0.4	8	#3

(-) Favorite Underdog (+)
-4.5 +4.5

2016 Weekly Betting Lines (wks 1-16)

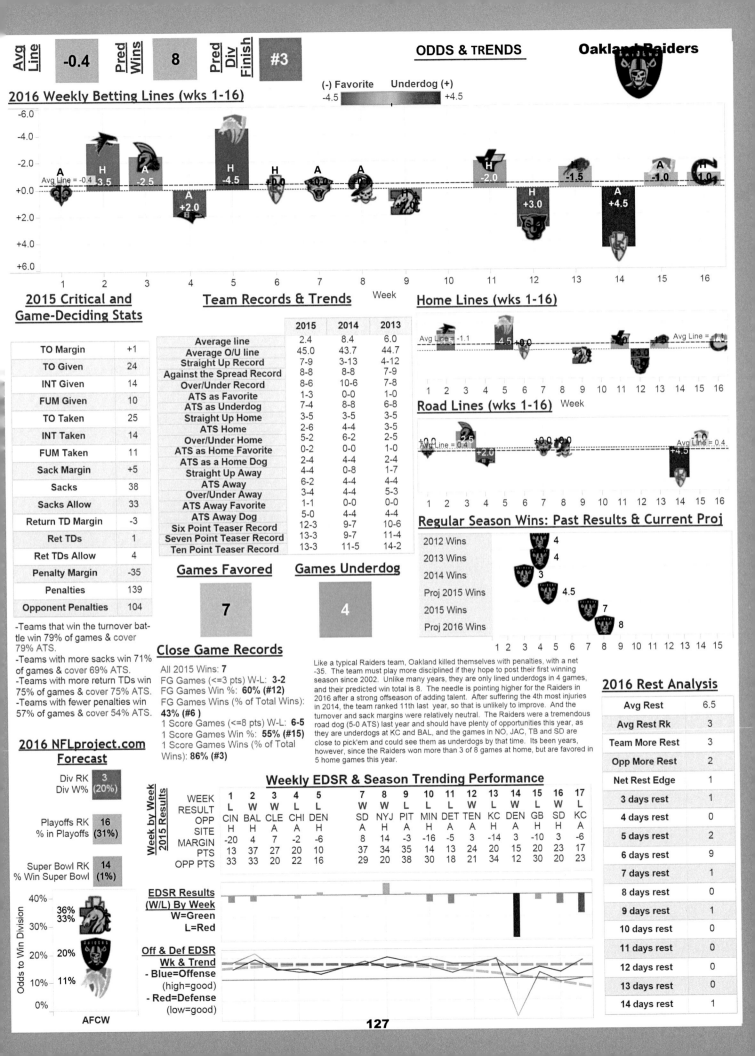

Avg Line = -0.4

Week: 1 2 3 4 5 6 7 8 9 10 11 12 13 14 15 16

Lines by week: A, H 3.5, H -2.5, A +2.0, H -4.5, H +0.0, A +0.0, A +0.0, H +2.0, (9), H -2.0, H +3.0, H -1.5, A +4.5, A -1.0, H -1.0

2015 Critical and Game-Deciding Stats

TO Margin	+1
TO Given	24
INT Given	14
FUM Given	10
TO Taken	25
INT Taken	14
FUM Taken	11
Sack Margin	+5
Sacks	38
Sacks Allow	33
Return TD Margin	-3
Ret TDs	1
Ret TDs Allow	4
Penalty Margin	-35
Penalties	139
Opponent Penalties	104

-Teams that win the turnover battle win 79% of games & cover 79% ATS.
-Teams with more sacks win 71% of games & cover 69% ATS.
-Teams with more return TDs win 75% of games & cover 75% ATS.
-Teams with fewer penalties win 57% of games & cover 54% ATS.

2016 NFLproject.com Forecast

Div RK	3
Div W%	(20%)
Playoffs RK	16
% in Playoffs	(31%)
Super Bowl RK	14
% Win Super Bowl	(1%)

Odds to Win Division
40% 36%
33%
30% 20%
20%
10% 11%
0%
AFCW

Team Records & Trends

	2015	2014	2013
Average line	2.4	8.4	6.0
Average O/U line	45.0	43.7	44.7
Straight Up Record	7-9	3-13	4-12
Against the Spread Record	8-8	8-8	7-9
Over/Under Record	8-6	10-6	7-8
ATS as Favorite	1-3	0-0	1-0
ATS as Underdog	7-4	8-8	6-8
Straight Up Home	3-5	3-5	3-5
ATS Home	2-6	4-4	3-5
Over/Under Home	5-2	6-2	2-5
ATS as Home Favorite	0-2	0-0	1-0
ATS as a Home Dog	2-4	4-4	2-4
Straight Up Away	4-4	0-8	1-7
ATS Away	6-2	4-4	4-4
Over/Under Away	3-4	4-4	5-3
ATS Away Favorite	1-1	0-0	0-0
ATS Away Dog	5-0	4-4	4-4
Six Point Teaser Record	12-3	9-7	10-6
Seven Point Teaser Record	13-3	9-7	11-4
Ten Point Teaser Record	13-3	11-5	14-2

Games Favored
7

Games Underdog
4

Close Game Records

All 2015 Wins: 7
FG Games (<=3 pts) W-L: 3-2
FG Games Win %: 60% (#12)
FG Games Wins (% of Total Wins): 43% (#6)
1 Score Games (<=8 pts) W-L: 6-5
1 Score Games Win %: 55% (#15)
1 Score Games Wins (% of Total Wins): 86% (#3)

Home Lines (wks 1-16)

Avg Line = -1.1

Week: 1 2 3 4 5 6 7 8 9 10 11 12 13 14 15 16

Road Lines (wks 1-16)

Week
Avg Line = 0.4
Avg Line = 0.4.

Week: 1 2 3 4 5 6 7 8 9 10 11 12 13 14 15 16

Regular Season Wins: Past Results & Current Proj

2012 Wins	4
2013 Wins	4
2014 Wins	3
Proj 2015 Wins	4.5
2015 Wins	7
Proj 2016 Wins	8

1 2 3 4 5 6 7 8 9 10 11 12 13 14 15

Like a typical Raiders team, Oakland killed themselves with penalties, with a net -35. The team must play more disciplined if they hope to post their first winning season since 2002. Unlike many years, they are only lined underdogs in 4 games, and their predicted win total is 8. The needle is pointing higher for the Raiders in 2016 after a strong offseason of adding talent. After suffering the 4th most injuries in 2014, the team ranked 11th last year, so that is unlikely to improve. And the turnover and sack margins were relatively neutral. The Raiders were a tremendous road dog (5-0 ATS) last year and should have plenty of opportunities this year, as they are underdogs at KC and BAL, and the games in NO, JAC, TB and SD are close to pick'em and could see them as underdogs by that time. Its been years, however, since the Raiders won more than 3 of 8 games at home, but are favored in 5 home games this year.

2016 Rest Analysis

Avg Rest	6.5
Avg Rest Rk	3
Team More Rest	3
Opp More Rest	2
Net Rest Edge	1
3 days rest	1
4 days rest	0
5 days rest	2
6 days rest	9
7 days rest	1
8 days rest	0
9 days rest	1
10 days rest	0
11 days rest	0
12 days rest	0
13 days rest	0
14 days rest	1

Weekly EDSR & Season Trending Performance

WEEK	1	2	3	4	5	7	8	9	10	11	12	13	14	15	16	17
RESULT	L	W	W	L	L	W	W	L	L	L	W	L	W	L	W	L
OPP	CIN	BAL	CLE	CHI	DEN	SD	NYJ	PIT	MIN	DET	TEN	KC	DEN	GB	SD	KC
SITE	H	H	A	A	H	A	H	A	H	A	H	A	H	A	H	A
MARGIN	-20	4	7	-2	-6	8	14	-3	-16	-5	3	-14	3	-10	3	-6
PTS	13	37	27	20	10	37	34	35	14	13	24	20	15	20	23	17
OPP PTS	33	33	20	22	16	29	20	38	30	18	21	34	12	30	20	23

Week by Week 2015 Results

EDSR Results (W/L) By Week
W=Green
L=Red

Off & Def EDSR
Wk & Trend
- Blue=Offense
(high=good)
- Red=Defense
(low=good)

STATS & VISUALIZATIONS

Oakland Raiders

Directional Passer Rating Achieved

Receiver	Short Left	Short Middle	Short Right	Deep Left	Deep Middle	Deep Right
Michael Crabtree	97	79	82	0	158	91
Amari Cooper	77	118	58	81	0	127
Mychal Rivera	89	100	82	0	158	63
Seth Roberts	111	64	36		118	109
Clive Walford	78	75	77	42	56	153
Andre Holmes	39	146	92	39	87	76
Lee Smith	96	81	127			
Rod Streater			100			

Directional Frequency by Receiver

Receiver	Short Left	Short Middle	Short Right	Deep Left	Deep Middle	Deep Right
Michael Crabtree	24%	33%	37%	14%	32%	33%
Amari Cooper	35%	20%	26%	36%	14%	26%
Mychal Rivera	8%	11%	10%	11%	9%	11%
Seth Roberts	18%	17%	6%		27%	5%
Clive Walford	9%	11%	10%	18%	9%	12%
Andre Holmes	3%	5%	6%	21%	9%	12%
Lee Smith	3%	4%	4%			
Rod Streater				1%		

Defense Passer Rating Allowed

Short Left	Short Middle	Short Right	Deep Left	Deep Middle	Deep Right
94	113	89	29	95	35

Derek Carr - 1st Down RTG

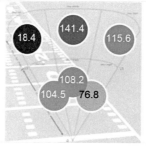

Derek Carr - 3rd Down RTG

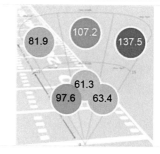

Derek Carr - 2nd Down RTG

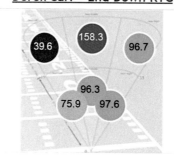

Derek Carr - Overall RTG

Pass Offense Play Success Rate

41%	45%	37%	48%	47%
57%	68%	59%	55%	62%
39%	36%	50%	58%	35%

Offensive Rush Directional Yds/Carry

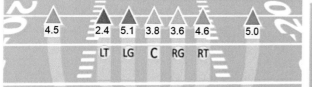

4.5 2.4 5.1 3.8 3.6 4.6 5.0
LT LG C RG RT

Offensive Rush Frequency of Direction

37 32 47 121 48 36 37
LT LG C RG RT

Offensive Explosive Runs by Direction

6 3 12 2 5 5
LT LG C RG RT

Defensive Rush Directional Yds/Carry

5.5 2.9 4.3 4.0 5.2 2.4 6.1
LT LG C RG RT

2nd & Short RUN (1D or not)

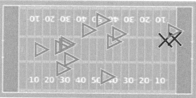

2nd & Short RUN Stats

Run Conv Rk	1D% Run	NFL 1D% Run Avg	Run Freq	NFL Run Freq Avg
3	86%	69%	70%	64%

2nd & Short PASS (1D or not)

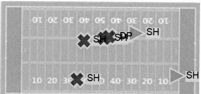

2nd & Short PASS Stats

Pass Conv Rk	1D% Pass	NFL 1D% Pass Avg	Pass Freq	NFL Pass Freq Avg
30	33%	55%	30%	36%

Pass Offense Yds/Play

4.8	7.3	4.1	4.9	4.5
8.7	10.4	8.8	10.5	6.4
6.7	4.1	8.9	9.6	3.1

Off. Directional Tendency (% of Plays Left, Middle or Right)

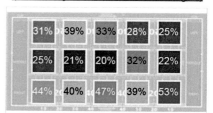

31%	39%	33%	28%	25%
25%	21%	20%	32%	22%
44%	40%	47%	39%	53%

Off. Directional Pass Rate (% of Plays which are Passes)

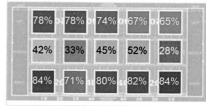

78%	78%	74%	67%	65%
42%	33%	45%	52%	28%
84%	71%	80%	82%	84%

128

San Diego Chargers

Coaches

Head Coach: Mike McCoy (4th yr)
OC: Ken Whisenhunt (TEN HC) (1st yr)
DC: John Pagano (5th yr)

Forecast 2016 Wins

6.5

Past Records

2015: 4-12
2014: 9-7
2013: 9-7

Opponent Strength
Easy — Hard

2016 Schedule & Week by Week Strength of Schedule

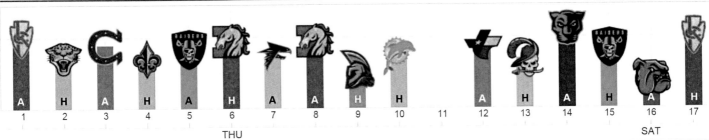

	A	H	A	H	A	H	A	A	H	H		A	H	A	H	A	H
	1	2	3	4	5	6	7	8	9	10	11	12	13	14	15	16	17

THU   SAT

2016 Overview

The NFL is a passing league. But teams are still allowed to call run plays. And given current defenses, there are definitely situations where running the football is substantially more efficient than passing. Teams still must main balance to find success. Teams who struggle in the run game on both sides of the ball are doomed, even in the modern era. Three teams last year finished 24th or worse in rush efficiency both offensively and defensively: The 3-13 Titans, 4-12 Chargers and 8-8 Falcons. The Chargers actually finished 31st in rush offense and 32nd in rush defense. The implications are disastrous:

When you can't stop the run, often you'll lose close games if you trail and cannot get the opposing offense off the field. Last year teams lost an average of 4 games by one score or less. But sure enough, the 4 worst teams in run defense lost an average of almost 7 games by one score or less, with the Chargers losing 9 games by one score or less. When you can't run efficiently, often you won't be able to salt away games you should easily win by simply chewing up clock and flipping field possession in the 4th quarter. Last year teams that led after 3 quarters won 81% of their games (83% long term since 2000). But sure enough, of the 4 worst teams in run offense, 3 finished at .500 or worse even when leading after 3 quarters. Only 5 teams were in this .500 or worse category last year, and the Titans, Jaguars and Chargers were among the teams with bad run offenses that could not win games that they led through 3 quarters.

The number one priority for the Chargers in 2016 must be to run and defend the run. Intelligently, they added run stopping along the defensive line via DT Brandon Mebane in free agency, and added depth along the offensive line in the draft and free agency. But a lot of pressure will fall onto last season's 15th overall selection, RB Melvin Gordon. Recall that the Chargers traded up to acquire Gordon, sending the 17th overall plus their 4th and 5th round selections to move up two spots to draft Gordon. By all accounts, Gordon was a disaster his rookie season. Playing directly into the narrative of being unable to run the game out, Gordon averaged less than 2.5 yds/carry if leading or tied in the game. On the critical 3rd down, he averaged just 2.2 yds/carry. And in opposing territory, he was given 55 carries. He turned just 6 into first downs, recorded zero touchdowns, and averaged less than 2.4 yds/carry.

Unfortunately, history does not bode well for a big bounce back. Very few first round running backs recorded max-5 rushing TDs and max-3.48 yds/carry in their rookie year. The list is littered with players who never lived up to expectations in the NFL. Players like Jahvid Best, Lawrence Phillips, Tim Biakabutuka and Tyrone Wheatley. Gordon also fumbled 6 times, and had microfracture knee surgery this offseason. If Gordon can't step up in 2016, the season will again fall to Philip Rivers targeting Keenan Allen at a ridiculous rate. Allen's 89 targets led the Chargers, but he played in only 8 games before being injured. He averaged 11 targets, 8 catches and 90 yards per game before his injury. As much work as the offense needs on the ground, the defense was even more of a problem in 2015. They lost their captain in the secondary when Eric Weddle went to the Ravens, but this defensive unit must play significantly better in 2016 if the Chargers want any hope of competing in what could be a very tight AFC West.

Strength of Schedule In Detail

True Strength of Schedule Rank: 18

Hardest Stretches (1=Hard, 32=Easy)
Hardest 3 wk Stretch Rk:	28
Hardest 4 wk Stretch Rk:	27
Hardest 5 wk Stretch Rk:	29

Easiest Stretches (1=Easy, 32=Hard)
Easiest 3 wk Stretch Rk:	32
Easiest 4 wk Stretch Rk:	24
Easiest 5 wk Stretch Rk:	26

Playing the Titans and Browns out of division always will lighten a team's Strength of Schedule, and San Diego is fortunate in that respect. The Chargers, once an exciting nationally televised team, plays just one primetime game this year on Thursday (wk 6) vs the Broncos. San Diego won't be able to get too comfortable this year, as they play just one set of back-to-back home games this year, and it's not until weeks 9 and 10.

2015 Play Tendencies

All Pass %	64%
All Pass Rk	5
All Rush %	36%
All Rush Rk	28
1 Score Pass %	65%
1 Score Pass Rk	2
2014 1 Score Pass %	59%
2014 1 Score Pass Rk	11
Pass Increase %	6%
Pass Increase Rk	5
1 Score Rush %	35%
1 Score Rush Rk	31
Up Pass %	62%
Up Pass Rk	1
Up Rush %	38%
Up Rush Rk	32
Down Pass %	66%
Down Pass Rk	22
Down Rush %	34%
Down Rush Rk	11

They Chargers went from passing 59% in one score games in 2014 to 65% last year. That 6% jump was 5th most of any team, and pushed the Chargers to being the 2nd most pass heavy team in the NFL. Primarily, this was because of a pathetic run game. The run game was so bad, that even when the Chargers had a lead, they still passed the ball 62% of the time, the most in the NFL. For comparison, when trailing they passed 66%.

2015 Offensive Advanced Metrics

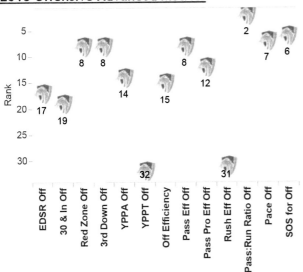

It's hard to be balanced when your run game is literally 2nd worst in the NFL and you find yourself trailing often on the scoreboard thanks to a terrible defense. Compounding things are that same defense ranked dead last vs the run, allowing opponents with a lead to run the air out of the ball. And that is, in part, why the Chargers went 3-9 last year in games decided by one-score or less. Overall offensively, they were not terrible. They went up against the 6th toughest schedule and produced above average numbers in most areas. But they were 17th in EDSR and 15th in overall efficiency. The Chargers must improve their yds/point efficiency, which was dead last in the NFL. Some of that was the result of turnovers off of longer drives: when Rivers threw an interception last year, on average it came after 5 plays, which was the 6th most in the NFL. Defensively, they must be more stout vs the run and find a way to rush the passer more efficiently.

2015 Defensive Advanced Metrics

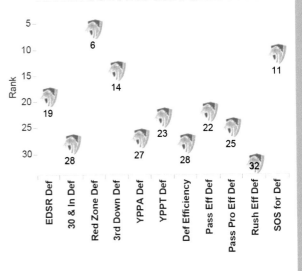

Drafted Players

PERSONNEL & SPENDING — San Diego Chargers

Rnd.	Pick #	Pos.	Player	College
1	3	DE	Joey Bosa	Ohio State
2	35	TE	Hunter Henry	Arkansas
3	66	C	Max Tuerk	USC
4	102	OLB	Joshua Perry	Ohio State
5	175	OLB	Jatavis Brown	Akron
6	179	P	Drew Kaser	Texas A&M
6	198	FB	Derek Watt	Wisconsin
7	224	G	Donavon Clark	Michigan State

Free Agents/Trades Added

Player (Position)

Brandon Mebane DT
Casey Hayward CB
Dwight Lowery S
Jeff Cumberland TE
Matt Slauson G
Travis Benjamin WR

Other Signed

Player (Position)

Adrian McDonald S
Carlos Wray DT
Chris Landrum LB
Chris Swain RB
DeAndre Reaves WR
Dominique Williams WR
Jamaal Jones WR
Kenneth Farrow RB
Larry Scott CB
Matt Weiser TE
Mike Bercovici QB
Mike McQueen T
Sebastian Johansson G
Shaq Petteway LB
Spencer Pulley C
Terrell Chestnut CB
Trevor Williams CB
Tyler Johnstone T
Tyler Marcordes LB
Vi Teofilo G
Zeth Ramsay T

2015 Players Lost

Transaction	Player (Position)
Cut	Brad Sorensen QB
	Brock Hekking LB
	Bryn Renner QB
	Chi Chi Ariguzo LB
	Donald Brown RB
	Donald Butler LB
	Kavell Conner LB
	Michael Huey G
	Mike Scifres P
	Sebastian Johansson G
Declared Free Agent	Brandian Ross S
	Eric Weddle S
	Jeff Linkenbach G
	Kendall Reyes DE
	Ladarius Green TE

- When a team cannot run the football nor defend the run, and thus can't hold leads or prevent teams from running out the clock, it is no surprise the team will finish poorly in close games. San Diego went 3-9 in one-score games last year. What is a surprise, however, is that such a team would want to lock in a skinny, diminutive WR in free agency for cap hits of $6M on average, with $13M guaranteed over the next two years.

- The prime reason the Chargers were able to make that move was because the let Eric Weddle leave and sign with the Baltimore Ravens. Why is that the prime reason? Take a look at the contracts: Weddle is averaging $6.5M against the cap, and his contract likewise is guaranteed for $13M. They are very similar deals from that perspective.

- Apart from their very poor run offense, their defense was their biggest problem in 2015. Particularly against the run. The team attempted to address that problem head on, by signing the Seattle Seahawks' best rush defender, DT Brandon Mebane, and drafting Joey Bosa 3rd overall. They also struggled to rush the passer. Bosa should help there as well, and the Chargers hope their 4th and 5th round picks will as well, snagging two OLBs: Joshua Perry and Jatavis Brown.

- Part of the big problem offensively was injuries along the line. In fact, the Chargers have been one of the most injured teams the last 2 years. They hope the combination of offensive line depth with their 3rd pick C Max Tuerk and G Matt Slauson, acquired via free agency, will help if the line struggles with injury in 2016.

- Fortunately for the Chargers, expensive QB Philip Rivers cap hits actually get cheaper after this year. Unlike many QB contracts, which spiral out of control at their conclusion, such as Drew Brees and his $30M figure this season, Rivers ($21M this year) drops to $18.5 in 2017, and increases by exactly $1M in each of the next two years, such that in 2019, he hits the cap for only $20.5M.

Lineup & 2016 Cap Hit

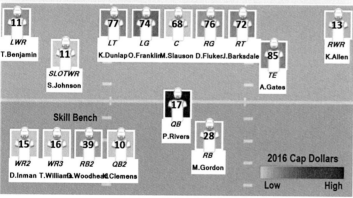

2016 Cap Dollars: Low — High

Skill Bench

Health Overall & by Unit (2015 v 2014)

2015 Rk	27
2015 AGL	89
Off Rk	26
Def Rk	10
2014 Rk	31
2014 AGL	119

2016 Positional Spending

	All OFF	QB	OL	RB	WR	TE	All DEF	DL	LB	CB	S
2015 Rk	7	2	21	9	27	4	27	24	19	22	6
Rank	10	9	11	16	23	11	22	15	23	10	23
Total	82.5M	22.3M	29.8M	7.4M	13.7M	9.4M	65.9M	20.2M	16.4M	21.9M	7.3M

2016 Offseason Spending

Total Spent	Total Spent Rk	Free Agents #	Free Agents $	Free Agents $ Rk	Waiver #	Waiver $	Waiver $ Rk	Extended #	Sum of Extended $	Sum of Drafted $	Undrafted #	Undrafted $
208M	11	10	69M	13	10	6M	31	3	80M	19M	21	34M

2015 Stats & Fantasy Production

Pos	Player	Ov. Rank	Pos. Rk	Age	Gms	St	Pass Comp	Pass Att	Pass Yds	Pass TD	Pass Int	Rush Att	Rush Yds	Rush YPA	Rush TD	Targ	Recp	Rec Yds	Rec YPC	Rec TDs	Draft King Pts	Fan Duel Pts
QB	Philip Rivers	74	11	34	16	16	437	661	4,792	29	13	17	28	2							299	294
RB	Danny Woodhead	33	11	30	16	1						98	336	3	3	106	80	755	9	6	249	203
	Melvin Gordon		53	22	14	13						184	641	3		37	33	192	6		118	92
	Donald Brown		78	28	9	2						59	229	4	1	13	8	88	11		49	42
	Branden Oliver		100	24	8	1						31	108	3		15	13	112	9		41	29
WR	Keenan Allen		47	23	8	8										89	67	725	11	4	166	128
	Malcom Floyd		64	34	15	13										68	30	561	19	3	106	87
	Steve Johnson		69	29	10	8										65	45	497	11	3	116	90
	Dontrelle Inman		71	26	14	7										63	35	486	14	3	104	82
	Javontee Herndon		134	24	8	2						1	13	13		33	24	195	8		47	31
TE	Antonio Gates	69	11	35	11	4										85	56	630	11	5	152	121
	Ladarius Green		19	25	13	11										63	37	429	12	4	111	89

Avg Line	Pred Wins	Pred Div Finish
+2.0	6.5	#4

2016 Weekly Betting Lines (wks 1-16)

(-) Favorite — Underdog (+)
-4.5 — +10.0

Scale: -6.0, -4.0, -2.0, +0.0, +2.0, +4.0, +6.0, +8.0, +10.0, +12.0

Avg Line = 2.0

Week 1-16 lines:
- Wk1: A +7.0
- Wk2: H -2.5
- Wk3: A +5.5
- Wk4: H -3.0
- Wk5: A +4.5
- Wk6: H +3.0
- Wk7: A +3.0
- Wk8: A +7.0
- Wk9: H -4.5
- Wk10: H -1.0
- Wk12: A +4.5, -2.0
- Wk14: A +10.0
- Wk15: A (Raiders)
- Wk16: -2.0

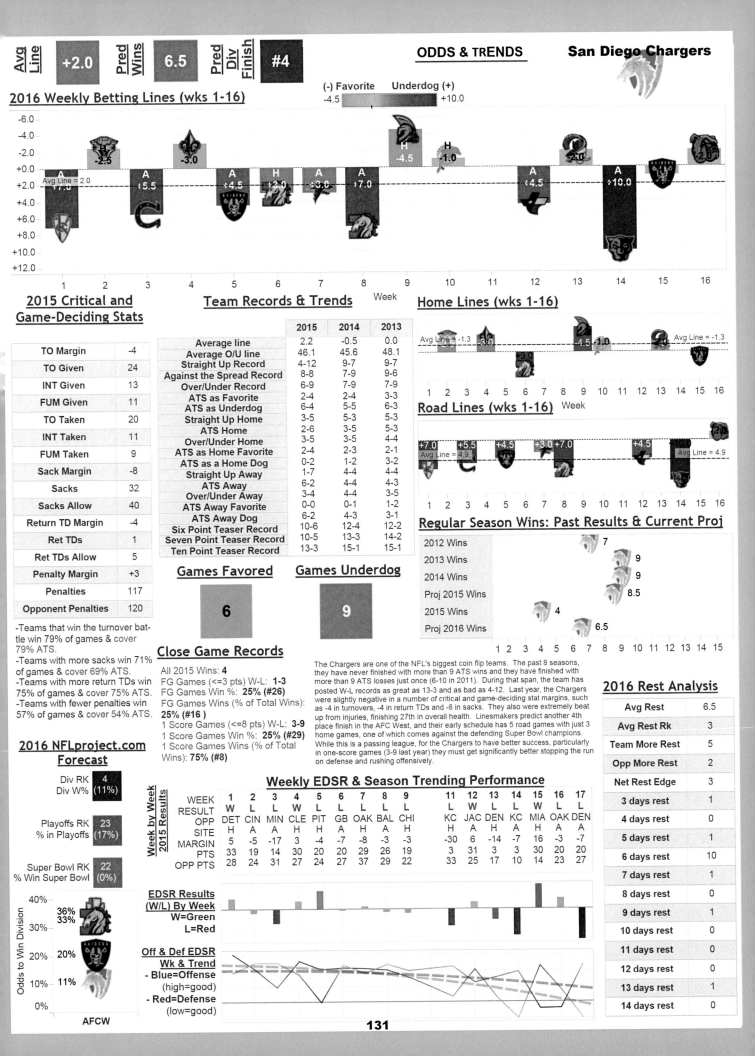

2015 Critical and Game-Deciding Stats

TO Margin	-4
TO Given	24
INT Given	13
FUM Given	11
TO Taken	20
INT Taken	11
FUM Taken	9
Sack Margin	-8
Sacks	32
Sacks Allow	40
Return TD Margin	-4
Ret TDs	1
Ret TDs Allow	5
Penalty Margin	+3
Penalties	117
Opponent Penalties	120

-Teams that win the turnover battle win 79% of games & cover 79% ATS.
-Teams with more sacks win 71% of games & cover 69% ATS.
-Teams with more return TDs win 75% of games & cover 75% ATS.
-Teams with fewer penalties win 57% of games & cover 54% ATS.

2016 NFLproject.com Forecast

Div RK: 4
Div W% (11%)

Playoffs RK: 23
% in Playoffs (17%)

Super Bowl RK: 22
% Win Super Bowl (0%)

Odds to Win Division:
- 36%
- 33%
- 20%
- 11%

AFCW

Team Records & Trends

	2015	2014	2013
Average line	2.2	-0.5	0.0
Average O/U line	46.1	45.6	48.1
Straight Up Record	4-12	9-7	9-7
Against the Spread Record	8-8	7-9	9-6
Over/Under Record	6-9	7-9	7-9
ATS as Favorite	2-4	2-4	3-3
ATS as Underdog	6-4	5-5	6-3
Straight Up Home	3-5	5-3	5-3
ATS Home	2-6	3-5	5-3
Over/Under Home	3-5	3-5	4-4
ATS as Home Favorite	2-4	2-3	2-1
ATS as a Home Dog	0-2	1-2	3-2
Straight Up Away	1-7	4-4	4-4
ATS Away	6-2	4-4	4-3
Over/Under Away	3-4	4-4	3-5
ATS Away Favorite	0-0	0-1	1-2
ATS Away Dog	6-2	4-3	3-1
Six Point Teaser Record	10-6	12-4	12-2
Seven Point Teaser Record	10-5	13-3	14-2
Ten Point Teaser Record	13-3	15-1	15-1

Games Favored
6

Games Underdog
9

Close Game Records

All 2015 Wins: 4
FG Games (<=3 pts) W-L: 1-3
FG Games Win %: 25% (#26)
FG Games Wins (% of Total Wins): 25% (#16)
1 Score Games (<=8 pts) W-L: 3-9
1 Score Games Win %: 25% (#29)
1 Score Games Wins (% of Total Wins): 75% (#8)

Home Lines (wks 1-16)

Avg Line = -1.3

- -3.0
- -4.5, -1.0
- -3.0

Week 1-16

Road Lines (wks 1-16)

Avg Line = 4.9

- +7.0
- +5.5
- +4.5
- +3.0 +7.0
- +4.5

Week 1-16

Regular Season Wins: Past Results & Current Proj

	Wins
2012 Wins	7
2013 Wins	9
2014 Wins	9
Proj 2015 Wins	8.5
2015 Wins	4
Proj 2016 Wins	6.5

Scale: 1 2 3 4 5 6 7 8 9 10 11 12 13 14 15

The Chargers are one of the NFL's biggest coin flip teams. The past 8 seasons, they have never finished with more than 9 ATS wins and they have finished with more than 9 ATS losses just once (6-10 in 2011). During that span, the team has posted W-L records as great as 13-3 and as bad as 4-12. Last year, the Chargers were slightly negative in a number of critical and game-deciding stat margins, such as -4 in turnovers, -4 in return TDs and -8 in sacks. They also were extremely beat up from injuries, finishing 27th in overall health. Linesmakers predict another 4th place finish in the AFC West, and their early schedule has 5 road games with just 3 home games, one of which comes against the defending Super Bowl champions. While this is a passing league, for the Chargers to have better success, particularly in one-score games (3-9 last year) they must get significantly better stopping the run on defense and rushing offensively.

2016 Rest Analysis

Avg Rest	6.5
Avg Rest Rk	3
Team More Rest	5
Opp More Rest	2
Net Rest Edge	3
3 days rest	1
4 days rest	0
5 days rest	1
6 days rest	10
7 days rest	1
8 days rest	0
9 days rest	1
10 days rest	0
11 days rest	0
12 days rest	0
13 days rest	1
14 days rest	0

Weekly EDSR & Season Trending Performance

2015 Results Week by Week:

WEEK	1	2	3	4	5	6	7	8	9	11	12	13	14	15	16	17
RESULT	W	L	L	W	L	L	L	L	L	L	W	L	L	W	L	L
OPP	DET	CIN	MIN	CLE	PIT	GB	OAK	BAL	CHI	KC	JAC	DEN	KC	MIA	OAK	DEN
SITE	H	A	A	H	A	H	H	A	H	A	H	A	H	H	A	A
MARGIN	5	-5	-17	3	-4	-7	-8	-3	-3	-30	6	-14	-7	16	-3	-7
PTS	33	19	14	30	20	20	29	26	19	3	31	3	3	30	20	20
OPP PTS	28	24	31	27	24	27	37	29	22	33	25	17	10	14	23	27

EDSR Results (W/L) By Week
W=Green
L=Red

Off & Def EDSR Wk & Trend
- Blue=Offense (high=good)
- Red=Defense (low=good)

All visualizations courtesy of SharpFootballStats.com. See Table of Contents for definition of stats & coding used. See SharpFootballStats.com for interactive visualizations which break data into more segments, allow customization & user download. Updated weekly throughout the 2016 NFL season.

STATS & VISUALIZATIONS San Diego Chargers

Directional Passer Rating Achieved

Receiver	Short Left	Short Middle	Short Right	Deep Left	Deep Middle	Deep Right
Keenan Allen	106	75	77	116	158	132
Antonio Gates	127	100	81	95	77	82
Steve Johnson	109	49	111	118	39	118
Ladarius Green	86	116	81	47		139
Dontrelle Inman	89	100	133	83	43	61
Malcom Floyd	64	104	51	60	72	56
Javontee Herndon	73	90	100			39
John Phillips	100	126	100			
Tyrell Williams	108			39	81	39
David Johnson	83		39			
Vincent Brown			39			118

Directional Frequency by Receiver

Receiver	Short Left	Short Middle	Short Right	Deep Left	Deep Middle	Deep Right
Keenan Allen	23%	18%	18%	15%	14%	10%
Antonio Gates	14%	28%	18%	6%	10%	12%
Steve Johnson	15%	14%	18%	6%	5%	2%
Ladarius Green	13%	17%	11%	15%		12%
Dontrelle Inman	14%	9%	11%	21%	10%	20%
Malcom Floyd	8%	6%	11%	33%	48%	37%
Javontee Herndon	10%	3%	10%			2%
John Phillips	2%	6%	1%			
Tyrell Williams	1%			3%	14%	2%
David Johnson	1%		1%			
Vincent Brown			1%			2%

Defense Passer Rating Allowed

Short Left	Short Middle	Short Right	Deep Left	Deep Middle	Deep Right
108	93	94	88	112	50

Offensive Rush Directional Yds/Carry

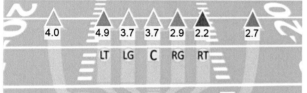

4.0 | 4.9 | 3.7 | 3.7 | 2.9 | 2.2 | 2.7
LT | LG | C | RG | RT

Offensive Rush Frequency of Direction

38 | 39 | 37 | 168 | 37 | 35 | 31
LT | LG | C | RG | RT

Offensive Explosive Runs by Direction

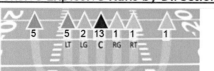

5 | 5 | 2 | 13 | 1 | 1 | 1
LT | LG | C | RG | RT

Defensive Rush Directional Yds/Carry

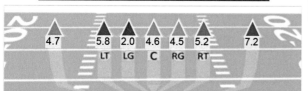

4.7 | 5.8 | 2.0 | 4.6 | 4.5 | 5.2 | 7.2
LT | LG | C | RG | RT

Philip Rivers - 1st Down RTG

56.9 | 87.5 | 69.2 | 90.9 | 87.9 | 82.2

Philip Rivers - 2nd Down RTG

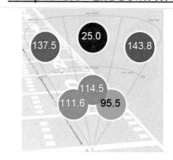

137.5 | 25.0 | 143.8 | 114.5 | 111.6 | 95.5

SHARP FOOTBALL STATS

2nd & Short RUN (1D or not)

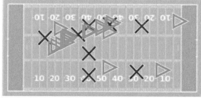

2nd & Short RUN Stats

Run Conv Rk	1D% Run	NFL 1D% Run Avg	Run Freq	NFL Run Freq Avg
14	70%	69%	71%	64%

2nd & Short PASS (1D or not)

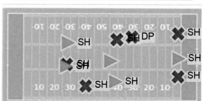

2nd & Short PASS Stats

Pass Conv Rk	1D% Pass	NFL 1D% Pass Avg	Pass Freq	NFL Pass Freq Avg
25	46%	55%	29%	36%

Philip Rivers - 3rd Down RTG

56.3 | 95.8 | 53.7 | 73.2 | 98.6 | 104.5

Philip Rivers - Overall RTG

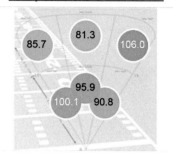

85.7 | 81.3 | 106.0 | 95.9 | 100.1 | 90.8

Pass Offense Play Success Rate

56%	60%	45%	31%	58%
53%	74%	53%	62%	45%
56%	52%	43%	45%	52%

Pass Offense Yds/Play

6.7	8.2	5.8	4.7	5.3
12.3	10.4	7.8	7.5	5.2
7.6	8.7	6.5	7.0	5.6

Off. Directional Tendency
(% of Plays Left, Middle or Right)

38%	37%	38%	43%	35%
25%	30%	24%	18%	29%
38%	32%	37%	39%	36%

Off. Directional Pass Rate
(% of Plays which are Passes)

81%	68%	77%	88%	72%
43%	43%	37%	34%	47%
78%	75%	80%	80%	82%

Indianapolis Colts

Coaches

Head Coach: Chuck Pagano (5th yr)
OC: Rob Chudzinski (2nd yr)
DC: Ted Monachino (BAL LB) (1st yr)

Forecast 2016 Wins

9

Past Records

2015: 8-8
2014: 11-5
2013: 11-5

Opponent Strength
Easy   Hard

2016 Schedule & Week by Week Strength of Schedule

H	A	H	A	H	A	A	H	A		H	H	A	H	A	A	H
1	2	3	4	5	6	7	8	9	10	11	12	13	14	15	16	17

LON — SNF — TKG — MNF — SAT

2016 Overview

The story of the Indianapolis Colts is as much about building a roster as it is about the plays they call and the victories they pile up. Which team do you think sported the most expensive defense in 2015? That question sounds impressive, doesn't it? The "most expensive defense" sounds like a good thing. Like owning the most expensive car or the most expensive diamond ring or the largest house. However, another way to phrase that same question: which team's salary cap was most hamstrung by cap allocation to the defensive side of the ball? Now it suddenly sounds bad. But it's all about the way you look at the situation. Unfortunately for Colts fans, when Ryan Grigson took over in 2012 as the Colts GM, he had a very precise philosophy which he didn't stray from in his first 3 years. And that cost the Colts in those years as well as carried over to 2015. Fortunately, he has appeared to turn a page, but first let's answer the questions posed above.

The Colts fielded the most expensive defense in 2015. And from 2013 through 2015, they allocated the 2nd most salary cap dollars to the defensive side of the ball in the NFL (Bengals #1). The reason for this was the strategy from Ryan Grigson. Draft offense, buy defense. From 2012 through 2014, Grigson's first 3 years in Indianapolis, he made 22 draft picks and used just 7 of them on defense. Only 2 defensive players he drafted started more than 1 game. Instead of drafting them, he bought them. In those 3 years, he signed in free agency the following defensive players: Cory Redding, Justin King, Tom Zbikowski, Brandon McKinney, LaRon Landry, Aubrayo Franklin, Erik Walden, Greg Toler, Ricky Jean Francois, Lawrence Sidbury, D'Qwell Jackson, Arthur Jones, Mike Adams, and Colt Anderson.

The biggest problem there is more than ever, drafting players is far cheaper than buying them in free agency. Since the 2011 new CBA, slotted contracts and 5th year options have allowed the smartest teams to stockpile draft picks, let free agents walk in exchange for compensatory selections, and build through the draft on the cheap, while retaining services of a few, key pieces. Another problem is that most free agents that are big signings end up withering after a year or two and then find themselves looking for a new job after getting cut.

The best thing Grigson ever did was the one thing that required him to not make a single decision. And that was to draft Andrew Luck 1st overall in 2012. Luck was served up on a silver platter. And despite how Grigson tried to buy defense to see immediate success, Luck himself was a large part of the reason the Colts went 11-5 from 2012 through 2014. That and playing in the AFC South. Clearly the Colts have Luck in the long term plans, and Luck's ability to use his brain and his legs to escape and extend plays will make him a valuable piece to build around for years. It seems like Grigson finally might have turned the corner in understanding how to build his defense, but success through the draft certainly doesn't happen overnight unless it's via a new quarterback. Grigson must continue to patiently build the team through the draft and by making smart, efficient decisions.

Strength of Schedule In Detail

True Strength of Schedule Rank: 20

Hardest Stretches *(1=Hard, 32=Easy)*
Hardest 3 wk Stretch Rk: 28
Hardest 4 wk Stretch Rk: 15
Hardest 5 wk Stretch Rk: 13

Easiest Stretches *(1=Easy, 32=Hard)*
Easiest 3 wk Stretch Rk: 17
Easiest 4 wk Stretch Rk: 17
Easiest 5 wk Stretch Rk: 7

Apart from a week 2 game in Denver, the first five games for the Colts looks manageable, and is the 6th easiest start for any team. The interesting aspect is the end of that stretch, as they are the first team to play in London (week 4 vs JAC) and then play the very next week (home vs CHI). Such travel and lack of rest could be tough for them, and they follow that game vs the Bears up with back to back road games (@ HOU, @ TEN) and won't get a bye until they play two more very challenging opponents (KC, GB).

2015 Play Tendencies

All Pass %	62%
All Pass Rk	10
All Rush %	38%
All Rush Rk	23
1 Score Pass %	58%
1 Score Pass Rk	20
2014 1 Score Pass %	61%
2014 1 Score Pass Rk	6
Pass Increase %	-3%
Pass Increase Rk	27
1 Score Rush %	42%
1 Score Rush Rk	13
Up Pass %	51%
Up Pass Rk	12
Up Rush %	49%
Up Rush Rk	21
Down Pass %	70%
Down Pass Rk	9
Down Rush %	30%
Down Rush Rk	24

The Colts were so dependent on Andrew Luck in the past, and in 2014 they passed the ball 61% of the time in one-score games, 6th most in the NFL. The decreased that figure down to 58% and 20th in the NFL last year. If Luck returns healthy, expect the Colts to get right back to throwing on over 60% of their play calls, particularly if 1st round pick C Ryan Kelly can provide effective pass blocking up the middle for Luck.

2015 Offensive Advanced Metrics

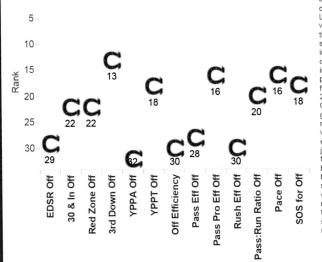

It is almost appropriate to toss out the entire 2015 Colts metrics analysis because they have depended so much on Andrew Luck the last several years, that when he plays in only 7 games, the team is inevitably going to struggle that season. After year in, year out 11 win seasons, they dropped to 8-8. Naturally, the impact was felt most in the passing game, where they finished dead last in yds/att, and 28th in pass efficiency. Opponents didn't fear the pass game, and they snuffed out the mediocre-to-begin run game, which finished 3rd worst in efficiency. The Colts converted just 56% of 2nd and short runs to first down, 28th in the NFL, 13% below average. Considering how bad the offense was overall, it's a surprise the Colts didn't fare worse defensively across the metrics spectrum. The team was terrible in several key areas, such as pass rush efficiency, and red zone defensive efficiency.

2015 Defensive Advanced Metrics

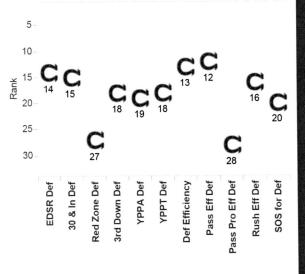

Drafted Players — 2016 Draft Grade: #12 (3.1/4)

Rnd.	Pick #	Pos.	Player	College
1	18	C	Ryan Kelly	Alabama
2	57	CB	T. J. Green	Clemson
3	82	OT	Le'Raven Clark	Texas Tech
4	116	DT	Hassan Ridgeway	Texas
4	125	OLB	Antonio Morrison	Florida
5	155	OT	Joe Haeg	North Dakota State
7	239	LB	Trevor Bates	Maine
7	248	C	Austin Blythe	Iowa

Lineup & 2016 Cap Hit

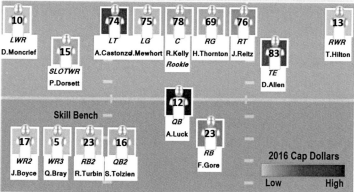

Defense
- FS — C.Geathers 42
- SS — M.Adams 76
- LB — N.Irving 55
- LB — D.Jackson 52
- RCB — V.Davis 21
- SLOTCB — P.Robinson 26
- OLB — R.Mathis 98
- NT — D.Parry 54
- DE — K.Langford 90
- OLB — E.Walden 93
- LCB — D.Smith 30

Offense
- LWR — D.Moncrief 10
- SLOTWR — P.Dorsett 15
- LT — A.Castonzo 74
- LG — J.Mewhort 75
- C — R.Kelly 78 (Rookie)
- RG — H.Thornton 69
- RT — J.Reitz 76
- TE — D.Allen 83
- RWR — T.Hilton 13
- QB — A.Luck 12
- RB — F.Gore 23

Skill Bench
- WR2 — J.Boyce 17
- WR3 — Q.Bray 5
- RB2 — R.Turbin 23
- QB2 — S.Tolzien 16

2016 Cap Dollars: Low — High

PERSONNEL & SPENDING

Free Agents/Trades Added

Player (Position)
- Brian Tyms WR
- Jordan Todman RB
- Patrick Robinson CB
- Robert Turbin RB
- Scott Tolzien QB

Other Signed

Player (Position)
- Adam Redmond G
- Andrew Williamson S
- Anthony Sarao LB
- Chester Rogers WR
- Chris Milton DB
- Curt Maggitt LB
- Daniel Davie CB
- Danny Anthrop WR
- Darion Griswold TE
- Darius White CB
- Davante Harris T
- Delvon Simmons DT
- Frankie Williams CB
- Isiah Cage G
- Jeremy Vujnovich T
- Josh Ferguson RB
- Marcus Leak WR
- Mekale McKay WR
- Michael Miller TE
- Ron Thompson LB
- Stefan McClure S
- Sterling Bailey DE
- Tevaun Smith WR

2015 Players Lost

Transaction	Player (Position)
Cut	Akeem Davis S
	Andre Johnson WR
	Andy Studebaker LB
	Anthony Sarao LB
	Ben Heenan G
	Bjoern Werner LB
	Cameron Clear TE
	Davante Harris T
	Eze Obiora LB
	Forrest Hill C
	Jonathan Newsome LB
	Josh Freeman QB
	Josh Mitchell CB
	Khaled Holmes C
	Mike McFarland TE
	Mitchell Van Dyk T
	Pierce Burton T
	Ryan Lindley QB
	Coby Fleener TE
Declared Free Agent	Jerrell Freeman LB
Retired	Matt Hasselbeck QB

- The Colts 2015 tight end cap hit ranked 24th in the NFL, as one of the less expensive teams. They didn't sign Coby Fleener and he left for a huge deal in New Orleans, but they did sign Dwayne Allen for a whopping $8.9M cap hit in 2016, and suddenly the Colts are spending 5th most in tight ends this season based on cap space. They still are lucky to have Andrew Luck on his rookie deal, because soon his cap hit will launch significantly higher.

- The Colts absolutely must figure out a way to better run the football in 2016. If the offense returns to a pass heavy style, the Colts could run into a defense that is playing pass more frequently, setting up +EV situations. While last year for the Colts certainly should not be predictive for 2016, they still ranked dead last in rushing efficiency in the red zone, with just 31% of their plays graded as successful. The NFL's best was at 58%, and the average team was at 47%. The Colts biggest weapon down there is Andrew Luck, who averaged nearly 4.6 YPA in 2014, but the remainder of the RB corps has been quite bad.

- It wasn't just in the red zone. Rushing on 2nd and short is one of the highest percentage situations to move the sticks, yet the Colts ranked 28th last year in their conversion rate, and the last 3 years the Colts rank 7th worst in the NFL.

- Ryan Grigson finally took a step back from the table and didn't go crazy in free agency. Prior to 2015, Grigson's tenure has seen the team spend 80% of their draft capital on offense, and 20% on defense. In turn, they received 85% of their drafted starts on the offensive side of the ball. Grigson drafted just 7 defensive players out of 23% of his selections, and of the 7 defensive players he drafted, only 2 started more than 1 game. In 2015, he drafted 5 defensive players and 3 of the 5 started more than 1 game. This past draft, he added 4 more defensive players. With the amount of cap the Colts will soon have tied up at QB, they will need a stable of cheaper, productive defensive players & you can only find that kind on their rookie deal from the draft.

Health Overall & by Unit (2015 v 2014)

2015 Rk	17
2015 AGL	65
Off Rk	6
Def Rk	26
2014 Rk	30
2014 AGL	105

2016 Positional Spending

	All OFF	QB	OL	RB	WR	TE	All DEF	DL	LB	CB	S
2015 Rk	29	18	29	13	14	24	1	23	1	6	23
Rank	15	19	24	18	15	5	21	30	5	16	27
Total	78.8M	18.6M	23.6M	6.7M	17.9M	11.9M	67.6M	12.8M	29.5M	19.7M	5.6M

2016 Offseason Spending

Total Spent	Total Spent Rk	Free Agents #	Free Agents $	Free Agents $ Rk	Waiver #	Waiver $	Waiver $ Rk	Extended #	Sum of Extended $	Sum of Drafted $	Undrafted #	Undrafted $
256M	5	8	21M	27	10	12M	18	3	158M	31M	21	34M

2015 Stats & Fantasy Production

Pos	Player	Ov. Rank	Pos. Rk	Age	Gms	St	Pass Comp	Pass Att	Pass Yds	Pass TD	Pass Int	Rush Att	Rush Yds	Rush YPA	Rush TD	Targ	Recp	Rec Yds	Rec YPC	Rec TDs	Draft King Pts	Fan Duel Pts
QB	Andrew Luck	28		26	7	7	162	293	1,881	15	12	33	196	6							148	141
	Matt Hasselbeck	35		40	8	8	156	256	1,690	9	5	16	15	1							101	96
RB	Frank Gore	36	12	32	16	16						260	967	4	6	58	34	267	8	1	202	176
	Ahmad Bradshaw		83	29	6							31	85	3		14	10	64	6	3	43	38
WR	T.Y. Hilton*	54	22	26	16	15										134	69	1,124	16	5	214	177
	Donte Moncrief		38	22	16	10										105	64	733	11	6	176	141
	Andre Johnson		58	34	16	14										77	41	503	12	4	118	95
	Phillip Dorsett		111	22	11							3	17	6		39	18	225	13	1	47	32
	Griff Whalen		125	25	14											26	19	205	11	1	47	32
TE	Coby Fleener		22	27	16	11										84	54	491	9	3	126	96
	Dwayne Allen		60	25	13	12						1	1	1		29	16	109	7	1	36	25

Avg Line	-0.8	Pred Wins	9	Pred Div Finish	#1

(-) Favorite   Underdog (+)
-8.0   +6.0

2016 Weekly Betting Lines (wks 1-16)

Avg Line = -0.8

H -5.5 · A +5.0 · A -3.5 · H -3.5 · A -3.5 · H -1.0 · A +6.0 · H -8.0 · A +2.0 · A +4.0

Weeks: 1 2 3 4 5 6 7 8 9 10 11 12 13 14 15 16

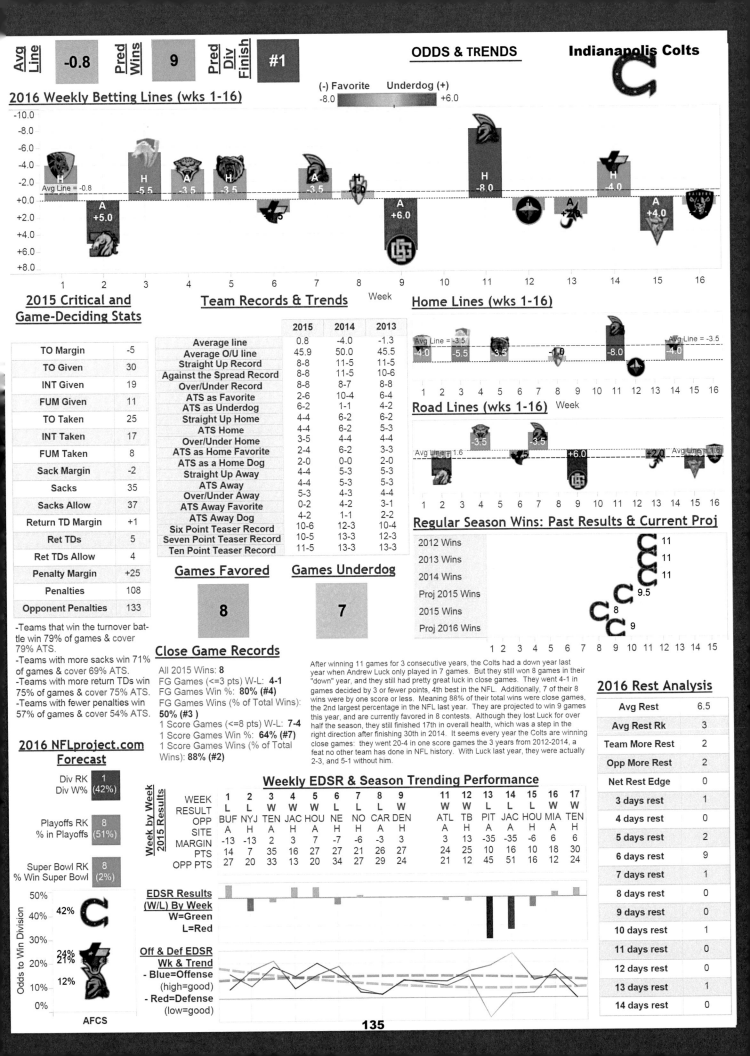

2015 Critical and Game-Deciding Stats

TO Margin	-5
TO Given	30
INT Given	19
FUM Given	11
TO Taken	25
INT Taken	17
FUM Taken	8
Sack Margin	-2
Sacks	35
Sacks Allow	37
Return TD Margin	+1
Ret TDs	5
Ret TDs Allow	4
Penalty Margin	+25
Penalties	108
Opponent Penalties	133

-Teams that win the turnover battle win 79% of games & cover 79% ATS.
-Teams with more sacks win 71% of games & cover 69% ATS.
-Teams with more return TDs win 75% of games & cover 75% ATS.
-Teams with fewer penalties win 57% of games & cover 54% ATS.

2016 NFLproject.com Forecast

Div RK	1
Div W%	(42%)

Playoffs RK	8
% in Playoffs	(51%)

Super Bowl RK	8
% Win Super Bowl	(2%)

Odds to Win Division
50%
42%
40%
30%
24%
21%
20%
12%
10%
0%

AFCS

Team Records & Trends

	2015	2014	2013
Average line	0.8	-4.0	-1.3
Average O/U line	45.9	50.0	45.5
Straight Up Record	8-8	11-5	11-5
Against the Spread Record	8-8	11-5	10-6
Over/Under Record	8-8	8-7	8-8
ATS as Favorite	2-6	10-4	6-4
ATS as Underdog	6-2	1-1	4-2
Straight Up Home	4-4	6-2	6-2
ATS Home	4-4	6-2	5-3
Over/Under Home	3-5	4-4	4-4
ATS as Home Favorite	2-4	6-2	3-3
ATS as a Home Dog	2-0	0-0	2-0
Straight Up Away	4-4	5-3	5-3
ATS Away	4-4	5-3	5-3
Over/Under Away	5-3	4-3	4-4
ATS Away Favorite	0-2	4-2	3-1
ATS Away Dog	4-2	1-1	2-2
Six Point Teaser Record	10-6	12-3	10-4
Seven Point Teaser Record	10-5	13-3	12-3
Ten Point Teaser Record	11-5	13-3	13-3

Games Favored

8

Games Underdog

7

Close Game Records

All 2015 Wins: **8**
FG Games (<=3 pts) W-L: **4-1**
FG Games Win %: **80% (#4)**
FG Games Wins (% of Total Wins): **50% (#3)**
1 Score Games (<=8 pts) W-L: **7-4**
1 Score Games Win %: **64% (#7)**
1 Score Games Wins (% of Total Wins): **88% (#2)**

Home Lines (wks 1-16)

Avg Line = -3.5
-4.0 · -5.5 · -3.5 · -1.0 · -8.0 · -4.0

1 2 3 4 5 6 7 8 9 10 11 12 13 14 15 16
Week

Road Lines (wks 1-16)   Week

Avg Line = 1.6
-3.5 · -3.5 · +5 · +6.0 · +2.0

1 2 3 4 5 6 7 8 9 10 11 12 13 14 15 16

Regular Season Wins: Past Results & Current Proj

2012 Wins	11
2013 Wins	11
2014 Wins	11
Proj 2015 Wins	9.5
2015 Wins	8
Proj 2016 Wins	9

1 2 3 4 5 6 7 8 9 10 11 12 13 14 15

After winning 11 games for 3 consecutive years, the Colts had a down year last year when Andrew Luck only played in 7 games. But they still won 8 games in their "down" year, and they still had pretty great luck in close games. They went 4-1 in games decided by 3 or fewer points, 4th best in the NFL. Additionally, 7 of their 8 wins were by one score or less. Meaning 88% of their total wins were close games, the 2nd largest percentage in the NFL last year. They are projected to win 9 games this year, and are currently favored in 8 contests. Although they lost Luck for over half the season, they still finished 17th in overall health, which was a step in the right direction after finishing 30th in 2014. It seems every year the Colts are winning close games: they went 20-4 in one score games the 3 years from 2012-2014, a feat no other team has done in NFL history. With Luck last year, they were actually 2-3, and 5-1 without him.

2016 Rest Analysis

Avg Rest	6.5
Avg Rest Rk	3
Team More Rest	2
Opp More Rest	2
Net Rest Edge	0
3 days rest	1
4 days rest	0
5 days rest	2
6 days rest	9
7 days rest	1
8 days rest	0
9 days rest	0
10 days rest	1
11 days rest	0
12 days rest	0
13 days rest	1
14 days rest	0

Weekly EDSR & Season Trending Performance

WEEK	1	2	3	4	5	6	7	8	9		11	12	13	14	15	16	17
RESULT	L	L	W	W	W	L	L	L	W		W	W	L	L	L	W	W
OPP	BUF	NYJ	TEN	JAC	HOU	NE	NO	CAR	DEN		ATL	TB	PIT	JAC	HOU	MIA	TEN
SITE	A	H	A	H	A	H	H	A	H		A	H	A	A	H	A	H
MARGIN	-13	-13	2	3	7	-7	-6	-3	3		3	13	-35	-35	-6	6	6
PTS	14	7	35	16	27	27	21	26	27		24	25	10	16	10	18	30
OPP PTS	27	20	33	13	20	34	27	29	24		21	12	45	51	16	12	24

Week by Week 2015 Results

EDSR Results (W/L) By Week
W=Green
L=Red

Off & Def EDSR Wk & Trend
- Blue=Offense (high=good)
- Red=Defense (low=good)

All visualizations courtesy of SharpFootballStats.com. See Table of Contents for definition of stats & coding used. See SharpFootballStats.com for interactive visualizations which break data into more segments, allow customization & user download. Updated weekly throughout the 2016 NFL season.

STATS & VISUALIZATIONS

Indianapolis Colts

Directional Passer Rating Achieved

Receiver	Short Left	Short Middle	Short Right	Deep Left	Deep Middle	Deep Right
Ty Hilton	54	83	60	116	16	71
Donte Moncrief	94	145	63	60	95	15
Coby Fleener	87	80	51	65	114	42
Andre Johnson	75	90	97	96	109	55
Griff Whalen	9	108	75	118	158	
Phillip Dorsett	95	84	60	44	103	4
Dwayne Allen	114	95	53			39
Jack Doyle	79	108	129			

Directional Frequency by Receiver

Receiver	Short Left	Short Middle	Short Right	Deep Left	Deep Middle	Deep Right
Ty Hilton	13%	20%	35%	43%	19%	33%
Donte Moncrief	33%	20%	12%	17%	19%	20%
Coby Fleener	20%	21%	15%	6%	24%	13%
Andre Johnson	14%	14%	13%	23%	14%	18%
Griff Whalen	4%	9%	7%	2%	5%	
Phillip Dorsett	6%	8%	6%	9%	19%	13%
Dwayne Allen	7%	6%	8%			4%
Jack Doyle	4%	2%	4%			

Defense Passer Rating Allowed

Short Left	Short Middle	Short Right	Deep Left	Deep Middle	Deep Right
101	103	95	44	70	83

Offensive Rush Directional Yds/Carry

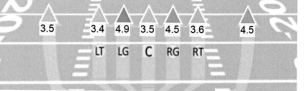

3.5	3.4	4.9	3.5	4.5	3.6	4.5
	LT	LG	C	RG	RT	

Offensive Rush Frequency of Direction

40	32	38	145	39	37	46
	LT	LG	C	RG	RT	

Offensive Explosive Runs by Direction

5	3	3	12	3	2	7
	LT	LG	C	RG	RT	

Defensive Rush Directional Yds/Carry

5.3	4.1	2.0	4.9	4.0	5.0	4.5
	LT	LG	C	RG	RT	

Andrew Luck - 1st Down RTG

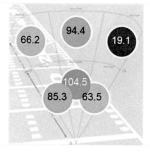

66.2 / 94.4 / 19.1 / 104.5 / 85.3 / 63.5

Andrew Luck - 2nd Down RTG

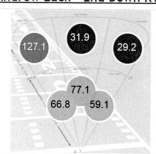

127.1 / 31.9 / 29.2 / 77.1 / 66.8 / 59.1

Andrew Luck - 3rd Down RTG

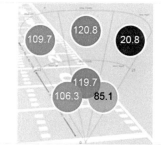

109.7 / 120.8 / 20.8 / 119.7 / 106.3 / 85.1

Andrew Luck - Overall RTG

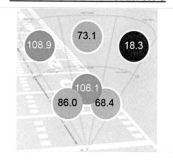

108.9 / 73.1 / 18.3 / 106.1 / 86.0 / 68.4

2nd & Short RUN (1D or not)

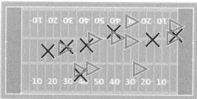

2nd & Short RUN Stats

Run Conv Rk	1D% Run	NFL 1D% Run Avg	Run Freq	NFL Run Freq Avg
28	56%	69%	49%	64%

2nd & Short PASS (1D or not)

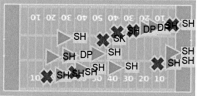

2nd & Short PASS Stats

Pass Conv Rk	1D% Pass	NFL 1D% Pass Avg	Pass Freq	NFL Pass Freq Avg
9	58%	55%	51%	36%

Pass Offense Play Success Rate

60%	49%	46%	43%	55%
39%	47%	67%	39%	63%
31%	47%	36%	50%	41%

Pass Offense Yds/Play

9.6	7.1	7.2	6.2	4.3
6.3	5.5	10.7	8.1	4.9
4.6	6.7	6.7	5.1	3.3

Off. Directional Tendency (% of Plays Left, Middle or Right)

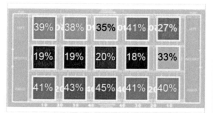

39%	38%	35%	41%	27%
19%	19%	20%	18%	33%
41%	43%	45%	41%	40%

Off. Directional Pass Rate (% of Plays which are Passes)

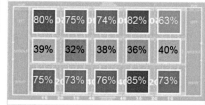

80%	75%	74%	82%	63%
39%	32%	38%	36%	40%
75%	73%	76%	85%	73%

SHARP FOOTBALL STATS

Houston Texans

Coaches

Head Coach: Bill O'Brien (3rd yr)
OC: George Godsey (2nd yr)
DC: Romeo Crennel (3rd yr)

Forecast 2016 Wins

8.5

Past Records

2015: 9-7
2014: 9-7
2013: 2-14

Opponent Strength
Easy — Hard

2016 Schedule & Week by Week Strength of Schedule

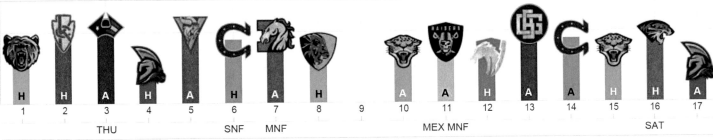

H	H	A	H	A	H	A	H		A	A	H	A	A	H	H	A
1	2	3	4	5	6	7	8	9	10	11	12	13	14	15	16	17

THU   SNF MNF   MEX MNF   SAT

2016 Overview

For several years now, the best part about being on the Texans has been playing in the AFC South. And that won't change this year. When you win 75% of divisional games the last several years, you're exactly halfway toward a winning season in just 37.5% of your annual schedule. But the reality of the 2016 Texans is that the season will hinge on the risky signing of QB Brock Osweiler. While HC Bill O'Brien has been trigger happy with his starting QB since taking over the reigns in Houston, with Ryan Fitzpatrick, Case Keenum, Ryan Mallett, Brian Hoyer, T.J. Yates and Brandon Weeden getting starts in the last 2 years, prior to that the franchise was dedicated to their starting QBs. From inception in 2002 through 2006, the team started 1st overall draft pick David Carr in 75 of 80 possible starts (94%). While the next QB, Matt Schaub, was injured in 2007 and 2008 (and thus started 22 of 32 games), from 2009 through 2012, Schaub started in 58 of 64 possible starts (91%) before getting benched in 2013.

Since 2013, the team has seen 8 QBs start over the 3 years, with two others playing at some point in the game, and no QB started more than 25% of their total games (Fitzpatrick started 12 of the team's 48 regular season games). Clearly, the Texans are looking for that next QB that can saddle up for years to come. Bill O'Brien thinks he found it in Brock Osweiler. They certainly are paying him as such. The Texans shelled out a 4 year, $62M contract for Matt Schaub in 2012, with a guaranteed $29M. After just 2 years, the Texans were done with him and traded Schaub to the Raiders. Their other moves (Fitzpatrick at 2 yrs, $7.25M and Hoyer at 2 yrs, $10.5M) since pale in comparison to the 4 year, $72M contract for Osweiler which includes $37M guaranteed.

At some point, the Texans are likely to transition from a defense-driven team to one which will be forced to rely on its offense more. Remarkably, when holding opponents to below 21 points last year, the Texans went 9-0. When allowing more than 21 points, the Texans went 0-7. They were the only team in the NFL to see such a result. The last 2 years they are 17-2 when holding opponents to below 21 points and 0-13 when allowing more than 21 points. The problem is, even though J.J. Watt is tremendous, looking ahead it is unreasonable to imagine the Texans can continue to hold opponent's below 21 points considering average scoring has been over 21 points per game since 2007. Their defense was the 3rd healthiest in 2015 and is the 7th most expensive in 2016. They did not add much to the defense this offseason, and to expect continued great health is unlikely.

One way for the offense to excel is to be extremely balanced. And by adding RB Lamar Miller, they have a chance to be balanced. Miller was severely underutilized the last few years, but has solid upside. As we know, starting early and playing well on the early downs (1st or 2nd) is huge in terms of efficiency. Last year, Miller's 561 yards on 102 carries (5.5 YPC) led the NFL on early down runs in the first half. The last time O'Brien had a healthy RB was 2014, the same year he had Ryan Fitzpatrick. O'Brien called 52% run in one-score games, the most run-heavy attack of any team the last 3 years. A fresh Lamar Miller will take some burden away from Osweiler and help the Texans offense do what it needs to do to win games, which increasingly may need to be by outscoring their opponent.

Strength of Schedule In Detail

True Strength of Schedule Rank: 10

Hardest Stretches *(1=Hard, 32=Easy)*
Hardest 3 wk Stretch Rk:	**15**
Hardest 4 wk Stretch Rk:	**21**
Hardest 5 wk Stretch Rk:	**10**

Easiest Stretches *(1=Easy, 32=Hard)*
Easiest 3 wk Stretch Rk:	**25**
Easiest 4 wk Stretch Rk:	**29**
Easiest 5 wk Stretch Rk:	**32**

Winning the AFC South for the third time in franchise history gave the Texans the Patriots and Bengals in 2016. The fixed schedule rotation gave the Texans the NFC North and the AFC West. The only reason their overall schedule is not more difficult is four games vs the Titans and Jaguars. They do get to start the year off with three of four home games, one of six teams with that benefit. And instead of playing in Oakland week 11, they play Oakland in Mexico. The Texans almost swept the AFC South the last two years, but their struggles have some in their non-division slate, where they are 10-21 (32%) the last three years, and 4-11 (27%) on the road. This year, success won't come easily, with games at the Patriots, Vikings, Broncos, Packers and Raiders.

2015 Play Tendencies

All Pass %	58%
All Pass Rk	20
All Rush %	42%
All Rush Rk	13
1 Score Pass %	59%
1 Score Pass Rk	16
2014 1 Score Pass %	48%
2014 1 Score Pass Rk	32
Pass Increase %	11%
Pass Increase Rk	1
1 Score Rush %	41%
1 Score Rush Rk	17
Up Pass %	46%
Up Pass Rk	25
Up Rush %	54%
Up Rush Rk	8
Down Pass %	67%
Down Pass Rk	19
Down Rush %	33%
Down Rush Rk	14

The Texans actually passed the ball slightly more last year despite juggling between Brian Hoyer and Ryan Mallett, but that was in large part because of their RB situation. Arian Foster played in 4 games, and they juggled between Alfred Blue, Jonathan Grimes and Chris Polk the rest of the time. Overall they were about league average, but it was a "pick your poison" situation for Bill O'Brien. With Brock Osweiler & Lamar Miller, we should see O'Brien's true colors show through.

2015 Offensive Advanced Metrics

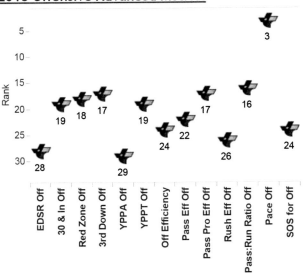

As has been the case for several seasons, the Texans strength continued to be their defense, while their offense (and in particular the passing game) struggled. The Texans were 4th in defensive EDSR but only 28th offensively. They were 10th in yds/pass allowed but 29th in offensive yds/pass. Overall their schedule should have been dealt with adequately. After two tough defenses (KC, CAR) to start the season, they faced a schedule replete with struggling defenses including #32 (NO), #26 (JAC), #25 (MIA), #24 (BUF), #23 (TEN) and #22 (ATL). Against that schedule, there was no reason the pass offense should struggle, as they faced #32, #31, #29, #26 and #24 in pass defense and many middling pass defenses. If Brock Osweiler can help the pass offense, it will be interesting to watch Lamar Miller in the rush offense. HC Bill O'Brien last had a healthy RB in 2014, and he ran the ball 52% of play calls in one-score games, most in the NFL the last 3 years.

2015 Defensive Advanced Metrics

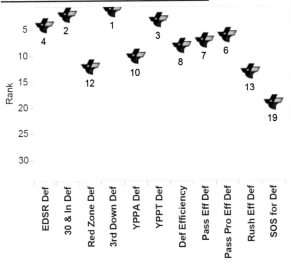

Drafted Players   2016 Draft Grade: **#8** (3.2/4)   PERSONNEL & SPENDING   Houston Texans

Rnd.	Pick #	Pos.	Player	College
1	21	WR	Will Fuller	Notre Dame
2	50	C	Nick Martin	Notre Dame
3	85	WR	Braxton Miller	Ohio State
4	119	RB	Tyler Ervin	San Jose State
5	159	S	K. J. Dillon	West Virginia
5	166	DT	D. J. Reader	Clemson

Free Agents/Trades Added

Player (Position)

Antonio Allen S

Brock Osweiler QB

Jeff Allen G

Lamar Miller RB

Quintin Demps S

Tony Bergstrom C

Other Signed

Player (Position)

Arturo Uzdavinis T
Brennan Scarlett LB
Cleveland Wallace III CB
Duke Thomas CB
Eric Lee LB
Joel Heath DE
Ka'imi Fairbairn K
Richard Leonard CB
Richard Mullaney WR
Ryan Langford LB
Shakeel Rashad LB
Soma Vainuku RB
Stephen Anderson TE
Tevin Jones WR
Tyrell Blanks WR
Ufomba Kamalu DE
Wendall Williams WR

2015 Players Lost

Transaction	Player (Position)
Cut	Arian Foster RB
	B.J. Daniels QB
	Brian Hoyer QB
	Eric Lee LB
	Garrett Graham TE
	Rahim Moore S
Declared Free Agent	Ben Jones C
	Jared Crick DE
	Nate Washington WR

- Not pulling any punches, Bill O'Brien has been a miserable evaluator of QB talent thus far in Houston. In 2014 he signed Ryan Fitzpatrick to a multi-year deal, and then traded him after one season. That same year, in order, he: drafted Tom Savage, traded away TJ Yates, traded for Ryan Mallett, waived Case Keenum, signed Thaddeu Lewis, then re-signed Case Keenum. Last year, it didn't get much better. He took Ryan Mallett, who he traded for, and signed him to a multi year deal with guaranteed money, but then released him during the season. He cut Thaddeus Lewis who he signed the prior year. He traded away Case Keenum, who he signed the prior year. He signed Brian Hoyer to a multi-year deal with $4.75M guaranteed, Kevin Rodgers and TJ Yates (who he traded away the prior year), and finally, claimed Brandon Weeden off of waivers.
- If QBs were drugs, O'Brien's friends and family would be having an intervention for the poor man. The QBs he's acquired are not good QBs. But it's not as if he drafts one, realizes they aren't good, and cuts them. He trades for them. He will sign them off waivers (one man's trash is another man's treasure), practice with them, realize they aren't good & cut them, and then sign them again.
- However, no intervention was scheduled and this past offseason, O'Brien signed Brock Osweiler to a 4 year, $72M deal with $37M guaranteed. Osweiler is a QB who is entering his 5th year, with a total of 7 starts in his career, and whose ratings are below average. O'Brien then cut Brian Hoyer, so despite 9 starts as part of a multi-year deal, Hoyer walked away with his 2015 salary and $4.75M guaranteed.
- On the positive, the move to acquire the underused Lamar Miller was intelligent given the fact Osweiler will now be under center. Miller was not used intelligently in Miami and I think he'll get plenty of touches in Houston., running behind the 5th most expensive offensive line.

Lineup & 2016 Cap Hit

Health Overall & by Unit (2015 v 2014)

2015 Rk	16
2015 AGL	65
Off Rk	25
Def Rk	3
2014 Rk	11
2014 AGL	60

2016 Positional Spending

	All OFF	QB	OL	RB	WR	TE	All DEF	DL	LB	CB	S
2015 Rk	27	25	13	5	31	18	9	14	10	4	28
Rank	27	23	5	14	30	32	7	14	7	14	26
Total	69.5M	14.4M	33.8M	8.5M	9.9M	3.0M	83.1M	27.0M	27.6M	22.0M	6.5M

2016 Offseason Spending

Total Spent	Total Spent Rk	Free Agents #	Free Agents $	Free Agents $ Rk	Waiver #	Waiver $	Waiver $ Rk	Extended #	Sum of Extended $	Sum of Drafted $	Undrafted #	Undrafted $
215M	9	8	139M	4	16	18M	10	1	6M	26M	16	26M

2015 Stats & Fantasy Production

Pos	Player	Ov. Rank	Pos. Rk	Age	Gms	St	Pass Comp	Pass Att	Pass Yds	Pass TD	Pass Int	Rush Att	Rush Yds	Rush YPA	Rush TD	Targ	Recp	Rec Yds	Rec YPC	Rec TDs	Draft King Pts	Fan Duel Pts
QB	Brian Hoyer		25	30	11	9	224	369	2,606	19	7	15	44	3							179	174
RB	Alfred Blue		39	24	15	9						183	698	4	2	16	15	109	7	1	119	104
	Jonathan Grimes		60	26	14						1	56	282	5	1	31	26	173	7	1	92	73
	Chris Polk		65	26	15	2						99	334	3	1	28	16	109	7	1	78	64
	Arian Foster		66	29	4	4						63	163	3		28	22	227	10	2	84	66
WR	DeAndre Hopkins*	10	6	23	16	16										192	111	1,521	14	11	334	276
	Nate Washington		50	32	14	14										94	47	658	14	4	140	113
	Cecil Shorts		68	28	11	4	1	1	21	1		10	47	5		75	42	484	12	2	114	89
	Jaelen Strong		102	21	10	1										24	14	161	12	3	51	41
TE	Ryan Griffin		38	25	9	4										34	20	251	13	2	60	47
	C.J. Fiedorowicz		53	24	16	14										24	17	167	10	1	42	29

ODDS & TRENDS — Houston Texans

Avg Line	+0.5	Pred Wins	8.5	Pred Div Finish	#2

2016 Weekly Betting Lines (wks 1-16)

(-) Favorite   Underdog (+)
-7.0   +8.0

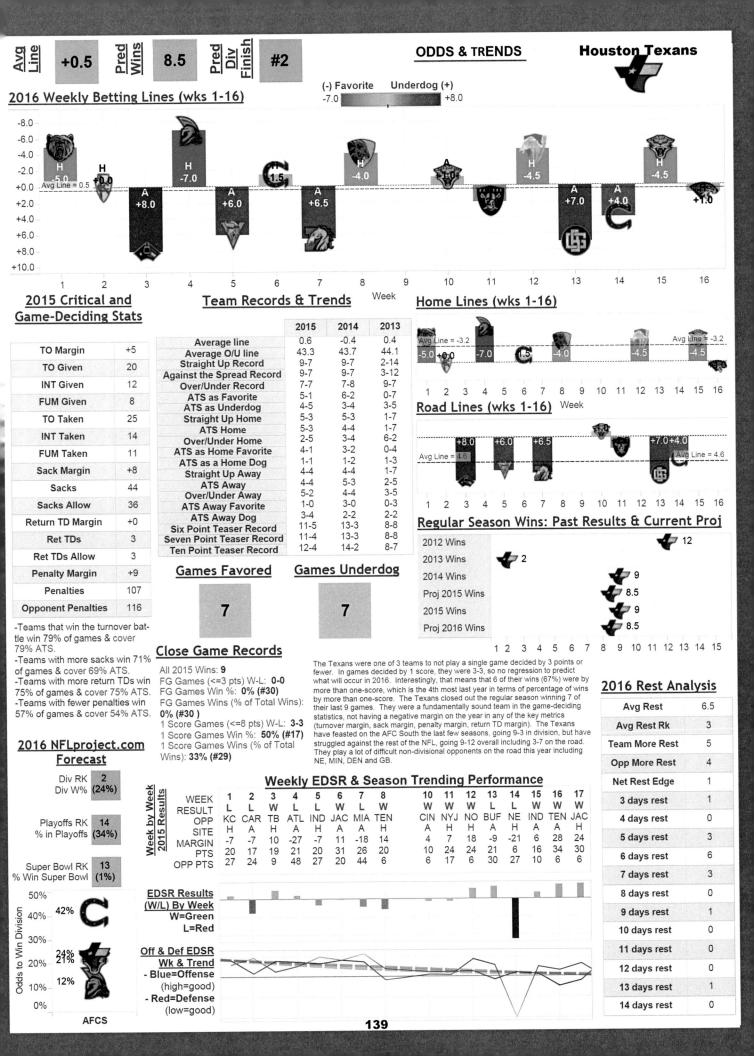

Week 1–16 lines:
- Wk1 H -5.0
- Wk2 H +0.0
- Wk3 A +8.0
- Wk4 H -7.0
- Wk5 A +6.0
- Wk6 C 1.5
- Wk7 A +6.5
- Wk8 H -4.0
- Wk10 A
- Wk11 H -4.5
- Wk12 A +7.0
- Wk13 A +4.0
- Wk14
- Wk15 H -4.5
- Wk16 +1.0

Avg Line = 0.5

2015 Critical and Game-Deciding Stats

TO Margin	+5
TO Given	20
INT Given	12
FUM Given	8
TO Taken	25
INT Taken	14
FUM Taken	11
Sack Margin	+8
Sacks	44
Sacks Allow	36
Return TD Margin	+0
Ret TDs	3
Ret TDs Allow	3
Penalty Margin	+9
Penalties	107
Opponent Penalties	116

-Teams that win the turnover battle win 79% of games & cover 79% ATS.
-Teams with more sacks win 71% of games & cover 69% ATS.
-Teams with more return TDs win 75% of games & cover 75% ATS.
-Teams with fewer penalties win 57% of games & cover 54% ATS.

2016 NFLproject.com Forecast

Div RK	2
Div W%	(24%)
Playoffs RK	14
% in Playoffs	(34%)
Super Bowl RK	13
% Win Super Bowl	(1%)

Odds to Win Division
42%
24%
21%
12%
AFCS

Team Records & Trends

	2015	2014	2013
Average line	0.6	-0.4	0.4
Average O/U line	43.3	43.7	44.1
Straight Up Record	9-7	9-7	2-14
Against the Spread Record	9-7	9-7	3-12
Over/Under Record	7-7	7-8	9-7
ATS as Favorite	5-1	6-2	0-7
ATS as Underdog	4-5	3-4	3-5
Straight Up Home	5-3	5-3	1-7
ATS Home	5-3	4-4	1-7
Over/Under Home	2-5	3-4	6-2
ATS as Home Favorite	4-1	3-2	0-4
ATS as a Home Dog	1-1	1-2	1-3
Straight Up Away	4-4	4-4	1-7
ATS Away	4-4	5-3	2-5
Over/Under Away	5-2	4-4	3-5
ATS Away Favorite	1-0	3-0	0-3
ATS Away Dog	3-4	2-2	2-2
Six Point Teaser Record	11-5	13-3	8-8
Seven Point Teaser Record	11-4	13-3	8-8
Ten Point Teaser Record	12-4	14-2	8-7

Games Favored
7

Games Underdog
7

Close Game Records

All 2015 Wins: 9
FG Games (<=3 pts) W-L: 0-0
FG Games Win %: 0% (#30)
FG Games Wins (% of Total Wins): 0% (#30)
1 Score Games (<=8 pts) W-L: 3-3
1 Score Games Win %: 50% (#17)
1 Score Games Wins (% of Total Wins): 33% (#29)

Home Lines (wks 1-16)

Avg Line = -3.2
-5.0 +0.0 -7.0 1.5 -4.0 -4.5 -4.5
Avg Line = -3.2

Road Lines (wks 1-16)

Avg Line = 4.6
+8.0 +6.0 +6.5 +7.0 +4.0
Avg Line = 4.6

Regular Season Wins: Past Results & Current Proj

2012 Wins	12
2013 Wins	2
2014 Wins	9
Proj 2015 Wins	8.5
2015 Wins	9
Proj 2016 Wins	8.5

The Texans were one of 3 teams to not play a single game decided by 3 points or fewer. In games decided by 1 score, they were 3-3, so no regression to predict what will occur in 2016. Interestingly, that means that 6 of their wins (67%) were by more than one-score, which is the 4th most last year in terms of percentage of wins by more than one-score. The Texans closed out the regular season winning 7 of their last 9 games. They were a fundamentally sound team in the game-deciding statistics, not having a negative margin on the year in any of the key metrics (turnover margin, sack margin, penalty margin, return TD margin). The Texans have feasted on the AFC South the last few seasons, going 9-3 in division, but have struggled against the rest of the NFL, going 9-12 overall including 3-7 on the road. They play a lot of difficult non-divisional opponents on the road this year including NE, MIN, DEN and GB.

2016 Rest Analysis

Avg Rest	6.5
Avg Rest Rk	3
Team More Rest	5
Opp More Rest	4
Net Rest Edge	1
3 days rest	1
4 days rest	0
5 days rest	3
6 days rest	6
7 days rest	3
8 days rest	0
9 days rest	1
10 days rest	0
11 days rest	0
12 days rest	0
13 days rest	1
14 days rest	0

Weekly EDSR & Season Trending Performance

WEEK	1	2	3	4	5	6	7	8		10	11	12	13	14	15	16	17
RESULT	L	L	W	L	L	W	L	W		W	W	W	L	L	W	W	W
OPP	KC	CAR	TB	ATL	IND	JAC	MIA	TEN		CIN	NYJ	NO	BUF	NE	IND	TEN	JAC
SITE	H	A	H	A	H	A	A	H		A	H	A	H	A	H	A	H
MARGIN	-7	-7	10	-27	-7	11	-18	14		4	7	18	-9	-21	6	28	24
PTS	20	17	19	21	20	31	26	20		10	24	24	21	6	16	34	30
OPP PTS	27	24	9	48	27	20	44	6		6	17	6	30	27	10	6	6

EDSR Results (W/L) By Week — W=Green, L=Red

Off & Def EDSR Wk & Trend — Blue=Offense (high=good), Red=Defense (low=good)

139

STATS & VISUALIZATIONS

Houston Texans

Directional Passer Rating Achieved

Receiver	Short Left	Short Middle	Short Right	Deep Left	Deep Middle	Deep Right
DeAndre Hopkins	93	68	94	60	128	110
Nate Washington	76	47	79	83	149	42
Cecil Shorts	73	109	82	109	0	61
Ryan Griffin	70	116	113	87	39	39
C.J. Fiedorowicz	26	110	114			
Jaelen Strong	135	102	89	39	158	5
Keith Mumphery	50	95	64	39	0	118
Garrett Graham	56	33	39	39	39	39
Chandler Worthy	79		72			

Directional Frequency by Receiver

Receiver	Short Left	Short Middle	Short Right	Deep Left	Deep Middle	Deep Right
DeAndre Hopkins	41%	26%	33%	57%	36%	53%
Nate Washington	15%	22%	21%	18%	12%	20%
Cecil Shorts	15%	21%	15%	6%	20%	7%
Ryan Griffin	9%	10%	8%	4%	12%	2%
C.J. Fiedorowicz	4%	4%	9%			
Jaelen Strong	6%	2%	4%	4%	4%	9%
Keith Mumphery	7%	2%	6%	8%	12%	4%
Garrett Graham	1%	11%	2%	2%	4%	4%
Chandler Worthy	1%		2%			

Defense Passer Rating Allowed

Short Left	Short Middle	Short Right	Deep Left	Deep Middle	Deep Right
98	87	79	60	80	53

Offensive Rush Directional Yds/Carry

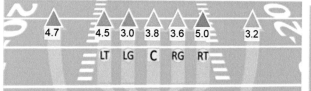

4.7	4.5	3.0	3.8	3.6	5.0	3.2
	LT	LG	C	RG	RT	

Offensive Rush Frequency of Direction

44	54	58	154	54	61	51
	LT	LG	C	RG	RT	

Offensive Explosive Runs by Direction

7	8	3	11	4	7	5
	LT	LG	C	RG	RT	

Defensive Rush Directional Yds/Carry

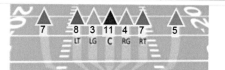

5.2	2.0	4.0	3.6	4.7	5.0	5.7
	LT	LG	C	RG	RT	

Brock Osweiler - 1st Down RTG

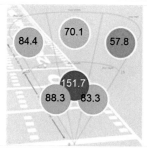

84.4, 70.1, 57.8, 151.7, 88.3, 83.3

Brock Osweiler - 2nd Down RTG

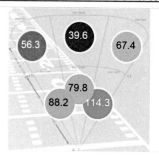

56.3, 39.6, 67.4, 79.8, 88.2, 114.3

2nd & Short RUN (1D or not)

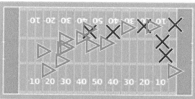

2nd & Short RUN Stats

Run Conv Rk	1D% Run	NFL 1D% Run Avg	Run Freq	NFL Run Freq Avg
17	68%	69%	61%	64%

2nd & Short PASS (1D or not)

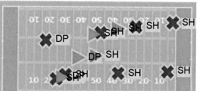

2nd & Short PASS Stats

Pass Conv Rk	1D% Pass	NFL 1D% Pass Avg	Pass Freq	NFL Pass Freq Avg
28	42%	55%	39%	36%

Brock Osweiler - 3rd Down RTG

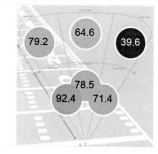

79.2, 64.6, 39.6, 78.5, 92.4, 71.4

Brock Osweiler - Overall RTG

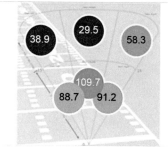

38.9, 29.5, 58.3, 109.7, 88.7, 91.2

Pass Offense Play Success Rate

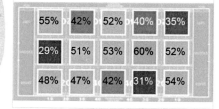

55%	42%	52%	40%	35%
29%	51%	53%	60%	52%
48%	47%	42%	31%	54%

Pass Offense Yds/Play

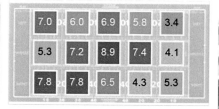

7.0	6.0	6.9	5.8	3.4
5.3	7.2	8.9	7.4	4.1
7.8	7.8	6.5	4.3	5.3

Off. Directional Tendency (% of Plays Left, Middle or Right)

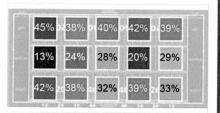

45%	38%	40%	42%	39%
13%	24%	28%	20%	29%
42%	38%	32%	39%	33%

Off. Directional Pass Rate (% of Plays which are Passes)

78%	73%	74%	62%	78%
16%	41%	47%	32%	41%
65%	67%	71%	72%	65%

Jacksonville Jaguars

Coaches
Head Coach: Gus Bradley (4th yr)
OC: Greg Olson (2nd yr)
DC: Todd Walsh (JAC DL) (1st yr)

Forecast 2016 Wins
7

Past Records
2015: 5-11
2014: 3-13
2013: 4-12

Opponent Strength
Easy ——— Hard

2016 Schedule & Week by Week Strength of Schedule

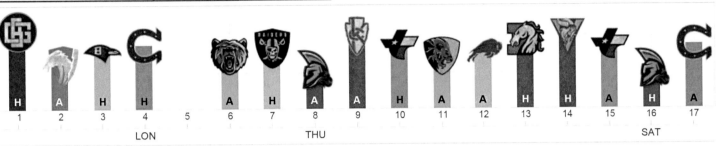

H	A	H	H		A	A	A	A	H	A	A	H	H	A	H	A
1	2	3	4	5	6	7	8	9	10	11	12	13	14	15	16	17

LON (wk 7) · THU (wk 8) · SAT (wk 16)

2016 Overview

For years the Jaguars have been the trendy pick to overachieve after years of posting poor records. Unfortunately, they have never exceeded even 5 wins since 2010, and their last winning season was 2007. The Jaguars made two splashes this offseason. Historically one splash flops, the other earns solid scores. The Jaguars outspent every other team in free agency and it really wasn't close between Jacksonville and even the #3 team. Malik Jackson, Kelvin Beachum, Tashaun Gipson, Chris Ivory and Prince Amukamara. Historically, spending free agency money does not pay off. It seems impossible for it to not help, but when so much of a team's salary cap gets allocated to a handful of new players, it's difficult to build enough depth or hunger to translate into wins.

Fortunately, the Jaguars had an incredible draft and get back 1st round pick from 2015 Dante Fowler as well. Though Jalen Ramsey had surgery to repair his torn meniscus in May, he should be on track to be fine for training camp. They added Myles Jack at the top of the 2nd round. Those 3 players are immediate impact players for the 2016 defense at a very inexpensive price. Factor in that of their first 5 draft picks, all 5 were on the defensive side of the ball, and you can see that through the combination of the draft & free agency, the Jaguars miserable 2015 defense will look (and hopefully perform) much different in 2016. The end result is the Jaguars moved from the 13th most expensive defense to the 2nd most expensive. Defensively, the team has a mix of young and hungry players looking to make a mark blended with veteran players who just received huge paydays. Offensively, the unit is extremely young and raw, built around 3rd year QB Blake Bortles.

The Jaguars should have 3 more years with a QB who is hitting the cap well below what he'll hit it in his 2nd deal. So the question comes: if not now, when? If the Jaguars can't use the massive free agency expenditures to win this year or use it as a platform to make the playoffs in 2017, will it ever happen for Gus Bradley? It is very unlikely that the talent they acquired in free agency sticks around for 3+ yrs.

The modern NFL is a passing league. Looking at teams who improved by approx 5+ wins from one year to the next the last 5 yrs, almost all of them did it via a QB change in that QB's first year: Kirk Cousins, Ryan Fitzpatrick (w NYJ & HOU, in Bowles' 1st & O'Brien's 1st), Carson Palmer (Arians' 1st), Nick Foles (Kelly's 1st) Robert Griffin III, Alex Smith (Reid's 1st), Peyton Manning, Andrew Luck and Andy Dalton. These QBs came in and took their team's from a losing record to a winning one by gaining 5+ more wins vs the prior yr. The only other teams who made such an achievement without a QB change were the 2011 49ers (Harbaugh's 1st), the 2012 Vikings, the 2013 Panthers and the 2015 Panthers. All 3 teams were built on with a run game and strong defense. While the Jaguars want to develop Bortles, they would be wise to let the run game take more off his plate in 2016. The introduction of Chris Ivory should help fix the NFL's worst short yardage game, and make the entire offense more efficient. If the Bradley can take all the new defensive pieces and get them to gel in short order, the defense could improve enough to turn the Jaguars into a winning team. But it won't be easy, and while I think they will improve, the hype surrounding this team for 2016 may be tough to live up to.

Strength of Schedule In Detail

True Strength of Schedule Rank: 14

Hardest Stretches (1=Hard, 32=Easy)
Hardest 3 wk Stretch Rk:	18
Hardest 4 wk Stretch Rk:	23
Hardest 5 wk Stretch Rk:	24

Easiest Stretches (1=Easy, 32=Hard)
Easiest 3 wk Stretch Rk:	21
Easiest 4 wk Stretch Rk:	30
Easiest 5 wk Stretch Rk:	27

Jacksonville's ranking is deceptive – it's not more difficult simply because they play the Titans twice. But looking at the visualization on my website, this schedule is rough. They lose a home game due to playing it in London, and their short week before their Thursday night game in Tennessee kicks off a stretch which sees them play four road games in five weeks. They bring the year to a close with a daunting 5 game stretch which features the Broncos, Vikings, Texans and Colts, but statistically doesn't rank as bad because they play the "easier" game vs the Titans in Jacksonville. Last year the Jaguars played the 31st rated schedule of opposing offenses, but even still, their defense was absolutely terrible. They allowed the Titans, Buccaneers, Texans, Chargers, Bills and Jets to put up 42, 38, 31, 31, 31, and 28 points. The positive for Jacksonville is looking across their schedule, the highest scoring offenses from 2015 they face are the Chiefs and Bills, so that's saying something.

2015 Play Tendencies

All Pass %	65%
All Pass Rk	2
All Rush %	35%
All Rush Rk	31
1 Score Pass %	60%
1 Score Pass Rk	12
2014 1 Score Pass %	60%
2014 1 Score Pass Rk	8
Pass Increase %	1%
Pass Increase Rk	16
1 Score Rush %	40%
1 Score Rush Rk	21
Up Pass %	48%
Up Pass Rk	16
Up Rush %	52%
Up Rush Rk	17
Down Pass %	71%
Down Pass Rk	8
Down Rush %	29%
Down Rush Rk	25

Due to such terrible defense, particularly on 3rd down and in the red zone, the Jaguars had to pass a lot as they trailed a lot. They passed 2nd most of any team, which was a boon to any fantasy enthusiast. But even in one score games, they passed 62% of the time. This, in part, because they were absolutely miserable when handing off to run the football. They were the NFL's worst short yardage run offense.

2015 Offensive Advanced Metrics

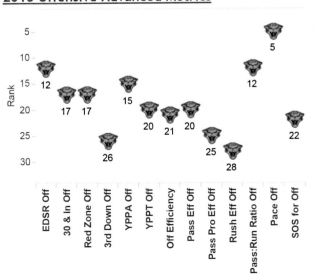

In 2015 Blake Bortles put up big numbers, as did Allen Robinson, but they weren't very efficient numbers. In total, both ranked top 5 from a fantasy-points perspective, but the Jaguars were 20th in pass efficiency and 15th in yds/pass. The Jaguars scored 23 or fewer points in 10 of their 16 games, but against some of the NFL's worst pass defenses, including New Orleans, Tennessee and Tampa Bay, the Jags put up over 27+ points in 5 games, including a 51 point outburst against the Matt Hasselbeck-led Colts. The 2016 Jaguars are being discussed as one of the better paper-defenses in the NFL, so that would be a total reversal from what they did in 2015. They ranked in the bottom 5 in most key metrics, including 31st in pass defense efficiency. And that was against the NFL's 2nd easiest schedule of opposing offenses. The Jags faced Matt Hasselbeck, Brian Hoyer & Marcus Mariota in 6 games, as well as the rookie Jameis Winston & backup QB EJ Manuel.

2015 Defensive Advanced Metrics

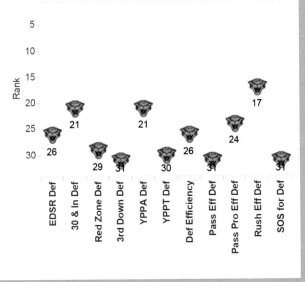

Drafted Players

2016 Draft Grade: #1 (3.7/4)

Rnd.	Pick #	Pos.	Player	College
1	5	CB	Jalen Ramsey	Florida State
2	36	OLB	Myles Jack	UCLA
3	69	DE	Yannick Ngakoue	Maryland
4	103	DT	Sheldon Day	Notre Dame
6	181	DE	Tyrone Holmes	Montana
6	201	QB	Brandon Allen	Arkansas
7	226	DE	Jonathan Woodard	Central Arkansas

PERSONNEL & SPENDING — Jacksonville Jaguars

Free Agents/Trades Added

Player (Position)
Brad Nortman P
Chris Ivory RB
Jeff Linkenbach G
Kelvin Beachum T
Mackenzy Bernadeau G
Malik Jackson DT
Prince Amukamara CB
Tashaun Gipson S

Other Signed

Player (Position)
Bjoern Werner LB
Braedon Bowman TE
Brian Boddy-Calhoun CB
Jaden Oberkrom K
Jamal Robinson WR
Jarrod Wilson S
Jeff Linkenbach G
Max Wittek QB
Mike Hilton CB
Pearce Slater T
Rashod Hill T

2015 Players Lost

Transaction	Player (Position)
Cut	Chance Casey CB
	Chris Clemons DE
	Damian Copeland WR
	Jaden Oberkrom K
	Sergio Brown S
	Toby Gerhart RB
	Zane Beadles G
Declared Free Agent	Andre Branch DE
	Stefen Wisniewski C
Retired	Tanner Hawkinson T

-With Blake Bortles still in his rookie deal, but exhibiting strong abilities, including a rating of over 100 on deep passes (one of the best in the NFL last season) the Jaguars have a lot to look forward to in the 2016 season. Despite their amazing talent at the WR position, they are spending the 4th least cap dollars on the position this year, with youngsters Allen Robinson, Allen Hurns both under the age of 25.

-In large part due to spending the most of any team in the NFL in free agency ($228M) the Jaguars are now the 2nd most expensive defense in the NFL. In came $85.5M Malik Jackson and S Tashaun Gipson, in addition to CB Prince Amukamara.

-To blend with those new pieces via free agency, the Jaguars welcome last year's #3 overall draft pick, edge rusher Dante Fowler Jr, who missed last year with an ACL tear. Then comes their insane haul of the #5 overall pick CB Jalen Ramsey and #36 overall pick LB Myles Jack. The Jaguars went on to add four more defensive players in the draft, thus drafting just one offensive player (QB Brandon Allen) and 6 defensive players. They made their point clear as day - last year's defensive numbers would not cut it, and they used all means possible to improve the talent and let HC Gus Bradley teach & mold them in his image.

-CB Jalen Ramsey had the highest SPARQ score and highest PFF grade of any cornerback in the 2016 NFL Draft.

-While talking about the Jaguars aggressive moves defensively in free agency is fun to discuss and exciting to visualize, spending significant free agency capital (particularly signing a player after he wins a Super Bowl) almost always is a failure.

-Specifically, I question signing RB Chris Ivory to a massive $32M deal. JAC needed help in the run game, but the dollars spent at the RB position are hard to stomach & will be very intrigued to see how Chris Ivory fares in short yardage situations.

Lineup & 2016 Cap Hit

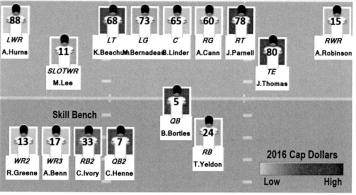

Health Overall & by Unit (2015 v 2014)

2015 Rk	20
2015 AGL	69
Off Rk	12
Def Rk	27
2014 Rk	20
2014 AGL	78

2016 Positional Spending

	All OFF	QB	OL	RB	WR	TE	All DEF	DL	LB	CB	S
2015 Rk	14	22	9	14	29	1	13	3	22	23	26
Rank	29	25	16	19	29	3	2	1	28	18	18
Total	74.4M	11.3M	26.6M	6.7M	17.0M	12.8M	90.5M	44.2M	14.3M	22.0M	10.0M

2016 Offseason Spending

Total Spent	Total Spent Rk	Free Agents #	Free Agents $	Free Agents $ Rk	Waiver #	Waiver $	Waiver $ Rk	Extended #	Sum of Extended $	Sum of Drafted $	Undrafted #	Undrafted $
354M	2	11	230M	1	16	20M	6	2	49M	40M	9	15M

2015 Stats & Fantasy Production

Pos	Player	Ov. Rank	Pos. Rk	Age	Gms	St	Pass Comp	Pass Att	Pass Yds	Pass TD	Pass Int	Rush Att	Rush Yds	Rush YPA	Rush TD	Targ	Recp	Rec Yds	Rec YPC	Rec TDs	Draft King Pts	Fan Duel Pts
QB	Blake Bortles	34	4	23	16	16	355	606	4,428	35	18	52	310	6	2						343	332
RB	T.J. Yeldon		27	22	12	12						182	740	4	2	46	36	279	8	1	162	138
	Denard Robinson		72	25	13	3						67	266	4	1	30	21	164	8		75	58
WR	Allen Robinson*	7	4	22	16	16										151	80	1,400	18	14	307	264
	Allen Hurns	35	14	24	15	14										105	64	1,031	16	10	229	193
	Bryan Walters	95	28	11	1	1					1					45	32	368	12	1	78	59
	Marqise Lee	109	24	10	1							5	38	8		32	13	191	13		47	36
	Rashad Greene	123	23	9												35	19	93	5	2	46	37
TE	Julius Thomas	15	27	12	11											80	46	455	10	5	125	99
	Clay Harbor	51	28	15	2											20	14	149	11	1	40	30
	Marcedes Lewis	52	31	16	16											37	16	226	14		42	31

ODDS & TRENDS — Jacksonville Jaguars

Avg Line +2.4	**Pred Wins** 7	**Pred Div Finish** #3	

2016 Weekly Betting Lines (wks 1-16)

(-) Favorite   Underdog (+)
-4.5 ———— +7.0

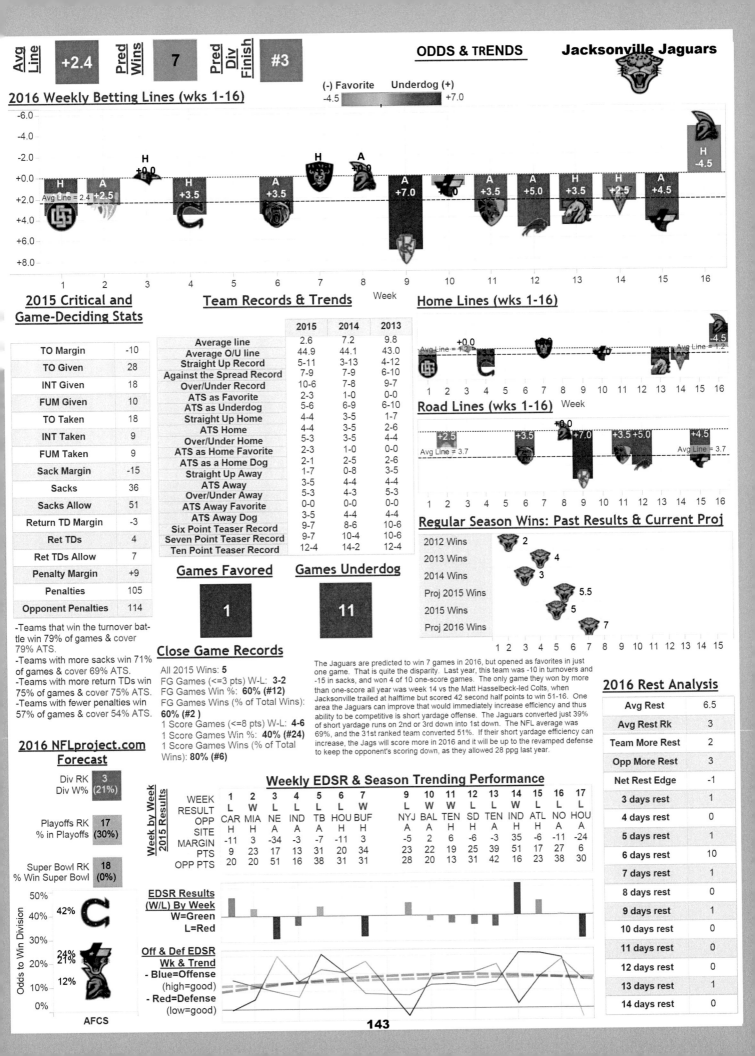

Week: 1 2 3 4 5 6 7 8 9 10 11 12 13 14 15 16

Lines by week:
- 1: H
- 2: A +2.5
- 3: H +0.0
- 4: H +3.5
- 6: A +3.5
- 7: H (Raiders)
- 8: A +0.0
- 9: A +7.0
- 10: +0.0
- 11: A +3.5
- 12: A +5.0
- 13: H +3.5
- 14: H +2.5
- 15: A +4.5
- 16: H -4.5

Avg Line = 2.4

2015 Critical and Game-Deciding Stats

TO Margin	-10
TO Given	28
INT Given	18
FUM Given	10
TO Taken	18
INT Taken	9
FUM Taken	9
Sack Margin	-15
Sacks	36
Sacks Allow	51
Return TD Margin	-3
Ret TDs	4
Ret TDs Allow	7
Penalty Margin	+9
Penalties	105
Opponent Penalties	114

-Teams that win the turnover battle win 79% of games & cover 79% ATS.
-Teams with more sacks win 71% of games & cover 69% ATS.
-Teams with more return TDs win 75% of games & cover 75% ATS.
-Teams with fewer penalties win 57% of games & cover 54% ATS.

2016 NFLproject.com Forecast

Div RK	3
Div W%	(21%)
Playoffs RK	17
% in Playoffs	(30%)
Super Bowl RK	18
% Win Super Bowl	(0%)

Odds to Win Division — AFCS
- 42% C
- 24%
- 21%
- 12%

Team Records & Trends

	2015	2014	2013
Average line	2.6	7.2	9.8
Average O/U line	44.9	44.1	43.0
Straight Up Record	5-11	3-13	4-12
Against the Spread Record	7-9	7-9	6-10
Over/Under Record	10-6	7-8	9-7
ATS as Favorite	2-3	1-0	0-0
ATS as Underdog	5-6	6-9	6-10
Straight Up Home	4-4	3-5	1-7
ATS Home	4-4	3-5	2-6
Over/Under Home	5-3	3-5	4-4
ATS as Home Favorite	2-3	1-0	0-0
ATS as a Home Dog	2-1	2-5	2-6
Straight Up Away	1-7	0-8	3-5
ATS Away	3-5	4-4	4-4
Over/Under Away	5-3	4-3	5-3
ATS Away Favorite	0-0	0-0	0-0
ATS Away Dog	3-5	4-4	4-4
Six Point Teaser Record	9-7	8-6	10-6
Seven Point Teaser Record	9-7	10-4	10-6
Ten Point Teaser Record	12-4	14-2	12-4

Games Favored
1

Games Underdog
11

Close Game Records

All 2015 Wins: 5
FG Games (<=3 pts) W-L: 3-2
FG Games Win %: 60% (#12)
FG Games Wins (% of Total Wins): 60% (#2)
1 Score Games (<=8 pts) W-L: 4-6
1 Score Games Win %: 40% (#24)
1 Score Games Wins (% of Total Wins): 80% (#6)

The Jaguars are predicted to win 7 games in 2016, but opened as favorites in just one game. That is quite the disparity. Last year, this team was -10 in turnovers and -15 in sacks, and won 4 of 10 one-score games. The only game they won by more than one-score all year was week 14 vs the Matt Hasselbeck-led Colts, when Jacksonville trailed at halftime but scored 42 second half points to win 51-16. One area the Jaguars can improve that would immediately increase efficiency and thus their ability to be competitive is short yardage offense. The Jaguars converted just 39% of short yardage runs on 2nd or 3rd down into 1st down. The NFL average was 69%, and the 31st ranked team converted 51%. If their short yardage efficiency can increase, the Jags will score more in 2016 and it will be up to the revamped defense to keep the opponent's scoring down, as they allowed 28 ppg last year.

Home Lines (wks 1-16)

Avg Line = 1.2
Week

Road Lines (wks 1-16)

+2.5, +3.5, +0.0, +7.0, +3.5, +5.0, +4.5
Avg Line = 3.7

Regular Season Wins: Past Results & Current Proj

2012 Wins	2
2013 Wins	4
2014 Wins	3
Proj 2015 Wins	5.5
2015 Wins	5
Proj 2016 Wins	7

1 2 3 4 5 6 7 8 9 10 11 12 13 14 15

2016 Rest Analysis

Avg Rest	6.5
Avg Rest Rk	3
Team More Rest	2
Opp More Rest	3
Net Rest Edge	-1
3 days rest	1
4 days rest	0
5 days rest	1
6 days rest	10
7 days rest	1
8 days rest	0
9 days rest	1
10 days rest	0
11 days rest	0
12 days rest	0
13 days rest	0
14 days rest	0

Weekly EDSR & Season Trending Performance

WEEK	1	2	3	4	5	6	7	9	10	11	12	13	14	15	16	17
RESULT	L	W	L	L	L	L	W	L	W	W	L	L	W	L	L	L
OPP	CAR	MIA	NE	IND	TB	HOU	BUF	NYJ	BAL	TEN	SD	TEN	IND	ATL	NO	HOU
SITE	H	H	A	A	H	H	H	A	A	H	A	H	H	A	H	A
MARGIN	-11	3	-34	-3	-7	-11	3	-5	2	6	-6	-3	35	-6	-11	-24
PTS	9	23	17	13	31	20	34	23	22	19	25	39	51	17	27	6
OPP PTS	20	20	51	16	38	31	31	28	20	13	31	42	16	23	38	30

(Week by Week 2015 Results)

EDSR Results (W/L) By Week W=Green L=Red

Off & Def EDSR Wk & Trend
- Blue=Offense (high=good)
- Red=Defense (low=good)

STATS & VISUALIZATIONS

Jacksonville Jaguars

Directional Passer Rating Achieved

Receiver	Short Left	Short Middle	Short Right	Deep Left	Deep Middle	Deep Right
Allen Robinson	60	130	87	103	90	70
Allen Hurns	50	152	69	118	137	117
Julius Thomas	90	102	56	40	109	39
Bryan Walters	88	104	64	158	116	118
Rashad Greene	105	97	70		39	39
Marcedes Lewis	42	47	39		56	39
Marqise Lee	56	83	109	39	52	39
Clay Harbor	64	90	86		118	118
Nic Jacobs				56	39	

Directional Frequency by Receiver

Receiver	Short Left	Short Middle	Short Right	Deep Left	Deep Middle	Deep Right
Allen Robinson	19%	18%	29%	54%	24%	54%
Allen Hurns	15%	17%	24%	24%	26%	24%
Julius Thomas	21%	23%	13%	14%	9%	5%
Bryan Walters	12%	9%	10%	4%	12%	2%
Rashad Greene	10%	5%	8%		6%	7%
Marcedes Lewis	13%	10%	5%		12%	2%
Marqise Lee	3%	11%	8%	2%	9%	5%
Clay Harbor	6%	7%	3%		3%	2%
Nic Jacobs				1%	2%	

Defense Passer Rating Allowed

Short Left	Short Middle	Short Right	Deep Left	Deep Middle	Deep Right
91	126	80	103	127	71

Offensive Rush Directional Yds/Carry

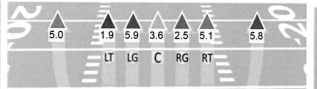

	LT	LG	C	RG	RT	
5.0	1.9	5.9	3.6	2.5	5.1	5.8

Offensive Rush Frequency of Direction

	LT	LG	C	RG	RT	
53	19	30	136	39	19	52

Offensive Explosive Runs by Direction

	LT	LG	C	RG	RT	
13	4	14	2	2		9

Defensive Rush Directional Yds/Carry

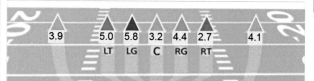

	LT	LG	C	RG	RT	
3.9	5.0	5.8	3.2	4.4	2.7	4.1

Blake Bortles - 1st Down RTG

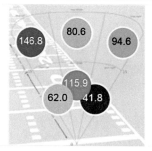

146.8 80.6 94.6
115.9
62.0 41.8

Blake Bortles - 3rd Down RTG

58.0 129.2 53.6
131.3
45.8 68.9

Blake Bortles - 2nd Down RTG

93.8 104.2 96.3
104.7
111.0 112.8

Blake Bortles - Overall RTG

109.2 100.1 90.3
114.9
77.7 74.4

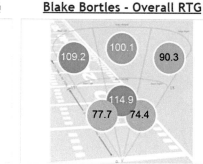

2nd & Short RUN (1D or not)

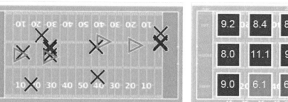

2nd & Short RUN Stats

Run Conv Rk	1D% Run	NFL 1D% Run Avg	Run Freq	NFL Run Freq Avg
32	25%	69%	43%	64%

2nd & Short PASS (1D or not)

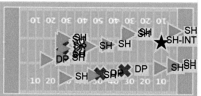

2nd & Short PASS Stats

Pass Conv Rk	1D% Pass	NFL 1D% Pass Avg	Pass Freq	NFL Pass Freq Avg
3	76%	55%	57%	36%

Pass Offense Play Success Rate

34%	47%	53%	50%	46%
56%	68%	61%	56%	61%
46%	43%	40%	53%	45%

Pass Offense Yds/Play

9.2	8.4	8.7	5.7	3.6
8.0	11.1	9.1	8.1	6.1
9.0	6.1	6.9	7.7	3.1

Off. Directional Tendency (% of Plays Left, Middle or Right)

37%	31%	34%	40%	31%
22%	23%	25%	24%	25%
41%	46%	41%	36%	44%

Off. Directional Pass Rate (% of Plays which are Passes)

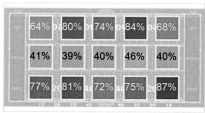

64%	80%	74%	84%	68%
41%	39%	40%	46%	40%
77%	81%	72%	75%	87%

Tennessee Titans

Coaches

Head Coach: Mike Mularkey (TEN TE) (1st yr)
OC: Terry Robiskie (ATL WR) (1st yr)
DC: Ray Horton (3rd yr)

Forecast 2016 Wins

5.5

Past Records

2015: 3-13
2014: 2-14
2013: 7-9

Opponent Strength
Easy — Hard

2016 Schedule & Week by Week Strength of Schedule

H	H	H	A	A		H	H	A	H	A	A		H	A	A	H
1	2	3	4	5	6	7	8	9	10	11	12	13	14	15	16	17

THU   SAT

2016 Overview

For just the second time in the last 25 years, an NFL team ended the season allowing 30 or more points to opponents in their last five games of the year. It was an ending most fans in Tennessee would like to forget. The Titans allowed 423 points last year (just over 26 per gm). Remarkably, five teams allowed more points. But unlike teams like the Saints, Giants and Eagles, who are capable of outscoring opponents to make up for defensive issues, the Titans don't have that type of offense. The Titans have won just 2 of 27 games (7%) when allowing over 14 points in a game the last two seasons, the worst mark in the NFL (by far).

Tennessee needed a move to help both sides of the ball, and they hope they made the right one in trading for DeMarco Murray. In doing so they hope to do their best impression of the 2014 Dallas Cowboys. The parallels, beyond the same running back, are interesting: the 2013 Cowboys defense ranked 30th in efficiency, allowed the 2nd most yds/drive & 3rd most points/drive. To improve in 2014 they altered their offense to help their defense. In 2013, in one-score games, the Cowboys called 66% pass plays (2nd most). They shifted in 2014 to call 50% runs, the 4th largest run rate in the NFL. It was a 16% shift from pass to run. It enabled Dallas to use up over 3 mins/drive (2nd best). They gained almost 36 yds/drive (4th best). By gaining more yards and eating more clock, the Cowboys inevitably were more efficient at scoring, so their defense was not playing in large deficits as often. The defense was fresher, and opponents had to play more desperate offensively given their own limited time of possession and game score. That resulted in takeaways for the defense, and they stole 0.17 turnovers/drive, the most of any team in the NFL (and the team who wins the turnover battle wins 79% of games).

The 2015 Titans were more pass heavy than average when Mariota was healthy, calling pass plays 61% of the time in one-score games through week 5, a high rate for a rookie QB. After his injury they dropped that rate to 57%. While it helped save Mariota from more hits, the Titans' run game was missing in action. In those 7 games, handoffs to running backs in one-score games generated just 2.9 yds/carry (NFL avg was 4 yds/carry). Due to this inefficiency the Titans faced third and long often. Tennessee averaged 7.8 yards to go on 3rd down, the third worst distance to go in the NFL. Inevitably the Titans had the second highest rate of 3-and-outs in the NFL last year, and the 26th rated time of possession per drive.

Murray should help the Titans in all of these areas if run plays are called to his strengths: run the ball more efficiently, call more runs and increase time of possession. It will also result in more manageable third downs. Even in a bad 2015 season, Murray was the best short yardage RB in the NFL last season. While in theory this move could help the Titans both offensively and defensively, producing a record like that of the 2014 Dallas Cowboys is a stretch because of two factors. The Cowboys also have a better offensive line and they have a veteran, savvy quarterback in Tony Romo. The Titans hope one day Marcus Mariota can emulate Tony Romo, but he has a long way to go. Even if not an exact replication, any change that mimics the 2014 Cowboys would benefit the Titans' offense and defense alike.

Strength of Schedule In Detail

True Strength of Schedule Rank: 17

Hardest Stretches *(1=Hard, 32=Easy)*
Hardest 3 wk Stretch Rk:	27
Hardest 4 wk Stretch Rk:	24
Hardest 5 wk Stretch Rk:	30

Easiest Stretches *(1=Easy, 32=Hard)*
Easiest 3 wk Stretch Rk:	13
Easiest 4 wk Stretch Rk:	4
Easiest 5 wk Stretch Rk:	2

Ranking with the 3rd hardest ending to the year (vs DEN, @ KC, @ JAX, vs HOU), Tennessee must make a mark earlier in the season. They have a chance during a very nice 5-week stretch from weeks 5-9, which is the 2nd easiest 5-week stretch of any team (@ MIA, vs CLE, vs IND, vs JAX, @ SD) and features a 3-game home stand.

2015 Play Tendencies

All Pass %	62%
All Pass Rk	11
All Rush %	38%
All Rush Rk	22
1 Score Pass %	58%
1 Score Pass Rk	18
2014 1 Score Pass %	57%
2014 1 Score Pass Rk	18
Pass Increase %	1%
Pass Increase Rk	14
1 Score Rush %	42%
1 Score Rush Rk	15
Up Pass %	45%
Up Pass Rk	26
Up Rush %	55%
Up Rush Rk	7
Down Pass %	68%
Down Pass Rk	15
Down Rush %	32%
Down Rush Rk	18

Ideally, the Titans would have run the football more often but the problem was they trailed often. When leading, the Titans ran the ball 55% of the time, 7th most in the NFL. Their pass frequency in one score games was essentially identical to what it was in 2014, so they didn't necessarily shield the young Mariota any more than prior QBs. They tried to stay balanced even when down, passing just 15th most often.

2015 Offensive Advanced Metrics

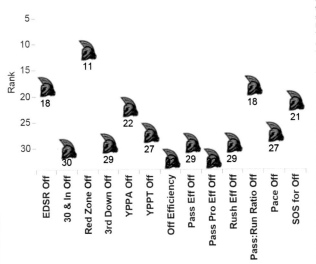

Suggesting that the Titans struggled last year would be an understatement. Offensively, that shouldn't come as much of a surprise. No team in 2015 had a less expensive offensive roster. They had a rookie QB under center, who then was injured due to protection issues. Their leading RB was 24 year old Antonio Andrews. Their leading WR was 22 year old Dorial Green-Beckham. So it's no surprise they ranked dead last in overall offensive efficiency and dead last in pass protection, even against a below average schedule. On the bright side, they finished 18th in EDSR and 11th in the red zone. What is more of a surprise is how bad their defense was, given the fact the unit was the 10th most expensive in 2015. The unit struggled almost everywhere, but was put in bad spots thanks to the offense, which the poor yds/point ranking shows. They certainly did not live up to their billing from a cost perspective - but 15th in EDSR defense was a positive.

2015 Defensive Advanced Metrics

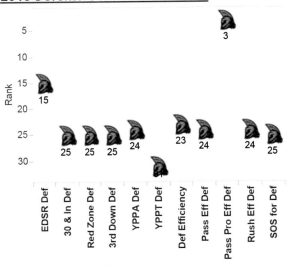

145

Drafted Players

2016 Draft Grade: #14 (3.1/4)

Rnd.	Pick #	Pos.	Player	College
1	8	OT	Jack Conklin	Michigan State
2	33	OLB	Kevin Dodd	Clemson
2	43	DT	Austin Johnson	Penn State
2	45	RB	Derrick Henry	Alabama
3	64	S	Kevin Byard	Middle Tennessee State
5	140	WR	Tajae Sharpe	UMass
5	157	CB	LeShaun Sims	Southern Utah
6	193	G	Sebastian Tretola	Arkansas
7	222	OLB	Aaron Wallace	UCLA
7	253	CB	Kalan Reed	Southern Miss

PERSONNEL & SPENDING — Tennessee Titans

Free Agents/Trades Added

Player (Position)
Antwon Blake CB
Ben Jones C
Brice McCain CB
DeMarco Murray RB
Matt Cassel QB
Rashad Johnson S
Rishard Matthews WR
Sean Spence LB

Other Signed

Player (Position)
Aldrick Rosas K
Alex Ellis TE
Antwaun Woods NT
Ben Roberts WR
Bennett Okotcha CB
Iosia Iosia DE
Lamarcus Brutus S
Mehdi Abdesmad DE
Mike Smith DE
Morgan Burns CB
Nick Ritcher T
Rashon Ceaser WR
Sam Bergen RB
Sam Carlson T
Terrell Lathan DE
Tyler Marz T

2015 Players Lost

Transaction	Player (Position)
Cut	Brice McCain CB
	Damaris Johnson WR
	Iosia Iosia DE
	Kevin Greene TE
	Michael Griffin S
	Rashon Ceaser WR
	Steven Clarke CB
	Zach Mettenberger QB
Declared Free Agent	Coty Sensabaugh CB

- 2016 should show whether DeMarco Murray was a product of the line in Dallas, or if 2015 in Philadelphia was just a horrible season for him and most every Eagles player. Murray averaged just 3.6 yds/carry in Philadelphia, but between the scheme and the usage, he was not handled well by Chip Kelly.
- Last year DeMarco Murray had 15 carries on 3rd or 4th down with 1-2 yards to go. He gained first downs all 15 times. He helped the Eagles (as a team) to convert 89% on such plays, the best rate in the NFL on such plays. The NFL average was a 69% conversion rate. The Titans were dead last in the NFL, converting only 37% on 3rd or 4th down with 1-2 yards to go.
- The Titans traded away their 1st overall draft pick this past season, and so far GM Jon Robinson has made multiple moves that bleed intelligence and savvy, when so many GMs seemingly don't understand worth and value.
- That said, the move to sign Mike Mularkey as the HC after letting him take over mid-season last year was a move that did not impress. While building around the offensive line & letting the run game assist a young QB sounds good in theory, the manner in which the Titans are built financially does not reflect that same strategy.
- The 2014 Cowboys, who the 2016 Titans may be attempting to replicate, had one of the least expensive defenses in the NFL, which was inexpensive throughout except at the CB position, where they spent the most of any team. They needed the offense (which was the more expensive unit) to carry the load and let the CBs make plays with a lead.
- The Titans have one of the most expensive defenses in the NFL & their offense is 26th (OLine = 25th). It will be hard for that line to perform well enough to play the style that the 2014 Cowboys played, so the Titans will need their own identity. If they can't produce points & can't control the clock well enough, they'll employ a more aerial attack to score faster, which goes against the philosophy they seem to desire under HC Mike Mularkey.

Lineup & 2016 Cap Hit

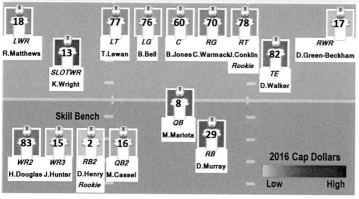

Health Overall & by Unit (2015 v 2014)

2015 Rk	18
2015 AGL	65
Off Rk	20
Def Rk	13
2014 Rk	22
2014 AGL	80

2016 Positional Spending

	All OFF	QB	OL	RB	WR	TE	All DEF	DL	LB	CB	S
2015 Rk	32	30	31	32	20	5	10	13	17	11	4
Rank	26	27	28	9	9	7	10	16	8	9	17
Total	74.5M	8.0M	20.9M	10.1M	22.5M	12.9M	80.1M	22.6M	24.6M	22.0M	10.9M

2016 Offseason Spending

Total Spent	Total Spent Rk	Free Agents #	Free Agents $	Free Agents $ Rk	Waiver #	Waiver $	Waiver $ Rk	Extended #	Sum of Extended $	Sum of Drafted $	Undrafted #	Undrafted $
150M	21	8	53M	17	8	11M	20	3	18M	44M	16	24M

2015 Stats & Fantasy Production

Pos	Player	Ov. Rank	Pos. Rk	Age	Gms	St	Pass Comp	Pass Att	Pass Yds	Pass TD	Pass Int	Rush Att	Rush Yds	Rush YPA	Rush TD	Targ	Recp	Rec Yds	Rec YPC	Rec TDs	Draft King Pts	Fan Duel Pts
QB	Marcus Mariota		22	22	12	12	230	370	2,818	19	10	34	252	7	2	1	1	41	41	1	227	215
	Zach Mettenberger		40	24	7	4	101	166	935	4	7	9	8	1	1						54	49
RB	Antonio Andrews		44	24	14	10	1	1	41	1		143	520	4	3	29	21	174	8		119	102
	Dexter McCluster		61	27	11	2						55	247	4		41	31	260	8	1	100	76
	Bishop Sankey		75	23	13	3						47	193	4		22	14	139	10	1	64	50
WR	Dorial Green-Beckha..		54	22	16	5										67	32	549	17	4	116	97
	Kendall Wright		74	26	10	9						5	17	3		60	36	408	11	3	100	79
	Harry Douglas		87	31	14	12						1	-6	-6		72	36	411	11	2	69	69
	Justin Hunter		104	24	9	5										31	22	264	12	1	57	43
TE	Delanie Walker*	19	5	31	15	10						1	36	36		133	94	1,088	12	6	247	197
	Anthony Fasano		36	31	16	11										42	26	289	11	2	70	54
	Craig Stevens		46	31	16	11										16	12	121	10	2	39	30

ODDS & TRENDS — Tennessee Titans

Avg Line	Pred Wins	Pred Div Finish
+4.5	5.5	#4

2016 Weekly Betting Lines (wks 1-16)

(-) Favorite Underdog (+)
-3.5 ————— +9.0

Weekly lines:
- Wk 1: H +3.0
- Wk 2: A +5.0
- Wk 3: H
- Wk 4: A +7.0
- Wk 5: A +5.5
- Wk 6: H -3.5
- Wk 7: H +3.5
- Wk 8: H 0.0
- Wk 9: A +4.5
- Wk 10: H +7.5
- Wk 11: A +8.0
- Wk 12: A +5.0
- Wk 14: H +5.5
- Wk 15: A +9.0
- Wk 16: A +4.5

Avg Line = 4.5

Scale: -4.0, -2.0, +0.0, +4.0, +6.0, +8.0, +10.0
Weeks: 1 2 3 4 5 6 7 8 9 10 11 12 13 14 15 16

2015 Critical and Game-Deciding Stats

TO Margin	-14
TO Given	33
INT Given	17
FUM Given	16
TO Taken	19
INT Taken	11
FUM Taken	8
Sack Margin	-15
Sacks	39
Sacks Allow	54
Return TD Margin	-4
Ret TDs	2
Ret TDs Allow	6
Penalty Margin	+19
Penalties	93
Opponent Penalties	112

-Teams that win the turnover battle win 79% of games & cover 79% ATS.
-Teams with more sacks win 71% of games & cover 69% ATS.
-Teams with more return TDs win 75% of games & cover 75% ATS.
-Teams with fewer penalties win 57% of games & cover 54% ATS.

2016 NFLproject.com Forecast

Div RK	4
Div W%	(12%)
Playoffs RK	20
% in Playoffs	(18%)
Super Bowl RK	26
% Win Super Bowl	(0%)

Odds to Win Division (AFCS): 42%, 24%, 21%, 12%
Scale: 0% 10% 20% 30% 40% 50%

Team Records & Trends

	2015	2014	2013
Average line	3.7	4.3	1.2
Average O/U line	43.7	44.6	42.8
Straight Up Record	3-13	2-14	7-9
Against the Spread Record	6-10	3-13	6-9
Over/Under Record	7-6	6-10	9-6
ATS as Favorite	1-1	0-2	3-3
ATS as Underdog	5-8	3-10	3-6
Straight Up Home	1-7	1-7	3-5
ATS Home	4-4	1-7	1-6
Over/Under Home	3-3	3-5	6-2
ATS as Home Favorite	1-1	0-2	1-2
ATS as a Home Dog	3-3	1-4	0-4
Straight Up Away	2-6	1-7	4-4
ATS Away	2-6	2-6	5-3
Over/Under Away	4-3	3-5	3-4
ATS Away Favorite	0-0	0-0	2-1
ATS Away Dog	2-5	2-6	3-2
Six Point Teaser Record	10-6	8-8	12-3
Seven Point Teaser Record	10-6	8-8	13-3
Ten Point Teaser Record	10-5	10-6	13-2

Games Favored: 1

Games Underdog: 13

Close Game Records

All 2015 Wins: **3**
FG Games (<=3 pts) W-L: **1-4**
FG Games Win %: **20% (#28)**
FG Games Wins (% of Total Wins): **33% (#8)**
1 Score Games (<=8 pts) W-L: **2-6**
1 Score Games Win %: **25% (#29)**
1 Score Games Wins (% of Total Wins): **67% (#15)**

Home Lines (wks 1-16)

Avg Line = 2.6
Lines: 3.5, -3.5, +0.0
Weeks: 1 2 3 4 5 6 7 8 9 10 11 12 13 14 15 16

Road Lines (wks 1-16)

Avg Line = 6.1
Lines: +5.0, +7.0, +5.5, +4.5, +8.0, +5.0, +9.0, +4.5
Weeks: 1 2 3 4 5 6 7 8 9 10 11 12 13 14 15 16

Regular Season Wins: Past Results & Current Proj

2012 Wins	6
2013 Wins	7
2014 Wins	2
Proj 2015 Wins	5
2015 Wins	3
Proj 2016 Wins	5.5

Scale: 1 2 3 4 5 6 7 8 9 10 11 12 13 14 15

The Titans are projected to win more games in 2016 than in 2013 and 2014 combined. That said, they still are projected to finish last in the AFC South thanks to the projected improvement of the Jacksonville Jaguars. Playing a big role in their poor performance last year, on top of their massive inefficiencies on both sides of the ball, was their performance in critical stats such as turnover margin (-14), sack margin (-15) and return TD margin (-4). Even a team with average efficiency would lose with that type of performance in those key metrics. The Titans must improve not just efficiency, but those areas as well. Projected to win 5.5 games, they opened as favorites in just 1 game this year, a home game against the Browns. The Titans are a combined 2-14 at home the last two seasons, so they haven't given the home crowd much to cheer for. The additions of RBs DeMarco Murray and Derrick Henry should improve the potency of the run game & hopefully lead to a trickle down affect of overall improvement on both sides of the ball.

2016 Rest Analysis

Avg Rest	6.5
Avg Rest Rk	3
Team More Rest	2
Opp More Rest	4
Net Rest Edge	-2
3 days rest	1
4 days rest	0
5 days rest	1
6 days rest	10
7 days rest	1
8 days rest	0
9 days rest	1
10 days rest	0
11 days rest	0
12 days rest	0
13 days rest	1
14 days rest	0

Weekly EDSR & Season Trending Performance

Week by Week 2015 Results	1	2	3	5	6	7	8	9	10	11	12	13	14	15	16	17
RESULT	W	L	L	L	L	L	L	W	L	L	L	W	L	L	L	L
OPP	TB	CLE	IND	BUF	MIA	ATL	HOU	NO	CAR	JAC	OAK	JAC	NYJ	NE	HOU	IND
SITE	A	A	H	H	H	A	A	A	H	A	H	A	H	A	A	A
MARGIN	28	-14	-2	-1	-28	-3	-14	6	-17	-6	-3	3	-22	-17	-28	-6
PTS	42	14	33	13	10	7	6	34	10	13	21	42	8	16	6	24
OPP PTS	14	28	35	14	38	10	20	28	27	19	24	39	30	33	34	30

EDSR Results (W/L) By Week
W=Green
L=Red

Off & Def EDSR Wk & Trend
- Blue=Offense (high=good)
- Red=Defense (low=good)

147

STATS & VISUALIZATIONS

Tennessee Titans

Directional Passer Rating Achieved

Receiver	Short Left	Short Middle	Short Right	Deep Left	Deep Middle	Deep Right
Delanie Walker	92	136	58	109	94	104
Harry Douglas	117	72	85	39	39	17
Kendall Wright	113	46	116	0	122	54
Dorial Green-Beckha..	97	121	75	14	158	38
Anthony Fasano	109	63	73	53		56
Justin Hunter	91	118	125	109	39	91
Craig Stevens	79	148	69	118	158	
Jalston Fowler	100		136			
Chase Coffman	118	95	56			
Phillip Supernaw	39	100	116			
Andrew Turzilli			95	118		
Tre McBride	122		39			39
Rico Richardson			39	39		39

Marcus Mariota – 1st Down RTG
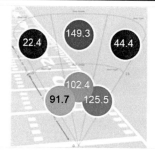

Marcus Mariota – 3rd Down RTG
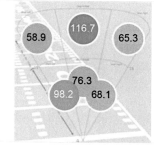

Directional Frequency by Receiver

Receiver	Short Left	Short Middle	Short Right	Deep Left	Deep Middle	Deep Right
Delanie Walker	31%	42%	28%	19%	33%	13%
Harry Douglas	14%	11%	20%	21%	11%	18%
Kendall Wright	16%	19%	7%	21%	11%	8%
Dorial Green-Beckham	14%	8%	11%	21%	28%	37%
Anthony Fasano	10%	9%	12%	6%		8%
Justin Hunter	9%	3%	8%	6%	11%	5%
Craig Stevens	2%	4%	6%	2%	6%	
Jalston Fowler	1%		4%			
Chase Coffman	1%	3%	1%			
Phillip Supernaw	1%	1%	1%			
Andrew Turzilli			1%	2%		
Tre McBride	2%		1%			3%
Rico Richardson			1%	2%		8%

Marcus Mariota – 2nd Down RTG
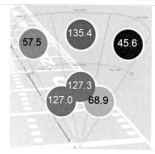

Marcus Mariota – Overall RTG
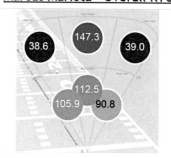

Defense Passer Rating Allowed

Short Left	Short Middle	Short Right	Deep Left	Deep Middle	Deep Right
104	88	103	99	144	118

Pass Offense Play Success Rate

54%	38%	41%	41%	50%
56%	54%	61%	53%	60%
41%	51%	41%	46%	52%

Offensive Rush Directional Yds/Carry
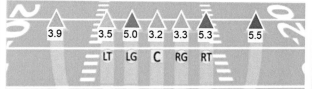

2nd & Short RUN (1D or not)
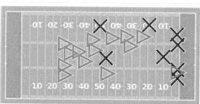

Pass Offense Yds/Play

9.7	6.8	5.6	6.2	5.0
8.2	7.0	12.4	8.2	6.7
6.5	6.8	6.9	6.4	4.1

2nd & Short RUN Stats

Run Conv Rk	1D% Run	NFL 1D% Run Avg	Run Freq	NFL Run Freq Avg
24	64%	69%	63%	64%

Offensive Rush Frequency of Direction

Off. Directional Tendency (% of Plays Left, Middle or Right)

37%	32%	32%	44%	42%
23%	25%	31%	21%	24%
40%	43%	38%	36%	34%

Offensive Explosive Runs by Direction
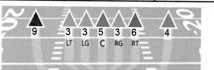

2nd & Short PASS (1D or not)
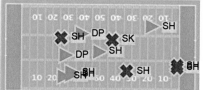

Off. Directional Pass Rate (% of Plays which are Passes)

62%	68%	62%	70%	74%
38%	45%	50%	36%	36%
68%	86%	65%	65%	70%

Defensive Rush Directional Yds/Carry
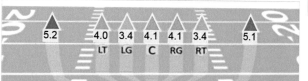

2nd & Short PASS Stats

Pass Conv Rk	1D% Pass	NFL 1D% Pass Avg	Pass Freq	NFL Pass Freq Avg
19	54%	55%	37%	36%

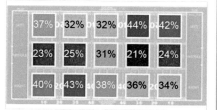

the **Sharp Football Analysis Podcast**

subscribe

feat. the Rearviewmirror...

What you think you saw vs what REALLY happened in last week's NFL games

-Analytics Rewind every <u>Tuesday</u>-
Featuring the Rearviewmirror segment
-Deeper than the score... deeper than the boxscore
-Advanced Metrics & Analytics
-Why teams won or lost
-What to take away from the games
-Weekly News & Headlines
-Early Down Success Rate: Top 5 / Bottom 5 / Rise or Fall
-Division & Playoff Projections via NFLproject.com
-Key Injuries – Effect & Impact
-Early look ahead to next week

-Preview & DFS every <u>Friday</u>-
Featuring Evan Silva of Rotoworld.com
Preview the upcoming week with full game breakdowns of
the key player and team matchups:
-Which players will have the biggest edges
-Which games are most likely to be fantasy gold
-Which games you should steer clear of
-Evan Silva's top recommendations
-1 Full Hour (maybe more) of NFL technical preview from
2 of the best in their field

Website Recommendations for 2016

1. **SharpFootballAnalysis.com** – visit the site, check out the free material and research from the blog articles, join up for the season. Best of all, pay NOTHING now and NOTHING until the end of the 2016 season.
2. **SharpFootballStats.com** – the most visually advanced NFL stats site. All visualizations fully interactive and customizable. The one spot you need to visit each week for updated info and research at your fingertips to make the process faster, more productive, and more educational.
3. **NFLproject.com** – weekly projections with new model runs, delivered in an easy to understand manner.
4. **Rotoworld.com** – For accurate player news and great NFL previews from Evan Silva

Other sites which are a good source for research & information:
- ProFootballFocus.com
- FootballOutisders.com
- Rotoviz.com
- FantasyLabs.com
- Rotogrinders.com

- FantasyInsiders.com
- Numberfire.com
- 4for4.com
- ESPN Chalk
- Sportsline.com

Podcast Recommendations for 2016

1. **Sharp Football Analysis Podcast**

Others with good X & O breakdown:
- Rotoworld Football Podcast
- Chalk Talk: Doug Farrar Football Podcast
- Roughing the Passer Podcast

Others with good analysis for DFS:
- Fantasy Feast: Eatin' with Ross Tucker
- Fantasyland

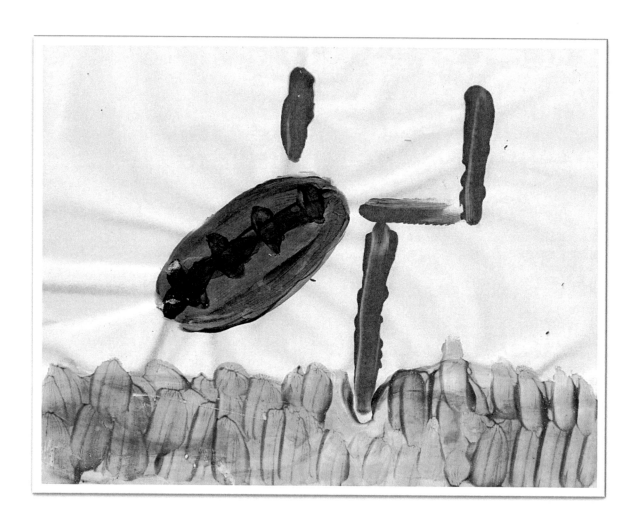

Thank you for checking out Warren Sharp's 2016 Football Preview!

If you enjoyed it or learned from it, please recommend it to a friend. Or share with your followers on Twitter or Facebook. Tag me @SharpFootball on Twitter with a photo of your copy and I'll give it a re-tweet.

Let's try to spread the word that analytics are educational, informative and useful. They help understanding and improve efficiency. And if viewed the right way, they actually can make things easier to understand and retain, while saving time.

Enjoy the 2016 football season and I hope to see you around this fall, interacting on Twitter and following along on my projects at Sharp Football Stats. Keep up with my weekly analysis during the season on my podcast, the Sharp Football Analysis Podcast. And don't miss my detailed, weekly game predictions over at SharpFootballAnalysis.com. Have a great and safe summer – it will be football season before you know it!

Best,
Warren

33727286R00085